RETAIL
MARKETING

Eighth Edition

RETAIL MARKETING

For Employees, Managers, and Entrepreneurs

Eighth Edition

Warren G. Meyer

University of Minnesota
Minneapolis, Minnesota

Donald P. Kohns

University of North Dakota
Grand Forks, North Dakota

E. Edward Harris

Northern Illinois University
DeKalb, Illinois

James R. Stone, III

University of Minnesota
St. Paul, Minnesota

GLENCOE

Macmillan/McGraw-Hill

Lake Forest, Illinois   Columbus, Ohio
Mission Hills, California   Peoria, Illinois

Sponsoring Editor: Sylvia L. Weber
Editing Supervisor: Melonie Parnes
Design and Art Supervisor: Nancy Axelrod
Production Supervisor: Mirabel Flores
Photo Editor: Rosemarie Rossi

Text Designer: Gail Schneider
Cover Photo: James Nazz

Library of Congress Cataloging-in-Publication Data

Retail marketing.

   Rev. ed. of: Retailing / Warren G. Meyer,
   Peter G. Haines, E. Edward Harris, c1982.
   Includes index.
   1. Retail trade.   2. Marketing.   I. Meyer,
Warren G.   II. Meyer, Warren G.   Retailing.
HF5429.R52   1988   658.8'7   87-26073
ISBN 0-07-041698-2

The manuscript for this book was processed electronically.

RETAIL MARKETING, For Employees, Managers, and Entrepreneurs

Eighth Edition

   6 7 8 9 0 VNHVNH   9 5 4 3 2 1

ISBN 0-07-041698-2

ABOUT THE AUTHORS

WARREN G. MEYER is professor emeritus at the University of Minnesota, where he organized the first distributive teacher education program. His earlier experience as a marketing educator includes teaching positions at the secondary, postsecondary, and adult levels in Wisconsin and Kansas. He was state supervisor for distributive education in Kansas. Professor Meyer also served as a vocational education consultant to the U.S. Department of State in West Germany. As a marketing practitioner he has held positions in department and specialty stores and in a service business.

Among Professor Meyer's honors are the Academy of Distributive Teacher Education Award, the John Robert Gregg Award in Business Education, the Distributive Education Professional Development Award (DEPDA), and life membership in the Distributive Education Clubs of America.

He has served as vice president for distributive education in the American Vocational Association, was a charter member of the AVA Research Committee, and president of the Council for Distributive Teacher Education, the Minnesota Business Education Association, and the Minnesota Distributive Education Association.

An author of *Retailing: Principles and Practices* since the fourth edition, Professor Meyer is also an author of *Merchandising,* published by Gregg/McGraw-Hill.

E. EDWARD HARRIS is professor of Marketing and Entrepreneurial Education at Northern Illinois University. In 1963 Dr. Harris received the Outstanding Service Award from the Distributive Education Clubs of America; he also was the recipient of the 1986 Distinguished Service Award from the Marketing Education Association. In 1987 he received the Freedom Foundation National Award for Excellence in Economic Education. He is listed in *Who's Who in America, Who's Who in the World,* and various other national and international references.

Dr. Harris serves on the Governor's Small Business Advisory Board in the state of Illinois and has served as a consultant for numerous businesses and organizations in more than 25 states and foreign countries.

In addition to his contributions to *Retailing: Principles and Practices* since the sixth edition, Dr. Harris is the author of *Marketing Research,* also published by Gregg/McGraw-Hill.

DONALD P. KOHNS is professor of Marketing Education at the University of North Dakota. Previously he was a teacher-coordinator of Marketing Education in Wisconsin and Minnesota. During that time he served as Wisconsin Delta Epsilon Chi coordinator-representative and was president of the Minnesota Association of Marketing Educators. He has written several curriculum guides focusing on marketing model store programs and small business management and has coordinated a Marketing Educator/Small Business Counselor Training Program which involved several different states. Currently, Dr. Kohns is an Active Corps of Executives (ACE) Counselor for the Small Business

Administration. He also serves as a Board Representative for the MarkED Resource Center (IDECC) and is developing state curriculum guides in the area of secondary marketing education and entrepreneurship.

JAMES R. STONE III is a marketing educator at the University of Minnesota. A former high school and adult marketing educator in Virginia, Dr. Stone also has ten years of experience in retail marketing management. Dr. Stone's involvement in research and development in curriculum and program design includes directing the project to develop a state curriculum guide for marketing education in Wisconsin. He was the Consensus Committee Chair at the 1984 National Marketing Education Curriculum Conference and is Chair of the Marketing Education Research Committee. A two-time recipient of the Neal E. Vivian Research Award in Marketing and Distributive Education, he is also active in the Marketing Education Association, the American Marketing Association, the American Society for Training and Development, the American Vocational Association, Professional Sales Association, and several other professional organizations.

RICHARD D. ASHMUN served for 23 years as professor and program coordinator for marketing education in the Department of Vocational and Technical Education at the University of Minnesota. He was president of the Council of Distributive Teacher Educators and the Minnesota Vocational Association. Dr. Ashmun is an honorary life member of Minnesota DECA and the Minneapolis-St. Paul Sales and Marketing Executives.

Besides coauthoring *Problems and Projects for Retail Marketing* with Donald Kohns, Dr. Ashmun is an author of *Selling: Principles and Practices* and *Exploratory Business,* both published by Gregg/McGraw-Hill.

PREFACE

One crucial constant in the people-oriented field of marketing is change. Changing consumer wants and needs demand timely responses from competing marketers — retail marketers in particular. Fortunately, new technologies enable retail marketers to meet consumer demands. The eighth edition of *Retail Marketing* has been tailored to help career-minded retail marketing students prepare for entry and advancement in this dynamic field.

Like retail marketing itself, this text has undergone major revisions to meet the needs of its market. Changes have been made throughout the text to reflect the current use of computer technology by retailers. The change in the title of the eighth edition from *Retailing* to *Retail Marketing* reflects the growing awareness among marketing educators — as well as practitioners — of the advantages of applying marketing principles in the retail setting. The new subtitle, *For Employees, Managers, and Entrepreneurs,* indicates the level of career development to which readers may aspire. Special attention is focused on entrepreneurship, an appealing option to many marketing students.

The broad scope of retail marketing is emphasized throughout the book. Teachers will notice the repeated use of the phrase "product or service," which reminds readers that retail marketing includes service retailers as well as retailers of products. Attention is also given to nonstore retailing and to the activities of businesses not usually thought of as retail institutions, such as not-for-profit organizations and providers of health care, and other professional services.

Organization

The improved grid format of organization in the eighth edition gives the students a perspective of the task of preparing for a career in retail marketing. It enables them to visualize the total spectrum of needed competencies so that they can trace their learning progress. Thus, it can be used in goal orientation and could augment student motivation. Teachers who have used this text before will note that the grid has been simplified. Coverage of career selection, which is an important element in career preparation, is integrated into the grid as a competency band. The chapters and units in the new edition are numbered horizontally across each of the seven competency bands, rather than vertically by level of learning.

The grid format also facilitates course planning for either the teachers who concentrate on one competency area at a time (following the horizontal sequence) or those who use the cyclical approach (following the vertical order of the three sections), which focuses on each of the three career development levels in turn: Section A — Getting Started in a Retail Marketing Career, Section B — Becoming a Career Employee/Retail Marketing Specialist, and Section C — Advancing Toward Management and Entrepreneurship.

The seven horizontal competency bands cover the foundations and functions of retail marketing. Treatment corresponds to the core curriculum framework developed by the National Council for Marketing Education (NCME). The competencies identified by the Marketing Education Resource Center (MarkED) (formerly the Interstate Distributive Education Curriculum Consortium (IDECC)) as being relevant to the NCME model are fully covered. Adherence to this model ensures that the text responds to the curriculum needs of marketing education classes across the country. The focus is on skills and understandings that retailers seek in their employees.

Competencies are approached in the approximate sequence that they are encountered on the job. To ensure transfer of learning, the authors not only tell the student how a task is performed but also explain why it is done and, in many instances, why it is done differently in various job settings. In this way, the text prepares the student to cope with a variety of situations that may arise on the job.

The information is presented in a lively and involving way. The text "talks" to the student in simple, interesting language. It presents the material from the student's perspective at the three levels of vocational development.

Teaching and Learning Aids

The activities provided both at the end of each chapter and at the end of each unit serve to implement and to supplement what is learned from reading the text. There are two end-of-chapter activities.

■ *Trade Talk* To understand retailing, the student must understand the language of retailing. Vital retailing terms used in this exercise appear in boldface type where they are defined in the text.

■ *Can You Answer These?* The questions in this section are based on the facts presented in the chapter. The questions serve several purposes: students find them a valuable study guide, and teachers find them a valuable measure of how well students can recall the infor-

mation in each chapter. The questions focus on points that guide the students toward achievement of the behavorial objectives for the chapter. These objectives are enumerated in the teacher's manual.

In addition to the activities at the end of each chapter, there are also four types of end-of-unit activities.

■ *Retail Marketing Cases* The Retail Marketing cases provide opportunities for students to analyze what they have learned and apply it to new situations. In solving these cases, students practice decision making.

■ *Problems* A variety of activities are included in this section. Some are designed to help students organize their learning by completing charts. Others involve mathematical computations or completion of forms to solve practical problems that retailers typically face.

■ *Projects* Each project is designed to take students out of the classroom and into the world of retailing, where they can apply what they learn in class to what is happening on the job.

■ *Business Plan Assignments* In the final competency band, Planning for Entrepreneurship, the end-of-unit activities take the form of business plan assignments. Each assignment relates to a chapter in the unit, and together, the completed assignments form a business plan, suitable for presentation to potential financial backers.

Support Materials

The supplementary materials described below have been developed to enhance the teaching of retail marketing with this text.

Problems and Projects for Retail Marketing

Two correlated student activity manuals accompany the textbook. The first manual contains student activities for Units 1 through 12, and the second manual, for Units 13 through 21. Each unit includes four types of activities designed to supplement and enrich the learning experiences provided in the textbook. The first section deals with vocabulary, using games and puzzles to maintain students' interest. The second section reviews the key points of the unit by means of short-answer objective questions. The third and fourth sections contain the working forms for the cases and problems in the textbook as well as supplementary cases and problems. The fifth and final section provides work space for the unit projects and the format for additional projects.

Software

To familiarize the students with retail applications of computer technology, software is being introduced with the eighth edition of this program. Two simulations are available on a single disk, in Apple and IBM versions, with corresponding print material provided in the student activity manuals. The first simulation, The Right Job, deals with applying for a job from the viewpoint of two potential retail employees. The simulation includes such considerations as compensation, nonfinancial factors, and qualifications. The Buy Right simulation gives students an opportunity to experience the results of merchandising decisions as they select products for their target market and vendors from whom to buy.

Objective Tests

A set of objective tests is also available. It includes a test for each of the 21 units as well as midterm and final examinations. Each test contains three types of objective questions and is equipped with easy-to-score answer columns.

Teacher's Manual and Key

The teacher's manual and key offers detailed guidelines for organizing the course and suggestions for teaching it most effectively. Options are discussed for one- and two-semester courses and for progressing through the foundations and functions of marketing (by following the sequence of horizontal bands in the table of contents) or using the stages of a career sequence (shown vertically on the table of contents grid). Recommendations are also given for teaching a specialized concentration on entrepreneurship in retailing. Specific, detailed teaching suggestions are provided for each unit as are additional learning activities. The teacher's manual and key also contains answers to all questions in the textbook, student activity manual, and objective tests.

Warren G. Meyer
E. Edward Harris
Donald P. Kohns
James R. Stone III

ACKNOWLEDGMENTS

The authors are appreciative of the many contributions of the late G. Henry Richert to the first six editions of this text and grateful to the many other marketing educators and retailing practitioners who have made subsequent contributions. The following reviewers of the seventh edition provided many useful recommendations for revisions:

Deborah S. Curlette, Crestwood High School, Atlanta, Georgia

Roberta Haynes, Shawnee Mission West High School, Shawnee Mission, Kansas

Gail Honea, Virginia Commwealth University, Richmond, Virginia

Dr. Carl F. Lebowitz, New York University, New York, New York

Dr. William T. Price, Virginia Polytechnic Institute and State University, Blacksburg, Virginia

The manuscript for the present edition has benefited from the valuable suggestions of the following reviewers:

Ginger Anderson, Marketing on the Mall, Bellevue Public Schools, Bellevue, Washington

Dr. M. Catherine Ashmore, National Center for Research in Vocational Education, Columbus, Ohio

Mary Jo Bracken, Solomon Juneau Business High School, Milwaukee, Wisconsin

Betty Fotheringham, Winston Churchill High School, Potomac, Maryland

Sallie Hook, University of South Carolina, Columbia, South Carolina

Dr. John McGinnis, Montclair State College, Upper Montclair, New Jersey

Douglas L. Roeseler, Henry Ford High School, Detroit, Michigan

Jean A. Samples, University of Houston, Houston, Texas

Adelaide Wortham, Detroit Public Schools, Detroit, Michigan

The authors are also pleased to acknowledge the participation in this project of Dr. Richard D. Ashmun, coauthor with Dr. Donald P. Kohns of the student activity manuals, and of Dr. John McGinnis, who developed the Buy Right simulation. Thanks go to Mark Michelman for his assistance in the preparation of the objective tests.

Photo Credits

Courtesy of Advertising Images, Inc.: 401. © Jules Allen: 25 (bottom left), 40, 148. Developed by J. Walter Thompson for the American Red Cross: 49. © Phillip Andersen: 130. Peter Arnold, Inc.: © H. Gritscher: 172; © Malcolm S. Kirk: 193; © Marilyn Sanders: 5 (top left). © Sybil Shelton: 17, 279; © Erika Stone: 115; © Bruno J. Zehnder: 5 (top right). Courtesy of Associated Credit Bureaus, Inc.: 293. Courtesy of L.S. Ayres & Co.: 370. Produced by Kracauer and Marvin Advertising Inc. for Benihana of Tokyo, Inc.: 275. Courtesy of Best Products Co. Inc.: 20 (top left). Courtesy of Bloomingdale's: 365. Courtesy of Caldor, a division of the May Department Stores Company: 20 (top right), 227. © Giuseppe Cavalieri: 5 (bottom right). © John Cavanaugh: 168. Courtesy of *Chain Store Age Executive*, June 1984: 414. Courtesy of The Clay Hand Gallery: 138. Courtesy of Cohoes Specialty Stores: 355. © The Corporate Level: 91, 387. Courtesy of The Dallas Apparel Mart, a Division of the Dallas Market Center: 482. Courtesy of Dayton Hudson Corporation: 10, 369 (top left). Courtesy of Dayton Hudson Department Store Company: 369 (middle left). Courtesy of Distributive Education Clubs of America: 27. Courtesy of Dunkin' Donuts: 344. © Estée Lauder, Inc.: 341. Courtesy of Expressions Custom Furniture: 565. © Will Faller: 25 (top left, top right), 165, 535. Courtesy of Federal Express Corp.: 48. Fundamental Photographs: (Kip Peticolas) 244 (bottom). Courtesy of GMAC: 291. Courtesy of WR Grace & Co.: 536 (bottom). UPC markings courtesy of Grey Advertising, Inc.: 419. © Richard Hackett: 25 (bottom middle), 43, 46, 57, 190, 200, 252, 264, 276, 283, 309, 315, 321, 328 (top left, bottom right), 346, (Urban Outfitters) 369 (middle right, bottom left) 375 (top), 426, 470, 474, 553. © Jane Hamilton-Merritt: 236. Courtesy of E.E. Harris: 20 (bottom right). Courtesy of City of Hartford, CT, Health Department and Bureau of Licences: 117. Courtesy of Health and Tennis Corporation of America: 402. Courtesy of D.H. Holmes Co., Ltd.: 391. © Honeywell Ball Inc.: 25 (bottom right). © IBM: 434 (right), 477. The Image Bank: © Steve Dunwell: 5 (bottom left); © Gary Gradstone: 244 (top left). © David M. Hamilton: 369 (bottom right); © William Rivelli: 369 (top right). Courtesy of Japan Air Lines: 272.

Courtesy of K&B Inc.: 337. Courtesy of Kentucky Fried Chicken Corp.: 300. Reprinted with special permission of King Features Syndicate, Inc.: 64. Courtesy of Kinney Shoe Corporation: 532. Courtesy of K mart Corporation, Troy, Michigan: 536 (top). Courtesy of The Landing at Behrman Place, a development by Brim & Associates, Inc.: 151 (top). Courtesy of Julie Laurence Ideas in Furniture, reprinted from the TV Shopper: 359. Narda Lebo: 141, 240, 334, 506. Courtesy of The Limited, Inc.: 113. © Long John Silver: 366. Reprinted with permission from *Retail Store Planning & Design Manual* by Michael Lopez, published by the National Retail Merchants Association, New York, NY: 533. Courtesy of Manhattan Savings Bank: 328 (top right). © Randy Matusow: 255. Courtesy of National Association of Retail Grocers: 262. National Business Systems: 436. *Nation's Business* (T. Michael Keza) 501: 514. © NCR Corporation, Dayton, Ohio: 434 (left). Courtesy of Neiman-Marcus: 305. Courtesy of NORAND: 462 (right). Courtesy of J.C. Penney Company, Inc.: 53 (top), 154. © James H. Pickerell: 505. Courtesy of Patrick Media Group, Inc.: 328 (bottom left), 354, 527. Photo Researchers, Inc., © David A. Frazier: 260; © Guy Gillette: 374; © F. Grunzweig: 367 (top); © Susan Kuklin: 367 (bottom); © The Photo Works: 375 (bottom), 565; © Barbara Reis: 134; *Southern Living*: 472; © Teri Leigh Stretford: 163. © Elizabeth Richter: 328 (middle), 423. Courtesy of Recognition Products, Inc.: 462 (left). Courtesy of Sanger Harris: 20 (bottom left), 215. Courtesy of Sears, Roebuck and Co.: 53 (bottom), 121, 244 (top right), 281. Courtesy of Sesame Place, Langhorne, PA: 349. Courtesy of Harry A. Shaud Real Estate: 151 (bottom). © Nate Silverstein: 5 (top left), 247. Courtesy of Stern's Department Store: 493. Courtesy of Stowe, Vermont/ Brownell: 78. Courtesy of Target Stores: 105. Courtesy of Telaction Corporation: 128. Courtesy of Thompson Associates: 524. Courtesy of Touro Infirmary: 338. Courtesy of Toys "R" Us: 94, 398. Courtesy of The Travelers Companies: 510. © 1983 United Features Syndicate, Inc.: 86. © Michael Weisbrot: 123. Woodfin Camp & Assoc., © Ira Berger, 1981: 455; © Michal Heron: 329; © William Strode: 318.

T·A·B·L·E O·F CONTENTS

C O M P E T E N C Y B A N D

COMPETENCY BAND

CAREERS IN RETAIL MARKETING

Life is made up of a large number of minor decisions and a very small number of major ones. Selecting a career is one of the most important decisions that we ever make. In fact, it has been predicted that we may change our careers three to five times.

To be happy in our lives we need to be doing things we enjoy both at work and in our leisure time. We can do a lot to plan for a successful career if we are willing to spend the time now and not delay until it is too late. We can begin by selecting a type of work that will be enjoyable and give us a chance to prove ourselves.

There are many ways to begin searching for a career with a future. Your friends, parents, teachers, and counselors may be able to help you learn more about your interests and about the types of careers that might be of interest to you. Getting ahead depends a lot on you and what you put into your career.

Marketing is one career field you may want to look at carefully. By the year 2000, approximately one-third of all people will be employed in the field of marketing. By 1995, retail marketing will employ more people than any other occupation in America, with 21.3 million jobs projected.

One of the most exciting benefits of retail marketing as a career is the almost unbelievable number of opportunities, either working for someone else or owning your own business. Retail marketing jobs range from part-time sales clerks to store managers to business owners. In this competency band, you will learn more about the possibilities that await you if you choose this career path.

U·N·I·T 1
EXPLORING RETAIL MARKETING

C·H·A·P·T·E·R

1 *What is Retail Marketing?*

Welcome to the world of retail marketing. It's a fascinating, people-oriented business, based on service to consumers like you. This book is designed to guide you through a study of this retail link in a chain of marketing institutions.

Retailing operates in an environment of attractive products and helpful services. Wherever you turn in retailing, you can find something interesting to look at, to explore, and often to purchase. We live in an age that is rich with products and services for most people to buy. (**Products** are goods grown or manufactured and available for sale; **services** are benefits or satisfactions that improve the appearance, health, comfort, or peace of mind of their users.) Most of these products and services reach you through retail marketers.

Retail marketing is more than an interesting subject to study; it is a vital part of our way of life. You've been involved with retailing most of your life. Chances are that one of your first purchases was made in a retail store where you bought candy, a toy for yourself, or a gift for someone else. You may recall your first trip to the barber or beauty shop to get your hair cut, or going to one of your first movies. Now, hardly a day passes that you don't enter a retail establishment of some kind. Farming, manufacturing, and other kinds of production are very important enterprises, but they are of little value unless the results of their labor are distributed (marketed) and consumed or used. Without marketing, they could not survive very long.

THE WORK OF RETAIL MARKETING

Business has two basic functions: (1) production of goods and services and (2) marketing goods and services. **Production** refers to creating, growing, processing, or

4   Unit 1   Exploring Retail Marketing

Retail marketing involves many activities and occurs in a variety of settings.

manufacturing. After a product or service has been produced or a service has been made available, it must be bought or sold in the marketplace. A **marketplace** is any point at which ownership changes hands.

A simple definition of **marketing** is the process of determining and satisfying the needs and wants of those who consume the products and services. Marketing activities really begin with an understanding of consumer needs and wants. They end after the customer has made a purchase and is satisfied with what he or she has purchased. A **customer** is the person who buys or rents products or services. Frequently the customer and the **consumer**—the person who uses the product or services—are the same. However, sometimes a person will buy something for someone else to use.

Successful retailers select the kinds of consumers they aim to serve, and these consumers become their **target population**—the people for whom they buy merchandise or design services. They don't just start a business and hope for customers. Identifying a target population to serve is critical because no retailer, even the giant companies, can effectively serve all kinds of consumers and make a profit. Keep this idea in mind as you study retail marketing.

Also bear in mind that in a free enterprise economic system a fair profit is an essential element. For the present time, **profit** may be defined as the amount of money left over from income after subtracting expenses. Profit, sometimes referred to as the bottom line, is the reward for business success. It will be discussed further in Chapter 10.

Retail Marketers

Retail marketing (retailing for short) is only one kind of marketing—the last link in the marketing chain of distributors, beginning with the producer and ending with the consumer. The chain may be long or short, depending on the number of "middlemen" between producer and consumer. **Retail marketing** includes all functions or activities involved in selling (or renting) goods and services to end-users, including households, individuals, and others who are purchasing goods and services for final consumption.

Retailing activities include purchasing goods and services for sale, storing, displaying, pricing, advertising, selling, financing, servicing, and other activities necessary to complete the sale with buyers. The retailer occupies the place in the channel of distribution that connects with the final consumer. The goal of retailing is to make a profit by serving the needs and wants of consumers for products and services. Thus, the key to making a profit in retailing rests with the retailer's ability to serve "targeted" groups of consumers.

The Retail Marketing Function

The retail marketing function is sometimes performed by producers, manufacturers, and wholesalers. Here are some examples of how they carry out the retail marketing function. Producers may sell vegetables at roadside stands. Manufacturers may sell cosmetics directly to the home through sales representatives or catalogs. Wholesalers may sell packaged foods through vending machines. Producers, manufacturers, and wholesalers may sell services, such as repair services, to final consumers. However, the vast majority of retail marketing is done by retailers who specialize in the field of retailing.

The **wholesale marketing function** is performed by businesses that buy products, generally in large quantities, and sell them, usually in smaller quantities, to retailers or to industrial users and other businesses rather than to consumers. However, many wholesalers also sell some of their products to consumers. Classification as a wholesaler or a retailer depends on which type of purchaser accounts for more than half of the seller's sales.

Channels of Distribution

Channels of distribution are the different paths that goods pass through in moving from the producer to the consumer. The decisions about which channels to use are important ones; some products and services are best sold one way, others another way. The usual distribution channels for consumer goods are shown in the illustration below.

The most direct channel for distributing consumer goods is the first, from the producer directly to the consumer. If you send away to a producer or manufacturer for something you see advertised in a magazine, you're using this channel. Most small service businesses, such as dry cleaners and beauty shops, use this channel. This channel gives the producer great control over the condition and price of the goods, along with a larger share of the profit. However, it does limit the number of customers and may be more costly, unless there is quite a large-scale distribution. This channel is the one used by manufacturers who establish their own retail stores for their goods, such as Kinney Shoes, Goodyear Tires, and Radio Shack computers.

Sometimes, of course, there's a sales intermediary in the channel acting as spokesperson for the producer. Many personal and home-use items, such as Amway and Avon products, are sold door to door, for example, rather than in stores. To overcome negative reactions to door-to-door selling, some manufacturers of art, clothing, and costume jewelry prefer to have their representatives arrange for home parties at which their products may be displayed and sold. Tupperware is probably the best known of the products sold this way; however, cookware and

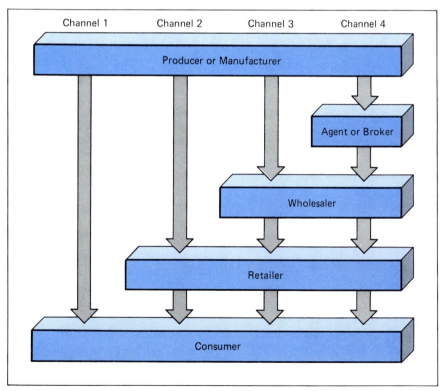

The channel of distribution from producer to consumer may be direct, or there may be one or more middlemen.

home-decorating parties are quite popular.

Food stores are examples of participants in the second channel, from the producer to the retailer to the customer. For example, Wonder Bread sells its bakery goods directly to large retailers, who then sell it to consumers. This channel provides wider coverage and potentially greater sales, but the producer begins to lose a little control over price and distribution.

The route from producer to wholesaler to retailer to consumer, the third channel, is still the most-used channel for goods that are sold by independent retailers, such as department, drug, and hardware stores. It's more reasonable, for instance, for a wholesaler to purchase large quantities of nuts and bolts and then resell them in usable quantities to hardware stores. This channel is probably the most economical one for the producer, for less personal selling, credit, and accounting are required.

In some instances, the fourth channel, from producer to agent or broker to wholesaler to retailer to customer, is used. This route tends to be used for specialized products of which there are only a few producers. The **agent** or **broker** is a representative who doesn't take title to or possession of the products but only brings the buyer and seller together. For instance, if the farmers waited to find buyers when strawberries began to mature in Florida, the berries might spoil. Instead, the strawberries are loaded into refrigerated railroad cars and shipped to Chicago. While the berries are in transit, brokers find wholesalers who want them. Then the berries are diverted to the buyer.

A company producing consumer goods might adopt two or more of these channels. For example, it could sell directly to chains and large independent stores, while at the same time using wholesalers to sell to small independent retailers.

The Retail Marketing Cycle

The work of retail marketing can be viewed as a cycle that begins with the identification of consumer needs and wants and ends with making sure that consumers are satisfied. Here is a brief description of each of the five elements of the **retail marketing cycle**. It will help you to understand what a good retailer really does for his or her clientele.

1. *Identifying target population needs and wants.* What kinds of products and services are needed and wanted? What sizes, shapes, and how many of each? When and where are they wanted?

2. *Determining what price to charge.* Are customers willing and able to pay enough to cover the costs to the retailer plus a fair profit?

3. *Telling consumers about products and services.* Where should they be advertised? Is personal salesmanship needed? How should the product or service be displayed?

4. *Getting the goods from producer to consumer.* What means of transportation should be used? How should financing be handled? Regarding services, should consumers come

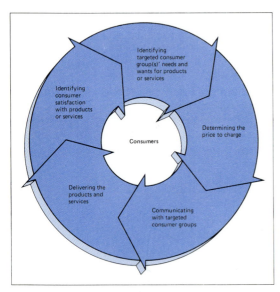

The retail marketing cycle shows that retail marketing revolves around the consumer.

to the service center or should the provider make house calls?

5. *Making sure that customers are satisfied.* Is the product or service really filling the intended need or want? Do the experiences of customers indicate that changes should be made?

CONTRIBUTIONS OF RETAIL MARKETING

Have you ever wondered how retailers decide what type and variety of products and services they should sell or offer? It is the consumer, the retail marketer's real boss, who helps make this decision. If consumers approve of what is done, they reward the retail marketer with their continued business. A retailer can't survive very long without such votes of confidence from consumers. Therefore, retailers are forced to change their ways of serving their customers; if they don't, a competitor will replace them. Retail marketing is what it is today because of this competition to gain the consumer's favor.

In our ever-changing society, the needs and wants of consumers don't remain the same. Technology, lifestyles, fashion, and many other factors affect consumer needs and wants. Think about the changes in retailing that have taken place since you were a child. What does all this mean? Just this: Retailing is dynamic—exciting to progressive merchants. There's hardly a dull moment. The key to success is flexibility and willingness to change with the times. In fact, progressive retailers themselves often start changes.

Firms such as Dayton-Hudson Corporation in Minneapolis, Minnesota, have formalized statements such as the one shown on page 10, in which they identify the contributions their firm plans to make. These contributions normally fall into three major categories: economic, social, and civic.

Economic Contributions

Retailing serves the economic needs of consumers in four ways:

1. By supplying the right goods and services when and where they are needed with little or no delay.

2. By making it easy to select and compare the features, quality, and prices of the goods and services consumers want.

3. By keeping prices low in order to compete for the consumers' dollars.

4. By helping to raise the American standard of living. (**Standard of living** is a term that refers to how well people live. It is measured by the amount and quality of goods and services that people have or use.)

Supplying Consumer Needs One of the most important consumer needs that retailing fulfills is making products and services available where and when they are needed. Imagine for a minute that you need a new pair of athletic shoes and there are no retailers nearby where you could compare styles and prices and get the proper fit. Think of how long it would take and how much it would cost to find and deal with shoe manufacturers in faraway places who might be able to satisfy your needs.

Retailers are purchasing agents for their customers. Retailers assemble the required products and provide the services needed when and where consumers want them. Thus, retail marketing businesses are nearly everywhere today. Most people can buy just about everything they want within a short distance of their homes.

Helping Consumers Buy Consumers may demand more than the mere availability of goods at convenient locations. They nearly always want to shop where it is easy to select and compare the features, quality, and prices of the products and services they are interested in. Therefore, retailers compete to win the favor of potential customers by making

Our Mission

We are in business to please our customers.

- By giving them the value they seek in terms of quality merchandise that is both fashion-right and competitively priced.

- By having the most wanted merchandise in stock -- in depth -- in our stores.

- By giving them a total shopping experience that meets their expectations for service, convenience, environment and ethical standards.

Everything we do -- throughout our organization -- should support and enhance the accomplishment of this mission.

Serving Society

We believe the business of business is serving society, not just making money. Profit is the means and measure of our service, but not an end in itself.

Our ultimate success depends on serving four major publics, and none at the expense of the other: customers, employees, shareholders and communities.

We strive to serve our communities because we know that a community's health ultimately affects our "bottom line," just as surely as our merchandising and management practices do.

Corporate public involvement is a fully integrated, fully committed, fully professional part of our strategy and operations.

- We annually budget an amount equal to five percent of our federally taxable income for community giving. We focus our giving in arts and social action programs.

- We maintain open lines of communication between business and government to achieve mutual respect and credibility.

- We encourage our people -- throughout our organization -- to give their time, talent and expertise.

At Dayton Hudson, we believe that our personal and financial involvement in community giving, community development and government affairs all help us manage our business better.

Community involvement helps us manage change.

Making The Difference With People

Our employees make it possible for Dayton Hudson to serve others: our customers, stockholders and communities.

They are the people who make the difference in our performance.

That's why we insist on competitive compensation, regular performance appraisal, systematic training and development. That's why we prefer to promote from within.

While no employer can guarantee job security, we want our people -- at all levels -- to have the opportunity for stable, long-term careers.

We comply -- voluntarily and fully -- with the law, and with good personnel practices. We provide equal opportunity. We are committed to affirmative action.

Throughout Dayton Hudson, we seek a work atmosphere that encourages employee initiative and input. And which fosters trust and creativity.

Spelling out our responsibilities to our employees is one thing. Living up to them is quite another. We're far from perfect, and we aim to get better.

Merchandising The Business

At Dayton Hudson, our objective is to serve our customers better than our competitors.

We believe that what the customer looks for -- in deciding where to shop -- can be summed up in one word: value.

Our merchandising philosophy identifies five major elements of value:

- Quality
- Competitive Price
- Dominance
- Fashion
- Convenience

We expect each of our companies to define "value" as it applies to them, and to determine what role it plays in their merchandise strategy.

We expect our companies to use the principles of Trend Merchandising to identify where their customer's emphasis on value is, and how it is changing.

Trend Merchandising helps us to determine what's becoming more important to the customer, and what's becoming less important -- so we can allocate our limited resources accordingly.

Measuring Business Performance

Dayton Hudson aims to be a premier investment. That means giving our shareholders a superior return on their investment.

To do that, we strive for premier performance -- as measured against standards recognized by the financial community, and as compared with our retail competitors.

One of the corporation's most important responsibilities is the objective measurement of performance.

For us, the two most important measures are Growth in Earnings and Return on Investment.

Because it tells the most about our performance, ROI is central to achieving our financial objectives. It helps us decide:

- Which capital projects to fund.
- Which strategies to approve.
- Which operating companies merit additional investment.

ROI is to the financial side of our business what "value" is to the merchandising side.

These excerpts from Dayton-Hudson Corporation's Management Perspectives Executive Summary describe the firm's principles concerning its relationship to its four publics.

easy shopping possible. Retail marketing will continue to be a vital service as long as consumers want to compare the features, qualities, and prices of the products and services they buy.

Fair Pricing   A third way in which retailing serves consumers' economic needs is by keeping prices low. Studies have shown that marketing through retailers is generally less costly than direct marketing by manufacturers to consumers. Relatively few types of products are sold directly to consumers. Cosmetics, cookware, and encyclopedias are examples of such products. In our economic system, retailers compete vigorously with each other for consumer dollars by keeping prices low for products and services of similar quality. Many of the techniques that retailers use to compete successfully with each other are discussed throughout this book.

Improving the Standard of Living   As the final link in the marketing process between producers and consumers, retailers strongly influence what people buy and consume. So retail marketing helps to improve America's standard of living. Were it not for all the sales promotion efforts of retailers (together with those of producers, manufacturers, and wholesalers), Americans wouldn't enjoy one of the world's highest standards of living. These promotional efforts through the use of television, newspapers, and direct mail brochures not only inform potential customers of the availability of new and improved products and services but motivate consumers to buy. The end results are increased sales and a higher standard of living.

Another way in which retail marketing contributes to maintaining our high standard of living is by making mass production possible. (**Mass production** is the efficient, high-volume manufacture of large amounts of goods.) Mass production wouldn't work without an effective retailing system to distribute the mass-produced products to consumers. For example, the ability of our factories to produce millions of computers would be of little value if there weren't an efficient way of getting those computers to consumers.

Social and Civic Contributions

In less visible ways, retail marketing also contributes to our social life and welfare as well as to our economic well-being. Here are two examples of this function. Throughout the ages, the marketplace has been a social gathering spot as well as a place to bargain and buy goods. Retailers today encourage people to meet at shopping centers and individual places of business. They do this by providing a variety of opportunities for customers to relax.

Also, retailers support worthy civic and cultural enterprises such as the United Fund and other community projects. They work hard at becoming an integral part of the community. They know that a better community is a good investment.

TRADE TALK

Define each term and use it in a sentence.

Agent	Products
Broker	Profit
Channels of	Retail marketing
distribution	Retail marketing
Consumer	cycle
Customer	Target population
Marketplace	Services
Marketing	Standard of living
Mass production	Wholesale marketing
Production	function

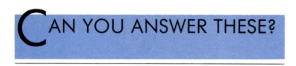

CAN YOU ANSWER THESE?

1. List the five elements of the retail marketing cycle.

2. How does retailing serve the economic needs of consumers?

3. What are the two basic functions of business?

4. Name four channels of distribution.

5. What is the major reason why retailers are in business?

C·H·A·P·T·E·R

2 Classifying Product and Service Retailers

Retail marketing ranges from the neighborhood lemonade stand to the 200,000-square-foot "hypermarket." America's largest retailer, Sears Roebuck and Co., provides an example of the scope. In addition to operating 800 stores and 700 catalog sales offices, Sears also operates Allstate Insurance, Dean Witter Financial Services, and Coldwell Banker Real Estate.

The 20 largest retailers in the United States are listed in Table 1. The latest U.S. Department of Commerce figures show that retail store sales were over $950 billion and non-store sales more than $60 billion.

Retail marketing businesses can be classified according to the following five categories:

1. Type of ownership
2. Products or services sold
3. Non-store retailing
4. Pricing strategy
5. Location

None of these five classifications is meant to be all-encompassing. The intention is simply to provide you with several bases for better understanding the broad field of retail marketing.

TYPES OF OWNERSHIP

Almost all retail businesses can be classified as independents, as a part of a corporate chain, or as a franchise. This is true whether a firm sells products or services. The independent is the most common type of ownership; however, it accounts for only one-fourth of sales.

Independent Retailers and Franchises

An **independent retail firm** is a retail outlet owned and operated independently and without affiliation. Many independent retailers, however, want some of the advantages that chains enjoy. For example, they want discounts for buying merchandise in quantity, assistance in developing effective advertising and sales promotion plans, and help in designing sound accounting and records-control systems. In order to obtain these advantages, independent retailers are willing to give up some of their independence.

Joining a **voluntary chain** such as ACE Hardware or IGA Food Stores is one means

TABLE 1 / THE 20 LARGEST RETAILERS—1988

	Company	Sales (000)	Number of Employees
1.	Sears Roebuck (Chicago)	$50,251,000	520,000
2.	K Mart (Troy, MI)	27,301,000	355,000
3.	Wal-Mart Stores (Bentonville, AR)	20,649,000	223,000
4.	Kroger (Cincinnati)	19,053,000	160,000
5.	American Stores (Irvine, CA)	18,478,400	165,000
6.	J.C. Penney (Dallas)	14,833,000	190,000
7.	Safeway Stores (Oakland, CA)	13,612,400	107,200
8.	Dayton Hudson (Minneapolis)	12,204,000	135,000
9.	May Department Stores (St. Louis)	11,921,000	152,000
10.	Great Atlantic & Pacific Tea (Montvale, NJ)	9,531,800	83,000
11.	Winn-Dixie Stores (Jacksonville, FL)	9,007,700	83,800
12.	F.W. Woolworth (New York)	8,088,000	132,185
13.	Southland (Dallas)	7,950,300	50,724
14.	Marriott (Bethesda, MD)	7,370,000	229,600
15.	Melville (Harrison, NY)	6,780,400	96,500
16.	Albertson's (Boise, ID)	6,773,100	50,000
17.	R.H. Macy (New York)	5,729,100	70,000
18.	McDonald's (Oak Brook, IL)	5,566,300	169,000
19.	Montgomery Ward Holding (Chicago)	5,371,000	49,200
20.	Walgreen (Deerfield, IL)	4,883,500	45,000

Source: *Fortune*, June 5, 1989, pp. 378–379.

of gaining some of the advantages of the retail chains while at the same time remaining independent. One of the advantages of purchasing a retail store franchise from a corporate franchisor is staying independent but benefiting from the brand name and experience of the chain. **Franchising** is a contractual agreement in which a parent company (franchisor) grants a small company or individual (franchisee) the right to do business under specified conditions.

Although independent retailers remain independent under these plans, they do sacrifice some of their freedom.

Franchising will be discussed in detail in Chapter 9 together with additional ownership and management opportunities.

Corporate Chains

A **corporate chain** is a group of two or more businesses linked together under one man-

agement and owned by a group of stockholders. For example, J.C. Penney is owned by a group of stockholders who select officers. The officers make decisions as to where new businesses will be located. The units in the chain are centrally owned and managed and usually sell more or less the same products and services.

The advantages of the corporate chain stem largely from its high sales volume, capacity to buy in huge quantities, and ability to employ workers with specialized talents to develop sales promotional materials. Because chains order large quantities, they receive discounts from their suppliers. The size of the corporation also permits hiring a central staff of specialists who plan the advertising and other aspects of sales promotion. Other specialists at the headquarter's office control the inventory of the outlets. In addition, the central management staff coordinates the overall operation and assists local managers.

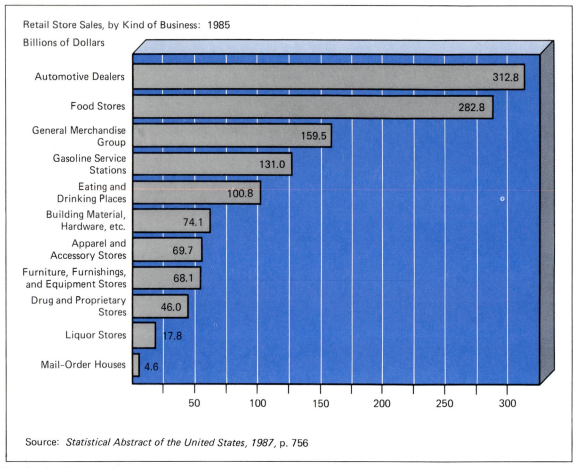

Retail Store Sales, by Kind of Business: 1985

Billions of Dollars

Kind of Business	Value
Automotive Dealers	312.8
Food Stores	282.8
General Merchandise Group	159.5
Gasoline Service Stations	131.0
Eating and Drinking Places	100.8
Building Material, Hardware, etc.	74.1
Apparel and Accessory Stores	69.7
Furniture, Furnishings, and Equipment Stores	68.1
Drug and Proprietary Stores	46.0
Liquor Stores	17.8
Mail-Order Houses	4.6

Source: *Statistical Abstract of the United States, 1987,* p. 756

Retail sales, by kind of business, 1985.

PRODUCTS OR SERVICES SOLD

One way of distinguishing among retailers is according to whether they sell services or products. The graph above identifies some of the most common types of retail products and service businesses.

Service Retailing

Service retailers are growing more rapidly in the United States than product retailers. Service retailing includes not only business firms but also not-for-profit organizations such as zoos, public transportation, and libraries.

There are three types of service retailing: (1) **Rented-goods services**, in which customers rent and use products; (2) **owned-goods services**, in which products owned by consumers are repaired, improved, or maintained; and (3) **non-goods services**, in which intangible personal services (rather than products) are offered to consumers.

Some examples of rented-goods services are rental cars, carpet cleaner rentals, and apartment rentals. In each case, a tangible product is leased for a fee for a specified period of time. The consumer may use the product, but ownership is not obtained.

Governments, as well as commercial businesses, market retail services.

Owned-goods services involve an alteration of some type in a product already owned by the customer. Examples are repair services (automobiles, watches, and appliances), lawn care, car wash, furniture upholstering, and dry cleaning. In this category, a service is provided to improve an owned good, and the retailer undertaking the service never owns the product.

Non-goods services are those where no tangible products are involved, and the retailer offers personal services requiring the use of his or her time for a fee. Some examples are baby-sitter, chauffeur, tutor, travel guide, barber, and beautician. In each instance, a personal service is provided, the sellers offer their expertise for a specified period of time, and a fee is paid to them.

The basic difference between the marketing of products and services is that retailers of products buy an inventory of goods for resale, while the service retailer concentrates on the material and labor needed to produce and sell services. Retailers of products emphasize the functions of buying, stocking, displaying, and selling merchandise, while the service business emphasizes the actual performance of the service.

The marketing characteristics of services differ significantly from those of products, as shown below:

■ The buyer of a service is often called a client and not a customer.
■ The amount paid for services is usually expressed as rates, fees, admissions, charges, or tuition and not in terms of price.
■ Standards are not precise, because many services cannot be mass produced.
■ Price-setting practices vary greatly.
■ Surpluses cannot be inventoried; therefore, services are highly perishable.

Product Retailing

Retailers can also be classified by type of products sold. Some of the most common types of product retail businesses include department stores, specialty stores, catalog stores, and food and drug stores.

Department Stores The U.S. Department of Commerce defines a **department store** as a retail establishment that employs at least 25 people and has sales of apparel and household linens amounting to 20 percent or more of total sales. A department store, the Department of Commerce also states, must sell items in each of the following lines of merchandise: (1) furniture, home furnishings, and appliances; (2) general apparel for the family; and (3) household linens and fabrics.

The modern department store also sells services such as gift wrapping, jewelry repair, and hair styling. Large department stores are organized into main divisions and departments. Each division combines a number of departments selling related lines of merchandise. For example, the home products division has departments such as furniture, appliances, lamps, and housewares.

A departmentalized retail store that makes it a policy to sell limited assortments of merchandise at reduced prices is known as a **discount department store**. Some well-known discount department stores are K mart, Wal-Mart, Venture, and Target.

Specialty Stores A **specialty store** typically concentrates on a few types of merchandise. Examples include The Limited (women's apparel), Computer Land (small computers), Toys "R" Us (toys), Gordon's (jewelry), and Singer Sewing Centers (sewing machines). Specialty stores are frequently located in large shopping malls.

Several other types of specialty retailers have experienced rapid expansion. These include hobby and craft centers (Tandycrafts), home decorating specialty stores (Color Tile), paint and decorating supermarkets (Sherwin-Williams home decorating centers),

home improvement centers (Wolohan), and superhardware stores (ACE Hardware).

Catalog Showrooms **Catalog showrooms** offer low prices, national brands, and small shopping areas with warehouse space adjacent to retail display areas. Typically shoppers review the widely distributed catalogs before visiting the store. The buyer must complete an order blank, which is processed before the item is provided to the buyer at a central location. By limiting displays, catalog showrooms reduce theft losses. Operating costs also are kept low by keeping the staff small. Examples of firms include Best Products, Service Merchandise, and Modern Merchandising.

Food and Drug Retailers The three major types of food and drug retailers are supermarket and superdrug stores, convenience stores, and combination stores. **Supermarket** and **superdrug stores** are large stores that sell high-volume foods or drugs at low prices. Customers select merchandise from aisles and place it in carts for movement to checkout counters. Examples of food supermarkets are Safeway, A&P, and Winn-Dixie. Drug chains include SuperX, Walgreen, Perry, and Osco. Drug stores sell general merchandise lines in addition to prescription and health and beauty aids. Most food and drug supermarkets are part of regional or national chains. Few single independently owned grocery or drug stores exist today.

A **convenience store** is a retail firm like 7-Eleven or Magic Mart that is located in residential neighborhoods because it appeals to consumers who want to shop when other stores are closed. Such consumers want to purchase quickly a limited number of products—such as a loaf of bread, a quart of milk, or a newspaper—close to home. Many food retailers such as Red Owl, Dominicks, and Jewel have their own convenience-type stores. Many combination grocery and drug stores carry many of the items that both supermarket and superdrug stores offer. **Combination stores** are larger than conventional supermarket or superdrug stores, but they are similar regarding pricing strategies and operating practices. The term **superstore** is also used to describe these large combination food and nonfood retailers. They range in size from 35,000 to 60,000 square feet. Several food chains are building combination-type stores. Giant superstores called **hypermarkets** or **warehouse retailers** have become popular in Europe and are gaining popularity in America under various names such as Warehouse Club, Price, and Unity. These combination supermarket and discount department stores are larger than U.S. combination stores and superstores (100,000 to 200,000 square feet), and the merchandise mix is expanded to include appliances, clothing, and several other nonfood and nondrug items. Operating in low-rent warehouse facilities exceeding 100,000 square feet, they recruit members selectively to include local retailers and professionals and employees of certain banks, utilities, and government offices. Some small retailers find items priced so low that they buy large quantities for resale.

Stores are not the only setting in which retail marketing occurs.

retailing. However, it has been estimated that non-store retailing has been growing at least three to four times the rate of store retailing. Several factors help to explain the popularity of catalog and other forms of non-store retailing. One reason is the rapid increase in the number of families in which both spouses work, limiting the amount of shopping time available but providing the income for more expensive non-store purchases.

NON-STORE RETAILING

Non-store retailers sell products and services by methods such as direct selling, machine vending, mail-order retailing, and electronic techniques. Flea markets, garage sales, farmers' markets, and other non-store retailing outlets are also quite common in many communities. Increasingly, products and services are also sold through telephone soliciting.

Approximately 80 percent of all retailing takes place in retail stores. The remaining 20 percent is done in various kinds of non-store

Telephone and Media Retailers

Telephone and media retailers use telephone contact and advertising media such as television, radio, newspapers, and magazines to inform and persuade consumers to buy their products. Television advertisements often are used in combination with toll-free telephone numbers (numbers with an 800 area code) to market cookware, records, tools, and a wide variety of other products.

Telephone marketing, or telemarketing, has become one of the fastest-growing methods of marketing a wide variety of products, including insurance, cameras, stocks, political candidates, and charities. One estimate places telemarketing sales of goods and services at $75 billion annually, expanding 15 to 20 percent a year. Although more expensive than direct or media advertising, telemarketing is much less expensive than face-to-face selling. Many industrial product marketers are also using telemarketing.

Vending Machines

Vending machines are an important part of retailing, dispensing everything from food and beverages to entertainment and insurance. Modern electronic vending machines are capable of performing a variety of tasks. Some of the new soft drink machines can even talk electronically. Vending machines are located in banks, supermarkets, hotels, offices, and schools. Typically, the products dispensed by machine cost more than if they were purchased in a store. For example, postage stamps from a machine in a hotel lobby cost more than stamps purchased at a U.S. Post Office.

Mail Order

Mail-order retailing experienced explosive growth during the last decade, although it has been around for approximately 100 years. In 1985, 5 billion copies of 4000 different catalogs were placed in mailboxes. Consumers made 15 percent of their purchases by mail in 1986; and, because catalog orders are growing faster than in-store purchases, it is estimated that 20 percent of all retail transactions will be made by mail by the end of the decade.

Direct Selling

Marketing goods directly to the consumer in the home or place of business is known as **direct selling**. Products commonly sold by this method include cosmetics, encyclopedias, and cookware. Sales representatives in

this field are often paid according to the sales volume of the products they sell. Other sales representatives are independent business people who buy the merchandise they sell. These sales representatives may make their sales by telephone, by home visits that have been arranged by telephone or mail, or by going directly to the home without any previous contact with the customer.

Some of these retailers, such as Fuller Brush, Avon Cosmetics, and World Book Encyclopedia, call on individual households. Others, such as Tupperware, persuade a household member to invite friends to a party at which goods are displayed.

Another direct selling method is street selling. Street salespeople range from drivers of ice cream trucks to vendors who set up booths on busy street corners to sell flowers, toys, foods, and novelty items.

Electronic Shopping

Videotex is a system for use by households and businesses to retrieve information from remote data bases using a terminal or television set and telephone lines. Videotex can be described as the generic term for a developing, interactive medium that delivers text and visual information directly to consumers. It can be used to reach audiences in both home and business markets. The user interacts with the system via a hand-held keypad, pushbutton console, or keyboard. Desired information is retrieved by user command from one or more public or private data bases through telephone lines, cable or broadcast signals, with text or graphics displayed on a television screen or other video device.

Viewtron, AT&T's first full-service, commercial videotex offering, went into operation in October 1983 in several Florida cities. The system can perform a number of functions including electronic banking and shopping.

CompuSave Corporation offers terminals built into free-standing kiosks (boxlike structures) that do duty as portable catalog show-

The price range of the products and services sold is an important part of a retailer's image. Generally, the higher the quality of the goods and services, the more convenience, customer service, and luxury environment are offered.

rooms, selling more than 3000 hardgood items at discounts of 20 to 40 percent. The supermarket chain, Stop & Shop, has already bought the idea and is beginning to install the kiosks in its stores.

■

PRICING STRATEGY

Retailers offer a wide spectrum of prices from low to high. Substantial variations in the price of the same brand can be found among retailers. Four catagories of retailers represent the range of pricing strategies used by retailers. **Full-markup retailers** price to maintain a substantial difference between the cost of merchandise to themselves and the selling price to their customers. Typically, department stores and specialty stores offer a variety of services, including attractive and conveniently located stores, to make it worthwhile to customers to patronize their businesses despite the prices.

Other retailers, such as discounters, pose an increasing threat to retailers who charge full price. Discounters often are located near full-price retailers and use low prices to attract business from full-price department and specialty stores. Warehouse retailers offer lower prices than discounters in stores that consciously present a "stripped-down" image. Finally, **off-price** or **factory outlets** operate at the low end of the pricing spectrum, marketing merchandise that may be irregular (containing minor imperfections), manufacturers' closeouts, or otherwise purchased at low cost to the off-price retailer. Examples of retailers using various pricing strategies are shown on page 19.

■

LOCATION

Retailers also can be classified according to where they are located. Retailers are most commonly located in the following three geographic locations:

- Downtown central business districts
- Strip developments
- Shopping centers

Some businesses are also located alone throughout a city and in rural areas.

Central Business District Retailers

During the last 25 years many retailers have moved from downtown to suburban locations, following the movement of people from central city locations. Several factors were responsible for this decline, including traffic congestion, lack of parking, crime, and the convenience of suburban shopping. In several cities, urban renewal programs are revitalizing retailing at downtown locations.

Single Store and Strip Retailers

Some retailers locate away from groups of stores because they can obtain store space at reasonable rates and shoppers are willing to travel to single store locations. Retailers also often are found along street and highway segments called **strip developments**. For example, such strips frequently are found at the edge of cities.

Shopping Center Retailers

Shopping centers range from small neighborhood retail store developments with adjacent parking to large, multilevel regional shopping malls. Major features of shopping centers are that they are planned by a developer and space is leased to different retailers. The objective is to obtain a group of retailers that cover a wide range of retail product lines and services.

Define each term and use it in a sentence.

Catalog showrooms
Combination store
Convenience store
Corporate chain
Department store
Direct selling
Discount depart-
    ment store
Factory outlet
Franchising
Full-markup
    retailers
Hypermarkets
Independent retail
    firm

Non-goods services
Non-store retailers
Off-price outlets
Owned-goods services
Rented-goods services
Shopping center
Specialty store
Strip developments
Superdrug store
Supermarket
Superstore
Videotex
Voluntary chain
Warehouse retailers

1. What are five ways in which retail marketing businesses can be classified?

2. Name and describe three types of service retailers.

3. Explain telemarketing and media retailing and give examples of products sold this way.

4. Describe videotex and how it relates to retailing.

5. How does the retailing of services differ from product retailing?

6. What advantages do chain store retailers enjoy over independents?

C·H·A·P·T·E·R

3 *Preparing for a Career in Retail Marketing*

Brenda Donahue had never taken a course in retail marketing or any other business subject. When she graduated from high school, Brenda didn't know what kind of work she wanted to do and had difficulty finding a job. Finally, with the help of her sister, she managed to get a job at the discount department store where her sister worked. After 8 months, she became dissatisfied with the job and decided to look for one that she would like better and would pay her a higher salary.

She found a job as a salesperson at a children's store. Even though the basic pay was the same as at the discount store, she thought that through commissions she might be able to earn more money. After holding this job for a year Brenda realized that she wanted to manage or own a store one day. She wanted more responsibility, a higher income, and an opportunity for career advancement.

Brenda decided to enroll in the retailing management program at her local commu-

nity college, which had a marketing on-the-job training program. During the next 2 years, she worked part-time at the children's store learning the business and completed her 2-year degree program in retail management. Now, after 9 years, she is a partner in the store where she received her on-the-job training. Brenda hopes to buy out her partner when he retires within the next few years.

Yes, Brenda was smart to realize she'd need special training to get a job in the retail marketing business that would both satisfy her and provide the advancement she wanted. If she hadn't seen this, she might have continued moving from job to job without getting any satisfaction from any of them. Or she might even have become unemployed, as were many of her friends. But you are even more fortunate than Brenda, because you are studying retailing now.

YOU HAVE A HEAD START

You have an advantage over Brenda and the million or so young people who will join the labor force each year, because you're learning about jobs and careers while you are still in school. You still have time to learn about yourself, decide what you want from a career, try out different jobs, see how you like them, and investigate various careers.

Careers versus Jobs

When Brenda realized that she wanted to manage or own a children's store, she was deciding on a career goal. It took her more time to choose and prepare for her career than to select the jobs that she'd previously held.

Brenda recognized the difference between holding a job and pursuing a career. A **job** is a collection of tasks, duties, and responsibil-

ities. A **career** is the series of jobs held and the specialized occupational education received by a person during a person's lifetime.

Career Ladders and Lattices

In the course of a career, you will have several different jobs. If you plan each wisely, each job can be satisfying in itself. These jobs can also provide the experience necessary for getting ahead, or climbing up the career ladder. A **career ladder** is made up of a series of jobs at different occupational levels that lead to an occupational goal. The first rung on the career ladder consists of an entry-level job, the base on which to build a career in a particular field. On higher rungs of the ladder are career-level jobs. These jobs require more skill, knowledge, and responsibility than entry-level jobs. Some people find self-fulfillment in career-level jobs. Others use them as rungs on the way to management-level positions.

In a career, not every step is a step up. Sometimes people have to move sideways in order to achieve their career goals. For example, if you wanted to be a store manager,

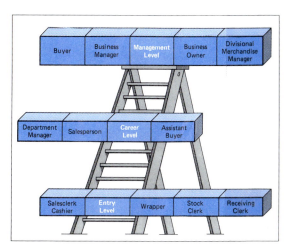

Throughout your career in retailing, you may move up the career ladder and across career lattices.

you would probably need experience in many jobs at the same level. You might begin with an entry-level job in receiving and then move to a job at the same level in sales. This type of sideways move is known as a **career lattice**.

It takes certain competencies and personal qualities to achieve success at each point on the ladder or lattice. In this book, **competency** means knowledge, attitudes, and skills needed on the job in order to be a satisfactory and satisfied worker. Some people learn too late in life that they either are not willing to follow the steps required in pursuing a certain career goal or that they don't have the competencies necessary to achieve that goal. But you have an advantage: You can form your career goal now while you're still in school.

■

EMPLOYMENT OPPORTUNITIES

Retailing is clearly a career field with opportunities for growth and advancement. It is made up of a large number of small businesses, a relatively small number of medium-size firms, and a small number of giant distributors. So, as a source of employment, retailing has many possibilities. The extent of career opportunities is suggested by the following statistics:

■ More than 1.9 million retailers operate in the United States.

■ One of seven working persons is employed in retailing.

■ Nearly one of five employees in retailing is a manager, so many opportunities for advancement are available.

■ By the year 2000, approximately 80 percent of Americans will be employed in marketing and service occupations. Almost 4 million new service jobs will be created. Table

Table 1 on page 24, shows the projected job growth for some of the most common retailing jobs. The demand for salespeople will remain strong despite the increasing automation of selling practices.

Retailing is a field in which you can work almost anywhere you like, because every community has some retail businesses. In a large city or small town there will generally be a retail job for a qualified person. You'll find that the work environment is nearly always pleasant.

Employment opportunities in retailing are excellent for young people of either sex. Advancement is usually rapid if you're qualified and willing to learn, accept responsibility, and work hard. The percentage of supervisory and managerial positions is very high compared to other occupational areas. Most people who become small business owners do so through retailing. Usually retailing is easy to enter, although the risk of failure is often quite high.

On the other hand, any field with all these advantages and as easy to enter as retailing attracts many people. Therefore, as a beginner, you may earn relatively low wages and there may be strong competition from other employees. Your hours and days of employment will depend on the type of job you hold in retailing. If you decide on a job in selling, your hours may be irregular and you may work on weekends.

Is retailing the right area of employment for you? It all depends on your abilities and what you want from your work. Retailing is such a broad occupational area and the jobs are so diverse that there are positions that fit almost any combination of work needs. Your selection of a career goal in retailing will be a matter of identifying the particular broad area that matches your interests and needs best. (Also bear in mind that most of the skills required for success in retail marketing can also be used in many other types of businesses.)

TABLE 1 / PROJECTED 1995 EMPLOYMENT

Occupation	Change in Total Employment (in thousands)	Percentage of Total Job Growth	Percentage Change Since 1985
Salesworker*	1,119	4.4	29.0
Cashiers	774	2.9	47.4
Sales clerk	685	2.7	23.5
Sales representative	386	1.5	29.3

Source: U.S. Bureau of Labor Statistics.
* Referred to in this text as "salespersons." See Chapter 28.

TABLE 2 / RETAIL TRADE EMPLOYMENT 1980–1986

	1980	1986	Change
Total retail trade	15,005,000	16,917,000	11.3%
Department stores	11,730,700	2,009,000	13.9
Variety stores	266,500	223,700	−16.1
Food stores	2,318,700	2,876,000	19.4
Men's and boys' apparel	137,800	108,900	−28.9
Women's ready-to-wear	252,000	391,900	35.7
Furniture stores	271,000	269,400	−0.6
Household appliances	84,000	86,300	2.7
Eating and drinking places	2,191,000	5,746,000	262.2
Drug stores	426,000	556,300	30.6

Source: U.S. Department of Commerce, *U.S. Industrial Outlook, 1986* (Washington, D.C.: U.S. Government Printing Office, 1977), p. 57-1; and U.S. Department of Labor, *Employment and Earnings* (Washington, D.C.: U.S. Government Printing Office, June 1986), pp. 69–70.

■

BROAD AREAS OF RETAIL MARKETING

Retail occupations can be grouped into five broad areas, or divisions, corresponding to the operating divisions of many retail businesses.

These are as follows:

1. Merchandising
2. Promotion
3. Operations
4. Finance and control
5. Personnel

Merchandising

Merchandising deals with the buying and selling of goods and services. Throughout this book you will hear about providing the customer with the right goods and services at the right place, at the right time, at the right price, and in the right quantities. Merchandising is a highly people-oriented area that includes occupations such as salesperson, buyer, fashion coordinator, and merchandise manager. Do you think any of these occupations seem right for you? Merchandising will be discussed further in Chapters 51–57. Chapters 28–37 discuss personal selling in more detail.

There are five broad areas of retailing. In which area would you like to work?

Promotion

Any activity that helps build sales is a form of **promotion**. Advertising, display, special promotions, and publicity all fit into this area. People in the sales promotion area are creative. Are you inclined to be creative? Do you like to draw, write, take photographs, and think up ideas? If you do, then promotion could be the area in retailing that matches your aptitudes. Promotion is presented in greater detail in Chapters 38–46.

Operations

The **operations** area involves activities related to operation of the physical plant and the physical handling of merchandise (for example, receiving and marking). It also involves responsibility for such services as delivery, adjustments, alterations, security, maintenance, supplies, fixtures, and equipment. Operations personnel set the stage for the sale. How do you feel about working behind the scenes in a store? Are you good at working with equipment? If your answer is "yes," then operations might be the retailing area that you'd like to investigate further as you read Chapters 47–50.

Finance and Control

The **finance and control** area relates to the management of income and expenditures. Finance and control could be your opportunity in retailing if you enjoy working with figures. Workers in this area deal with activities such as financing the business, accounting, budgeting, cashiering, customer credit and collections, cost control, expense control, office management, and other operations that involve money. You will have an opportunity to learn more about finance and control in Chapters 57–65.

Personnel

Workers in the **personnel** area are responsible for the selection, training, placement, advancement, and welfare of all employees. The area includes employee relations, counseling, health and welfare benefits, and executive development. If you like to work with people, this area would be a good place for you to begin your career in retailing. Personnel-related topics are covered in various parts of this book, including Chapters 19–27.

■

STEPS TO FOLLOW

Retailing has other attractive features apart from the variety of jobs that it can offer you. It is easy to gain entrance into the retail field. You may not have to pass a required entrance examination, spend years studying, or get a college degree. However, to advance to management positions in large firms, it may be necessary to obtain a professional degree. There are many ways for you to prepare for a career in retailing.

You can apply for an entry-level job without any formal preparation and depend only on the training provided by your employer. That has been the common practice in the past and it is still common today. The advantage of this approach is immediate employment. Limited opportunity for growth and advancement is the major drawback.

A better way to launch your retailing career is to build a sound foundation through formal retail marketing instruction in school. During such training you can test your interests and abilities as well as gain an insight into the satisfactions and way of life associated with the areas of retailing. In this way, you can develop and evaluate a more realistic career plan. This career plan can serve to guide you and perhaps motivate you to study further if you decide that a career in retail marketing will satisfy your interest, aptitudes, and work needs.

To start your retail training in high school, you can participate in the marketing education program. Some of these programs provide opportunities for students to enter into supervised on-the-job training that combines classroom and part-time job experience. When you graduate, you can either enter full-time employment or enter a postsecondary marketing education program.

At the post-high school level, many communities offer programs in marketing education through community colleges and technical institutes. These institutions stress preparation for middle-level management and usually specialize in fields such as food marketing, fashion merchandising, wholesaling, real estate, insurance, and hotel-motel management. Many local school districts, colleges, and universities offer adult education courses through day and/or evening classes to update and upgrade the skills of people who are already employed.

Your success in retail marketing will depend a great deal on your willingness to prepare for a career. As you study this book, try to picture yourself in the occupations associated with the aspect of retailing being discussed. Think about each occupation, what

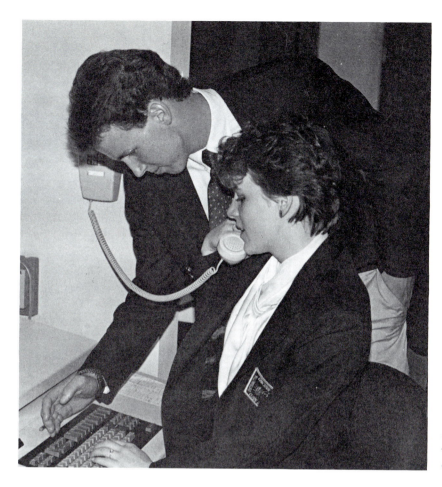

Your high school marketing education program, including such activities as membership in DECA (Distributive Education Clubs of America), can give you a solid foundation on which to build a career in retail marketing.

it involves, what it requires from you, and how it matches your interests, aptitudes, and lifestyle needs.

TRADE TALK

Define each term and use it in a sentence.

Career	Job
Career ladder	Merchandising
Career lattice	Operations
Competency	Personnel
Finance and control	Promotion

CAN YOU ANSWER THESE?

1. What is the best way to launch a career in retailing?

2. What percentage of the American workforce will be employed in the field of marketing by the year 2000?

3. What is the best way to launch a career in retail marketing?

4. What are the five broad areas of retail marketing?

5. What will your success in the field of retail marketing depend upon?

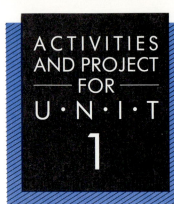

RETAIL MARKETING CASE

The climate-controlled shopping mall offering a vast array of merchandise and prices has become a favorite American shopping place. In 1976, however, Sol and Robert E. Price began a different kind of retailing in San Diego. They created a warehouse operation where shoppers contend with drafts when the weather is cool and with stuffy humidity when it is hot.

Workers scoot around the floor on electric dollies, moving in boxes of merchandise. Customers take their purchases to checkout lines. There are no charge accounts, and no credit cards are accepted. But the warehouse store offers rock-bottom prices.

The primary market of the Price Club was the small business person who did not have an efficient way of buying many items wholesale, and government employees.

A typical Price Club has 100,000 square feet and covers about 2.3 acres. It stocks only 4000 items at one time, which is one-tenth of the products carried by a K mart store. Brands change from week to week, depending on the best buys the Price Club management can find.

The limited selection has made for very efficient retailing. An average retailer will turn over inventory four times a year, but the Price Club will turn over inventory between 15 and 18 times a year. Merchandise can be sold at 20 to 40 percent below the prices offered by supermarket and discount stores. Some Price Club stores are doing ten times the volume of the average discount store.

In the 1980s a dozen other companies including Zayre, Wal-Mart, and Pay-n-Save opened warehouse outlets. Membership clubs can now be found in about 50 percent of the 100 largest markets in the country.

1. What are the keys to success of warehouse clubs?

2. Make a list of the many different types of retail outlets where a consumer can buy the following items in your community or shopping area: stereos, prescription drugs and over-the-counter medicines, toys, jewelry, clothes, and food.

3. What factors influence where a consumer will buy each of the items above (price, service, quality, etc.)?

PROJECT: PLANNING YOUR CAREER

YOUR PROJECT GOAL

Given the desire to identify your goals, list and describe five possible careers in retailing that might help you fulfill your personal goals.

PROCEDURE

1. On a separate sheet of paper, list the following questions under the major heading, "Interests." Leave 3 inches of space, for your interests may change and you will want to record these changes.

    a. Which school subjects do you like best? Why do you prefer them?

    b. Which school subjects do you like least? Why do you dislike them?

    c. What hobbies and leisure-time activities do you enjoy?

    d. Which extracurricular school activities do you especially like to take part in? Why do you enjoy them?

    e. Are there any extracurricular activities in which you are not taking part but would like to do so? Why?

2. Arrange an appointment with your guidance counselor to achieve the following purposes:

    a. Obtain from your counselor information about your interests or aptitudes that may assist you in learning more about yourself.

    b. Discuss with your counselor what you can do to learn about your interests and aptitudes.

    c. Make plans for carrying out the recommendations of your guidance counselor in order to learn more about yourself and your possible career choices.

3. On an additional sheet of paper headed "Goals," leave approximately 3 inches of space for each of the following:

    a. List five or six goals that you want to achieve in a career.

    b. Arrange these goals in order of importance to you.

    c. Explain why you feel that each of the goals is important to you and why some are more important than others.

4. On an additional sheet of paper, write the heading, "Potential Careers."

    a. List these career goals toward which you might like to work. At least one of these should be in the field of retail marketing. (Note: *The Occupational Outlook Handbook* and *The Dictionary of Occupational Titles*, career literature, and discussions with retailers, the marketing education teacher-coordinator, your teachers, and personnel at the state employment service may be of help to you in selecting these goals.)

    b. Prepare a list of advantages and disadvantages and an explanation of the future opportunities of each of the career positions you selected.

Note: This project is related to Chapter 6 of this book, which you may want to look at now. Be sure to save this project for use with the project in Unit 2.

EVALUATION

Your plan will be evaluated on neatness and completeness of the information that you are able to gather and record about your interests, aptitudes, goals, and potential career.

U·N·I·T 2

STARTING YOUR CAREER

4 Getting a Job in Retail Marketing

Paul Gibson was less than 200 feet away from Lorenzo Computer Sales and Service in the Palm Tree Shopping Center. As he walked in the shadows of the buildings, perspiration spread over the palms of his hands. He went over his appointment for what seemed like the hundredth time: owner . . . Mr. Terrence Lorenzo . . . 3:00 p.m. . . . 315 Palm Tree Avenue.

For nearly all job applicants, the first try is a fuzzy blend of faces, forms, pens, rooms, and butterflies. And Paul's experience was no exception. "I can remember looking at my application," he said later, "and thinking nobody could be more scared than Paul Gibson." Yet he was confident because he had prepared carefully for this day.

Paul was interviewed and tested and was hired for the job he wanted. What did Paul Gibson do to help ensure that he would be successful in getting that job?

CHOOSING THE TYPE OF RETAIL BUSINESS

First, Paul studied the various types of retail businesses that would give him the satisfaction he wanted. He asked himself questions such as "Which kind of retail business will help me advance toward my career goal?" When answering this question, Paul kept in mind the types of products and services sold, the experiences offered, and the level of customer service required; these would determine to some extent the type of people with whom he would be working. How did Paul go about finding out which type of retail business was best for him? Factors such as the following are important in helping you choose the type of retail business that's right for you.

Past Work Experience

Retail experience—part-time or full-time—will help you identify the kind of work you like best. For example, if you've worked part-time as a salesperson during the Christmas season, that can be a valuable experience.

If you're looking for part-time jobs in retailing, naturally you want to work in the kinds of retail businesses that interest you most. But some businesses have more part-time jobs than others. In general, department stores, supermarkets, and fast food businesses hire the largest number of part-time staff.

Paul studied marketing education in high school, so he had opportunities to learn about careers in marketing and to work part-time in the school store. In the school store, he learned how to order, stock, display, and sell various types of merchandise to his classmates. He also learned how to use a computer to keep a record of the inventory.

Interests, Hobbies, and Education

You can use your interests, hobbies, and education as a guide to the kind of job that will give you the greatest rewards and satisfactions. A hobby often gives you special knowledge and skills that you can put to good use in retailing. An interest in flowers or gardening may lead to a job in a florist shop. An interest in fashion may lead to a position in a dress shop. An interest in mechanics may lead to a job in an auto-accessories store.

In what courses in school have you been successful? You might be able to use them successfully in some jobs. For example, did you develop an understanding of the principles of color and design in art courses? If so, you can use these skills in interesting positions in merchandise display, advertising, and selling. Accounting and mathematics courses may bring out an aptitude for figures that can be used in retailing.

Paul had learned from his marketing education experience that he wanted to run a computer store someday. But first, Paul knew, he had to learn how to be a good employee.

Benefits Offered

When you are choosing a place to work, you should become familiar with the wages, working conditions, and various benefits (vacations, retirement, hospitalization, and life insurance) offered. The opportunity to advance on the job, to learn, and to gain valuable experience should be considered ahead of other factors. But the benefits offered may be a deciding influence if everything else is nearly equal. Some firms offer excellent training courses and employee development and promotion programs. Accepting few benefits and a small salary in the beginning can be justified if you gain good experience that may be used later to obtain a better position or eventually start your own business.

MAKING THE EMPLOYMENT CONTACT

Once you have narrowed the list of possible jobs to the ones that interest you most, consider ways to contact prospective employers. There are many ways to go about locating the job you would like to have. A recent survey of employees showed that the five leading job sources were:

1. Hearing about the job from friends, relatives of employees, and teachers
2. Applying for a job without knowing if the opening was available
3. Reading newspaper advertisements
4. Visiting a state employment job service agency
5. Visiting a private employment agency

Let Friends Help

Is it unreasonable to ask friends or relatives to let you know about job openings? Some people think so, feeling that they don't need help or that using "pull" is wrong. Letting friends help you is not necessarily using pull—most jobs are obtained only if the applicants really merit them. An introduction or recommendation from a mutual friend is simply one way of meeting the employer. It is, therefore, wise to allow friends to assist you when they have contacts that you don't have.

Among those friends is your marketing education instructor. Paul Gibson knew that his marketing education teacher, Mr. Spano, was well acquainted with many of the business leaders in the community. Some of these leaders had visited the marketing education class as guest speakers.

Prepare a Letter of Application

A **letter of application** is a written request applying for a job. A properly prepared letter of application is one of the best methods of finding out if a particular firm has a current or anticipated job opening. Employers may receive hundreds of letters of application. But they select only a few of the best candidates for interviews, basing their selection on the candidates' letters of application.

First, employers look for letters that are attractive. The importance of this first impression cannot be stressed too much. Second, employers look for attention to the following points when reading the letter:

■ Is it free from errors in grammar, spelling, and punctuation?
■ Is it free from typing errors?
■ Is it a fair presentation of the applicant's strengths and what he or she has to offer?

Paul had prepared the first copy of his letter of application for Mr. Spano, his marketing education teacher-coordinator. You can also ask business or English teachers or business people to examine your letters of application and offer suggestions for improvement. A copy of Paul's letter of application is shown on page 33.

Check the Help Wanted Advertisements

The **help wanted advertisements** in the local newspapers are very good sources of information about retailing jobs. The help wanted columns contain many **blind ads**, which are ads that give only a post office box number and do not identify the employer. Such advertisements protect the employer from having to interview many unqualified people.

Following the directions in the advertisement is considered very important by the employer. For example, don't telephone in response to an advertisement unless the ad directs you to do so.

Check With Employment Agencies

There are several types of employment agencies that will help you find a job. The largest public agencies are the employment services operated by state governments in cooperation with the federal government. They are well informed of the employment picture both locally and statewide.

Most cities have one or more private employment agencies that are good sources of jobs. Private employment agencies operate to make a profit. The job hunter or the employer pays the agency a fee, usually a percentage of the first year's salary. When dealing with a private agency, be very sure that you understand who is to pay the fee and how much is being charged.

■

HANDLING THE INTERVIEW

To convince an employer that it will be to the advantage of the company to hire you, you must demonstrate your interest in the job and make the interviewer aware of your talents and capabilities. The interviewer will

```
                                        62-64 Almeria Boulevard
                                        Dallas, TX 75200
                                        March 18, 19--


        Mr. Terrence Lorenzo
        Lorenzo Computer Store
        315 Palm Tree Avenue
        Dallas, Texas 75200

        Dear Mr. Lorenzo:

        Please consider my application for a position with your firm.  I've had
        special training in the high school marketing education program and ex-
        perience in the school store.  This training, combined with my interest
        in computers, makes me an enthusiastic candidate for a job with the
        Lorenzo Computer Store.

        You will see from my personal data sheet, enclosed, that I have enrolled
        in such high school courses as business data processing, marketing, re-
        tailing, and the Marketing Education Project Laboratory to help me pre-
        pare to pursue my career goal.

        I would appreciate an interview with you, at your convenience, to dis-
        cuss my qualifications personally.  Please call me at 555-9362 any
        weekday evening between 7 and 9 to arrange an appointment.  I am looking
        forward to hearing from you.

                                        Sincerely yours,

                                        Paul E. Gibson

                                        Paul E. Gibson

        Enclosure
```

This letter may serve as a model as you develop your own letter of application.

begin to form an impression of you from the moment you meet. Here are a few tips to help you make that impression a favorable one.

Apply in Person

Never apply for a job by telephone unless you are instructed by an employer to do so. While you can sometimes make an appoint-ment by telephone, it's better to show up in person. You will usually be told whom to see. If you're not, ask for the employment or personnel office. When going for the inter-view, always go alone—never take a friend or relative with you. If you bring someone along, an interviewer might get the impres-sion that you lack self-confidence and inde-pendence. And that's not a good first impres-sion.

Make a Good First Impression

No matter what kind of job you are applying for, dress appropriately for the type of business. Avoid outfits that are too casual, too formal, or that call attention to themselves. Clean, freshly pressed clothes are a must. Of course, all interviewees should be immaculately clean. One way to determine whether or not you look right is to go to a place where you would like to work. Notice how the workers there look.

If you look right and know it and if you feel good, the chances are that you will also act right. Acting right means many things. It means walking with a firm, sure step—not shambling along with stooped shoulders. It means sitting straight—not slouching. And it means being able to read or sit quietly until your turn for an interview comes—not whistling or talking. It may mean just being patient and not looking bored if you have to wait.

Additional ways to make a good first impression include arriving 5 to 10 minutes early and being respectful to the receptionist and interviewer. Study company brochures, promotional materials, or catalogs if they are available in the reception room. You may be able to comment on these materials during the job interview.

Prepare a Personal Data Sheet

One of the best ways to present your talents and interests is by using a **personal data sheet**, or **resume**. This is an outline of information about you as a potential employee. It presents such facts as your name, address, and telephone number. And it describes your career goal, education, work experience, and personal interests. It may also provide the names and addresses of several references—such as teachers, former employers or club advisers—who are willing to discuss your work. Some applicants simply use the line "References furnished on request." A copy of Paul's well-planned personal data sheet is shown on page 35. Be sure that your personal data sheet is neatly typed. Ask someone to proofread the data sheet to eliminate any errors.

Bring a copy of your personal data sheet to the interview, even if you have previously submitted one to the employer. If you are asked to fill out an application, you will find it convenient to have the facts already written out. Personal data sheets also provide employers with information that they could not obtain from an application form alone. In a large company, the interviewer may not have seen your personal data sheet before the interview.

Handle the Application Form With Care

As a job applicant, you will nearly always be asked to fill out the official application form of the firm. A **job application form** asks the applicant for information similar to that provided in a personal data sheet. Take this form seriously. Your qualifications may be judged by the care with which you complete it. Failure to follow directions or carelessness in completing the form has cost many applicants a chance at a job.

Interviewers use the completed form as a source of information from which to ask pertinent questions concerning education, experience, and personal data. So information on the form should be complete and accurate. Your application form remains a permanent record in the files of the firm, and falsifying it, purposely or through carelessness, is a dangerous practice that can leave a bad mark on your record.

As a job applicant, you'll usually be asked to provide names of people to act as references. Courtesy demands that you ask such people in advance for permission to use their names. Double-check that you use the correct spelling of their names. Although a friend can be listed as a character reference, it is better to list people who know and will hon-

```
                        Paul E. Gibson

                    62-64 Almeria Boulevard
                      Dallas, TX 75200
                       (214) 555-9362


      CAREER GOAL

      Computer store manager

      EDUCATION

      Will be graduated from Monterey High School, June 6, 19--, with a major
      in marketing education
      Business subjects studied:  business data processing, general business,
      marketing, retailing, Marketing Education Project Laboratory.

      EXPERIENCE

      Salesperson and Inventory Control Specialist:  Marketing Education
      School Store, Monterey High School, 19 Columbine Boulevard, Dallas,
      Texas, 75200, September 19-- to June 19--

      ACTIVITIES AND INTERESTS

      Computer Club-president
      Distributive Education Clubs of America-vice president of local chapter
      Monterey High School football team-comanager
      Hobbies include computer games and football

      REFERENCES

      Mr. Harold O'Shea (neighbor), owner, Lincoln Drugstore,
      1094 Hazelwood Drive, Dallas, Texas 75200
      Mr. Harlowe Davis (principal), Monterey High School,
      19 Columbine Boulevard, Dallas, Texas 75200
      Mr. Jose Spano (marketing education teacher-coordinator),
      Monterey High School, 19 Columbine Boulevard, Dallas, Texas 75200
```

Your personal data sheet summarizes your qualifications. Organize the information in a way that will market your abilities.

estly say what you can do. The reference who can only say, "Well, he's a really nice guy" or "She's a pleasant girl" does the applicant little good. Above all, don't list a relative as a reference.

Examples of references include teachers, school principals, neighbors, members of the clergy, counselors, and employers. If you leave one job and go to another to better

yourself, ask your former employer to serve as a reference for you. This is a good way to keep your reference list current.

Here are some tips to keep in mind as you prepare an application form:

■ Carefully read everything on the application before starting to fill in the blanks. You will avoid making mistakes and give the impression of being a careful worker. For names, dates, and correct spelling, refer to your personal data sheet.

■ Neatly print on the form with a pen unless directions tell you otherwise.

■ Answer every question that applies to you. For those that do not apply, write the word "none" or draw a line in the blank to show that you didn't overlook it.

■ Ask the person who gave you the application form any questions that you may have about it, for example, whether you may use abbreviations.

■ List all types of education, on-the-job training, or hobbies that have given you skills for any type of work for which you are applying.

■ Accurately and completely describe your previous work experience, because employers prefer to hire applicants with skill, ability, and experience.

A copy of Paul Gibson's completed application is shown on page 37.

Be Sharp for the Interview

When you are called into the interviewer's office, move in with poise and confidence. If you receive an offer for a handshake, make it a firm one, but don't take the lead. Don't sit down until you are asked. When seated, try to sit up straight with both hands in front of you. When you speak, try to speak clearly and enunciate carefully. Take time to explain your statements so that your interviewer understands you fully. You may be expected to respond to a wide variety of questions about the business, yourself, and your future plans. So try to be prepared for questions such as the following:

■ Why do you want to work for this company?
■ Why do you like retailing?
■ What kind of work do you want?
■ Would you rather sell or be in a nonselling position?
■ Why do you think you are qualified for the job for which you are applying?

■ What job would you like to have 5 years from today?
■ What can you do for us?
■ What salary do you expect?
■ What leadership positions did you have in school?
■ Have you belonged to school and community youth organizations?
■ Do you have any health problems?

The personal qualities that most employers look for are sincerity and earnestness. They also look for a degree of confidence. But remember, too much confidence may seem like conceit to many people. You may find the following suggestions helpful: Be pleasant and friendly during the interview. Show that you are interested in learning and in a future in retailing. Stress your strong points but do not hide your weaknesses. Emphasize your reliability and dependability. Don't be afraid to ask the interviewer a question if you have a concern. Last, recognize when the interview is at an end, thank the interviewer, and leave promptly.

A survey of employers showed that the ten leading reasons given for rejecting job applicants after the job interview were:

1. Little interest or poor reason for wanting a job.
2. Applicant has a past history of job hopping.
3. Inability of applicant to communicate during job interview.
4. Poor health record.
5. Immaturity (other than chronological age).
6. Sloppy personal appearance.
7. Poor manners and irritating mannerisms.
8. Unpleasant personality
9. Lack of job-related skills.
10. Job application poorly filled out.

Be Prepared for Tests

Some large firms give tests in addition to interviews. Often, tests of basic arithmetic

EMPLOYMENT APPLICATION

NAME _Paul_ _E._ _Gibson_ ADDRESS _62-64 Almeria Blvd._ APT. NO. _—_
First Name   Middle Initial   Last Name

SOCIAL SECURITY NO

CITY _Dallas_ STATE _TX_ ZIP _75200_ AREA CODE _214_ TEL # _555-9362_ | 0 0 0 | 1 0 | 1 0 0 0 |

AVAILABILITY:

	M	T	W	T	F	S	S
From	5	5	5	5	5	9	—
To	9	9	9	9	9	9	—

ARE YOU LEGALLY ABLE TO BE EMPLOYED IN THE U.S.? ☒YES ☐NO

PART TIME ☒HOURS FULL TIME ☐AVAILABLE:

HOW FAR DO YOU LIVE FROM STORE? _1 ½ miles_

HOW WILL YOU GET TO WORK? _Bus or Walk_

SCHOOL MOST RECENTLY ATTENDED:
NAME _Monterey High School_ ADDRESS _19 Columbine Blvd._

TEACHER OR COUNSELOR _Jose Spano_ LAST GRADE COMPLETED _11_ GRADE POINT AVERAGE _3.1_

GRADUATED? ☐YES ☒NO NOW ENROLLED? ☒YES ☐NO

MOST RECENT EMPLOYMENT

COMPANY _Monterey High School_ ADDRESS _19 Columbine Blvd._ PHONE # _555-4566_
POSITION _Bookstore_ _Salesperson in_ SUPERVISOR _J. Spano_ DATES WORKED: FROM _9/7/--_ TO _Present_
WAGE _$3.10 per hr._ REASON FOR LEAVING _Graduation_

COMPANY _—_ ADDRESS _____ PHONE # _____
POSITION _____ SUPERVISOR _____ DATES WORKED: FROM _____ TO _____
WAGE _____ REASON FOR LEAVING _____

U.S. MILITARY:
SERVED? ☐YES ☒NO

ARE YOU A MEMBER OF AN ACTIVE RESERVE OR NATIONAL GUARD UNIT? ☐YES ☒NO

PHYSICAL:
ANY HEALTH OR PHYSICAL LIMITATIONS WHICH COULD AFFECT YOUR EMPLOYMENT? ☐YES ☒NO

IF ANY SUCH HEALTH OR PHYSICAL LIMITATIONS EXIST, PLEASE EXPLAIN _—_

DURING THE PAST 7 YEARS, HAVE YOU EVER BEEN CONVICTED OF A FELONY? ☐YES ☒NO

IF YES, DESCRIBE IN FULL _____

BONDING INFORMATION
1. Have you ever been short in your accounts in your present or past employment? ..... ☐Yes ☒No
2. Has any company ever refused to issue or carry a Bond for you? . . . . ☐Yes ☒No
3. Have you ever been discharged from any employment? . . . . ☐Yes ☒No

I HEREBY BIND MYSELF, my heirs, executors and administrators to indemnify and keep indemnified and/or reimburse THE INSURANCE COMPANY for any and all loss, costs, and expenses incurred or sustained by it or for which, by reason of any act of mine, it may become liable under this bond or any other bond issued by it.

UNDER STATE LAW an employer may not require or demand any applicant for employment or prospective employment or any employee to submit to or take a polygraph, lie detector or similar test or examination as a condition of employment or continued employment. Any employer who violates this provision is guilty of a misdemeanor and subject to a fine not to exceed $100.

I CERTIFY THAT THIS INFORMATION IS ACCURATE AND COMPLETE to the best of my knowledge.

DATE _4/15/--_ SIGNATURE _Paul E. Gibson_

This application expires in 30 days.

In case of emergency phone _555-9362_

Complete a job application neatly and accurately. It represents you to the prospective employer.

are used to eliminate those who are weak in this skill. Tests of clerical ability, such as number matching, may be given to applicants for nonselling positions. Tests of "manual dexterity" (the ability to use one's hands skillfully) are sometimes used in selecting people for positions. A few firms use tests to judge aptitude for leadership and honesty.

Do the best you can on such tests, because they are another way in which the employer is evaluating you. Remember that your interview, personal data sheet, job application form, and test results are the ways you have of presenting yourself to the employer.

A GOOD LAST IMPRESSION

Once the interview and testing procedure have been completed, you have an opportunity to make a good last impression. When the interview is over, rise and shake hands with the interviewer and express your appreciation for this opportunity. On your way out of the office, also thank the receptionist.

Within a day or two of your interview, write a short, sincere thank-you letter or note to your prospective employer to express your appreciation.

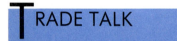

TRADE TALK

Define each term and use it in a sentence.

Blind ad   Help wanted advertisements

Job application form   Personal data sheet
Letter of application   Resume

CAN YOU ANSWER THESE?

1. Why is it particularly wise to use a letter of application?

2. What are the six tips for preparing an application form?

3. Is it wise to have friends help you find a job in retailing? If so, why?

4. What kinds of questions may be asked of you during a job interview?

5. List several kinds of unsuitable job interview behaviors.

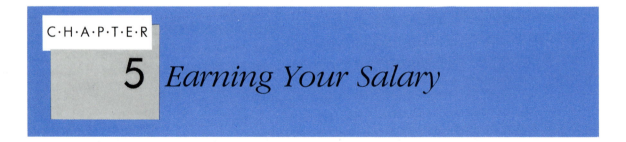

C·H·A·P·T·E·R 5 *Earning Your Salary*

Paul Gibson was looking forward to Friday because it was payday. This was indeed a special day for Paul, because for the first time he would receive a paycheck.

As Paul slowly opened the envelope, his mind wandered for a second and focused on the new printer he wanted to buy for his computer. As he finally got the envelope open, he noticed that he had both a check and a paycheck stub. "Hmmm," he said to himself, "this is complicated—what do all

these numbers mean? Why doesn't my check include all the money I thought I had earned? It's more than $35 short!" Paul then began to recall some of the things that he had learned in school, and again when he was hired, about federal and state taxes, Social Security deductions, the various wage plans, and how pay is computed.

This chapter focuses on these and similar items related to getting paid and earning your salary.

HOW EMPLOYEES ARE PAID

Several methods are used to pay retail employees. These methods vary according to the type of business, the kind of work done, quantity and quality of work, and the amount of responsibility carried. For example, the amount of money earned by those engaged in sales work usually depends on how much they sell. Retail marketing employees who don't sell directly to customers are usually paid an hourly, weekly, or monthly wage.

Straight Salary

A beginner like Paul is likely to be paid a straight salary, which is usually received in the form of a check every week or every other week. A **straight salary** means being paid a fixed number of dollars an hour for a fixed number of hours a week—for example, $4.00 per hour for a 40-hour week. So if Paul works 40 hours a week at $4.00 per hour, his earnings amount to $160. If he works more than 40 hours, he may earn $1\frac{1}{2}$ times his regular rate for every hour over 40 hours. Suppose that Paul worked 48 hours one week. The example below shows how his wages would be figured:

40 hours at $4.00 an hour	$160
8 hours at $6.00 an hour ($1\frac{1}{2}$ X $4.00)	48
Total week's earnings	$208

Most nonselling employees—and many salespeople—are paid by the straight salary method. Many beginning employees in retailing start out by receiving the federal minimum wage. The **federal minimum wage**, which is covered by the Federal Labor Standards Act, is the lowest amount that businesses operating in more than one state are allowed to pay their employees. This federal law also established 40 hours per week as the maximum number of hours that people can work at their basic wage rates. For any additional time worked, a worker must be paid time and a half. Most states also have minimum wage laws. These laws apply to firms that do business within a state (mostly small firms) that do not come under the federal law.

Straight Commission

Some salespeople are not paid a salary at all. They are paid entirely on commission. In retailing, a **commission** is a percentage of the total amount of sales that the employee makes during the employee's pay period. If, for example, your commission is 5 percent of sales and you sell $8000 worth of merchandise or services in a week, your total income for the week is $400. Commission rates vary, but a rate of between 5 and 8 percent is common when that is the only pay you receive. This is known as **straight commission**. Straight commission selling occurs most often in furniture stores, appliance stores, automobile dealerships, and other establishments that carry high-priced merchandise. Insurance and real estate agents are examples of salespeople in service businesses who usually sell on straight commission.

Salary Plus Commission

As an incentive to increase sales, many salespeople are paid a straight salary plus a commission. Although commission rates vary, 1 percent is most common for merchandising employees who also receive a straight salary.

Assume that a salesperson's regular salary is $200 a week plus 2 percent commission and that the salesperson sells merchandise or services amounting to $3000 during the week. The example below shows how the salary is figured:

Regular salary	$200
Commission (2 percent of $3000 total sales)	60
Total week's earnings	$260

Quota

Under the **quota**, salespeople are paid a straight salary but are also given a bonus for sales exceeding a predetermined quota. The quota is set by the store management. Salespeople get a percentage of all sales above that quota. Suppose that a salesperson's quota is $4000 and the bonus is 2 percent. If the salesperson sells $4800 worth of merchandise, he or she draws a bonus on the $800 above the quota, or $16 (2 percent of $800). Of course, the salesperson gets a regular salary, too.

Premium Money

Sometimes salespeople are paid an extra amount for selling a particular item that is hard to sell. This extra amount is sometimes called **premium money** (PM) and is paid in addition to other compensation. (PMs are also called "spiffs" or pin money.)

The amount of the premium for each sale varies—from as little as 10 cents to $200 or more. Premium money gives salespeople an incentive to sell slow-moving merchandise or merchandise that may take an extra effort on the part of the salesperson, such as initialed jewelry that the salesperson must take time to engrave. Sometimes this plan is discouraged by retailers to avoid the risk that customers might be sold something they don't really want, leading to loss of the customer's goodwill.

Fringe Benefits

In addition to wages paid to the employee, retailers also offer several benefits called **fringe benefits**. These are advantages that the company provides for its employees in addition to financial compensation for work. The number of benefits retailers offer varies from one retail establishment to another. Generally speaking, the larger the firm, the more benefits offered. Benefits should be counted as a part of your total income. These benefits may include the following:

■ Employee discounts of from 10 to 20 percent on merchandise and services

Fringe benefits add to the financial compensation provided by a salary. For example, an employer may pay for a medical plan, saving the employees that expense.

■ Medical, dental, and hospitalization insurance
■ Paid vacations (usually 1 week's vacation after 1 year of employment and up to 4 weeks' vacation after several years of employment)
■ Group insurance plans whereby life insurance can be purchased by employees at a lower cost than they could obtain elsewhere
■ Retirement plans whereby the firm and the employee contribute to a fund that will provide an income upon retirement
■ Worker's compensation and unemployment insurance as required by law
■ Social, recreational, and educational activities of various kinds

HOW PAY IS COMPUTED

The amount of money you earn on your job is called **gross pay**. This is the amount earned before anything is subtracted from your check. There are always some deductions from your pay, however. Once all these deductions have been subtracted from your gross pay, you realize your **take-home pay**, or net pay.

Income Tax Deduction

There is a federal law that requires employers to hold back some of each employee's wages for payment of income tax. This is called **withholding tax**. When Paul started to work, he filled out a W-4 form—an Employee's Withholding Allowance Certificate. This form lets his employer know how much of his pay must be withheld for federal income taxes. The amount of federal income tax withheld depends on the amount of money earned and the number of tax exemptions claimed. **Tax exemptions** are allowances for people who rely on the wage earner for food, clothing, and shelter. Every wage earner can claim one exemption for himself or herself. Parents can claim their dependent children. Paul could claim only himself as an exemption.

Anyone who has an income of more than a specified amount a year must file a federal income tax return. This return must be filed by April 15 of the year following that in which the income was earned. Shortly after January 1, wage earners receive from their employers a W-2 form which tells how much they earned and how much tax was withheld. Taxpayers who had more of their income withheld than the amount they owed receive a refund. However, to get these taxes refunded, the wage earner must file a federal income tax return. The money is not refunded automatically.

Taxpayers who owe more than the amount withheld must pay the additional amount due when they file their income tax form. Because Paul started his new job in October, his income for the year was small and therefore more money was withheld than he owed. So Paul should file a federal income tax return to receive a refund for the taxes that were withheld from his October, November, and December paychecks. Many cities and states also have an income tax, and employers are required to withhold income for these taxes also. Employees must file separate returns with the state and/or city.

Social Security Tax Deduction

In addition to income tax, Paul and all other people employed in retailing have to pay **Social Security tax**, which is also referred to as FICA (Federal Insurance Contributions Act). Social Security is a federal program that provides cash payments to workers who retire or become disabled or to the families of deceased workers. Both employees and employers contribute to the fund. The sum of money that is taken out of each employee's paycheck is matched by the employer and sent to the federal government.

Other Deductions

The number of other deductions from your paycheck will usually depend on your wishes. If you decide to participate in the company's retirement plan when you become eligible, a certain amount may be taken from your paycheck for your retirement fund. Whether or not you take out medical or life insurance is usually up to you. Most employees think that it is a bargain and choose to have the cost of the insurance deducted from their pay by their employer. If you belong to a union, you may ask your employer to deduct your union dues from your check. Some employees have the contributions that they make to various community groups, such as the United Fund, deducted regularly from their paychecks.

DOING THE BEST JOB POSSIBLE

Once you have obtained a job and received a few paychecks, you might find yourself catching your breath and wondering, "Where do I go from here?" That's a good question to ask yourself. But on a new job, your most important concern should be how to do the best job possible so that you can truthfully

Period Ending	Hours Worked	Regular	Overtime	Total	Withholding	FICA	Insurance	Other	Total	Amount	Ck. No.
2/9/--	40	390.00	--	390.00	44.00	29.29	12.00	10.00	95.29	294.71	978
		Earnings			Deductions					Net Pay	

Employees Pay Statement
Detach and retain for your records.

Abbott Company
Nashville, TN

- -

Abbott Company
205 West Sixth
Nashville, TN 37202

Payroll
Check   No. 978 $\frac{87-21}{640}$

Feb. 16   19 --

**Pay To
The Order Of** _William Proudfoot_ ——————————————— $ 294.71

Two hundred ninety-four and 71/100--- Dollars

COUNTY BANK
635 South Walnut Street
NASHVILLE, TN 37205

Sharon Knox

⑈0640⑈0021⑈ 324⑈0340⑈

The stub of a paycheck shows all the deductions that affect the amount of an employee's take-home pay.

say, "I earned my salary."

First of all, always be sure you arrive at the job on time. If you work for a large company, check to see which door you should enter, and—if necessary—sign in. Be sure you arrive at work dressed appropriately. Just as soon as possible, learn about all of the company rules and policies. Mr. Lorenzo, Paul's employer, gave him a very simple and useful set of rules concerning his firm.

Handling Mistakes

During the first few weeks on a job, almost everything will be new to you. And you are bound to make mistakes because there are so many things to learn. However, to make as few mistakes as possible, try to listen carefully to instructions from your supervisor. Ask questions if you don't understand what is expected of you. If you do make a mistake, report it to your supervisor. Try to learn from

your mistakes so that you don't make them a second time. But don't get discouraged. Smile, you'll catch on in a while!

Keeping Busy

Often, a supervisor can't tell exactly how long it will take to do a job. Sometimes, as a new employee, you'll complete jobs before your supervisor returns. When this happens, observe the work that experienced employees perform, and as you "learn the ropes," keep your eyes open for work that needs to be done. As you find time, learn to accomplish this work without being told. A supervisor will learn how much work you can do and will assign it as she or he gets to know you better.

Employers do expect a full day's work for a full day's pay. A supervisor will expect you to think for yourself and show an interest in your work by keeping busy.

Accepting Responsibility

You are usually hired to work a predetermined number of hours each week. Sometimes, though, there are a number of small jobs remaining at the end of your work period that you can do without taking much time or effort. If you leave without doing them, your supervisor probably won't complain. But if you stay just a few minutes, finish the job, and leave a clean work area, you can be sure that your efforts will be noticed. Your supervisor will know that you're really interested in your work and will be glad you were hired. Even after the first day, your supervisor may realize that you're a good worker and may be somebody to look at for possible promotion!

Developing Good Work Habits

It's a good idea to ask yourself each day on the job what new things you learned to do, what tasks you learned to do better, and which ones still need improvement. (A task is something you are assigned to do as a part of your job.) Asking for an opinion or for help will show that you are interested in doing your job well and that you are anxious to please. It will also encourage some supervisors to help you advance to a better job.

Extra effort can earn you recognition as a valuable employee.

Remember that for the first few weeks on a new job, you are investing your time and your employer's time, money, and effort in training you. You may have to learn a great deal before you can turn out a full day's work that's equal to the work of most experienced employees. Also, as you do your job, keep in mind that you're building your reputation as a worker. Paul was off to a good start and is now in the process of planning for what he hopes will be a raise and promotion.

TRADE TALK

Define each term and use it in a sentence.

Commission
Federal minimum
  wage
Fringe benefits
Gross pay
Premium money
Quota

Social Security tax
Straight commission
Straight salary
Take-home pay
Tax exemption
Withholding tax

CAN YOU ANSWER THESE?

1. List five examples of possible deductions that can be made from a paycheck and that would therefore decrease take-home pay.

2. What federal taxes are required to be subtracted from your paycheck?

3. Why do some employees prefer to earn a straight commission?

4. What should you do if you do make a mistake?

5. Why should you ask for your supervisor's opinion or assistance?

6 *Planning for Career Advancement*

Setting the stage for a possible promotion begins with your first job. Use the suggestions in this chapter as guides to help you to plan for career advancement.

Like Paul Gibson, many young people first enter the work force in the field of retail marketing. Retailers like Mr. Lorenzo always seem to need fresh and enthusiastic help for sales or stock work. That is how Paul got his start with Lorenzo Computer Sales and Service. He had little selling experience, but his knowledge of computers, his pleasant manner, and his retail marketing class experience landed him the position. At first, he did only stock work. By handling the incoming merchandise he gradually became familiar with the different hardware and software lines Mr. Lorenzo carried. Paul spent most of his free time at home experimenting with his computer and reading computer magazines. He attended all of the weekly sales meetings that he could. He listened carefully to the explanations of the features and benefits of new merchandise. He heard about the problems and successes of the salespeople. Gradually, he began to join in the sessions. He shared his ideas on novel ways to use various computer programs with the group. Paul was promoted to a salesperson. Paul was delighted because he now had the opportunity to earn more money through commissions and bonuses.

Paul found that he enjoyed working with his customers. He got the chance to exhibit his expertise. He guided people in their buying decisions; and most especially, he got hooked on the thrill of satisfying customer's needs. Paul realized that he wanted a career in retail marketing. He confided this ambition to Mr. Lorenzo and asked for suggestions to help achieve this goal. He was advised to take business and marketing courses and to look into the marketing education program at Palm Valley Community College.

Next year Paul plans to take Mr. Lorenzo's advice and enroll in a two-year degree program in marketing at the community college. He will continue to work part-time for Mr. Lorenzo and learn the computer store business in greater detail. Upon graduation he plans to get a job as an assistant manager of a larger computer store. His course work will help prepare him for the various areas of responsibility such as personnel, merchandising, finance and control, operations, and promotion. By the time he is 30, he hopes to own his own business.

Will Paul succeed in achieving his career goal? Will the career plan he developed in the marketing education program ever be fully realized? As President Lyndon Johnson once said, "Dreams give mobility to a purpose." Paul and thousands of young people each year have their dreams, and you can too.

■

QUALITIES NEEDED FOR PROMOTION AND SUCCESS

If Paul were like most workers who are promoted from entry-level jobs, he could have been promoted for a number of reasons. Research has shown that the most common reason people are promoted is because of their ability to perform their entry-level jobs in an efficient and effective manner.

Qualities Needed for Success

To succeed in an entry-level position in retail marketing, you must have the following personal qualities:

- Ability to work with people
- Ability to listen and follow directions
- Honesty and personal integrity
- Determination to follow company policies
- Devotion to job, enthusiasm, initiative, and a positive outlook on life
- Adaptability
- Loyalty to employer
- Determination to stay in the field of retailing
- Willingness to assume responsibility

Qualities Needed for Promotion

If you want to be promoted in retail marketing, you'll need additional qualities. Eight of the most important qualities needed for promotion are as follows:

- Drive to work (produce) at a consistently high level
- Persistence to see a task through to completion (that is, to get the job done!)
- Tenacity to stay with a problem and solve it
- Ability to work rapidly and accurately
- Adaptability to change and ability to work in difficult situations
- Supervisory skills, including ability to manage time and organize work so that things get done
- Skill in using oral and written communications
- Potential for assuming additional responsibility

RETAIL MARKETING JOB OPPORTUNITIES

There is an incredibly wide variety of job opportunities in retailing, a fact that few people, even those engaged in retailing, realize. Here are some of the categories of retail employment with the best opportunities for jobs and self-employment:

- Advertising and display services
- Apparel and accessories
- Automotive and petroleum
- Financial services
- Floristry, farm, and garden supplies
- Food marketing
- Food service marketing
- General merchandise
- Hardware and building materials
- Home furnishing
- Hotel, motel, and lodging services
- Insurance
- Personal and business services
- Real estate
- Recreation
- Transportation and travel

PRODUCT-ORIENTED CAREERS

The four areas of product retailing that employ the largest number of people are:

1. General merchandise
2. Apparel and accessories
3. Automotive and petroleum
4. Food marketing

It makes sense to learn more about the types of jobs at the various employment levels and which jobs offer the greatest promotional opportunities. Note that experience in one field of retailing is usually helpful in other fields. For example, what you've learned as a salesperson in a general merchandise firm would be valuable in a furniture store.

General Merchandise

Today more than 2.6 million people are employed in many types of general merchandise stores, including department stores, discount stores, and mail-order houses. Almost 70 percent of these employees are women. The fastest-growing area of the general merchandise retailing industry is the mail-order category.

As a salesperson in a department store, you'll usually begin in housewares or some other department where a customer needs little assistance. As you gain experience, you'll

Mail-order retailing is a rapidly growing part of the general merchandise retailing and apparel and accessories industries.

move to positions of greater responsibility, selling high-priced items such as furniture.

There are many career ladders in the merchandise retailing area. If you demonstrate that you're a good salesperson, you'll have the opportunity to advance in the field.

Apparel and Accessories

You can find career opportunities in six kinds of apparel and accessory businesses. These are men's and boys' clothing and furnishings, women's ready-to-wear, women's accessories and cosmetics, children's and infant's wear, family clothing, and miscellaneous apparel and accessory businesses.

If you're a successful salesperson, chances are that you'll be promoted to higher-level positions in retailing. In the apparel and accessory field, if you've mastered all the competencies required of a good salesperson, you'll probably be on your way to success. The outlook for women is particularly bright, as more than 65 percent of all employees in the industry are women.

Food Marketing

Food marketing is the nation's largest business, with annual sales reaching an all-time peak each year. The typical American family spends approximately 25 percent of its income on food. Today, the average consumer enjoys more and better food than at any other time. And the increasing number of packaged meals continue to make living easier.

But food marketing is not all that is going on in supermarkets today. Major supermarket chains throughout the country have expanded and diversified their product lines to include general merchandise items. Supermarket shoppers are filling up their shopping carts with hardware, cosmetics, greeting cards, toys, and plants as well as food. This trend toward one-stop convenience shopping continues to provide additional career opportunities for you as the industry grows at a rapid pace.

In this farmers' market, the channel of distribution is direct from producer to consumer.

Another trend is the growing number of specialized food stores and farmer's markets.

Automotive and Petroleum Retailing

There are almost 2 million employees in the retailing area of the automotive and petroleum industry. You might prefer to enter automotive retailing as a salesperson for a tire, battery, and accessory (TBA) store. Some of these outlets are departments or branches of department stores. Others are independent stores.

If you have the ability and desire to continue a career in the tire, battery, and accessory field, you may be able to move to a management-level position. Other higher-level jobs include those of parts buyer or store manager or owner.

The position of automobile salesperson is one of the most common entry-level jobs in automotive retailing.

If you succeed in automobile selling, you'll be financially rewarded. And if you want to step up to management, you may become a

sales manager or, in a large agency, a general manager. If you can raise the necessary capital, you could purchase your own dealership.

■

RETAIL SERVICE-ORIENTED CAREERS

To satisfy consumers, retailers of services must be as enterprising as retailers of products. Successful service retailers are willing to tailor their services to fit their customers' wishes. For example, because of customer demand, a dry-cleaning business might offer clothes repair and alteration services.

Nine of the fastest-growing service career areas will now be explored.

Food Service

Today, the growing trend toward eating out is being met by an increase in the number of restaurants, cafeterias, and drive-ins. In addition, the number of caterers providing food and service for small or large parties has grown. Because of the rapid expansion of the food service industry, the number of jobs in the industry is rising. This could be the retailing area where you'd like to begin your career.

Financial Service

Consumers are demanding more and more financial services from banks, savings and loan associations, insurance companies, stockbrokers, small loan companies, credit unions, and finance firms. Financial service businesses are responding to this demand by increasing both the types of services they provide to the public and the number of retailing functions they perform. Because they must engage in sales promotion to make consumers aware of the benefits they can provide, these businesses can offer you many job opportunities if you're interested in selling financial services.

Recreation and Tourism

Some of the most popular types of recreation and tourism businesses are bowling lanes, boating marinas, golf courses, country clubs, theaters, hobby shops, amusement parks, travel agencies, and travel clubs. These firms continually engage in sales promotion campaigns. Customer reaction is what matters most in recreation and tourism retailing. Your study of retailing can also prepare you for careers in the recreation and tourism services industry.

Transportation Service

One of the main functions of airlines, railroads, bus companies, and car rental firms is to transport the customer from one place to another. These firms, however, also recommend accommodations, arrange seating space, sell tickets, and make adjustments in travel arrangements. All these are retailing functions. The career opportunities for you in transportation services are extensive and previous retail experiences can be directly related to this career field.

But service businesses that transport travelers are only part of the overall transportation picture. A transportation network made up of various freight carriers stretches across this country. Part of the freight carrier's business is the retail marketing of transportation services. There are millions of jobs in thousands of companies that are involved in such diverse activities as transporting goods by air, rail, truck, and water. These include dispatchers, route planners, and sales representatives.

Lodging Service

Americans travel extensively for both business and pleasure, and the lodging industry has grown to meet their need for places to stay. The industry must provide dining and recreation facilities as well as sleeping rooms. In fact, only half the income of a large hotel or motel comes from the sale of lodging

THE RED CROSS COURSE CATALOG

A Guide to Health, Safety, Youth, and Life-style Courses

First Aid

A Healthy Life-style

Swimming and Lifesaving

Cardiopulmonary Resuscitation (CPR)

Boating Safety, Boating Fun

Family Health

Courses for Young People

Instructor Training Program

American Red Cross

The American Red Cross, a not-for-profit organization, is marketing a service when it distributes this course catalog.

space. The rest comes from providing food, beverages, and recreation. And it also comes from supplying services such as laundry and dry cleaning and from the shops that rent space on the premises. All these services will provide job opportunities for you when you have completed your training.

Not all travelers sleep indoors. Millions of people go on camping trips each year. Another retailing market is flourishing among travelers with trailers who rent space in state and private parks.

Repair and Maintenance Services

The more customers buy mechanical products, the more they need repair services. They need people to fix cars, computers, and television sets. Most repair service workers are skilled; they have had mechanical or technical training. When they meet customers, they are also selling their firm's services. Also, repair service workers have an important role to play in building and maintaining customer goodwill because they are often in direct contact with customers. So customers view them not only as repair workers but as the firm itself. During the past few years, there has also been a significant increase in maintenance-type service firms such as car washes and cleaning services. If you'd like a career that combines working with things and with people, it might be worthwhile to investigate further the repair and maintenance area of retailing.

Rental Services

Not very many years ago, a consumer could rent only a house or apartment. Today there are service businesses that specialize in renting almost anything: cars, trucks, ten-ton cranes—or paintings to hang on the living room wall or plants and fish tanks or videotape equipment.

Retail rental services must carry the products and equipment local customers want, or they will soon be out of business. They advertise continually so that potential customers—who often decide that they need something on the spur of the moment—will remember the name of the firm and where to obtain the desired rental products and services.

Personal Service

Personal retail service businesses are concerned with individual care. Laundries, nurs-

Businesses offering overnight delivery of letters and packages to retail customers have grown in number in recent years.

ery schools, barber shops, health spas and gyms, photography studios, shoe repair shops, and suntanning spas are all examples of personal service businesses. Personal service businesses combine product and service production functions. For example, on the service productions end, dry cleaners employ spotters. On the selling end, they employ salespeople at their counters to meet the customer and sell their service. Does the area of personal services retailing appeal to you? Many of the owners of small businesses today were employees just a few years ago.

CAN YOU ANSWER THESE?

1. List eight important qualities that a person should develop in order to succeed and gain a promotion.
2. What are the four areas of retailing that employ the largest number of people?
3. What is the fastest growing area of general merchandising?
4. Name three services that might be rented.
5. When should you plan for promotion?

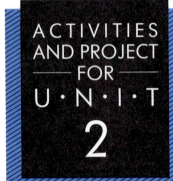

ACTIVITIES AND PROJECT FOR U·N·I·T 2

RETAIL MARKETING CASE

Mary Long owns an older motel on the outskirts of a small city on one of the main highways leading from the west to the east coast of Florida. In recent years, several franchised outlets of major motel chains, notably Holiday Inn and Ramada Inn, have opened in the same general area. With their modern facilities, and especially their toll-free reservation service, they have drastically cut into Mary Long's business.

Mary realizes that to be competitive in terms of facilities would require a major investment in rebuilding and modernizing. Such an investment could not even assure that the competitive problem would be solved, since these chain motels have engendered brand loyalty on a national scale. In defense against the chain motels, some independent motel operators have joined motel associations such as Quality Inns and Best Western Motels. These permit the member firms to benefit from joint advertising expenditures, a recognized national or regional sign and motif, a uniform and carefully maintained reputation for quality and service, some interaction with other motel operators and their problems and solutions, as well as certain managerial and accounting aids. Furthermore, they provide a somewhat similar reservation service to that of the motel chains. However, to join such an association would also require a considerable investment in remodeling an older motel and bringing it up to the standards required for membership.

What would you advise Mary Long to do at this point? Defend your recommendations as persuasively as possible.

PROBLEMS

1. Rule a form similar to the one below. Check the help wanted advertisements in your local newspaper to locate job opportunities in retailing. Then list the current full-time and part-time openings for a person like yourself and the wages currently being offered for beginners of your age and experience. If wages are not listed, indicate this with an (X) symbol. Many job listings may not include wage information.

Job Opening	Beginning Wage

2. Select one of the jobs you have listed that would be consistent with your career goals and prepare a personal data sheet that you could use to apply for the job. Be sure to include the following information:

Name
Address
Telephone
Career goal
Education
Experience
Activities and interests

PROJECT: RETAIL MARKETING CAREER PLAN

YOUR PROJECT GOAL

Using the Unit 1 Project, "Planning Your Career," select the most desirable retailing career for yourself, outline the steps for preparing a career in retail marketing, and prepare a career plan and schedule that you intend to follow as you pursue your career.

PROCEDURE

Before starting this project, you will need the project for Unit 1 entitled "Planning Your Career," which you completed and had evaluated by your instructor.

1. Review the project that you completed for Unit 1 and select a retail marketing career that you, your teacher, and your counselor feel you can realistically pursue successfully.
2. On an additional sheet of paper, write the heading "Jobs and Job Descriptions."
   a. Identify the jobs and the number of different positions you may have to hold during your career.
   b. Prepare a brief description of each of the jobs identified above. You may find the *Dictionary of Occupational Titles* helpful in terms of job information and of how to prepare such a description.
3. Draw a chart or diagram and place each of the jobs identified in Step 2 on it. Attach a tentative timetable and an explanation of the plan you intend to follow as you pursue your career.
4. Hand in this completed project to your instructor together with the project for Unit 1.

EVALUATION

Your career ladder will be evaluated on the completeness of the information that you compiled in Steps 1–3 and on its neatness.

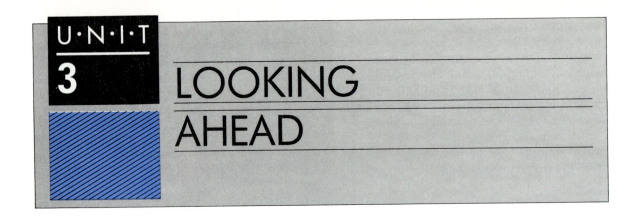

U·N·I·T
3
LOOKING AHEAD

7 *Ownership and Management Opportunities*

What do the following famous businesses have in common: Sears Roebuck and Co., J.C. Penney, Wal-Mart, Holiday Inn, and McDonald's? They all started as very small businesses and grew to corporate giants.

In 1902, with just $500, James Cash Penney opened his first store, The Golden Rule Store, in Kemmerer, Wyoming. This store consisted of one room on the street level and an attic in a wooden building without plumbing. Today, J.C. Penney employs more than 175,000 people and has sales of nearly $14 billion.

In 1954, Ray Kroc talked the McDonald brothers into letting him franchise their restaurant idea nationally. Today, the familiar golden arches of McDonald's can be seen around the world.

Richard Sears started his business career by selling watches to farmers in the Chicago area. Now Sears Roebuck has sales of nearly $41 billion and 465,000 employees worldwide.

Sam Walton, a former J.C. Penney employee, started Wal-Mart stores in 1962 in Bentonville, Arkansas. By 1986, Mr. Walton was listed as the richest man in America.

How much do you know about the retailers in your community? How did they get started? How are their businesses organized?

In many respects, the small business owner represents what people around the world believe to be the typical American. These people think that our business owners possess the basic American traits of independence, self-expression, initiative, inventiveness, industriousness, persistence, and dedication to free enterprise.

Small businesses make up 97 percent of all U.S. businesses. More than 50 percent of all small businesses in America are retail or service businesses. Around 600,000 new firms

J.C. Penney, a giant among general merchandise retailers today, started out as the Golden Rule Store. Sears Roebuck and Co. also began as a small business.

are started each year in America, but half will fail within a year.

Also, not all individuals who go into retail business for themselves are successful the first time. For example, F. W. Woolworth failed three times before he learned to broaden his assortment of merchandise, to sell 10-cent as well as 5-cent items, and to locate his stores in areas where many potential customers would pass by the store.

In this chapter, we will look at retail businesses by forms of ownership: individual proprietorship, partnership, and corporation. In Chapter 9 we will look at franchising, and other ideas about owning your own business will be presented.

OVERVIEW OF TYPES OF BUSINESS OWNERSHIP

Many businesses begin as individual proprietorships and as they grow larger are organized as partnerships or corporations. Before we discuss specific types of retail store ownership, a brief description should be made of the three ways in which a business may be organized. Table 1 summarizes the three types of business ownership.

Sole Proprietorship

First, a business may be started as a **sole** or **individual proprietorship**. This means that one person owns the business, investing both money and time. The owner makes decisions about the business and assumes personal responsibility for its debts. Most small retail establishments, and some moderate-sized ones, are sole proprietorships.

Partnership

A business may also start as a **partnership**, a form of organization in which two or more people invest their money and time. On the basis of a partnership contract, the partners agree on how the business is to be operated, the amount of time each partner is to devote to it, and how profits and losses are to be shared. The partners are personally liable for the debts of the partnership. As with sole proprietorships, most retail partnerships are small establishments.

Corporation

The third way in which a business may be organized is as a corporation. The owners who invest in the company are called **shareholders**, but they do not necessarily share in its management. Instead, major decisions are made by a board of directors, with day-to-day operations made by executives and other employees. A major advantage of owning stock in a corporation is that shareholders have **limited liability**; that is, their personal responsibility for the company's debts is limited to the amount of their investment. Virtually all large retail organizations are corporations, and some small retailers are family-owned corporations with only a few shareholders.

Scope of Retail Businesses by Type of Organization

Table 2 contains a breakdown of retailing firms in 1982 by type of business organization. It also lists business income for each type. It is interesting to note that while sole proprietorships accounted for 69.5 percent of all retail firms, their share of total receipts was only 6.3 percent. On the other hand, corporations, with 20.1 percent of the total

TABLE 1 / TYPES OF BUSINESS OWNERSHIP

	Sole Proprietorship	Partnership	Corporation
Ownership	Single owner	Two or more partners	Stockholders
Investment	Money and time	Money and time	Money
Decisions made by	Owner	Partners	Board of directors and executives
Owner responsibility for debts	Unlimited (one person)	Unlimited	Limited to amount of investment

number of retail businesses, had 90 percent of the receipts. Obviously, sole proprietorships dominate the field of retailing in number of enterprises, while corporations garner the lion's share of sales volume. Table 2 also indicates that partnerships, with 10.4 percent of the total number of firms, registered only 3.7 percent of the receipts.

Each form of business ownership has advantages and disadvantages. Although no one form is better than another, a particular form of ownership may be better for certain types of owners and certain types of businesses. How these work is shown in the following story about Julie Weiner and her successes in the retail florist industry.

■

INDIVIDUAL PROPRIETORSHIP

While in high school Julie Weiner worked part time for a local florist. She liked the work so much that she wanted to become a full-time florist after graduation and continue as a retail florist. Julie had begun to dream of owning her own florist shop. She wanted to be her own boss, try out some of her own designs, and earn more than she thought she could make working for someone else. She saved as much money as she could, borrowed some from a local bank, and managed to establish credit with several wholesale florists. These resources allowed her to rent a small shop in the south part of town.

Pros and Cons of an Individual Proprietorship

After her initial excitement over owning her own store, Julie began to discover some realities about being an individual owner. She found that she had less time to relax and was seeing less of her family and friends, because she had to work very long hours. She also found herself doing a good deal of worrying about the success of the store and often wondered whether it would provide adequate income and security.

Julie saw that in many ways, working for someone else had been less troublesome than being her own boss. There were fewer responsibilities and worries. Nevertheless, every time she considered her situation, Julie was pleased with being on her own. She had found that there were many advantages to being an individual owner.

Simple Organization There was little red tape to organizing the business that Julie started. There were few legal problems and no approval by outside parties. She simply obtained the necessary money and began her operations. Ease of organization is one of the reasons most businesses start out as individual proprietorships.

Freedom of Action Julie could make her own decisions; it was not necessary to ask anyone when she wanted to try something new or give up something that was not profitable. She had complete authority.

TABLE 2 / SOLE PROPRIETORSHIPS, PARTNERSHIPS, AND CORPORATIONS IN THE RETAILING INDUSTRY—NUMBER AND RECEIPTS

Type of Business Organization	Number	Percent of Total	Business Receipts (billions)	Percent of Total
Single proprietorship	10,106,000	69.5	$ 433.7	6.3
Partnership	1,514,000	10.4	251.6	3.7
Corporation	2,925,000	20.1	6157.0	90.0

Unshared Profits If Julie succeeds in her store, she can keep all profits herself; she does not have to share them with anyone. However, if the business fails—which is a possibility—Julie must suffer the loss.

Taxes Although Julie had to pay taxes on her income, the individual proprietorship is not taxed in the same way as more complex types of businesses. For example, the individual owner does not have to pay an income tax on the business separate from personal income tax. The total amount of tax paid, therefore, tends to be much smaller than that paid by more complex businesses.

Personal Pride of Ownership Many people like to be their own boss. The owner of a business can take pride in the fact that success in the venture is a personal one. The person can say "This is mine—I did it myself." Pride of ownership can be one of the most rewarding aspects of being on one's own.

Characteristics of an Individual Proprietorship

Most individual proprietorships are small. A small business can be started with a modest investment plus credit from banks and suppliers. Most individual proprietorships are owner operated. Although other employees may work in the business, most owners of such businesses cannot afford to hire many additional employees. The owner works in the business and supervises its operation. Because this results in personal contact between customers and owner, individualized service is often a feature of sole proprietorships.

■

PARTNERSHIP

When Julie's floral shop started to make a sizable profit, she started to think about expanding. She knew she had almost reached maximum sales volume selling cut flowers and floral arrangements alone. There was only one way Julie thought she could increase sales. She didn't carry any live plants or gift items. Customers continually asked her for gift cards or houseplants.

Julie knew these items would sell if she could get them. Establishing a plant department would be a lot of work. She would have to find a new supplier and redo the store to make room for the plants, which would cost a lot of money. Furthermore, Julie knew little about buying and taking care of plants, or about promoting them to customers.

The more Julie thought about it, the more necessary she thought this move would be if she was going to expand her business. Since she lacked the capital and knowledge she needed, she started to think about forming a partnership.

After a good deal of searching and inquiring, Julie met Linda James, who had studied about plants and flowers in school. Linda had some money saved up and had long hoped to go into business for herself. She and Julie decided to form a partnership. They agreed on the amount that Linda would invest in the business, how the responsibilities would be divided in operating the store, and how the profits would be distributed between them. These decisions were put in the form of a contract—called articles of copartnership—and both Julie and Linda signed it. They were in business.

Characteristics of a Partnership

Many retailers form partnerships rather than start individual proprietorships, because two or three people can usually assemble a great deal more money than one person. Then, too, each partner can contribute to the business a special skill the others may not have. In many partnerships, in fact, each partner is a specialist and takes care of a different aspect of the business. In Julie's and Linda's store, it was agreed that Linda would run the plant department because she knew more about it than Julie. This experience and know-how were just as important to Julie as the money that Linda had invested. In the typical partnership, all partners share in managing the business, and all have a say in any decisions that are made.

Pros and Cons of a Partnership

Both Julie and Linda discovered that there are certain drawbacks to being someone's partner. To begin with, they found that they did not always agree on how their business should be run. Being involved in a partnership means sharing authority with others who do not always see things from your point of view. It also means taking a chance on your partners' honesty, willingness to work, and ability to do what they have promised to do.

Being someone's partner, then, means an end to total business independence; each partner is dependent on the others in important ways. In a partnership, each partner is responsible for the business decisions made by the others. An agreement made by one partner is binding on all other partners. This means that if one partner makes a poor decision, the other partners face the consequences as well. Each partner is also liable for the debts of the other as far as the business is concerned. The death, serious illness, or withdrawal of one or more partners can strain a business to the point where the owners are forced to dissolve it. The law requires that a business be reorganized whenever partners leave the business or whenever new partners are added.

In spite of these disadvantages, both Julie and Linda were mature enough in their attitudes toward each other and conscientious enough in their attitudes toward their partnership to have a successful relationship. As they worked together, they were pleased to discover that a partnership offered a number of advantages.

More Capital Available   Two or more people can usually assemble more capital than one person can. This makes it possible to start a larger business, have more capital for expansion, and have reserve funds to fall back on. Likewise, if the business suffers a loss, both partners share the burden of the loss.

Better Management   Each person in a partnership usually has a special skill that the others lack. One may be a specialist in accounting and finance, another in advertising and promotion, and still another in buying and merchandising. These combinations of

Each member of a partnership can bring his or her special skills to the business.

skills lead to better operating procedures and better management.

Greater Interest in the Business
When a person becomes a partner, there is a much keener interest in the success of the business than when a person is merely an employee. For this reason, partners usually work harder, make a greater effort to keep costs down, and use their imagination more creatively.

Relatively Simple Organization
It is not difficult to organize a partnership as compared with a corporation. There are few regulations to be dealt with, and the cost of setting up the partnership is relatively small. A lawyer usually prepares a legal document stating the agreements made by each partner.

Low Taxes
Just as in the individual proprietorship, a partnership enjoys a tax advantage, for the business is not taxed separately on its income.

■

CORPORATION

Julie and Linda prospered in their partnership. The plant department made a handsome profit. They remodeled and expanded the store, and they also added several new lines of plant supplies that turned out to be profitable. But they were still not satisfied. They knew that they would do a much greater volume of business if they opened an additional store in a new shopping center. However, this would require a great deal more capital than Julie and Linda could raise, even if they sold their present store (which they did not want to do). The additional store would require a good deal of money, not only for the fixtures and another floral cooler but also for the merchandise. Moreover, a large staff would be required to operate the store—salespeople, bookkeepers, cashiers, and department managers would have to be hired. Julie and Linda would also have to hire someone to manage the present store.

It would be extremely difficult for Julie and Linda to borrow a sum large enough—$100,000 or more—to start and to organize such an operation. If, however, they were to find 20 people willing to invest $5000 each (with the expectation of making a profit on their investment), their problem would be solved. So, to raise the capital for the new store Julie and Linda decided to form a corporation.

Characteristics of a Corporation

A **corporation** is a form of business ownership that operates under a charter. The **charter** is a legal document that permits the corporation to sell shares of stock, each share representing part ownership of the business. The shareholders, or owners of the business, elect a board of directors to decide upon the policies of the business. The elected board of directors has the responsibility for appointing the top executives to manage the firm.

A corporation may have any number of owners. Some corporations have only a few shareholders, often members of the same family. Other corporations have as many as 100,000 or more shareholders (also called stockholders). Since Julie and Linda are now accountable to other shareholders, they will no longer be as independent as when they were partners—they will actually be employees of the corporation. However, they will still have a major voice in the business, will draw attractive salaries, and will share in the profits of the business by receiving dividends on their investment in the stock.

Pros and Cons of a Corporation

Before Julie and Linda formed a corporation, they found that corporations have several advantages over the other forms of ownership. They could understand why corporate form of ownership is increasing in popularity. Some of its advantages follow.

Limited Liability   Each shareholder is liable for debts only to the extent of the original purchase of stock. In contrast, in a partnership, each partner is responsible for all obligations of the firm.

Designated Officers Make Legal Contracts   As partners, Julie and Linda could make agreements for which the other partner was responsible. Since there is no one owner in a corporation, only designated officers can make a contract that will bind the company and all its owners (shareholders).

Continuity   When an individual proprietor or a partner dies, the business is often forced to close. This is not true of a corporation. The life of a corporation is not affected by death or disability of an owner; a corporation continues to exist for as long as it operates at a profit.

Growth Possibilities   A corporation can usually expand rather easily. If the firm wants to build new stores or take on new lines and needs a great deal of money to do so, it can offer stock or sell bonds to the public and obtain the capital needed.

Expert Management and Economic Operations   The large corporation can afford to hire a variety of skilled personnel. The large corporation can also save money by purchasing goods in large quantities and by organizing its operations efficiently.

■

CHOOSING A FORM OF OWNERSHIP

There are several factors to consider when choosing a form of ownership. These factors include (1) the type of business, (2) the degree to which the owners wish to take part in the management of the business, (3) the amount of capital needed for the business, (4) the extent of risk or liability the owners wish to assume, and (5) the owners' experiences.

TRADE TALK

Define each term and use it in a sentence.

Charter	Limited liability
Corporation	Partnership
Individual proprietorship	Shareholders
	Sole proprietorship

CAN YOU ANSWER THESE?

1. What are the advantages of the type of ownership called an individual proprietorship?

2. Why would people choose to organize a business as a partnership rather than as an individual proprietorship?

3. One advantage of a corporation is limited liability. Why is this so important?

4. What type of organization is best if a business requires a large amount of capital? Why?

5. What form of ownership is least common in the retail industry? What are some advantages of this form of ownership?

8 *Preparing for Management*

Lee Iacocca, Vince Lombardi, and Mary Kay Ash have at least one thing in common: They are all managers. Lee Iacocca is president of Chrysler Corporation, Vince Lombardi is a Hall of Fame football coach from the Green Bay Packers, and Mary Kay Ash is president of Mary Kay Cosmetics.

The importance of management cannot be overestimated. Dun & Bradstreet reports show that the most frequent cause of business failure is "poor management." When asked about their career objectives, a large number of business students say, "I want to be a manager."

Management is the achievement of organizational objectives through people and other resources. The manager's job is to combine human and technical resources in the best way to achieve these objectives.

This chapter examines the levels of management in a typical organization. The managerial functions of planning, organizing, staffing, and controlling are described, and the areas of leadership aptitude and styles are explored.

■

LEVELS OF MANAGEMENT

The local 7-Eleven store has a very simple organization—a manager and an assistant manager or two. In contrast, larger Safeway stores have a store manager, assistant managers, department heads, and other supervisory personnel. Are all of these people managers? The answer is yes, since all are engaged in combining human and other resources to achieve company objectives.

There are three major levels of management personnel: top management, middle management, and supervisory-level management.

Top Management

The highest level of management is referred to as **top management**. In the headquarters of a large retail firm such as K mart or Hertz, top management consists of the president and other key company executives. These people devote time to developing long-range plans for the company. In a small, locally managed retail service business, the store manager may be the only top-level manager.

Middle-Level Management

The second level of management in a firm is frequently referred to as **middle-level management**. People in jobs such as assistant manager in a local retail store or regional manager or manager for a large firm are considered to be middle-level management. These individuals are responsible for implementing the plans of top management.

Supervisory-Level Management

Supervisory-level management includes people who are directly responsible for details of assigning workers to specific jobs and evaluating their performance. These first-level management personnel are responsible for putting into action the plans developed by middle-level management.

■

FUNCTIONS OF MANAGEMENT

Managers at all levels perform the following five functions: planning, organizing, staffing, directing, and controlling. The diagram below shows how these functions interrelate.

Managers *plan* when they decide what to do and how to do it. Managers *organize* when they group work to be done into logical units or departments. Managers *staff* when they select and assign people to do the work. Man-

agers *direct* when they communicate to personnel how to perform the work. And managers *control* when they determine if the work is accomplished as planned.

Planning

The management process begins with **planning**, or deciding what work will be done and how it will be accomplished. Planning sets the stage for what will be done. Every plan should be:

■ Written—We are all familiar with the types of communication gaps that can arise when managers give instructions orally.

■ Comprehensive, yet also as simple as possible—The plan should cover the main situ-

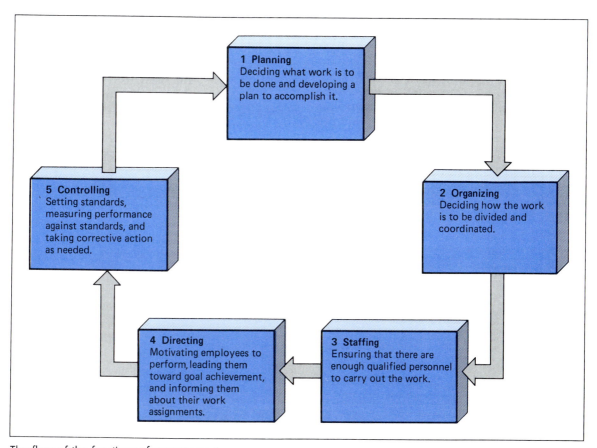

The flow of the functions of management.

ations likely to arise but should not try to cover every possible situation. Such an attempt generally results in an overly complex plan, with the result that many people misinterpret of fail to grasp the plan.

■ Flexible—While flexibility will vary with the level of management, even when rules are stated very clearly, it should be possible to modify them in unusual circumstances.

■ Revised regularly—Because conditions change, a good practice is to review all plans at least annually and to revise them when necessary.

■ Communicated—It may seem obvious that managers should explain plans to the people who are to carry them out, but often they do not. A good question for managers to ask themselves is, "Does everyone understand the message?"

Organizing

Organizing is the management function of deciding how to divide and coordinate work. It is the process of grouping activities, assigning responsibility, and establishing working relationships that enable employees to work with maximum efficiency and effectiveness.

Organizing is more complex in a large business than in a small one. Sam, a store manager with only five employees, is organizing the business when he says, "Roger, you're in charge of all supplies and materials; handle them the best way you can. When you have problems, bring them to me. And when I'm not here, you're in charge of the entire department. Mary, your job is to handle all telephone selling. When I'm here, bring your questions to me; but when I'm gone, ask Roger what to do."

In a large company, where employees must perform hundreds or thousands of jobs, organization is naturally much more complicated. The manager must decide:

■ How to divide the work among the employees and exactly what work each individual is to perform

■ What responsibility and authority each employee should have
■ To whom each employee will report—that is, establish the chain of command
■ How to coordinate the work done by individuals and groups of employees

When employees know exactly what management expects of them and to whom they report, they are much more likely to operate as a team working toward common goals. When things are disorganized, employees are more likely to resemble a confused mob than a team. Though inefficient organization is not always obvious, it often causes friction among employees and may result in unsatisfactory service to the customer.

Staffing

Staffing is the managerial function of selecting, training, compensating, and evaluating people so that they perform the work according to established standards. In a large firm a personnel department may handle much of the work involved in staffing. It may also be responsible for providing employee benefits and services and for maintaining health and safety programs.

Personnel management, sometimes called human resource management, is the process of providing an organization with qualified employees and maintaining an atmosphere in which they will be productive and loyal. Personnel management focuses on relating people to the work the firm expects them to do.

Directing

Motivating employees, leading them toward common goals, and informing them about their work assignments are aspects of the management function of **directing.**

Team spirit is essential in any organization. To get the job done, employees have to get along and watch out for each other. Hall of Fame Coach Vince Lombardi, in commenting on team play, said, "Each player has to be thinking about the next guy and saying to himself, 'If I don't block that man, he is going to get his legs broken. I have to do my job well in order that he can do his.' "

Lee Iacocca believes that cooperation and concern for other people and other departments is just as important for corporate greatness as it is for sports greatness. He says, "The whole function of an executive is to motivate other people, and if a manager has trouble getting along with other people, he's [or she's] in the wrong place."

Controlling

Controlling is the managerial function of setting standards for work, measuring actual performance against the standards, and correcting the situation if performance does not meet the standards. For example, if a standard says that sales should be $20,000 a week but sales are actually only $15,000, the manager must decide what should be done to raise actual performance from $15,000 to $20,000. There are three major steps in the control process: setting standards, measuring performance against the standards, and taking corrective action.

Set Standards   The first step in the control process is to set a **standard**—a preestablished performance level. Managers must ask themselves, "What level of quality should we supply—low, medium, or high?"

Consider two companies that have decided to sell carpet cleaning services. Company A sees its target market as the customer who chooses a brand primarily on the basis of price rather than quality. This company will probably provide a medium- to low-quality service. For example, delivery may be slow. Repairs might not be offered. Company B, in contrast, seeks to appeal to people who are discriminating in quality and not price conscious. Therefore, it will probably provide a service of high or very high quality and will charge accordingly.

Provide a Measure of Actual Performance Against the Standards   Step 2 in the control process is **measurement of performance** against standards. It involves comparing what the standards accomplished with what managers hoped to accomplish with the standards. Performance measurement is always the middle step in the control process, following the setting of standards and before corrective action.

Measuring performance is essential for two reasons: First, a standard obviously serves no purpose unless one determines to what degree it is met. Second, measurement of performance tells managers when corrective action, the third step in the control process, is necessary. Without measuring performance, managers have no way of answering such key questions as, "How well are we doing" and "What should we do to improve performance?"

Take Corrective Action   The first two steps in the control process—setting standards and measuring performance against standards—have little value unless the manager takes **corrective action**, or devises a plan to make performance meet the standards.

Corrective action takes many forms. Consider, for example, the performance standard, "No stealing." Evidence indicates that merchandise is being stolen by personnel. Unless something is done, the control process (inventory recordkeeping) is pointless.

Consider another example: Ray Jones sells stationery products. His assigned quota is 2000 units per month, but he sells only 1000 units. Some forms of corrective action are: lower the standard to 1000 units; assign Ray to a different department; enlarge his present territory; give him more training; have him sell a different combination of products; or terminate him.

Good managers should be simultaneously tender and tough. Mary Kay Ash believes in identifying problems to her employees but, more important, she believes in helping them to solve those problems. She thinks that managers should approach employee problems by placing themselves in the other person's shoes, then working together with the employee to solve the problem. That way the boss comes across not as a harsh critic but as a helpful friend. Such an approach, she believes, encourages employees to do their best to keep from letting the manager down. Other ideas for taking corrective action are discussed in Chapter 25.

■

IS RETAIL MANAGEMENT FOR YOU?

What if you do not plan to become a manager? What if you do hope to become one someday, but you are now in a junior position? You should still learn as much about management skills as you can. Manager or not, you will have to work with and within organizations all your life. To do so effectively, even at the level of an individual contributor, you have to learn how to manage.

Characteristics of Good Managers

Management is an art, and there is no exact prescription for developing that art. However, effective managers seem to have the following six qualities:

1. *Ability to inspire others*—Effective managers can excite people about the task to be done.

2. *A good understanding of what makes people tick*—Effective managers work hard to understand their employees.

3. *Ability to communicate effectively*—This is especially true of the spoken word.

4. *Credibility*—Effective managers come across so that employees believe what they say.

5. *Ability to set an example for others to follow*—Effective managers work hard so that employees will work hard.

6. *Ability to take full responsibility*—Managers don't blame others when things go wrong.

Many good managers firmly believe that the only way you can motivate people is to communicate with them. Successful managers will tell you to be direct and straightforward: The best way to motivate employees is to let them know what the plan is so they can be part of it. People want to know what the goals of the company are—what its future plans are, and how they fit into those plans. Lee Iacocca encourages his employees to make suggestions and contributions that

What are the competencies of a good manager?

will help the company in some way. To Iacocca, listening is just as important as talking. In fact, he believes that the ability of management to listen well is the difference between a mediocre company and a great one.

When employees come up with a good idea, managers should make sure that their efforts are appreciated and that the employees are thanked. Otherwise, employees may not find it worthwhile to share their future ideas.

Similarly, Mary Kay Ash maintains that people come first in her company. She and her managers strive hard to keep a family-like atmosphere. It is their top priority and it works very well for them. One technique that Mary Kay uses when meeting people is to imagine them wearing a sign saying, "Make me feel important."

Mary Kay's special approach to management is applying the Golden Rule. Here are some other practices she considers important. Mary Kay believes that most managers underuse praise, which is unfortunate. She has found praise not only to be an incredibly effective motivator but also a way to show sincere appreciation for a subordinate's efforts. She also thinks that it is important to show praise and recognition to her people in front of their peers. Some examples of how she does this include recognition of top producers (on stage) at her seminars and coverage of exceptional employees (including photographs) in her monthly magazine, *Applause*.

The Mary Kay Company also shows appreciation in tangible ways. Salespeople are called "beauty consultants," and when a consultant does her first $100 show, she receives a ribbon. For other achievements, consultants receive mink coats, diamond rings, first-class trips abroad, a diamond bumblebee, and of course, the highly visible pink Cadillac.

TRADE TALK

Define each term and use it in a sentence.

Controlling	Personnel
Corrective action	management
Management	Planning
Measurement of	Staffing
performance	Standard
Middle-level	Supervisory-level
management	management
Organizing	Top management

CAN YOU ANSWER THESE?

1. What are the three levels of management?

2. What are the five major functions of management?

3. Why is the organization function of management in a large firm more difficult than in a smaller one?

4. What are the six qualities of a good manager?

5. What level of management would best describe a department head?

9 *Preparing for Entrepreneurship*

More and more Americans are saying good-bye to their jobs and investing their time and money in a business of their own. It's a sweet dream that works out well for many Americans. Unfortunately, starting a business has never been more risky than in the 1980s, with eight out of ten new firms failing within 5 years. In fact, figuring out "what's hot" or "what's not" sometimes dictates success or failure.

■

IS ENTREPRENEURSHIP FOR YOU?

The chance to be independent and succeed on one's own appeals to many Americans. They see an opportunity to gain special compensations—high income, personal growth, the experience of being in charge, a chance to try out their own ideas, and the opportunity to choose their own work hours. Other reasons given by people who go into business for themselves include being able to supplement their incomes, to fill an immediate need for a job, to build a business for their children, and to prove their own ability to make business decisions.

The term entrepreneur comes from the French and means "one who assumes the risk of a business." In this book we will use a broader definition. **Entrepreneurs** are individuals who organize, manage, and assume the risks of a business for the purpose of making a profit.

What Makes an Entrepreneur Successful?

When this country was in its early stages of development, almost anyone with a little money and some merchandise or a saleable service still could make a living running a shop. But this is no longer true. To be a successful retailer takes more than money, resources, and a place to do business. Today's successful entrepreneur must have well-defined traits, competencies, and resources. Some of these qualifications have been discussed earlier. Additional ones are presented in this chapter.

Retailing is a people business. So the needs of people, more than products or services, are the entrepreneur's stock in trade. The first qualification of a successful retail entrepreneur is a genuine interest in what people need. That is the main reason that successful retailers make it a point to talk to many of the customers who come into their places of business.

In addition to a deep concern for people, entrepreneurs can be characterized by the following managerial abilities (items 1–6) and traits (items 7–15):

1. Organizing ability
2. Ability to absorb setbacks and bounce back
3. Problem-solving ability
4. Human relations ability
5. Communications ability
6. Ability to make sound decisions and to take full responsibility for decisions made

7. Realistic expectations about the amount of work required and willingness to work long hours

8. Persistence and patience to wait until the business really becomes successful

9. Ambition, energy, and drive

10. A sense of independence and self-confidence

11. Technical knowledge of how to operate the retail business

12. Enthusiasm

13. Willingness to take a chance

14. Common sense

15. Good health

Why Do Businesses Fail?

It's a good idea to gain an understanding of why businesses fail in order to avoid some possible pitfalls. Studies show that the greatest number of retail businesses fail during the first 2 years. They also show that if a business operates successfully for 5 years, its chances for continued success are much better. The Small Business Administration estimates that at least 90 percent of all business failures can be attributed to bad management—inexperience or incompetence. The factors that cause businesses to fail can be categorized into the following four areas: (1) inadequate planning, (2) inadequate financing, (3) obsolete methods, and (4) personal factors. Examples of each of these factors were presented in a U.S. Office of Education Curriculum Project as follows:

1. Inadequate planning
   a. Lack of economic knowledge about trading area
   b. Poor selection of location
   c. Failure to foresee major marketing opportunities
   d. Failure to plan properly for financial needs
   e. Failure to anticipate personnel requirements
   f. Inadequate advertising strategy and planning

2. Inadequate financing
   a. Inadequate funds to purchase equipment needed
   b. Inadequate capital reserves to withstand slow business period
   c. Insufficient funds to purchase adequate inventory
   d. Insufficient funds to obtain best location

3. Obsolete methods
   a. Poor expense controls
   b. Poor inventory controls
   c. Poor accounts receivable controls (too many outstanding bills)
   d. Poor personnel policy
   e. Poor cost records and pricing methods
   f. Lack of modern equipment

4. Personal factors
   a. Poor knowledge of business
   b. Unwillingness to accept advice
   c. Unwillingness to work long hours
   d. Contentment with things as they are
   e. Excessive expenditures in good and bad economic periods

Should You Go Into Business for Yourself?

Before answering this question and reading further, you may want to take a few minutes to review Chapter 3, "Preparing for a Career in Retail Marketing" and the career project you prepared at the end of Unit 1.

Successful entrepreneurs believe that examining one's skills, abilities, and experience is essential. They believe that any prospective entrepreneur should determine what he or she wants out of life and how much he or she is willing to sacrifice to achieve these goals. They recognize that they must be qualified for their intended field or type of business, physically, by experience, by education, by learning capacity, and financially. The successful entrepreneur must be able to give positive answers to some personal questions, such as: What will be the effects of this decision on my family? How will this new life-

Are You a Self-Starter?

I do things my own way. Nobody needs to tell me to get going.	If someone gets me started, I keep going all right.	Easy does it. I don't exert myself unless I have to.

How Do You Feel about Other People?

I like people. I can get along with just about anybody.	I have plenty of friends. I don't need anyone else.	Most people annoy me.

Can You Lead Others?

I can get most people to go along without much difficulty.	I can get people to do things if I drive them.	I let someone else get things moving.

Can You Take Responsibility?

I like to take charge and see things through.	I'll take over if I have to, but I'd rather let someone else be responsible.	There's always some eager beaver around wanting to show off. I say let him.

How Good an Organizer Are You?

I like to have a plan before I start. I'm usually the one to get things lined up.	I do all right unless things get too mixed up. Then I stop.	I just take things as they come.

How Good a Worker Are You?

I can keep going as long as necessary. I don't mind working hard.	I'll work hard for a while, but when I've had enough, that's it!	I can't see that hard work gets you anywhere.

How Good Is Your Health?

I never tire.	I have enough energy for most things I want to do.	I run out of energy sooner than most of my friends seem to.

Review this rating scale for personal traits important to an entrepreneur. Do you think the person who checked this scale is suited for a career in entrepreneurship? Now rate yourself on this scale.

style affect them? Do they understand the risks and sacrifices, and will they support my efforts?

■

IS FRANCHISING YOUR ROUTE TO ENTREPRENEURSHIP?

Say the word "franchise," and most people think of fast food—McDonald's, Kentucky Fried Chicken, or Godfather's Pizza. But franchising touches almost everything.

We buy homes from franchised real estate agents and drive in cars purchased from franchised car dealers. We have our hair cut, clothes laundered, homes cleaned, and income taxes prepared by local merchants linked to famous franchise networks.

Walk down any street in the United States and you will feel a sense of familiarity. Dunkin Donuts on the East Coast taste the same as on the West Coast. Century 21 real estate agents sell log homes in New England and oceanside condominiums in California. Jazzercise clients work out to the same routine in studios from New York to Alaska.

The growth of franchising—the method companies use to sell individuals the licensing rights to distribute their products or services—knows no limit. Sales at nearly 500,000 franchised units topped $575 billion in 1986, which was 72 percent above those at the start of the 1980s, according to the U.S. Department of Commerce. Futurist John Naisbitt predicts that franchise sales will approach $2.5 trillion in the next 25 years. The figure on page 69 shows that one-third of all retail sales in America are done through franchise businesses.

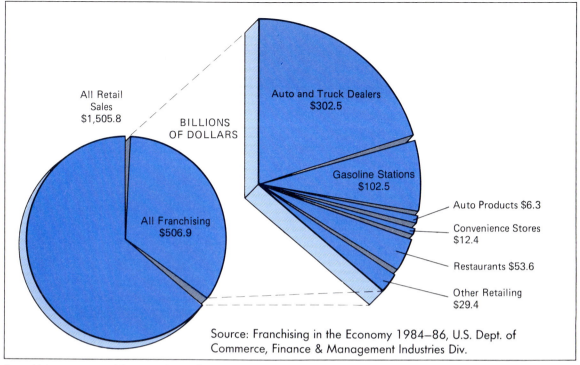

All Retail Sales
$1,505.8

BILLIONS OF DOLLARS

All Franchising
$506.9

Auto and Truck Dealers
$302.5

Gasoline Stations
$102.5

Auto Products $6.3

Convenience Stores
$12.4

Restaurants $53.6

Other Retailing
$29.4

Source: Franchising in the Economy 1984–86, U.S. Dept. of Commerce, Finance & Management Industries Div.

Franchising accounted for one-third of retail sales in the mid-1980s.

What Is Franchising?

In Chapter 2 we defined franchising as a contractual agreement in which a parent company (**franchisor**) grants a small company or individual (**franchisee**) the right to do business under specified conditions. The length of time for which a franchise agreement is valid is called the **contract period**. It may run from 5 years to perpetuity. Most agreements run 20 years. After the period has ended, the franchisor often has the right to buy back or resell the unit.

In the simplest form, a franchisor owns the right to a name or trademark and sells that right to a franchisee. This is known as **product trade-name franchising.** In the more complex form, **business format franchising**, a broader and ongoing relationship exists between the two parties. Business format franchises often provide a full range of services, including site selection, training, product supply, marketing plans, and even financing. Generally, a franchisee sells goods or services supplied by the franchisor or sells goods or services that meet the franchisor's quality standards.

The spectacular growth of franchising represents the rapid rise of two trends: the rush by individuals to become their own bosses and the need of companies to find cheaper, more efficient ways to expand.

Perhaps the major reason for the growth of franchising is that it offers people the opportunity to own their own businesses while still enjoying many of the advantages of a corporate chain operation. Some of these advantages are group buying power, promotional support, financial aid, help in finding a good location, detailed product information, the use of a well-known name, managerial training, and supervision of operations.

The franchisor's return from the franchise takes one or more of the following forms:

1. A **franchise fee**. A one-time, front-end fee that franchisees pay directly to the franchisor to be part of the franchise system. The fee reimburses the franchisor for the costs of locating, qualifying, and training new franchisees.

2. A **royalty**. An annual fee, between 1 percent and 20 percent of the franchisee's sales, that is payable to the franchisor. These payments represent the costs of doing business as part of the franchise organization.

3. An **advertising fee**. An annual fee, usually less than 3 percent of sales, that goes toward corporate advertising.

4. Profits from the sale of equipment, supplies, or finished products or services to the franchisee.

Not all franchises are winners, of course. But compared with other small businesses, the survival odds are better in franchising. Many figures show that only 5 percent of all franchises are discontinued every year, compared to 50 percent of independent start-ups.

Two organizations that help control franchising are the Federal Trade Commission and the International Franchise Association. The **Federal Trade Commission** is a government agency with headquarters in Washington, D.C. In 1979 the FTC issued a guide of trade regulation rules, disclosure requirements, and prohibitions concerning franchising and other business opportunity ventures. The **International Franchise Association (IFA)** is the Washington, D.C.-based trade association that represents franchisors. The IFA requires its members to follow a rigid code of ethics, but the fact that a company is a member of the IFA does not make it reputable.

Though it may be the safest way to enter business, franchising is not the cheapest. Some analysts estimate it costs between 10 percent and 30 percent more to buy a franchise than to start a business from scratch.

Although the success rate for franchise-owned businesses is significantly better than for many other start-up businesses, success is not guaranteed. One of the biggest mistakes an entrepreneur can make is to be in a hurry to get into business. Although most franchises are managed by reputable individuals, as in all industries, some are not. Also, some franchises could be poorly managed and financially weak.

Let's start by taking a careful look at the advantages and disadvantages of franchising.

What Are the Advantages of Franchising?

According to the U.S. Small Business Administration, the franchise has several advantages over the independent retailer. These are as follows:

■ *Reputation*. In an established and well-known franchise system, the new franchisee does not have to work to establish the firm's reputation. The product or service being offered is one that the public has already accepted.

■ *Working Capital*. It takes less money to operate a franchise business because the franchisor provides the franchisee with good inventory controls and other means of reducing expenses. When necessary, the franchisor may also provide financial assistance for operating expenses.

■ *Experience*. The advice provided by the franchisor makes up for the new owner's inexperience.

■ *Management assistance*. The owner of a small independent store has to be a jack-of-all-trades, and even an experienced retailer may not be an expert in all aspects of financing, record keeping, marketing, and sales promotion. The better franchising companies provide the franchisee with continuing assistance in these areas.

■ *Profits*. Assuming reasonable franchise fees and supply arrangements, the franchisee can usually expect a reasonable margin of profit because the business is run with the efficiency of a chain.

■ *Motivation*. Because the franchisee and the franchisor both benefit from the success of the operation, both work hard to achieve it.

What Are the Disadvantages of Franchising?

There are also disadvantages for the retailer in franchising. The Small Business Administration lists the following drawbacks:

■ *Fees*. The fees the franchisor charges for the use of the firm's name, the prices charged for supplies, and other charges may be too high for a particular locality. So they may result in losses or low profit margins for the retailer.

■ *Less independence*. Because the franchisee must follow the franchisor's pattern of operation, the retailer loses some independence.

■ *Standardization*. Procedures are standardized, and franchisees don't get much of a chance to use their own ideas.

■ *Slowness*. Because of size, a franchisor may be slow to get in on a new idea or adapt methods to meet changed conditions.

■ *Cancellation*. It's difficult and expensive to cancel a franchise agreement without the cooperation of the franchisor.

How to Learn More About Franchising

The U.S. Small Business Administration offers the following advice and recommends these sources of information:

■ A directory of franchisors, such as the Franchise Opportunities Handbook (published by the U.S. Department of Commerce and available from The Superintendent of Documents, U.S. Government Printing Office, Washing-

ton, D.C. 20402). Others are available at your library.

■ The disclosure document. A Federal Trade Commission (FTC) rule requires that franchise and business opportunity sellers provide certain information to help you in your decision. The FTC rule requires the franchisor to provide a detailed disclosure document at least 10 days before you pay any money or legally commit yourself to a purchase. This document includes 20 important items of information, such as:

1. Names, addresses, and telephone numbers of other purchasers
2. A fully audited financial statement of the seller
3. The background and experience of the key executives
4. The cost required to start and maintain the business
5. The responsibilities you and the seller will share once you buy

■ Current franchisees. Talk to other owners and ask them about their experiences regarding earnings, claims, and information in the disclosure document. Be certain that you talk to franchisees and not company-owned outlets.

■ Other references. You should get more information and publications from the U.S. Small Business Administration, the Federal Trade Commission, the Better Business Bureau, the local Chamber of Commerce and associations, such as the International Franchise Association (1025 Connecticut Ave., N.W., Washington, D̸ ͢0036).

■ Professional adv ͢ ⁻⁻ you have had consider; and legal training, countant, and a b⟋ you and go over and proposed money and tim⟨ late may save yͻ investment.

72

TRADE TALK

Define each term and use it in a sentence.

Advertising fee
Business format
  franchising
Contract period
Entrepreneurs
Federal Trade
  Commission
Franchise fee
Franchisee
Franchisor
International Franchise
  Association
Product trade-name
  franchising
Royalty

CAN YOU ANSWER THESE?

1. Besides a genuine concern for people, what are three managerial abilities that an entrepreneur should have to be successful?

2. What are the four main factors that cause businesses to fail?

3. What are the four ways franchisors can receive a return from the franchisee?

4. What do you believe are the most important advantages and disadvantages of franchising to the franchisee? Explain your answer.

5. What are two important sources for finding more information on franchising?

ACTIVITIES AND PROJECT FOR U·N·I·T 3

RETAIL MARKETING CASE

Beth Elliott owned a small neighborhood apparel store in Detroit. The business, operated as an individual proprietorship with two full-time employees in addition to Beth, was profitable and well established.

Brent Reed, a long-time friend of Beth's, n employed by a specialty mail-order 5 years when he suggested that he t a mail-order business of their own, to be called the Green-Z Company. Since Beth had already been considering expanding her business, she agreed to Brent's suggestion.

A verbal understanding was reached to the effect that Beth would be paid back the money she put into the business before a 50–50 sharing plan was begun. Brent quit the mail-order house where he had been working and devoted all his time to preparing a catalog and mailing list and to similar duties. He did an excellent job of getting current price quotations from potential suppliers of the articles listed in the catalog. He made no effort, however, to obtain firm price commitments on any given quantity of goods or for any specified period of time.

For several years preceding Beth's and Brent's venture, prices had been fairly stable with a slight tendency to decline. However, just as their catalog was mailed, conditions changed and prices rose because of inflation. The Green-Z Company received orders that emptied its small inventories within a week. It soon became clear that many of its goods could no longer be obtained at prices that allowed any profit. So closing the business was inevitable.

Forms were quickly printed to accompany refunds on all future orders, and notices of dissolution were sent to the entire mailing list. Beth paid the printer and all expenses connected with winding up the affairs of the company. Her total loss was close to $5000. They agreed that Brent would eventually repay half of this amount.

Fortunately, Beth was able to settle the affairs of her retail store business. Brent soon had another job. Both had learned a lesson about partnerships.

1. Since Brent was the mail-order expert, was it fair for Beth to suffer the entire financial loss?

2. What would you have done had you been in Beth's shoes?

3. Under the circumstances described in the case, should the Green-Z Company have been incorporated? If it had been, what effects would that have had on the outcome of the business?

4. What lesson did Beth and Brent learn about partnerships?

PROBLEM

Rule a form similar to the following. In the left column, write the letter of each of the following business organization characteristics: (0) two or more people combine their money and skills; (a) a board of directors is elected; (b) a contract is drawn up on how responsibilities and profits will be shared; (c) the owner is boss; (d) the business is formed more easily than other forms of business; (e) capital is obtained by selling shares of stock; (f) the business is dissolved upon the death of an owner; (g) only designated officers can make a contract; (h) the owner assumes all risks; and (i) the business requires a written state charter. In the right column, give the appropriate form of business organization for each characteristic listed.

Business Organization Characteristic	Type of Ownership
Example: (0)	Partnership

 PROJECT: FRANCHISING

YOUR PROJECT GOAL
Compare and contrast two franchise organizations from the viewpoint of a prospective franchisee.

PROCEDURE
Interview two franchisees in your community that deal with the same type of goods or services. For example, you may want to compare McDonald's with Burger King, or Howard Johnson's with Holiday Inn. Compare the two in terms of necessary money and experience; employment and training opportunities for learning the business; the franchisee's satisfaction or dissatisfaction with the franchisor and company policies.

EVALUATION
You will be evaluated on the thoroughness of your investigation.

MARKETING AND ECONOMICS

Success in marketing, as in most other career fields, is based on acquiring basic knowledge, skills, and attitudes. In the field of retail marketing these foundations include understanding the role of profit, learning about consumers and their needs, and becoming familiar with the role of government in retailing.

Retail marketing is changing so rapidly that some retail businesses that were very profitable just a few years ago have now disappeared, and exciting new businesses have taken their place. Specialty retailers serving carefully targeted customers are on the increase in America. Retailers who know how to blend the factors in their marketing mix as carefully as a good cook are the ones most likely to succeed.

Creating a retail marketing plan is the first step to success in retailing. Increasingly, the planning process is being recognized as being just as important in retailing as it is in other kinds of businesses. The planning techniques learned by developing an overall retail marketing plan will be most helpful in preparing strategies for selling, sales promotion, merchandising, and small business ownership.

EXAMINING THE MARKETING CONCEPT

C·H·A·P·T·E·R

10 *Private Enterprise and Profits*

Michael Lopez had worked for Mrs. Rodriguez, owner of Toy World, for about a year. He enjoyed working and learning about the latest toys. He noticed that Mrs. Rodriguez often worked long hours, especially during holidays. Michael wondered why Mrs. Rodriguez didn't just get a job and work for somebody else and not have to worry about her business and all its day-to-day decisions. He decided that he would talk to her and find out why people like her are in retailing.

He learned that Mrs. Rodriguez likes her job for several reasons, most of which are personal. But, like so many people in retailing, she has a sense of social service too, and she gets satisfaction from pleasing her customers.

From a personal viewpoint, she likes to "do her thing"—be her own boss, performing a variety of tasks. She enjoys the freedom to use her abilities as she wishes and to exercise her creative talents. The opportunity

to work with people, being in a pleasant work environment, and enjoying a certain amount of social status are pleasing. Also, from an economic viewpoint, she likes the way she is compensated for her work—being paid for her creativity and the risks she takes.

From the standpoint of society, Mrs. Rodriguez serves two groups of people: her customers and her employees. Her customers receive products and services for the money they spend. Her employees gain an opportunity to earn a living. In her role as a retailer, Mrs. Rodriguez stands between the producer and the consumer. If her business is to succeed, it must respond to the needs of its customers. Survival also depends on the productivity of the workers who serve those customers, and on competitive prices. For Mrs. Rodriguez to stay in business, a profit must be made.

Mrs. Rodriguez's business is a small part of the American economic system, but her store and the many other retail marketing businesses in the country play a significant role.

■

ECONOMIC SYSTEMS

Economics is the management of human (people) and material (money, land, and similar physical possessions) resources of society. Every society faces the need to make economic choices. Why? Because none ever has enough resources to provide every person with what he or she needs—or wants.

The basic resource questions are: (1) what to produce; (2) how much to produce; (3) who is to get what and how much. In making these choices, societies from earliest times have been guided by custom, tradition, or a central authority such as a king or ruler. In socialist (nonmarket) economies those decisions are still left largely to the government.

How these questions are answered depends on the economic system of the particular country. There are two basic ways by which economic systems may be organized—capitalism and socialism. Under **capitalism** the means of producing and distributing goods are privately owned and controlled. Under the economic system of **socialism** the means of production and distribution are owned and controlled by the government. In practice the economic systems functioning in most countries of the world today have elements of both private and government ownership and control. However, among the major industrial nations, the economic systems are quite different.

Capitalism

In the United States the economic system might be characterized as capitalistic. In general, the means of production and distribution are owned and controlled by the citizens and not the government. Private profit is an incentive to business to supply the goods and services desired by customers.

Socialism

The political-economic system in the Soviet Union is commonly called communism. **Communism** is an economic system in which the government dictates the economic activity in which individuals may engage. The central government owns—and very carefully controls—almost all the means of production. The concept of private profit is lacking in economic planning and motivation. There is a high degree of government planning for the economy at the national level, and economic objectives are set by government planning agencies. These agencies tend to emphasize the production of industrial and military goods rather than consumer goods. Because of this, a high percentage of resources are directed toward military equipment, and consumers do not have many choices of consumer products.

■

THE AMERICAN ECONOMIC SYSTEM

The American economic system is sometimes called the **modified free enterprise** or **private enterprise system**. It is called "free" because individual freedoms are an important part of it. Each American is "free" to go into whatever business he or she chooses. People are "free" to choose whatever area of employment they wish. It is called "private" because most businesses are privately owned and operated, not run by the government. It is called "modified" because the government controls some of its actions. For example, it is against the law to sell goods that are harmful to people, such as narcotics. Other names used for our economic system are "capitalism" and "market economy."

In a **market economy** the consumers vote in the marketplace (through buying or not buying) to determine the nature and the prices of goods and services produced. The law of **supply and demand** says that the supply of a good or service will tend to increase when the demand is great and fall when the demand is low. For example, when consumers shop for winter clothing in the fall, retailers increase their supply of this merchandise and charge full price for it. At the end of the season, demand decreases and retailers stock fewer winter clothes. They reduce prices to attract customers. The **price** is the amount of money exchanged for goods and services. But prices are more than expressions of value. They also reflect changing conditions of supply and demand. And so the price mechanism serves as a guide for the quantity, the quality, and kinds of goods and services to be produced.

There are six important elements of the American economic system.

1. Economic freedom
2. The market
3. Competition
4. Risk
5. Profit
6. The role of government

Each of these elements will be discussed in this chapter.

Economic Freedom

Many of our freedoms are economic freedoms. Individuals have the freedom to go into business if they wish. Employees have freedom to bargain with their employers for wages, benefits, and working conditions. Workers have the freedom to choose the type of work they do. We have the freedom to

How does the law of supply and demand affect the price of children's skiing lessons?

own private property; businesses and individuals can buy or sell property without government permission. As consumers, we have the freedom to purchase the goods and services we want. So the private enterprise system gives businesses as well as consumers many freedoms.

Retailers have the freedom to compete with each other for consumer dollars. They have the freedom to make profits (or incur losses), and they can do various things with those profits.

As a retailer, Mrs. Rodriguez has many economic freedoms. She can buy goods and services of her own choosing. She can develop advertising techniques to suit her needs. Lowering or raising her prices are her own decisions. And, as well as going into business, Mrs. Rodriguez can go out of business if she chooses.

What Is a Market?

The **market** is made up of people who need or want a product or service and who have the money and authority to buy it. Markets consist of buyers and sellers, but for the most part they are defined in terms of those who purchase certain types of goods and services. A market is made up of people with purchasing power, the authority to buy and the willingness to buy goods and services. For example, the market for inexpensive compact automobiles is much different from the market for luxury automobiles such as Cadillacs. The market is the mechanism that answers those questions on what to produce, how much, and for whom. It controls the changing relationships between buyers and sellers, with each trying to do what he or she thinks is best. Buyers compete with each other to obtain goods and services at the most favorable price. Sellers compete to dispose of their goods or services on the most favorable terms.

Supply and Demand   In the private enterprise system the economy is organized as a system of markets in which buyers and sellers exchange money for goods and services. The market price that results from these exchanges reflects the actions of the buyers and sellers. The market functions to match the supply and demand for each type of product or service. As a consumer you strongly influence what will be produced by exerting economic power in purchasing a product or service or passing it by for a competing product or service.

Nobody designed the market system; it evolved. And yet the market system works and involves millions of individuals and businesses. Take, for example, the economic life of a large city such as New York or Chicago. Overnight, foods and goods necessary to the city's survival are delivered in the right quantities and right kinds to thousands of restaurants, supermarkets, and stores. It is an enormous operation, requiring a large number of individual decisions. And yet most citizens take for granted that their needs will be supplied.

Pricing   A market economy is an economic system in which prices determine how resources will be used. Prices also determine how the products produced will be distributed.

Buyer demand is governed, in part, by pricing, and, in part, by preference. But demand also refers to the quantities of goods and services people are willing and able to buy at a certain time and price.

So, too, with the word supply. Supply refers not only to particular goods and services that may be offered at a certain price, but also to the quantity of goods and services offered in a range of prices.

When demand is strong, buyers compete for the same goods and services, bidding prices upward, which, in turn, increases the producer's potential for profit. This added incentive for profit encourages business to increase production. And often, still other producers enter the market, further increasing the supply.

Then, as more goods are offered consumers, competition among the sellers tends to drive prices downward. Thus, in a market economy there is a strong balance between supply and demand.

Competition

Competition is the force that makes the American free enterprise system work. **Competition** can be defined as rivalry among firms to attract and serve customers in hopes of making a profit. It constantly generates improvements in the ways retailers distribute goods and services to their customers. Retailers compete with one another in satisfying the changing needs of consumer groups. And they try to get consumers to buy products and services from their particular business. Retailers do this by special advertising, various types of sales promotions, lowering prices, improving services, and various other activities. So the name of the game is: "the right products and services at the right price."

Risk

Risk is always present in business activity. Firms do not know if they will earn a profit or how much it will be. **Risk** is the uncertainty of attempting to earn a profit. It is also the uncertainty of the amount of expected profit or loss. The person who starts a business thinks the expected profit is worth the risk involved. In general, the greater the expected profit, the greater is the risk.

Of the thousands of firms that fail every year, most are new firms. Their owners probably saw less risk and more reward than was really there. Even big, established firms sometimes fail.

In a way, the "right to fail" in a business is just as important as the right to pursue profit. If all Americans avoided all risk, nothing new would happen. We would still be using horses and buggies instead of air transportation to travel.

Profit

Another important characteristic of capitalism is the profit motive. Profit is defined as the money difference between what it costs to produce and sell a product or service and the income from its sale.

Simply stated, profit is what is left over after the bills are paid. For a business to earn a profit, it must take in more money than it spends in costs. These costs include materials, employee salaries, and sales expenses, including the owners' salaries. Subtract these costs from income and you get net profit—what is sometimes called the "bottom line." The free enterprise system is popularly known as the profit system. More realistically, it might be called the profit-and-loss system. Without profit, an enterprise falters and dies. Thus, profit becomes the reward for a successful business operation. Without the lure of profit, the owners of businesses would not be willing to take the risks that are always possible in operating a business.

The profit motive as the key to the American economic system will be discussed in greater detail in a later section of this chapter.

The Role of Government

In the American free enterprise system, the major role of government is to protect our individual rights, ensure fair competition, and promote public welfare. In recent years, the role of government in our economic system has grown. Over the past 70 years, government on all levels—federal, state, and local—has become an increasingly important part of our economic system. The Employment Act of 1946 made the federal government even more responsible for the care of our economic system. This act called for the government to encourage a healthy economy and good business conditions. The purpose of the legislation was to encourage as many people as possible to have jobs with incomes at increasing levels.

Government often affects a nation's economic system. For example, the Soviet Union does not give priority to consumer likes and dislikes when making economic decisions. Instead, special committees decide what and how much to produce and sell in retail firms. The same is true of the People's Republic of China and other communist countries. These countries use government policies to decide who gets certain goods and services and where they are sold.

Retailers in our economic system relate to government in a number of ways. Minimum-wage laws require at least a certain wage rate for employees. Other laws require periodic inspection by health officials if a retailer sells food or beverages. To go into business, in certain cities, one must pay a fee for a license. Retailers must be aware of government rules that affect their businesses. The role of government in retailing will be discussed further in the latter part of this chapter and in Chapter 15.

■

RETAIL MARKETING IN THE AMERICAN ECONOMIC SYSTEM

Michael, who was curious about Mrs. Rodriguez's love of business, might wonder how the American economic system functions. He could look at his parents going to work, or Mrs. Rodriguez stocking her shelves, or a city ambulance going to a hospital. All these activities represent economic activities. But what does the whole economy look like? How do the many different parts of an economy work together? How does money function in the economy? These and many other economic questions can be answered by studying the circular flow in the American economic system.

There are three main groups of people in the circular flow: business, consumers, and

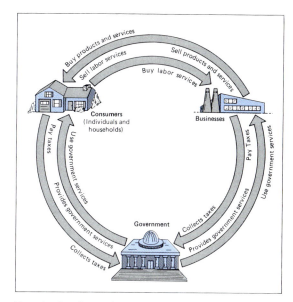

The circular flow of our economic system.

government. Businesses consist of all producers and sellers of goods and services. Consumers are all people who buy and use goods and services. There are three levels of government: federal, state, and local.

Here is how these groups work together. Among businesses, consumers, and government, both money and goods and services change hands. For example, consumers exchange money in payment for goods and services supplied by business. Wages flow from businesses to employees, who are also consumers, in payment for the labor services they provide.

The Role of Government in Retail Marketing

How does government fit into our picture of an economic system? Government performs the following six activities in our economy: (1) collecting taxes, (2) providing services, (3) maintaining the market system, (4) maintaining a competitive environment, (5) redistributing income, and (6) providing economic stability. Collecting taxes and providing services are presented below, and four additional activities of government will be discussed in Chapter 15.

Different levels of government collect different types of taxes. The local, or city, government may collect water and sewer taxes from Mrs. Rodriguez. The local, or county, government may collect a property tax based on the value of her store. Income taxes are collected by the federal government and sometimes by state and local governments. Also, most states have sales taxes, which Mrs. Rodriguez collects from customers.

What does the government do with the taxes it collects? It provides goods and services, including fire and police protection, education, public health programs, the maintenance of competitive markets, highways, bridges, airports, and public parks.

Now you have seen how our free enterprise system works. Each of its parts is important to our country's strength. But what keeps the system going? For example, why do retailers want to keep providing us with products and services? And why do people go into business? Some of these questions were answered briefly at the beginning of this chapter. The next sections answer them in greater detail.

The Role of Profit in Retail Marketing

Our country has many different kinds of businesses. Some are large, like Sears Roebuck, McDonald's, or Hertz. Others are smaller, owned by one person such as Mrs. Rodriguez. Some businesses, such as car washes, sell only services. Others, such as large department stores, may sell both products and services. Why were these businesses started? What keeps them going for many years?

As we mentioned earlier, there are two basic reasons for going into business. One is the personal satisfaction of being in charge of a business a person can call her or his own. A second reason is the desire to earn profits. What are profits?

Let's go back to Mrs. Rodriguez's toy shop. Profit starts with income. Mrs. Rodriguez receives money from her customers when she sells them toys. This is called **income**. Is this profit? No, because as Mrs. Rodriguez owns a business, she has to pay out money from that income. She must pay a mortgage on the store building. The store uses electricity, for which she pays the power company. Wages to her salespeople are another cost of doing business. She must also pay for the merchandise she sells to her customers. All these costs are called **expenses**. Profit is the amount of money left over from income after subtracting expenses. A retail business must have profits or it will eventually close its doors.

Profits can be measured and evaluated in three ways: as a percentage of sales, as a percentage of assets, and as a return on investment. Each way of considering profit serves a different purpose.

Profits on Sales   Profit as a percentage of sales can tell management the ability of a business to control expenses and get the most sales profit for each dollar spent on the sales effort. For example, if Mrs. Rodriguez earned profits of $15,000 after selling $300,000 worth of toys last year, her profits as a percentage of sales would be 5 percent. She would calculate it this way:

$$\frac{\text{Total Profits}}{\text{Total Sales}} = \frac{\$15,000}{\$300,000} = 0.05 = 5\%$$

Profits on Assets   Profits as a percentage of assets tell management how well the business's assets are contributing to its well-being. **Assets** are things the business owns, such as store fixtures and stock. This measure of profits tells if a business is getting its money's worth from what it owns. Are all the store fixtures, sales representatives' cars, and neon signs contributing to profits, or are they unnecessary to the business? If Mrs. Rodriguez's store assets were worth $150,000 and she had a $15,000 profit last year, her profit as a percentage of assets would be 10 percent. She would calculate it like this:

$$\frac{\text{Total Profits}}{\text{Total Assets}} = \frac{\$15,000}{\$150,000} = 0.10 = 10\%$$

Profits on Investment Another way to measure profits is in relation to the amount of money the owners have invested in the business. This measure of profits is called **return on investment**. Suppose that Mrs. Rodriguez had invested $75,000 of her own money and had also borrowed $25,000 from a bank to start her business. If she had earned profits of $15,000, she would figure her return on investment as follows:

$$\frac{\text{Total Profits}}{\text{Total Investment}} = \frac{\$15,000}{\$100,000} = 0.15 = 15\%$$

Mrs. Rodriguez earned 15 percent on the money she invested in her business.

Results of each measure of profit can be used in a number of ways. For example, Mrs. Rodriguez could compare them to last year's figures. She could also compare them to the figures of similar businesses to see how she is doing in terms of her competition. These measures of profit provide guideposts to Mrs. Rodriguez on how well she is doing. They provide owners and managers with a "thermometer." They let managers know if they are on the right track in effecting good retail management.

What Profits Represent

Mrs. Rodriguez prefers the freedom of owning her own business. Because she is the owner, she can do what she wants with the profits of her store. She may want to return the profits to the business, perhaps using them to expand it. This is called **reinvestment**, or returning the profits to the business. Or she might wish to keep the profits for her personal use, perhaps to buy a new car.

Profit, then, represents the money that business owners receive in return for the money they risk by going into business. Rather than investing their money in a business, they could put it into a savings account and be assured of earning interest. Business profits, however, usually provide the owners

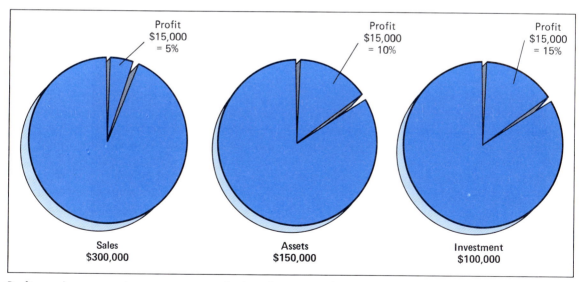

Profits can be measured as a percentage of sales, of assets, or of investment.

with more money than the interest they could earn in a savings account. But first, of course, they have to be willing to take the risk of owning a business. Profit is never a "sure thing" for business. Owners always have to live with the possibility that their business may make no profits. In fact, if their business expenses are greater than their income, they will not only fail to make any profit, they will suffer a loss.

Profits and Free Enterprise

What things determine whether a business will make a profit or take a loss? Mrs. Rodriguez will have to make sure her prices are high enough to cover her expenses and that she has an adequate sales volume. But she must also be careful not to price her goods too high. Why? Her customers might go to other toy stores. She must also watch her expenses. If they are too high, she may not have enough income to make a profit. Sometimes poor local business economic conditions that she cannot control, such as a local factory closing, also will affect profit.

Retail marketing businesses are a very important part of our economic system. They provide us with both goods and services. Retail businesses hire people to work for them and serve as sources of income. Yet, to have businesses, there must be profits. Profits are the reward for the efforts of running a business effectively and for the risks of owning a business. Without profits, few or no businesses would exist. Profits are the lifeblood of our free enterprise system. The source of profits is income from the sale of goods and services after expenses are paid. When consumers buy goods and services from Mrs. Rodriguez's shop, they provide her with a reason to stay in business. Consumers, by

deciding to buy a particular brand name at a particular store, are an important force in the American economic system. Profits provide the basis of future economic growth when owners reinvest them in their businesses.

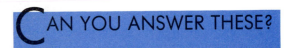

TRADE TALK

Define each term and use it in a sentence.

Assets	Modified free
Capitalism	enterprise
Communism	Price
Competition	Private enterprise
Economics	Reinvestment
Expenses	Return on investment
Income	Risk
Market	Socialism
Market economy	Supply and demand

CAN YOU ANSWER THESE?

1. What is profit, and why is it so essential to a retailer?

2. What are two roles of government in our American free enterprise system?

3. What are the names of the basic economic systems, and how do they differ?

4. List the five characteristics of the American economic system.

5. How does reinvestment relate to profit?

11 Serving the Changing Consumer Market

Christmas 1983 is likely to be remembered as the year of the Cabbage Patch Kids. It was a crazy time. Children all over America threatened to turn against Santa Claus if they did not receive one of the homely, soft dolls that were all the rage. Parents, in turn, assaulted salespeople and each other so that their children would not be disappointed on Christmas morning.

Mrs. Rodriguez ordered a large number of Cabbage Patch Kids for her toy store because marketing research studies conducted by Coleco Industries, manufacturers of the dolls, predicted the tremendous success. They found that adults and children alike reacted enthusiastically to the prospect of being able to "adopt" a plain one-of-a-kind "baby" doll, and this spurred the sales. Incidentally, at the same time Coleco toys were such a success, many other toys were just sitting on the shelf because there was a major oversupply of toys. Michael remembered back to 1983 and to Cabbage Patch Kids that his sisters had and the problems his parents had in buying them. He also remembered how many stores that sold toys had a bad year because the economy was not very strong.

Mrs. Rodriguez always emphasized to Michael the importance of understanding and serving the changing needs and wants of consumers. **Consumers** are all people who buy and use products and services. So the consumer market is made up of people with needs to satisfy and money to spend. Everyone is part of the consumer market, because everyone spends money. But people differ in the amount of money they have to spend and in the things they are willing to purchase. Retailers who know what their customers want to buy have a head start in planning, buying, promotion, and the future of their businesses.

In short, retailers study the makeup of their consumer markets and try to determine what their customers will buy and how much they are likely to spend for different products or services.

■

THE MARKETING CONCEPT

The American Marketing Association defines **marketing** as the process of planning and executing the conception, pricing, promotion, and distribution of ideas, goods, and services to create exchanges that satisfy individual and organizational objectives. The marketing process begins with the idea of a product or service in the mind of the marketer and ends with satisfied customers. It includes all marketers, embracing producers and manufacturers as well as wholesalers and retailers. The process includes the marketing of ideas as well as goods and services.

In Chapter 1 we looked at the work of retail marketing and the contributions of retailing. In this chapter we will look at the changing field of marketing and the changing needs of consumers. Marketing has changed dramatically in the last half century, as rapid technological advances and increased competition for customers have forced many firms to be aggressive simply to stay alive. Historically, some businesses have tended to direct their efforts toward marketing the very best product or service. This emphasis is known as **production-oriented marketing**. Other firms have concentrated on using television, newspaper advertising, and other sales promotion efforts. **Sales-oriented marketing** became more important as the supply of products and services exceeded the demand.

Today, however, it is increasingly being recognized that the businesses that succeed are those that are most successful in implementing the marketing concept. The **marketing concept** holds that the key to success is determining the needs and wants of consumers and providing the desired satisfaction more effectively and more efficiently than competitors. Examples of firms that have been successful in implementing the marketing concept and how they do it will now be presented.

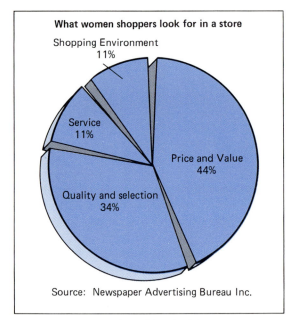

Source: Newspaper Advertising Bureau Inc.

A recent survey conducted by the Newspaper Advertising Bureau, Inc. has found out what women shoppers look for in a store.

Requirements of the Retail Marketing Concept

Customer satisfaction, the process of meeting customer needs, is what business is all about. Retailers who know about their customers and how to serve them will be successful more often than those who do not give proper attention to these critical tasks. The retail marketing concept includes the following three requirements: (1) customer orientation, (2) coordinated effort, and (3) profit orientation.

Customer Orientation   A retailer must determine the characteristics and needs of customers. More and more retailers have implemented the requirements of the retail marketing concept. For example, J.C. Penney's motto clearly illustrates an application of the retail marketing concept: "To do all in our power to pack the customer's dollar full of value, quality and satisfaction."

What do you think of Nancy's marketing idea?

Consumers today increasingly want to get the very best buy for their money and at the same time be able to do one-stop shopping, which cuts down on the number of trips they have to make.

But, consumers are constantly changing. Retail marketers who know what product or service their customers want to buy, where they want to buy it, what price they will pay, and how to promote sales are most likely to succeed in the highly competitive field of retailing.

Coordinated Effort The most successful retailers are those who are able to coordinate plans and organize activities to maximize efficiency.

Retailers can adopt the marketing concept most effectively if they plan carefully. Customer characteristics and needs are researched. Changes in customers, the economy, competition, and so on, are studied. Plans are based on profitability rather than on sales. Strategies for doing this are presented in Units 5 and 6.

Profit Orientation A retailer must strive to generate sales while attaining acceptable profits. Unfortunately, the retail marketing concept is not understood and used by all retailers. Many retailers lack a systematic plan for increasing profits. Because they manage their business costs poorly, they tend to increase sales at the expense of profits. Too often, retailers are not receptive to change, or new customer services are ignored by retailers, or one retailer initiates a new strategy and competitors blindly follow. All too frequently, unsuccessful retailers rely only on the reports of suppliers or their own past sales and do not conduct research on the future preferences of their consumers. This lack of knowledge about the profit picture can be fatal for a retailer. Maintaining sales is important, but profit is even more important.

The Four P's of the Marketing Mix

A convenient way to study—and practice—marketing is to understand the **four P's**: *prod*uct, *p*rice, *p*lace, and *p*romotion. The combination of the four P's forms the **marketing mix**, whose purpose is to satisfy consumer demand. Using the four P's, a retailer of athletic shoes, for example, would answer questions such as:

■ What kinds of shoes—tennis, jogging, football, and so on—should we sell? (product)
■ What price should we charge? (price)
■ Where should we sell the shoes—in our stores (and, if so, where in each store), by direct mail, and so on? (place)
■ How should we tell consumers about our shoes—radio, TV, brochures, and so forth? What selling points should we stress? (promotion)

The following diagram illustrates how retailers implement the marketing mix to achieve the goal of consumer satisfaction.

Throughout this book you will have an opportunity to learn how to use the four P's

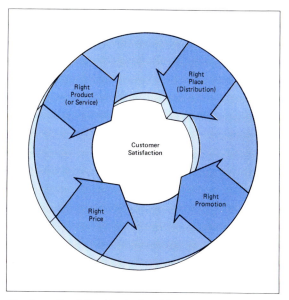

The Four Ps of the Marketing Mix.

of marketing in planning for a career in retail marketing. In Chapters 13 and 17 you will learn how retailers use the four P's of marketing in creating an effective retail marketing mix.

Retail marketers constantly study the makeup of their consumer markets and try to determine what their customers will buy and how much they are likely to spend for various products or services. They do this by studying population changes and income and spending patterns.

Retailers need to concentrate particularly on those consumers they serve in their retail trading area. A **retail trade area** is the geographic area from which a retailer secures sales.

■

POPULATION CHANGES

A logical place to start the study of the market is with a study of the total population. In 1967, there were 200 million people and by 2000, there will be 270 million people living in the United States. Even though the birth rate has been declining since the 1960s and is expected to stay at its present low level, the population is growing. People are living longer.

Consumer buying patterns will be important to retailers everywhere. Some of the things that influence buying patterns in this country have to do with age, metropolitan-suburban growth patterns, changes in number and size of households, and how frequently people move. All these things are discussed in the following sections.

Changes in Proportion of Age Groups

Retailers watch national, regional, state, and district changes in the proportion of age groups in their trading areas. The sharp change from the baby boom years of the late 1940s and 1950s through the 1960s to the baby bust years that began in the 1970s will soon be reflected in a much smaller pool of teenagers. This change will affect retailers, both as employers and as sellers of goods and services. By the year 2000, the percentage of teenagers and young adults (aged 15 to 29) will drop from almost 50 percent of the total population to 43 percent. So those retailers selling products and services such as sportswear, pizzas, and stereo records to consumers in this age group will be strongly affected.

Workers ages 25–44 will constitute more than half of the workforce by 1990. The number of people in the 31–56 age group is increasing as a percentage of America's total population and is expected to have grown by 20 million people by the year 1995. The growth of the population in this age group will mean increased sales for retailers of travel and leisure services, food services, home products, health services, furniture, and appliances.

The ranks of over-65 Americans will increase from 11 percent of the population now to 16 percent by 2020. The number of individuals over 85 will increase 79 percent by 1995. Retailers of services such as home security systems and health care products will have increased opportunities.

Shift of Population to Suburban Areas

The rate of population shifts from cities to rural areas, which reversed a 200-year American trend when they began in the 1970s, will decrease. Cities, whose unattractiveness as places to live drove families to the suburbs in the 1950s and 1960s, are gaining new appeal for today's younger workers.

Local shifts in population are especially important in retail marketing. For example, the average earnings of suburban families are one-fifth higher than the earnings of city families. So, of course, suburban families usually spend more money than city families.

In general, the increase of the number of people living in suburban areas is expected to continue as the number of people living in big cities declines. In many large cities, however, the population migration to the suburbs shows signs of leveling off and in some cases reversing itself. As a result, retailers are helping to rebuild downtown areas in cities such as Detroit, Kansas City, Philadelphia, Atlanta, Minneapolis, Baltimore and Washington, D.C.

Standard Metropolitan Statistical Areas

To describe larger central cities and surrounding suburbs, the federal government uses the term **Standard Metropolitan Statistical Area (SMSA)**. An SMSA consists of a county or a group of adjoining counties with a total population of at least 100,000 plus a central city with a minimum population of 50,000 (or two nearby cities with a combined population of 50,000). An SMSA may span several states. For example, the New York City SMSA includes areas in the states of New York, Connecticut, New Jersey, and Pennsylvania.

There are 257 SMSAs in the United States today, and 75 percent of the population lives in them. These areas have proved to be good markets for retailers. The continued general growth of SMSAs means that more and more retailers will have to locate in suburban areas. And it also means that retailers will have to satisfy an increased consumer demand for items such as home- and lawn-care products, home furnishings, snow blowers, home freezers, do-it-yourself products, and home entertainment and recreational items.

Inner City

As middle-income families move to the suburbs, the economic makeup of the inner city changes a great deal. Retailers in many central cities have to adapt their businesses to an entirely different consumer group. Retailers who are familiar with one set of buying patterns have to learn about and cater to an entirely different set. This is because families that remain in the city or new families that move in often have less money to spend.

Changes in Number and Size of Households

Every time a person or a family sets up a new household, retailers of real estate, furniture, and household appliances and equipment have another potential customer.

The number of households will grow another 20 percent over the next 10 years, to a U.S. total of 96 million, continuing a long-term expansion that began after World War II. The size of the households will decrease. This is expected because of three major trends: (1) the tendency of young single people to live apart from their parents, (2) the larger number of senior citizens who live apart from their adult children, and (3) the rising divorce rate.

By 1995, 27 percent of U.S. households will consist of single individuals—30 million of them—constituting a market for goods and services far different from that offered by the traditional standard family unit of a mother, father, and two children.

For retailers, the number of households dealt with is often more important than the size of each household. For example, even if three households consist of only one person each, a salesperson may sell one blender to each of them, or three blenders in all. However, it is highly unlikely that the salesperson will sell three blenders to one household that consists of three or more people. Retailers of furniture, housewares, and similar products and services essential for setting up a household can profit from this trend.

Mobility of Population

Americans are a mobile people. No longer is it taken for granted that people will stay in the town where they were born. In fact, approximately 20 percent of Americans change their addresses each year. In about 60 percent of these cases, the move is a local one. But in 40 percent of the instances, the move is to another state or county. So in a short period of time, the nation's population will be redistributed, with some regions growing more rapidly than others. The population of the Pacific Southwest and Florida is expected to increase faster than elsewhere.

Impact on Retailing The mobility of the population may cause some retailers to face the prospect of losing 20 percent of their customers every year. However, they do have the opportunity of gaining some new customers. To attract the new group, they must be alert to what goods and services are wanted. If they find that the new consumers in their community are very different from the old, and if the retailers do not wish to make major changes in the nature of their businesses, they, too, should consider moving to new areas.

New Opportunities for Retailers In areas where the population is growing, retailers who have the greatest opportunity to take advantage of the mobility factor include:

■ Retailers who sell well-known brands and those who operate easily recognized franchises.
■ Retailers of rental services. Many newcomers prefer to rent expensive items, such as refrigerators and stoves, rather than purchase them. They are reluctant to purchase when they think that they might have to move again soon.
■ Retailers of clothing and home products. Newcomers purchase these types of items to make the adjustments required by climate and type of living.
■ Retailers who advertise extensively and are a part of a nationwide credit plan. Newcomers often have to locate products and services they need quickly but cannot pay for them until a later date, when they have recovered financially from the cost of moving.

INCOME AND SPENDING

When retailers want to increase their share of the consumer market, they must study not only population factors but also consumer income and how it is used. There are many kinds of income. **Personal income** is the amount of money a person receives from any source. Salary or professional fees, dividends from stocks, interest on savings, and Social Security are some sources of personal income. **Disposable income** is personal income minus all federal, state, and local taxes. **Discretionary income** is the amount of money left after essential expenses have been met. Essential expenses include such items as food, clothing, rent, home mortgages, household utilities, local transportation, insurance, debt payments, and health care.

To retailers, discretionary income indicates the consumer's financial ability to purchase nonessential products and services. The amount of discretionary income consumers have is not necessarily the amount of money they will spend—they might save it, for example. However, it is the amount they could spend if they wished to do so. Discretionary income is also affected by the number of working members in a family. For example, a family that includes more than one working person will often have greater discretionary income.

American families spend about 12 percent of their income for clothing and accessories, 20 percent on food and beverages, 9 percent on medical and personal care, 5 percent on household furnishings and equipment, and 24 percent on housing. This does not mean that all families spend the same amount of money. Although a family with an income of $40,000 and one with an income of $20,000 may both spend 4 percent of their income on recreation, the dollar amount in one case would be $1600 and $800 in the other.

Three major factors are increasingly having a major impact on the total amount of money that consumers spend for various products and services. These factors are inflation, the changing role of women, and changing family income patterns.

Inflation

During periods of inflation, or sharp increases in the costs of products and services, consumers can't spend as much, simply because the purchasing power of their dollars has decreased. For example, consumers who, before inflation, could afford to eat out at least once or twice a week may have to cut out this expense during inflationary periods because they have to spend more of their income on more costly essential items, such as clothes and transportation. Thus inflation reduces consumers' discretionary income and has a major effect on retailers who sell nonessential products and services.

Changing Role of Women

Women will represent more than 47 percent of the workforce by 1995, compared with 32 percent in 1960. The percentage of women in the 25–34 age group who have attended college is already much higher than in the 35-plus group. These better-educated young women are likely to want careers in which they can command higher wages than their predecessors and to resist taking what has traditionally been considered "women's work." Eight to 10 percent of women now in their 20s will never marry, compared with only 4 percent of women who were in their 20s during the 1950s.

Less Time to Shop   Growth in the number of women who are workers, wives, and mothers all at the same time is more and more important to retailers. These women have less time to shop and are therefore less likely to go from store to store looking for bargains during regular store hours, especially when purchasing basic, inexpensive items, such as milk, bread, or detergent. People who

The growing number of career-minded women has increased the market for the goods and services that this group of consumers want. The business suit modeled here is featured in The Corporate Level of Carson, Pirie, Scott, Chicago, a store-within-a-store that caters to business executives and professionals.

work—both men and women—are likely to go to stores that are nearby, easy to get to, or open during the evening hours, or they will buy through the mail or over the telephone. They usually prefer one-stop shopping even if it means paying higher prices.

Spending Patterns   Working people who can afford to do so spend larger amounts of money for time-saving products, services, and leisure products. Such products and services include major appliances, household equipment, repair service and rentals, sporting goods, travel, ready-made clothing, prepared and convenience foods, and restaurant meals. One implication of this for retailers is that when they advertise, they will now need to appeal to working women as well as to men.

Changing Family Income Patterns

Retailers need to study how income is distributed throughout various regions of the country and various segments of the population. The information from such studies can be extremely valuable to retailers in long-range planning.

Living standards have almost doubled in the past 35 years in America. By 1990, about one-fourth of the households in the United States are expected to have incomes of $35,000 or more, based on the value of a dollar in 1980. This anticipated increase in higher-income households is largely a result of the big population growth predicted for the 25–45 age group—the big spenders. We will still have low-income families; however, far fewer will be below the poverty level.

In 1965 more than 40 percent of all families earned less than $15,000, and only 22 percent earned over $25,000. By 1990 almost 65 percent of all families are expected to be earning more than $15,000 and 42 percent more than $25,000.

In this chapter, you have been given an overall view of the changing consumer market, how this affects retailers, and what they can do to keep ahead and take advantage of such changes to better serve their customers. In Chapter 12, you'll learn about the behavior of consumers and their lifestyles.

TRADE TALK

Define each term and use it in a sentence.

Consumers	Production-oriented
Customer	marketing
satisfaction	Retail trading area
Dicretionary income	Sales-oriented
Disposaable income	marketing
Four P's	Standard Metropolitan
Marketing concept	Statistical Area
Marketing mix	(SMSA)
Personal income	

CAN YOU ANSWER THESE?

1. Explain the marketing concept.
2. What is the significance of SMSAs for marketing research?
3. How is household composition expected to change in the years ahead?
4. How will the changing role of working women affect retailing?
5. Which age group of the population is expected to increase the most in years ahead, and how will this change affect retail planning?

CHAPTER

12 *Consumer Behavior and Lifestyles*

Michael Lopez's family moved to Chicago, Illinois, from Atlanta, Georgia, and so he had to find a new job. Luckily, he found a job opening at a newly opened retail store, Kids "R" Us, a children's clothing subsidiary of Toys "R" Us. Michael felt confident that Mrs.

Rodriguez had taught him well and that he could handle any situation. However, Michael did not relate well with the Chicago customers. He felt uncomfortable selling to people who were in such a hurry and did not want to talk. Further, Michael couldn't figure out why Kids "R" Us existed. He felt that a clothing section in Toys "R" Us would have been more than enough. Needless to say, these occurrences limited Michael's success in his new job in Chicago.

Realizing that he could not succeed in his new job without help, Michael called Mrs. Rodriguez for some advice. Mrs. Rodriguez asked Michael some important questions about his new job—Who buys their products? How do they buy? When do they buy? Where do they buy? Why do they buy? Michael was confused; he never thought much about the people he sold products to in the store.

CONSUMER DIFFERENCES

Mrs. Rodriguez knew she had her job cut out for her to set Michael straight. She realized that consumers are very different. Each consumer is influenced by a number of different factors (for example, age, education, where he or she lives, religion, friends, or organizations to which the person belongs). She decided to explain to Michael how consumers differ from each other, then how retailers who know this information can reach groups of these consumers most effectively.

Psychological Differences

Consumers have certain beliefs, attitudes, and motivations that influence what they buy. People's **attitudes** (how they feel about something) are influenced by their **beliefs** (religious or moral values), as well as their **social culture** (the way they interact with family, teachers, clergy, relatives, and friends).

Individual attitudes will influence how they feel about a product or service and the retailer who sells it.

Why are consumers motivated toward buying products? Consumers are motivated to respond to their needs and desires. When people have a gap between what they want and what they have, a need or desire forms. Consumers will buy when they are sufficiently pressed by those needs to act. For example, if you feel hungry, eventually the need for food will cause you to fill that gap by eating something.

Social Differences

Consumers differ by how they relate to their families, friends, teachers, and organizations to which they belong. As they grew up, their family might have consisted of mother, father, brother, sister, uncles, aunts, and grandparents. Over the years family size has declined, as has the family's influence. The relationships we develop with our families has a great deal of influence on our buying, whether we buy to please our parents, to be like them, or in rebellion against them.

Furthermore, the relationships or dealings that we have with friends, teachers, clergy, or social groups (organizations) also influence our buying. Consumers do not buy things only to please themselves but also to please others. Throughout most of their lives, people develop role models or aspire to be like the people they most admire. These aspirations thus influence the type of products they buy.

REACHING CONSUMERS THROUGH MARKET SEGMENTATION

After Mrs. Rodriguez explained these differences to Michael, he asked, "How can I use

Why would the management of Toys "R" Us open a separate children's clothing store division?

Unit 4   Examining the Marketing Concept

this information to reach consumers?" Mrs. Rodriguez explained that many businesses look at consumers in small groups, called market segments. A **market segment** is a group of consumers with similar characteristics. For example, the people who shop at Kids "R" Us are usually young parents who purchase clothing for their children.

Marketing segmentation, dividing the markets into parts, is used by businesspeople to improve their marketing efforts. If the managers at Kids "R" Us did not know that young parents were the market for their products, they could waste their advertising and promotional efforts. Their advertising could appear on radio stations that these parents rarely listen to.

In retailing, there are four types of segmentation strategies. These strategies are demographic, geographic, behavioral, and usage.

Demographics

Consumers in a market can be identified and reached based on demographics. **Demographics** refers to the study of population characteristics, such as age, sex, education, income, race, mobility, occupation, marital status, family size, religion, and social class. In the previous chapter many of the changes in these characteristics were addressed.

One or a number of these characteristics can be used in both identifying and reaching consumers. For example, the best potential consumers for Cabbage Patch dolls might have female children under the age of 12 and a family income high enough to be able to pay the high price for the funny-faced dolls. What unique characteristic does this group possess? Answering this qustion gives some ideas on how to reach this target group.

Geographic Variables

Geographic variables are the basic characteristics of regions, states, cities, counties, and towns. Some of the important considerations might be residency (urban, suburban, or rural), city or county size, climate, or population. Certain products sell very well based on geographic considerations. For example, retailers use the climate information about an area to determine when to make new winter clothing lines available. Furthermore, certain parts of the country have different taste preferences. Interestingly, Dr. Pepper soft drink sells three times better in the Southwest than in other parts of the country.

Consumer Behavior

Many products can be sold to people based on how they behave. **Consumer behavior** is the act(s) of individuals in obtaining and using economic goods and services, including the decision processes that precede and determine these acts. Segmenting based on behavior is influenced by the characteristics of motivation, attitudes, learning, personality, perception, and lifestyle.

Lifestyle can be generally defined by the attitudes, interests, and opinions of the potential customer. Such variables as an interest in hunting, attitude toward the role of women in society, and opinion on the importance of dressing well can be used to understand the consumer better.

The owner or manager of a small retail business will need to understand personally the lifestyles of the neighborhood. The management of larger firms can take advantage of lifestyle research designed to identify segments and ascertain their size and the things they want in a retail business.

Certain types of people consume certain products. For example, weight-conscious individuals have made good sellers of all kinds of low-calorie or weight-reducing products and services. Many retailers now offer a wide selection of these products and services for consumers to choose from, including everything from diet drinks to diet and health centers.

Usage

The amount and manner in which a product or service is used, called **usage segmentation**, is one way of defining market segments. Some of the characteristics related to usage are volume usage, brand loyalty, benefits desired, and price sensitivity. For example, strategies can be developed to make heavy users more brand loyal, medium users buy more often, and light users at least to try the business's product. Based on the consumer usage of products and services, retailers try to position themselves to maximize their profits. **Positioning** refers to how customers view a retailer in the marketplace. For example, Kids "R" Us could be viewed in any of the following ways:

Position 1: A firm that offers high quality-products and services sold and a great deal of customer service

Position 2: A firm that offers low quality products and services sold and a great deal of customer service

Position 3: A firm that offers low quality products and services sold and limited customer service

Position 4: A firm that offers high quality products and services sold and very little customer service.

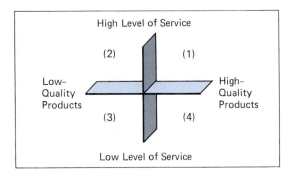

If Kids "R" Us is viewed as fitting in position 4, it may want to reposition itself closer to position 1. It could increase the number of helpers in the store or highlight service in its radio commercials. The purpose of posi-

The Left Hand's market niche is left-handed people.

tioning is to create a **niche** in the market where the competition will be less severe.

◼

TARGETING MARKET SEGMENTS

Targeting takes place when retailers direct their efforts toward meeting specific consumer needs and wants. If retailers can find these unfilled gaps that exist, they can then segment the market and target their efforts at a specific group of consumers. It really depends on how a market can be segmented and how the retailer can develop the attributes that give them a competitive advantage.

Michael asked, "How narrow can a segment be? When is a consumer group too small to be profitable?" In many cases, the smaller the better. **Niche marketing**, the hottest trend in retailing today, has proved that segments can be divided and subdivided into highly specialized bands. Some of the most successful merchants now limit their appeal not to gender or age alone, but to subgroups including large-sized men, petite girls, and working women. Each consumer category views the specialty store as being more attuned to its needs in terms of the best goods and services.

Distinguishing Your Product or Service

One of the key techniques used by retailers is to make certain segments of the market believe that their product or service is the best for them. This is done using various techniques to achieve product or service differentiation. **Product or service differentiation** is the process of distinguishing one product or service from another using techniques such as brand name, design, capabilities, color, taste, or price.

Michael was amazed; he now understood why Kids "R" Us was separate from Toys "R" Us. He learned that they were trying to differentiate themselves from the toy market but still remain identified with the children's market. The strength of the identification from Toys "R" Us carried over in consumers' minds into their clothing operation. What Kids "R" Us had done was identify a segment and then position itself against competitors to gain a distinct advantage.

Targeting Consumer Differences

Mrs. Rodriguez reminded Michael that the many consumer differences were not just identified for retail store positioning. They were also identified so that he would realize that people in Atlanta are different from people in Chicago. There are geographic, attitude, value, and social differences that make people in one part of the country different from those in another. Furthermore, Michael realized that even in Chicago, people are going to differ depending on where they live, their religion, and other factors. He realized that all people are different. These people differences require that retailers remain very flexible.

Michael was confused. Why should retailers be flexible once they have identified their markets? Mrs. Rodriguez explained that even though you have a feeling for your identified markets, those markets are constantly changing (consumers move to a certain part of the city or suburbs away from your business). It

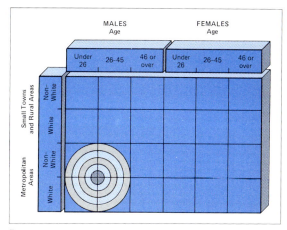

Targeting market segments for men's sportswear.

is important that retailers always keep on top of market changes. Furthermore, right now a retailer might be successfully satisfying a certain niche, but what if the needs of people change or another retailer closes the market gap? If retailers are not flexible, they will find themselves out of business very quickly, because they could be offering products or services that are not satisfying enough consumer needs and wants to remain profitable.

Michael thanked Mrs. Rodriguez for explaining consumer differences and segmenting to him. He knew it was time to go to work, and he knew today would be different. He decided that he would adapt to his different consumers. In the end, Michael became a store manager for Kids "R" Us. His co-workers always seem to be amazed at how well Michael dealt with customers. When asked how he did it, Michael always replied, "I had a good teacher," and he smiled, thinking of Mrs. Rodriguez.

TRADE TALK

Define each term and use it in a sentence.

Attitudes	Consumer behavior
Beliefs	Demographics

Geographic variables	Positioning
Lifestyle	Product service
Market segment	differentiation
Market segmentation	Social culture
Niche	Targeting
Niche marketing	Usage segmentation

CAN YOU ANSWER THESE?

1. What are the four segmenting strategies used in retailing?

2. Why are consumers differences important to retailers?

3. Why must retailers be flexible in analyzing their markets?

4. Give two examples of how lifestyles can be used in market segmenting.

5. List two geographic variables used in the chapter.

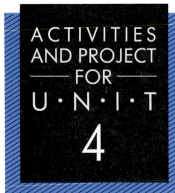

ACTIVITIES AND PROJECT FOR U·N·I·T 4

RETAIL MARKETING CASE

Blue jeans, an American classic in casual apparel, had their origin during the California gold rush days. Levi Strauss, a young immigrant, traveled to San Francisco in 1850 with plans to become a dry-goods merchandiser. He manufactured and sold his now famous blue jeans in response to the needs of the prospectors for sturdy, long-wearing work pants. Today Levi Strauss & Company has annual sales exceeding $2 billion. The market for blue jeans has grown to such an extent that it has attracted other manufactur-

ers. The best-known competing brands are Wrangler and Lee. On a national scale, about 10 percent of the jeans market buys designer jeans, bearing such names as Calvin Klein, Jordache, and Sasson, among others.

Ron Schultz owns a small family apparel store in a town of 20,000, about 45 miles south of Pittsburgh, Pennsylvania. The town is suffering from the decline of the steel industry, the major business of the area, and the population is aging as the young adults move elsewhere to seek employment.

1. What percentage of Ron's stock of jeans should be devoted to each of the following categories? Explain your reasons.

a. Men's basic jeans (Levi's, Wrangler, Lee, and so on)

b. Men's designer jeans

c. Women's basic jeans

d. Women's designer jeans

e. Infants', toddlers', and children's basic jeans

f. Infants', toddlers', and children's designer jeans

2. How should Ron's stock of jeans compare to his stock of business-and dresswear?

PROBLEM

In Chapter 11 the four P's of marketing were discussed. Rule a form similar to the following. Identify two products and two services that you use and write the name of each product or service in one of the four spaces provided on the left side. Indicate under each of the four P's the percentage of each that accounts for purchasing decisions. The total of your four P's should equal 100 percent.

How would these percentages differ if a person 50 years of age were the consumer? Why?

Name of Product or Service	Product	Price	Place	Promotion
Example: Records/tapes	60%	5%	10%	25%
Example: Fast food	30%	5%	60%	5%

PROJECT: CLASS MARKET SURVEY

YOUR PROJECT GOAL

Given a market (your class), survey a sample to identify demographic and psychographic characteristics.

PROCEDURE

Interview approximately 20 of your classmates. For each classmate record the responses to the questions below. After you have completed your survey, tally the responses. Give the results to your instructor along with your recommendations for products and services to be sold to your classmates.

1. Are you male or female?

2. Is your age 15 or younger, 16, 17, 18, 19, or older?

3. How many people are in your immediate family—2, 3, 4, 5, 6, or more?

4. Are you employed?

5. Which do you spend most of your own money for, essentials (food, clothes) or nonessentials (movies, records, videos)?

Based on the information you have collected, list three products or services that you believe would sell well to your class. Give reasons for each choice.

Now you may turn this in to your instructor. When it is returned to you, save it for use in Unit 5.

EVALUATION

Your plan will be evaluated on neatness and the completeness of the information that you are able to gather and record.

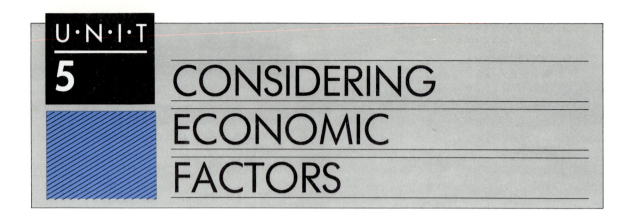

U·N·I·T
5
CONSIDERING ECONOMIC FACTORS

C·H·A·P·T·E·R
13 *Obtaining Marketing Information*

Salesperson: Why do you have those new ski gloves marked to sell for $39.00? Haven't we been selling them for $37.95?

Department Head: They're a good value, and most customers won't know that they were ever sold for less.

Salesperson: Why not sell them for the lower price? Won't we sell more?

Department Head: I doubt it; the customer who buys a pair of these gloves has enough money that the price difference won't mean that much.

Who is right? And what could the salesperson and the department head do to determine who is right? Could they study the past sales record of differently priced ski gloves? Could they find out the income class of their customers by studying credit records? Could they try out both prices to see which yields the greater profit? Could they visit competitors to find what price they are charging for the ski gloves? Or, at different times, might they run two advertisements for the gloves, one at each price, and then compare the num-

ber of customers who responded to each advertisement? Yes, the salesperson and department head could do a number of different things to find out who is correct. All these activities are examples of marketing research that retailers can perform to help them make valid marketing decisions.

Marketing research is the gathering, recording, and analyzing of facts relating to the sale of products and services to consumers. Some retailers tend to look upon marketing research as something they cannot afford to pay for and cannot possibly do themselves. However, marketing research can often be of major assistance to retailers by taking much of the "guesswork" out of making decisions.

WHY USE MARKETING RESEARCH?

One of the greatest needs of retailers is adequate, accurate, and current information on

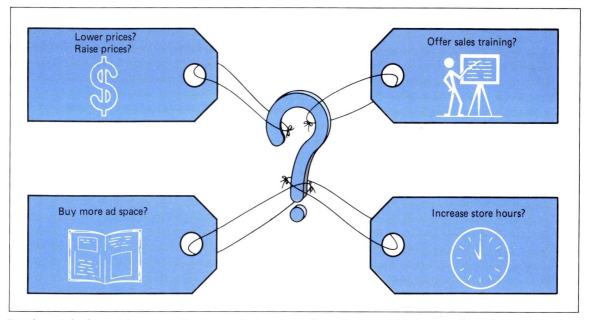

Retailers and other marketers conduct research to gather information on which they can base decisions.

which to base decisions concerning the marketing of their products and services. Retailers need to have answers to such questions as: Who is apt to buy my products or services? Where are these customers located? How often will they buy? In what amounts? What styles and colors do they prefer? What sizes are needed? Only after these questions are answered can the retailer make decisions.

A study conducted by the American Marketing Association showed that more than half the retailers involved in the study were engaged in the following seven types of research activities:

■ Forecasting sales—How much will a firm make in sales during the coming year? What will customer traffic be like in 2 years?

■ Measuring market potential—What is the potential for sales in various departments and in geographic areas?

■ Determining the characteristics of a market—What are the customers like in terms of age, income, occupation, and geographic location, and what kinds and types of firms are competing for their purchases?

■ Analyzing market size—What is the total sales potential for a product or service?

■ Making sales analyses—What kinds of products or services are being purchased in which locations by what kinds of customers because of what types of promotion?

■ Making location analyses—Is a firm in a good location? Or, if a new location is to be added, where should it be located?

■ Conducting product-mix studies—Is the quality of a product or service adequate? Is a product packaged properly? Is a brand recognized and approved? What kinds of services should be provided?

The Marketing Research Process

A systematic approach to marketing research is most likely to yield useful information so that objective decisions can be made. The six steps of the marketing research process are described below.

Define the Problem In this step, the problem is stated clearly and accurately in

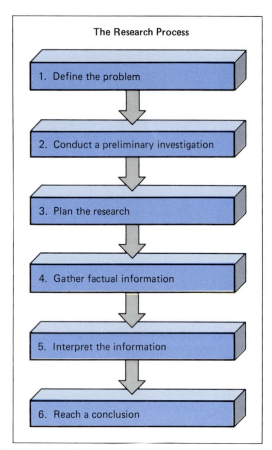

The Research Process

1. Define the problem

2. Conduct a preliminary investigation

3. Plan the research

4. Gather factual information

5. Interpret the information

6. Reach a conclusion

The six steps of the research process provide information that leads to action.

order to determine what issues are involved in the research, what questions should be asked, and what types of solutions are needed. It is a crucial step and should not be rushed. Time and money spent to determine the exact nature of the problem frequently saves more time and money in later steps of research.

Conduct a Preliminary Investigation

The objective of a preliminary investigation is to develop a sharper definition of the problem and a set of tentative answers. These tentative answers are developed by examining the internal facts and the published data and by talking with people who have some

experience with the problem. These answers are tested by further research to determine which ones appear to be the solution to the problem.

Plan the Research   At this stage, the researcher knows what facts are needed to resolve the identified problem and what information is available to help. A plan is then prepared on how best to use existing data, what additional information will be needed, and how the data should be gathered.

Gather Factual Information   Once the basic research plan has been completed, the information can be collected by methods such as mail, telephone, observation, or personal interviews. The choice depends on the plan and the available sources of information.

Interpret the Information   Facts by themselves do not always provide a sound solution to the market research problem. They must be interpreted so as to determine what choices are available to the retailer.

Reach a Conclusion   Sometimes the conclusion is obvious when the facts are interpreted. According to the facts, the logical thing to do is such and such. In some cases, however, reaching a conclusion may not be so easy because there are gaps in the information or other factors that are difficult to evaluate. If and when the evidence is insufficient, it is important to say so when drawing a conclusion.

Marketing Research in Retailing

Reseach activities may be performed by retailers themselves, by their employees, or by outside agencies. Today, large and small retailers are spending more time, money, and effort on research than was dreamed of only a few years ago. Much of the research is simple and quite informal. The use of relatively inexpensive computerized information systems has made marketing research a reality for most retailers.

Retailers in small firms are particularly interested in research that will provide the information they need to make decisions that will lead to improved sales and higher profits. For example, the data gathered on sales records may be used as part of the research. Employees who do recordkeeping, work with personnel, serve customers, deal with suppliers, or promote products or services all have the opportunity to provide or gather information that will be helpful in the marketing research process. To improve their merchandise, service, and customer communications, many retailers rely on stock-control records, customers' complaints and suggestions, records showing reasons for returned goods, and customer service and credit records.

In large retailing organizations, a department may be established to plan, coordinate, and conduct various types of research activities. Also, large retail firms are increasing their research on customer attitudes regarding products, services, prices, advertising, and business hours. These firms, and all progressive retailers, are anxious to maintain a good public image.

The large retail firms also conduct research to determine the ideal locations for new outlets. For example, they take counts of pedestrian and automobile traffic, carefully analyze where people are and will be living, and obtain information from shopping surveys.

Progressive retailers of all sizes conduct studies to determine where to locate departments within their businesses and where to place and promote products in services within the departments. They test various pricing plans, display methods, and advertising techniques to find those that will increase sales and profits. For example, one retailer conducted a study to determine the productivity of salespeople in large and small department stores.

SOURCES OF RESEARCH DATA

Two major types of data are extremely valuable for marketing researchers—primary data and secondary data. **Primary data** are the original facts that researchers collect. For example, suppose that Gene Moreno, owner of a rental car business, wanted to know how many people in a particular community would consider renting a car under certain circumstances during the next 3 years. To get this information, he would probably have to conduct his own study. However, before researchers invest time and money on a new study, they usually check to see whether their questions can be answered by secondary data. **Secondary data** are facts that have already been gathered for other purposes. For example, suppose that researchers wanted to know how many people lived in a particular community in 1970, 1980, 1990. They would look up the information in the Census of Population, a report prepared by the U.S. Bureau of the Census, which constitutes secondary data.

Secondary Data

There are two types of secondary data: internal data and external data. **Internal data** are facts, figures, and other information available within the firm, business, or industry that a researcher is investigating. There is almost no limit to the types of internal data available. Some of the most common types are salespeople's reports, invoices, records of shipments, statements, and all types of budget reports.

Many firms use computerized inventory-control systems to store their internal data. When managers and other employees need information on which to base decisions, they can get it quickly from the firm's system.

For example, suppose that you are the buyer for a retail store and you must decide what merchandise should be ordered for the coming season. You have to determine what styles of merchandise should be ordered, how much of each style will be needed, and whether some product lines should be expanded while others are eliminated. You have a big responsibility. Your decisions will be extremely important to the success of the store, for the store needs enough merchandise to meet customers' needs through the entire season. If you order too much, the store will be forced to take unplanned price reductions at the end of the season to move the unsold items. By consulting internal data, you can make wise and accurate decisions.

A computer has an almost unlimited capacity for aiding retail managers. It can provide not only accurate inventory-control records on stock counts but also information on employee theft, the effectiveness of displays, fashion trends, and so on. More and more, inventory-control systems are being used in making decisions about expanding a product line, identifying potential problem areas, and determining when merchandise should be placed on sale. No matter what a researcher's problem, one very important source of internal data is the firm's inventory-control system.

External data are facts, figures, and other information obtained from sources outside a firm or an industry. Examples of external data classification are:

■ **Census data**—information collected by the U.S. Bureau of the Census
■ **Registration data**—information collected and reported regularly through legal requirements or legislative procedure, for example, the number of automobiles registered in a given area
■ **Research and project data**—project reports published in books, encyclopedias, bulletins, monographs, periodicals, and newsletters

■ **Commercial data**—information collected and sold on a subscription basis.

Primary Data

When retailers cannot find out what they want to know from existing information, they gather their own data. The way they do this depends on such factors as the information needed and the objectivity and precision required. Often, retailers may know the best method for obtaining the information they need, but they must also consider the time, money, personnel, and facilities available for gathering the information. Taking into account their research objectives and the resources available, retailers may choose one or a combination of three basic methods of gathering primary data: by survey, by observation, and by experimentation.

The Survey Method The process of gathering data using a variety of methods such as personal interviews, mail questionnaires, and telephone interviews is known as the **survey method**. When it is not economical to survey the total population, a sample is drawn. A **sample** is a limited number of representative members selected from a large group. The sample chosen is expected to represent the viewpoints of the total population. The surveys with which many people in the United States are most familiar are the public opinion polls that attempt to predict the outcome of presidential elections. These polls show the usefulness of the survey method for learning people's beliefs, opinions, and personal tastes. Personal interviews, telephone surveys, and mail questionnaires are three basic techniques used in the survey method for gathering data.

Personal interviewing, though not always practical, is usually the best way to conduct a survey. Collecting information through personal interviews allows retailers an opportunity to ask consumers questions while they are in the store and when their thoughts about the firm are fresh in mind. Another advantage is that interviewers can ask follow-up questions relating to the consumers' responses to earlier questions. In this way, therefore, it is possible to obtain information that is precise and complete.

One of the most widely used applications of the personal interview technique is the "walkout" study. With this technique, every person leaving the business without a purchase is interviewed about why he or she didn't buy anything.

Another way to get the direct opinions of customers is to establish a consumer panel. A **consumer panel** consists of a selected group of customers who work with the business's management and buyers in helping to make product and service selections. The panel may be a small group that is representative of the firm's customers, or it may be a special group, such as teenagers or college students.

Another application of the interview technique is the **shopping list study**. With this technique, the customer's shopping list is compared with actual purchases. The purchases that were not on the shopping list are studied to find out whether the customer who bought them was influenced by displays and other business motivators. Similarly, if items on the list were not purchased, the reason why is determined. This technique is used a great deal by food stores to measure purchases made on impulse.

Telephone surveys can usually be handled less expensively and in a shorter period of time than either face-to-face interviews or mail questionnaires. As with personal interviews, it is possible to obtain direct responses. Because of the relatively low cost of telephoning and the relative ease of administering such a survey, this technique is being used more and more. But a telephone survey may be inaccurate. It is difficult to get a representative sample of the population, because some people do not have telephones or have unlisted numbers, while others may refuse to cooperate with survey interviews.

Dear customer, please tell me...

I hope you will tell me how you feel about Target.
I'll personally review your comments and see that you receive a response to specific concerns or questions.
I look forward to hearing from you.
— Bruce G. Allbright

	You Are The Best	Good, But No Better Than Your Competition	Need A Lot Of Improvement
Shopping Convenience Good store layout, can quickly find what I need	☐	☐	☐
Apparel Value The quality, look and price of apparel is a good value	☐	☐	☐
In Stock On items I want every day	☐	☐	☐
In Stock On ad merchandise	☐	☐	☐
Checkout Checkout operation is quick, accurate and makes me feel like my business is appreciated	☐	☐	☐
Policies Store has good policies on things like refunds, exchanges, check cashing, and rain checks	☐	☐	☐
Assistance Can get help when I need it	☐	☐	☐
Employees They are courteous and make me feel like I am important	☐	☐	☐
Overall My overall impression of shopping at Target	☐	☐	☐

Time Shopped
☐ Weekday ☐ Morning ☐ Afternoon ☐ Evening
☐ Weekend ☐ Morning ☐ Afternoon ☐ Evening

Comments: ______________________

☐ I would like a reply ☐ I don't need a reply

Name

Address

City State Zip

Telephone number

Retail businesses ask their customers for evaluations by using reply cards such as the one shown here. Similar surveys are conducted by restaurants, hotels, airlines, and other service retailers.

The mail questionnaire would be an excellent technique of gathering information if respondents always cooperated fully. Typically, though, only 10 percent of the people surveyed do cooperate. An advantage to such questionnaires, however, is that respondents can think carefully about their answers. Also, respondents need not be concerned with impressing the interviewer, so their answers may be more objective. On the other hand, conversation may clarify questions and answers that mail questionnaires do not. This factor, together with high mailing costs and the lack of cooperation that makes the results of mail surveys questionable, has led to a greatly diminished use of the mail-survey technique.

Mail surveys have yielded excellent returns for retailers who immediately follow up services such as delivery, appliance repairs, and carpet cleaning with postcards containing a few key questions. These brief mailed questionnaires help retailers keep a constant record of the treatment of their customers and the quality of their service.

The Observation Method

The observation method of obtaining primary data is probably one of the oldest known research methods. For thousands of years, people have been observing others and drawing conclusions from what they see. Small retailers have counted on this method extensively in training their personnel, in determining what they should do to improve their business, and in identifying their customer wants.

Creative researchers can think of many methods to use in observing people. Many retailers subscribe to shopping services to determine the effectiveness of their salespeople. With this method, unknown shoppers come into the store, are waited on by the salesperson, make a purchase, pay for the purchase, and leave the store with the purchase. After the shoppers leave, they record the salesperson's behavior and any other information they may have been instructed to observe. Retailers use the information received to improve the effectiveness of their salespeople.

Trained interviewers often use observation in combination with personal interviews. Observations of consumer behavior during the interview can be recorded on interviewers' reports, along with answers to the questions asked.

Experimentation

Experimentation is a useful method when retailers want to learn about cause and effect. It is especially useful if they want to test something new, such as a display, a price, a promotional plan, a product, a store layout, or shopping hours. Experimentation has an advantage over observation: Experimentation can be conducted under controlled conditions, whereas observation cannot. This enables researchers to identify the reasons for behavior. For example, retailers can observe the number of people who buy a product at a certain price, but they cannot determine whether price is an important reason for buying the product. If they experiment and raise the price while keeping constant other factors such as placement of the product on the shelf, amount of advertising, and assortment of sizes and colors, they can find out if a change in price influences the sale of the product.

Because experimentation usually takes place without consulting with the subjects, it is possible to find out what people's true reactions are. For example, if customers are asked if they are willing to pay a certain price for a new product, they may say yes or no. But if they were to see the product in the store or catalog at that price, they might act differently.

There are a number of disadvantages to the experimental method, however. The major problem is controlling the conditions that affect the experiment. Some variable factors—such as competition, economic conditions, laws, political conditions, and cultural and social environment—cannot be controlled by researchers. Also, a well-planned experiment may require more time or money than the average retailer has available. The tests and the analysis of the results may take several months. But time is an important factor in retailing, especially when competitors are doing things rapidly. The costs of a retailer's experiment include both the costs of planning and administering the experiment and the costs of the retailing activity being tested.

■

USING INFORMATION

Once data have been collected, whether primary or secondary sources or both are used, the information must be organized, analyzed, and put to use. No matter how elaborate or simple the project is, the data must be accurate, precise, and easy to understand. For example, a written questionnaire might include a question like the one shown below:

1. Why did you shop in this store for a dishwasher?
   a. Saw newspaper advertisement
   b. Advised by a friend
   c. Regular customer
   d. Other (specify)

Researchers may tabulate hundreds of answers to this question—along with other answers in the survey—and may organize the information in tables, charts, and graphs. The responses or observations of the subjects are tallied according to such categories as "shopped in this store because saw newspaper ad" and "regular customer." Then the researchers can calculate the percentage of the sample population that fits into each category.

Once the facts have been assembled, they can be compared and conclusions can be drawn. For example, the owner of an appliance store may check sales figures before and after advertising a dishwasher in the newspaper. The two sets of sales figures do not reveal very much information individually. But when retailers compare them, they can draw conclusions about the effect of their ads on their sales.

The analysis or interpretation of data is the basis for decision making, and the purpose of research is, after all, to provide information to guide retailers' actions.

TRADE TALK

Define each term and use it in a sentence.

Census data
Commercial data
Consumer panel
External data
Internal data
Marketing research
Primary data
Registration data
Research and project data
Sample
Secondary data
Shopping list study
Survey method
Telephone surveys

CAN YOU ANSWER THESE?

1. What are the six steps in the marketing research process?
2. What are the two sources of secondary data?
3. When does a retailer usually gather primary data?
4. Why aren't mailed questionnaires used more frequently?
5. What is the major advantage of experimentation as a method of gathering primary data?

14 *Marketing Environments*

Smart retailers plan for success by combining the four P's—product, price, place, and promotion—into a marketing mix that is aimed at their target customers. Thorough research helps retailers focus on their market, and careful control and adjustment of the marketing mix sharpens their aim. Sometimes, however, even the best planners miss the mark. Why? Consumers are a moving target. They, and the retailers who aim to reach them, are influenced by factors beyond the retailers' control. These factors, make up the **external marketing environment:**

■ Economic factors—including economic conditions that have an effect on the customer's ability and willingness to buy and the retail marketers' ability to serve their needs and wants.

■ Social factors—including consumers' social and cultural values, the consumer movement, and environmental concerns.

■ Legal factors—including government regulations and policies that affect marketing.

In Chapter 10, we briefly discussed a number of these environmental factors. In this chapter, we will address additional key economic factors, and in Chapter 15, societal and legal considerations will be presented.

■

BASIC ECONOMIC CONSIDERATIONS

Understanding economics is important for every person. High taxes, unemployment, and inflated prices are only a few economic issues. Each of these issues affects us directly. For example, citizens are asked to pay taxes to support government programs and national defense efforts. Because most people must work for money to provide a living, unemployment creates serious economic problems. Retired people often have trouble meeting their living expenses because their retirement income does not keep up with rising prices. Each of these situations illustrates the importance of economics in our daily life. These factors also affect retailers, because if consumers do not have money they cannot buy goods and services.

Gross National Product

The American economy produces thousands of different types of goods and services, ranging from needles and pins to cars and electronic games, and services from haircuts to health care and rock concerts.

Before goods and services can be supplied, business and industry must organize production. Productivity, which contributes to the abundance of our material welfare, is based on three factors:

1. Land, which describes natural resources, whose form, condition, and location are changed by . . .

2. Labor, which includes the employment of and reward for all types of physical and mental human effort, and . . .

3. Capital, which consists of the tools, plants, and equipment used to produce and distribute goods and services.

Increased productivity results from the effective use of human energy applied to more efficient tools. Productivity is greatest in competitive societies where economic decisions are made in the marketplace by individuals and business organizations rather than by governments.

How well the American economy works as it produces these goods and services can be determined partly from the **gross national product (GNP)**. The GNP represents the total money value of all goods and services produced in a specific time period. Dividing GNP by total population yields a per-capita (per-person) GNP. A country with a high per-capita GNP is usually better off economically than one with a low per-capita GNP.

Inflation and Productivity

Even though America's standard of living is high, inflation and productivity are important economic concerns. If inflation is high and productivity is low, these two factors when combined will lower our nation's standard of living.

When the price of food, gasoline, or medical service goes up, it is not necessarily bad. After all, a higher price means more money for someone. It is bad, however, when the general level of all prices goes up. That is **inflation**, meaning that everybody's money buys fewer goods and services. For example, a family of four earning $15,000 in 1980 had to earn $25,000 in 1986 to maintain its 1980 buying power. The amount of money soared, creating an illusion that people almost always improve their standard of living. However, actual buying power did not increase.

Productivity is one way to help control inflation. **Productivity** is a measure of the relationship between what is produced and what is used to produce it—in other words, the relation of output to input. When a person produces more output with the same amount of input, that represents a gain in productivity.

Productive workers can be paid more wages without causing inflation because they are producing more. Traditionally, America has had a high productivity growth rate—at least until the 1970s. Then our productivity growth rate slowed at a time when inflation rates started rising. These two factors combined to seriously affect our economy and our standard of living. This trend must be reversed if America is to strengthen its economy, improve the quality of life of its citizens, and compete with other nations in world markets.

■

COSTS AND BENEFITS OF MARKETING

One of the major criticisms of American marketing is that it is costly and wasteful. Many critics feel that marketing costs are excessive when they make up as much as half the retail price of a consumer product. One of the major difficulties here is that marketing provides services, which are intangible and therefore hard to pinpoint. Just how much is it worth to be able to shop 24 hours a day? What price would you put on the convenience of being able to purchase records and tapes when you want them? Such questions are difficult—perhaps impossible—to answer.

Why Have Marketing Costs Increased?

Here are some reasons for the general increase in marketing costs over the years.

1. Consumer demands for such services as conveniently located, pleasant shopping centers, wide assortments of attractively displayed merchandise, credit, merchandise-return privileges, guarantees and warranties, after-sale service, and free delivery all add to marketing costs.

2. Rapidly increasing costs of energy, labor, transportation, packaging materials, labels, and most other inputs used by suppliers of goods and services have directly increased marketing costs.

3. Government regulations on packaging, labeling, grading, and a host of other marketing activities have increased the benefits of marketing, but they have increased its cost as well.

What Are Benefits of Marketing?

Though critics tend to focus on the costs of marketing, they do not deny that it serves a useful purpose. Some of the benefits of marketing activities include the following:

■ Development of new or improved products. Marketing research discovers consumers' changing needs and wants and translates them into new or improved products and services. The consumer gains through increased want satisfaction, often at lower prices.

■ Creation of jobs. The jobs provided by approximately 2 million retailers, 400,000 wholesalers, 22,000 transportation companies, and thousands of advertising agencies are directly related to marketing.

■ Improved standard of living. By creating and delivering an immense variety of goods and services, marketing improves the standard of living.

■ Creation of time, place, and possession utility. Marketing provides goods and services where and when customers want them.

How Does Marketing Create Utility?

Marketing, like manufacturing and other means of producing goods and services, adds utility. **Utility** is the power of a good or service to satisfy a human need. A lunch at a fast food restaurant, an overnight stay at a motel, and a new automobile all satisfy human needs. Each possesses utility. There are four kinds of utility. One of these is created primarily by the production process, and three are created by marketing.

Form utility is created by converting production inputs into finished products. Marketing research contributes to decisions about the form the finished product should take. A newly manufactured automobile in a factory in Detroit has form utility. If a customer for the automobile was from Detroit,

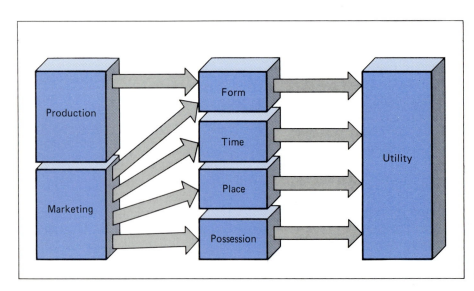

Marketing creates
four types of utility.

the car could satisfy the consumer's need and want. However, Detroit has just a very small percentage of the total population of America.

The three kinds of utility that are created by marketing are place utility, time utility, and possession utility. **Place utility** is created by making a product available at a location where customers wish to purchase it. Our automobile was given place utility when it was shipped to an automobile dealer someplace in America.

Time utility is created by making a product available when customers wish to purchase it. For example, an automobile might be manufactured in February but not displayed until April, when consumers start thinking about buying a new car. By storing the automobile until it is wanted, the manufacturer or retailer provides time utility.

Possession utility is created by transferring title (or ownership) of a product to the buyer. For some products this is simple, with the transfer taking place through a sales slip or receipt. For such products as automobiles, the transfer of title is a more complex process.

Time, place, and possession utility have real value in terms of both money and convenience. This value is created and added to goods and services through a wide variety of marketing activities.

■

FUNCTIONS OF MARKETING

As you have already learned, marketing is more than just selling. It is a very complex activity that reaches into many aspects of a business and its dealings with consumers. Marketing can be classified into nine functions as follows:

1. Marketing information management
2. Product or service planning
3. Purchasing or buying

4. Pricing
5. Selling
6. Promotion
7. Distribution
8. Financing
9. Risk management

The functions of marketing include all of the activities involved in getting goods from producers to consumers. Activities that are similar in purpose are referred to as a **function**. Some functions are performed by manufacturers, some by wholesalers, still others by retailers. All of these functions add to the utility created by marketing. Let us look at how marketing is involved in each of these activities.

Marketing Information Management

Marketing research is the primary marketing activity in which retail marketers are constantly seeking out information on what products and services should be offered and which consumers will buy them.

Marketing information management includes providing efficiently and effectively information to help make marketing decisions. Marketing information was discussed in Chapter 13 and will be discussed further in Chapter 17.

Product or Service Planning

Product or service planning is the process of developing the product or service mix in response to market opportunities. Skill in performing this function includes the ability to:

■ Conduct market opportunity analysis studies

■ Perform product or service planning activities

■ Work with the various components of the product or service mix so as to position and achieve a desired image

■ Determine quality assurance, grades and standards, warranties and guarantees
■ Conduct product or service performance evaluation

Purchasing or Buying

In making their own buying decisions, retail marketers must study how and why consumers buy certain products and services. The study of consumer or buyer behavior is critical to the firm's overall success. Some retail service businesses must purchase component parts, raw materials, and equipment. For example, restaurant managers must know what foods are popular with their customers in order to purchase appropriate ingredients. Cooking utensils, appliances, and supplies must also be purchased for use in preparing and serving the food. Retail buyers of goods have to choose the styles and designs they believe will sell the following season.

Purchasing or buying includes skill and knowledge of the planning and procedures necessary to obtain goods and services for use in the business or for resale. This includes (1) determining needs, (2) identifying sources, (3) purchasing or buying activities, and (4) management of the purchasing or buying function. See Unit 18.

Pricing

To maximize sales, goods and services must be priced appropriately. The demand for most products or services varies inversely with price. This means that when price goes up, demand usually goes down; when price goes down, demand usually goes up.

The pricing function includes determining a price for a product or service on which buyer and seller can agree. This includes: (1) determining selling prices, (2) adjusting selling prices, and (3) understanding the effects of credit on price. See Unit 17.

Selling

Selling is often seen as the core of the marketing function. All the other marketing activities ultimately aim at selling goods and services to produce income. All retail marketers must "sell" their goods or services to someone if they are to succeed. Selling is usually done through the organization's promotional strategy. Personal selling and sales promotion are the standard sales tools.

Responding to consumer needs and wants through planned, personalized communications in order to influence purchase decisions and ensure satisfaction is addressed extensively in Units 10, 11, and 12.

Promotion

Promotion (advertising, display, and so on), involves organizations communicating information about products, services, images, and/or ideas to influence consumer behavior. A major portion of this book has been devoted to promotion, including Units 13, 14, and 15.

Distribution

Marketing activities associated with the physical movement or transfer of ownership of a product or service from producer to consumer are classified under the distribution function. Two of the activities under the distribution function that are particularly important for retail marketers are transportation and storage. Goods cannot be sold without transporting them to the point of sale and then to the ultimate consumer. Careful management of the transportation of products can bring significant savings in the cost of selling them. The vast network of transportation systems in the United States enables many firms to centralize their distribution facilities. This helps them to serve even customers in remote areas economically. Many retail marketers provide their own transportation.

A large retailing firm may have its own storage and transportation facilities to get merchandise to its customers quickly and efficiently.

Storage is required to keep goods until they are to be made available to consumers. Some goods, such as agricultural produce, must be stored because they are produced seasonally. Many retailers store goods near their consumers in order to avoid delays in transportation.

Financing

The financing function involves handling and recording all money receipts, payments, and credit transactions. It also includes locating possible sources of capital to cover initial expenses until profits can be earned through sales. Most retailer marketers must pay for their goods and services before they receive payment from customers. This requires financing. Money is often borrowed to pay for the products or services so that an adequate inventory can be maintained.

Activities that must be performed include: (1) budgeting for financial needs, (2) obtain-ing business credit, and (3) extending credit to consumers.

Risk Management

Whenever goods or services are produced or bought to be sold, there is the risk that they cannot be sold profitably. Risk taking, then, is an inevitable function in any marketing activity.

Risk management is the managing of marketing activities to optimize the relations of potential loss to gain. Risk management will be discussed further in the next section of this chapter.

■

RISK MANAGEMENT

It is said that "Nothing is certain except death and taxes." Retailers live with still another certainty—that of risk on products and services that they own. They also cannot be certain if their business will succeed and which competing ones will fail. In Chapter 10 we defined risk as the uncertainty of earning a profit.

Dealing With Risk

The three basic ways to deal with business risks are: (1) reduce the risk; (2) transfer the risk to someone else whenever possible, by carrying insurance; and (3) save to cover possible future losses. The best solution is often a combination of these approaches.

The simplest method is to reduce the risk through the use of the marketing research process described in Chapter 13. For example, keeping good sales and inventory records can avoid risks associated with having too much stock on hand at the end of each selling season.

Risk transfer means shifting the risk to an organization outside the business that agrees to shoulder the risk of others. The best-known form of risk transfer is **insurance**, by which an insurance company agrees, for a fee (a premium), to pay an agreed sum of money for a given loss. Examples of insurance include automobile, health, life, property, and liability insurance.

Property and liability insurance provide protection against loss of, or damage to, property itself and against any liability caused by owning the property. A **property loss** is a financial loss resulting from fire, theft, vandalism, or other destructive damage to property. A **liability loss** is a financial loss suffered when a person's or business's property causes damage or injury to another person. Examples are injury to a customer caused by a product or service you sold, or a broken leg suffered by someone who slipped in your parking lot.

Some types of risks can be minimized by saving money in advance to cover a possible risk. For example, instead of paying a high insurance premium to cover all possible dam-

ages to delivery trucks, a retailer might take out insurance just for the damage costs over $1000.

Types of Business Risks

The four types of risks the retailer may face include: (1) marketing-centered risks, (2) customer-centered risks, (3) property-centered risks, and (4) employee-centered risks.

Marketing-Centered Risks   Changes in consumer demand are very difficult to predict. One part of demand, individual preference for a good or a service, can be changed by many factors. Many products are popular for only a short period of time. The sales of roller skates or home video recorders, for example, will depend on their popularity among consumers.

The ability of consumers to buy goods and services also changes. Unemployment and inflation are two conditions that change the buying power of consumers and therefore add to the risks of retailers. Changing conditions might also interfere with retailers' efforts. A change in the sales tax, for example, might cause changes in shopping patterns.

Think about the risks undertaken by the owner of a record store. The owner must try to figure out what styles of music and what recording artists will be good sellers. Furthermore, the number of albums sold is influenced by forces that are beyond the control of the record store owner. The selection of music played by local radio stations is one factor that enters the situation. Or the appearance of a band at a local concert might bring about a sudden demand for that group's albums.

Customer-Centered Risks   Customers are the source of profit for business, but they also are the center of ever-increasing amounts of business risk. Much of this risk is attributable to personal injury, product liability, and bad debts. Most customer-centered risks are insurable, and smart retailers buy insurance to be able to pay for personal injury and product liability suits against their business. **Personal injury suits** can be reduced by practicing good business housekeeping. For example, if the aisles of a store are free of cartons and other obstacles, customers are less likely to stumble.

Customers' bills that cannot be collected are called **bad debts**. Bad debts are an un-avoidable risk associated with credit selling. Most customers will pay their bills with no more than a friendly reminder. A few customers will intentionally try to avoid payment.

Property-Centered Risks   In contrast to marketing-centered and customer-centered risks, property-centered risks involve highly visible assets such as buildings and vehicles. When these physical assets are lost, they are quickly missed. Most property-centered risks, however, are insurable. Examples of property-centered risks include fires, floods, tornadoes, business interruption, burglary, and shoplifting. In Chapter 49 security risks, including shoplifting, are discussed.

Employee-Centered Risks   Employee-centered losses occur indirectly due to employees' personal circumstances or directly through employee actions against the business. A physically sick or injured employee is an example of an indirect loss. An employee strike, on the other hand, is a direct action against the business and is a major concern for many businesses.

Thefts by employees may include not only cash but also merchandise, tools, and such supplies as stamps. There is always the risk of forgery, raising of checks, or other illegal practices. The trusted bookkeeper may enter into a deal with an outsider to arrange for payment of bogus invoices or invoices of double or triple the correct amount. In addition to

Property centered risks, such as a fire, could wipe out a business if it were not insured.

insuring employees, the firm's major protection against fraud is a system of internal checks or control.

TRADE TALK

Define each term and use it in a sentence.

Bad debts	Personal injury
External marketing	suits
environment	Place utility
Form utility	Possession utility
Function	Productivity
Gross national	Property loss
product (GNP)	Risk transfer
Inflation	Time utility
Insurance	Utility
Liability loss	

C·H·A·P·T·E·R

15 Government's Role in Retail Marketing

■ You walk into a drug store, buy a bottle of capsules, carry it home, and take the recommended dosage. How can you be sure the drug you took is safe—that the contents of the bottle haven't been tampered with? Americans found themselves asking this question when seven people in the Chicago area died after taking Extra Strength Tylenol capsules laced with cyanide.

■ A national retail firm was ordered by the Federal Trade Commission (FTC) to stop advertising a washing machine at a very low price. Evidence showed that the company discouraged sales personnel from selling this advertised product and instead urged them to sell higher-priced washers.

■ A woman who wanted to start a small dress shop in her house was denied permission to do so because of local zoning laws.

■ A community was declared a disaster area by the President of the United States, making 25 small retail business owners eligible for low-cost loans to reconstruct their stores, which had been severely damaged by a flood.

These four different cases show the types of social and legal factors that take place on the local, state, and national levels. They are examples of the roles of government in retail marketing.

Years ago, large manufacturers were able to obtain unfair prices for the goods and services they produced, and at times they sold products that were unsafe to use. Eventually, legislators at various government levels were persuaded to pass laws governing business practices.

These government laws both assist and control business. So a knowledge of existing government legislation is an important part of any retailer's education. Government laws and legislation affect business location and operation, retail prices, advertising, competition, products and services offered, and the channels of distribution.

In Chapter 10, we discussed two of the roles of government—collecting taxes and providing services. Additional roles of government include: maintaining the market system, maintaining a competitive environment, redistributing income, and maintaining economic stability.

MAINTAINING THE MARKET SYSTEM

Government takes steps such as protecting private property, guarding against unfair practices, and generally helping to ensure that the market system is given a chance to work. Each level of government uses those techniques that best serve the needs of a majority of the citizens within its jurisdiction.

Local Government

Many county, city, and township governments are concerned with making sure that all retail marketers follow proper business practices. One way governments do this is by issuing business licenses. Other methods that governments use include enforcing zoning and building laws and imposing restric-

tions on direct-to-the-home and on-the-street selling.

Licenses   The **business license**, which is required by many communities, is legal or official permission to operate a business. It is an effective method of local regulation because it can be taken back if the business does not meet the standards of operation that the community requires.

Local officials usually require companies to obtain a license if their business is one that affects the health and well-being of consumers. Examples are restaurants, barber shops, beauty shops, and health and reducing studios. Usually, these types of businesses must pass periodic inspections, and sometimes they are restricted to certain days and hours of operation.

Zoning and Building Laws   Other local ordinances that concern the retailer are zoning and building laws. **Zoning laws** restrict the types of business that may operate on a particular piece of property or in a certain area. Such laws may prevent retailers from locating their business on a site they have chosen. So retailers should always check

In some places, a restaurant must meet certain standards to qualify for a business license.

with their local zoning board before deciding where to locate their places of business. Zoning laws also protect individuals located in residential areas from having undesirable commercial firms within the area.

Building ordinances are requirements for the construction or remodeling of buildings. In most communities, a building must meet certain construction standards in plumbing, electricity, and fireproofing. A building permit will not be granted if the building plan does not meet these standards, which are designed to ensure consumer safety.

Direct-to-the-Home Selling Restrictions

In many localities, retailers who use direct-to-the-home salespeople have to obey additional regulations. Some communities require licenses for such salespeople; others have laws that prohibit salespeople from entering premises without the prior consent of the occupant. Such licensing is intended to protect residents from door-to-door salespeople who use deceptive selling techniques.

State Government

State governments have, over the years, passed various types of laws that have affected retailers. Examples of state legislative efforts include involvement in areas such as sales taxes, unfair trade practices, fraud and usury laws, and licenses and charters. Some states try to attract business by lowering their taxes, or they try to keep certain kinds of business out by raising taxes.

Sales Taxes

State governments and sometimes local governments use retail sales as a source of tax revenue. In fact, by collecting sales taxes, retailers in some states collect more than half of all the revenues for their state. In some states, local sales taxes are added to the state sales tax. Retailers must collect both these taxes from customers and are accountable to the state and local governments. State retail sales taxes may also make it difficult for retailers in areas that border another state to compete with neigh-

TABLE 1 / IMPORTANT CONSUMER PROTECTION LEGISLATION

Year	Name of Law	Purpose and Function
Product Safety		
1962	Food and Drug Amendments	Requires pretesting of drugs for safety and effectiveness and labeling of drugs by generic name.
1966	Child Protection Act	Bans sale of hazardous toys and articles.
1967	Flammable Fabrics Act	Broadens federal authority to set safety standards for inflammable fabrics, including clothing and household products.
1968	Federal Hazardous Substances Act	Requires retailers to prominently display a sign informing consumers of the fact that certain hazardous products are sold in their store.
	Toy Safety Act	Requires retailers to give consumers a refund if a toy is found to be dangerous.
1970	Public Health Smoking Act	Extends warning about the hazards of cigarette smoking.
	Poison Prevention Packing Act	Authorizes standards for child-resistant packaging of hazardous substances.
1972	Consumer Product Safety Act	Establishes a commission to set safety standards for consumer products and bans products presenting undue risk of injury.
1975	Auto Recall Repair Law	Requires tire, auto, and replacement-part makers to offer refund, replacement, or refund options on defective products.

TABLE 1 (*continued*)

Marketing Credibility

1939	Wool Products Labeling Act	Requires that information about the textiles fiber content be included on a tag or label together with care instructions.
1958	Textile Fiber Products Identification Act	Requires that information about the textile's fiber content be included on a tag or label together with care instructions.
1966	Fair Packaging and Labeling Act	Requires producers to state what a package contains, how much it contains, and who made the product.
1975	Magnuson-Moss Warranty Act	Requires clearly understandable and accurate wording in ordinary language with every term and condition spelled out in writing for all warranties.

Fair Payment Arrangements

1968	Consumer Credit Protection Act (Truth-in-Lending)	Requires full disclosure of terms and conditions of finance charges in credit transactions.
1971	Fair Credit Reporting Act	Protects consumers from inaccurate or obsolete information in their credit records. Guarantees the consumer's right to know what personal data are being reported.
1975	Equal Credit Opportunity Act	Makes it illegal for banks, retailers, and other lenders to deny or terminate credit on the basis of age, color, marital status, national origin, sex, or because one is on welfare.
	Fair Credit Billing Act	Sets up billing dispute settlement procedures and requires prompt correction of billing mistakes.
1978	Fair Debt Collection Practices Act	Protects consumers from being threatened, harassed, or otherwise abused by debt collectors.
	Electronic Funds Transfer Act	Provides protection for consumers if EFT transaction card is lost or stolen.

boring merchants across the state line. This is especially true if the adjoining state has a lower sales tax.

Unfair Trade Practices A wide variety of unfair trade practice legislation has been passed at various times. However, some of the laws are not enforced effectively. The most common unfair trade practice acts now in force are related to minimum markup. These laws affect the amount that retailers may raise the selling price of goods over what they paid. The purpose of such laws is to prevent retailers from underselling their competitors unfairly. In most states, however, the

law allows exceptions. Most of these laws are not strictly enforced, but they must still be considered by retailers.

Most states also have laws to control false and misleading advertising. These laws vary greatly from state to state, but they all make it illegal for advertisers to deceive the consumer. Some states also have **blue laws**, which prohibit selling certain types of products, such as alcoholic beverages, on Sunday.

Fraud and Usury Most states have laws against fraud and usury. **Fraud** is an act of deceit by which someone seeks to gain some unfair or dishonest advantage. **Usury** is the charging of interest in excess of a legal rate. Laws against both fraud and usury have been in existence for many years, and emphasis on enforcing them more effectively has increased.

Licenses and Charters   Some states require certain businesses to be licensed. Among the retailers who have to obtain licenses are real estate agents, barber shop and beauty shop operators, motor vehicle dealers, funeral directors, and pharmacists.

States also regulate the right to establish certain businesses. For example, banks, insurance companies, and telephone, gas, and electric companies must be chartered by the state. (A **charter** is a written document granting the right of organization and other privileges and specifying the form of organization and operation.) In most states, the purposes for which these businesses may be formed are limited, and the period of residence of the incorporators and the amount of capital required are specified by law.

Federal Government

In response to consumer demand, the federal government has established regulations to control various types of business activities. The federal government also issues currency and regulates the money supply.

Consumer Rights   In 1962, President John F. Kennedy, in an address to Congress, proclaimed that consumers have four basic rights:

1. *The right to safety.* We live in an affluent nation, where mass production and complicated distribution systems have increased the possibility of dangerous products being manufactured and sold. The right to safety means that the consumers have a right to be protected against danger from inferior products and deceptive industry practices.

2. *The right to be informed.* Consumers are entitled to complete and accurate product information so that they can make an informed choice among available products. Consumers must be protected against fraudulent, deceitful, or misleading information, advertising, or labeling.

3. *The right to choose.* Consumers have a right to spend their money on any legal product or service they choose. They are further entitled to choose from a variety of products and services of satisfactory quality that are competitively priced.

4. *The right to be heard.* Consumers' views should be given consideration by retailers, manufacturers, and government alike. Consumers' interests are entitled to receive sympathetic consideration by government bodies in the formation and administration of policy on consumer issues.

As a result of federal consumer protective legislation, retailers have to be aware of and follow many rules and regulations that deal with consumer purchasing. The federal laws—as well as their purposes and functions—that retailers should know about are given in summary form in Table 1. These laws, of course, do not affect every retailer.

Two laws that are of major importance to retail marketers are the Fair Packaging and Labeling Act and the Magnuson-Moss Warranty Act.

Fair Packaging and Labeling   The Fair Packaging and Labeling Act has many implications for retailers. This act requires that packaged consumer products used in interstate commerce be honestly and informatively labeled. Some of the major provisions are that labels must:

■ Identify the commodity and give the name and place of business of the manufacturer, packer, or distributor
■ Give the common name of the product and list the ingredients in order of their importance

- Contain a statement of net contents in units appropriate for the product in a uniform location on the principal display panel
- Be free of such misleading terms as "jumbo pound" and "giant quart"
- Give the net quantity per serving if the number of servings is stated
- Show dating of products to indicate freshness

This law also prohibits packaging the product with an unnecessary amount of packing material or air space.

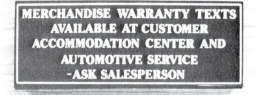

Retailers need to know about the warranties for products they sell because consumers have the right to review the warranty before they buy.

Magnuson-Moss Warranty Act The Magnuson-Moss Warranty Act of 1975 gave the Federal Trade Commission the power to require clearly understandable and accurate wording in warranties. A **warranty**, also called a **guarantee,** is an agreement that the manufacturer will be responsible for any defects in a product and will replace or repair a product that is faulty. Warranties on consumer products that cost more than $10 must be available for consumers to look at before they buy. Consumers can also force manufacturers to keep their warranty promises. The Magnuson-Moss Warranty Act specifically requires that all warranties must be easy to read and understand.

■

MAINTAINING COMPETITION

To make sure that the market system will keep working efficiently, government takes steps to maintain competition.

Competitive markets have a number of attractive features. Competition makes producers more efficient and more responsive to the wants of consumers. Initiative and enterprise are encouraged and often rewarded with success. And with competition, many people take part in the economic decision-making process.

However, the logic of competition must be considered. People compete in order to win. When some people win, it may become impossible for other people to compete on an equal basis. For example, if a company is successful, it might begin to receive favorable treatment when buying raw materials. If other companies wish to enter the same area of business, they may be unable to buy the raw materials at such favorable rates. Maintaining effective competitive markets is something that government must handle.

At the close of the nineteenth century, small businesses were threatened by the unfair business practices of large corporations. There were complaints that corporations were seeking a monopoly of trade. (A **monopoly** is the control of the supply of a product or service by one person or group of people.) In response to these complaints, the federal government passed the Sherman Antitrust Act in 1890 and the Clayton Act in 1914. The Clayton Act was passed in an attempt to curb efforts of large organizations to drive smaller ones out of business.

Federal Trade Commission (FTC)

In 1914, the Federal Trade Commission Act was passed to set up the legal structure for enforcing the Sherman Act, the Clayton Act, and similar legislation. Retailers can be found guilty of restricting trade if they perform any of the following:

1. Pressuring manufacturers not to sell to competitive retailers

2. Buying out other retail firms to substantially reduce competition

3. Agreeing with other retailers to fix the prices of goods they sell for the purpose of restricting price competition

4. Underselling retailers in one area of the country, for the purpose of forcing competitors out of business, and at the same time selling the same products at higher prices in other parts of the country.

Robinson-Patman Act

Another federal law that is of major importance to retailers is the Robinson-Patman Act of 1936. This act was intended to curb the price advantages enjoyed by large retailers. It specifically prohibits manufacturers from giving and retailers from taking the following:

1. Discounts for purchases unless they are justified by a reduction in costs or expenses for the product

2. Discounts in the form of agents' or brokers' fees, unless these are available to all buyers

3. Unequal advertising, display, sales assistance, and other promotional allowances

The Robinson-Patman Act does not make all price differences illegal. For example, it is legal for one retailer to be charged a lower price than another for the same product if the manufacturer can prove that it costs less to sell it to the first retailer. Also, discounts are legal for such practices as prompt payment and buying in large quantity, and it is usually the large retailer who can take advantage of such discounts.

U.S. Small Business Administration

The U.S. **Small Business Administration (SBA)** is a federal agency, created by Congress in 1953 to assist, counsel, and champion the millions of American small businesses that are the backbone of this country's competitive free-enterprise economy.

The mission of the SBA, simply put, is to help people get into business and to stay in business. To do this, the SBA acts as an advocate for small business; at the direction of Congress, the agency espouses the cause of small business, explains small business's role and contributions to our society and economy, and advocates programs and policies that will help small business. The SBA performs this advocacy role in close coordination with other federal agencies; with Congress; and with financial, educational, professional, and trade institutions and associations.

The agency also provides prospective, new, and established persons in the small business community with financial assistance, management counseling, and training. The SBA also helps get and direct government procurement contracts for small firms.

The agency makes special efforts to assist women, minorities, the handicapped, and veterans to get into business and stay in business, because such persons long have faced unusual difficulties in the private marketplace.

■

INCOME REDISTRIBUTION

Even competitive markets may lead to inequalities in wealth and income. To limit these inequalities, government has tried to provide some means of income redistribution. Using tax revenues, government has developed certain welfare programs. Such programs provide at least a limited income for people who are not able to work or who cannot find work. Government programs in education, housing, and health care also help to remove income inequalities. Ability-to-pay taxes also help to limit inequalities in income.

Most Americans agree that taxation is necessary, but there is little agreement as to how heavily individuals and businesses should be taxed. And some people are against government's using taxation as a way to redistribute income. However, many people feel that income redistribution is necessary to make sure that economic power remains widespread.

The federal government is playing an increasingly important role in supervising the welfare of employees. There are many employee welfare regulations designed to protect or benefit workers, and they all affect the way retailers run their businesses. The following sections discuss various types of federally funded programs designed to redistribute income and provide for the welfare of millions of Americans.

Fair Labor Standards Act

The Fair Labor Standards Act of 1938 established a minimum wage, maximum hours, the principle of equal pay for equal work, and child labor laws.

The child labor section of the act states that 14- and 15-year-olds may work in a number of jobs in retailing. They may do clerical, cashiering, or sales work. They may pack and carry orders. They may work in a kitchen, do

Food stamps are an example of a federal government program of income redistribution.

cleanup work, pump gasoline, and clean and polish cars. But they may work only at certain times if they are employed in a business subject to federal labor laws. In addition, they must obtain a proof-of-age certificate, sometimes called a worker's permit.

Occupational Safety and Health Act (OSHA)

The Occupational Safety and Health Act requires all employers to provide their employees with a safe place in which to work. The act specifies certain safety and health standards that employers must obey. For example, aisles and passageways must be kept clear and in good repair, with no obstructions that could create a hazard. Retail employers must also eliminate slippery floors, poorly lighted stairways, torn or unanchored floor coverings, and loose wires.

Social Security Act

Social Security is a federal government program set up under the Social Security Act of 1935. It provides cash payments and hospital care to retired or disabled workers and their dependents and to survivors of deceased workers. The benefits are paid for by a tax based on the worker's salary. Employer and employee each pay half the tax. Anyone who is engaged in a business must make allowances for the expense of providing these and similar benefits for employees.

Employee Retirement Income Security Act (ERISA)

This act was passed in 1975 to establish guidelines for starting and administering employee retirement funds or pensions. The purpose of the legislation is to ensure that when employees retire, their pension funds will be available to fulfill the contractual retirement agreement.

Wagner Act

The Wagner Act of 1935, also known as the National Labor Relations Act, guarantees the rights of workers to organize unions, bargain with employers, and choose which unions to join. It outlaws such unfair employer labor practices as penalizing workers for belonging to unions and closing or threatening to close firms if employees join a union.

Taft-Hartley Act

The Taft-Hartley Act of 1947 modified the Wagner Act by enabling states to adopt right-to-work laws. A **right-to-work law** is a law under which union membership is not required for employment. This means that in states where right-to-work laws have been passed, neither labor nor management can require an individual to join a union as a condition of employment.

Civil Rights Act

The Fair Employment Practices section of the Civil Rights Act of 1964 makes it illegal for employers to refuse to hire or promote employees because of their race, color, religion, sex, or national origin. It also outlaws segregation of workers on any of these grounds.

■

MAINTAINING ECONOMIC STABILITY

Another function of government is to take steps to ensure the stability of the American economy. By and large, the level of business activity in an economy increases when households, businesses, and government agencies spend more. When they spend less, the level of business activity declines and the level of unemployment rises.

Full Employment

To stabilize the economy, government tries to achieve relatively full employment at a relatively stable price level. Government uses **fiscal policies**—taxation and spending—and **monetary policies**—controlling the supply of money and credit—to achieve economic stability. If the level of business activity is low, the federal government might increase its spending, cut taxes, or increase the money supply.

Increasingly, local communities and states are developing strategies to attract new business and industry and to retain existing businesses so as to improve employment opportunities.

Fighting Inflation

To fight inflation, government might cut its spending, increase taxes, or reduce the money supply. Sometimes, govenment implements a combination of these strategies. In a modern industrial society, achieving economic stability is a task our government feels it must fulfill.

TRADE TALK

Define each term and use it in a sentence.

Blue laws	Monetary policies
Building	Monopoly
ordinances	Right-to-work law
Business license	Smal Business
Charter	Administration (SBA)
Fiscal policies	usury
Fraud	Warranty
Guarantee	Zoning laws

CAN YOU ANSWER THESE?

1. What are the six roles of government in retail marketing?

2. How does government legislation affect retailing?

3. How are local governments involved in retailing?

4. How can the SBA help retailers?

5. What are three rights of consumers?

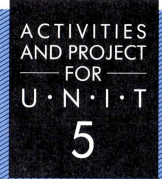

ACTIVITIES AND PROJECT FOR U·N·I·T 5

RETAIL MARKETING CASE

Murray's, an independent department store in a downtown area, has decided to update its men's department. The department will now have to be more competitive with three new stores located in the shopping center on the edge of town: a large chain store, a men's specialty store, and a discount store.

Murray's menswear department chiefly handles work clothes. Research carried out by some of its staff revealed that its competitors stock not only work clothes but also an assortment of sports clothes and other items. The large chain store turned out to be Murray's largest competitor because of the work clothes that it carries in its men's department. The men's specialty store carries a complete line of fashion clothes for men, but it does not carry any work clothes. The discount store carries a large variety of clothing, but it carries its stock in small quantities only. Its prices are lower than those of the other two stores.

The research staff at Murray's drew up the chart on page 126, which analyzes the merchandise lines and prices involved. With the information they have obtained, they are now ready to consider such measures as adding or dropping lines, adjusting prices, and developing a new image for the store.

1. Is the research conducted by the staff at Murray's as complete as it should be? Why or why not? If not, what additional research should have been done?

2. Is it always advisable to do what competitors do? Why or why not?

3. What changes do you think should should be made at Murray's? Why?

PRODUCT LINE AND PRICE COMPARISON

Item	Murray's	Chain Store	Discount Store	Specialty Store
Belts		$ 6–$ 8	$ 4–$ 8	$ 8–$ 12
Cufflinks		$ 5–$ 9	$ 5–$ 9	$ 7–$ 17
Dress slacks		$ 8–$ 16	$ 8–$ 16	$ 17–47
Gloves	$ 2.55–$ 7	$ 4–$ 8	$ 4–$ 8	$ 10–$ 22
Jeans		$ 9–$ 12	$ 9–$ 12	$ 17–$ 47
Shop aprons	$ 3.50		$ 3	
Socks	$ 2.95–$ 3.95	$ 2.65–$ 3	$ 2.49–$ 3	$ 3.25
Sport coats		$ 27–$ 42	$ 22	$ 37 and up
Sport shirts	$ 6–$ 8	$ 6–$ 11	$ 5–$ 9	$ 8–$ 19
Suits		$ 42 and up		$ 57 and up
Sweaters		$ 10–$ 17	$ 7–$ 14	$ 16–$ 62
Ties		$ 4–$ 7	$ 3–$ 5	$ 6–$ 14
Underwear	$ 4.98	$ 4.98	$ 4–$ 5	$ 6
Work pants	$ 7–$ 14	$ 8–$ 11	$ 6–$ 8	
Work shirts	$ 5–$ 9	$ 6–$ 9	$ 5–$ 7	
Work socks	$ 3–$ 4			

PROJECT: MARKETING RESEARCH

YOUR PROJECT GOAL

Given a retailing problem, you will review the results of a survey questionnaire, interpret them, and use your interpretation to make recommendations to solve the problem.

PROCEDURE

In Unit 4 you conducted a class marketing survey. Secure a copy of that project to use with this project. Now, assume that you have been called to a meeting of your local Chamber of Commerce. Three retailers are considering expanding their businesses and want your help. These companies are interested in attracting the business of *your* classmates.

(a) A mail-order clothing company is considering expanding its junior department to include business suits.
(b) A reasonably-priced family restaurant is considering removing three of its booths and adding a take-out section.
(c) A small record store is considering expanding into the vacant store next door and opening a "Putting on the Hits" studio. Customers could select a record and the studio would prepare a video tape that looked as if the customer was singing the song on the record.

1. Write a paragraph that summarizes the results of your survey. Present the results of each of your categories in both total numbers and in percentages.
2. Decide which of the three businesses you will advise.
3. Explain why you would or would not recommend expansion, *basing your advice on the results of your survey.*
4. Do you believe your classmates' responses would be typical of all students in your school? Would they be typical of all high school students? Why or why not?

EVALUATION

You will be evaluated on how effectively you can use the data you gathered in Unit 4.

U·N·I·T 6
DEVELOPING RETAIL MARKETING STRATEGIES

C·H·A·P·T·E·R

16 *Retail Marketing Trends*

■ In the Civic Center in Hartford, Connecticut, a frantic office worker on her way to the bank rushes up to the Avon Beauty Express, a telephone booth-sized electronic kiosk (boxlike structure) in the center's shopping mall. She orders $50 of her usual make-up, skin-care products, and perfume, plus some cologne for her husband—all without a store, a salesperson, or a hassle. Elapsed time: 3 minutes.

■ In Los Angeles, customers of P.U.F.F.S., a California-based manufacturer of upholstered furniture with its own retail stores, see customized furniture and room settings on a wide screen, electronic projection system in a corner of the store. A salesperson operates the computer-driven system, which shows various combinations of furniture in room settings of the customer's choice.

■ At a Sears Roebuck and Co. store in San Diego, California, electronic kiosks guide customers through basic information on its financial services and a wide range of fashions, giving customers printouts of their choices to take to salespeople. Other customers can also view and order Sears products from their home TV sets.

These examples of current trends show how retailers respond to the challenges of marketing in the late twentieth century. Some 47 percent of personal income is presently spent on retail goods, but this percentage has slipped from 62 percent in 1948. Taxes, housing, medical services, and other expenses are taking an ever-larger share of the consumer dollar. As retailers compete for the rest, a number of trends can be seen.

Malcolm P. McNair, a noted marketing scholar, has suggested that the rise and fall of forms of retailing follows a cycle called the **wheel of retailing**. According to this theory, new concepts win acceptance through low costs and low prices. As they mature, product lines, services, and features are add-

Interactive TV home shopping is a trend brought about by the technology of cable TV access and touch tone telephones.

purchased by value-conscious "baby boom" families, individuals with limited incomes, and other individuals who are concerned with price. **Fashion goods**, on the other hand, are products that are higher-priced and appeal to consumers with higher disposable incomes. The term "fashion" refers to the popularity of a particular style of merchandise. Fashion goods are more commonly purchased by lifestyle-oriented, two-income families or single people with larger salaries.

In this chapter we will look at the environmental trends that are likely to have the greatest impact on retail marketing in the future. We will examine some of the strategies retail marketers will employ in response to these trends. The major environmental trends that we will consider can be grouped according to whether they are brought about by changing technology or changing consumers.

ed. This makes the concepts more attractive, but it also raises their costs. At some point stores face new, lower-cost competitors.

Electronic selling is just coming onto the scene. Off-price clothing stores (stores that sell name-brand clothes at lower than regular price) are in a stage of rapid growth. Discount stores and supermarkets have reached maturity. Department stores seem to be in a stage of decline.

No single retailer can hope to be all things to all customers. The industry is segmenting into a wide variety of sales outlets, which can be grouped under two headings: commodity, or basic resources, and fashion resources. Tomorrow's consumers will be divided into those who want recognizable national brands at the lowest prices and those who are willing to pay for up-to-the-minute fashion and services.

The term **commodity goods** can be used to describe those goods that are competitively priced but serve the basic needs of consumers. They will be more commonly

■

CHANGING TECHNOLOGY

The technological revolution has brought many electronic devices to the aid of the retailer. Smart machines now help at the checkout stand, process credit-card transactions, do billings, and maintain inventory-control records.

These systems are now used throughout the marketplace, from neighborhood groceries and restaurants to such specialized retailers as computer stores, to department stores, and to mail-order operations. These devices enable retailers to identify and serve specific market segments at a profit—a task that would have seemed impossible a few years ago. By improving the mechanics of their operation, retailers can better concentrate on their primary function: selling.

New ways of communicating will change the very appearance of the retail business. Tomorrow's retail stores will not always fit our image of a dress boutique or a bookshop. Walking in and touching things may be impossible or impractical in many cases. Many purchases can and will be completed remotely through interactive video systems, computer networks, or telephones. Banks are rapidly adopting the concept of electronic service, as are some travel agencies. There is no reason to assume that other services, such as insurance or legal and accounting services, could not be marketed the same way.

Electronic Shopping

The explosive growth of electronic shopping, which has paralleled the development of home computers and videotext services, will bring profound changes to the retail industry. Retailers will have to take a triple-threat approach to selling, using a combination of stores, mail-order catalogs, and electronic shopping services to attract more quality- and value-conscious shoppers.

Consumers across the country will be able to sign onto a computer, either in their homes or at a special kiosk in their favorite store, look at pictures and read detailed descriptions of selected merchandise, comparison shop for features and prices, and then use their credit cards to order, all in a matter of minutes, and all by spending little or no time in a retail store. Electronic retailing is expected to grow from $285 million in sales in 1985 to $55 billion by the year 2000.

Like the telephone in the early 1900s, the automated teller machine (ATM) in the 1970s, and electronic funds transfer in the 1980s, electronic shopping is clearly the wave of the future. But it is one that will take time to reach and be accepted by the average consumer. ATM-style shopping kiosks in public buildings, retail stores, employee cafeterias, hotels, banks, and shopping malls will fuel the continued growth of electronic shopping. Most industry observers agree that such growth will come slowly, possibly beginning to take off in the late 1980s.

Shopping in Public Places The heart of the electronic kiosk, which is about the size of a telephone booth, is a touch-sensitive screen similar to a television screen. By touching defined areas on the screen, a shopper chooses, "menus," or departments to browse in, and then progressively narrows the field to the item he or she wants to buy.

Once the merchandise is selected, the shopper runs a credit card through a reader, and types in the billing and shipping address. Most companies' main computers process the orders the same night and send them out by parcel service the next day.

Some of the prime reasons for the growing acceptance of electronic shopping are the increase in the number of women who work outside the home, the inconvenience of in-store shopping, and the shortage of knowledgeable salespeople.

The impact of electronic shopping kiosks on retailers will be seen first and most dramatically in mail-order operations. It is predicted that electronic shopping kiosks could nearly double mail order's current 8.5 percent share of general-merchandise sales. Electronic shopping will change the basic economics of the mail-order business, driving costs down and increasing the size potential.

But the growth of companies such as CompuSave Corporation shows just how far and how fast electronic retailing is spreading to conventional stores, giving even small convenience stores a chance to become large, general-merchandise retailers. Currently, California-based CompuSave's electronic kiosks sell more than 2000 brand-name items—including televisions, cameras, VCRs, and household appliances. The kiosks enable retailers to accomplish a great deal in less than 6 square feet of space: big-ticket, space-eating goods, such as electronic equipment and furniture, can be ordered directly from a single, central warehouse, avoiding the need for more space in new stores.

In-Home Shopping While the idea of electronically shopping for a TV or a stereo system within the comforts of one's own living room may once have seemed a bit far-fetched, shop-at-home services may well have a dramatic effect on retailing over the next decade.

Research shows that 45 percent of U.S. consumers would subscribe to an at-home shopping service, and that 25 percent would use it regularly. Estimates of purchases by in-home electronic shopping by the year 2000 range from $18 billion to $55 billion.

Many retailers believe that the spread of cable television and video catalogs will revolutionize sales and promotion methods. Cable television (CATV) is expected to reach 50 percent of U.S. households by the year 2000. Similarly, by 1990, many Americans will own videocassette and videodisc players.

Video ordering systems will open the way for nonstore selling on a massive scale. All consumers will have to do is turn on the television, request to see a product or service, and immediately contact the retail store or its warehouse. Staple items will be more readily adaptable to this form of shopping than most other types of products.

The cable television shopping system works as follows. First, the consumer orders by punching a product code number into a home computer console and indicating the quantity desired. Regular repeat purchases are made through a special code number, programmed especially for the consumer. Weekly specials are shown on a teleshopper screen. It is possible for a consumer to complete all purchases in 10 to 15 minutes.

Second, accompanying the ordering system is an order-processing, delivery, and billing system that records, interprets, and processes an order, schedules delivery, and posts transactions in a checkless account. This system eliminates waiting lines, traffic jams, and parking problems.

In the future, a number of technological developments will allow shop-at-home services to capture a larger share of business. Eventually, erasable videodiscs will enable retailers to send customers an entire store catalog via a modem. This will increase the popularity of shopping at home. However, electronic shopping and other new ways to see merchandise will never eliminate traditional retailers' sales totally. Electronic shopping isn't likely to account for more than 10 percent of all general retail sales. In fact, more and more, videotex services enable retailers to advertise merchandise, allowing a store to be open 24 hours a day without increasing overhead.

Home shopping via CATV.

Electronic Funds Transfer

To retailers, **electronic funds transfer (EFT)** refers to the transfer of money to the store's bank account from a customer's bank account. There is a growing interest in EFT because it's a time-saving device for both consumers and retailers. From the consumer's point of view, EFT saves time and makes shopping easier, because it eliminates the need to write checks to pay for orders. From the retailers' point of view, EFT represents a fast and safe method of making sales.

Although a large number of retail experts feel that individual-store credit cards and accounts will be eliminated through the use of a centralized, nationwide credit and banking system, consumers have been more reluctant to accept the concept of the electronic transfer of funds. Some consumers don't like the idea of not having canceled checks to use in balancing their checkbooks; others prefer to deal with humans rather than machines; still others are concerned about the possibility of computer error or the invasion of privacy.

Some of the developments facing retailers from the growing electronic funds transfer system include the following:

1. More retailers will accept credit cards other than their own, single-purpose retailer cards.

2. Customer loyalty to a retailer will be reduced, because customers will use credit cards accepted by a number of retailers rather than the retailer's single-purpose card.

3. Retail operating expenses will be reduced. Collection, bad debts, and so on will no longer be retailer problems.

4. Banking operations will increase in many nonbank settings, such as supermarkets and department stores.

5. Bank personnel will be decreased.

6. Banking services will be available 24 hours per day, 7 days a week.

7. Electronic shopping will be facilitated.

Automated Self-Service Machines

Banking isn't the only service business that will be automated in the years ahead. Self-service machines are already beginning to be used to handle rental-car returns, register and check out hotel guests, and even dispense ski-lift tickets.

Airline tickets are dispensed automatically to credit-card customers who punch flight information into self-service computer terminals at the airport. Automotive service stations sell gasoline to customers who use bank cards and automated pumps. Companies in many retail service industries agree that the consumer will see a great deal of automation in the next 10 years.

Specialization

The electronic revolution has contributed to another trend in retailing: specialization. Prepackaging technology and electronic support systems enable the retail marketer to operate more efficiently and profitably than ever before.

The rapid growth of specialty retailing has been aided by the growth of shopping centers, which provide fertile ground for many small store owners. Malls often give specialty stores preferred leasing arrangements. This ensures a diverse assortment of businesses for the shopping complex. The variety of specialty shops brings more shoppers.

Shopping centers in all different sizes, shapes, and forms are emerging to serve the various needs of consumers, many of whom like to make shopping a pleasant experience. Shopping centers are increasingly being built in new and renovated downtown areas, in suburbs, in small and large communities, and in historic and other tourist areas. The range of products and services sold continues to change rapidly.

Shopping centers in the United States are still expanding, and most are prospering. Approximately 40 percent of all retail sales made in this country now take place in shopping centers. By the year 2000, it is estimated that more than 50 percent of retail sales will take place in shopping centers.

One of the trends in retailing today is to convert an existing building into many specialty shops. These are self-contained shops that specialize in items ranging from stationery to gourmet food. Also, the types of retail establishments located in shopping centers are changing drastically. Among the trends that are surfacing are a greater variety of eating places, more service businesses, more entertainment facilities, and more shops showing up-to-date fashions.

The growth of shopping centers will continue through the year 1990. By the year 2000, experts predict, the rate will decline, in part because of increasing land and construction costs and in part because of the very cost of doing business.

Some centers are already in trouble because of poor management, a poor regional economy, or poor planning. Some of these centers will ultimately fail.

■

CHANGING CONSUMERS

Technological changes affecting the marketplace are often responses to changes indicated by consumer attitudes and wants. Perceptive marketers have reacted to those attitudes and wants with such successes as fast-food restaurants, instant cameras, and designer jeans. Equally notable failures have included paper dresses, personal fallout shelters, and frozen "TV breakfasts."

Understanding the consumer will be increasingly critical. Consumers of the 2000s will be more educated, demanding, and individualistic than any previous generation. These factors will have perhaps the greatest impact on tomorrow's marketplace. Even though consumers may not have specific knowledge of a product or service, their increasing knowledge about the marketplace in general makes it essential that salespeople demonstrate a knowledge of what they are selling.

Consumers are particularly cautious when venturing into specialized markets—sound systems, cameras, and home computers, for example. When they seriously consider buying such expensive and complex items, they try to make themselves at least as knowledgeable as the salesperson, if not more so. Be-

cause they have a keen interest in a particular product, they research the market, read the literature, and then formulate specific questions. Ultimately, they will buy where their questions are answered and where they feel that the sales staff is competent. Vague answers and ignorance are sure to send them to another seller.

Consumers will increasingly expect retailers to stand behind their products' performance and are already less prone to accept advertising claims without proof. Retailers will need to emphasize quality, value, and service, not only in their advertising but in the store itself. Retailers must increasingly cast themselves in the role of consumer advocates—helping individual customers overcome specific problems rather than simply selling a product or service. This modern philosophy of selling is discussed in greater detail in the Selling Band.

The consumers of the 2000s will be more interested in developing a unique personal style than their parents were. Consumers see themselves as individuals with special needs, and they are less likely to adopt a lifestyle or buy a product they are not comfortable with. They surround themselves with goods and services that reflect who they are rather than what is merely in vogue, and they will often wait rather than accept a compromise.

Now that we have taken a quick look at the behavior of the intelligent consumer of the future, let us look specifically at some of the changes in consumers such as demographics, education, and the new consumer types.

Changing Demographics

Several key changes in the U.S. population, estimated to be 274 million by 2004, will take place in the next 20 years. Four of these changes are:

■ Baby boomers will have aged to 35–55 and account for about 30 percent of the U.S. population.
■ Households will be considerably smaller, averaging 2.5 people.

- Sixty percent of all women will be working outside the home.
- Nearly one-fourth of all households will have annual incomes above $50,000 in constant (inflation-adjusted) dollars.

Consumers are also becoming increasingly educated. By the year 1990, 35 percent of the nation's adults will have college training, as opposed to 18 percent in 1965. In addition, since those with more education have higher incomes, it is likely that by 1990, half of all consumer dollars will be spent by those who have at least some college education. The percentage of college-educated individuals is increasing due to changing values as well as the increasing need for better-trained employees in today's sophisticated business enterprises. In addition to formal education, educational television, news, and other activities have increased the general level of knowledge and awareness among consumers. Corporate training programs and various types of adult education courses are also moving the market in this direction. Increasing education has changed the expectations and values of consumers. It has, in general, led to more innovation and to new value structures in the population.

Changing Consumer Values

Values among the population are shifting toward "people over things." Traditional values and the work ethic are on the decline. Quality of life rather than quantity of material possessions is becoming a preference of an increasing number of consumers. People are learning to get pleasure from nonmaterial experiences.

The role of women in society is also shifting dramatically. This is consistent with the increasing number of women in the workforce. In comparison to women who have not pursued a career, working women tend to be more:

1. Appearance-conscious (concerned with fashion and dress)

2. Interested in maintaining a youthful posture

3. Confident and individualistic

4. Concerned with the convenience and ease of performing household duties

5. Knowledgeable and demanding as consumers

6. Interested in leisure and travel

7. Concerned with improving themselves and their educational background

8. Interested in equal rights

9. Indifferent to small price differences among stores or products

The trend toward fitness in the society will continue to grow. A rich, full life is becoming more important. This involves a healthy diet, decreasing consumption of alcohol, and other health-related moves.

New Types of Consumers

Many new types of consumers are emerging as a result of the various forces present in the market. For example, the **buy-for-one consumers** will become increasingly important. They spend their money differently, buying in smaller packages, and seeking more services than shoppers who buy for a family. There will also be an increasing number of **stability-seeking consumers**. These consumers seek a return to yesterday, life simplification, a return to nature, and various hobbies with similar emphasis. A third type is the **get-your-money's-worth consumer**, who is more motivated by the total cost concept: Many substitute labor for dollar cost, buying such things as self-service gas. The **less-for-less consumer** purchases such things as powdered drinks and no-name brand foods. The **time-buying consumer** is another trend to be found in the marketplace. Eating out, convenience store shopping, buying microwave ovens and food processors, and catalog shopping are all examples of the increased concern on the part of many consumers for the poverty of time. Many shoppers are willing to pay extra in

Time buying consumers are willing to spend their money on products and services that save them time.

order to save time that they can then use for other pursuits.

The new consumers will bring special challenges to the retail marketer of the decades ahead:

■ Consumers are much more discriminating in their visits to a retailer, better informed, and much more aware of what products and values are likely to be available from the retailer's competitors.

■ Convenience has become much more important in shopping. To some shoppers, convenience does not merely mean a retailer near one's place of residence. It may mean shopping on the way to work or during one's lunch hour, shopping where one can buy many things from the same retailer, or shopping in a mall where various errands can be accomplished, parking the car only once. Convenience may involve shopping from catalogs or electronic media at home or at some other nonstore location.

■ Business loyalty tends to be of much less importance than in a former era, because of the more widespread distribution of many well-known brands, which can now be obtained from different kinds of outlets with various forms of pricing structures.

■ Consumers have become much more value-sensitive. This means that they are somewhat less interested in low prices for items purchased than they are in the value received for the expenditure made.

■ Discretionary expenditures are much more carefully considered by consumers. Many sources of consumer shopping information indicate a large number of consumers willing to shop only from carefully prepared lists.

In Chapters 11 and 12 we discussed some key retail marketing strategies that will continue to be the wave of the future, such as positioning, targeting, niche marketing, segmentation, and differentiation.

■

CHANGING RETAIL MARKETING STRATEGIES

Changes both in technology and consumer attitudes and needs are of major importance to retail marketing. Some general strategies that retail marketers will employ to cope with these changes include the following:

1. Closer attention to the selection of merchandise and services and more frequent review of the selections to make sure they meet customer wants. This strategy may help a retailer attract new consumer types, such as buy-for-one consumers. Responding to the needs of these consumers will require carrying more items in smaller quantities.

2. Larger assortments create an even greater need for good inventory control and management.

3. Make shopping easier for the consumer by consolidating departments or product or service lines.

4. Review the attitudes and buying habits of local customers regularly, perhaps with periodic use of marketing surveys.

5. Study changes in floor traffic and adjust business hours and personnel accordingly. Because consumers are consolidating their shopping trips, floor traffic has dropped in the morning and early afternoon, but increased in the late afternoon (after work), evening, and weekends.

Specific retail marketing strategies that will be discussed in the next few pages include:

- Specialty and lifestyle retail marketing
- International marketing
- Self-service techniques and scrambled merchandising
- Improving productivity
- Home-based retail businesses

Specialty and Lifestyle Retail Marketing

A few years back, all family shopping was bundled in the hands of one member, the lady of the house, and stores were designed, stocked, and located to be arenas for family shopping, where one woman could find everything she needed for the entire family. But when the lady of the house went out to take a job, the family began to unbundle—family members began doing things for themselves at home—and everybody started to shop.

When family members shop for themselves, and know precisely what they want, a traditional department store becomes less useful—and a specialty store, which offers a concentrated and wide selection of a specific category of goods, becomes more useful. This approach, known as **positioned retailing**, consists of identifying a target market segment and developing a unique retail offering, designed to meet the segment's needs. The retailer positions for one specific seg-

ment and not the mass market. Positioning creates a high level of loyalty and protects a retailer from competitors who try to serve larger market segments.

Positioned retailing will have a large impact in the future. It will lead some firms with broad target markets (such as department and discount stores) to nonprice competition and more specific target focusing. The growth of boutiques and specialty stores, and of department stores with small, self-contained departments is expected to continue. And the department-store concept of one-stop shopping may change to that of the one-stop shopping center.

The trend toward positioning to specialized market segments is clear, and it will carry over to all types of retail service marketing. More and more retail businesses in malls and departments in department stores are focusing their efforts on attracting specific lifestyle segments rather than on people who simply wish to purchase a specific kind of merchandise or service. For example, one new type of store in the 1980s, the computer store, has combined advances in technology with changing lifestyles to become a success in the retail industry. In addition to catering to small businesses, these stores cater to computer hobbyists. Other examples of stores catering to special segments include those that serve large and tall customers, petites, senior citizens, or children.

As consumers continue to adopt more individual lifestyles and buying patterns, more attention will be focused on the home, with large sales growth in household appliances, electronic communications and home-entertainment gear.

Nationwide, markets for goods such as sports equipment, cameras, and even some apparel will increase in the next 20 years. There's an increased demand for this type of goods by the baby-boomers, who will have money to spend because more women will be working. In addition, the minority population—predominantly blacks and Hispanics—will continue to rise dramatically.

Many of the most profound changes will occur in the do-it-yourself industry, widely expected to be booming by 2004. Homeowners' tastes and wants will be driven more by the European lifestyle than by the California lifestyle.

Primary ingredients in the more European lifestyle include:

■ Smaller living spaces, with the dream house no longer a ranch home in suburbia but a condominium, townhouse, or row house

■ More emphasis on interior fashion as a way of showing the owner's lifestyle

■ Homeowners who are willing to spend more of their leisure time, which will also increase, on household projects

Self-Service Techniques and Scrambled Merchandise

One of the most significant trends in merchandising for the past three decades has been the increased use of self-service and self-selection. Self-service has reduced the amount of labor needed and let the store serve more customers more quickly. Indeed, mass merchandising is not really possible without some degree of self-service. **Mass merchandising** involves retailers presenting a discount image, handling three or more merchandise lines, and having 10,000 square feet or more of floor space. Because mass merchants have relatively low operating costs, achieve economies in operations, and appeal to price-conscious consumers, their continuing popularity is forecasted. Mass merchants include traditional discount stores, combination stores, superstores, and warehouse outlets.

Customers must be willing to do some things for themselves in the store if huge volumes of goods are to be moved out. Today self-service has invaded just about every type of business imaginable: discount houses, drug and hardware stores, garden supply centers. The retailer encourages customers to serve themselves and bring the goods to a checkout counter whenever possible.

Scrambled merchandising, also called mixed merchandising, has become so common that few people think much about it. It is the offering of a wide assortment of goods by one store. Supermarkets led the way. They proved to the marketing world that when there is a flow of shoppers through a store, they will buy a wide variety of merchandise if that merchandise fits into their buying patterns. The woman buying groceries is willing to buy drugs, housewares, hardware, and even certain types of inexpensive clothing.

Supermarket techniques, which provide shoppers with carts, will continue to grow in many types of retailing. Specialty stores selling merchandise such as paints and home improvements, discount books, auto repair and replacement parts, toys, sporting goods, and children's clothing are all moving in this direction. The trend toward self-service is likely to accelerate in both large and small stores.

Discount department stores and hypermarkets will continue to play a major role in the sale of commodity goods and services. However, for many consumers and types of products and services, personalizing selling service is the wave of the future, as we have noted in the previous section.

Improving Productivity

Retail marketing in the decades ahead will direct more attention toward increasing productivity. Increased productivity means more output per unit of input, and this will become an even more important goal by the year 2000. The key controllable inputs in a retail operation are personnel (40 to 50 percent of operating expenses), inventory (40 to 50 percent of total assets), and facilities (5 to 15 percent of total expenses). To increase productivity, retailers will need to use personnel more efficiently, control inventories more effectively, and make better use of the space.

It is difficult to improve productivity simply by trying harder; it usually requires doing things differently. For example, retailers are getting suppliers to provide more services, freeing store personnel for other tasks. Self-service and automated inventory control also cut labor costs.

Retailing will have an increased number of trained managers and owners. The days of predominance by small stores with sole proprietors who have not been trained are coming to a close. Franchises and major corporations are increasingly involved in the education of their personnel. This will likely bring more emphasis on such concepts as return on investment, management by objectives, and management information systems. An increased use of more sophisticated management techniques will alter the type of personnel needed to run retail operations in the decades ahead.

International Marketing

In the future, retailing in the United States will become even more intertwined with the economic activities of other countries. Companies from Europe, the Middle East, and the Orient will invest more heavily in the U.S. retail industry. Retailing innovations from other countries will be introduced into this country's economy. Additionally, many U.S. retailers will expand into international markets. Many companies are already moving in this direction, and more will follow in the years ahead.

International marketing includes all marketing that involves exchanges across national boundaries. Thus a firm is engaged in international marketing when it buys some portion of its input from, or sells some portion of its output to, an organization located in a foreign country.

Exporting is selling and shipping raw materials or products to other nations. Coca-Cola, for example, exports its product to a number of countries, for sale to the local population.

Importing is purchasing raw materials or products in other nations and bringing them into one's own country. Thus, buyers for a department store may purchase crystal in Ireland or shoes in Italy and ship them back to the United States for resale.

Importing and exporting are the principal activities in international trade. They give rise to an important concept called the balance of trade. A nation's **balance of trade** is the total value of its exports less the total value of its imports, over some period of time. If a country imports more than it exports, its balance of trade is negative and is said to be unfavorable. (A negative balance of trade is unfavorable because the country must export money to pay for its excess imports.) A **trade deficit** is an unfavorable balance of trade.

On the other hand, when a country exports more than it imports, it is said to have a **favorable balance of trade**. This has consistently been the case for Japan over the last two decades or so.

A nation's **balance of payments** is the total flow of money into the country less the total flow of money out of the country, over a given period of time. Balance of payments is a much broader concept than balance of trade. It includes imports and exports, of course, but it also includes investments, money spent by foreign tourists, payments by foreign governments, and all other receipts and payments.

A continual deficit in a nation's balance of payments (a negative balance) can cause other nations to lose confidence in its economy. A continual surplus (a positive balance) can indicate that the country encourages exports but limits imports by imposing trade restrictions.

Many U.S. retailers are looking for expansion into foreign markets. Kentucky Fried Chicken, 7-Eleven, Burger King, and McDonald's are examples of retailers now operating in foreign markets.

A large number of foreign retailers have entered the United States in order to appeal to the world's most affluent mass market. The following have major interests in American retailers:

■ Wienerwald of Switzerland, which owns Lums restaurants, International House of Pancakes (IHOP), Love's Wood Pit Barbecue restaurants, Copper Penny restaurants, and Ranch House restaurants.
■ Tengelmann of Germany, which owns A&P supermarkets.
■ Imasco of Canada, which owns Hardee's fast-food restaurants, Shoppers Drug Mart, and Tinderbox tobacco stores.

Home-Based Businesses

Ten years ago, working from home was primarily a way to "moonlight" (work at a second job) in order to earn the extra money needed to keep up with bills. While many people still moonlight, a more significant trend has been that more are working at home full-time. This is causing an explosion of home-based businesses in this country. Today experts estimate that as many as 20 percent of new small business enterprises are operated out of the owner's home.

For many years home-based business was considered to be for women only. But today many factors are leading both men and women to work from their homes. Some find it difficult or too costly to commute each day and believe they can be equally productive by working at home.

Many people have succeeded in unusual businesses: One man, a former bookstore manager, now sells only "hard-to-find" books from his home; another began a computer information service; and a woman has a thriving catering service offering the same goodies she once served her house guests.

Electronic Cottage   A new development in home-based business is the advent of electronic telecommuters—employees who keep in touch with their offices by computers, word processors, and telephones located in their homes. It is estimated that there will be more than 5 million home-based telecommuters before 1990.

Swap Shops, Flea Markets, and Garage Sales   Call them sporadic, informal retail institutions, call them bazaars, call them what you will, casual markets are now quite substantial. They have developed in response to an economic need. People have surplus goods that still have value. They don't want to throw the goods and their value away.

This potter offers unique merchandise and the opportunity for the customer to see how it is produced.

Formal institutions have been created to accommodate these rather informal types of sales. Entrepreneurs lease parking lots and sublet small spaces each Saturday and Sunday to people who have something to sell. On an average Sunday, 100 vendors or more will have goods on display, and thousands of shoppers will survey the goods. Garage sales have become so common that some cities are beginning to regulate and tax them.

In a very real way, entrepreneurs are moving into these areas and formalizing them. They operate like just another retail business.

Artisan Shops　The number of artists in business for themselves continues to multiply as American consumers spend more and more of their dollars on home-made goods and services. Most people enjoy watching a craftsperson at work. They enjoy buying and using goods that they saw being made by people whom they know. The personal touch is not yet dead. It lives in the artisan shops.

Successful Retail Marketing Strategies

The retail marketer must learn how to deal with change. Effective understanding and management of change will be the major internal challenge for tomorrow's retailer and the basis for success in tomorrow's marketplace.

William R. Davidson, of Management Horizons, Inc., believes that the winning retailers of the future share three major traits:

Market drive. Winners will be preoccupied with consumer needs, offering more of something (value, fashion, or convenience) than other stores.

Technological leadership. Winning retailers will not merely automate what was done manually before but will provide an integrated management information system, linking distribution centers with the headquarters-based buying and financial functions.

Strategic planning. Successful retailers will be committed to a clearly defined mission with long-range goals, staking out "where they want to be."

In the next two chapters we will look at how retailers can develop the information systems and the retail marketing plans that are essential for success.

Define each term and use it in a sentence.

Balance of payments
Balance of trade
Buy-for-one consumers
Commodity goods
Electronic Funds Transfer (EFT)
Exporting
Fashion goods
Favorable balance of trade
Get-your-money's-worth consumer
Importing
International marketing
Less-for-less consumer
Mass merchandising
Positioned retailing
Scrambled merchandising
Stability-seeking consumers
Time-buying consumer
Trade deficit
Wheel of retailing

CAN YOU ANSWER THESE?

1. What are three important advantages to electronic shopping?

2. What are two of the future implications of the growing electronic funds transfer system?

3. What are three expected consumer demographic changes in the years ahead?

4. How is international marketing generally expected to change in the future?

5. How are home-based businesses changing?

6. What three major traits will the winning retailers of the future need to have?

17 *The Marketing Information System*

Why do you buy from one retailer in preference to another? Why do you avoid buying from some retailers in your community? Did you hear something bad about them or about their personnel? Did you have an unpleasant experience yourself? Do you think retailers in your community are aware of how you and other people feel about their companies? By finding the answers to these questions, retailers can shed light on some of their major problems.

The most critical problem that retailers experience is how best to identify and satisfy the ever-changing needs and wants of customers. In meeting these challenges, retailers who have the attitude that the customer is the boss are most likely to succeed. They will ensure that they and their employees always remember that the business exists for the customer, not the customer for the business. This means that retailers will be able to provide the products and services their customers want at prices they are willing to pay and at places where it is convenient for them to buy. The advertising and sales promotion techniques that a successful retailer uses will make customers aware of the business as the place where their needs and wants can be fulfilled.

■

THE RETAILING MIX

Every retail firm caters to its own clientele. These regular customers of a retail firm are changing constantly. The need to keep up-to-date information about customers' needs and wants is increasingly being recognized. To provide what customers desire, retailers develop a **retailing mix**. This is a combination of a product or service sold at the right price, in a particular place, and promoted to attract customers. The four P's of the retailing mix described in Chapter 11—product, price, place, and promotion—must be combined in such a way that they work together to serve customers and earn a profit.

Combining the Ingredients

Julie Paper sells a particular brand of badminton set in her two sporting goods stores. She knows that the set is a quality product, and that badminton is a popular game. But these two facts won't assure her of selling the sets profitably. The product is only one ingredient of the retailing mix. Julie must also think about the best place to sell it. At her downtown store, customers may buy a badminton set once in a while, so Julie keeps only a few sets in stock at that store. Julie keeps the bulk of her supply at her suburban branch store, because she reasons that the demand will be greater there. She realizes that many people who live in the suburbs have lawns on which to play badminton, and also that they're more likely to shop for badminton sets in her suburban store than in her downtown store. Julie must also think about "place" within her suburban store. She must locate the sets where customers can find them easily—near the tennis equipment, for example.

To let her customers know that the product is available, Julie must also include promotion in the retailing mix. She can, for example, display a badminton set in the store so that customers can examine the equipment. And Julie can attract people to the store by advertising the set in her spring catalog and in the local newspaper.

When Julie considered price, she found that the badminton set sold very well at $19.95. However, she would have to sell the set at $25 or more to allow for sufficient profit. But when she priced it at $25, it sold poorly.

As you can see, even though three of the four P's work well together, the mix is unsatisfactory. In this instance, the product, promotion, and place are attractive to customers. But the high price has discouraged them from buying badminton sets in Julie's store. To solve this problem, Julie must adjust the combination of her retailing mix.

Adjusting the Combination

What can Julie Paper do to achieve a satisfactory retailing mix? Should she sell a different, less expensive brand of badminton set? If she increases her promotion efforts, could she convince customers to buy the present brand at the higher price? Can she afford to accept a loss on badminton sets if the lower price attracts customers to the store and they buy other products as well? There are many ways Julie can adjust the four P's of her retailing mix to achieve a profit. However, whichever choice she makes, all four P's must work well together in satisfying her customers.

Making a wise decision requires information. Julie must know how her customers act in order to determine which changes in her retailing mix are likely to bring the most profitable results. For this necessary information, retailers rely on marketing research.

Retailers need information about their target customer in order to plan a successful marketing mix.

Obtaining Marketing Information

Retail marketers need information to help them answer the following types of questions:

1. Who are the target group of customers for this business, or the people we want as our clientele?
2. Where should the business be located?
3. What hours should the store or other place of business be open?
4. What should be done to improve sales of various products or services?
5. What price lines should be carried in stock?
6. When and where should a new product or service be offered?
7. What services do customers expect?
8. Where can expenses be reduced without losing sales?

It's almost impossible for any retailer to gather this information without some help. Wise retailers gather information from as many different sources as they can. And they consider many alternatives before making a decision. For example, they use trained market researchers, credit managers, buyers, department heads, and salespeople to help them gather data. And often, retailers will also, from time to time, call on any one of their employees for the information they need. But they must always be sure that the information employees provide is objective and accurate.

In Chapter 13 we discussed the marketing research process and how it is used to help make decisions. As was also discussed in Chapter 13, the sources of information that retailers use to help them learn about their customers can be divided into two main groups: primary sources and secondary sources. In this chapter we will look at how retail marketers can obtain and use information from various sources as a part of a marketing information system.

■
MARKETING INFORMATION PLANNING

Information for marketing decision making must be planned, not left to chance. Retail marketers need timely, accurate, and relevant information, yet they want to avoid confusion. Achieving these objectives means that the flow of information from the various sources to the retailers who use it must be controlled. Meeting this challenge is the purpose of marketing information planning. Let us see how this planning works.

How Marketing Information Is Obtained

Information begins as facts and opinions about the marketing environment that we call data. Facts are numbers, words, or symbols that describe something about activities, transactions, or events that have happened or are happening now. For example, the number, names, and characteristics of competitors; the number and characteristics of customers; and last quarter's percent growth in the economy are a few of the many facts that are used by retailers. Opinions are ideas that people believe or are their predictions of events. A study that asks customers whether they will buy a product or service in the future yields opinion data. Because these customers have not actually bought at the time of the study, they can only render an opinion about future behavior.

Types of Marketing Information

Information planning requires knowing where data are located and how they are obtained. Essentially, marketing data have three main sources: (1) secondary data in the retail marketer's files and records, (2) secondary data gathered from various external sources, and (3) primary data gathered by marketing research. Gathering primary data was discussed in Chapter 13.

Internal Secondary Data Every organization daily accumulates and records an amazing amount of data. **Internal secondary data** describes the transactions and activities of a company, including orders, shipments, purchases, inventory, accounts receivable, expenditures, and previous studies. Retailers store internal data in many places—accounting records, department files, internal correspondence (letters, memoranda, and reports), and even in employees' minds. By keeping track of sales through detailed records, retailers get an idea of customers' likes and dislikes. As retailers study their records, for example, they may discover that a good number of people in the area hardly ever come to their place of business. Why? Often only one or two unsatisfactory practices are enough to drive some people away. A disagreeable cashier, for example, may cause customers to think unkindly of the entire business.

Realizing the importance of information from customers, retail firms are increasingly making efforts to learn all they can about their customers' likes and dislikes regarding the firm's policies, merchandise, services, and personnel. For example, complaints from regular customers can help retailers identify specific needs and wants. Even customers who say they shop for only one or two things that they can't get elsewhere provide excellent information. Such comments make the retailer aware of bad experiences the customers may have had or something unfavorable they may have heard about the business. Unfortunately, many customers don't complain, no matter what kind of service they get. Instead of complaining, they simply never come back.

External Secondary Data Although considerable amounts of secondary data are available internally, even more data are available from external sources. So much is available at little or no cost that the retailer faces the problem of being overwhelmed by the amount of data available from many sources.

External secondary data can be classified according to the source of the data: government sources and private sources.

Government Sources. Various government agencies are the nation's most important sources of secondary data, and the most frequently used data are census data. The most commonly used data base is the Census of Population. The information is available for use without charge at local libraries, and it can also be purchased on computer tapes for a nominal fee. The Census of Population is so detailed that population characteristics for large cities are available by city block. Data are available on age, sex, race, citizenship, education levels, occupation, employment status, and income.

The Census Bureau also conducts a Census of Housing, which provides such information as the value of homes in a particular geographic area, the number of rooms, the type of structure, the occupants' race, and the year the home was built. This information can be used by retailers to target specific kinds of potential shoppers.

Other government reports include the Census of Business, the Census of Manufacturers, and the Census of Agriculture. So many censuses are produced by the government each year that many firms purchase its guidebook, *Catalog of U.S. Census Publications*, in order to keep abreast of current publications. Other government sources include the *Statistical Abstract of the United States*, the *Survey of Current Business*, the monthly *Federal Reserve Bulletin*, and the *Monthly Labor Review*. State and city governments are still other important sources of information.

Private Sources. A number of private organizations provide information for retailer marketers. Trade associations are excellent resources. A **trade association** is a group of people in the same business who join together to pool their knowledge and search for solutions to common problems. Many associations have been formed on local, state, and national levels by retailers who sell similar products or services. Others have been formed to represent all the retailers in a certain area of a community. Many trade associations provide excellent sources of information about consumers, such as what types and prices of products or services they are buying or intend to buy in the months ahead. Trade associations publish magazines or newsletters in specialized areas such as hardware, supermarket, franchising, furniture, department stores, apparel and accessory stores. The following list gives examples of associations that publish a variety of information that is useful for retail marketers:

American Management Association
American Marketing Association
Better Business Bureau
Chamber of Commerce
Conference Board
Direct Marketing Association
Food Marketing Institute
International Association of Chain Stores

International Council of Shopping Centers
International Franchise Association
Marketing Science Institute
National Mass Retailing Institute
National Retail Furniture Association
National Retail Hardware Association
National Retail Merchants Association
Point-of-Purchase Advertising Institute
Radio Advertising Bureau
Supermarket Institute

Retailers also learn a great deal about consumers' needs and wants by studying research reports. Manufacturers, wholesalers, and advertising agencies spend huge sums of money on research to find better ways of distributing the product and services they sell. Also, other information about consumer preferences can be obtained from articles in trade magazines, reports of government studies, articles in the business and financial sections of metropolitan newspapers, and consumer magazines. Table 1 lists some of the more

TABLE 1
PUBLICATIONS THAT PROVIDE INFORMATION FOR RETAIL MARKETERS

Periodicals	Description
Advertising	Semiweekly magazine of advertising, with application to retailing
Business Week	Weekly magazine, with articles on all phases of business
Chain Store Age	Monthly magazine, which specializes in information about chain stores
Journal of Marketing	Quarterly magazine, with developments in all areas of marketing
Journal of Retailing	Quarterly magazine, with developments in all aspects of retailing
Journal of Small Business Management	Quarterly magazine, of interest to retailers and all other kinds of small business managers
Retail Control	Monthly magazine, with focus on credit, store security, and inventory management
Sales and Marketing Management	Monthly magazine, of interest to retailers: annual survey of buyer power by county (based on income, retail sales, and population in each county)
Stores	Monthly magazine, for members of the National Retail Merchants' Association, with emphasis on store management

commonly read periodicals that help retailers stay up to date about the changing needs and wants of their consumers:

Several national firms offer information to businesses on a subscription basis:

A. C. Nielsen Company conducts a Retail Index service, providing continuous data on food, drug, cosmetic, toiletry, and other similar products sold in food stores and drug stores.

Audits and Surveys provides a physical audit of merchandise in stores.

Market Research Corporation of America examines purchasing behavior via a large consumer panel, and computes consumer and store data.

R. L. Polk provides mailing lists and automobile registrations.

Selling Area—Marketing, Inc. (SAMI) gathers information on the flow of products to retail outlets.

Standard Rate and Data Service collects information on advertising rates for various media. Consumer data include income, retail sales, and so on.

Table 2, on page 146, lists some additional sources of information available through private firms.

HOW A MARKETING INFORMATION SYSTEM OPERATES

A **marketing information system** (MIS) is a computer-based system for managing marketing information that is gathered continually from internal and external sources. A computer is essential to a marketing information system because of the amount of data the system must accept, store, sort, and retrieve. Also essential is the continual collection of data, so that the system incorporates the most up-to-date information.

A Simple Concept

In concept (and with a computer), the operation of a marketing information system is relatively simple. Data from a variety of sources are fed into the system. For example, secondary data from internal sources include sales figures; advertising costs; inventory levels; and information on customer satisfaction with business. Data from secondary external sources concern the firm's suppliers and middlemen, trade associations, and economic conditions. All these data are stored and processed within the marketing information system. Its output is a flow of facts and figures in the form that is most useful for marketing decision making. Among this information might be daily sales reports by department and product or service, forecasts of sales or buying trends, and reports on the effectiveness of particular marketing strategies. Both the information output and its form depend on the requirements of the individual firm. As needed, primary data could be gathered as described in Chapter 13, and included in the marketing information systems.

A Practical Application

A marketing information system can help retailers monitor performance during and after implementing a strategy. Initially, information helps set standards for evaluating performance. With standards in place, information is collected at regular intervals (daily, weekly, monthly, quarterly) to show how well actual performance compares with these standards. For example, retailers can routinely use order records to study trends in sales. The information can help them compare performance of the company's marketing program to sales objectives or standards and take action to promote improvements.

Zales Jewelry constantly uses its marketing information system to supply information for decisions about the relocation of stores. Here are some typical questions the MIS helps to answer.

TABLE 2 / SOURCES OF RETAIL MARKET INFORMATION AVAILABLE THROUGH PRIVATE FIRMS

Source	Type of Information
Editor & Publisher's *Market Guide*	Information on more than 1500 individual geographic areas, including location, transportation facilities, population, households, banking, passenger automobile registration, utilities, principal industries, climate, and retail trade.
Sales & Marketing Management Magazine's *Survey of Buying Power Data Service* and *Survey of Buying Power Forecasting Service*	Data on population, households, effective buying income, retail sales, and a buying power index for both the United States and Canada. Geographic subdivisions covered include states, counties, and metropolitan areas. The data service has current statistics, and the forecasting service makes future projections.
Standard & Poor's Industry Surveys	Data on 69 U.S. industries. Prospects for the future as well as historical trends and problems are reviewed. Also includes a comparative analysis of selected companies in the industry.
Standard Rate and Data Services	Data on cost of advertising space in various publications such as newspapers, magazines, radio, and television; their circulations; and demographic and socioeconomic data on areas.
Rand McNally and Company's *Commercial Atlas and Marketing Guide*	Demographic and socioeconomic data on states and cities.
Simmons Market Research Bureau's *The Study of Media and Markets*	Results of Simmons' annual survey of product and media usage by people in the United States. The results of each survey are published in 40 volumes organized by product. Each report provides data on demographic and socioeconomic characteristics of product and media users.
Dun & Bradstreet's *Key Business Ratios*	Data are reported on selected business ratios for wholesaling, retailing, manufacturing, and service industries.

■ Where do target customers live and shop?
■ Which and how many retailers serve the target customers' needs?
■ Is the area's target segment growing?
■ Are there enough customers in the area to support another store?
■ Can the market be entered without taking sales from existing Zales Jewelry stores?

■ Can the store expect to be profitable in the area?

Our discussion of a marketing information system demonstrates the contribution that information makes to retailing. In the next chapter we will look at the retail marketing plan.

Define each term and use it in a sentence.

External secondary data
Internal secondary data
Marketing information system
Retailing mix
Trade association

1. What is the most crucial problem retailers face?
2. What kinds of questions must retailers be able to answer?
3. What are the three main sources of marketing information data?
4. What are three examples of government sources of secondary data?
5. Why is a computer essential for implementing a marketing information system?

C·H·A·P·T·E·R

18 *Creating a Marketing Plan*

A major responsibility of retail marketing managers and owners is to plan, implement and evaluate their organization's marketing plan—in other words, to manage the marketing aspects of their business. Because retailing is a form of marketing, a retail business's marketing plan is central to the firm's success.

A retail marketing plan is an overall plan for providing goods and/or services to consumers for a profit. Normally, this plan will cover 1 year. However, planning may cover longer or shorter periods of time. Simply stated, planning is drawing from the past to decide in the present what to do in the future. People who plan tend to get things done.

BENEFITS OF A RETAIL MARKETING PLAN

A carefully prepared marketing plan yields several benefits for the retail marketer. First, it provides a critical analysis of the business operation, its clientele, and the marketing environment. Second, it specifies the marketing objectives in terms of sales volume, profit, and desired corporate image. Third, it furnishes guidelines for using the four Ps of marketing in reaching these objectives. Fourth, it supplies a systematic procedure for evaluating the firm's success and for making adjustments. Thus, this essential document enables a retail marketer to anticipate and often avoid crises.

It is important to note that the various parts of the retail marketing plan depend on each other. Most firms start off with a general plan that will become increasingly specific over time. The marketing plan can be prepared by the retailer, consultants, or a collaboration of the two. After a retail marketing plan has been prepared, it must then be implemented in the marketplace. To do this, the retailer needs an organization to put the strategy into action. The results should then be monitored and adjustments made as necessary.

Now that you know what a marketing plan is and what it does, let's look at its preparation and use. The five major phases of implementing a marketing plan are: (1) analyzing the situation, (2) preparing marketing objectives, (3) determining how to achieve objectives, (4) implementing retail marketing tactics, and (5) evaluating progress and making adjustments.

A situation analysis includes a study of the environment. What influence might the construction of a luxury apartment building have on the retail businesses in the area?

■

ANALYZING THE SITUATION

A **situation analysis** is a review of the company's existing marketing program. By analyzing where the firm has been and where it is now, the retailer can determine where the business should go in the future. A situation analysis normally includes study of the environmental forces that surround the retailer. These include the economic conditions that we discussed in Chapter 14 and the role of government, which we examined in Chapter 15. These factors are major influences that shape and direct a retailer's marketing effort. A situation analysis also includes a detailed review of the retailer's present marketing mix—its product and pricing situation, its distribution system (place), and its promotion program.

Situation analysis is the objective evaluation of the opportunities and potential problems facing a retailer. It seeks to answer two key questions: Where is the retail marketer now, and in what direction should the business be headed? To answer these questions the retailer needs a good knowledge of the retail environment and the characteristics, expectations, and images that consumers have of the business. This information is basic to setting realistic goals and planning a successful retail mix.

■

PREPARING OBJECTIVES

Objectives are the measurable goals that the retailer hopes to attain within a specified period of time. A retailer may be concerned with one or more of the following objectives: (1) sales (including growth, stability, market share), (2) profit (including level and return on investment), (3) image and satisfaction of public (including customers and general public).

The objectives a retailer selects will determine the direction of the overall marketing plan. The retailer who clearly defines objectives and develops strategies to achieve them improves chances for success.

An example of a retail firm that has clearly specified objectives and has established strategies to achieve them is Wal-Mart, a discount chain that operates largely in smaller and medium-sized communities of 5000–30,000 people. Wal-Mart's sales growth plan calls for doubling sales every 2 to 3 years. It opens between 100 and 125 new stores a year and has attained a sales growth of 17 percent in stores that are at least 1 year old. This is double the retail industry average and is due to Wal-Mart's choice of towns (which other merchants tend to avoid), its knowledge of local markets, and new types of retail institutions such as buying clubs (Sam's Wholesale Club).

Sales Objectives

Sales objectives are those concerned with the sales volume of a retailer. Growth, stability, and/or market share are the sales objectives most often sought by retailers.

Some retailers set growth as a top priority. Under this objective, a firm is interested in expanding operations and increasing sales. For example, a retailer that does well often becomes interested in opening new units and increasing sales volume.

However, too active a pursuit of expansion can result in problems. Many retailers who are successful in their current business fail when they open new units. Sales growth is an important goal for large and small retailers, but growth should not be too fast or exclude the consideration of other objectives.

Stability in annual sales and profits is the objective of a wide range of retailers. These companies place their emphasis on maintaining their sales volume, market share, price lines, and so on. Small retailers are often interested in stable sales that will enable them to make a satisfactory living every year. Other retailers develop a loyal following of consumers and are intent not on expanding but on maintaining the services that attracted their original consumers.

Another objective of large retailers is market share. **Market share** is the percentage of total industry sales contributed by one company. Small retailers are usually more concerned with competition across the street or down the block than with market share.

Profit Objectives

Profitability means that the retailer wants to attain at least a minimum level of profits during a designated time period, usually a year. Profits may be expressed in dollars or as a percentage of sales. The computation of the various types of profit was discussed in Chapter 10.

A satisfactory rate of return is determined ahead of time by the company, and this rate is compared with the actual rate of return at the end of the year. Many retailers have policies that lead to small annual increases in sales and profits, rather than policies of introducing innovative ideas that might lead to ups and downs in company sales and profits. Stable earnings for the retailer is a sign of good management.

Increased efficiency in promotion is an objective of many retailers. A retailer with sales of $1 million and promotional expenses of $500,000 has an efficiency rating of 50 percent. Fifty cents of every sales dollar are contributed to nonselling costs such as merchandise purchases, and 50 cents go for promotional expenses. The retailer might set as an objective for next year an increase in promotional efficiency to 80 percent. On sales of $1 million, promotional expenses would have to be reduced to $200,000. In this instance, 80 cents of every sales dollar are contributed to nonselling costs and profits; only 20 cents go for promotional expenses. The increase in efficiency will lead to an overall increase in the retailer's profits.

Image and Satisfaction of Public Objectives

Image refers to how a firm is viewed by consumers and others. A firm may be viewed as ethical or unethical, caring of consumers or indifferent, offering bargains or being high priced, and so on. Retailers are concerned with the way they are viewed and set as an objective the creation of the image they want. The key to a successful image is that the consumer views the business in the manner the retailer intends.

Consumer satisfaction is an objective that most firms desire to achieve. They can easily accomplish this by creating a company philosophy that is consumer oriented. If the consumer is satisfied, the other objectives will be accomplished.

Good supplier relations are also important. If favorable prices, new products, good return policies, prompt shipments, and cooperation are to be received, retailers must understand and work with suppliers, such as manufacturers and wholesalers. Because suppliers perform many functions for small retailers, good relations are particularly important for them.

■

DETERMINING HOW TO ACHIEVE OBJECTIVES

The next step in preparing a retail marketing plan is to determine how to achieve stated objectives. In developing strategies to achieve the objectives, retailers must consider both the controllable elements (the four P's of marketing mix) and the uncontrollable elements (the consumer, competition, technology, and so on) that were presented in Chapters 14 and 15. Now let's look at how the retail marketing mix—the controllable elements—is employed by successful retailers to meet their objectives.

The consumer group that a retailer tries to satisfy is called the **target market**. In selecting this target market, the retailer can utilize any of three techniques: (1) to sell products to a broad spectrum of consumers, the **mass market**; (2) to zero in on one specific market, market segmentation; or (3) to use niche marketing strategies, in which the retailer attempts to capture several market segments at the same time, using different offerings for each.

For example, most conventional supermarkets and traditional shoe stores, such as Kinney's, define their target markets in very broad terms. These stores have several different product lines and stock many kinds of items at a variety of prices. On the other hand, the small boutique or a clothing store for large and tall men exemplifies the retailer who selects a well-defined and narrow consumer group. Both of these shops have a narrow product assortment because they attract a certain type of customer, not everyone. Most department stores seek multiple market segments. These stores cater to several different groups of consumers and provide unique products and services for each group. For example, women's clothing may be subdivided into several distinctive boutiques scattered throughout a department store. Large retail chains frequently have divisions that appeal to different market segments.

The selection and clear statement of a target market give direction to a retailer's choice of (1) products and services, (2) physical facilities (place), (3) price, and (4) promotion efforts. Having a clear direction enables the firm to stress its competitive advantages and direct its financial resources. Although all of these are important, the concept of competitive advantage is too often over-

These retailers both sell rental housing, but each appeals to a different target market.

looked. The choice of a target market and its satisfaction by a unique retail offering are necessary for success.

To attract customers and thus create sales, the retailer needs to establish a program that meets the expectations of target customers better than its competition does. In addition to attracting customers, the retail mix must be created with two primary objectives—sales and profit—in mind.

Potential customers can be affected by any or all of the components of the retail marketing mix. In deciding with which retailer to do business, the customer has access to the retail mix of various competitors. The alternative retail mixes are actually all that a customer can see of the various retail businesses. These are the only factors that are visible to the public; thus, the only way that a retailer can influence business choice and patronage is by adjusting the retail mix—the four P's of marketing.

The four P's of retail marketing mix are briefly described below to set the stage for you to begin to prepare a marketing plan.

Product and Service

A vital part of the retail mix is the merchandise and services to be carried. The retailer must decide (1) what items to carry, (2) from whom to buy, and (3) when and how much to reorder. Buying the right items in the right quantities to meet the needs and expectations of the retailer's target customers is critical.

Decisions must be made about the following matters:

■ Breadth of the assortment (the number of different product or service categories a retailer handles)
■ Depth of the assortment (the completeness of stock within a given product category)
■ Policies outlining how innovative the retailer is going to be in introducing new products or services
■ Criteria for buying decisions (how often, terms, and so on)
■ Forecasting, budgeting, and retail accounting procedures

- The level of inventory (average stock on hand) for each type of product that is stocked
- Control or evaluation procedures in order to measure the success or failure of each product or service offered for sale

In effect, a retailer is a purchasing agent for a group of potential customers. If a significant number of customers don't like the retailer's merchandise or services, sales and profit will fall below the desired levels. Chapter 56 contains a detailed presentation of how to prepare a merchandise plan.

Place—Physical Facilities

The location of the retail firm and the physical layout are crucial because of the fact that most types of retailers have a relatively large number of competitors. Therefore, customers usually don't have to go very far to find what they want. Most shoppers are convenience-oriented at least to some degree; thus, finding the right location is often a key to the success or failure of a retailer. Selecting the right location is becoming an increasingly complex task as populations shift and the retail trade is geographically spread over larger areas.

Retailers have several location and operations decisions to make. The general area and the specific site must be determined. Competitors, transportation, number of people, type of neighborhood, nearness to suppliers, and so on, should all be considered when picking a business location. The terms of the lease on the building (such as amount of rent, flexibility and length of contract) must be evaluated, and a buy-or-rent decision must be made about a building. The size and type of building and the fixtures need to be chosen next.

After a location has been selected, the retail store must be designed and its layout established. The way a store is physically arranged can affect its convenience for shoppers, the atmosphere and image it projects, as well as the sales and service of individual items. The policies and plans related to the physical facilities will be discussed in various chapters of this book, including a special emphasis on small business planning in Chapters 61 and 62.

Price

After the merchandise or service has been selected, the retailer must plan the pricing component of the retail mix. The retailer has two levels of decision relative to pricing. The first decision is to establish a basic pricing strategy, which involves the extent to which price will be used as a tool to attract customers. Retailers can use low prices to attract customers or, alternatively, they can use other means (convenience, quality, good service, and so forth) to attract customers while maintaining higher margins. Second, after the pricing strategy is set, decisions must be made relative to markups and markdowns needed to put the strategy into effect.

Retailers can choose from several pricing techniques. They can decide what level of prices to charge: low, medium, or high. Which of these levels is consistent with the retailer's image and the quality of the products or services offered? The method of payment, such as cash only or cash plus credit, must be planned. Many retailers today allow credit purchases. Billing terms must also be determined: length of deferred payments and the resultant interest charges; the use of COD; discounts for cash or early payments.

Pricing policies will be discussed in detail in Chapter 55.

Promotion

After the product or service is priced and is in place for sale, the customer must be informed and persuaded to buy. This is the job of promotion. The three primary tools of promotion are advertising, visual merchandising, and personal selling. Creative promotion can be used to create excitement and project a desirable store image.

Image is critical to the success of a retailer. If potential customers do not see the firm in the manner intended by the retailer, then the retailer will not succeed. Therefore, a distinctive image (consistent with the desires of the target market) must be sought. This image can be created through the use of several techniques.

The physical appearance of the retail store helps to project the image. A prestige business creates and upholds its image through plush carpeting, wide aisles, attractive displays, and hidden price tags. A discounter creates and upholds image through bare floors, crowded displays, obvious price tags, and self-service. Color arrangements, scents, music, and type of sales personnel also contribute to a retailer's image. The construction of the physical exterior contributes to the image or atmosphere of the store. It is the first part of the business a consumer sees. Layout and displays are other contributors to atmosphere.

Customer services and community relations should also be used as tools in creating a favorable retailer image. Customer services include parking, gift wrapping, liberal return policy, extended hours during special seasons, layaway plans, alterations, use of credit cards, and telephone and mail sales.

Proper use of promotional techniques can help lead to profitable retailing. These techniques range from very inexpensive flyers delivered door to door for a supermarket or take-out restaurant, to very expensive national advertising campaigns for a franchise chain. Various types of paid promotion are available to retailers. Mass advertising (television, radio, magazines, billboards, direct mail, and most often, newspapers) allows the retailer to direct one message to a large number of consumers. Personal selling enables the retailer to create a one-to-one relationship with consumers. Special promotional events provide added persuasion in attracting and satisfying the customer. In addition to these forms of paid promotion, retail businesses are promoted by free publicity through news reports and announcements of their community service and other projects. These promotional activities are examined in detail in the Selling and Promotion Bands.

An interesting illustration of how one retailer is attempting to use its retail mix to change its image and attract increased sales is provided by J.C. Penney's fashion gamble. Penney had been America's number two volume retailer behind Sears for many years, selling private-label goods on a price basis in bargain-basement surroundings in small towns. In 1976, however, a fast-moving K mart took over the number two spot. Due to these competitive pressures and various social changes, Penney's management is attempting to transform the company into a chain of moderate-priced department stores with a heavy emphasis on higher-priced fashionable merchandise in hard goods, housewares, and especially apparel. This is a complete break with the previous store image.

Penney had established itself solidly in the large urban shopping centers, but the old image and much of the old retail mix had remained. Management felt that it knew the consumers and that finding the right item had become more important than price to its target consumers. Thus Penney made a decision to change its whole approach to retailing. This meant changing the store's layouts, merchandise mix, buying and pricing structure, advertising, and personnel. Today, the long pipe racks of polyester staple goods—jammed together in wearying sameness and starkly lit by fluorescent tubes—have all gone. In their place are women's apparel departments—softly lit and carpeted—where cashmere sweaters, wool skirts, soft-style silk blouses, and even some $4000 mink coats are attractively displayed.

■

IMPLEMENTING RETAIL MARKETING TACTICS

At this point the development of the overall strategy for the marketing plan has been com-

Getting back
to basics in
100% cotton from
St. John's Bay.
Like these
Ultimate Pants
that virtually need
no ironing. And this
great fatigue sweater.
Each in the classic
colors for fall.
Pants $30.
Sweater $33.
They just may become
a fundamental part
of your life.
You're looking
smarter than ever at
JCPenney.

Available at most large stores
and through the JCPenney Catalog.
Prices Higher in Alaska.
© 1987 JCPenney Co., Inc.

J.C. Penney changed the promotion part of its marketing mix as part of its image change. The theme "You're looking smarter than ever" appears in Penney newspaper ads and on its TV commercials.

pleted. The next step is to undertake the activities necessary to carry out the plan. These action steps are called **tactics** and involve the daily and short-run operations of the retail business. In this chapter and throughout this book, hundreds of retail marketing tactics, from buying to promotion, are discussed, and more will be presented as you continue to prepare for management and ownership.

Retailers will want to be particularly responsive to the uncontrollable environment that surrounds them. Consumer demands, competitive action, and government control especially need to be considered in the retailer's tactical decisions. The secret of successful retailing is constructing a sound strategy and fine tuning it as changes occur. A retailer who stands still is often moving backward. Changes in strategy are often necessary as the marketing environment changes.

■

EVALUATE PROGRESS AND MAKE ADJUSTMENTS

Once the retail marketing plan has been developed and the tactics implemented, the plan must be evaluated continuously and necessary adjustments made. Periodically, a retailer may want to conduct a retail audit. A **retail audit** is a systematic, critical, unbiased review and evaluation. Objectives, strategy, implementation, and organization are each evaluated.

154

A retail audit consists of six steps: (1) determining who does the audit, (2) determining when and how often it is conducted, (3) determining areas to be audited, (4) developing audit forms, (5) conducting the audit, and (6) reporting to management. After management reads the audit report, the necessary revisions in strategy are made.

Small retailers may want to consider using the Small Business Administration booklet entitled *Management Audit for Small Retailers*, series number 31, 3rd edition.

TRADE TALK

Define each term and use it in a sentence.

Market share   Mass market

Objectives   Situation analysis
Profitability   Tactics
Retail audit   Target market

CAN YOU ANSWER THESE?

1. What are the major benefits of having a retail marketing plan?

2. What are the five components of the retail marketing plan?

3. Which two key questions are answered during the situation analysis?

4. What are the three major objectives that should be addressed in a marketing plan?

5. Why is a retail audit conducted?

ACTIVITIES AND PROJECT FOR U·N·I·T 6

RETAIL MARKETING CASE

Diane Roth owns and operates a moderate-sized drug store in Atlanta, Georgia. The store has been open since 1971 and attracts a loyal, but small, clientele. While Diane continues to earn solid profits, competition from supermarkets, stationery stores, off-price chains, and others is increasing rapidly.

In response, Diane's store began to carry a variety of goods, everything from cosmetics, stationery, and greeting cards to toys, batteries, and small appliances.

Recently, Diane started an intensive evaluation of the store that focused on the merchandise lines and the individual items being sold. For each category of merchandise, the analysis included sales, gross margin (profit), and percent of floor space, as shown in Table 1, on page 156.

A new product line of inexpensive watches

is under consideration. In order to add this line, an existing product category must be dropped. The watches have the characteristics presented in Table 2.

1. Which product line should be dropped in order to add watches? Why? What are the risks of this?

2. What other factors should Diane consider before adding the watch line, aside from those shown in Table 2?

TABLE 1 / DIANE ROTH'S DRUG STORE

	Appliances	Batteries, Film, etc.	Cosmetics, Health Care	Stationery, Cards	Toys, Gifts	Total Store
Annual sales						
Past	$20,000	$35,000	$75,000	$47,000	$32,000	$320,000
Current	$20,000	$40,000	$75,000	$50,000	$28,000	$340,000
Future	$20,000	$45,000	$75,000	$50,000	$25,000	$350,000
Gross margin (percent)	26	32	25	35	34	30
Floor space (percent of total selling space)	10	5	25	15	10	100.0

TABLE 2 / PROPOSED WATCH LINE

Models	Three men's and three women's—two of each to be quartz and one to be digital
Brand	Timex
Price range	$25 to $60
Estimated annual sales	$30,000
Gross margin (percent)	30
Floor space (percent of total selling space)	5

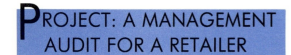

PROJECT: A MANAGEMENT AUDIT FOR A RETAILER

YOUR PROJECT GOAL
Evaluate the management of a retail business.

PROCEDURE
In Unit 5 you conducted marketing research and prepared a report for a retailer that in-

cluded a series of recommendations. Secure a copy of this report from your teacher. Evaluate that retail business or another retail business that you are knowledgeable about. Interview the owner, manager, or another key individual, using the questions below. When you have completed your evaluation, prepare a two-page written report in which you highlight the strengths of the retail business and make recommendations for improvement.

Interview Questions*

Answer yes or no to each question.

A Look at Yourself and Your Ability to Grow

1. Do you keep abreast of changes in your field by subscribing to leading trade and general business publications?

2. Do you plan for a profit (your net income) above a reasonable salary for yourself as manager?

3. Are you an active member of a trade association?

Customer Relations

1. Do you purposely cater to selected groups of customers rather than to all groups?

2. Do you have a clear picture of the store image you seek to implant in the minds of your customers?

3. Do you evaluate your own performance by asking customers about their likes and dislikes and by shopping competitors to compare their assortment, prices, and promotion methods with your own?

---

*Adapted from John W. Wingate and Elmer O. Schaller, *Management Audit for Small Retailers* (Washington, D.C.: Small Business Administration, Small Business Management Series No. 31, 3rd ed., 1977).

Insurance

1. Is your business insurance handled by a conscientious and knowledgeable agent?

2. Have you updated your insurance needs to assure adequate protection for buildings, equipment, merchandise, and other assets, as well as for public liability?

Planning for Growth

1. Over the past few years, have you done very much long-range planning for growth?

2. When you find that change is called for, do you act decisively and creatively?

3. Do you make most of your changes after thoughtful analysis or as reactions to crises?

4. Are you grooming someone to succeed you as manager in the not-too-distant future?

EVALUATION

You will be evaluated on the completeness of your report.

COMPETENCY BAND

HUMAN RESOURCES

Alex was considered extremely efficient in his job of receiving and processing shipments of computers and computer parts. He had been hired originally because of recommendations from the teachers of his computer classes. He enjoyed working with computers and knew a great deal about them. It seemed an ideal part-time job for Alex. But he was unhappy in his job, and this was evident to everyone around him.

His co-workers found it very difficult to get to know Alex. He rarely spoke to people, and when he did, he was not very pleasant. When his supervisor gave him instruction or criticism, he would have a wisecrack in response. When a co-worker asked for help, Alex would ridicule the co-worker and boast about how efficient he was and how he didn't need anyone's help.

After about 3 months, Alex was fired. Although Alex was very qualified and good at his job, his supervisor found it better for the company to terminate Alex's employment. In fact, most people who are fired from a job are fired not because they cannot do the job, but because they cannot get along with co-workers, supervisors, or customers.

In retail marketing more than in many other businesses, success means much more than just knowing the technical aspects of your job. Success in retail marketing requires good *human relations* skills, good *communication* skills, and a positive attitude. Retail marketing is a people business.

ASSESSING YOUR INTERPERSONAL SKILLS

C·H·A·P·T·E·R

19 *Understanding Yourself*

There is no field of work where human relations are more important than retail marketing. The entire process, from the point of production to the point of distribution to the final consumer, is built on personal relationships. These relationships exist between customers and salespeople, between employees and supervisors, and among employees themselves.

Eighty percent of people who are fired from a job are fired because of a human relations problem of one type or another. The failure to develop and practice good human relations skills can have a negative impact on your career in retail marketing. If you are a rude salesperson, customers will shop elsewhere or avoid you. If you don't cooperate with your fellow employees, your satisfaction with your job will suffer. If you fail to work as a team member, you will most likely be denied promotions and raises, even if you know your job very well.

Human relations are personal and working relationships among people. Good human

relations means good working relationships among people. If you are going to succeed in retail marketing, there are many people with whom you must have good relationships. Developing these relationships requires as much skill as any other part of the job.

Specific techniques for improving your human relations skills will be addressed in more detail in Chapter 20. But before you can appreciate those techniques, it is important for you to do a little self-analysis and answer the question: "How can I learn to be successful working with people in retail marketing?"

■

LEARNING TO BE SUCCESSFUL

If you are the type of person who reaches out to learn, then you are already on your way to succeeding in retail marketing. Continued learning—about yourself, about others, and about your job—is critical to success. By setting attainable goals and striving to achieve them, you will begin to develop your potential and gain self-confidence. But remember, no one is successful all of the time. You, like other successful people before you, must be willing to risk failure in order to experience success.

You can learn to be successful in your retail marketing career by understanding more about yourself and how others see you; by learning how to handle failure, how to develop your potential, how to motivate yourself to achieve, and why you need to continue your learning.

Understanding Yourself

S. S. Kresge, a famous retail marketer, lived to be nearly 100 years old. When Harvard University awarded him an honorary degree to recognize his accomplishments, he responded with a speech. He stood up and said, "I never made a dime talking" and then sat down. It was probably the shortest speech ever delivered at that university—maybe one of the most sensible. Kresge made some $200 million in his lifetime and gave most of it away. He is quoted as saying, "I have a simple philosophy: Go early to bed; get up early; don't eat too much; work hard; help people; don't let anything get your goat; tend to your own business; be enthusiastic; and always keep God in mind." S. S. Kresge surely had a clear understanding of himself and his place in the world.*

To work successfully with other people, you must first understand yourself. How you see yourself will affect your success on the job. There may be a difference between how you see yourself and how others see you. Your employer, co-workers, and customers look at you (and judge you!) based on various characteristics: your general behavior, your attitude, and your performance on the

job. Other characteristics such as appearance and communication skills also affect how people will judge you; these are discussed in Chapter 23.

Behavior is a term often used to describe how a person acts in the presence of others. An attitude reflects how one thinks about something or someone. Your attitude can be shown through your behavior or actions. In fact, behavior is often thought of as the acting-out of attitudes.

Some behaviors are appreciated by others; other behaviors are not. Sometimes a behavior is appreciated at first, but later it is not. Behavior must be appropriate to the situation. For example, there are times when you can be playful, but there are other times when you must be serious.

Table 1 lists some, though not all, behaviors and attitudes your co-workers, supervisors, and customers will find desirable. To learn more about yourself, think about each one and think about which you have and which you need to improve upon. Can you think of any you could add to this list?

Handling Failure

People who start businesses must have a strong sense of self-confidence. **Self-confidence** is an inner feeling of trust, reliance, and assurance about your own abilities. One study of successful small business owners found that they have averaged between three and four failures in business before they achieved success. But they continued to try and ultimately achieved their goals. Successful people believe that failure is simply an opportunity to learn.

The key to dealing with failure is learning from it. This means that you should expect failure and rejection. Remember, nobody wins them all. Even the famous baseball player, Babe Ruth, struck out 1330 times. Charles Dickens, the author of *A Christmas Carol* and many other books, saw many of his books rejected before they were finally accepted.

Anger and frustration often result from fail-

---

*From Norman Vincent Peale, *Enthusiasm Makes the Difference*, Prentice-Hall, Englewood Cliffs, N.J., 1967, pp. 223–224.

TABLE 1 / VALUED BEHAVIORS AND ATTITUDES

Attitude or Behavior	Definition
Trustworthiness	Others can believe in you
Respectfulness	Polite, courteous, mannerly
Cheerfulness	Full of good spirits, happy
Compassion	Having or showing sympathy
Dependability	Being reliable
Enthusiasm	Filled with zest, optimism
Helpfulness	Being of service to others
Modesty	Unassuming, humble, not boastful
Independence	Making up your own mind, not following the crowd
Open-mindedness	Willing to accept another's point of view, willing to learn from others
Friendliness	Kindly, neighborly, cordial
Patience	Composed, enduring calmly without complaining or losing self-control
Persistence	Intense motivation to accomplish objectives
Self-acceptance	Believing in yourself and striving to achieve your true potential
Sense of humor	Perceiving the fun of things
Sensitivity	Being aware of others' feelings
Tolerance	Respecting the rights and opinions of others when they are different from yours
Initiative	Originating new ideas and thinking without being urged

ure. Use these emotions to your advantage. They are part of everyday life. Cope with anger and frustration by turning them into positive energy. Let them motivate you.

Don't let rejection or failure in one area of your life spread to everything you do. If you suffer failure in one class, it does not mean you cannot excel in another. If your friend ends a relationship with you, it does not mean that you are not doing a good job at work.

Study the negative qualities of the experience. Rejection is sometimes the ultimate compliment. Perhaps your boss lacks the imagination to appreciate your creativity. After a fair-minded examination, you may be able to tell yourself that if your boss cannot recognize your potential and rejects you, he or she is the loser.

Use the rejection or failure to learn more about your weaknesses. This will allow you to convert those weaknesses to strengths. If you are turned down for a job, ask the interviewer for some solid suggestions on how you can improve your performance in future interviews. And remember: A rejection is simply the start of another opportunity.

Developing Your Potential

You are a potential success waiting to happen. You are a future business leader, political leader, or social leader. You can be all these things if you begin to develop a plan for yourself. While no plan is foolproof, there are some basic things you can do.

Begin by setting goals. Decide what you want to accomplish and by when. You may find it helpful to carry a notebook. Use it to chart your daily progress toward the specific goals you have set.

Develop your skill and craftsmanship in your chosen field of work. Become the expert. If you want to run a business, learn all you can about business. Real professionals work very hard at their craft.

Broaden your interests by reading or developing a creative hobby. Relate new things you learn from reading to what you already know. This will broaden your mind and make you a more interesting person.

A sense of humor will help put life in its proper perspective. How you view life and how you let events affect you are indicators of how well developed your inner sense of humor is. Humor is a great way to handle the frustrations that are part of everyday life. Learn to take a smile break each day. And while you are at it, daydream in your free moments. Don't get bogged down in the routine of school and work. Give your mind a chance to explore, to dream.

Learn to be observant and to recognize trends that may affect your areas of interest.

Keep your senses sharp and alert. Observe your surroundings closely. Listen skillfully. Remember, success comes to those who recognize possibilities.

Finally, create a mental image of success. Picture yourself accomplishing the goals you want to achieve. Dwight Stones, a famous high jumper, was one of the first to use this technique. Before each jump, he pictured in his mind every step he would take; how he would plant each foot, and how he would float over the bar. Then he would take off on his run.

■

MOTIVATING YOURSELF TO ACHIEVE

No one else can motivate you. Motivation is an internal activity. Others can create the climate in which you can be motivated, but only you possess the power to motivate yourself. Self-motivation requires goals. To be motivated, you must know something about yourself and also become enthusiastic about being motivated.

Increasing Your Motivation

The following suggestions are designed to help you increase your motivation. The process begins with you. If you want to be motivated, you will be. If you do not, all the aids in the world cannot help you. But if you possess the four D's of success, you can be motivated:

Discipline—a trained condition of order and obedience
Dedication—a complete concentration of energy to a purpose
Desire—a strong hope
Determination—a firm commitment

If you have discipline, dedication, desire, and determination, you will find the following seven suggestions helpful.

1. Care enough about yourself to want to improve.

2. Listen actively to discover your needs, wants, and problems.

3. Learn more of your own strengths and weaknesses and learn to like yourself.

4. Involve others and obtain their ideas and suggestions.

5. Give encouragement to and build on the strengths of others.

6. Make sure you acknowledge other people's performance according to the effort they have put into a job or task.

7. Do not demand perfection, but expect excellence.

Continuing Your Education

Learning can be described as a spiral process that begins with you, the learner, and continues throughout your lifetime. In retail marketing, learning is an activity that never ends because of the rapid and continuous changes that are always occurring.

The spiral begins with you and change. Something changes in your life. Perhaps you are preparing to leave high school and need a good occupation, one with a future. This creates a desire to learn something new—how to get a job or professional selling skills. You begin to learn, make mistakes, perhaps even fail. But as you gain experience, you will gain confidence.

As you become secure with this newly acquired knowledge or skill, you will move toward achieving your goals. As you begin to achieve your goals, you will set new goals. These new goals represent change. Some change may come from the outside. New changes in technology, society, or in your job may cause you to add to or modify your goals. This change, regardless of its source, will cause the spiral to begin again. This process goes on throughout your lifetime. You will find that you will need to continue your learning through training provided by your employer; formal education provided by vocational-technical schools, community col-

leges, four-year colleges, or professional schools; and, informal learning directed by yourself.

Change is inevitable. Facing change with a positive learning attitude is what separates the successful person from the unsuccessful person.

■

HUMAN RELATIONS IN RETAIL MARKETING

Retail marketers practice good human relations to achieve three goals: (1) gaining the cooperation of others, (2) increasing productivity through people, and (3) increasing job satisfaction. Each of these three goals can lead you to success in a career in retail marketing.

Gaining the Cooperation of Others

Other people are important to your success in retail marketing. Because you are in the "people" business, cooperation from your co-workers and supervisors is a must.

You can show cooperation with co-workers by helping out when your work is completed and they are still working. This leads to reciprocal behavior. **Reciprocal behavior** means that when you need help the next time, the person you have helped will very likely pitch in and help you. In a well-managed business, a spirit of teamwork is always evident. Just as in playing baseball, volleyball, or hockey, each person knows that his or her success depends on cooperation and help from others. Stockclerks make sure that goods are available when the salesperson needs them. Salespeople cooperate with buyers by noting customer preferences and regularly communicating them to the buyers. Salespeople cooperate with each other by sharing leads, duties, and information.

Success in retail marketing is built on cooperation between employees and supervisors.

Cooperation with supervisors and managers is more than simply following instructions. It involves doing everything you can to help make their job easier. Showing that you are part of the team will gain cooperation from supervisors when you need their help.

Increasing Productivity through People

The primary motivation for any business is to make a profit. One of the key factors in earning a profit is the productivity of employees. Some research suggests that when people cooperate with each other on the job and work together as a team, productivity increases.

That is why successful retail marketers constantly try to improve the work environment through policies, regulations, and working conditions. This leads to improved employee relations. Good employee relations, in turn, lead to increased productivity through lower employee absenteeism, lower employee turnover, and a greater employee commitment to the success of the business.

Increasing Job Satisfaction

Practicing good human relations skills ultimately will contribute to your own personal sense of satisfaction with your job. Job satisfaction is a result of many things: your attitude, your relations with co-workers and supervisors, and working conditions. Although you cannot control working conditions, you can control the quality of co-worker and supervisor relationships and your attitude.

Employers provide opportunities in the form of jobs. They establish a framework for these opportunities by defining the tasks and duties you are responsible for, and the rules and regulations under which you will work. Because retail marketing is a dynamic field, it is impossible for an employer to foresee all possibilities and create rules and regulations for every eventuality.

Many times you will be supervised by more than one person or by different people at different times. This means that you must remain flexible enough to fit into new job situations, work with several supervisors at one time, or with different supervisors at different times. Maintaining this flexibility will help increase your job satisfaction.

In this chapter you've been given some suggestions on how to achieve success in retail marketing. The key to these suggestions is that *you* are ultimately responsible for your own success. In the next two chapters you'll gain an understanding of how to get along with co-workers and supervisors by examining their expectations. In Chapter 21 you will explore the communication process and the communication skills that can improve human relations.

TRADE TALK

Define each term and use it in a sentence.

Behavior	Reciprocal behavior
Human relations	Self-confidence

CAN YOU ANSWER THESE?

1. What are the three goals of human relations?

2. Why are most people fired from their jobs?

3. What are five attitudes or behaviors you should try to develop?

4. What are five rules for handling failure?

5. What are the four D's of success?

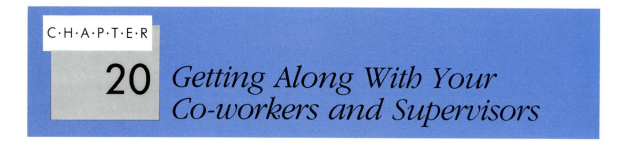

C·H·A·P·T·E·R

20 *Getting Along With Your Co-workers and Supervisors*

"A man without a smiling face must not open a shop." This ancient Chinese proverb has been passed on for many years, along with such sayings as, "Always treat other people as you want to be treated," "Courtesy is contagious," and "Before you criticize, walk a mile in the other person's shoes." These and other sayings you have heard are simple ways of remembering how to get along with other people. They are guides for effective human relations.

As noted in Chapter 19, human relations skills are essential in retail marketing, because this is a people business. Employers will accept a lack of some retailing skills and knowledge in a beginner who is still learning the retail marketing field, but they will not overlook the inability to get along with others.

People learn how to get along with others by solving human relations problems. Some respond to problems of getting along by running away from them: They run away from home, they skip school, or they quit their jobs. These avoidance behaviors do not solve the problems. They usually create new prob-

lems. In the long run, human relations problems need to be dealt with directly. This is an important difference between someone who will be successful in retail marketing and someone who will not: The successful person tries to resolve human relations problems; the other type of person runs away or just quits.

Employers don't like to hire people who run away from difficult situations. For example, most retail marketers will avoid hiring people who have quit school. They feel that someone who has quit in one situation may be in the habit of walking out on problems rather than trying to cope with them. When starting a retail marketing job, it's not unusual to find that a great many adjustments have to be made. Co-workers will be new and often different people. They may be older, of a different race or religion, or may hold different values than you do. Adjusting to them will help achieve good human relations. Adjustments cannot be avoided: The beginning retail marketing employee will have to face them and deal with them.

HUMAN RELATIONS STARTS WITH "YOU"

If you get the chance some time, try tape recording one of your conversations. You will be amazed to hear how often the word "I" is used. This reflects a very human characteristic of being more interested in ourselves than in others. Dale Carnegie once said that you can make more friends in 2 months by becoming interested in other people than you can in 2 years by trying to get other people interested in you. In order to make and keep friends, try using the word "I" less and "we" or "you" more. Your choice of words is a good starting point for improving human relations. To help you do this, try memorizing the following list:

The six most important words: "I admit I made a mistake."
The five most important words: "You did a good job."
The four most important words: "What is your opinion?"
The three most important words: "If you please."
The two most important words: "Thank you."
The one most important word: "We"
The least important word: "I"

But how can you become more aware of others? One rule is always to make the other person (rather than yourself) the center of conversation.

Associations with others will be generally pleasant when both parties demonstrate concern and thoughtfulness. However, coping with an unpleasant person will require working extra hard to create a positive human relations environment. "Telling that person off" will simply make matters worse. In these situations tolerance, understanding, and a good bit of self-control will prove more beneficial in the long run. People who are moody, unpleasant, or troublesome cannot be changed overnight.

Throughout your career in retail marketing, you'll encounter people who may seem impossible to get along with. They may be customers, co-workers, or supervisors. Their thoughts, actions, and emotions may not make sense to you. Do not be too quick to react to their behavior. No two people are alike in how they respond to things going on around them. Their behavior should not control your behavior. If they cause you to get angry or upset, you are letting their behavior control yours. In a very real sense, you are giving up control of your life to someone else.

When you find yourself at odds with your supervisors, co-workers, or customers, try to understand them and use the opportunity to learn as much as possible about their points of view. If it is necessary to confront the person making you angry, do it in a positive way. Psychologists have suggested using three "I" statements. For example, if a co-worker has not been pulling his share of stock work, tell him what is upsetting you: "I resent that you stood around talking to your girlfriend while we were supposed to be putting away the shipment." Then follow this with what you expect from the person: "I want you to help with this; it's hard work." Finally, it is important to mention something you appreciate about the person or the situation: "I know this is a boring part of the job, but it will all go faster if each of us helps." This procedure may not be as immediately satisfying as yelling at your co-worker, but in the long run it will maintain positive human relations and get the work done.

WHAT YOU AND YOUR EMPLOYER CAN EXPECT

When you go to work for someone, whether it is baby sitting, mowing lawns, working in a store, or delivering pizza, you have entered into an agreement. The agreement has two parts: (1) what you agree to provide, and (2) what the employer agrees to provide. It is very rare in beginning jobs for these agreements to be written down. As you advance in your career you may be asked to sign a written contract detailing the agreement. But whether the agreement is written or not, both parties have certain expectations of the other.

What You Can Expect From an Employer

A good human relations environment is created when an employer provides a good place to work. Obviously, the employer should inform you what the wage or salary will be for the job and the conditions of employment. But the successful retail marketer knows that employees expect more than just a salary. They know that to obtain and keep good employees, they must provide favorable working conditions, fringe benefits, and a chance for personal growth.

Favorable Working Conditions Favorable working conditions include such things as a safe working environment. Often, an employer will conduct special training programs to inform you about safety on the job. This has become such an important area in recent

Many employers provide facilities such as employee cafeterias.

years that there are now special businesses that exist solely to advise other businesses about safety on the job.

Most employers recognize the value of providing for the employees' comfort during the working day. Employee lounges or cafeterias are often provided where employees can take breaks. Some businesses provide day-care facilities for working parents. Because of the shortage of workers in some cities, companies like McDonald's are even providing free transportation to workers who live far from the immediate area of the store.

Fringe Benefits Employers provide a number of material benefits beyond the paycheck. Some, such as worker's compensation, are required by law. Worker's compensation is insurance against potential financial losses resulting from accidents on the job. If you injure yourself on the job, worker's compensation will pay your hospital bills. Under some conditions, this same insurance may pay you for retraining. Unemployment insurance is also required by law and is a fund designed to pay you a set amount of money if you are out of work for reasons beyond your control.

But there are many other types of fringe benefits that employers may provide. Most employers provide a retirement program for their long-term employees; profit sharing, which means that the company invests a percentage of its profits in a pension fund you can draw upon at retirement; sick leave, vacation leave, and employee discounts. Many businesses provide gyms and workout rooms on site.

Chance for Personal Growth Forward-thinking retail firms recognize that the individual employee is a valuable asset. They will invest large amounts of money in employee training and development programs. Business and industry spend more than $100 billion a year on such activities. These programs make it possible for you to learn new jobs so that you can advance, and learn new skills and techniques so that you can improve your performance on your current job. Some businesses even provide the opportunity for you to continue your formal education at their expense.

Businesses will provide these and many other kinds of benefits in order to improve the working conditions of their employees. They know that these will help improve the human relations environment in the business. In turn, however, employers have many expectations of you.

What an Employer Can Expect From You

Employers know from experience that the personal qualities of each employee have a lot to do with how the employee gets along with co-workers, supervisors, and customers. Many research studies have tried to identify what these qualities are. We have already discussed some valued behaviors and attitudes in Chapter 19. The following are other qualities employers have indicated they believe to be important to success in retail marketing. Many people label these qualities "occupational survival skills" because they are so important to surviving on the job. You will need to develop all of these qualities.

Desire to Work The desire to work includes knowing how to work as well as wanting to work. Employees who work only for the money are less desirable than employees who work because they like the job and consider work to be a meaningful part of their lives. They see the job as an opportunity. Money may be important, but money in itself is not enough.

Knowing how to work implies understanding the job. It means showing good work habits, such as keeping busy and finding tasks to do without having to be told what to do.

Industriousness **Industriousness** is steady, earnest, diligent effort. It is often stated as "doing a full day's work for a full day's pay." Industrious workers attend to what they are supposed to be doing. They work as hard when they are alone as when someone is watching. They avoid such behavior as "clock watching," taking extra-long breaks, talking on the business phone to their friends, and other actions designed to avoid work.

Integrity **Integrity** includes morality, honesty, and ethical conduct. It means being truthful, trustworthy, sincere, fair, and straightforward in your relationships with your employer and others. It also includes refraining from lying, stealing (time, money, or merchandise), cheating, or taking advantage of the company.

This suggests that you should never take unfair advantage of your discount privileges, for example, by helping your friends obtain merchandise at less than the ticketed price. It means that you do not waste time on the job when no one is watching, or abuse sick-leave privileges. Stealing time from an employer is just as bad as stealing money.

Integrity also means getting to work on time, and being absent only when absolutely necessary. It means accepting responsibility for errors you make. It means keeping promises you make.

Loyalty **Loyalty** means keeping confidential any information about a business that is not supposed to be public knowledge. In this day of sharp competition, trade secrets are very important to the survival and success of a business. You should try to represent the firm in the best possible manner at all times.

As a loyal employee you won't criticize the business, its policies, its personnel, or its merchandise or services. You may disagree with some things that are done by the firm you work for, and you can discuss them with your supervisor, but you should not discuss them with others. Not all businesses or businesspeople deserve your loyalty. If you find yourself in a position where you cannot maintain a sense of loyalty, you should look for another job.

Cooperation
Cooperation means acting or working together with others for mutual benefit. The difference between a good retail firm and a poor one is often reflected in the cooperation, or lack of it, among the people who work there. When people help each other, working as a team, the department or company will function smoothly. When there is no cooperation, jobs become grudging chores.

Initiative
Initiative is shown by those who see a job that needs to be done and go ahead and do it without being told to do so. Personnel directors frequently point out that initiative is a prime requirement in the selection of people for supervisory and management training. Demonstrating initiative is important in all types of work, but more so in smaller firms where duties are usually less well defined and there is often less supervision than in large firms.

Tact
The ability to say and do the right thing at the right time is called **tact**. Tact is particularly needed when you are dealing with people who have strong opinions, people who are upset about something (such as a customer with a problem), people who have grievances, or people who are just having a bad day. Customers, co-workers, and supervisors don't like to be contradicted in other than a pleasant, tactful manner.

Empathy
The ability to feel the way another person does, or **empathy,** is important in relating tactfully to someone. If you think carefully about what to say so as not to hurt their feelings or embarrass them, then you will be able to handle delicate situations and sensitive individuals. It will also show that you have good control over your actions and emotions. Empathy also means treating people as you would like to be treated. Teasing and making smart remarks may seem funny at the time, but sometimes such behavior can be very irritating.

Enthusiasm
Enthusiasm is particularly valued by employers, because they know that an enthusiastic employee works hard. People show enthusiasm in many ways. Having a ready smile for customers and co-workers, being aware of what is going on around you, and quickly jumping into new tasks without argument are all examples of enthusiasm. Showing pride in your work and your business is also a way of showing enthusiasm.

Enthusiasm is especially important for the professional salesperson. Enthusiasm is contagious, and it helps convince customers to buy. If you demonstrate a positive attitude toward your products, services, and company, customers will more likely believe in you and will more likely buy from you.

Willingness to Accept Change
Because marketing is a dynamic and rapidly changing field, employers value people who can accept change and welcome it rather than resist it.

Many people have a difficult time accepting change. Perhaps it is because change means something new and unknown, and they see that as a threat to their sense of security. This is a very normal reaction.

Some changes are very small and are easily dealt with such as the introduction of a new sales ticket. Other changes may be great and more difficult to deal with. For example, over the past decade many businesses have installed microcomputers to help increase productivity, reduce errors, or improve business performance. This may require additional training and perhaps even a revision of a person's job responsibilities. Yet without this change the business may not be able to remain competitive. Employers expect employees to adapt to change regardless of how large or small the change may be.

■

WHAT CO-WORKERS CAN EXPECT FROM YOU

Carefully considering how to be more thoughtful toward others can help you achieve better human relations. It has already been mentioned that you should show genuine concern for others. Here are five additional keys for good human relations with co-workers: (1) treat people as individuals, (2) never pass the buck, (3) observe rules, (4) carry your own weight, and (5) work as part of a team.

Treat Co-Workers as Individuals

No two co-workers are the same. They come in all colors, shapes, sizes, personalities, and with a variety of outlooks on life. Some may have problems that show up on the job as unpleasant behavior. Try to show empathy by mentally putting yourself in their positions. Suppose that a co-worker (or your supervisor, for that matter) came storming into your work area and began yelling at you about some minor problem. Try to think about why the co-worker is acting this way. Has he or she just been chewed out by the supervisor? Is the person not feeling well? What might have caused the outburst? Instead of becoming angry and yelling back, stay calm and try to help your co-worker regain composure.

Learn names. People like to hear their names. Also, find out something about each person you work with that you can talk about (family, pets, favorite sports, car, and so on). Use this information to start conversations when it is appropriate: "Say, Jim, have you been able to get the part you needed for your car?" Remember, showing sincere interest in others is a sure way to improve human relations.

Never Pass the Buck

Blaming someone else for your mistakes is called *passing the buck*. This is a sure way to become unpopular with your co-workers. Those who can stand on their own two feet, do their job well, do their fair share of the work, and admit when they have made an error are normally liked by their co-workers. Everybody makes mistakes sometimes, so by admitting mistakes and errors you show confidence, and that will be appreciated by your co-workers.

Observe Rules

Most organizations have two types of rules: written and unwritten. Observing these rules helps improve human relations and helps make a business run smoothly.

Written rules are often provided in the form of an employee handbook. They typically include rules on work breaks, pay periods, vacation, sick leave, and other policies. As a new employee, you will have much greater success getting along with your co-workers if you read and carefully follow your company's handbook for employees.

Unwritten rules are often developed over time and become part of tradition in an organization. Even though they are not written, they may be as important as the written rules. These unwritten rules may determine who gets to go on break first, how overtime is dealt with, or who has first rights to customers in certain areas of the store.

Carry Your Own Weight

You must do your share of the work in order to get along with others. Nobody likes someone who dumps his or her responsibilities onto someone else.

One way to make sure you are doing your fair share is to review your job description. A **job description** outlines your specific tasks and responsibilities. However, many retail marketers do not provide job descriptions for all of their positions. The best way to find out what is your fair share is to ask someone. You should ask what is expected of you as well as what is not expected of you. Do not be afraid to ask questions, because all the long-term employees have started a new job sometime in their life, so they all have experienced what you are experiencing.

Work as Part of the Team

Teamwork requires that you sacrifice a little of yourself to help others accomplish something. This is part of getting along with others. Here are some tips on things you can do to improve the spirit of teamwork.

Accept Praise Gracefully When you are praised by your supervisor, look at him or her and simply say thank you. Don't then go around bragging about your personal success. Word of it will eventually get out, from others.

Share the Credit Rarely do people accomplish anything by themselves. Sometimes you receive credit for what you and others have done. Accept credit for what you have done, but be sure to tell about how the others contributed to the success.

Cooperation and teamwork benefit all the members of the team.

Praise Others Individuals like to hear nice things about themselves. When you recognize the accomplishments of others, do it with sincerity and because you want to. Do not do it because you expect something in return. Insincerity is easily recognized and can damage your relations with others.

Don't Flaunt Special Privileges When you obtain special privileges or additional responsibilities (this will happen as you advance in your career), don't brag about it in front of your co-workers. You should be proud of your accomplishments, but resist showing off.

Help Everyone Be a Winner In order for you to get ahead, someone else does not have to fall behind. It is possible, and indeed likely, that when one person advances, others can advance. The idea of teamwork is that each person helps the other. Another person's success is your success when a genuine sense of team spirit is present. Your efforts to help others succeed is a mark of leadership. Leadership is a highly valued skill by retail marketers and can lead to promotion.

Now that you have completed this chapter, you should have a better understanding of the value of good human relations on the job. In the next chapter you will have the opportunity to find out how good communications skills can improve human relations.

TRADE TALK

Define each term and use it in a sentence.

Cooperation	Integrity
Empathy	Loyalty
Industriousness	Tact

CAN YOU ANSWER THESE?

1. Describe one basic rule for good human relations.

2. How can you show genuine interest in others?

3. What do you have a right to expect from an employer?

4. What does an employer have a right to expect from you?

5. What are five strategies for improving human relations with co-workers?

C·H·A·P·T·E·R

21 *Communicating Effectively*

"What we have here is a failure to communicate!" How often have you heard such a phrase? Many problems in retail marketing arise because of poor communications. This is true in large corporations as well as small entrepreneurial enterprises. As business managers have begun to recognize the problems associated with poor communications, many are beginning to provide training programs in communication skills—listening, speaking, reading, and writing.

Effective personal communication is critical at all levels of retail marketing. Sam Walton, president of Wal-Mart stores, a discount retail chain, personally visits between 6 and 12 stores each week. As he visits in one of the more than 500 chain stores, he talks with employees at all levels about the business, about their concerns and their ideas. He knows hundreds of his employees on a first-name basis. Walton's personal communication style is largely responsible for Wal-Mart becoming one of the fastest-growing discount chains in the United States.

HOW COMMUNICATION HAPPENS

Communication has many meanings, but for our purposes, we will define **communication** as the two-way movement or sharing of information, opinions, and ideas that results in understanding between a sender and a receiver. You will note that this definition means more than just simply giving information.

Many people think that just telling someone something is communication. It is not. Communication involves the opportunity for the receiver of the information to clarify the message. This requires the active involvement of more than one person. Understanding is the other part of the definition. This means that the person sending the message and the person receiving the message share the same meaning or understanding of the message. This is the source of many human relations problems, as people often place different meanings on messages because of a variety of barriers that will be discussed in this chapter.

A Model of Communication

Effective communications is made up of four parts: a sender of the message, the message, a receiver, and feedback. It works this way. Suppose that you are a salesperson of major appliances. A customer approaches and you begin a sales conversation. During the conversation you will select words to communicate information, ideas, and opinions (message) about your brand of appliances. During the conversation the customer asks questions or responds to your questions (feedback). **Feedback** is a response necessary to make sure the message has been understood. This helps you more clearly identify how you can help the customer make a good buying decision. A simplified model of this process is shown below.

But life is rarely this simple. People view the world through perceptual screens. **Perceptual screens** are filters through which

people give meaning to messages. Typical screens that affect the communication process include emotions, attitudes, nonverbal clues, and role expectations. These cause the communication process to be more complex. Most communication really looks like the figure on page 175.

Now let's look at that sales transaction again. You communicate a message about your appliances. Your selection of words to use are the result of how you may feel at the moment (emotion), what you think about the particular appliance the customer is interested in (attitude), how you view the customer (role expectation), and how interested the customer appears to be in the product or service (nonverbal clues). Customers, in turn, interpret what you say based on how they feel at the moment (emotions), their feelings about the product or the store (attitudes), their perception of you as a salesperson (role expectation), and how interested you appear in meeting their needs (nonverbal clues). It is because of the these screens that communication breaks down and human relations problems begin. Let's look at each part of the model in terms of possible barriers to effective communication.

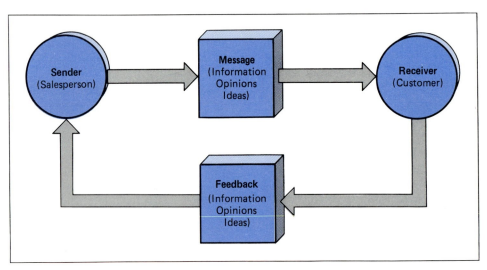

Simple communications model.

Unit 7   Assessing Your Interpersonal Skills

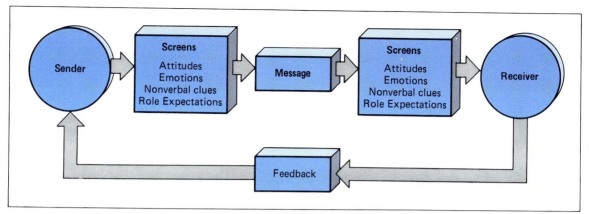

Complex communication model.

Barriers to Effective Communication

Each element of the communication model above is an opportunity for communication to succeed or to fail. Your use of words, your display of emotion, your attitude, your role expectations, and your nonverbal communication all affect the quality of the communication process.

Words   Words carry at least two meanings: the explicit meaning found in a dictionary (denotation), and the meaning associated with the word (connotation). Many times words have more than one explicit dictionary meaning. For example, the word "market" has at least nine different meanings. The word "lead" has more than 80. The 500 most common words in the English language have more than 14,000 different meanings.

Many words are associated with strong emotions. The connotation of the word salesperson is different to different people, usually as a result of their past experiences with salespeople.

The English language is constantly changing, and new words are being created all of the time. The increasing importance of technology in our society is reflected in the use of such words or phrases as "interface" and "dialog" (both mean to talk to someone else); "high-tech" (loosely refers to any computer-based business); and "overload" (you have too much work to handle). These words and many others are referred to as jargon. **Jargon** is specialized vocabulary used by people who have a common interest. Think of all the phrases from sports, government, and your own circle of friends that have meaning to others in the same field, but do not communicate to people outside the field. Effective communication avoids the use of jargon and instead relies on the use of commonly understood, standard English.

Emotions   Strong feelings about something can often cause a listener not to hear what a speaker is actually saying. It can cause an angry listener to ignore the message, or it may cause the listener to accept uncritically what the speaker is saying if the listener is carried away by the speaker's eloquence. Either way, the listener is not paying attention to the content of the message, but rather to his or her own feelings about it.

Emotions trigger emotions in other people. If a customer is angry about poor service, missing parts, or another problem, the poorly trained salesperson often reacts with anger, turning the discussion into an argument and creating a human relations problem. That salesperson may win the argument but lose the customer. The salesperson who is sensitive to the customer's needs, remaining calm and courteous, can probably save the sale and, in the process, save the customer for the business.

Role Expectations   **Role expectations** refer to what sorts of behavior people expect in others. You have certain expectations concerning how you expect your teachers to act, how you expect your supervisor to act, and so on. In turn, supervisors, customers, and co-workers have expectations of how you should act.

Sometimes these expectations can disrupt effective communications. Customers may expect to find someone older than you selling a particular product or service. Thus, when you approach them to provide service, they may not listen to your message but instead focus their attention on your youth. There was once a store manager for a major shoestore chain who was promoted to manager just after he turned 21. Unfortunately, he looked younger than his age, and older customers frequently asked to talk to the "real manager" when they had a problem, not expecting someone who looked so young to have such responsibility. Rather than argue with the customers and create a human relations problem, he would have one of his older, more mature employees handle the situation after first giving the older employee his instructions.

Frequently in retail marketing, someone you have worked with as a co-worker is promoted to become your supervisor. It can be very difficult for you to accept the former co-worker in his or her new role.

Attitudes   Your attitudes are displayed by the way you act, look, or otherwise demonstrate your feelings toward a subject. They can be a barrier to communications by altering what the listener hears in a message. Many customers believe that the salesperson is going to sell them something they do not want. Such an attitude creates barriers to effective communication that limit the salesperson's ability to provide good service.

Positive attitudes can facilitate good communication. A salesperson with a positive attitude can often overcome many of the barriers to effective communication. People with positive attitudes are generally more liked by others than people with negative attitudes.

Nonverbal Clues   **Nonverbal clues** are how you communicate with body movement. Examples of nonverbal clues are smiling, frowning, looking around (when you should be focusing on the speaker), slouching, and looking at your watch when someone is talking to you. All of these gestures communicate more to someone than the words you use. When listeners feel that the nonverbal clues are consistent with the words used to communicate, they will tend to trust the speaker more. When the nonverbal clues are inconsistent with the verbal message, they will believe the nonverbal clues.

Now let's look at the brief exchange between salesperson and customer again. Each of the elements of the communication model represents a potential barrier to communication. Effective human relations will result when the salesperson actively uses each as an opportunity to improve communications. By being sensitive to the customer, and being conscious of—and controlling—his or her own attitudes, emotions, and nonverbal clues, the salesperson can enhance communications and improve human relations.

■

BECOMING A BETTER LISTENER

The Greek philosopher Epictetus observed, "Nature has given to men one tongue but two ears, that we may hear from others twice as much as we speak." How much of the time do you listen? Do you learn more when you are talking or when you are listening? Good listeners respect the other person's right to express an opinion. Good listeners are also interested in comparing points of view and in learning from others rather than defending their own position. And good listeners are patient.

The Importance of Good Listening

It has been said that hearing is with ears, listening is with the mind. This suggests that a good listener thinks about what is being said. Listening is much more than just hearing. Listening is an active process and is a skill that can be learned, just like good speaking. Successful people in retail marketing spend much more time listening than in any other form of communication, as shown in the following illustration.

In spite of the amount of time people spend listening, most do it poorly. Why? Experts in communication suggest that there are reasons why people are poor listeners: (1) people think faster than they talk; (2) people are planning a reply while the speaker is still speaking; and (3) emotions, attitudes, and role expectations block out certain messages. Since we have already talked about the problem of emotions, attitudes, and role expectations, let's look more closely at reasons 1 and 2.

People Think Faster Than They Speak
The average person speaks at a rate of about 125 words a minute. When you are excited, you will talk a little faster. Yet most people have the ability to process 500 words a minute. The brain gets bored with this extra capacity and frequently turns attention to other things.

People Plan a Reply While the Speaker Is Speaking
One of the traits of humans is that we are all egocentric. **Egocentric** means that we think of everything in relation to ourselves. So when someone talks to us, we often pretend to listen but are really waiting to jump in with what we think is important or with our own story. Some of the extra capacity of the brain is being devoted to planning our reply instead of concentrating on what the speaker is saying.

Developing good listening skills is critical for success in retail marketing. Employers often complain that employees do not follow directions well. Part of the reason is that the employees do not actively engage in listening.

In developing effective human relations, careful listening is very important. Effective listening can provide managers and supervisors with insights into employees' problems. Effective listening can provide employees with a better understanding of their jobs and of the people with whom they work. And in retail marketing, listening will help all workers relate better to that especially important partner in communication—the customer.

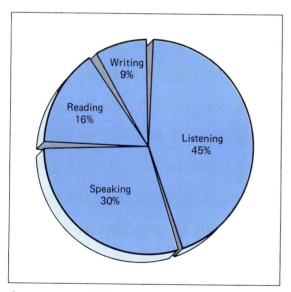

Communication skills used during an average workday.

Improving Your Listening Skills

Although there are no hard-and-fast rules for effective listening that will always work, there are a number of general rules that will help you become a better listener.

1. Listen for facts and feelings. When people speak, they often communicate how they feel as well as factual information. It is important to be able to separate the two.

2. Become actively involved. Nodding your head occasionally or saying things like "I see" or "I understand" indicate that you are paying attention and are actively involved in the conversation.

3. Eliminate distractions. Focus on the speaker. Turn off background noise (radio or TV, for example) if possible. Move closer to the speaker or change to a quieter location.

4. Don't anticipate. Do not plan your reply while the speaker is speaking. Resist the temptation to complete the speaker's sentences or jump to conclusions. Most important, don't interrupt a speaker. A little silence now and then in the conversation is not a problem.

5. Avoid prejudging the speaker. Regardless of what you may feel about the speaker, focus on what he or she is trying to say, not the delivery, appearance, or other distractions.

6. Clarify. Ask questions. Good listeners make sure they understand the terms and concepts the speaker is using.

7. Give immediate feedback. One way to ensure real understanding is to immediately restate the communication. Even the best listener will occasionally misinterpret the spoken word, so it's important to repeat the message to the sender. Simple feedback such as "In other words, you want me to . . ." or "What I hear you saying is . . ." is often all that is necessary.

Sometimes when you do not understand what the speaker has said, you can provide feedback by using "I" statements. Rather than say, "you were not very clear," you could say, "I feel as if I missed something. . . ."

BECOMING A BETTER SPEAKER

The most important thing to remember when you are communicating through speaking is to think before you speak. Think about whom you are speaking to, the extent of their knowledge of the subject, and what it will take to gain and keep their attention.

In dealing with customers, remember that words and phrases you and your friends use will very likely not communicate much to older people. Poor or awkward grammar and poor enunciation or pronunciation may give them a bad opinion of you and your firm.

Remember that communication is a two-way process. So allow your listeners to express *their* ideas. For example, listen to customers when they express their needs and seek out the merchandise or services that answer these needs. Don't get upset if their opinions differ from yours. Avoid showing frustration, anger, or bluntly contradicting your listeners. Instead, clarify your key points and end your message with a summary. If you have carefully thought through what you said in a polite, courteous manner, you'll be most effective in gaining the confidence of your listeners. This will be discussed in greater detail in Unit 11.

USING NONVERBAL COMMUNICATION

Nonverbal communication is defined as messages without words. It is sometimes called body language or surface language. It is all of the nonverbal things that you do with your head, arms, hands, legs, feet, and facial expressions that communicate meaning to others. As noted earlier, this is an important component of how we communicate meaning to others. Experts claim that half of what we communicate is transmitted using nonverbal channels of communication such as posture, facial expressions, and gestures. Another 40 percent is conveyed by our tone of voice. The actual words we use communicate only 10 percent of our total meaning.

As noted earlier, when there is an inconsistency between what we are saying and what we are showing with our body language, people tend to believe the nonverbal communication. The problem is that much of this communication occurs at a subconscious level. That is, we are not aware we are doing it. This means that the effective communicator will have to work at ensuring consistency between what he or she is saying and the nonverbal clues he or she may be sending out. Generally, body language is thought of in terms of three types of behaviors: gestures, eye contact, and use of personal space.

Gestures

The gestures you use and the body posture you assume when speaking or listening to others constantly send messages to people about how you are reacting to them. No one gesture will mean the same thing all of the time, but gestures are seen by and reacted to by your listener or speaker.

When someone is speaking to you, do you turn a shoulder toward the speaker? Do you fold your arms, or sit with one leg crossed over the other? These are ways of communicating that you are closed to the speaker. Or do you face the speaker, sit with your body turned toward him or her, and have your arms unfolded? This communicates an openness toward the speaker.

Our posture communicates much. A slouchy posture communicates indifference. Sitting on the edge of the chair instead of in the middle communicates anxiety. A salesperson leaning against a wall or counter while talking to a customer communicates lack of interest. In retail marketing it is important to communicate interest in the customer from the moment he or she walks in the door. Many potential customers are lost as a result of nonverbal messages that say, "go away and don't bother me."

Eye Contact

The poets have said that the eyes are the windows to the soul. This may or may not be true, but the eyes certainly transmit more information than any other part of the body. Most cultures have unwritten rules concerning eye contact, such as "It is impolite to stare."

Generally, in business, direct eye contact is considered important. Most businesspeople mistrust someone who does not look them in the eye when they are introduced, when they are talking, or when they are responding to questions. Although this is true for most people in our country, it may not be true for all. Some minority cultures consider it impolite to look someone directly in the eye. It may be considered rude for young people to look their elders directly in the eye during conversation. If you have difficulty looking someone directly in the eyes during conversation, work on developing your ability to do so. In the world of business, it will help improve how people think about you.

Use of Personal Space

People are affected by the physical distance between themselves and others. We all need a certain amount of room between us and someone else. The amount of room we need depends on the social situation. This room, or territory, is often called **personal space**.

For most Americans, the personal space required extends up to about 18 inches past our bodies. The area inside this space is reserved for only our closest friends and loved ones. Others who enter this space for more than a brief moment (shaking hands, for example) are perceived as being aggressive, and people generally react negatively to such behavior.

Some experts suggest there are other zones of space beyond personal space. *Social space* is the next ring outward from our bodies, where conversation occurs with strangers. It is a distance ranging from around 1½ feet to 4 feet. In this space you are close enough for a conversation but far enough away to maintain your privacy. Of course, where you are affects how you react to the closeness of others. Intrusion into one's personal space is accepted on crowded elevators. However, if only you were on an elevator and another person got on and stood close to you, you would probably feel very uncomfortable.

Like eye contact, however, the amount of personal space required is sometimes a result of culture. Many people from Latin America think that North Americans are cold and stand-offish, because Latin Americans generally prefer to stand only a foot apart while talking, and North Americans typically prefer 2 to 3 feet of distance. So it is important for you to know and understand the cultural aspects of personal space.

■

HOW COMMUNICATION WORKS IN ORGANIZATIONS

Successful retail marketing organizations, large or small, depend on cooperation. Good communication helps build cooperation and a positive human relations environment by permitting communication to flow in both directions. People need to know what is expected of them in their jobs, why the organization exists, and how they are expected to communicate.

It is important, particularly for new employees, to learn quickly about the organization, the new job, and their responsibilities. Most businesses have a formal organization chart that shows how communication is supposed to flow. All organizations have an informal organization that provides another means of communication flow. As an employee you must know how to use both.

Formal Communication

The formal communication process allows a business to operate quickly and smoothly. This process is usually expressed in the form of an **organization chart**, such as the one for a small hotel chain shown on page 181. The black lines connecting the boxes show who has authority over whom and who reports to whom. Those higher on the chart have authority over those lower on the chart. The chart also shows areas of responsibility. For example, the vice president for marketing has responsibility for advertising and sales.

In the formal organization, lines of communication follow the lines of the organizational chart. For example, if the general manager wanted to change the policy on how to handle discounts for military and government personnel, notice of the change will flow down from (1) the general manager to (2) the hotel manager to (3) the shift supervisor to (4) the clerks. What this shows is that official communication comes to an employee from his or her immediate supervisor. While you may hear about it from someone else, it is not official until it comes from a supervisor. Official communication generally includes messages about such things as:

- Change in working conditions
- Change in company policies
- Promotions
- Employee evaluations
- Sales goals

Official communications also flow upward following the same lines shown on the organization chart. If you are a clerk at the front desk in a hotel and you have an idea on how to improve the flow of paperwork during busy periods, you would communicate this to your immediate supervisor, the shift supervisor. In turn, the idea would be communicated to the hotel manager. Depending on the nature of the idea, it might stop there for action, or it might continue up the line of communication. Failure to follow these lines of communication can create tremendous human relations problems. "Going over the head" of your supervisor is frowned upon and can often result in problems for you on the job.

Informal Communication

Every organization has informal lines of communication. These are established because groups within an organization may have common social background (grew up together), something in common (all go to the same school), the same religion, or some other unifying factor.

The name usually associated with informal communications is "the grapevine." The term dates back to the American Civil War. At that time, the telegraph was relatively new, and wires were strung through trees, bushes, and along fences—much like grapevines. Secret messages were transmitted over the telegraph. Today, the term grapevine has come to mean all unofficial messages.

Unlike official communications, the grapevine does not follow the lines on an organization chart. Let's look at the organization chart for the hotel chain again, but this time focus on the informal channels of communi-

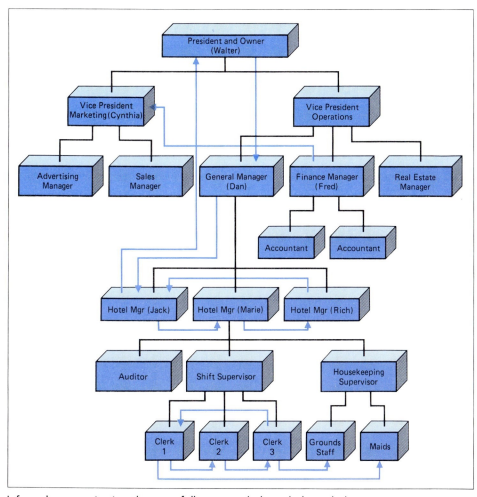

Informal communication does not follow an orderly path through the organization.

cation, represented by the colored lines with arrows. Walter, who owns the company, has known Jack, the hotel manager, since Jack was a kid, and they frequently have lunch together. Jack, Marie, and Rick all share the same responsibilities, and so they communicate often about business. Fred, the finance manager, and Cynthia, the vice president for marketing, grew up together, and their families often socialize. Dan, the general manager, goes to the same church as Jack. You can see that a web of informal communications quickly grows up around any type of organization.

But is the information that goes through the grapevine accurate? Some experts suggest that informal messages are about 80 percent accurate. This sounds good, unless you consider that, to be effective, communications must be 100 percent accurate! Otherwise, messages are distorted, exaggerated, or abbreviated and will cause human relations problems. Remember, you can only be sure of a message if it comes through official lines of communication.

TRADE TALK

Define each term and use it in a sentence.

Communication	Nonverbal communication
Egocentric	Organization chart
Feedback	Perceptual screens
Jargon	Personal space
Nonverbal clues	Role expectations

CAN YOU ANSWER THESE?

1. What are the basic elements of the communication model?
2. What are four typical barriers to good communications?
3. What nonverbal clues can affect the meaning of communication?
4. What are six ways you can improve your listening skills?
5. What is the difference between formal and informal communications in an organization?

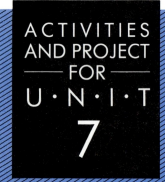

ACTIVITIES AND PROJECT — FOR — U·N·I·T 7

RETAIL MARKETING CASES

1. Jacqueline Braun had been working at Frank's Hardware for about 2 weeks. On her first day of work, the store manager, Lester McCallum, explained in great detail the procedures to follow when customers wanted to use VISA or MasterCard to pay for purchases. Jacqueline was very nervous that first day and didn't concentrate on everything Mr. McCallum had told her. She also didn't fully understand all of the instructions. Mr. McCallum assumed that Jacqueline understood all of the processes. However, when Mr. McCallum checked on Jacqueline the next day,

he found that she was making costly errors. He reprimanded her. Now he finds she is still making the same kind of errors.

1. What communication skills did Jacqueline neglect?

2. Why do you think she had communications problems?

3. What communication skills did Mr. McCallum neglect when training Jacqueline?

4. What would you recommend to Jacqueline and Mr. McCallum to improve future communications?

2. Michael was president of the Marketing Club. One of their annual activities was to raise money for the Jerry Lewis Telethon for muscular distrophy. Mike and the other officers of the club organized the fundraiser, and the club members conducted the event. The fundraiser collected more money that year than ever before, and the club received special recognition at the school's spring awards assembly. Mike was called to the stage to receive a certificate. Mike accepted the certificate for himself and then showed it off to his friends during the day.

1. Did Mike do the right thing in accepting the certificate for himself?

2. What problems do you see this causing?

3. How did Mike make the problem worse?

4. How should Mike have handled the award?

PROJECT: QUALITIES FOR SUCCESSFUL RETAILING EMPLOYEES

YOUR PROJECT GOAL

Identify the personal qualities that employers in retail marketing consider to be important for career success.

PROCEDURE

1. Identify a retail marketing career area of interest to you. With your instructor's permission, contact a manager, business owner, or other person with supervisory responsibility in the career area you have identified. Make an appointment to conduct an interview with this person.

2. Prepare a list of qualities you think might be important to career success. In your interview, show the list to the interviewee and ask if he or she would add any other qualities to the list.

3. Then ask the interviewee to rank each quality in terms of importance. Place a "1" next to a quality the employer feels is critical to success, a "2" next to a quality that is helpful but not critical, a "3" next to a quality that is useful, and a "4" next to a quality that is nice to have.

4. Ask the interviewee what types of education and other experience he or she feels is necessary for a person to pursue a career in retail marketing.

5. When you have completed the interview, think about the information you have obtained. Why are some qualities considered more important than others? Prepare a short report on qualities and experiences that your interviewee has identified as necessary for a career in retail marketing.

6. Compare your conclusions with those of others in your class.

EVALUATION

You will be evaluated on:

1. The reasons by which you justified the different ratings among qualities for success.

2. How well you combined information on qualities for success and education and other experience required for career success in retail marketing.

ENHANCING YOUR CUSTOMER RELATIONS

22 *Developing a Customer Service Attitude*

When John came home, he was obviously angry. "I'll never shop at that store again!" John's roommate, Sean, asked what had happened. "Those people think they're doing me a favor when I spend my money there. First of all, it took a good 10 minutes to get a salesperson's attention. They were much more interested in talking to each other than to me. Then the jerk made me feel stupid when I asked him some questions about cable hookups for my VCR. I asked him because he's supposed to be the expert. I'll never go back there."

John experienced something that happens all too often in retail marketing—poor customer service attitude. It is estimated that this type of behavior costs stores millions of dollars every year.

By now you should be able to see the importance of customers to the success of a business and to your opportunity for employment. You will agree that customers are the most important element in a business, and it quite literally pays for you to concentrate on developing good relations with customers. This chapter is devoted to helping you develop a positive customer service attitude that will increase your chances for a successful career in retail marketing.

■

WHY CUSTOMERS PATRONIZE YOUR BUSINESS

There will always be competitors for your customers. Someone can always sell what you sell for less. Someone can always offer substitute products or other brands. This is what our free enterprise system is all about. Competition is what influences most business decisions. So why should a person buy from your business?

There are three main reasons why customers initially buy from and continue to patronize your business: (1) products and services offered for sale; (2) sales-supporting services provided before, during, and after the sale; and (3) goodwill. Customers patronize a business for some or all of these reasons.

Products and Services Offered

Customers are initially attracted by the products or services provided by your business. A customer may be looking for a product that is sold by a number of retailers, such as a clock or radio, or something unique, such as a monogrammed wristwatch. If someone is looking for something that a number of stores sell, then he or she may be attracted by price. If the product is unique, the customer may be attracted by availability.

Regardless of what brings them into the store, customers keep coming back because of the availability of suitable products or services. Few firms stay in business long if what they sell is inferior. The goods and services must do what the seller claims they will do, and they must be safe for the consumer to use. Most important, the product or service must satisfy the customers' needs.

Businesses that sell services provide something that is intangible. **Intangibles** are things you cannot touch, feel, or otherwise possess, such as hair styling, a plane ride, music lessons, or the opportunity to play a video game. Even though they are intangible, they still must be safe for consumer use, satisfy the consumer's needs, and be offered at a profitable selling price.

Sales-Supporting Services

Many companies provide services to complement the products they sell. Such services are referred to as **sales-supporting services**. These services may be provided before, during, or after the sale. Unlike services offered for sale and priced to generate profit, sales-supporting services are frequently provided at no cost or on a cost-recovery basis.

Cost recovery means that the fee charged is intended only to cover the cost of providing the service and does not generate profit.

Sales-supporting services increase sales of the firm's products by building customer goodwill, bringing customers into the place of business, or making a product more attractive. For example, real estate agents are in a unique position to provide service before a sale is actually made. People moving into a new community often obtain information about the community from realtors before they even arrive. Fabric stores will often have interior design consultants available during a sale. Appliance stores, electronic stores, and automobile dealerships usually provide repair services after a sale. And furniture stores will usually deliver furniture after a sale is made. Successful retail marketers recognize that effective customer relations are built on providing quality products. But in addition to products, quality services are also necessary to retain customer loyalty.

The Whirlpool Corporation, a major manufacturer of appliances, conducted a study of consumer attitudes recently. Among its many findings are the following:

■ 73 percent of those polled said that the availability of local services was a factor in their decision to buy.

■ There were mixed reviews of the quality of specific services: 50 percent felt automobile repair services had declined; 24 percent felt that service for appliances had declined; 18 percent felt that service provided by home electronics businesses had declined; and 12 percent felt that service at the supermarket had declined.

What these poll results suggest is that customer service is an important part of developing a positive customer relations strategy. The study also suggests that there is a market for a business willing to offer service after the sale as a high priority.

The various services that businesses provide after the sale must be fairly priced and provide additional customer satisfaction. This improves the image of the business in the customer's eyes.

Goodwill

Goodwill is the positive feeling that people have toward a particular business. Goodwill is the product of many factors, but it is certainly generated by friendliness, honesty, and courtesy on the part of a business's employees. Customers prefer to shop where they feel they are valued. But the important thing to remember is that a business does not generate goodwill. The people who work for the business generate goodwill.

People who work for a business create goodwill in many ways. It might be something as simple as a friendly smile and greeting when the customer enters the store. It might be a sincerely helpful attitude. It might be remembering customer names and the products or services a particular customer prefers. Other ways in which you can develop goodwill are discussed in Chapter 35.

Goodwill generated by employees of a business is long remembered by customers. When customers enter a place of business—a hotel, a shoe store, a dry cleaner—they are there because they have needs and wants the retail marketer can fill. Customers expect to pay for assistance in solving their problems. But they expect more for their hard-earned money than just a product in return. They expect to be shown that their patronage is valued.

■

SOURCES OF CUSTOMER COMPLAINTS

There are many sources of customer complaints, although recent research has suggested some common problem areas. A study by a national insurance company on consumer attitudes found that:

■ 73 percent felt products did not last as long as they did 10 years ago.

■ 64 percent said they had difficulty getting products repaired.
■ 61 percent thought the quality of goods and services had worsened.
■ 50 percent believed they got a "worse deal" in the marketplace than they got 10 years ago.

Although the retail marketer has only limited control over some of these factors, a well-developed customer service program, supported by employees with a good customer service attitude, can create a loyal customer base.

Customers will often tell their friends about how they feel they were treated by a retailer without any prompting from the retailer. This is called **word-of-mouth advertising**. However there is a catch to word-of-mouth advertising. Some research suggests that customers who are satisfied with how the business treated them will tell up to three other people. Dissatisfied customers will tell up to 12 other people. So word-of-mouth advertising can work for or against a business, depending on how the customer felt he or she was treated. Many customers complain about other problems as well. Typical comments include reference to:

■ Delivery problems
■ Installation problems
■ Lack of information on product use
■ Problems with enforcement of warranties
■ Lack of knowledge on the part of the salesperson
■ Indifferent attitude on the part of store personnel

This final complaint is one that deserves special attention. *Stores Magazine*, a trade journal for the retail marketer, several years ago found that 68 percent of those customers who stopped shopping at a particular store did so because of what they perceived as indifference on the part of store personnel. **Indifference** is a lack of concern, interest, or feeling. This means that if we look at all of the reasons why someone does not shop at a

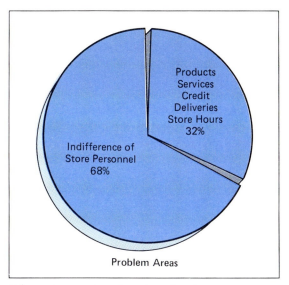

Products
Services
Credit
Deliveries
Store Hours
32%

Indifference of
Store Personnel
68%

Problem Areas

Why customers stop shopping at a store.

particular store, the biggest single problem is store personnel who don't care about the customer.

SERVING DIFFICULT CUSTOMERS

One of the exciting aspects of working in retail marketing is the opportunity to interact with many types of people. Most are pleasant and will respond positively to your efforts to help them. Inevitably, you will encounter customers who are difficult to work with. While some retail employees try to avoid difficult customers, the professional retail marketer recognizes that difficult customers are simply a special challenge.

Top-performing salespeople will tell you that difficult customers frequently become excellent, steady clients. They especially appreciate the seller's understanding in contrast with the usual behaviors of inept sales personnel. Moreover, they are inclined to tell their friends about the unique service they received.

Practicing the Customer Service Attitude

There are many ways to classify difficult customers. Some are argumentative, others are complainers, some are nontalkers, still others are know-it-alls. At least they seem to be that way during a given personal contact. So don't stereotype a person because of a single encounter. Keep in mind that on a particular occasion you may show similar behaviors. While you should be very cautious in classifying people, it is useful to recognize that some customers present special problems in effective communication.

When attempting to work with difficult customers, it is important to remain calm and courteous. Losing your temper will most likely lose a customer. Try to listen carefully to what the customer is actually saying and reduce the barriers to communication discussed in Chapter 21. Finally, do not avoid attempting to help the difficult customer. By offering courteous, helpful service, you will build clientele for your business.

The general suggestions offered above should be practiced with all customers. More specific suggestions for dealing with particular types of difficult customers are offered below.

Argumentative Customers

The argumentative customer is aggressive and will question or disagree with most statements the salesperson may make. This type of customer will try to put the salesperson on the defensive by pointing out the salesperson's mistakes.

The first thing to remember with this type of customer is not to let yourself be drawn into an argument. Try to improve the situation by using a soft voice, humor, or flattery. Inviting the customer's opinion is a good strategy. "You certainly seem to know cameras, Mr. Adler. Which have you found to get the best results?" Sometimes it might even be necessary to excuse yourself temporarily if the customer has really caused you to become angry. It might even be useful to turn the customer over to another salesperson. It is important that you seek out points of agreement. Try to be patient, sincere, and respectful. Base your responses on points of agreement between you.

Constant Complainers

Some customers will complain about everything associated with a business: the products, the service, the prices, and so forth. Yet they continue to return. Typical phrases used by this type of customer include "I know you don't have my size . . .," "The prices here are always increasing . . .," "Nobody here seems to know what they're doing . . . ." They seem to enjoy complaining and do it frequently.

With this type of customer, it is important to separate real complaints from phoney complaints. Clarify the true nature of the complaint by asking questions. Do not give advice to this type of customer. He or she will come running back to tell you how your advice was followed and how it didn't work.

Non-Talking Customers

Sometimes your customers may be shy, insecure, or sensitive. He or she may seem indifferent while you are speaking and may be reluctant to answer questions. In spite of the difficulty in communicating with these customers, they still require the services of competent retail marketers.

Patience will be required when working with this type of customer. You will most likely need to make an extra effort to help the customer feel comfortable. Generally, it is helpful to ask questions that require short answers. As you obtain responses, stress their agreement on key selling points.

Know-It-All Customers

The know-it-all customer will claim to know more about your business and products than you do. This type of customer will try to manipulate you by reciting facts, figures, or logic. Know-it-all customers will have all the answers. They tend to be overly self-confident and pushy. These customers can be very frustrating to try to help.

With these customers, it is important to let them do the talking. By letting them feel that they are in charge, they will ultimately sell themselves. Try agreeing with what they say. Or, when they venture an opinion, thank them for the information. Other techniques that may prove helpful include asking their advice, complimenting and praising them, and trying to present any decision as theirs.

A positive customer service attitude toward know-it-alls—in fact toward all your customers—is likely to win their patronage and enhance our career potential in retail marketing.

TRADE TALK

Define each term and use it in a sentence.

Cost recovery   Intangibles
Goodwill   Sales-supporting services
Indifference   Word-of-mouth advertising

CAN YOU ANSWER THESE?

1. Why are customers important to a business?

2. Why are customers important to your opportunity for employment and advancement?

3. What are three reasons why customers shop at a particular place of business?

4. What are three sources of customer complaints?

5. What is the benefit to a business of developing a pro-customer attitude?

6. What is the single biggest reason why people stop shopping at a particular store?

7. Identify four types of difficult customers and how you can work with each.

C·H·A·P·T·E·R

23 *Creating a Positive First Impression*

"First impressions are lasting impressions." You have heard this since you were very young. Unfortunately—or fortunately—it is true. Research by social scientists over the past decade has shown that people do tend to hang on to first impressions. They have also found that first impressions are formed very quickly, often in a matter of seconds. Impressions of you may be formed even before you have a chance to say anything! This chapter treats the way first impressions are formed and how a successful retail marketing employee can use this knowledge to his or her advantage.

■

THE IMPORTANCE OF FIRST IMPRESSIONS

Martha Framboski came to work on her day off to help out. Her employer at the jewelry store in Tyson's Mall appreciated her willingness to work. Because she wasn't "officially" working, she wore jeans and an old sweatshirt. She assumed that she would be working in the stockroom, so she felt her casual clothing was appropriate. She had been working about 2 hours when the store became very busy, and, as she was moving stock onto the sales floor, she offered to help a customer who was standing next to the diamond rings.

The woman she approached was obviously put off by her appearance. After a very few words, lasting no more than a minute, the woman left the store. Martha watched her go across the mall to another jewelry store.

Even though Martha was trying to be helpful, her casual appearance was perceived unfavorably by the customer. Regardless of how knowledgeable Martha was about the rings, this customer felt that someone dressed in jeans could not help her make a buying decision involving hundreds of dollars.

First impressions are formed by more than a person's appearance. Jason was planning a trip to Baltimore, Maryland, Washington, D.C., and northern Virginia. He decided to fly into Baltimore-Washington International Airport, rent a compact car, and drive to his various destinations. He called one of the larger car rental agencies and was greeted by a "Can I help you" spoken in an indifferent tone of voice. Jason told the rental agent what he wanted. The agent replied irritably, "We don't allow compact cars for interstate trips; you'll have to rent a full-sized car." The tone of the agent's voice seemed to communicate that the agent was criticizing Jason for not knowing this particular company's rental policy. Because of this curt remark, Jason felt that the employee did not care if he obtained Jason's business or not. This conversation lasted about half a minute. Jason thanked the agent for his time and then called another car rental agency.

Appearance and tone of voice are just two of the factors that can influence a first impression.

The Primacy Effect

Experts call the tendency to form impressions quickly upon an initial meeting a **primacy effect**. The primacy effect forms a mental framework from which a person judges all future behavior. Future behavior that contradicts initial impressions is often ignored or interpreted through this framework. This means that customers who are put off by a business's personnel due to a negative first impression will most likely not return. These first impressions are often formed in 1 minute or less.

It is very easy to say to yourself that this isn't fair. Martha was just trying to be helpful. The car rental agent might just have been having a bad day. This may be true, but it is irrelevant. Customers usually are not interested in the employee's problems or motives for working. They are interested in making their purchases where they believe their business is appreciated and where they will be assisted by competent personnel.

Stereotypes

Initial impressions are formed as a result of both assumptions and facts. People tend to rely more on assumptions than facts, however. Very often these assumptions are based on stereotypes. **Stereotypes** are beliefs about people, groups, or ideas that do not allow for individuality or critical judgment. As we grow up, we come by these beliefs from family, friends, and the community in which we live.

Some of the more common stereotypes held today include:

- Fat people are jolly.
- All jocks are dumb.
- Science club members are superintelligent.

You have only one chance to make a good first impression.

- Japanese are very industrious.
- Italians are very emotional.

Again, we can argue that stereotypes are not fair. This is true. But the retail marketer cannot change how customers deal with stereotypes. What the retail marketer can do is recognize what creates good first impressions and refrain from reinforcing negative stereotypes.

■

FACTORS INFLUENCING FIRST IMPRESSIONS

How people react to you in a retail marketing setting is a result of many factors. The combination of these factors creates your personal image. Just as the business that employs you has an image, so do you as an individual. In retail marketing the image that you project to customers is a major part of the customers' image of the business you represent. A positive image results when customers feel comfortable with you or feel good about you. A negative image is formed when people feel uncomfortable with you.

When you project a positive image, you can set the stage for success for yourself and your employer. When you project a negative image, you are most likely setting the stage for failure. The image you project is a result of how knowledgeable you are about your job. It's also based on your past performance, your attitude toward customers, your manners, and your personal appearance.

Knowledge of Your Job

People like to shop where they believe the salespeople and other retail marketing employees know what they are doing. During the past 15 years, there has been considerable growth in discount stores. Discount stores offer merchandise at lower prices than regular retail stores. However, the trade-off is in lower levels of service, and in the case of some such stores, fewer salespersons who have experience in using the materials they sell. Many customers are willing to go to smaller, independent hardware stores, for instance, where prices may be higher because they can find store personnel who are knowledgeable about the products sold and how to use them.

You can improve your personal image with customers as well as your store's image with customers by working at becoming knowledgeable about the products and services you sell. Ways you can actively seek out information about your products and services are discussed in more detail in Chapter 29. Your ability to respond intelligently to questions about your products and services will help you create a positive first impression with customers.

Past Performance

Customers are influenced by the past performance of employees in your company as well

as by your past performance. They form an image of your business and often communicate this to their friends, based on a variety of behaviors. Your past helpfulness, honesty in dealing with the customer, and the attitude you projected while you were working with the customer all contribute to their memories of your past performance.

Attitudes toward Customers

Are you negative or positive in your approach to customers? Attitudes are contagious. If you are positive, polite, and pleasant, you will find that those around you—including customers—will behave in much the same way. As discussed earlier, people look for behavior clues to determine what your attitude is.

Remember, you are always communicating when you are with customers. Based on what you communicate, they will decide if you have a positive or negative attitude. Sometimes they may misread your attitude because of your behavior.

Customers are sensitive to several common behavior clues that determine if you have a positive attitude. For example, do you show that you:

- Are willing to see the other side?
- Do not complain or make excuses?
- Have a friendly, pleasant expression?
- Are ready to accept responsibility for errors?
- Are not critical of others?
- Are respectful of others?

If you can impart these behaviors, even when you are having a "bad day," then customers will perceive you as a person with a positive attitude. It is not always easy, but it is always rewarding.

Manners

"Please," "Thank you," "Yes sir," "No ma'am." These are some of the magic words that your parents told you will open doors. **Manners**, sometimes referred to as etiquette, are the socially acceptable ways of relating to other people. The lack of appropriate manners can serve as a barrier to developing a positive first impression.

Jonathan Swift, a famous author and social commentator, noted that good manners is the art of making people comfortable. He said that whoever makes the most people comfortable has the best manners. Practicing good manners—making those around you feel comfortable—is the best way to develop a positive first impression.

It is very important for you to understand the types of behaviors that cause people to be uncomfortable. Armed with this knowledge, you can work on avoiding such behaviors. While the social situation will govern what manners are appropriate, some general rules apply in the retail marketing setting.

1. When you first meet people, you should avoid calling them by their first names. This means that you should use a person's title: Ms., Mrs., Mr., Dr., or Miss. The use of such titles is a measure of your respect for that person. When the other person says, "Oh, you can call me John" or "You can call me Susan," then it is all right to use the first name. The general rule is to keep the relationship formal until invited to do otherwise.

2. The use of obscenities is always offensive. Foul language is always inappropriate in the retail marketing setting. It instantly communicates a lack of respect. Most people generally view a person who uses obscene language as ignorant and unworthy of respect. Comments or jokes that are racist, sexist, or disparage any ethnic or religious group are also inappropriate in the work setting. Off-color comments about a customer or co-worker are highly offensive. Such comments may cause the speaker to become the subject of a legal action. They may also get the speaker fired.

3. Keep your opinions regarding controversial issues to yourself. It is not a good idea to express strong opinions about debatable issues when you are working with customers. Wearing political buttons, religious symbols, or anything that identifies you with an issue should be avoided while at work. There is rarely a safe position to take, and you run the risk of offending someone.

4. The practice of smoking is viewed with disapproval by a growing number of people. It is usually advisable not to smoke in the presence of others. Smoking is bad for your health. It is also bad for anyone else who has to breathe the smoke. If you smoke, you have made a decision that will affect your health. But others should not have to suffer from your decision. In many places it is illegal to smoke at the workplace. People who do not smoke will appreciate your consideration in not smoking around them.

5. Say "thank you" often. A simple, sincere thank you can mean a lot to others. Not saying thank you when you should can create human relations problems. The customer who spends money at your place of business wants to know that his or her patronage is appreciated.

6. Avoid personal habits that may offend others. Sometimes a very small habit can be annoying to someone else. Chewing gum, biting your fingernails, putting on makeup in public, or scratching your head are examples of habits some people find annoying. There are no doubt many more. Being conscious of your own habits and controlling them can help ensure that you will not unknowingly offend someone.

Manners are critical to creating a positive first impression. Following the rules above will help you to be viewed positively by customers and supervisors.

Personal Appearance

"Discrimination by appearance in the business world is a fact of life." This comment comes from a famous author, Egon Von Furstenberg, who offers advice to business executives on dress. What he is saying is that people make many assumptions about you based on the clothes you wear. While this may not seem fair, it is a fact of business life.

It is amazing what sort of assumptions people will make. They will make assumptions about your economic situation, level of education, trustworthiness, social position, level of sophistication, social background, success, and your moral character.

Clothing and appearance are among the most important criteria we use to judge people. This means that you must consider very carefully how you dress in the retail marketing setting. In many cases, the choice of clothing is made for you. If you work for McDonald's, Burger King, or any of the other fast-food restaurant operations, you will wear some type of uniform. This is partly because research has shown that in the service industries, people work better in a uniform. Wearing a uniform creates a bond among workers. It creates a feeling of being part of a group. Other service industries such as hotels, banks, some retail establishments, airlines, and many other people-oriented businesses provide uniforms for their employees.

But for most retail marketers, the choice of clothing they wear is their own. Selecting the correct type of clothing can be difficult. Some organizations have written policies detailing what is to be worn to work, but this is unusual.

Customer expectations concerning clothing and grooming are unconscious. That means that customers are not immediately aware of what their expectations are. They are just turned off or become confused when a retail marketing employee is dressed in a way they did not expect. There are three business-related factors and three personal guidelines for you to consider in deciding what to wear.

Merchandise or Services Sold by Your Firm
If you work in a tire store, customers will not expect you to wear a three-piece suit. They will expect you to wear clothing that is neat, clean, and businesslike, perhaps with a necktie (for men). If you work in a

real estate office or a bank, customers expect males to wear conservative business suits. They expect women to be similarly dressed, perhaps in a gray or blue skirted suit. A woman will not be taken seriously if she chooses to wear clothing described as cute, frilly, or too feminine. Blue jeans are never acceptable.

However, if you work in a store that sells sportswear, then you will probably be expected to wear clothing similar to that sold by the store. Casual clothing will be quite acceptable. People who work in hardware stores, feed stores, or other retail establishments where more durable clothing is required may find it appropriate to wear more casual clothing. It is always important to discuss this with your employer.

Expectations of the Customer Served
Who is your customer? How do your customers dress? People are more likely to buy

The products or services you sell affect the type of clothing you should wear. A chimney sweep is expected to be sooty, but most retailing jobs require a clean, neat appearance.

from someone they perceive as being like themselves. Are your clients very conservative in their dress? Then you should be as well. Are your clients very casual in their dress? Then so should you be. In some instances a business may offer the same product or service to different types of customers. A real estate agent showing a couple with small children a home in the suburbs should wear conservative business attire. However, a real estate agent working with a farmer might find the farmer uncomfortable around someone dressed in a suit. In this case, more casual attire would be appropriate.

Desired Image in Your Line of Work

Because clothing has such an impact on image, many firms will set standards for clothing worn by their employees. One clue to what is acceptable apparel is to look at how your fellow employees dress. Chances are, the clothing they wear reflects the image desired by that business.

Color of Your Clothing

Be cautious of the color of your clothing. Men, for example, should avoid bright red or green clothing. While women can wear these colors in some situations, they are usually considered too flashy for men. Select colors that will complement your hair color and skin tone. For example, some people cannot wear yellow, because when viewed against their skin, it makes them appear to be in poor health.

Wearing Jewelry

While wearing lots of rings or earrings may be fashionable among your friends, it could reduce your effectiveness in working with customers who may be distracted by multiple bracelets, rings, and necklaces. Remember, it is always more helpful to err on the side of conservative dress than to be viewed as too trendy in your attire.

Hair Styling

Customers in the retail marketing setting expect salespeople and other employees to be neatly groomed. Hair that is too long, too short, cut in extreme styles or dyed unnatural colors can put off many people. Keep in mind that you need to reduce barriers to creating positive first impressions, not increase them.

■

DEVELOPING A POSITIVE IMPRESSION

The importance of customers to the success of the business that employs you cannot be overstated. Without customers, there cannot be opportunities for employment.

The human relations that you try to develop with customers has a special name in retail marketing. It is called **customer relations**. Your ability to develop positive customer relations is highly valued by business managers and owners.

Customers will buy from your business for a number of reasons: products and services sold, sales-supporting services, and good feeling toward the business. However, they will often stop patronizing a particular business because of indifferent employees.

Your role as an employee in a retail marketing business is to maintain and improve good customer relations. One technique in this process is for you to make sure that you create a good first impression. This is not always easy, and it does require constant effort on your part.

In reviewing what contributes to the development of a positive first impression discussed in this chapter, six rules can be formulated:

1. Remember that the time you have to develop a positive first impression is very short. Sometimes it is less than 1 minute.

2. Avoid stereotyping your customers. Stereotypes may cause you to mistreat, misunderstand, or insult and lose a customer.

3. Be knowledgeable about the products and services sold by your business. Customers expect you to be the expert. Become one.

4. Maintain a positive attitude. When you walk through the door of your store and report for work, whatever else is going on in your life remains outside that door. While working, you need to show a positive attitude toward your job, your company, and most of all, toward your customer.

5. Practice good manners. Manners are the magic to creating and maintaining good customer relations.

6. Dress to meet your customers' and employer's expectations. Remember, how you look to someone will instantly communicate how you feel about him or her.

TRADE TALK

Define each term and use it in a sentence.

Customer relations	Primacy effect
Manners	Stereotypes

CAN YOU ANSWER THESE?

1. Why are first impressions important in retail marketing?

2. Why is it important to be aware of stereotypes?

3. Why would customers shop for merchandise where the price is higher than at a competitor's place of business?

4. List six rules leading to good manners.

5. What factors contribute to a positive first impression?

6. How does the primacy effect influence first impressions?

7. What are five behavior clues that indicate you have a positive attitude?

CHAPTER

24 *Communicating With Customers*

In the early 1970s, the Chrysler Corporation was in serious financial difficulty. The company president, Lee Iacocca, took to the airwaves to bring Chrysler's message directly to the American people. His style of communication, what he communicated verbally and nonverbally, has been credited with much of the success Chrysler has enjoyed since then.

Since that time, many other business executives have copied Iacocca's approach. You have probably seen the local automobile dealer, hardware store owner, TV store owner, and other retail marketers appearing in television commercials testifying for their companies. Some have been more successful than others.

These examples of communication via TV illustrate one important way that communication can influence customer behavior. In this chapter you will have the opportunity to study the reasons why some people are more effective in communicating than others. Successful communicators in retail marketing manifest four critical competencies: the ability to (1) recognize customer status preferences, (2) converse intelligently with customers, (3) use nonverbal communication properly, and (4) practice effective telephone techniques.

■

RECOGNIZING CUSTOMER STATUS PREFERENCES

A basic rule in retail marketing is that the customer is boss. You are the customer's employee, so to speak. You are supposed to behave the way the "boss" wants you to. Agree? Now, is this truly the case, or is that giving only lip service to customer relationships? What does "the customer is boss" really mean? Let's explore the concept. "The customer (boss) acts surprisingly different at times," says a retail worker who contacts customers daily. "Sometimes he or she looks down on me. Most of the time, however, the customer acts like a friend, and we seem to be on even ground. And sometimes customers even ask for an opinion about something in my field of expertise. I feel as if I'm the smart one in the driver's seat."

This retail worker has just given a clue to good communication with customers—or anyone else for that matter. She has just identified three types of face-to-face customer contacts—situations that good communicators instinctively recognize and keep in the back of their mind during a personal business contact. This feeling or understanding usually influences the communicator to react in conformance to the customer's preference. Let's look at the three customer preference situations more closely.

When the Customer Wants to Be Boss

Customers generally prefer to take charge in purchases when they have had satisfactory experience with a product or service and know its qualities well. Thus, most grocery shoppers like self-service stores where they are left alone to make their buying decisions. However, many customers, by nature, want to take the lead when purchasing almost any product or service, whether or not they are knowledgeable about it. The latter type often places the seller in a delicate situation that calls for diplomacy. Confrontation often leads to rejection, so effective sellers communicate in such a way that the customer is given credit for the knowledge that is imparted. Confrontation and conformance relationships are presented graphically below.

When the Customer Accepts You as Co-Equal

When dealing with customers your own age who need purchasing assistance or others who show co-equal status, you are in an ideal communication situation—that is, if you assume the role of a peer. Both customer and seller engage in assessing the situation at hand and move cooperatively through a series of buying decisions to a satisfactory solution. However, if the seller is an egotist and flaunts his or her superior knowledge, the transaction is likely to end without a purchase.

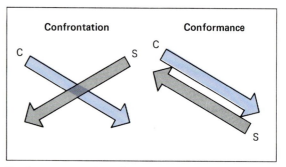

Confrontation and conformance relationships with customers who want to be the boss.

When the Customer Wants You to Lead

There are times when customers are poorly informed or ignorant about a product or service to be purchased, or they may be uncertain about a given buying decision and prefer to be helped. Effective sellers sense the purchaser's insecurity, and practice their creativity in coming to the rescue. However, sellers who lack the self-confidence to take the lead allow the customer to remain uncertain. Thus, sales are lost because the seller doesn't "close the sale."

Authorities agree that it is important to make the other person feel comfortable. This goal can be achieved only if the seller recognizes the customers status preference. Tuning in on customer preferences is discussed in Chapter 31.

Now that you understand the relationship between customer status preference and good communication, the following analysis of a business conversation will be more meaningful.

■

CONVERSING WITH CUSTOMERS

The most important thing to remember when you are talking to other people is simply this: Think before you speak. Think about your intended audience, who they are, the extent of their knowledge of the subject, and what it will take to capture their interest. This planning will help you to prepare a logically organized, clear, and brief message. As you think about what you are going to say, it is helpful to think about verbal communication in three parts. The diagram below shows how a typical verbal exchange with a customer flows. The first stage is the greeting. This is usually (but not always) followed by a conversation. In turn, this is followed by a goodbye stage.

The Greeting Stage

The greeting stage is often considered the most important part of verbal communication with the customer. If you do not handle the greeting well, you will often not be able to engage the customer in the conversation stage. You might simply cause the customer to say goodbye and leave.

In most cases, the actual words we use are not as important as the attitude we convey through our tone of voice. The feeling we put into the words, the warmth and genuine enthusiasm, will contribute to creating a positive first impression.

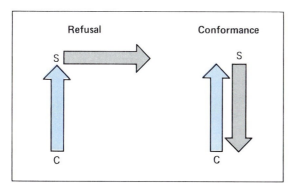

Refusal and conformance relationships with customers who want the seller to lead.

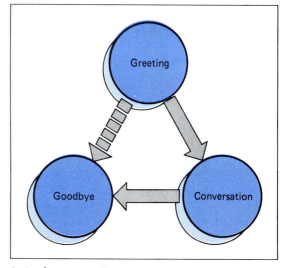

A simple conversation.

On the other hand, a cool or indifferent attitude may create a negative impression and make it difficult to provide good customer service.

Everyone wants to be treated as a unique individual. It is flattering to be given special attention. To do this with your greeting, look at the customer directly, making good eye contact. Try to put as much genuine personal warmth into your voice as possible. Sincerity is important in this process.

If you are in a selling situation, there are many ways you can greet the customer. These will be discussed in more detail in Chapter 30. But regardless of the technique used, it is vitally important to make each customer feel that he or she is a unique and special person.

The Conversation Stage

If you successfully engage the customer with your greeting, then you will move to the conversation stage. Conversations vary a great deal in length. If you are a salesperson, your conversation may have several distinct parts; these are discussed in Chapter 28. In most retail marketing situations, it is usually best not to spend a lot of time in "small talk." It is possible in your conversation to be both friendly and efficient.

There are three rules to follow during the conversation stage. You should demonstrate self-confidence, interest, and creativity. These S-I-C rules of conversation will help you establish a positive customer service attitude.

Self-confidence Self-confidence stems from many sources. As discussed in the previous chapter, customers expect salespeople and other employees to be knowledgeable about the products and services they sell. Being knowledgeable contributes to your sense of self-confidence.

You also need to be knowledgeable about the operation of your business. You need to be able to communicate such things as company policy to customers. Often employees who are not well trained will seem indifferent because they really don't know how to perform the duties associated with their job.

Your sense of self-confidence can be communicated through nonverbal communication.

Self-confident retail marketing employees are appreciated by customers. Your confidence in your ability to provide efficient service is the basis for any successful conversation with a customer.

Interest Showing interest in customers is one way of saying that you care about their problems. Perhaps the easiest way to demonstrate interest in your customers is by asking questions and being an attentive listener. Listening is a form of recognition. Positive recognition satisfies a very basic human need. It is hard to overemphasize the need people have to be listened to and to have their problems taken seriously.

Creativity Creativity in what you say is needed to treat each customer as a unique person. It is very easy to fall into the trap of saying the same thing to everyone. The cashier who routinely says "Thank you for shopping at . . ." or the salesperson who says "Can I help you?" to each new customer is not showing much creativity. When sales personnel fail to be creative, they soon become bored, and this boredom is then communicated to customers as indifference.

The Goodbye Stage

The goodbye stage is very important because it can put the seal on a successful exchange with the customer. It also represents your final opportunity to create a lasting positive impression.

Just as during the greeting stage, it is important to personalize how you say goodbye. In some retail stores, such as supermarkets, there is special training for cashiers and utility clerks or baggers because they have the final contact with customers.

One technique in personalizing the good-bye is to use the customer's name. You may obtain the customer's name during the greeting stage as you introduce yourself. If you don't know it, you may be able to learn it by looking at the credit card, personal check, or sometimes, the salescheck.

One final comment on saying goodbye. In many retail marketing situations, it is very appropriate to shake hands with a customer. The handshake should communicate warmth, interest, and an image of confidence in the transaction just completed.

Many people, particularly younger people, are hesitant to shake hands. A good handshake should be firm. Weak, limp, or "fishy" handshakes communicate a lack of self-confidence. Although the handshake should be firm, it should not be viewed as a contest of physical strength. Good eye contact is also important.

Of course, at all stages of this process, good manners are required. This means a sincere thank you is appropriate—even if the customer did not buy from you this time.

■

IMPROVING YOUR NONVERBAL COMMUNICATION

In Chapter 21 you learned that in the communication process, people often give nonverbal clues as to their attitude, their feelings, and what they really mean by what they are saying. You will recall that nonverbal communications are the messages that we send without words. These messages are communicated through the gestures we use, the posture we assume while talking, and the facial expressions we wear.

How we approach customers when they enter our place of business is an example of nonverbal communication. In many mall stores, for example, the salespeople tend to crowd around the entrance. They seem to be lying in wait for the next customer who dares enter the store. While it is always a good practice to give the customers prompt and undivided attention as soon as they appear, it's not a good idea to appear too anxious when a customer arrives. Every retail marketing business should have a well-thought-out strategy for greeting the customer, and you should follow management's policy. You can enhance customer relations by providing prompt but not pushy service, show a pleasant smile, and communicate your friendliness, enthusiasm, and self-confidence. This is discussed in more detail in Chapter 30.

■

USING THE TELEPHONE EFFECTIVELY

Telephones have become an important tool for retail marketers. Telephone shopping has become increasingly popular. More and more customers are "letting their fingers do the walking through the Yellow Pages" and placing orders over the telephone or are calling for information before they go shopping.

Catalog and telephone shopping have become increasingly important as a result of changes in the workforce. Because more women have entered the full-time workforce, it has been estimated that more than 11 billion hours of shopping time, worth $55 billion, has shifted from in-store shopping by the consumer to catalog shopping. Now, with home cable video shopping, specialty mail-order firms, and the increase in telemarketing, skill in efficiently using the telephone is required for success in retail marketing.

In addition to customer-initiated telephone calls for information and orders, businesses are increasing their use of telemarketing. **Telemarketing** means using the telephone to promote a business or to sell products and services. Currently, telemarketing is more widely used in businesses that sell to other businesses. But businesses that use the telephone to sell directly to retail customers are increasing. Regardless of whether the business or the customer initiates a telephone call, it is up to the retail marketer to make sure that this important communication tool is used correctly.

The Telephone Greeting Stage

Talking with customers via telephone involves the same three stages as talking with customers in person. But there are some differences. The first difference is that body language—gestures, posture, and facial expressions—is no longer an influence on the communication process. This means that the tone of your voice and the words you use take on additional importance.

When customers call, you can make them feel welcome. You should answer promptly and state the name of your business and your name. Giving your name personalizes the call and helps reduce barriers to communication.

Sometimes you will need to call customers. Perhaps their order has arrived or service on a product that they purchased has been completed. When you call, be sure to call at a convenient time (not during dinner time). Introduce yourself, give the name of your firm, and state your purpose in calling. Be brief but courteous.

Be friendly. Let your smile come through your voice. Make callers feel glad they patronized your business rather than the competition. Remember, the tone in your voice will communicate much more than the words you use.

The Telephone Conversation Stage

After you properly greet the customer, the conversation will begin. As you speak to the customer, your voice is your only tool of

Customers may not be able to see your smile on the telephone, but they will hear the pleasant, friendly tone of your voice.

communication. There are four ways to improve your telephone voice.

Alertness. You can demonstrate alertness by giving the customer your full attention.

Pleasantness. Your voice should communicate a pleasant tone. This helps build a positive image for your business. Pleasantness is contagious.

Distinctiveness. Speak clearly and distinctly. This is often referred to as **enunciation**. Good enunciation can reduce the problems caused by inexpensive telephones, which sometimes do not transmit sound as well as the better-made telephones.

Expressiveness. When talking on the telephone, you should use a normal range of tone for your voice. Avoid extremes of loudness or softness. Talk at a moderate rate, neither too fast nor too slow. Vary your

Unit 8   Enhancing Your Customer Relations

tone of voice to add vitality and interest to what you say.

Improving Your Telephone Reception

Reception of what you say will be improved if you follow the two-finger rule. You should be able to place two fingers between your lips and the speaker in the telephone. If your mouth is closer than that, it will cause your words to sound mumbled to the customer. When talking to customers, remember that poor or awkward grammar will slow down communication and reception and give the customer a bad opinion of your firm.

Coping with Interruptions

There are two special circumstances that may occur when using the telephone. The first happens when you may have to put the caller on hold while you check out stock or get information for the customer. A general rule of thumb is never to leave the customer on hold for more than 60 seconds. If it is going to be longer than that, return to the line with a progress report before the minute is up. Of course, always tell the customer you're putting him or her on hold and explain why.

The second circumstance that frequently occurs is that you take a call when you are working with another customer. First, be sure you properly excuse yourself to answer the telephone. Second, if you cannot handle the call quickly, you should either offer to call the customer back after explaining that you are busy, or suggest that the customer call you back at his or her convenience. Do not subject the customer who is present in your store to the annoyance of waiting while you help someone who called.

The Telephone Goodbye Stage

When closing a call, try your best to say goodbye in a way that will leave the caller feeling positive about the conversation. Whether you have been able to help the caller or not, it is important to thank the person for calling your business. Remember, even if you cannot help the customer, it is important to leave him or her feeling that yours is a business that cares.

It's a good idea to let the caller hang up first. Always put your receiver down gently.

You have now had the opportunity to study how to be more effective in communicating to customers, co-workers, and supervisors. Unit 9 will introduce you to how supervisors and managers supervise, train, and motivate employees, and the important role that communication plays in this process.

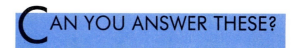

TRADE TALK

Define each term and use it in a sentence.

Enunciation   Telemarketing

CAN YOU ANSWER THESE?

1. What are the three stages of talking with a customer?

2. Explain the importance of the tone of your voice during conversation.

3. During the initial stage of talking to a customer, what are you trying to accomplish?

4. What are the S-I-C rules of conversation?

5. When talking on the telephone, what are four ways you can improve your telephone voice?

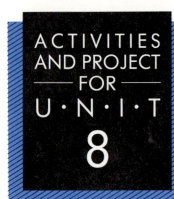

RETAIL MARKETING CASES

1. There are many opportunities for you to develop positive customer relations. In the following situations, think of what you might say to the customer. Remember, your goal in improving customer relations is to generate goodwill for the business and make the customers feel valued by your business.

Situation 1. You are currently working at the drug counter checking out customers. There is a long line and you have been unable to get the attention of your supervisor to help out. You've been working for quite a while without a break. An elderly customer is your next customer to check out and is fumbling around in her purse for her special senior citizen's discount card. She is getting more and more nervous and frustrated because the customers behind her are muttering about the poor service in your store. What do you say to the elderly customer?

Situation 2. You are a teller at Park Bank. Park is one of the larger banks in your city. It is often accused of being too big and ignoring its customers. A man approaches your station and begins by complaining about past service as he hands you a check to cash. In a voice that can be heard by others in the bank lobby, he says, "I don't know why I continue to do my banking here, I never get very good service." What do you say?

Situation 3. It is Monday evening and business has been slow. Your manager has let several of the part-time people go home and asked you to stay because you are one of her better salespeople. About 7 p.m. she steps out to get a cup of coffee. A few minutes later a customer comes in who seems to be just looking around but asks you many questions about your products. About 5 minutes after you begin talking to this customer, the telephone rings. You are in the store alone. What do you say?

When you answer the phone, it becomes quickly apparent that the caller is going to take some time to assist. What do you say to the caller? What do you say to the customer in the store?

2. As a new salesperson at Tyler's Men's Shop, you have been assigned to a more experienced salesperson for training. Tyler's sells higher-priced, quality menswear. Tyrone, the salesperson to whom you have been assigned, has been with the business for 6 years and has the reputation of being a very good salesperson.

Tyrone has been explaining store policies to you as well as describing how he approaches customers. He has told you that the typical Tyler's customer is in his late twenties to early thirties, a professional worker, and has a good income.

As you are talking, an older man walks into the store. He is poorly dressed and wearing dirty sneakers. As you start toward him to offer assistance, Tyrone grabs your arm and says, "Don't worry about him, he won't want anything we sell. And besides, he couldn't afford it anyway."

1. Identify the problem.
2. What are the important facts to be considered in this case?
3. List several possible ways this situation could be handled.
4. Which would you recommend? Why?

PROJECT: HOW CUSTOMERS EVALUATE RETAILING EMPLOYEES

YOUR PROJECT GOAL

You are to identify the qualities, characteristics, and attitudes of retail marketing employees that customers consider important when they decide which businesses they will patronize. Conduct a survey of at least 15 actual customers.

This is a type of marketing research on consumer attitudes and is often done to help retail marketers better understand their markets.

PROCEDURE

1. Identify at least two retail marketing career areas of interest to you. These areas might include banks, supermarkets, insurance agencies, restaurants, hotels, or clothing stores.
2. Develop a survey questionnaire. At the top of the page, write a question such as:

Which of the following personal characteristics of employees in (insert the type of business in the blank) would cause you to want to continue doing business there?

Prepare a list of ten qualities, characteristics, and attitudes that you believe customers will consider important in developing good customer relations. Write the list down the left-hand side of a page; next to each quality, draw a short blank line.

3. After creating your list, determine where you might find a group of customers who would patronize the two types of businesses you identified in Procedure 1. (This may be a shopping mall, shopping center, or other place.)
4. After checking with your teacher and the store or mall manager, arrange to spend time in the location where you will have the chance to meet potential customers of the businesses. It is helpful to do this activity with a partner.
5. You will want to interview at least 15 people. This means that you will want to have at least 15 questionnaires. The procedure for this survey is to:

a. Stop a person and introduce yourself. Explain that you are doing a class project and ask whether he or she would answer ten short questions. If the answer is yes, continue with the questions. If no, *politely* thank the person and look for another person. Remember—manners are important in this process.
b. When a person agrees to answer the questions, ask the person to rank each of the ten items for both types of businesses you have selected. Use the following scale. (1) This is very important. (2) This is important. (3) This is not very important. (4) I do not think about this at all. Put the number of the response the person has chosen in the blank next to each personal quality, attitude, or characteristic you listed.
c. Then ask the interviewee if there are any other personal qualities of employees that he or she considers important that you did not list. Write these down on a separate sheet of paper.
d. When you are finished, be sure to thank the interviewees for their time and their answers. Remember your manners.

6. When you have interviewed at least 15 people, compute the average ranking for each item. To compute the average ranking:

    a. Add all the actual scores you entered into a blank for each of the ten items.

    b. Divide that sum by the number of customers ranking that item (typically 15). This will give you an average ranking.

7. Which item had the lowest average ranking? Which item had the highest average ranking? Are there differences between the two types of businesses you selected to study? Discuss the results with your partner. Prepare a brief report on your results. In your report, be sure to:

    a. Explain how you conducted the interviews and your feelings about talking to people.

    b. Show which items were ranked highest and which items were ranked lowest.

    c. Discuss why you think some items were ranked higher than others.

    d. Discuss the differences or similarities between the two types of businesses you investigated.

    e. Explain why you think they were different or similar.

    f. Discuss what other items your interviewees added to your list.

8. In class discussion, you and your partner should present your findings and be prepared to discuss differences and similarities between your report and theirs.

EVALUATION

You will be evaluated on:

    1. Your selection of ten items to include in the survey

    2. How well you interpreted the results of your survey

    3. The quality of your written report

U·N·I·T
9

DEVELOPING RETAIL MARKETING PERSONNEL

C·H·A·P·T·E·R

25 *Supervising Retail Workers*

In this unit you'll begin to look at the job of being a supervisor in retail marketing. Although it may be a while before you actually become a supervisor, by understanding the process of supervision and the responsibilities of a retail supervisor, you'll learn more about what it takes to be a successful retail worker.

Approximately one out of every four people working in retail has some supervisory responsibility. If you were to ask any of them what their greatest problem is, they will most likely respond, "the people problem." As the illustration on this page shows, the higher the level of management, the more important knowledge of people and ability to work with people becomes.

People are the heart of any successful retail marketing business. A retail firm is only as good as the people who work there. That means that hiring and retaining quality personnel is the key to successful management of any size retail marketing business.

You will begin your study of this important part of operating a retail business by looking at supervision and the qualities of effective supervisors. In the next chapter you will have the opportunity to learn about train-

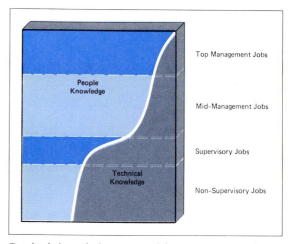

Total job knowledge required for success in retail marketing.

ing strategies. In the concluding chapter of this unit, you will see how supervisors can create a positive work environment through team building.

■

WHAT IS SUPERVISION?

The word supervision is made up of two parts: "super" and "vision." "Super" means superior. "Vision," in this context, means perspective as applied to a task to be performed. So **supervision** means the oversight of tasks, or more specifically, the management, direction, and oversight of others. Supervision is management at its closest point to people. "Supervisory-level management" is another term that is often used to describe the first level of management.

Like all aspects of modern life, ideas about what makes a person an effective supervisor are changing. Not too long ago, the authoritarian, task-oriented person was thought to be effective. Then some experts argued that a more relaxed, people-oriented type of person was effective. Today it is recognized that the most effective supervisors are people who can carefully balance the need to be oriented toward tasks and the need to be oriented toward people. This balanced approach is sometimes referred to as **results-oriented supervision**.

Providing Leadership

Being promoted to a position as supervisor does not automatically give you leadership. **Leadership** is the ability to influence the opinions, attitudes, and behavior of others. This means that anyone who is able to influence others toward some common objective is a leader.

Many new supervisors get started on the wrong foot because they don't realize that being named assistant manager or shift manager doesn't automatically make them a leader. They don't recognize that after they re-

ceive their promotion, they have to earn the acceptance of their work group before they can have any real influence on the group's behavior. There is a real difference between being a "boss" and a "leader."

John had been a salesperson at Chess King for 2 years. He had participated in the company's management training program and was promoted to assistant store manager when he was 19. As an employee, he was well liked by the other salespeople. After his promotion, things began to change. John felt that he could order people to do things—have them do what he didn't want to do. Initially the employees accepted his ordering them about, but very soon they began to complain to each other and then to the store manager. They felt that John did not know what he was doing and that he never listened to their ideas. The manager talked to John about the situation several times. Finally, the manager demoted John.

John had confused being the boss with being a leader. A boss orders, directs, threatens, and pushes employees. A leader obtains the group's trust and willingness to follow by earning their respect.

Becoming a Supervisor

Many people want to be supervisors. In retail marketing, there are many opportunities. But you must be prepared for them.

As the world around us becomes more complex, so does the job of supervisor. As a result, companies look for certain kinds of background in potential supervisors. Many young people who aspire to supervisory and management positions have found it valuable to take advanced training at postsecondary schools.

Other young people take advantage of the opportunities for management training provided by the companies for whom they work. In fact, there are more people involved every year in company training programs than are enrolled in all the colleges in the United States. Of course, retail marketing businesses place a very high value on work experience.

So, as you begin to think about supervision, think about how you will prepare yourself to take advantage of the opportunity when it comes. Begin now to plan for your continuing education and training. Also, begin now to plan to get the kind of occupational experiences that retail marketers will value.

■

WHAT A SUPERVISOR DOES

Supervisors have many responsibilities and duties. But the most important responsibility in retail marketing for a supervisor is to ensure that his or her work group is results-oriented. That means that the salespeople, stock clerks, cashiers, and other employees are making a positive contribution to the profitability of the business. This is number one. To accomplish this, the effective supervisor must be able to perform the following six duties: Supervisors must know their people, be able to plan their work, develop their personnel, communicate, maintain discipline, and prevent accidents.

Know Your People

As was noted earlier, retail marketing is a "people" business. In addition to the importance of relating well to customers, the retail supervisor must also relate well to the people he or she supervises. For some people this is easy. Others have to work hard at this. The effective supervisor has a sincere, active interest in people. As a supervisor, you will have to know the people you supervise as human beings. You should be aware of everything that might affect their job, their performance of that job, and their potential for development.

Although there are many things you will come to know about the people you supervise, the following list includes some of the more important information you will want to be sure to know about your employees.

Name. This sounds simple, but it is extremely important. Quickly learning an employee's name is a form of personal recognition that is important to everyone.

Job description. This is necessary so you will not have unreasonable expectations about what an employee is supposed to be doing. It is also important for the employee to understand and have this information. For example, in many retail firms, the stockpeople are not expected to provide backup help to the sales staff when it is very busy. In other situations, cashiers might be expected to provide such backup assistance during very busy times.

Education and work background. This will give you a clue to the person's interests and potential. It may also be useful to you in making specific assignments.

General physical condition. Having a sense of the person's health, physical condition, and handicaps will help you avoid situations in which the person may not be able to perform well. A person with a bad back should not be expected to lift heavy objects.

Work habits. Knowing a person's good and bad work habits will allow you to focus your supervision on improving the poor work habits and encouraging the good ones. If one of your salespeople is particularly good at demonstrating your primary lines of merchandise, you could have other salespeople observe his or her technique.

Relations with co-workers. Your awareness of friendships, personality clashes, and the like will help you in your supervision of the entire group. There are always going to be problems between and among individuals. Knowing where these are might influence your scheduling of your employees.

Aspirations and ambitions. Knowing where a person wants to go can help you spot opportunities where the person may be able to advance toward these goals. Hopefully, every one of your employees wants your job, or your supervisor's job. Every one of them should be given the opportunity to develop his or her other skills so that they can one day earn the promotion.

Hobbies and outside interests. Often a talent or skill a person uses in a hobby can be used to good advantage on the job. A person who likes to draw and knows art can be very helpful in planning and building displays.

There are other aspects of your employees' personalities that you will find useful to know in order to understand them better. As you gain experience in your role of supervisor, you will develop your own list. The more background you have about your employees, the better you will be able to relate to them as individuals, and the better you will be able to provide supervision.

Plan Your Work

Planning is the key to success in supervisory and management positions. People often resist planning, however, because it requires taking time away from activity. Activity is often confused with accomplishment. Some people believe that if they are not actively doing something, they are not accomplishing anything. This is not true. An hour spent in planning can very well save you 3 hours of activity.

Planning requires that you stop, sit down, and think. The process of planning is necessary to help you do a better job of supervising. Planning results in a more effective use of time and people. It will improve your business's profitability and your employees' morale.

Major planning tasks of a supervisor in retail marketing include: planning and organizing work, planning for personnel improvement, and planning your own time.

Planning and Organizing Work Retail supervisors have a primary responsibility for assigning people to specific duties. In a fast-food restaurant, for example, the supervisor must assign certain people to handle the shakes, others to work the registers, still others to prepare the food. When assigning tasks, the supervisor has to be certain that instructions are clear and assignments are being carried out.

Another responsibility is to schedule employee working hours. Every retail business must plan to have sufficient staff available to meet customer needs for assistance. This requires a careful analysis of past trends in business for certain days, weeks, and seasons, as well as time of day. It also requires that the supervisor project, or estimate, what staff needs will be in the future. Having too many people scheduled to work will reduce the business's profitability. Having too few people scheduled to work will cause customer relations problems and, in the end, reduce the business's profitability. So you can see the necessity of careful planning.

This can be seen in the following example. A major chain of automotive accessories stores uses a guide of 11 percent of gross sales for personnel costs. If Frank Murphy, the store manager, plans for gross sales of $30,000 next week, the personnel budge will be $3300 (because $30,000 X 0.11 = $3300). Frank would have to calculate the salary of all of the full-time employees and subtract that from the personnel budget, and then calculate how much part-time help can be scheduled during the coming week.

Planning for Personnel Improvement
There are two aspects of planning for personnel improvement. The first is to plan for improvement or changes in the work group in order to improve morale and productivity. The goal is to create an environment where people can work smarter, not harder. This might include planning for changes in assignments, procedures, or equipment (for example, the use of computerized cash registers).

The second aspect of this type of planning is planning opportunities for your employees to grow in job knowledge and skills. This may involve specific training in one position or rotation through a series of different jobs. The employee spends a short period of time in each.

Planning Your Own Time   "Time is money." You have no doubt heard that very often. But everyone has the same amount of time. Time is a major resource, and it must be planned carefully. The process of careful planning of your own time is often called **time management**. Time management is a way to gain control over your working day, rather than have it control you.

Time management begins by analyzing where you spend your time now. This is often done by keeping a log of your activities for a week. Such an analysis will often show where you are wasting time that could be better used for something else.

Another technique of time management is to develop a "things to do" list and assign each "to do" a grade of "A," "B," or "C." The "A's" are your top priority, the "B's" are next in priority, and the "C's" are least important. The rule is to work on and complete your A's, then work on your B's, then your C's. This assures that your most important tasks get done first.

Effective supervisors are effective managers of time. This is perhaps the most difficult skill to develop, but you can begin now, before you become a supervisor.

Develop Your Personnel

Developing your personnel involves several activities. Each of these activities has the same goal: to provide for the occupational growth of your employees. The first of these activities is training. Because of its importance, training will be discussed in detail in the next chapter.

Experience   Besides training, the supervisor needs to provide opportunities for employees to gain experiences that will be use-ful for occupational growth. This means that you will need to keep track of what experiences your employees have had. This is best done by keeping good records and using a long-range training plan for each of your employees. It also means that their assignments should include new experiences. This will give them a chance to learn new skills and also keep their jobs interesting.

Personal Growth   When an employee is given new tasks, it is important to provide close supervision. This will give you a chance to provide correction when necessary, and provide praise when appropriate. This will lead to an increase in the employee's self-confidence and ability to perform the task.

Feedback   **Supervisory feedback** may be defined as verbal and nonverbal communication to the employee about his or her performance. This is an important part of personnel development. All employees need feedback, and the newer they are, the more feedback they need.

To be effective, feedback must be continuous. It cannot be a one-shot activity on your part. It should be timely, honest, and specific to the situation. The type and methods of feedback that supervisors provide will be discussed in more detail in Chapter 27.

Communicate

You were introduced to a model of communication in Chapter 21. The process of communication is the same for supervisors and employees. However, the supervisor's ability to communicate is even more crucial to his or her success.

The supervisor functions as a channel of communication between the employees and management. He or she is the principal link between management and the employees, as shown in the illustration on page 210.

This role is often referred to as being a liaison. **Liaison** means a connection, or some-

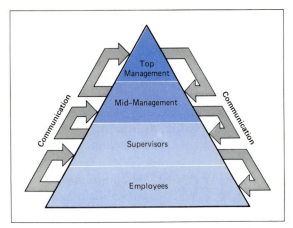

Supervisors are the principal link between employees and management.

one who serves as a connecting link. Supervisors are the connecting link between management and employees. Liaison involves interpreting management policies, explaining employee concerns to management, suggesting changes to management, hearing complaints, and handling grievances.

Interpreting Management Policies

The purpose of management policies is to ensure the same employee behavior throughout the firm. Accuracy in the interpretation of policies is, consequently, very important. Supervisors must understand the policy and interpret it in a straightforward manner. The interpretation of store policy is especially important when new employees are being trained, and it may be a sensitive task when employees don't follow policies.

Explaining Employee Concerns to Management

Explaining employee problems to management is an important supervisory function because profits depend so much on the productivity of the work group. If employee concerns are not met, productivity is likely to suffer.

Suggesting Changes to Management

In retail marketing, many excellent ideas originate from salespeople, customer relations specialists, cashiers, and others who have daily contact with customers. And some of the best ideas for improvements come from supervisors who have an overview of the daily work of employees. As a part of the management team, supervisors are in an excellent position to explain to top management the need for change and its possible beneficial results.

Hearing Complaints

Dealing with complaints is an important part of being a liaison. Complaints take many forms. Some may be about management, others about co-workers. Supervisors can handle both kinds of complaints effectively by carefully identifying the real problem, collecting the necessary facts about the problem, and making decisions about how best to resolve the problem. In some cases, this will involve upper management. In other cases, it may involve having two individuals sit down together and work out mutual problems. This requires careful listening and communication skills on the part of the supervisor.

Handling Grievances

A **grievance** is a real or imagined injustice. Grievances frequently develop from the repetition of an annoyance. Supervisors try to prevent a grievance by taking care of annoyances before they became grievances. Early attention to complaints is very important, because a grievance may spread to other employees and become a problem for the entire business.

Maintain Discipline

Discipline often has a bad connotation. Many people connect discipline to punishment. **Discipline** in supervision means maintaining a work environment where there is fair and impartial enforcement of rules and regulations and consistent treatment of all employees.

Discipline is easier to maintain when all employees are aware of what is expected of them and feel that they are a part of something important. People will strive to achieve when they know what is expected of them.

However, there are times when an employee needs to be corrected because of errors or poor performance. Following a few simple rules for correcting an employee will reduce the possibility of offending the employee or destroying his or her morale.

1. *Make sure everyone knows and understands work rules and regulations.* Never assume anything. Do not take it for granted that "everybody knows this." You cannot expect your employees to observe rules they don't know about.

2. *Be consistent in enforcing the rules.* This is very important and sometimes hard to do. However, inconsistency on your part will almost assure human relations problems in your work group. You cannot expect employees to observe rules you have "bent" for others.

3. *Control your emotions.* Sometimes it is easy to lose your temper when someone does something wrong. However, your loss of personal control will simply make the situation worse. What you say in anger will trigger a defensive response from the employee who made the error.

4. *Get all of the facts.* Before taking any action, make certain you know what actually happened and why it happened, with information from all individuals involved. Making decisions with only partial knowledge of the situation almost guarantees that the decision will be a poor one.

5. *Take action in time to be effective.* Disciplinary action, if it is to be corrective, must occur as close to the time of the problem as possible. This is so your action is closely associated in the employee's mind with the problem.

6. *Do it in private.* Once you have decided the appropriate disciplinary action to be taken, always do it in private. Never embarrass employees in front of their peers. This will create resentment and loss of respect and often lead to other unwanted behavior.

Prevent Accidents

An important responsibility of the retail marketing supervisor is to maintain a safe work environment. In addition to being concerned about their employees' well-being, the supervisor must remember that when employees are injured on the job, it costs the business money in terms of insurance and payments to the employee who misses work. It may also cost the business money because the employee is not there to provide service to customers.

Where there is potentially dangerous equipment, you must make certain that people are properly instructed in its use. For example, many grocery stores have machines that compress cardboard boxes for easy disposal. These machines can also compress human hands and arms! Some retail businesses use potentially harmful chemicals. Employees should be trained in the proper use and disposal of these chemicals.

Accidents occur as a result of human error and because of unsafe conditions. Both can be corrected.

Human Error   There are many types of human error. Some is deliberate, such as "horseplay," practical joking, operating equipment without authorization, or removing safety equipment. Other human error is not so deliberate, such as picking up heavy objects improperly, failing to use safety equipment, or using equipment improperly.

Many human error problems can be prevented through training. However, certain behavior, such as horseplay, must be stopped immediately and then dealt with privately.

Unsafe Conditions   Unsafe conditions include anything in the work environment that may cause an accident because it is broken, defective, not up to standards, or inadequate. Fire extinguishers that have not been recharged in over a year, missing guardrails leading down to a storeroom, inadequate lighting in a stairwell are all examples of unsafe conditions. These are all repairable by the supervisor or by someone hired by the supervisor or manager. Management's failure to fix unsafe conditions may result in injury to employees and customers. It may also result in lawsuits against the business if a serious injury occurs.

■

SUPERVISORY DECISION MAKING

One of the major tasks a supervisor faces on a daily basis is to make decisions. Problems arise and answers need to be found. Decision making is a skill that can be learned. A good decision maker is a person who has knowledge and applies intelligence to learning and practicing decision-making skills. For a supervisor, there is plenty of opportunity to practice decision-making skills. Effective supervisors continually learn from past experience in making decisions. Most decisions can be made by following a sequence of thinking processes or steps.

Define the Problem

The decision-making process begins with adequately defining the problem.

What people first notice when a problem arises is often a symptom. A **symptom** is a condition or event that accompanies something and indicates its existence. That means that a symptom is not the problem itself, it is just evidence of a problem.

For example, you supervise two people who are constantly arguing and cannot get along. This is a symptom. Without further investigation you might conclude that they are having a personality conflict. After checking into the situation, you find that what they argue about is who has responsibility over an area of the stock room. The problem, then, is not personality, but lack of clarification of

job duties. It is often stated that this simple process of defining the problem solves 80 percent of the problems.

Gather Facts and Analyze the Problem

After the problem has been defined, the next step is to analyze the problem. This sometimes occurs as you are defining the problem, as in the example above.

Let's assume that sales have been dropping lately. What's the problem? The problem is not declining sales; this is a symptom of something larger. It is possible that sales are declining because of an increase in the number of inexperienced salespeople on your staff. (There may be other problems as well.)

What facts might be helpful in understanding this problem? You would probably want to find out more about what the salespeople are doing while they are working with customers. You could examine their personnel files to determine how much sales training they have had. It might also be useful to talk with them about what they think might be helpful.

There may also be intangible facts to consider. How is their morale? Are there sufficient incentives for superior performance?

Develop Alternatives

Once you have defined the problem, gathered facts and analyzed them, you will be ready to consider alternative solutions. You should attempt to develop as many alternatives as time permits. The old way of doing things may no longer be appropriate, and new approaches may prove useful. Almost all problems have more than one solution.

It is usually appropriate to include your employees in this process. This might be accomplished through brainstorming with a group of your salespeople. Creative problem solving is a hallmark of the effective supervisor.

Evaluate the Alternatives

The ultimate purpose of decision making is to choose the specific course of action that will provide the most desired consequences and the fewest undesirable consequences. After developing the alternatives, the supervisor can mentally test each of them by considering what would happen if it were put into effect.

As the supervisor examines each alternative, certain factors should be considered. What is the degree of risk involved? All decisions involve risk, some more than others. What is the relationship between the time required to implement a decision and how economically it can be implemented?

In the example above, some possible alternatives might involve additional training, the addition of sales incentives, having more experienced salespeople work longer hours until the new salespeople gain experience, or laying off some of the inexperienced salespeople and trying to hire people with more experience. Each alternative has positive and negative consequences.

Select an Alternative

After developing and evaluating the alternatives, the supervisor must select the alternative that seems to be best. This is where the supervisor's willingness to accept responsibility is so important. In the final analysis, the supervisor has to make the decision. Supervisors rely on experience, intuition, advice from others, and experimentation.

Follow-Up and Evaluation

After a decision has been reached and specific actions taken, it is important to determine the results of your decision. Follow-up can take many forms. Depending on the nature of the decision, evaluation may take the form of a simple observation. In a more complex situation such as the one discussed above, a more formal assessment of changes in sales volume would be appropriate.

The important point is that no decision-making process is complete without some form of follow-up and appraisal of the actions taken. If the problem was solved or the situation improved, then the supervisor can feel confident that the decision was sound. If the problem continues or worsens, then the supervisor must start all over again, beginning with problem definition.

TRADE TALK

Define each term and use it in a sentence.

Discipline	Supervision
Grievance	Supervisory feedback
Leadership	Symptom
Liaison	Time management
Results-oriented supervision	

CAN YOU ANSWER THESE?

1. What is the difference between being a leader and being a boss?

2. How can you prepare to be a supervisor?

3. List six duties of a supervisor.

4. What are the qualifications required for a retail supervisor?

5. Outline the steps in supervisory decision making.

26 *Training Retail Marketing Employees*

One of the most important supervisory responsibilities is training employees. Regardless of the size of the firm, all employees require training at different stages of their employment with the organization. Sometimes this training is provided informally, through meetings and brief discussions with supervisors. At other times the training is more extensive and more formal.

Individual training is the most common type of training in retail marketing. When a new cashier is hired, someone must work with that person to help develop the necessary skills to operate the register efficiently. It may be the supervisor who assumes this task. At other times the supervisor may delegate this to another person, such as a senior cashier.

One problem with individual training is that many supervisors and more experienced employees know their job so well that they forget that newer employees may struggle with tasks the experienced person views as second-nature. Without proper training, simple tasks—such as completing a sales ticket—may prove to be very difficult. Mistakes by newer employees in completing a simple sales ticket may cause customer dissatisfaction, which will cost the store money and profit.

Reducing mistakes is just part of the reason for training employees. Other reasons include increasing worker productivity, improving relations with employees, and motivating the employee.

REASONS FOR EMPLOYEE TRAINING

Retail marketers usually look at training in terms of costs and benefits, just as they would any other operating function. Some firms follow a policy of promotion from within the company and invest heavily in training programs. Others try to hire people with related experience and provide little employee training. Nevertheless, recent studies have identified the lack of employee training as contributing to the failure of many small businesses. So businesses that do not invest in their employees are adding to the risk of business failure.

Increasing Worker Productivity

One way to reduce labor costs is to improve the effectiveness and efficiency of your employees. Much employee training in retail marketing is directed toward improving customer relations, improving technical skills (such as selling), and improving employee performance in regular job duties. As their employees improve their efficiency and effectiveness in each of these three areas, supervisors have more time to devote to their other duties. With improved employee performance, the business will realize more profits, fewer customer complaints, and more satisfied customers to build sales.

Training programs help employees become confident in their work because they can learn the company's policies and procedures.

Improving Relations with Employees

A good training program helps all employees to understand the firm's policies and practices. Also, employees will feel that they have a common purpose. And, of course, this means that the employees will project a consistent store image.

Well-trained employees are more self-confident, less defensive, and easier to work with than untrained workers. Also, they usually have greater respect for the firm and the role of management, their customers, and the merchandise and services they sell. Employee training leads to more worker satisfaction and this leads to greater commitment to the firm.

■

MOTIVATING RETAIL MARKETING EMPLOYEES

Training is a crucial part of creating a "motivational" climate for retail employees. To

understand how this works, it is useful to examine the concept of motivation in more detail.

Why People Work

You may have worked for someone either part time or full time. Have you ever thought about why you worked? Your immediate response is because you wanted to earn some money. This is a typical response for most people, particularly younger workers. However, people also work for other reasons.

Job Satisfiers People do work to earn money for the material things they want and need in life. People need food, shelter, clothing, and physical security. But there are other, equally important rewards that people obtain by working. These are what the experts call job satisfiers. **Job satisfiers** are the parts of a job that provide personal satisfaction and meet the employees' need for recognition, a sense of belonging, respect, and self-fulfillment. It is almost impossible to attach a dollar value to these needs.

Job Dissatisfiers One of the continuing arguments about the role of employee compensation is whether or not money will motivate an employee to be more productive. Although the argument may never be settled, research by business experts suggests that money is not much of a motivator. Research suggests, however, that money works as a job dissatisfier when the employee feels that he or she is underpaid. **Job dissatisfiers** are the parts of the job that cause a person to be unhappy in that job. If a dissatisfier is present, there is not much that will motivate a person to do a good job. Table 1 identifies 21 different kinds of job satisfiers and job dissatisfiers. As you can see, there are many more job satisfiers than job dissatisfiers.

If the salary paid does not meet your expectations or needs, a supervisor will have a very difficult time motivating you to improve your job performance. Increasing your sal-

TABLE 1 / JOB SATISFIERS AND DISSATISFIERS

Job- and Employee-Related Factors That May Increase Satisfaction	Job-Related Factors That May Cause Dissatisfaction*

The following may increase satisfaction and motivation if the supervisor builds each into the employee's job:
    Use of one's abilities
    Feeling of achievement
    Constant activity
    Opportunity for advancement
    Authority over others
    Personal autonomy
    Opportunity for creativity
    Independence in work activities
    Recognition for work done
    Responsibility
    Social contribution of work
    Social status
    Variety in work
	The following may create dissatisfaction if they are perceived as poor or inadequate by the employee:
	    Company policies and practices
	    Pay and compensation
	    Relations with co-workers
	    Job security
	    Technical supervision
	    General working conditions
	    General supervision

* *Remember*: If the employee feels that any of the dissatisfiers is inadequate or poor, it is unlikely that any of the satisfiers can be used by a supervisor to create a motivational climate. However, when the employee is generally happy with the level of the factors listed in the right-hand column, then a supervisor can use various job satisfiers to create a motivational climate.

ary will often have a short-term impact on your job performance. But paying employees more money (or reducing other dissatisfiers) rarely causes long-term improvement in job performance.

Developing a Motivational Work Environment

Motivating employees means providing them with the opportunity to get what they want in exchange for what the employer wants them to do. Different jobs require different kinds of skills, and in turn, offer different kinds of rewards.

As a worker, you will bring to a job your potential and a set of abilities. You seek certain rewards or satisfactions. Employers offer employment requiring certain skills and provide certain types of rewards and satisfactions. The key to successful supervision is to develop as close a match as possible between what the employee offers in abilities, poten-

tial, and needs, and what the job has to offer. This is where training becomes a valuable tool in supervision.

Looking again at Table 1, you will find many opportunities to enhance the job satisfiers and reduce the job dissatisfiers. Poor technical supervision is likely to be a job dissatisfier. However, an effective training program can reduce this dissatisfaction and make it easier for the supervisor to motivate a retail employee.

Training can also influence the job satisfiers. A well-designed training program can help individuals make better use of their abilities. Advanced training is usually required for promotion. Individual autonomy and independence can be increased with sufficient training of employees. Being selected to participate in training programs is a powerful form of recognition and can lead to additional responsibility. And finally, training can provide the opportunity for variety in people's work as they train to assume new duties.

It is important to stop at this point and consider another debate concerning motivation. That is, can a supervisor actually "motivate" an employee? The answer seems to be no. Motivation is something only the individual can do. **Motivation** is defined as the internal drive to accomplish a particular goal. Other people cannot motivate you; only you can do that. What supervisors can do is provide a working environment where individuals will want to motivate themselves. This is an important role of the retail supervisor. This is what is meant by supervisory motivation.

Motivation and Career Stage

Not all employees have the same perspective on work or the same career ambitions. So the importance that workers attach to their jobs varies a great deal. An employee's career ambition often explains his or her attitude toward work and provides clues for supervision and training strategies.

There are four stages of career orientation. These are discussed below in more detail.

Job Orientation   Employees in the job-orientation stage work primarily for the salary or benefits offered. Others may work simply to have something to do. Some will work part-time in addition to another full-time job. Their orientation is to the employment itself and what the employment provides them. They see their employment primarily as a job.

Task Orientation   Employees in the task-oriented stage enjoy working and take pride in being hard workers. They enjoy the tasks associated with the job and are not necessarily interested in advancement to another position.

Occupation Orientation   Occupation-oriented employees take great pride in the type of work they do—being a craftsperson,

sales representative, display person, and so on. They maintain high standards of performance in their work. They will often identify more with their occupation than with their employer.

Career Orientation   Career-oriented people are the professionals in the field. They love their work and usually feel strongly that they're making a contribution to society through their work. They work hard and have a strong commitment to their "profession." The advancement of their profession is as important as their own individual advancement.

Recognizing that people have different orientations to their work is important for effective supervision. Supervisors who know their employees and understand their work objectives are in a better position to identify appropriate training and, thus, are in a better position to create a motivational environment.

■

TYPES OF TRAINING PROGRAMS

Everyone benefits from well-designed training programs. Employees benefit because training increases their opportunities to obtain rewards from their work. Supervisors benefit because they have fewer problems to solve and because employees are more productive. Customers benefit because well-trained employees give more efficient service. The business owner benefits because a well-trained employee contributes to the profitability of the business.

To design an employee training program to meet the needs of all workers in a retail marketing firm, employers must understand the different types of training programs available. One method of classifying training program options is by occupational level or type of employee served.

Entry-Level Training

Training for new employees should be a mandatory part of any company training program. New employees need to feel comfortable and a part of the organization in as short a time as possible. They will need to know about such things as:

- Company policies and regulations
- Completing sales checks
- Operating cash registers
- Handling customer complaints
- Other systems within the business

Focusing on the "job survival" skills needed in a job will help the supervisor help the new employee reduce the anxiety associated with starting a new job.

This training may be formal or informal, depending on the size of the company, the experience of the new employee, and the nature of the job. But the important thing to remember is that all new employees will require some initial training to become part of an effective retail marketing team.

Career-Level Training

Even the best retail marketing employee occasionally needs to be provided with the opportunity to update his or her technical expertise. **Updating training** is designed to bring employees up to date on knowledge and skills needed in their present job. Because retail marketing is a dynamic, ever-changing industry, updating should be a continuous part of a retail business's training program.

Updating training may involve simple concepts such as changes in store procedures. The introduction of microcomputers over the past decade has resulted in much updating training in retail marketing. New products and services, changes in government regulations, and new strategies in personal selling all are potential updating training topics.

Upgrading training is usually designed to prepare trainees for promotion to higher positions. Most management training programs fit into this category. Upgrading training can also focus on better employees who have been selected to assume additional or different responsibilities regardless of level. This type of training may also provide greater depth in specific technical areas, leadership, or human relations.

Supervisory Training

Supervisory training is probably the most critical type of instruction because it has a strong effect on the workforce. Also, it occurs at a crucial time for young supervisors. Many of them make up their minds to continue or to end their retail marketing careers at this point.

Supervisory training usually includes topics such as techniques of effective supervision, training techniques, employer-employee relations, and the interpretation of company policies and regulations. Businesses regularly devote more of their training dollars to supervisory training than to any other area. This is strong evidence of the importance placed by businesses on the process of supervision.

Executive Development

Executive development is designed to enable operating and administrative managers to keep up with trends in retail marketing and to encourage creativity on the part of executives. It usually includes such topics as marketing, economics, finance, communications and human relations, telemarketing, civic responsibility, and other topics unique to retail marketing.

Executive development tends to use different kinds of training activities than those used in training at other occupational levels. Training at this level often includes conferences, regular college courses, retreats, travel, exchange programs, and other activities thought to be useful in developing leadership at the highest levels.

DESIGNING A TRAINING PROGRAM

Let's assume that you've been asked to help design a training program. As a supervisor, what steps would you follow in preparing the program? The ensuing discussion outlines a useful process that most retail marketers could pursue.

Identify Training Needs

The first step in developing a training program is to identify the specific needs that should be addressed. **Training needs** may be defined as the gap between what an employee can do (actual condition) and what the employee ought to be able to do (ideal condition). This is important because without a clear understanding of training needs, your training program will most likely not be effective.

One useful technique is to develop a skills inventory. A **skills inventory** is a listing of tasks or knowledge in which your employees should be competent. It is useful to develop skills inventories for each area of their job. The skills inventory on page 220 is typical for a retail salesperson.

Once the skills inventory is complete, the supervisor can evaluate each employee on his or her level of skill in this area. The difference between what the employee can do and should be able to do provides guidance for developing a training plan.

A second technique is to analyze **job performance**. Job performance is the actual behavior of an employee on the job. Through observation of the employee under actual work conditions, review of customer complaints, and review of other internal records, the trainer can identify sources of job performance problems and develop appropriate training.

A third strategy is more informal. Supervisors can ask their employees where they feel they need more training. This might be done informally through individual discussions or during group meetings. In large organizations, a formal survey might also be useful.

It is important to recognize that not all job performance problems can be solved with training. Many times the sources of the problems are unrelated to employee skill or expertise. Other obstacles to proper job performance may include scheduling problems, poor communications between management and employees, inadequate materials to do the job, or lack of adequate supervision. These problems require changes in the organization and are often referred to as **organizational development**.

Regardless of the method or methods used, no training should be attempted until a thorough needs assessment has been conducted. To conduct training without doing a needs assessment is to waste training dollars.

Develop the Training Program

After identifying the training needs of the employees and then deciding on a priority for training, the supervisor can design a training program. This step requires a series of decisions on the part of the person developing the training program.

Choose an Appropriate Instructional System The most widely used instructional systems are:

1. *On-the-job training (OJT).* **On-the-job training** is one-to-one training with an experienced employee or supervisor. Employees are immediately placed in the work situation and are trained as they go along. Virtually all retail marketers use some type of OJT, often in combination with other training systems.

2. *Company training classes.* These are classes organized and offered by the company. This is a popular system used by many major retailers.

PROFESSIONAL SALESPERSON SKILLS INVENTORY	Excellent	Good	Fair	Poor
CUSTOMER RELATIONS				
Explain the purpose and importance of selling	—	—	—	—
Explain the importance of integrity in selling	—	—	—	—
Observe company policies	—	—	—	—
Determine customer/client needs and buying motives	—	—	—	—
Use buying motives as basis of sales presentation	—	—	—	—
Address needs of individual personalities	—	—	—	—
Facilitate customer buying decisions	—	—	—	—
Question/Probe for information	—	—	—	—
Use appropriate timing	—	—	—	—
Handle customer/client objections	—	—	—	—
Explain the need for courtesy when dealing with difficult customers	—	—	—	—
Handle customer/client complaints	—	—	—	—
Maintain/use customer/client list	—	—	—	—
BASIC TRANSACTIONS				
Open the sales presentation	—	—	—	—
Use suggestion selling	—	—	—	—
Sell from displays	—	—	—	—
Close the sale	—	—	—	—
Wrap/package products	—	—	—	—
Explain sales quotas	—	—	—	—
Process mail/telephone orders	—	—	—	—
Arrange delivery of purchases	—	—	—	—
Arrange alterations	—	—	—	—
Process special orders	—	—	—	—
HANDLING MERCHANDISE				
Handle product properly	—	—	—	—
Demonstrate product	—	—	—	—
Involve customer/client in sale	—	—	—	—
MERCHANDISE INFORMATION				
Obtain product information from appropriate individuals	—	—	—	—
Obtain product information from sources on/with the item	—	—	—	—
Summarize the use of brand names in selling	—	—	—	—
Use company promotional material for selling information	—	—	—	—
Study competitors' promotions	—	—	—	—
Use feature/benefit selling	—	—	—	—
Explain the nature of a selling vocabulary	—	—	—	—
Suggest product substitutions	—	—	—	—
Determine size and fit (apparel)	—	—	—	—
Advise customers on current fashions (apparel)	—	—	—	—

A skills inventory for a retail salesperson.

3. *Public and private school courses.* Many retail marketers take advantage of regular courses offered in area vocational-technical colleges and private schools. Programs offering supervisory training, sales training, customer relations training, and the like are a cost-effective way to train employees. The companies usually pay their tuition.

4. *Correspondence courses.* Training by mail is useful in limited areas. It is used mostly in those areas that require the acquisition of knowledge rather than skill.

5. *Job rotation.* **Job rotation** is training in which an employee is placed into a different position and is expected to perform in that position or to learn it as if he or she were a new employee. After a limited period of time, the employee should be able to perform most of the duties of that job. This is a particularly useful instructional strategy where the supervisor wants people who can perform in several positions or where an individual is being prepared for advancement.

Identify Training Staff If formal training is required, many retail marketers hire professional trainers. This is particularly the case in organizations that do not have a for-

mal training department. For many smaller firms, much training is done using the OJT method or in small groups.

Many retail chain operations leave training up to the store manager. He or she is often ill-prepared to deliver effective training.

In OJT and group instruction, one effective instructional strategy, used extensively by the U.S. Army during World War II, is called the four-step method. To get the best results, instructors follow the steps outlined in Table 2.

TABLE 2 / THE FOUR STEPS OF ON-THE-JOB TRAINING*

Step	Purpose	How Accomplished
1. Prepare the learner.	To relieve tension. To establish training base. To arouse interest. To give him or her confidence.	Put him or her at ease. Find out what he or she already knows about task. Tell relation of task to mission. Tie task to his or her experience. Ensure that he or she is in a comfortable position to see you perform the task clearly.
2. Present the task.	To make sure he or she understands what to do and why. To ensure retention. To avoid giving him or her more than he or she can grasp.	Tell, show, illustrate, question carefully and patiently, use task analysis. Stress key points. Instruct clearly, completely, one step at a time. Keep your words to a minimum. Stress action words.
3. Try out learner's performance.	To be sure he or she has right method. To prevent wrong habit forming. To be sure he or she knows what he or she is doing and why. To test his or her knowledge. To avoid putting him or her on the job prematurely.	Have him or her perform the task and do not require that he or she explain what he or she is doing the first time through. If he or she makes a major error, assume the blame yourself and repeat as much of Step 2 as is necessary. Once he or she has performed the task correctly, have him or her do it again and this time have him or her explain the steps and key points as he or she does the task (most frequently neglected).

(*Table continues*)

TABLE 2 *(continued)*

Step	Purpose	How Accomplished
		Ask questions to ensure that key points are understood. Continue until you know that he or she knows.
4. Follow up.	To give him or her confidence. To be sure he or she takes no chances and knows he or she is not left alone. To be sure he or she stays on the beam. To show your confidence in him or her.	Put him or her on his or her own; praise as fitting. Encourage questions; tell him or her where he or she can get help. Check frequently at first. Gradually reduce amount of checking.

* This chart is used by the U.S. Army to guide on-the-job training of civilian employees.

Evaluating a Training Program

All training activities should be evaluated to determine if the training has accomplished the goals set as a result of the needs assessment. Evaluation should also determine if the methods used in the training were the most effective, and whether the cost of the training is worth the results.

Evaluation can take many forms. Sometimes a formal test is useful, particularly where knowledge was a goal. Trainees need to understand that these tests are not for a "grade" as in high school, but rather to determine if the training has been successful.

Some evaluations may use observation of the employee performing the tasks that were the object of the training. If customer relations was the object, then employees could be observed by their supervisors as they work with customers, to see if the employees have improved their customer relations skills.

When training methods are being evaluated, it's useful to keep track of which methods produced desired results and which did not. The results should be compared to the costs of the training method in terms of employees' time, staff time, and the money spent on the training.

TRADE TALK

Define each term and use it in a sentence.

Job dissatisfiers
Job performance
Job rotation
Job satisfiers
Motivation
On-the-job training

Organizational development
Skills inventory
Training needs
Updating training
Upgrading training

CAN YOU ANSWER THESE?

1. What are three reasons for employee training?

2. Identify the types of training that might be offered to employees at different occupational levels.

3. What are the three steps in the design of a training program?

4. What is a training need?

5. Identify the four steps of training useful in OJT and group instruction.

6. What are five factors that contribute to employee dissatisfaction?

7. What are five factors that might be used by a supervisor to create a motivational climate?

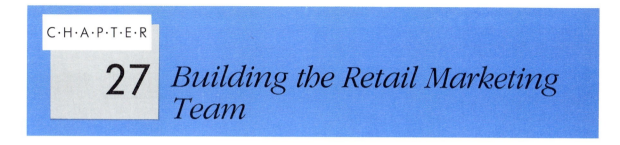

C·H·A·P·T·E·R

27 *Building the Retail Marketing Team*

Teams. Teamwork. These terms are becoming more important in today's business world. Most of us are familiar with sports teams. The U.S. Olympic volleyball team won the gold medal in 1986. Our Olympic hockey team won the gold medal in 1984. We have teams that win the Superbowl, the World Series, basketball championships, and many others. Regardless of the sport, successful teams share many common traits beyond having talent. Teams talk over plans and strategies together. They review films of their past performances. They identify mistakes and set goals for the next game. They share a common sense of direction.

Strategies used by successful teams have been recognized as valuable to the operation of a business. Where groups of people share a common sense of direction, talk over plans and strategies, review past performances, and set goals, they can create a sense of belonging to a team. This chapter will give you a chance to consider the concept of team building in retail marketing. How does management style relate to team building? What are the principles of team building? And what are the guidelines for team building? These questions will be discussed in detail. By the end of this chapter, you should be able to see the value of approaching supervision as an opportunity to create a winning retail marketing team.

■

MANAGEMENT STYLE

The emergence of management style as an important factor came about quite accidentally. In the early 1930s, a group of Harvard professors were interested in finding out if the amount of light in a factory influenced productivity. What they found puzzled them. Production increased if they increased the amount of light. It also increased if they decreased the amount of light. In fact, production continued to increase all during their study. About 2 weeks after they concluded their experiments, production returned to what it had been before the study.

Why did production fall back to preexperimental levels? After the experiment was completed, management and the supervisor went back to doing things the way they had been done before the experiment began!

So what caused these results? The researchers quickly concluded that lighting was not the cause. The answer? Production increased because the employees were given special treatment as part of the experiment. It made the employees feel that they were part of a team and that management cared about them. This phenomenon came to be known as the **Hawthorne effect**, named after the Western Electric plant in suburban Chicago where the experiment took place. These studies showed that it is possible to improve production by developing a spirit of teamwork. Certain factors were present during the experiment that led to increased production:

■ The supervisor had a personal interest in each person's achievement (he recorded changes in production).
■ He took pride in the record of the group.
■ He helped the group work together to set its own conditions of work.
■ He continually posted feedback on performance.
■ The group took pride in its own achievements and had the satisfaction of knowing that someone outside the group was interested in their performance.
■ The group did not feel pressured to make any changes.
■ The group was consulted before changes were made.
■ The group developed a sense of confidence.

These studies demonstrated that certain behaviors on the part of supervisors, or their **management style**, could influence production and productivity. Let's examine management style in more detail.

Theory X, Theory Y

One of the earliest theories of management style was suggested by Douglas McGregor. He argued that there were two types of management style, which he called Theory X and Theory Y. Each was an attempt to explain why managers behave in certain ways. According to McGregor, **Theory X managers** assume that people dislike work and will try to avoid it. These managers think that employees must constantly be told what to do and threatened with punishment to get them

to work toward achieving the organization's goals. This type of manager believes that the average person wants to avoid responsibility and prefers to be directed by someone else. Others have called this type of management authoritarian.

Theory Y managers, on the other hand, believe that work is as natural as play. They believe that people will exercise self-direction and self-control in the pursuit of objectives they feel a commitment to. This commitment is viewed as a result of the rewards they associate with achieving these objectives. The average person welcomes responsibility and is often frustrated by the lack of responsibility in his or her job. Some have interpreted this as a *laissez-faire* style of management or hands-off management. If employees are given the freedom, they will achieve company objectives.

Although neither style by itself is considered appropriate in today's business world, McGregor did contribute the concept of two important dimensions of management: concern for the needs of the organization and concern for the needs of people. These two themes were further developed by others.

Two-Dimensional Management

Many other theorists have suggested why some managers and supervisors are more effective than others. In understanding effective leadership behavior in business, authors such as Robert Blake and Jane Mouton, among others, suggested that there are two important dimensions. They labeled these concern for people and concern for production.

The relationship between these two dimensions is shown in the diagram on page 225. This figure shows how a manager's orientation toward these two traits determines his or her style. The 1,1 management style is often called low involvement or *laissez-faire*. A 9,1 management style shows a high concern for people and a low concern for production or structure. This will lead to a comfortable, friendly work situation. This style is

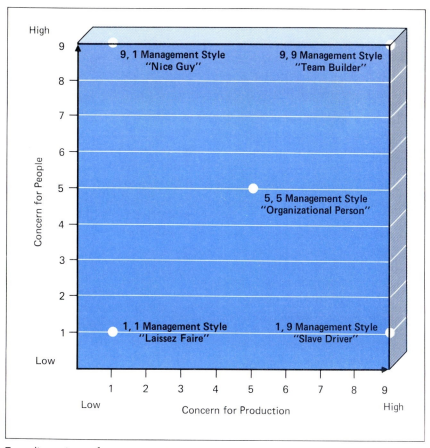

High

9   9, 1 Management Style   9, 9 Management Style
     "Nice Guy"   "Team Builder"

8

7

6

Concern for People

5   5, 5 Management Style
                                   "Organizational Person"

4

3

2

1   1, 1 Management Style   1, 9 Management Style
     "Laissez Faire"   "Slave Driver"

Low

     1   2   3   4   5   6   7   8   9
     Low   High
              Concern for Production

Two dimensions of management.

very close to Theory Y discussed earlier. The 1,9 management style, similar to Theory X, is mostly concerned with production and efficiency of operations. A style of 5,5 on this graph is a kind of compromise style, where the manager tries to balance these two dimensions at a minimal level or just enough to get by.

The team-building style (9,9) is one where the manager or supervisor has a high degree of concern for the people in the organization and a high degree of concern for the efficiency of business operations. This style, often called **team management**, stresses achievement at work through employees who are committed to the success of the organization. Teamwork will achieve production

through a high degree of shared responsibility, along with high participation, involvement, and commitment.

■

PRINCIPLES OF TEAM BUILDING

Effective supervisors and managers can look to the field of human relations for basic principles that will help them understand why a team-building style can be effective:

1. *People support what they create.* People are more productive and effective when they feel ownership or can identify with the goals of the organization. When they have participated in the development of these goals, and shared in the decision-making process, they feel ownership and will have a personal stake in achieving these goals.

2. *Mutual respect leads to trust and effective human relations.* When trust exists in an organization, it is easier to build a spirit of teamwork. Where there is mutual respect, a supervisor and employees can more openly discuss problems and find solutions that meet the organizaton's needs and the needs of the employees.

3. *Effective communication builds understanding between people.* As discussed earlier in this competency band, people need to communicate. This can happen only when there is sufficient trust and mutual respect.

4. *Handling conflict by direct problem solving promotes personal job satisfaction.* Conflict in an organization, either between employees or between supervisors and employees, is costly to an organization. It causes people to ignore their job responsibilities, lose sight of the organizational goals, and otherwise perform poorly. Conflict produces stress and may even affect personal health.

5. *Initiative is increased by having responsibility.* People want to control their own lives. When you are not permitted some control over your work situation, it is very likely that you will become frustrated and begin to resent working. However, when you are given responsibility for accomplishing goals you are committed to, you are more likely to demonstrate initiative and enjoy your job.

■

GUIDELINES FOR BUILDING A RETAIL MARKETING TEAM

Each of us has a style of management that we will use when we are in a position of responsibility. The style we have is a result of our personality, our upbringing, and our super-

visory role models. **Role models** are people whose behavior we observe and imitate. Regardless of how you acquire your style, you can improve upon it and become a team builder.

Improving Your People Dimension

If you find that you are more task-oriented, more concerned for production than people—1,9 management style—then you need to work on improving your people or consideration skills. There are several strategies you can use:

Recognize Accomplishments A famous expert on management, Kenneth Blanchard, once said, "Go out and catch someone doing some things right." As discussed earlier, people desire recognition in their job. Regardless of the job they perform, individual achievement should be noted and praised. When praise is given, it must be for real accomplishments, and it must be sincere.

Provide Opportunities for Early Success You have probably heard the old saying, "Nothing succeeds like success." This is true. As a supervisor, you should create situations where all your employees can experience success early in their jobs. This means that you should not overwhelm new employees with responsibilities, but break them in gradually. As they succeed at each new task, recognize their achievement and provide new challenges for them to master. Early success will build their self-confidence and foster a feeling of being contributing members of the retail marketing team.

Individualize Your Supervision Get to know your people. This was discussed in the previous chapter under duties of the supervisor. Sometimes it is helpful to have a card file containing information about your employees to help you remember important facts about them.

Recognition of an employee's performance encourages the employee to continue to perform well and sets an example for other employees.

Work at Communication When employees feel comfortable talking to the supervisor, team building is more likely to be possible. Open, honest communication is necessary to work out problems, create new solutions, and share ideas. Morale is improved by good communication, and productivity is closely linked to morale. Regular staff meetings before or after business hours are very helpful in encouraging employees to share ideas.

Improving Your Production Dimension

If you find that your style leans more toward concern for people over concern for production or structure, there are several strategies you can follow to improve the production dimension. Remember, team management requires a high degree of commitment to people and a high degree of commitment to task.

Clearly Define Goals Members of a team must know where they are heading. Successful sports teams regularly review past goals and set new ones. So do successful retail marketing teams. Groups are more effective when they know what the goals are and are aware of their progress toward the goals. A team management supervisor creates an environment where appropriate goals are set and understood.

Help Employees Set Their Own Goals Individuals know their own strengths and limitations better than anyone else. They should be encouraged to set their own personal goals in relation to the organizational goals.

The supervisor should meet and discuss personal goals with each employee and together agree on performance targets. There are many personal goals for members of a retail team, such as increasing sales, reducing expenses, lowering the amount of returned goods, improving accuracy in writing sales tickets, and so on. Once personal goals are set, they should be reviewed on a regular basis. New goals will emerge as old ones are achieved.

Provide Regular Feedback on Performance

Feedback is an important part of team building. Evaluating employees' performance is a daily and time-consuming part of the supervisor's role. It is critical for a new employee, but also important for a more experienced employee. You should always reward or reinforce the job behaviors that are desirable and correct those that are not.

When an employee does not measure up to the established standards, he or she should be held accountable. Never criticize a group for the failings of an individual. And never criticize an individual in front of the group. When it is necessary, direct your criticism at the poor performance, not at the employee as a person. Phrases like "You're a lousy salesperson, you just lost another sale" can destroy the concept of a retail marketing team. However, statements like "I think there were ways to have saved that sale," or "Let's talk about what might have gone wrong with your last customer," will maintain the employee's morale and still allow you to criticize poor selling performance. Again, this discussion should take place between you and the employee alone.

Balancing the Two Dimensions

Teams are groups of people. To be effective, a supervisor must be able to balance the people dimension and the production dimension within the group being supervised. It has been estimated that most managers spend between 50 and 90 percent of their working time in group activities. Effective managers and supervisors recognize that when groups work effectively as teams, they can produce more than as a collection of individuals. Nowhere is this more evident than at a Wal-Mart store, where employees are actively encouraged to submit ideas to their supervisors. Wal-Mart is a company that recognizes that

most of the good ideas come from the bottom up, beginning with the shelf stocker. The success of this firm is a direct result of implementing thousands of ideas contributed by employees.

■

CHARACTERISTICS OF A RETAIL MARKETING TEAM

How do you know when you have built an effective retail marketing team? Experts in this area suggest a number of observable characteristics. Among them are the following:

■ The goals or tasks are understood and accepted by the group. These goals are developed as a result of group discussion, and each person should have the opportunity to contribute his or her ideas.

■ There is a lot of discussion about work-related issues. All of the group participates, but their conversations stay directed toward the task at hand.

■ People listen to each other. Each person is allowed to express his or her ideas fully and others contribute to or react to the ideas.

■ There is often disagreement. There is enough trust in the group to permit open and honest disagreement. They do not try to cover or ignore conflict over ideas. But the conflict is over ideas, not between people.

■ The general atmosphere is informal and relaxed. It is a working environment where people are involved, interested, and certainly not bored.

■ People feel free to express their feelings as well as their ideas about the problem and how the group is handling the problem. In short, members of the team are not shy about expressing themselves in front of their team members.

You have now concluded your initial study of human resources and communications in retail marketing. By now you should have an understanding of the importance of human relations and communications in this dynamic field. When you begin working, your immediate need is to be able to get along with your co-workers, your supervisors and your customers. As you build your career in retail marketing, you will build your skill in human relations. Your understanding of customer expectations and how to improve communication with them is a beginning. Finally, you have had the opportunity to examine how successful retail marketers build a spirit of teamwork within their organization.

TRADE TALK

Define each term and use it in a sentence.

Hawthorne effect	Team management
Management style	Theory X managers
Role models	Theory Y managers

CAN YOU ANSWER THESE?

1. Describe the different assumptions underlying Theory X and Theory Y management styles.

2. How does the team management style relate to the two dimensions of management: people and production?

3. What five principles from human relations help explain why team management can be effective in retail marketing?

4. Suggest two strategies for improving your consideration dimension.

5. Suggest two strategies for improving your structure dimension.

6. Identify five characteristics of an effective retail marketing team.

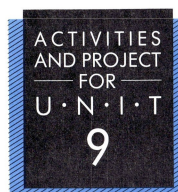

ACTIVITIES AND PROJECT FOR UNIT 9

RETAIL MARKETING CASES

1. Rosemary Cordova, supervisor of the small appliance department at Stein's Department Store, came into the office of Dawn Jackson, personnel manager of the company. "Dawn," said Rosemary, "I've got a problem with one of my salespeople and I need your help."

"What's the problem?" replied Dawn.

"It's Larry Wilson. He has been in my department for 2 years and I have been having trouble with him. Every time I give my salespeople a directive or some other instructions, they seem to check everything out with Larry first. You know, when I say I want something done, I expect it to be done. Most of the time they do end up following my directives, but I resent the fact that he seems to be the authority in my department and not me.

"Quite frankly, I've been trying to find a way to fire him, but so far I haven't had any luck. Anything I have thought of would surely end in a grievance. I know that the union would not object if I got rid of him, since he bugs them as much as he bugs me. He has never directly contradicted my orders or tried to sabotage what I wanted done. So I really don't have a case against him. I just don't know what to do."

1. What do you see as the problem?
2. If you were Dawn, what would you suggest?
3. If you were Larry, what would you suggest?
4. How would you describe Rosemary's management style?
5. If you were to suggest improvement in Rosemary's management style, what would you suggest?

2. You are the store manager for the Jeans Shack. This is one of 1200 retail units located across the United States. As a store manager, you are primarily responsible for supervising eight to ten retail employees. Because of the small size of the staff, there is no assistant store manager. You have only recently been promoted to this position from another store in the chain.

One of your part-time salespeople, Paula Black, is 19 and has a young child. She is one of your better workers. But she is almost always late for work. You have spoken to her about this many times, but nothing seems to work. She sometimes has trouble finding baby-sitters. Since she is employed full-time during the day, she is sometimes late leaving her other job. She also argues that she works twice as hard as anyone else and stays late to make up for her tardiness.

There is no question that she is the best salesperson you have and that she is better at putting stock on the floor and also at working the displays. You also know that she needs the extra income to help support her child.

One Thursday evening just before Christmas, it is very busy. The crew scheduled to get off at 6:00 p.m. is anxious to leave so they can do their Christmas shopping. Paula is late again, and you have to ask one of the day crew to stay until she comes. As you walk into the back room where your personnel check in, you overhear two of your full-time workers talking. "That Paula is getting preferred treatment. Why should she be given any favors? If I pulled those stunts, I'd be fired in a minute!"

Paula finally arrives, 30 minutes late. You feel you must do something.

1. Suggest three alternative actions you can take right now.
2. What would be the consequences of each of your proposed actions?
3. Select your best proposal and defend your choice.
4. How will you evaluate whether you made a good decision?
5. How can you prevent this type of thing from happening in the future?

PROJECT: DESIGNING A TRAINING PROGRAM

YOUR PROJECT GOAL
You will design a customer relations training program.

PROCEDURE
1. Identify a business in your career interest area.
2. Develop a plan for two alternative methods of collecting the information you will need to develop the training program.
3. Make an appointment with the manager of the business you identified in Procedure 1. You will need to have his or her permission to carry out the training needs assessment methods you identified in Procedure 2.

4. Once you have identified your customer relations training needs, you will need to plan a training program. Prepare a list of specific skills needing training, the methods you propose for the training, and the type of person or persons you would recommend to do the training.

5. Develop a plan for evaluating the success of your customer relations training program.

EVALUATION

You will be evaluated on the completeness of your training program. Specifically:

1. Did you identify the customer relations training needs adequately?

2. Are the training activities you propose appropriate for the needs you identified?

3. Is your plan for evaluating your training program appropriate?

SELLING

"Build a better mousetrap, and the world will beat a path to your door." WRONG! That line of thought has been the downfall of countless entrepreneurs the world over. Every year, thousands of ambitious people with great aspirations start retail goods and service ventures assuming that all they have to do to thrive is offer good merchandise or render a superior service. They assume that customers will recognize the quality of their product or service and rush in to satisfy their needs. It doesn't happen that way. The enterprise frequently fails.

This misconception has always handicapped venturesome business owners and managers, but it is much more lethal in today's marketplace. Recent data on retail marketing shows that only those firms that know how to merchandise (sell, in the broad sense) and how to promote (nonpersonal selling) survive very long.

There is no mystery in selling, nor are special talents needed to be successful. Selling is a competency area that is learned through continuous study and meaningful practical experience. It is a human relations business skill that is transferable from one marketing occupation to another and to many other occupational fields. Therefore, as a learner, an investment of your time now in the study of selling promises to yield rich rewards in terms of career progress and personal satisfaction. And there's no better place to start the learning process than in retailing, where the learner is so close to the final consumer.

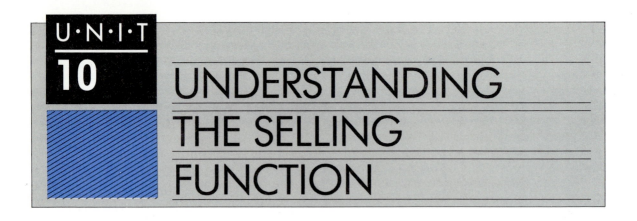

UNDERSTANDING THE SELLING FUNCTION

C·H·A·P·T·E·R

28 *Analyzing Retail Selling*

The basic activity in retail marketing, as well as in other kinds of marketing, is *selling*. In both personal selling and nonpersonal selling through the media and the mail, a value system and thought pattern make the entire marketing process click. This mental set is an essential element in mastering the *marketing concept* described earlier in this book.

■

ETHICS IN MARKETING PRACTICES

Both from the standpoint of the consumer and those who pursue careers in marketing goods and services, retailing has come a very long way in ethical practice during the twentieth century. Only a hundred years ago, many distributors were still following the policy of **caveat emptor** (say "ka'-ve-at emptor"), meaning "let the buyer beware." Some of

them even agreed in principle with the philosophy of P. T. Barnum, the circus tycoon, who said, "There's a sucker born every minute." Retailers who were situated where the competition was weak or nonexistent usually tended to follow the greedy way of doing business. However, the business climate has changed drastically since those early days.

Consumers no longer tolerate shady business practices, and competitors soon take over the trade of those who violate good business ethics. The demise of *caveat emptor* is largely attributed to: (1) disappearance of a seller's market, (2) greatly increased consumer knowledge, and (3) development of a new corporate conscience.

1. Today, the business environment is known as a buyer's market. A **buyer's market** is one in which purchasers of products or services are in control because the supply of products and services tends to exceed the demand for them. Even in a **seller's market**, in which demand is much greater than supply, ethical practices usually prevail. They prevail because retailers realize that customers have long memories and support the firms that treat them fairly regardless of market conditions.

2. An informed public, long-term profitability, and ethical business conduct are inseparable. (Bad ethics is bad business.) The ethical pursuit of profit in the United States is a fundamental requirement of sound business management. The basic reason for this gradual change in attitude rests with education—education of both buyers and sellers. Thanks to more education of greater numbers of people, and particularly to television and aggressive journalism, a consumer has access to almost unlimited information. As a result, institutions of every description—not just retailing—find their clients more sophisticated, more secure in their challenges, and sharper in their questioning than ever before.

3. Business managers are coming to realize that business is not a purely economic activity. More and more, they are developing a **corporate conscience**—a sense of responsibility to the community and to the society of which they are an integral part. They realize that consumers are not the only losers in the perilous world of *caveat emptor*; so are the businesses that fail to recognize the human relations factor in selling.

Ethics in Retail Selling

Do you know that the cost of attracting new customers is five times greater than the cost of retaining a customer? Do you know that, on average, a customer who is satisfied with your product or service will tell three other people? Do you know that if you can get dissatisfied customers to complain and then solve the problem, about 80 percent of them will remain your customers?

Even if you don't resolve the complaint satisfactorily, 54 percent will be repeat customers. However, if alienated customers don't complain, only about a third of them will ever come back. These conclusions, which were drawn from a national study, point up the importance of treating customers fairly and respectfully in all business contacts, especially during the selling process.

Without question, the current emphasis in retail marketing is on retaining present customers and winning their support in eliciting new ones. Successful long-term selling depends on customer assistance that is tailored to the customer's expectations—the kind that generates business. It's completely service oriented.

Serving today's customers is not a "telling" (persuading) situation; it's an "asking" business. It's a myth that in selling you have to "sell" anything to anybody. The really productive salespeople are those who help people buy. No one likes to be "sold" anything, but we do like to buy. Therefore, service-minded salespeople know what to do to lower the barriers between buyers and sellers and let people buy, helping them when they want assistance. Following the Golden Rule is one of the best tools a seller can use: Treat people as you yourself want to be treated. And "when in Rome, do as the Romans do."

Selling is an enjoyable calling when viewed as an opportunity to help individuals satisfy their needs and meet their expectations for goods and services. It's a socioeconomic service that propels a business enterprise. It's the human element in an economic transaction. Now let's see how it functions in retail marketing.

Basic Beliefs of Retail Selling

In a large, well-known New York department store, there was an extraordinary young menswear salesperson whose daily sales volume was always nearly twice that of any of the other 14 salespeople in the department. George Johnson consistently had a higher average-sale record than any of his co-workers. He also had a smaller percent-

All customers deserve a courteous salesperson.

age of returned merchandise than anyone else on the floor. And his relationships with the sales force and supervisory staff were excellent.

George wasn't the most handsome man in the department, but he dressed well and was well groomed. He was friendly, but not overly so. He wasn't especially talkative—he didn't spend a great deal of time with each customer. Yes, he was honest and reliable. But what made George such a successful salesperson?

There were many reasons. To begin with, George understood the basic beliefs of retail selling—and he practiced them, consciously at first, then as a matter of habit.

A CUSTOMER is not a cold statistic but a flesh-and-blood human being with feelings and emotions like our own.

A CUSTOMER is a person who brings us needs, wants, and expectations—it is our job to fill those needs and wants.

A CUSTOMER does us a favor when calling on us—we are not doing our customer a favor.

A CUSTOMER is not an interruption of our work but the purpose of it.

A CUSTOMER deserves the most courteous and attentive treatment we can give.

A CUSTOMER is part of our business—not an outsider.

A CUSTOMER is the most important person in any business.

These basic beliefs about customers are the essence of all retail sales transactions. No matter what the type of retail marketing, selling begins first with customer service.

All retail workers should understand how their jobs help to make sales take place. So even those retail workers who don't come into direct contact with customers should understand and practice the basic beliefs of retail selling. And they should know enough about the selling process to cooperate with those whose main job is selling.

Everybody Sells In today's retail market, everybody sells something. Selling is a teamwork task in which some workers utilize human resource skills, while others create and maintain an inviting shopping environment. Even customers take part in selling when they tell their friends or relatives to buy a certain product or shop at a certain store.

A large part of current retail selling is making it easy, pleasant, and economical for customers to buy—few sales would be made without this contribution. Some retail employees develop advertising to bring potential purchasers into the place of business. Some make displays that help sell merchandise. Some provide customer services such as credit. Some keep records, take care of stock, clean floors, do repair work, and perform a variety of services. And, of course, sales personnel serve customers during the final phase of the selling process.

Types of Retail Selling In the past, when retail selling was limited mainly to over-the-counter contacts with customers, it was relatively easy to analyze a sale. But today, nonpersonal selling methods have taken over a much larger role, and in some product and service lines, they embrace the entire selling process. Advertising and display now presell many products and services, so customers don't need as much assistance from salespeople. This change has made it fitting to view retail selling in two different ways: (1) as personal selling and (2) as nonpersonal selling, sometimes called mass selling. **Personal selling** is person-to-person selling to individuals or small groups. Sales personnel are involved in the selling process. **Nonpersonal selling** is selling to larger groups or segments of a market, excluding face-to-face contact with salespeople. It is the preselling of products and services through various forms of advertising and display without the use of salespeople. However, even though the aim of nonpersonal selling is to presell goods and services, some assistance from salespeople may be needed by customers after they are physically in the store or shop. And, of course, sales assistance is needed at the checkout counter.

Both types of selling require the basic beliefs discussed on page 237. But the ways in which those beliefs are applied to the personal and nonpersonal selling processes are very different. Likewise, both personal and nonpersonal selling are based on valid product or service analysis. The results of such analyses, however, are organized and applied in different ways. One must first understand the different types of goods and services.

Types of Goods and Services   Goods and services may be divided into three groups based on customer buying habits: (1) convenience goods and services, (2) shopping goods and services, and (3) specialty goods and services.

Consumers seldom want information from a salesperson about **convenience goods and services**. These are items such as candy, toothpaste, or film processing, which customers usually buy wherever and whenever

it's convenient. Customers, however, do want information and advice when purchasing **shopping goods and services**, such as dress clothing, refrigerators, or a new roof for their house, because these are things that they generally compare and shop for before purchasing. Certainly, an experienced homemaker wants no help when buying coffee but may require much information when purchasing a microwave oven. **Specialty goods and services** are those that attract consumers for some reason other than price. Customers will usually go out of their way to visit a retail firm where these products or services are available. Some typical specialty goods are high-quality watches, famous-label clothing, Disneyland entertainment, and a prominent architect's services.

Of course, not everyone has the same purchasing habits. Some people buy automobiles only after shopping carefully for them; then cars are shopping goods. Others decide the "make" or brand of car they want and go directly to the dealer who sells it—these cars are specialty goods. However, when classifying goods for merchandising purposes, retailers are concerned mainly with the majority of customers.

Now that you understand the types of goods and services, we can probe the two general categories of retail selling. Let's look at nonpersonal selling first, since it applies to a broad range of products and services.

■

NONPERSONAL SELLING

The form of nonpersonal selling most used by retailers is newspaper advertising. Much advertising is also placed in magazines, on television and radio, or carried through the mail.

Nonpersonal selling also includes favorable publicity in the news media, displays, public relations events, and special incentives. See Chapter 38 for more.

All of these nonpersonal sales devices have some common elements that influence the way in which sales goals are achieved. How this works is explained in the following pages.

Characteristics of Nonpersonal Selling

As mentioned earlier, nonpersonal selling is directed to target groups of people rather than to individuals (except for certain direct mail appeals). It applies to all types of products and services, ranging from rubber bands to real estate. It is used extensively in marketing convenience goods and services.

Compared to personal selling, nonpersonal selling allows the seller more time to think through a sales message. And it lends itself to market research. But once the message is released, it's relatively difficult to retract or change. Finally, except for mail orders, nonpersonal selling does not close many sales.

All these characteristics suggest a broad general approach when selling to large groups of customers. The mental stages experienced by a customer during a purchase, which are usually referred to as AIDCA, offer a sales approach that fits nonpersonal selling.

AIDCA Sales Analysis

Regardless of how long it takes them to buy a product or service, customers pass through a series of mental stages. But all these stages do not necessarily occur at the time of purchase. They are (1) attention, (2) interest, (3) desire, (4) conviction, and (5) action.

1. *Attention*: The first mental stage takes place when a prospective customer notices and pays attention to a product or service being offered for sale.

2. *Interest*: Customers reach the interest stage when they continue to give attention to the product or service and become motivated by a concern or curiosity about it.

3. *Desire*: Desire is developed the moment that customers feel that they will be lacking something if they can't have the product or service.

4. *Conviction*: Conviction grows out of a desire for the product or service. It's a mental stage at which prospective purchasers believe that there's more to gain by making the purchase than by not doing so. They are convinced that they should buy.

5. *Action*: This mental stage occurs when customers indicate a readiness to buy.

Sometimes an additional stage, "satisfaction," may be added to a final mental stage. Satisfaction may be described as a feeling of enjoyment or contentment regarding the purchase itself, the merchandise acquired, or the business firm and the salesperson who served the customer. If a customer is satisfied, repeat sales are frequently made.

If you begin your retail career in personal selling, you may find it difficult to use AIDCA to plan your sales. It may be helpful for you to think of the mental stages as intermediate objectives to be achieved as a sale progresses rather than as distinct steps of a sales transaction. AIDCA has high value in analyzing nonpersonal selling. If you become employed in that area, it will help you identify your role in the total retail marketing process.

■

PERSONAL SELLING

Personal selling will continue to improve its status in retailing as long as invention and technology increase the number of products and services on the market. As consumer purchasing becomes more complex, consumers will step up their demand for more consumer information and counseling, and they'll insist on better-trained retail salesworkers to help them buy wisely. This trend can be noted in shopping centers, where there is a growing number of specialty shops that feature full-service assistance. It's also manifest in the department store offering of personal shopping service for business people and in the 800 service numbers for computers and for mail-order businesses.

Although nonpersonal selling has modified the role of salespeople, it is raising the competency standards of all salesworkers in personal selling. For example, advertising and a pleasing shopping environment may provide the initial attraction to consumers. But salespeople, by the competency they possess, still play a large part in making customers want to return. Today's customer has so many kinds of merchandise from which to choose that buying frequently becomes more of an emotional than a rational process. "Satisfying" the customer is not enough, and it is being replaced with a commitment to *please the customer*.

Wise customers like to feel thrifty and clever when shopping in a discount house or catalog showroom. And they also like to feel secure and confident when shopping in a specialty store. So the consumer's selection of retail outlets varies between service and self-service outlets. So long as our economic system continues to offer these choices, there will always be a need for skillful personal selling.

Buying-Decision Sales Analysis

Skillful retail salespeople, consciously or without realizing it, use the customer's buying decisions as a tool in analyzing their sales and serving their customers. Here's how the system works: Every customer must make five major buying decisions during a purchase or there will be no sales transaction. Here are the decisions the customer must make and the questions that must be answered:

Need decision—What type of product or service do I need to solve this problem?
Product or service decision—Which product or service (and brand) should I buy?
Price decision—How much should I spend on the product or service?

Place decision—From which source should I buy it?
Time decision—When should I buy it?

It will be easy for you to learn the five buying decisions because you have made them many times—probably without realizing it.

Sequence of Decisions   Unlike the fixed sequence of the customer's mental stages (AIDCA), the order in which the decisions are made varies a great deal. The need decision is nearly always first in a rational purchase, but the other decisions may be made as soon as a need is recognized and when the customer has a strong preference for a particular brand. The place decision can be made at the time the need is recognized, or it can be delayed until the moment the purchase is actually made. The time decision may follow the need decision, or it may be postponed to the end of the transaction. And, of course, the price decision may be made at any time after the need is realized.

Where Decisions Are Made   A purchaser's buying decisions may be made almost anywhere. However, they are usually made at the point of sale or in the home, depending on the type of product or service. When purchasing low-priced convenience goods, customers frequently make all five buying decisions before entering the place of business. This happens because the customer has already purchased the item many times before. Purchases are made quickly. On the other hand, most of the buying decisions for shopping goods are usually made in the store. The larger the investment being considered, the more difficult the decisions become and the greater is the need for personal assistance with buying decisions.

Applications of Buying-Decision Sales Analyses   Manufacturers spend millions of dollars persuading consumers that they need certain types of products (need decision) and

The Need

"I need a new look ..."

The Product or Service

"This lipstick should be just the thing"

The Place

"I wonder whether this store is the right place to buy cosmetics ..."

The Price

"Five dollars seems a lot, but the color looks good"

The Time

"I could wait, but I'd better buy it today"

The five buying decisions your customer makes.

that they should buy a particular brand (product decision). Retailers do the same, but they also spend large amounts in satisfying consumers' price, place, and time decisions. Within retailing, salespeople spend a great deal of time helping their customers arrive at all five of the necessary buying decisions—to complete those that they have not yet made. So all types of marketers and all levels of retail workers find analysis of the five buying decisions useful. It is a customer-based sales analysis and planning method that is especially useful in this country, where customers cast economic votes both for products and services and for the retail marketers who meet their needs, wants, and expectations best.

Steps of a Sale

Now that you are aware of the mental stages experienced by customers during a purchase (AIDCA) and you understand the five buying decisions they must make before a purchase is completed, let's switch to the salesworker's perspective and identify the steps he or she normally takes during a sale. Just what does a retail salesperson do during a sale to get a prospective purchaser to buy shopping goods? What steps does an insurance agent take while selling protection to a prospect? Here are the common titles usually assigned to the sequence of steps (tasks) taken by a salesperson during a sale of shopping goods or services.

Preapproach
Approach
Identifying wants and needs
Presenting the product or service
Answering questions and objections
Suggestion selling
Closing the sale
Postsale services

Of course, all steps are not taken when selling convenience goods. Nor do they always take place when salespersons or sales representative sell.

LEVELS OF RETAIL SELLING OCCUPATIONS

A final item in building your foundation for learning the techniques of retail selling deals with the levels of retail selling occupations. Observe that the main differences among the levels of in-house jobs is the amount of buying assistance usually needed by customers. Note the relationship between the five buying decisions and the sales levels in the list that follows:

Salesclerk: All five buying decisions are made by the customer, usually without assistance. (The term "clerk" is derived from the word "clergy." During the Middle Ages, monks copied documents by hand. Thus, clerks are people who write orders or who ring them up on a register.)

Salesperson: The need, product, and time decisions are frequently made by customers, but they usually need help with item and price decisions.

Sales representative: Customers may need help with all five buying decisions, because the product or service requires a large investment. Numerous other titles for the position are used, such as sales agent, sales associate, account executive, and various kinds of counselors.

Some retailers refer to all salesworkers as sales associates. In this book we shall use the terms salespeople, salesworkers, and sales force to designate all sales employees who sell goods or services.

This occupational hierarchy explains, in part, the reasons underlying the differences in pay associated with the levels of sales occupations. Additional enlightenment about applications of the customer's mental stages (AIDCA) and the five buying decisions is given in later units of this book. You should now be prepared to develop the essential product and service competencies that will enable you to start your study of personal selling on the right foot.

TRADE TALK

Define each term and use it in a sentence.

Buyer's market	Salesperson
Caveat emptor	Sales representative
Convenience goods	Seller's market
and services	Shopping goods
Corporate conscience	and services
Nonpersonal selling	Specialty goods and
Personal selling	services
Salesclerk	

CAN YOU ANSWER THESE?

1. What were the causes of the demise of *caveat emptor*?

2. What are the characteristics of successful retail selling today?

3. What are the basic beliefs that characterize retail selling today?

4. What mental stages does a customer pass through when purchasing a product or service?

5. What are the buying decisions a purchaser must make during a purchase?

6. In which of the buying decisions does a salesclerk usually participate? A salesperson? A sales representative?

C·H·A·P·T·E·R

29 *Developing Product and Service Competencies*

You will recall from Chapter 28 that George Johnson didn't spend a great deal of time with each customer, yet he had a large customer following and the smallest percentage of returned goods in the menswear department. Obviously, the purchasers—who frequently had to wait while he finished with another customer—were pleased with his ability to help them select apparel that met or exceeded their expectations. In order to do that, George had to possess a high degree of product and service competency.

Therefore, George had to understand his customers' needs and wants very well, and he had to know the features and benefits of his products exceptionally well. In addition, he had to be a stock expert to be able to find a particular item quickly when he needed it for a customer.

Personal selling, merchandising, and sales promotion depend on the seller's ability to see products and services from the customer's viewpoint. This ability is the keystone of successful personal selling as well as of effective retail marketing. It is also the key to making product and service analyses and to constructing feature-benefit tables, on which this chapter focuses.

Product and service analyses and feature-benefit tables are tools used by salespeople to help them "tune in" on the purchaser's concerns when presenting merchandise or services to a customer. Both are springboards to marketing creativity.

Let's consider what causes customers to search for a given product or service. It's a condition that involves their needs, their wants, and their expectations.

UNDERSTANDING CUSTOMER NEEDS, WANTS, AND EXPECTATIONS

Customers' needs, wants, and expectations are motivators that prompt customers to do something about the condition or situation that causes them. A **need** is an unfulfilled requirement not necessarily demanding immediate supply, while a **want** or **desire** is an urge or craving to have a particular product or service. An **expectation** is the state of looking forward to the benefits resulting from a purchase. (Fulfilling expectations is a recent addition to the satisfactions that characterize the new marketing concept.)

If you are employed in a sales position, your first responsibility will be to master information about the products or services you sell. You will be required to know their location, their special features, and the benefits the customer receives from their use. The importance of this knowledge is the reason why, as a beginner in retail marketing, you may be assigned to stock work, or if you sell a service, to engaging in that service. For example, if you sell landscaping service, you would benefit from experience in doing landscaping work before you start selling the service.

Together with improving your sales and marketing abilities, product and service analysis will offer you personal satisfactions. For example, you'll get to know the merits of various brands, models, and services. And you'll learn how products should be used and cared for. You'll witness the satisfaction that customers receive from their purchases. This will give you a sense of social service in the people-oriented field of retail marketing. It will help you develop self-confidence and a sense of personal worth.

GETTING READY FOR A PRODUCT OR SERVICE ANALYSIS

To comprehend fully the procedure of product or service analysis construction, it is necessary to understand the three categories into which retail marketers group their offerings. You will recall the characteristics of the three categories of goods and services that were described in the preceding chapter—convenience, shopping, and specialty goods and services. It will be helpful to keep these categories in mind while preparing both your product or service analyses and your feature-benefit tables. The way the different types of products and services are marketed has a bearing on the selection of content while preparing the documents being discussed.

Marketing Convenience Goods and Services

Most convenience goods are presold through the media—newspapers, magazines, television, and radio—and through point-of-sale displays. Preselling reduces the need for person-to-person selling. Nevertheless, employees assigned to the sales floor must be able to locate items and identify services for customers, and also to answer brief questions. Thus, product or service analyses and feature-benefit tables have relatively little value to salesclerks, but they are of considerable worth to salespersons, sales representatives, and promotion personnel.

Can you identify the convenience goods, shopping goods, and specialty goods?

Marketing Shopping Goods and Services

Product or service analyses and feature-benefit tables are especially essential in selling shopping goods and services. Competition in shopping goods and services is based largely on strong buying appeals to consumers. These buying appeals are made through national magazine and TV advertising, personal sales service, and point-of-purchase displays. Merchandising and sales promotion personnel must thoroughly understand the products and services they sell in order to compete for the shopper's favor.

Marketing Specialty Goods and Services

To maintain the prestige of specialty goods, retailers continuously make their customers conscious of the products' unique features. So selling specialty goods usually requires even greater product or service analysis competency to reinforce the purchaser's confidence in the product or service. By and large, people who purchase specialty products and services tend to be highly discriminating customers who insist on the best service, so marketers take special precautions in training sales personnel to conform to their customers' expectations. Decision makers are likely to select a distinctive set of items when preparing a product or service analysis or feature-benefit table for specialty goods and services.

WHAT IS A PRODUCT OR SERVICE ANALYSIS?

A **product or service analysis** is a complete inventory of selling information about a product or service. It is used by all kinds of sellers—salespeople, merchandisers, and promotion personnel—in pursuing the marketing concept. Thus, product or service analysis starts with the identification of potential consumers and their needs and wants concerning a specific product or service. The logical way to analyze a product under the marketing concept is to answer questions that customers might consciously or unconsciously ask themselves during the buying process.

This approach consists of the following nine basic questions. These questions may be organized into an analytical checklist that can be modified to fit a particular product or service or group of products or services.

1. Is the product or service a convenience, shopping, or specialty item?

2. Who uses it? *(consumer characteristics)*
  a. Age, sex, marital status
  b. Approximate income level
  c. Occupational, social, and cultural background
  d. Fashion consciousness
  e. Other consumer characteristics

3. What do consumers want from it? *(need decision)*
  a. Appearance
  b. Comfort
  c. Distinctiveness
  d. Economy
  e. Prestige
  f. Protection
  g. Seasonality
  h. Security
  i. Sentiment
  j. Suitability
  k. Trade name
  l. Other satisfactions

4. How does the product or service satisfy user needs and wants? *(product or service decision)*
  a. Regular uses
  b. Advantages for each use
  c. Special or unusual uses
  d. Use with other products or services
  e. Objections raised by customers
  f. Disadvantages or limitations
  g. Special features

5. Why does the product or service satisfy consumer needs? *(brand decision, proofs)*
  a. Materials and methods used in manufacturing
  b. Quality of workmanship and construction
  c. Special features, processes, and finishes
  d. History of the product or service
  e. Availability of replacements
  f. Guarantee or warranty
  g. Other proofs

6. How much should be spent for the product or service? *(price decision)*
  a. Savings from use of product or service
  b. Potential value compared to other products or services
  c. Savings through cash payment
  d. Cost of upkeep or maintenance
  e. Competitors' prices
  f. Payment arrangements
  g. Market-price behavior
  h. Other price factors

7. Where should the product or service be purchased? *(source decision)*
    a. Company policy on customer satisfaction
    b. Customer services
    c. Quality of personal selling
    d. Other source factors
8. When should the product or service be purchased? *(time decision)*
    a. Times when the product or service is available or in season
    b. Stage of the fashion cycle
    c. Duration of sale or reduced prices
    d. Anticipated price change
    e. Time required for delivery
    f. Dates of related holidays and relevant events
    g. Other time factors
9. How should the product or service be used, cared for, or maintained? *(care and use decisions)*
    a. How to assemble the product
    b. Regular uses or applications of the product or service
    c. Special uses or applications
    d. When to use and when not to use the product or service
    e. Product care and maintenance
    f. Availability of repair service
    g. Other use and care factors

■

ACQUIRING PRODUCT OR SERVICE ANALYSIS COMPETENCY

What motivates superior merchandising personnel—salespeople in particular—to learn the basic facts about a product and keep on learning after the basic facts have been mastered? Where do they obtain the essential information? How do they develop skill in recalling and applying their knowledge when it is needed? The following sections answer these questions.

Learning to Like Product Analysis

First, superior performers like, or learn to like, the products or services they handle. This feeling grows as they gain more information. Knowledge produces enthusiasm; and enthusiasm helps sell goods and services. Salespeople receive personal satisfaction from being authorities on the products or services they sell. What may at first seem to be bothersome responsibility becomes an enjoyable challenge as they seek new sources of knowledge.

Sources of Information

The five basic sources of information are (1) direct experience, (2) other people, (3) consumer education information, (4) promotional materials, and (5) formal training.

Direct Experience Direct experience means personal contact with the product or service. The most effective direct experience is personal use of the product or service. Salespeople who use a product or service themselves are usually better informed and more enthusiastic about it. This is one reason why employers offer their staff discounts on the products they sell.

Another kind of direct experience is examining the product or service—comparing the various grades, styles, or models. This helps merchandising personnel to explain the differences to customers. Products or services may be studied while doing regular sales or stock duties, during business lulls, or during shopping trips.

Studying labels is also an excellent way to learn product and service information. As a modern merchandising tool, labels save time for both customers and salespeople.

Visits to trade shows, factories, and wholesale houses, when possible, provide valuable information. When salespeople know how products are made and distributed, they develop confidence in what they sell and in their ability to sell it.

Understanding the features of different models in a product line enables the salesperson to explain and demonstrate benefits to customers.

Other People One of the best ways to get product or service information is by talking to customers as well as to friends and relatives. Good salespeople encourage their customers and personal acquaintances to share their buying problems and their experiences with a particular product or service. By doing this they learn why customers prefer certain models, brands, and colors. For example, if you sell men's work overalls, it pays to know why some users prefer the high-back model to low-backs. Then you'll know what to recommend to future customers and probably reduce the amount of returned goods.

Experienced salespeople know and beginners soon learn that when it is done tactfully, asking their supervisors about a product or service brings good results. Successful merchandisers frequently spend part of their time on the sales floor selling and helping salespeople. Buyers, especially, have product information that is not available from other sources. For example, they probably have valuable information about the source and availability of products and services.

When possible, questioning vendor sales representatives and product or service demonstrators can be an excellent way of obtaining special information. New ideas and information may be obtained from these representatives because they come into contact with a variety of sales situations. A Chicago manufacturer of baked goods requests his sales representatives to spend some of their Saturdays behind the counters of retail stores so that they will be able to offer advice to the merchants they serve.

Obtaining product or service information from other people is a fast and easy method and often results in unique knowledge—the kind that individualizes sales and is appreciated by your customers. It often leads to additional sales. Try to develop your own technique for eliciting product and service information from others.

Consumer Education Information
The consumer movement has given rise to many ways of informing consumers about buying and using thousands of products. Consumer organizations, federal, state, and local governments, newspapers, radio and TV, and the marketers and merchandisers themselves engage in consumer education programs. For example, Consumers Union publishes *Consumer Reports*, which provides helpful buying guides and rates the various brands of products in a particular category. Knowledge of such ratings and the means of their derivation places the salesperson in good stead.

Promotional Materials Because product and service information is always changing, only the advertising and sales promotion media can supply the information a person would need to stay knowledgeable in a particular product or service area. Virtually all types of consumer advertising and displays are potential sources of information for product and service analysis. Their value lies mainly in the creativity used to persuade prospective customers. If you are at present engaged in selling, try using some of the information gleaned from a TV commercial advertising the product or service you sell.

When you are using a biased source such as promotional materials, it is necessary to separate facts from propaganda. In learning to identify basic product and service information, however, beginners in product analysis usually find the major mail-order catalogs to be a good starting point.

For their sales staffs, large manufacturers and some retailers prepare special sales training materials ranging from simple product manuals to costly visual materials and computer programs. Most of these sales training materials relate to specific products or services. Usually they are very effective.

Formal Training Some sales, merchandising, and sales promotion workers can take a shortcut to learning product and service analysis if they work for a company that of-

fers courses related to their line of work. Large department and specialty stores, franchising companies, and chain stores usually offer such courses.

Public schools also offer similar courses taught by well-qualified instructors who design the content to meet the needs of class members. Instructors preselect the necessary reading materials, which saves learners the time they would need to do this themselves. This type of guided study shortens the route to mastery of product analysis. Also, students are able to evaluate what they have learned and fill any gaps in their knowledge. Ask your teacher, vocational director, or an appropriate school administrator for information about available instruction.

If you aspire to high-level retail marketing positions in a large firm, you should investigate the means of preparation in appropriate postsecondary schools, colleges, and universities. Many of them will help you design a program to meet your special needs.

FEATURE-BENEFIT TABLE
Product/Service _____ (All-terrain Bicycle)

Features-Facts	Benefits
1. Wide, straight handlebars.	Allows rider to sit more upright than on a racing bike; rider can see better and exercise more control.
2. Rugged, easily modulated brakes.	Allows control and quick stops in all conditions.
3. High strength, light weight frame.	Withstands hardship of travel over rough terrain.
4. Low and low-low gears.	Permits pedaling at a normal pace while climbing mountains.
5. Fat tires with pronounced treads.	Plows through mud or rough terrain.
6. Quick adjustment for seat height.	An adjustment can be made without rider getting off the bike. Seat can be raised to permit full leg extension when climbing hills; seat can be lowered for better control in downhill riding.

Source: Based on Consumer Reports, February 1986, p. 97.

PREPARING FEATURE-BENEFIT TABLES

Now that you understand what a product-service analysis is and know where to get the necessary information to prepare one, an easy way to whet your appetite for developing product and service knowledge is to prepare a feature-benefit table. This is really a very simple offshoot of product and service analysis that many top salespeople use to help improve their productivity.

A **feature** is a specific fact about a product or service that describes it or a part of it. A **benefit** is a potential satisfaction or an advantage that a customer receives from a product or service. To be meaningful to a customer, the features of a product or service must be converted into specific benefits that fulfill the purchaser's needs, wants, and expectations. Customers buy what the product or service will do, rather than its features or facts about its history or manufacture.

Of course, more than one benefit may be derived from a single feature or fact. Since products and services usually embrace a number of features, which leads to even more benefits, a simple **feature-benefit table** may be prepared as a reference to be used in selling-oriented situations; see table on page 248. Customer benefits are based on customer buying motives, so checking the buying motives in the product-service analysis checklist questions on pages 245–246 may help you identify added benefits and even remind you of features previously overlooked.

Appropriate uses of the feature-benefit conversion table will be discussed a number of times in the chapters that follow. You will find it very helpful in making a merchandise approach, which you will learn about in the next chapter.

TRADE TALK

Define each term and use it in a sentence.

Benefit	Expectation
Desire	Feature
Feature-benefit table	Product or service analysis
Need	Want

CAN YOU ANSWER THESE?

1. What are the benefits to the business firm of preparing a product or service analysis? Benefits to the salesworker?

2. Why should retail salespeople, as well as management, understand the differences among convenience goods, shopping goods, and specialty goods?

3. What are the questions to be answered in a product or service analysis?

4. Which buying decisions can be answered with information from the product or service analysis?

5. How do successful salesworkers learn to like product and service analysis?

6. What are five good sources of product and service analysis information?

7. How does a salesworker use a feature-benefit table?

30 *Setting the Stage in Personal Selling*

As a Customer Assistant, your day begins as you enter the store through the Associate Entrance and proceed to the locker room. Here you will hang up your coat, put any valuables in your locker and put on your badge.

Once you have signed in on the time sheet, you will head straight for the sales floor. On your way, you will check the bulletin boards for any new associate information. You will also check the advertising boards for any advertised items that are in your department *and* in the rest of the store. Customers will ask you about advertised items in your department and other departments too. You need to be prepared to help find what they want.

Upon reaching your department, you will probably meet the merchandiser (your department head), the merchandising assistant or some other supervisor. You might talk about: where you should put the advertised items, what new items have come in, and what tasks need to be completed. A quick tour of the department will show you those items that have been discussed.

Although there are various assignments to be completed, the number one priority is to give the best customer service possible. All tasks you complete are related to sales in some way, but nothing is more important than the contact you have with each customer. The image you project and the way you act will reflect directly upon the J.C. Penney Company.*

---

*What's the Job Really Like? J.C. Penney Company, Inc., 1983.

These instructions, taken from a J.C. Penney booklet given to new employees, telegraph the image that the company intends to convey to its employees and customers. It implies the desired relationship between seller and purchaser by calling the salesperson a "customer assistant."

Even though you may work in marketing a retail service or are concerned with a small business, the concept revealed in the Penney booklet applies to your business. It will be developed more fully in the following steps of the selling process—the preapproach and the approach to the customer.

THE PREAPPROACH

The **preapproach** in personal selling includes all duties and responsibilities of a salesworker prior to meeting a customer. Its purpose is to help maximize sales by thorough preparation of the salesworker, the product or service, and the selling environment. If the sale is to take place on-site, the customer, even before seeing a salesworker, forms an impression of the company that affects the forthcoming business transaction. And, of course, when the eyes of buyer and seller meet, that initial impression is complete.

If the sale is to occur off-site, the sales representative prepares to meet the prospect by planning a presentation that is tailored to the prospect's needs. In either case, what happens when seller and buyer meet depends largely on the readiness for business achieved through the preapproach.

How do salespeople prepare to meet customers or prospects? The task entails two general responsibilities: (1) preparing yourself to meet the purchaser, and (2) ensuring that the selling environment—including the product or service—is ready for the personal contact.

Preparing Yourself to Meet the Purchaser

Preparing yourself to meet customers or clients (purchasers) entails a true service-oriented mentality. Just being courteous isn't enough to cause a customer to single you out and return to you on the next shopping trip. Customers can tell if you're sincere about serving them and whether or not you care about their needs and wants.

If you really care about customers, they'll go out of their way to please you (and you'll do the same). Caring makes selling pleasurable, whether you are dealing with products, services, or ideas. Studies show that the 20 percent of salespeople who make almost 80 percent of the total sales have a similar purpose in life—they want to make people feel good. And helping people make wise purchases contributes to their personal satisfaction. Consequently, they prepare an initial contact that communicates warmth and respect.

Both on-site and off-site sellers place high value on the first impressions that you studied in Chapter 23, so they check the appropriateness of their apparel and grooming.

Both types of salespeople check their firm's advertising to be informed about current values and prices; and they read competitors' ads as well. Some even shop the competitors in order to do a better job of counseling.

Good salespeople keep current on fashions and technology, and they read magazines and newspapers in order to serve their clientele effectively. All of these activities instill self-confidence in both kinds of sellers, and they furnish the knowledge needed for bona fide retail marketing service.

Preapproach activities of off-site sales representatives differ from those of their on-site counterparts because the buyer has the controlling voice in the location of the meeting. Therefore, the sales representatives' responsibilities rest primarily in gathering pertinent information about the prospect and planning a product or service presentation that is meaningful and saves time. Fortified with such knowledge, they are able to select appropriate promotional literature, samples, and other sales supporting materials for the pending demonstration.

Preparing the Selling Environment

Although the preapproach activities of off-site salespeople seem to have remained relatively constant in recent years, those of salesclerks and many salespersons have increased markedly. Many on-site salesworkers perform an important role in visual merchandising, selling through the use of sight only. Thus, in order to portray the product or service at its best, they are responsible for stocking and restocking displays and shelves, straightening stock, folding textile merchandise, checking supplies, adjusting price tickets, keeping the selling area neat and tidy, and many other seemingly stockkeeping tasks.

Getting the workplace ready and putting merchandise and supplemental sales equipment (such as measuring devices, sample books, and catalogs) back where they belong have become among the most important tasks in the preapproach.

If you sell products, knowing where your merchandise is kept in your department is just as important as knowing its advantages. If you cannot find an item, or if you take too long to find it, the customer will be exasperated. Also, customers lose confidence and often distrust salesworkers who do not know their stock. Knowing the location and/or availability of the product or service you sell pays

To attract customers to self-service displays, salespeople can prepare the merchandise and the selling area by dusting and cleaning them.

good dividends. Here are some of the advantages to a salesperson of knowing where stock is located:

■ You do not lose sales needlessly because you can't find an item.
■ You save time that may be used to serve other customers.
■ You are able to act incisively and in a businesslike manner, which encourages your customer to do likewise.
■ You inspire greater confidence on the part of customers.
■ Your self-confidence increases, and as a result, you sell better and with more assurance.

In a similar manner, a service salesworker will reap comparable benefits.

■

THE APPROACH

The following statement of a frustrated salesperson is not unusual.

> "When I notice that a customer is interested in something, I approach that customer, and in a pleasing voice I say, 'May I help you?' It seems that nine times out of ten the customer says, 'No thanks, I'm just looking,' and walks away. I suppose that I should be used to it by now, but it burns me up."

Why does the salesperson relating this experience get "burned up" because customers nearly always walk away? Why do they walk away?

This salesperson doesn't approach customers in an effective manner because the chances are that he is interrupting their thinking with "May I help you?"—a poor approach in this situation. Moreover, none of us likes to be sold anything, but we do like to buy. So, many customers will respond with the excuse, "I'm just looking."

Successful salespeople understand how customers like to be approached, the best time to approach them, and what to say and do while opening the sale. They realize that initiating the sales process calls for zeroing in on their customers' thoughts and feelings.

Objectives of the Approach

A great Finnish runner once confided that a race is won or lost during the first few seconds. Likewise, many sales are won or get off to a good start during those first few moments when buyer and seller meet. It's something like being introduced to a new acquaintance; you notice whether the handshake is hearty, whether the words of greeting are warm and friendly, whether the person seems genuinely interested in meeting you. That first impression, in many cases, determines whether you really like that person or not.

What really happens during that flash of time? What do you, the seller, want to accomplish? Defining the objectives and keeping them in mind is critical, because each meeting is different—the individuals, the time, and the situation vary widely, and if the seller is sincere about serving individuals, the approach should vary with each sale.

With goals firmly in mind, the seller senses what to do. Although goals may be adjusted to meet the current situation, the commonly accepted goals are the following:

1. Establish a friendly, receptive atmosphere.

2. Convey the impression that serving the buyer has top priority.

3. Instill confidence and generate trust in the seller.

4. Focus attention on the product or service and proceed with the buying decisions.

How Customers Want to Be Approached

A good clue to achieving the objectives of an approach is to consider your own feelings when being approached by a salesworker.

Customers usually enter a place of business because they want to purchase something, though sometimes they are only interested in getting ideas or information regarding a future purchase. Occasionally they're just looking around with the thought in mind that they may find a bargain. Whatever their reason for coming in, your job as a salesworker is to get in tune with their thinking and help them achieve *their* purpose.

Customers Like to Feel Welcome
Abraham Lincoln said, "If you would win a man to your cause, first convince him that you are his good friend." All good salesworkers have learned from experience the wisdom of Mr. Lincoln's suggestion. Even when everything seems to go wrong and they don't feel like being friendly, they make their customers feel that they are glad to see them.

Customers Want to Feel Important
Nearly all buyers think of themselves as being important, at least when shopping. When they have money to spend, they like to think that they are appreciated. Regardless of the customer's appearance, manner, or the quality of product or service they ask for, seasoned salespeople treat their customers respectfully and make them feel important from the very start, by making a courteous sales approach. This practice applies to children as well as adults.

Customers Like to Have Confidence in a Salesworker
Most customers feel that they work hard for their money and want to get as much as possible for it. For this reason they prefer salespeople who take a genuine interest in their problems. They like to believe that the seller is competent and

willing to help them select the product or service that, within the limits of their pocketbooks, will best meet their needs.

Customers Expect Prompt Attention

Even though they are just looking around, honest customers like to feel that their presence is known and appreciated. Attention is a subtle form of flattery. Time your approach to the customer's actions, as effective salesworkers do. When customers enter the selling area hurriedly and seem anxious to buy, approach them briskly. On the other hand, when customers come in and wander around in a leisurely way, approach them in an unhurried manner but with unmistakable interest. If customers just want to look around, encourage them to do so and point out something in particular to look at. It is important to observe tactfully the "just-looking" customer and watch for clues indicating that the customer is at the point of needing assistance.

Types of Approaches

The **approach** is the first direct contact with the customer during those few seconds when the seller and customer meet. If a salesperson is stationed behind a counter, the customer usually comes to the salesperson. More often, the salesperson is free to move around a given area and usually goes to any customer who enters the area.

There are three basic approaches—the greeting approach, the service approach, and the merchandise approach—plus the informal approach. Salespeople choose an approach according to the circumstances.

The Greeting Approach As its name suggests, the **greeting approach** involves addressing a customer or prospect—either with a general greeting such as "Good morning" or with a greeting and the customer's name—before the person has shown interest in any particular kind of product or service.

Either the buyer has just come to you, has just entered your department, or, if you are a sales representative, you are calling on the purchaser.

Words are only part of making buyers feel welcome, important, and confident in your ability to serve them well. The tone of your voice, your facial expression, and your inflections and gestures show your attitude and can help you make a natural, friendly approach.

Treat your customers as if they were guests in your home. Greet them by name if you can. Usually, the appropriate form of address to use is based on relative age: the first name for children; the social title (Mr., Dr., and so on) for people older than yourself. First names may be appropriate for people your age in some business firms, such as men's specialty shops. If you don't know your customer's name, you may say "Sir" or "Ma'am" or just "Good afternoon" or "Good evening." Customers will usually return your greeting and indicate what product or service interests them. If you know your customer's name, use it throughout the sale.

After you have greeted your customer, *wait*. Don't move, and don't say anything for about 4 seconds. This gives your customer a chance to respond. Within those 4 seconds, most customers will tell you what they want, thus putting you in a good position to continue the sale.

The Service Approach When you ask a polite question that indicates your willingness to be of service, you are using a **service approach**. Some firms that distribute mostly convenience goods insist on a service approach and usually encourage a greeting to go with it. However, "May I help you?" or "What can I do for you?" can become monotonous to customers and also make selling routine and uninteresting. "How can I help you?" is an open-ended question that is much better. "Good morning, is someone serving you?" is an acceptable question to a waiting customer.

Customers should be made to feel as welcome as a guest in your own home.

The Merchandise Approach When competent salespeople notice a customer paying attention, indicating interest in an item, they make a comment or ask a question that helps move the customer from the attention or interest stage to the desire stage. This reference to the product or service is called a **merchandise approach**. If the salesperson at the beginning of this discussion of the approach had used the merchandise approach, the customer might not have walked away. When applied skillfully, the merchandise approach is an effective tool to increase personal sales. For example, a fitting remark to a customer examining a pair of curtains made of polyester might be, "Those polyester curtains will look just as fresh after they have been washed many times." A few more comments may instill desire and convince the customer to take action.

The effectiveness of a merchandise approach depends on the appropriateness of your opening comments and how well they match what the customer is thinking at the time. You can usually get clues by observing the customer's behavior. For example, a customer who is examining a price tag is likely to be interested in price or size. One who is reading a label may be concerned about material, construction, or warranty. One who is handling an article may want to know about the quality of workmanship and material.

In the absence of a definite clue, you can direct the customer's attention to more general interests such as (1) popular items, (2) special values, and (3) items with unusual appeals. Your opening words should contain a special appeal to the customer's needs and quickly get the customer to transfer from the salesperson to the merchandise.

The merchandise approach holds great promise for successfully leading into a presentation of the product or service. It tends to preclude a negative response. Remember, once customers answer negatively to an approach, they usually put themselves on the defensive, and it may be difficult for them to reverse that position and admit that they have a question or would like some help. However, if you make an appropriate merchandise approach, it's irrational for a shopper to respond with "No, I'm just looking." When practicing this purchaser-oriented technique, keep in mind that its purpose is to serve the buyer by volunteering useful information pertaining to the wise purchase of a product or service and not to psychologically outwit the prospective purchaser.

The Informal Approach The **informal approach** is really a personalized greeting based on a preexisting relationship. For example, one might say to an acquaintance, "Hi, Claire, how are you today?" or to a steady customer, "Greetings, Mrs. Gross, did your daughter like that Boundary Waters sweater you purchased for her last week?" Any remark that makes the customer feel good will do, as long as it's in good taste.

When to Approach the Customer

Usually, the time to approach a customer is as soon as the customer enters the sales area. However, you may be busy serving another customer. In most cases it is wise to wait on customers in order of their arrival.

Even if you are busy with another customer, you should still acknowledge the arrival of the second customer. Exactly how you do this depends on which buying stage the first customer has reached.

If the first customer is just about ready to buy and requires your full attention, simply look up at the second customer, smile, nod, and concentrate on completing the first sale.

If the first customer still needs your attention but is not quite ready to buy, say to the second customer, "I (or somebody) will be with you in a moment."

If the first customer is still at an early buying stage and doesn't need your constant attention, excuse yourself from the first customer for a moment, greet the second customer, identify the latter's need, and then return to the first customer.

Sometimes you'll be able to wait on several customers at a time. For example, you may find this necessary when you're selling garments that need to be tried on or products the customer may want to consider carefully, such as wallpaper. However, you should begin to serve only as many customers as you can handle at once. A customer who feels neglected is likely to depart quickly—and often permanently.

This concludes your introduction to the important first steps in the personal selling process (the preapproach and the approach). The preapproach provides the assurance needed for an effective approach. And as you now know, selecting and executing the approach are important tasks because they set the stage for a selling process tailored to the individual customer.

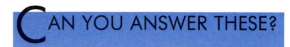
TRADE TALK

Define each term and use it in a sentence.

Approach	Merchandise approach
Greeting approach	Preapproach
Informal approach	Service approach

CAN YOU ANSWER THESE?

1. List four preapproach duties of a salesperson.

2. How do prudent salespeople prepare themselves for customer and client contacts? Prepare the product or service? Prepare the selling environment?

3. What are the objectives of an approach?

4. How do customers like to be approached? Expect to be approached?

5. Under what conditions should each of the four approaches be used?

6. Explain why an appropriate merchandise approach is more effective than other types of approaches and how experienced salespeople determine what to say.

7. How does a good salesperson know when to approach a customer?

8. What do salespeople who are busy with a customer say to customers who are waiting to be served?

Unit 10   Understanding the Selling Function

RETAIL MARKETING CASES

1. While studying this unit on understanding the selling process, Jon Hudson saw the value of knowing when to use the three types of sales analysis: the buying-decision approach, the mental-stages approach, and the steps-of-a-sale approach. He wanted to see which approach(es), if any, the salespeople, the promotion people, and the merchandising people were using.

Although obtaining valid answers to this question would require resources beyond those available, his instructor encouraged him to plan an informal study of a limited sample of retail workers on Main Street. If he were to conduct such a study, how would Jon proceed?

1. What kinds of businesses should be included in the survey?

2. Which job titles should be surveyed?

3. What should he know about each interviewee?

4. When and how should each interview be conducted?

5. What questions should be asked of the interviewees?

6. What else should Jon know?

7. What do you anticipate Jon would find out?

2. Amy Anderson was disappointed because she was assigned to stock work rather than to a selling position in a high-fashion women's wear specialty shop. She had prepared herself for sales work, hoping some day to own or manage a shop. When she was hired, the manager had said that it was store policy to start all sales and merchandising personnel in the stock room. Amy thought the idea was old-fashioned, but she took the job anyway.

1. Should Amy take a position about which she is not enthusiastic?

2. Will her attitude toward her job be reflected in her work? How?

3. What are the possible reasons why the management assigns new personnel to stock work?

4. How can stock work help Amy to prepare herself for a selling job?

5. What activities regarding product analysis would you recommend that she engage in? Regarding customer buying decisions?

PROBLEM

Rule a form similar to the one below. In the left column, write the letter of each of the following statements made by customers: (o) My hands seem a little rough. (a) I know Donaldson's has beautiful shoes, but I can't get there without a car. (b) My mother would be upset if I spent that much on a blouse. (c) I'm sick of wearing the same jacket winter after winter. (d) Only ten more shopping days until Christmas. (e) I like the blue in that rug, but I know my husband prefers brown. Then add the numbers of these questions made by salespersons: (1) That's a real value at that price, isn't it? (2) We have usually been able to find the right thing together, haven't we? (3) No wardrobe would be complete without a tuxedo, would it? (4) Of course, you will want to wear this sweater to the game Saturday, won't you? (5) That princess dress is certainly your style, isn't it? In the right column, indicate whether the statement relates to a need, produce, place, price, or time decision.

Statement or Question	Buying Decision
Example: 0	Need

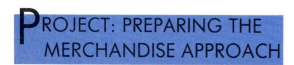

PROJECT: PREPARING THE MERCHANDISE APPROACH

YOUR PROJECT GOAL

Given two products or services and a product or service analysis sheet, interview five customers and determine whether, in each case, their reasons for buying revolved around a product or service feature or a personal benefit. Prepare an effective merchandise approach for each product or service.

PROCEDURE

1. Consult your teacher about your selection of two products or services that are suitable for your feature-benefit conversion table. Students who work in retail stores or service businesses should choose products or services they sell on their jobs.

2. Construct two feature-benefit tables like the one on page 248. Put one of the products or services you have chosen on each page.

3. For each product or service, interview five customers who have just purchased the product or service from you. (Students who are not employed in sales work may interview friends and relatives.) Ask each customer why he or she bought the product or service. If the reason is based on a product feature, record the particular feature in the right column; if it pertains to a benefit, record the particular benefit in the left column.

4. Circle those benefits and features that occur more than once.

5. Compare your lists with those of your classmates who selected the same product or service. On a separate sheet of paper, list all the circled items and rank them in order of their popularity.

6. Write as many effective opening remarks about the product or service as you can for use in making a merchandise approach. In doing so, use the most popular features and benefits.

7. Prepare a brief skit in which you assume that the customer is interested in either or both of two products. Have the salesperson use a merchandise approach that stresses the benefits and features you have found to be most popular in this project.

EVALUATION

You will be evaluated on your ability to match product or service features with customer-benefits in a merchandise approach that gets the customer's prompt attention, makes the customer feel welcome, important, confident in you, and focuses attention on the product or service.

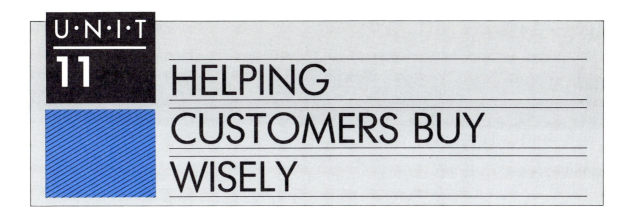

C·H·A·P·T·E·R

31 *Identifying Customer Wants and Needs*

One morning a smartly dressed young woman entered the men's furnishings department where Kevin Mills worked and asked to see some black neckties. Assuming that the tie was to be worn with a uniform, as is so often the case, Kevin took two black four-in-hand neckties from a rack—one a very serviceable Botany brand and the other a competitive but lesser-quality tie. Because he thought that the higher-priced tie was a much better value, Kevin took special pains to present it properly. He described its features and benefits in detail, showing the long staple wool bias-cut lining and the cravat construction, and he crumpled the tie to demonstrate its resistance to wrinkles.

After listening patiently to his sales talk, Kevin's customer said courteously, "I appreciate the information, young man, and normally I really would buy the better tie, but I'll take the inexpensive one today. You see, for my purpose it will serve just as well—my uncle's going to be buried in it."

■

THE TASK OF IDENTIFYING WANTS AND NEEDS

Certainly, Kevin's traumatic experience would never have happened to George Johnson, who was introduced to you in Chapter 28, because George realized fully the objectives and importance of properly identifying (not determining) customer wants and needs. George saw the purpose of Step 3 in the selling process like this:

■ To identify the satisfactions a customer seeks. (The identification process frequently continues into the next step of the sale.)
■ To give the customer confidence in the seller's ability to help solve his or her purchasing problem and feel that the salesperson cares.
■ To provide the salesperson with clues for a good presentation of the product or service.

Through meaningful past experiences, George knew that careful identification of the purchaser's wants and needs brought the following results that were appreciated by his customers, his employer, and his co-workers on the sales floor.

■ Saves the purchaser's time as well as that of the seller—both customer and salesperson benefit.

■ Prevents confusing the customer by introducing inappropriate items—both customer and salesperson benefit.

■ Reduces returned merchandise or cancelled sales—customer, employer, and salesperson all benefit.

■ Reduces stockwork, returning stock to where it belongs—co-workers and salesperson benefit.

■ Increases self-confidence and provides the personal satisfaction of performing a social service—everyone to whom the salesperson relates benefits from his or her behavior.

Identification of customer wants and needs is the most critical part of a sales transaction, both from the economic standpoint of maximizing sales and from the perspective of the salesperson's performing a social service. Everything that happens after Step 3 depends on it. And in highly competitive situations, alert, empathetic detection of wants is crucial to ensuring repeat sales.

■

FACTORS DETERMINING CUSTOMER WANTS AND NEEDS

Customers make purchases because they have a want or a need that they believe the purchase will satisfy. No matter how attractive the features of a product or service may be, if it does not satisfy a customer's particular want or need, he or she is unlikely to buy it. When a customer believes that a product or service does satisfy a want or need, then the sale should be closed.

Not all customers need help in making their selection, but to provide good customer service, be quick to recognize the customer who needs help.

Successful, experienced sales personnel instinctively recognize the difference between a specific customer's needs and his or her wants, and they serve their customers accordingly. Most sales transactions that take place on the sales floor involve serving customer wants, because most shoppers who come to a place of business know what they need. First, let's examine the matter of assessing a customer's wants and then talk about needs.

Differences in Awareness of Wants

If a customer's awareness of a need is strong enough to do something about it, it is termed a *want*. Customers can be divided into three groups according to the strength of their wants.

1. *Customers who know exactly what they want*: An example of such a customer is a nurse who needs new shoes for her work at a hospital, knows the brand, size, and width she wants, and asks for them. Most grocery purchases are made by customers who know exactly what they want.

2. *Customers who have a general idea of what they want*: They are not sure about the specific article or service they intend to buy and are open to suggestions. For example, when shopping for fashion clothing, customers usually know the occasion for which the garment will be worn, but they have not decided on the specific features it should have.

3. *Customers who have no particular need in mind*: They have given no thought to what they want. They enjoy shopping and, when approached properly, are open to suggestions. A service-minded salesperson is able to help "just-looking" customers identify their needs and wants.

Differences in Consciousness of Needs

Customers who contact the seller usually have well-defined needs. However, they may also have real needs but do not realize that they have those needs. Such needs are called **latent needs**. A conscious need, on the other hand, is one about which the customer is well aware. Successful salespeople assess their customers' concern for the need and provide the assistance needed to identify it. Through proper questions and alert listening (to be discussed later in this chapter), they work with their customers to arrive at the most appropriate product or service to fulfill their needs.

HOW TO IDENTIFY CUSTOMER WANTS AND NEEDS

Graciously assisting customers in defining their needs and in refining their wants is a "skill" that distinguishes professional sales personnel from their less sophisticated co-workers. It's a way of treating customers that elicits a warm relationship between buyer and seller. It's not just what the salesperson does; it's how the salesperson does it. It's empathy and a sincere desire to serve. Sometimes, it requires much patience.

Identifying customer's needs and wants takes keen perception. Here is how a top saleswoman responded to an oral interviewer who probed the techniques of helping customers buy:

> You make things harder for yourself if you don't study your customer. There are so many little things one notices that tell you right away how to act. For instance, the way they walk, what they look for, and how they talk. You can see a lot without your customer's knowing it if you know what to look for.

With the perceptive salesworker in mind, let's discuss the three kinds of sales situations described above, starting with what usually is the simplest case.

Serving Customers Who Know Exactly What They Want

It's easy to serve customers who know exactly what they want if you have the item or can deliver the service. If you can provide the requested product or service, you can quickly get the article or describe the service and find out whether some related product or service is needed. However, certain precautions may be necessary.

Verifying the Specifications Sometimes a customer wants a specific product or service but forgets one of the necessary specifications. Or you may suspect that one of the specifications is wrong—shoe size, for example. In either case, the specifications should be verified, for if the customer takes home the wrong product or orders the wrong service, you will not have succeeded in making a satisfactory sale.

Selling Substitute Products Most customers like to be served quickly, especially when they want a specific item. If you don't have the item they ask for, they will often accept your suggestion for something to take its place. Selling a product or service or a brand other than that requested by the customer is called **substitute selling**. When you do substitute selling, remember the following rules:

■ Be sure that the article you suggest as a substitute will serve the customer's needs as well as or better than the article requested.

■ Don't criticize the article originally requested. If you hint that the requested item is inferior, the customer might interpret your statement as an insult.

■ Here are six actions that you might take to sell a substituted item for the one originally requested:

1. Make a sincere attempt to locate the requested article if the firm carries the line of merchandise.

2. Bring out the substitute merchandise.

3. Tell the customer that it is not the brand, style, or color requested.

4. Inquire about the intended use of the article.

5. Point out the features that are similar to those in the requested article.

6. Point out additional features if the substitute article is of a better grade.

A customer will often accept a substitute if persuaded that it will satisfy his or her needs as well as or better than the product first requested.

Serving Customers Who Have a General Idea of Their Wants

Shopping goods and services are usually purchased by customers in this category. For example, a customer may be interested in buying a typewriter without having any particular size, model, or brand in mind. Here is how you would help this type of customer define needs and clarify wants.

Asking the Right Questions Success in serving an impartial customer depends largely on asking the right questions in the right way. There is certain information you'll always need before being able to select the appropriate product or service to present to a customer. For example, suppose that a customer says, "I'd like to look at a typewriter." Your first job is to determine how she or he intends to use that typewriter. You might ask the customer, "Something for your personal use?" The answer will enable you to pick out and show the models of typewriters most likely to satisfy that need. Questions about the use of a product or service are usually open questions. They create the impression that you're interested in solving the customer's problem and not trying to dismiss him or her.

Other factual questions, such as "leather or fabric?" when selling drivers' gloves, are used to advance the sale. Further questions may be used to test a customer's feelings and coax an opinion from a customer who talks very little. Directional questions may be used to speed up a purchase for a customer who is in a hurry.

Take care to avoid the impression that you are cross-examining the customer. Don't ask too many questions—you may lose the sale before you've even had a chance to present your product or service. Don't ask a long series of questions, such as "What size?" "What color?" "What kind of material?" "About how much would you like to pay?" Here are the dangers of these kinds of questions:

■ They may force the customer to make snap decisions concerning a point to which little thought has been given.
■ The answers to specific questions of this type usually restrict the variety of merchandise or services that may be presented.
■ Numerous direct questions increase the danger of being out of stock or not being able to provide the product or service.
■ The customer may feel that you don't want to present a broad selection.

Learning what questions to ask, when to ask them, and how to ask them requires concentrated study. Consider asking your teacher to share his or her knowledge of the art of questioning. Both selling and teaching depend a great deal on the use of thought-provoking questions.

Listen With Your Ears Listening will be one of your most valuable skills as a salesperson. It is important throughout the sale and is especially critical when you are identifying customer wants and needs.

Many times you will be able to appraise your customer's desires by listening carefully to what is being said and particularly to how it is said. If you're alert, the speed of speech, tone of voice, inflection given to certain words, and even the accent will be meaningful. The art of listening, which requires discipline and practice, is discussed in Chapter 23. A customer's silence isn't necessarily a sign of disapproval. A silent customer is communicating too. Silence may be another way of saying "Go ahead, I'm listening." Pause occasionally, so that you don't miss the customer's message.

Listen with Your Eyes Pay attention to your customer with your eyes as well as your ears. Customers may not say what they think or feel. Often you can gauge what might interest your customers by their body language. For example, it is an accepted fact that the pupils of people's eyes enlarge significantly when they see something that is especially pleasing. This involuntary reaction is far more reliable to the salesperson who observes it than any verbal statement.

If you think this knowledge gives you an advantage, you're right. You must remember, however, that your customers, if they are perceptive, can also use the technique on you.

If you don't look your customers in the eye as you are talking, they are likely to be suspicious of what you are saying. A straightforward, honest manner is vital.

The next time you have an opportunity to observe two or three good salespeople, study how they use their eyes to communicate and notice the way they actively participate when you do the talking. Compare their techniques.

Serving Customers Who Are Unaware of Their Needs

Customers who are unaware of their needs present an interesting challenge, even if you are an experienced salesperson or a sales representative. They really don't plan to buy. Their attention can be won relatively easily if they have just finished a purchase and you are able to make an appropriate suggestion—suggestion selling, a technique to be discussed later. It may be more difficult if they are in your place of business and "just looking." And it is a distinct challenge if you are a sales representative prospecting for customers with latent needs for life insurance, real estate, home improvements, education, or donations to a charity. House-to-house canvassing and telemarketing call for special techniques.

It is necessary to convince such customers that they have a need and explain to them how your product or service can satisfy that need. That entails high-level competencies.

You will recall from your study of the five buying decisions in Chapter 28 that a sales representative helps a customer make all five buying decisions, especially the need decision. After receiving favorable attention, the next step in selling products or services that

Sales representatives for financial services, real estate, and other services face a special challenge in customers who are unconscious of their need or do not know how to satisfy it.

require large investments such as insurance, financial assistance, and real estate is **qualifying the customer**—that is, obtaining the information needed to assess the customer's needs cooperatively. This may call for special training and, in some cases, certain education and licenses. Qualifying a customer's needs for a product or service demands all of the questioning, listening, and observation skills mentioned above.

In this chapter, you've learned how to identify customers' wants and needs. But to be a successful salesperson, you'll also want to know how to demonstrate products and services effectively and how to help customers make buying decisions, which are discussed in Chapters 32 and 33.

TRADE TALK

Define each term and use it in a sentence.

Latent needs
Qualifying the customer

Substitute selling

1. Why is the identification of the customer's wants and needs the most critical step in the sales process?

2. Why should salespeople be able to discern the difference between the purchaser's wants and needs? Which of these is most important in serving customers in today's market?

3. What are the essential differences when identifying the needs of customers who know exactly what they want, those who have a general idea about their wants, and those who are unaware of their needs?

4. What steps should be taken when substituting a product or service for one that you do not have?

5. List four suggestions for asking customers questions about their wants and needs?

6. List four examples of nonverbal clues that can help you interpret customer's reactions to your efforts to identify their wants and needs. What are the responsibility and procedure for serving customers who are unaware of their needs?

C·H·A·P·T·E·R
32 Demonstrating Products and Services

Two people were doing their weekly shopping in a supermarket. While passing through the central aisle, one of them put an attractive, brightly colored package of cereal from an eye-level shelf in her shopping cart and went quickly on her way. The other shopper stopped, compared the weight of the contents and prices of the various brands, checked the store coupons, chose the best buy, and crossed "cereal" off his shopping list.

The differences in the shopping habits of these two customers may seem unimportant to most people. But to retailers, the shopping habits of consumers are important. Retailers analyze consumer shopping habits to find the reasons why and how people buy. Knowledge of the satisfactions customers seek from a given product or service and priorities given to those potential satisfactions is the key to retail selling and sales promotion. These preferences are **buying motives**, or the needs and wants that cause people to buy.

A working knowledge of consumer buying motives will help you understand why an individual buys a certain product or service. It will also help you get a good start on a career in retail marketing. Applying your knowledge of consumer buying motives to retail activities is a basic competency, or skill, that all retail workers need—from entry-level to top-management positions. In today's fast-changing markets, all types of marketers are highly dependent on research concerning customer buying motives. So the time you spend studying why and how people buy will offer a good return on your investment.

■

WHY PEOPLE BUY

In Chapter 29, the feature-benefit technique was recommended as the preferred method of helping purchasers satisfy their product and service needs and wants. That procedure focuses the seller's attention on the interests and concerns of the primary decision maker and hopefully results in a mutually satisfactory buying decision. This chapter deals with the critical benefits component of the feature-benefit approach.

To a *novice* salesworker, matching benefits to the features of a product or service may seem a simple task. Selecting suitable benefits during a sales presentation is, however, more complex. Understanding customer benefits entails knowledge of the psychology of human needs and motivations to buy. Such knowledge is required if you are to be able to put yourself in the purchaser's shoes.

Understanding the psychology of differences in the behavior of customers, such as the two supermarket shoppers above, is crucial to successful retailing. Retail marketers must know why their customers or clients buy and how they buy in order to help them satisfy their product and service wants and needs.

Human Needs—What Comes First

For a long time, marketers have known that people assign priorities to their needs and alter their values when conditions change. Psychologists identify this phenomenon as the process of clarifying and ordering human needs. Keeping this concept in mind will help you tailor your sales presentations to your customers' needs and wants.

Everyone has certain physical and psychological needs that are vital to happiness. A. H.

Maslow named the following needs in order of their importance:

1. *Physical needs*: Food, drink, sex, and shelter are needs that people try to satisfy first.

2. *Safety needs*: Next, the individual seeks security, family stability, and protection from danger.

3. *Social or love needs*: These include the need for affection and social acceptance.

4. *Need for self-esteem*: People who feel socially accepted may then attempt to gain self-respect or self-esteem.

5. *Self-actualization*: People who reach this highest need level have achieved most of their life goals and want to express things in a personal way in their decisions and value judgments. They may donate money to causes that benefit others as well as themselves.

Psychologists believe that as soon as one of our needs is satisfied, another demands to be fulfilled. As long as a person is hungry or thirsty, for example, he or she will not spend time and energy seeking social acceptance. But when the physical needs have been met, social needs become important motivators.

From your experience, you can realize that people usually try to satisfy their needs on several of these levels at the same time. Also,

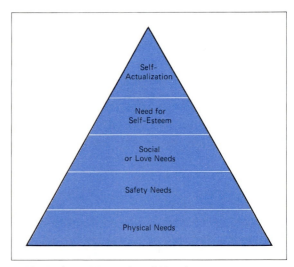

A. H. Maslow's Hierarchy of Needs

the needs on any given level are seldom satisfied completely; people are almost always ready to accept more affection, more security, and more money.

Lifestyle Affects Buying Motives The ways in which consumers interpret and satisfy their needs and wants depend on many factors: age, climate, cultural background, customs, group affiliations, income, occupation, resource availability, goals, and personal values are all important influences in making buying decisions. But as these factors change, of course, consumers' needs and wants also change.

Among the most consistent and rapidly changing areas of consumer needs and wants are those associated with lifestyle stages. (See Chapter 12.) As the age, income, and marital status of a consumer change, different needs and wants emerge. These changes in needs and wants are reflected in *consumer buying patterns*—the combination of products and services consumed. Table 1 shows the needs and wants that are likely to predominate among different consumer age groups along with the likely purchases during each life stage.

Consumer Preferences Shift Consciously or unconsciously, each consumer develops needs and wants and places them in order of importance. Consumers base the order of their needs and wants on their personal concepts of value and efficiency. When they make intelligent choices, they allow for emotional as well as clear-headed buying motives in satisfying their needs and wants.

A consumer's priorities may shift with each succeeding purchase of a product, because every new purchase affects his or her value system. Every purchase increases the con-

TABLE 1 / MAJOR MOTIVATION AND BUYING PATTERNS BY LIFE-CYCLE STAGE

Age Group	Major Needs and Wants	Buying Patterns
Children	Physical comfort and pleasure, affection	Toys, food, candy
Teenagers	Social (love) needs, pleasure, self-esteem	Clothes, cosmetics, recreation, education
Teenage parents	Security, shelter, family stability, social acceptance	Housing, food, baby products, insurance
Young couples without children	Self-esteem, social acceptance, pleasure	Car, furniture, TV, VCR, recreation, education
Young couples with children	Safety needs, family stability, affection, shelter	Insurance, home, toys, major appliances, car
Single working women with children	Food and shelter, security, affection	Children's needs, housing, insurance, education
Single working males and females	Self-esteem, social needs, self-actualization	Car, entertainment, education, travel
Middle-aged couple	Social acceptance, self-esteem, self-actualization, protection	New furniture and appliances, car, fancy foods, travel
Older married couple	Self-actualization, self-esteem, security, affection	Art, theater, donations, travel, recreation
Retired couple	Self-actualization, affection, protection from danger	Theater, travel, donations
Single older person	Physical comfort, safety, self-esteem, self-actualization	Medical care, housing, recreation, donations

sumer's desire to buy and consume more. And often, consumers make purchases in terms of the relationship of the product or service to an earlier transaction. If that experience was positive, chances are that consumers will try to repeat it. This is why management is so concerned about customer-oriented personal selling. Each sale affects the next one.

Values Control Buying Motives

There are many known and unknown forces that influence our buying motives. They determine the origin, intensity, and priority of consumer needs and wants. One known force is our value system.

Every customer has a different system of values. **Values** are convictions about things one considers good, important, or beautiful. Values may be moral, social, esthetic, cultural, or economic. They are learned from parents, teachers, friends, peers, clergy, and so on. Values are involved in every situation that calls for a choice.

Values come from many internal and external sources. Individual customers are products of their own cultural background and environment, and they are members of a number of social groups that influence their needs and wants.

Since customers usually come from a variety of cultural and group backgrounds, retailers cannot impose their values on their clientele. Nor is the retailer likely to do much about the external influences on individuals, such as their income and use of their time. However, the more a retailer understands human behavior, the greater is the likelihood of satisfying the needs of his or her clientele.

Types of Buying Motives

Buying motives can be divided into three broad categories: rational, emotional, and patronage motives. If you are engaged in personal selling or sales promotion tasks, it's important to know whether to appeal to rational motives or emotional motives and how to capitalize on patronage motives.

Rational Buying Motives

When consumer purchases involve carefully calculated reasoning, they are based on **rational buying motives**. They include such considerations as economy, efficiency, dependability, and saving of time, money, or space. Rational motives are always conscious. Many purchases are definitely based on rational motives. For example, the purchase of prescription drugs, men's socks, or school textbooks is nearly always based on rational motives.

Emotional Buying Motives

When consumer purchases involve feelings such as pride, comfort, and romance, they are based on **emotional buying motives**. These emotional motives may occur either independently or together with rational buying motives. The customer may or may not be conscious of them. Emotional motives may have a more important influence on buying decisions than do rational motives. In fact, many customers convince themselves that they are using rational motives while actually justifying an emotional purchase. For example, a customer may claim to be buying a Mercedes car for reliable performance when the real reason is prestige; here an emotional purchase is obviously being justified with a rational argument. Spur-of-the-moment purchases on impulse are frequently emotional.

Patronage Buying Motives

So far in this chapter we have discussed the customer's motives for buying certain products or services. But when the same or equally suitable purchases can be made in several business houses, the customer selects one of the sources for patronage reasons. **Patronage buying motives** are those that cause a customer to buy from one business instead of another. Patronage buying motives may be either rational or emotional.

Patronage buying motives stem from the firm's image in the trading area. In the mind of a consumer, a business firm's image may be judged on the basis of his or her value system or past experience with the company. For example, a customer may shop a certain business first because it is easy to return goods there. Table 2 lists various patronage motives together with examples of customer benefits associated with the motives.

TABLE 2 / RELATING PATRONAGE MOTIVES TO CUSTOMER BENEFITS

Patronage Motive	Customer Benefit
Customer policies	Satisfaction with goods and services, returns, and adjustments
Integrity	Fair dealing, truthful advertising, and reliability
Fashion cycle	Up-to-date merchandise and suitable styles
Quality of merchandise	Purity, freshness, and excellence of goods
Shopping atmosphere	Store layout, decor, noise factor, cleanliness, and lighting
Assortment policy	Number of lines stocked and adequacy of selection
Courteous treatment	Courtesy of sales staff and other personnel
Customer services	Credit, delivery, gift wrapping, and carry-out service

The percentage of sales completed in relation to the number of shoppers entering the place of business is related to the strength of a firm's appeal to the patronage motive. It is difficult to estimate what the percentage of sales closed should be; so much depends on what is being sold to whom. However, a rule of thumb is that more than 50 percent of the customers who enter the place of business should be sold something, and 70 to 80 percent is not an uncommon achievement. This is why management is so concerned about how customers are treated.

Getting Buying Motives to Work for You

Whether you are a salesperson or you have a nonsales job, when you're at work, always keep in mind that people buy for *their* reasons, not yours. And don't lose sight of the fact that people *hate* to be sold, but they *love* to buy.

Reflect for a moment on your own shopping experience. When you feel you're being sold, you question the intent of the other person and don't feel you're in control of what's happening.

How do successful retail marketers counteract this feeling? Merely by walking in the customer's shoes, you say. But that's not a simple thing to do. It means being mentally flexible to deal with the values, tastes, habits, manners, mannerisms, judgments, sense of humor, and idiosyncrasies of a broad spectrum of consumers. It means selecting the right benefits for the situation at hand. And it means communicating explicitly with the customer, client, or prospect, even using the customer's language, so to speak.

No, it's not acting; it's for real. And remember, you're not a missionary, you're a self-respecting servant.

■

HOW PEOPLE BUY

Here is what a top-ranked salesperson of a leading specialty store told a researcher about retail selling procedures:

Consumers are very different in their likes and dislikes and in the way they buy. The kind of selling attitude that would make me feel comfortable might offend a customer. What you have to do certainly is not to treat them exactly the same way you want to be treated, but rather to find out—as well as you can—how each customer wants to be served and then do it that way whether it's your way or not.

Most of us do not always understand why we behave as we do in the marketplace. We like to think that we make sensible decisions. But who hasn't regretted an impulsive purchase?

It's important for everyone in retailing to understand that everybody has changing moods and attitudes toward buying. Sometimes we hunt for the best price, gladly walking a mile to save a dollar. At other times, all we want is to save time. And then there are occasions when we want reassurance about quality and taste, and in our minds only certain retail firms can satisfy this need. All retail workers should take these changing customer behaviors into account.

In general, consumer buying practices can be separated into two categories: rational buying and impulse buying. But of course, there are many combinations of the two in between. Let's look at impulse buying first.

Impulse Buying

Unplanned purchasing based largely on an on-the-spot decision is called **impulse buying**. To avoid impulse buying would be *not* to make a spur-of-the-moment decision. The real issue about impulse buying isn't whether the purchase has been planned in advance but whether the purchase proves to be wise or foolish later on. Many impulse purchases prove to be good investments. Many meet an unclarified but real need. A customer may see something he or she had not planned to purchase, but this may be the exact item that, at some time in the past, he or she has

considered for future purchase. Upon seeing the item, the customer is reminded of this earlier thought or plan and is prompted to act on it.

In some cases, the customer may feel the need of a mental lift that the purchase of a given product or service might offer. Sometimes people are afraid to submit to their inner needs because it's difficult to rationalize many of them. But often these inner needs are being satisfied when an item is bought impulsively.

Rational Buying

You will recall from Chapter 29 that consumers act differently when buying convenience goods and services, shopping goods and services, and specialty goods and services. Also, it makes a great deal of difference whether they are in a hurry or can take their time. They act differently when purchasing a product or service they haven't used before or one that is new on the market. And they act differently when buying for themselves rather than for someone else.

Without doubt, the salesperson quoted above gave sound advice when suggesting that the first thing to do in personal retail selling is to find out how each customer wants to be treated. Knowing how people buy is an art and a science. The information that follows will help you cultivate the art and introduce you to the science of how and when people buy.

The Decision-Making Process Customers usually aren't aware of the mental stages through which they progress during the course of a sale except for the final stage—action, when they decide to end the transaction. On the other hand, they are often conscious of the buying decisions during an important purchase. Therefore, if selling is a matter of helping customers buy, let's concentrate on assisting them with buying decisions and winning their confidence.

Of course, little or no deliberation takes place when consumers buy on impulse. And there is very little thought given to the purchase of many convenience goods and services. But when financial resources are limited and a sizable expense is involved, consumers often think about a purchase for a considerable length of time.

Step 1. Normally, the first step consumers take in solving a purchasing problem is to clarify their need. You will recall from Chapter 31, on identifying customer wants and needs, that there are customers who know exactly what they want, those who have a general idea of their needs and wants, and those who are unaware of their needs. This is a critical step in the buying process because the remaining steps depend on its outcome. The amount of thought given to it varies markedly.

Step 2. The next step consumers take is to identify alternatives available to meet that need. As in Step 1, the difficulty of this task varies with the complexity of the buying problem. Sometimes there is no alternative product or service available, but often there are many.

Step 3. The third step consumers take is to gather information about each alternative. Consumers may make the operation simple or complex. Its degree of complexity depends on the consumer's sophistication, the availability of accurate information, the variety of choices available, and the prices of the product or service being considered.

Step 4. The last step consumers take is to choose the most appropriate alternative and take action. In this step, consumers weigh the evidence, then rank the alternatives on the basis of their concept of personal values and efficiency. When making an original purchase, consumers usually include a series of eliminations, first one item and then another, in making this final decision.

How the Ego Is Involved   A very important influence on consumer buying behavior is the consumer's concept of self, or the ego. The way consumers act and the decisions they make in the marketplace reflect what they think of themselves. From a retailer's viewpoint, protecting the customer's ego is *law*. Witness the old saying, "The customer is always right," which relates to that "law" of retail marketing.

How deeply a consumer's ego is involved in any given purchase depends on that person's value system, the kinds of products or services being purchased, and their treatment by the firm and the sales personnel. Some people are more concerned than others with possessions and personal services and become highly ego-involved in a purchase. Rightly or wrongly, many customers think that they are attractive to others because of their possessions.

When consumers purchase products, such as groceries, that call for little ego involvement, they generally use fewer steps of the decision-making process. But when they purchase products such as fashionable clothing or contract for interior decorating, where there is considerable ego involvement, they may use all the steps of the decision-making process. Regardless of the product or service being purchased, all consumers are influenced by a salesperson's attitude toward them. And all consumers feel somewhat flattered when a salesperson treats them with respect and shows a sincere interest in their problems.

Salespeople must be able to judge consumers' ego involvement in a purchase and provide the right amount of subtle reinforcement. Insincere bolstering of a customer's ego is almost sure to backfire.

WHY PEOPLE DON'T BUY

Consumers may choose between one brand or another, *or* they may decide not to buy at all. Selling is an interpersonal relationship. In this relationship, the purchaser's fears, prejudices, and attitude toward the company or the salesperson are just as important as his or her feeling about the product or service and its price. If customers have any doubts about their buying decision, the firm, or the salesperson, they may decide not to buy.

Fear of a Poor Decision

Customers may fear that a product will not look nice or perform as well as it did on the sales floor. They may also fear that they will look foolish in the eyes of a spouse or friends, or that they might have bought it for less elsewhere, and so on. Any of these fears may prevent customers from buying.

Fear of the Salesperson

Most customers fear the salesperson's expertise at the same time that they seek help. Right or wrong, your customers believe that you know more about your merchandise than they do. Also, they know who pays your salary and believe that you will place your employer's interest above theirs. Your task, therefore, is to convince customers that you are on their side, believing that there is more to be gained from satisfying them than from the profit of a single sale. It's a matter of trust. When dealing with customers, keep in mind that:

■ People will listen only when we've taken time to listen to them.
■ People will understand what we say only after they know we understand them and what they say.
■ People don't care about how much we know until they know how much we care.
■ Most people are concerned about themselves and what they are experiencing; but when they feel that we care about them, they will open up.

Demonstrating concern for customers helps to win their business.

■ People can hear six times faster than we can talk, so get to the point. It's what happens in the intervals while we drone on that usually loses our listeners.

How will you know if you're earning your customer's trust? You will know by how willing they are to share their situation with you. One of the most helpful values the seller provides is helping customers recognize what they really want.

Now that you understand the motives underlying consumer buying behavior and how consumers buy, you're ready to see how, as a retailer, you put this knowledge into practice during a sales presentation. Chapter 33 discusses how superior salespeople help customers make buying decisions.

TRADE TALK

Define each term and use it in a sentence.

Buying motives
Emotional buying
    motives
Impulse buying

Patronage buying
    motives
Rational buying motives
Values

CAN YOU ANSWER THESE?

1. What uses can retail marketing personnel make of their understanding of consumer buying motives?

2. What is the order of needs categories in A. H. Maslow's hierarchy of needs? How does a good salesperson use this knowledge?

3. What are the factors that affect a consumer's buying motives? Why do buying motives change?

4. Why is an understanding of the three types of buying motives important for retail personnel?

5. Why don't some people buy goods and services?

6. Why is it so important for a salesperson to show that he or she cares about the customer's needs and wants?

7. Why do consumers sometimes make impulsive purchases?

8. What are the mental steps a customer uses when making a rational purchase?

9. How is a customer's ego involved in making a purchase?

C·H·A·P·T·E·R

33 *Helping Customers Make Buying Decisions*

As a retail marketing student, what is your opinion of the following response of a specialty shop women's ready-to-wear salesperson to a researcher who was probing the secrets of superior salespeople?

I try to persuade a customer to get what is really becoming to her. I lead her to notice for herself that certain styles are not becoming to her.

I think it is my duty to speak up if what she chooses is the wrong thing, very unbecoming, or not the right size or color, or not durable enough for her purpose. If she is going to be sorry she bought it, she won't remember that she herself insisted on having it. She will blame me and the store. So I always try to show her, pleasantly and tactfully, why something else would answer better.

If a customer wants a thirty-six when she should wear a thirty-eight, don't contradict her, but tactfully lead her to try on the size you think she should wear.

Do you agree with the statement in principle? Does it conflict with the precept that the customer is always right? Is it better to lose a sale rather than sell a product or service that is not right for the customer?

Unfortunately, there are consumers who use poor judgment in selecting the goods and services they buy. But there are also salespeople whose judgment stems from their own preferences, which may or may not be right for the situation at hand. Thus, the issue above is not clear-cut.

Of course, good salespeople are not likely to encounter similar situations very often because they are skilled in identifying customers' needs and wants, and they know how to help their customers make buying decisions. They start their sales presentation from the customer's perspective in making buying decisions; they anticipate probable objections to the item being discussed; they answer questions prudently; and they tactfully guide their customers to satisfying decisions to buy or not to buy.

Attempting to impose the salesperson's will on customers (high-pressure selling) has always been distasteful to the customer and damaging to the business as well as to the salesperson. The key to today's personal selling is empathy—placing yourself mentally in the customer's shoes. Empathy implies:

■ A desire to please each customer
■ A willingness to consider each customer's buying problem
■ Respect for the customer's wants and preferences

PRESENTING THE PRODUCT OR SERVICE

Many customers need help with their purchasing problems. They need an advisor who knows all about the products or services they buy, and who can show them the product's features and benefits. This part of the selling task is called the **sales presentation**. It involves (1) choosing the right product or service to present, (2) dramatizing it, (3) involving the customer in the dramatization, and (4) emphasizing the customer benefits.

Choosing the Items to Present

In order to choose the right product or service to present to the customer or client, you, as a salesperson, must know the features and benefits of what you're selling and the major differences among similar items. No customer will expect you to know everything about every item in the department. But customers do expect you to be able to locate the desired information quickly if you don't have it.

When choosing items to present, you have to decide which ones to show first and how much merchandise to present at one time.

What to Present First   When determining what product/service to show first, experienced salespeople use the following guidelines:

■ If a customer asks for a particular style, color, price, model, or brand, show it immediately.
■ If the customer expresses no preference, inquire about the intended use and present what you think would be appropriate for that use.
■ If the customer gives no clue concerning price, show the medium price line first.
■ When in doubt, show the advertised or very popular items first.

How Much to Present   The following suggestions from experienced salespeople will help you to decide how many items to present:

■ Present enough items to allow the customer a reasonable choice. When selling goods such as shoes, show several styles.

- Indicate that you are interested in your customer's buying problem and that you are willing to present all suitable alternatives, but avoid overwhelming the customer with stock.
- If you display and describe your products or services effectively, you will not need to present every item you have to offer. Try to avoid unnecessary steps in getting more merchandise from stock.

Dramatizing the Product or Service

Customers are much more likely to move from the mental stage of interest to the point of wanting to own a product or service if you present the item vividly, bringing out its strong features and dramatizing its uses. Many customers are confused by the number of items they have seen; others haven't really concentrated on any product. When serving either kind, keep in mind the old maxim, "Actions speak louder than words."

The kinds of dramatization practices that add to the success of a sales presentation are (1) displaying the product effectively, (2) showing the product or service in use, (3) using descriptive language and appropriate gestures.

Displaying the Product Effectively

Displaying the product is an art in itself. It is said that the most effective display prop is the salesperson's hand. The manner in which you handle a product reveals your feeling toward it. For example, if you sell expensive jewelry, or fine china, carefully select each item from the display case or shelf. While showing it to a customer, handle it gently so that the customer feels this to be a very special product, one that the customer would like to own.

If an article is small, separate it from similar items. You may want to hand it to the customer so that attention is concentrated on that single item rather than on the entire display of merchandise. Listen to the advice of a ready-to-wear sales expert:

This chef knows the value of using showmanship to present his product.

When you try a dress on a customer, try to stand between her and the mirror until you have the dress fastened. If you do this she can't see the dress until it is on her. Then drop down and turn the hem to the proper length. If the skirt is too long, it makes the whole dress look bigger and often spoils a sale.

Showing the Product or Service in Use

Seeing is believing. Whenever possible, show your customers how the product will look when used. Show a towel over a towel bar and a rug spread on the floor. Put records on stereos, sew on a sewing machine, and turn on lamps. If you are a travel agent, show slides or brochures of vacation spots and hotels. These activities help customers see how the product or service will solve their buying problems.

Using Effective Language and Gestures

When you make your sales presentation, use simple, accurate language at all times. Avoid slang, because it makes a poor impression on customers and generally fails to convey meaning. Also, avoid words like "nice," "pretty," "fine," and "wonderful," which have very little meaning. Try to use stimulating adjectives and phrases that carry conviction. How much more effective it is to say, "See how smoothly this jacket fits across the shoulders," than to say, "It's a nice fit."

Communicating with gestures gives meaning to your words. Use your hands, arms, and face to express enthusiasm and to get and keep the customer's interest. Sincere enthusiasm is contagious. Hands play an important role in communication; they emphasize the spoken word, communicate feelings, and direct the customer's attention to the product.

Involving the Customer

Participation allows the customer to "experience" the product or service. Also, participation can change a customer's interest in an item into a desire for it. How customers act and feel and what they say while participating will reveal clues concerning their needs and wants. To involve customers, encourage them to talk and to participate physically by examining or demonstrating the product or service, using as many of the five senses as appropriate.

Appealing to the Five Senses   Competent salespeople help their customers make use of as many of the five senses as possible. Studies show that people receive ideas from their senses in the following proportions: sight, 87 percent; hearing, 7 percent; touch, 3 percent; smell, 2 percent; and taste, 1 percent. Of course, these percentages do not hold for certain categories of products such as food and cosmetics.

Sight. Sight is 27 times faster than hearing and has 22 times more impact; therefore, skillful salespeople take particular pains in showing their goods in an interesting, effective way. You may have noticed how a person selling diamonds uses soft, black velvet to display the stones. If you understand the principles of color, line, and design in selling, you'll have the advantage because you'll be able to show products and services in attractive ways.

Input from the five senses varies from one product or service to another and from one customer to another.

Hearing. Retailer marketers appeal to the sense of hearing in several ways: They use it through the spoken words of salespeople or through the loudspeakers that announce shoppers' specials. They use it through the sounds made by the products themselves, such as stereos and VCRs. And they use it through background music to establish a buying mood.

Touch. The sense of touch complements sight and hearing. By feeling a fabric, a customer can tell whether it's soft or stiff, smooth or rough, lightweight or heavy. When customers can handle a golf club, balance a hammer, or type on a typewriter, their sense of touch will satisfy their needs. Words cannot communicate those feelings accurately.

Smell. Obviously, the sense of smell is very important in selling products such as cosmetics and food. But we often do not realize that aroma plays an important part in creating a pleasant shopping environment for any product. This is the main reason why retailers are concerned about eliminating a musty warehouse odor, the fumes of gasoline, the odorous smell of decaying fruit, and of course offensive breath and body odors among employees.

Taste. Taste may be considered a minor factor in retail marketing except for food and a few other oral products. But within this field of goods it is virtually supreme. Neither color nor quality, nor any amount of oral persuasion about nourishing qualities, could make any headway with a customer who dislikes the taste of a food or drink.

Communicating with Customers Because customers react differently and say different things, you must vary your responses. Make sure that your comments suit each customer and each situation. If you talk too much, you may make your customers feel that you're more concerned with making a sale than you are about helping them. If you talk too little, you may cause a customer to think that you lack interest in the sale. After making a point, stop and let your customer ask a question. If the customer doesn't respond in some way, try asking a question that will direct attention to the product or service—"Do you think, Mrs. Smith, that this color will fit into your decor?"

ANSWERING CUSTOMERS' QUESTIONS AND OBJECTIONS

Why do consumers procrastinate, ask questions, and sometimes make excuses when making a purchase? Usually because they are ambivalent—they can't decide—or they don't want to be bothered. Much depends on the intensity of their wants for whatever you're selling and sometimes on personal reasons outside your control or knowledge. As a salesperson, your responsibility in helping customers buy is to appraise the customer's intent and respond in a positive manner, usually welcoming the customer's behavior. The important element in dealing with customer questions and objections is to maintain the customer's trust.

Appraising the Customer's Intent

Customers differ in the ways they reveal and conceal their objections to buying. Some are straightforward in expressing their feelings and come directly to the point that concerns them most. An objection based on an honestly felt misgiving about a purchase is called a **sincere objection**. Many customers refuse to reveal their true objections. They may be polite or timid. Or they may want you to give some good reason for their making the purchase. Concealing the real objection is called an **excuse**. For example, customers may say, "I don't intend to buy today," when they really mean that they are not satisfied with the article.

Anticipating Objections

Generally, the best way to deal with common, misconceived objections is to prevent them from arising by incorporating the answers into the presentation. Keep in mind that the customer's very act of raising an objection often magnifies that thought in the customer's mind. And talking about it too much can help increase the customer's negative attitude. Therefore, a good strategy may be to present product or service knowledge skillfully, answering objections before the customer has even thought of them.

Anticipating objections is particularly important when customers who have used a product for a long time are reluctant to accept a new model. It is your job to educate them about the new model so that they will accept it.

Dealing with Product or Service Disadvantages

It's almost impossible for a retail marketer to stock an assortment of items large enough to meet all customer needs and wants. So even the best salespeople encounter valid objections. If a customer has a serious objection to a product, it is far better to keep the customer's confidence than to try to force the customer into a sale. When appropriate, present the strong features of the item and show why these points are important. If the customer agrees, then you will make the sale. If the customer is not convinced, you may not make the sale, but the customer will remember your helpful interest in serving his or her needs.

Dealing with Sincere Objections

A customer's sincere objection offers the salesperson an opportunity to identify areas of doubt and to show the customer additional benefits that relate to the customer's concern. Listen very attentively to the customer's objection.

Most—but not all—sincere customer questions and objections relate to the customer's uncertainties concerning buying decisions. Failure to make one or more of the five buying decisions blocks the final commitment to buy. So it's the salesperson's responsibility to identify the missing decision(s) and supply the information needed to solve the buying problem. Thus, the first thing to do is to locate the missing link. This may require tactful questioning based on what transpired prior to the objection. Much depends on how well the salesperson handled the preceding steps of the sale, especially the identification of wants and needs. Here are some buying objections in the order most frequently heard:

Price (cost) objections. Most price objections are the result of customers' wanting to make the best buy possible in order to get the most for their money, rather than the inability to pay. In case of the former, stress quality of the product or service, its features and benefits, and customer services offered by the firm. If you feel that lack of funds is the root of the objection, you can suggest credit arrangements.

Product or service objections. Usually, product objections are valid expressions of concern about the offering itself. As a rule they relate to the quality of the item; its features, color, or size; service required; or brand preferences. Responses to objections are derived from the salesperson's knowledge of the item.

Place (company) objections. Place objections are usually the result of negative past experiences. If possible, identify the specific dissatisfaction and tactfully provide assurance of present and future service.

Time objections. Usually time objections are the most difficult objections to handle. They are frequently an excuse to cover up the real objection, but they may be legitimate. Point out the appropriate advantages of buying now—saving money and time, assuring an adequate supply, charge account availability, and so on.

Need objections. Possible conflicts may arise between a want and a need. Customer says, "I would like a food processor, but I don't really need it that badly." Or there's a possible conflict of needs: The customer says, "Yes, I need a leaf blower, but I need a chain saw more." Your job is to reinforce the need by stressing the benefits of the product and the value it offers, or try to sell the chain saw.

Procedure for Answering Objections

Experienced salespersons recommend the following procedures for answering objections:

1. *Listen carefully:* Don't interrupt the customer.

2. *Reinforce the customer's feelings:* You might say, "I'm glad you brought that up," "I can see why you feel that way," or "Many customers raise that point."

3. *Restate the objection:* This shows the customer that you understand it.

4. *Answer the objection honestly and continue with the sale.*

There are numerous ways of responding to a customer's objections, some of which may be called high-pressure, but the two preferred techniques are the inquiry and the "yes, but" response:

■ Inquiry: Asking customers to explain the objection. As customers attempt to explain, they often answer the objection or else show that it is not a serious one.

■ The "yes, but" response: Agreeing with the customer but presenting another angle. For example: *Customer*: "I can get it cheaper somewhere else." *Salesperson*: "Perhaps you can buy it cheaper, but is it really the same?"

The salesperson continues with features-benefits or calls attention to a customer accommodation service, such as being able to return the product.

Dealing with Excuses

Never ignore a customer's excuse. Instead, treat the customer courteously and try to find the underlying objection. The real objection will usually reveal itself as a result of your question, or it may come to light as the sale proceeds. The customer may state it differently, or you may detect it from the customer's remarks and actions. Here is an example of how you can use a question to help a customer complete the five buying decisions.

When a customer says, "I'm just looking," you may say, "Certainly, that's the best way to know what we have. Isn't this a great assortment of posters?"

Note that the salesperson followed the excuse with a question concerning a buying decision. The salesperson questioned the

Customers may be reluctant to give their real reason for not buying, especially if the price is more than they can afford.

source decision. Suppose that the customer had said, "Yes, but I really had something less expensive in mind." It would have been evident that the price decision had not been made, and you would have had to work on that buying decision.

■

TRADING UP

Trading up is the salesperson's effort to interest the customer in better-grade and more expensive goods than the customer expects to buy. When used properly, it is a legitimate customer service—far removed from the bait-and-switch tactics of shoddy merchandisers. Why does management encourage salespeople to sell better-grade goods and services? It is simply because the company usually makes more profit on the higher-priced items, and frequently the result is greater customer satisfaction. Retail marketers make very little profit on their low-priced specials.

The least costly items are often not the best value for the money in terms of the customer's use of the product. Many customers may be willing to pay higher prices if they believe that they will receive additional benefits for their money.

Why does a store stock several price lines of some of its products? One good reason is to serve customers who buy the product for different reasons or use it in different ways. For example, there are customers who are price-conscious. There are prestige-motivated buyers who insist on deluxe models. And there are those between these extremes. Therefore, several price lines may be stocked. So salespeople, more than ever before, have to be knowledgeable about more products and features, be familiar with more prices, and be in a position to explain the differences to customers.

You can master the techniques of trading up if you follow these rules.

1. Determine the customer's intended use of the product or service before you try to trade up. This enables you to help your customer find the best buy for the purpose. It also helps keep you from misjudging the consumer values the customer seeks.

2. Do not belittle the lower-priced item by suggesting that it is of inferior quality. If you do, and your customer does not want the higher-priced goods, you may spoil your chances of making a sale.

3. Lower-priced specials frequently are less functional, and once the customer realizes this, he or she may not be satisfied. Therefore, indicate the similar features of the better product, and call the customer's attention to its *additional* benefits.

4. If the store advertises a product, be fully prepared to sell and deliver it. Avoid any suggestion of the "bait-and-switch" selling technique in which customers are pressured into buying a higher-profit item; it is unethical as well as illegal.

Some customers cannot afford to pay a higher price, and in some situations the low-priced article may be satisfactory. One should not try to trade up if the customer does not really need the higher-priced item.

■

SELLING ADDITIONAL PRODUCTS OR SERVICES

Suggestion selling is a technique through which the salesworker gives the customer an idea that leads to the purchase of additional products or services.

In many sales transactions, customers need certain products in addition to the ones they came to purchase. They are frequently grateful for suggestions that will save them another shopping trip or a telephone call to the store. Also, many customers are interested in new products and opportunities to save money. They usually welcome useful suggestions from competent salespeople. So place yourself in the customer's shoes, and suggest appropriate additional products or services.

Types of Suggestion Selling

There are several types of suggestions that you can make to sell additional products or services. They include:

- Related products or services
- Larger quantities of an item
- New stock, products, and services
- Special values
- New or additional uses of products
- Products or services for special occasions

As a salesperson, you have to choose the type of suggestion that is practical for the situation.

Suggesting Related Items Items that can be used with the article or service the customer has purchased are called **related** or **companion products or services**. You'll succeed with this type of suggestion only if you know what you have in stock and have mastered your product or service knowledge. Related products or services help the customer in the following ways:

- Increase the value or pleasure derived from the original purchase. For example, shoe polish protects shoes.
- May be used with the original product or service. Brushes, paint thinner, and sandpaper are usually used with paint.
- May improve the appearance of the original item. Costume jewelry or a scarf is often used to accent a dress.

Suggesting Larger Quantities Suggesting a larger quantity of some items can save customers additional shopping trips because they will have a supply of the product on hand. Also, it may save them money. By suggesting a larger quantity of an item, you may be appealing to convenience or economy.

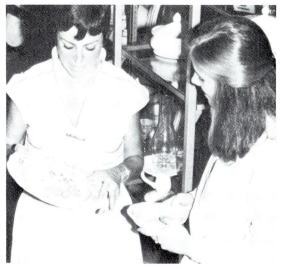

A salesperson may suggest an additional item or larger quantities before the completion of the sale. Customers appreciate suggestions that save them money, more shopping trips, or inconvenience.

Suggesting New Stock, Products, and Services Most customers will appreciate your telling them that new merchandise has been received by the store. For example, if you've just sold a suit to a customer, you might say, "We've just received our first shipment of fall coats. Would you like to see what they're wearing this year?"

Suggesting Special Values Stores often advertise goods or services at special low prices. End-of-season and pre-inventory sales help to empty the shelves of old merchandise and make room for new. To take advantage of these situations, suggest appropriate unadvertised specials that the customer may not have noticed.

Suggesting New or Additional Uses of Products Sometimes you can suggest a new use for products that will lead the customer to buy more then one item. For example, if you sell towels, you can show the customer a display featuring a beach robe made of towels.

Suggesting Products or Services for Special Occasions On holidays, when people buy gifts, alert salespeople make appropriate suggestions. When possible, remind customers of coming events.

When to Suggest Additional Purchases

A good time to suggest additional purchases is just after a customer has bought one item, while the customer is still in a buying mood. There are times, however, when you may suggest an additional item before completing the first sale. This occurs when the suggested item might increase the customer's desire for the original product or service. For example, if a customer is examining a man's dress shirt, an attractive necktie—knotted and laid in position on the shirt—might help the customer visualize the shirt in use.

Timing a suggestion is a matter of sensing your relationship to the customer and using good judgment. Occasionally, suggestion selling is appropriate after the salescheck is completed, particularly when there is a lull in business and the customer is waiting for the purchase to be wrapped.

How to Make Suggestions

A large percentage of successful suggestion sales depends on knowing not only when to suggest but to whom and how the suggestions is to be made. You can achieve good results by making certain that the conditions for making a suggestion are favorable. And you can also succeed by using the tested procedures that follow.

Conditions for Suggestion Selling Successful suggestion selling depends on the following conditions:

1. *The customer must need the suggested article.* Training and experience will enable you to sense what is best suited to a particular customer's need. You will be guided by your experience during earlier sales.

2. *The customer's attitude toward you should be positive.* You can pave the way toward acceptance by gaining the customer's confidence. A customer who suspects that you're more interested in making a sale than in being helpful is not likely to accept a suggestion.

3. *The suggestion should exclude opposing ideas.* For example, you would not say, "Would you like some shoe polish?" because of the opposing idea that the customer might have some at home. Rather, you might say, "This polish matches the color of your shoes exactly. If you polish them before you wear them, you'll be assured of a long shine."

Recommended Procedures for Suggestion Selling Here are three rules to follow when using suggestion selling. They will help you avoid any resentment on the part of the customer and will make your suggestions more welcome.

1. *Suggest a specific item.* You might say, "This fluid is recommended by the manufacturer of this copying machine." Don't say, "Do you need any cleaning fluid?"

2. *Explain the reason for the suggestion before making it.* Customers are willing to look at additional merchandise if they feel that you're trying to help them satisfy their needs. For example, "The trim on your bike will keep its shine longer if you use this special polish."

3. *Show and demonstrate the item.* The product will often speak for itself. If the article is handed to the customer, the customer can see it, feel it, and begin to think about owning it.

■

CLOSING THE SALE

The aim of the entire selling task is to guide the customer to a decision to buy, in other words, to *close the sale.* Frequently the customer says, "I'll take it," thereby closing the sale. But some customers will wait to be asked—even after they have made up their minds to buy—and you will have to close the sale.

Like many new salespeople, you might be afraid to close the sale. It might seem like asking a favor. You may fear that the customer's response will be negative. Or you might not want to hurry the customer and feel that the customer should always take the initiative. With experience, however, you will realize that some customers need help in making decisions, and you will close the sale with confidence.

When to Try for a Close

The best time to try for a close is when the customer seems receptive to making a favorable decision to buy. This may occur in a few minutes. Or it may not occur until the customer has returned several times to examine the product. The process by which you can test the readiness of the customer to buy is called a **trial close**. As an adept salesperson, your aim is to help the customer reach the point when a close can be attempted. Here are some ways you can make that happen.

Identifying Clues to Close   Watching the customer rather than the merchandise will help you to know when a customer is ready to make the final buying decision. Watch for the following clues:

■ When your customer looks pleased with an article and does not seem to be looking for more, ask for a decision.

■ When your customer shows interest in an article and appears annoyed if anything else is brought out, try for a decision.

■ The moment your customer begins to show signs of weariness or confusion, stop bringing out goods and try for a close.

■ Listen carefully for remarks such as "This is exactly the style I'm looking for," or "I don't like the price, but I do like the desk."

Acting on Closing Clues   When you see that the article will satisfy the customer's needs and wants, select one of these procedures leading to the close of the sale.

1. Try to identify the questionable buying decision that blocks the decision to buy. Testing for the product decision, you might say, "Those shoes certainly match your coat well, don't they?"

2. If the customer asks for your opinion, give it without hesitation and state the reason from the customer's viewpoint.

3. When you see that the customer is inclined toward a suitable choice, call attention to its advantages for the customer's need.

4. Without appearing to hurry the customer, lay aside or put away quietly articles that have not seemed to interest the customer.

How to Try for a Close

How do you go about the ticklish business of getting a customer to decide, of being helpful and yet not pressuring the customer?

First of all, don't be afraid to ask your customer for a decision. Many sales have been lost simply because salespeople have continued to talk when they should have tried to close the sale.

When a customer cannot seem to make a buying decision, the salesperson should attempt a trial close.

Start your trial close by making a comment or asking a question that invites agreement from the customer. When selling suits, you might say, "Don't you think this suit gives you dignity and distinction?" Agreement is a positive reaction. Having made one positive response, the customer is then in the right frame of mind to make a favorable decision to buy. The point should be one that seems to appeal to the customer most. Once the customer has voiced or nodded an agreement, you may assume that the customer's mind has been made up. So ask for some additional information that is needed to complete the sale. Typical questions are:

- Would you like this to be cash or charge?
- Do you want to take it with you?
- Will a half-dozen be enough, or should I send a dozen?

There is always the possibility that the customer will stop short at this point and say, "Wait a minute—I haven't made up my mind." But far more often the customer will take your question for granted and answer it without ever having said, "I'll take it."

What To Do After the Sale Is Made

Part of your selling personality should be a friendly interest in people. This should be as evident after the sale as when you are serving the customer.

First, show your appreciation. When a salesperson says sincerely, "It was a pleasure serving you," the customer is pleased.

Next, make some friendly remarks while completing the paperwork on the sale. Casual conversation helps create a friendly atmosphere.

When appropriate, try a sincere compliment. People like to hear genuine compliments about their children, their property, their taste, their judgments, or anything that concerns them.

What To Do if the Sale Is Not Made

It pays to be courteous, even if the customer doesn't make a purchase. Tell such customers that you were glad to help them. If they didn't find what they wanted, you'll be pleased to serve them when they return. Don't leave or turn away quickly. You may give them your card or your name and ask them to inquire for you.

Remember, your job is to offer service as well as to sell. Providing good service, regardless of whether it brings a sale today, can result in a future sale.

TRADE TALK

Define each term and use it in a sentence.

Excuse	Sincere objection
Related or companion products or services	Suggestion selling
	Trading up
Sales presentation	Trial close

CAN YOU ANSWER THESE?

1. How does a salesperson show empathy for a customer's buying problem? How does such empathy help the salesperson? Help the employer?

2. What guidelines do salespeople use in selecting goods or services to present to the customer?

3. How does a productive salesperson dramatize products or services for customers?

4. What is the basic difference in procedure between handling an excuse and dealing with sincere objections?

5. What are the four rules to follow in trading up?

6. What are the six types of suggestion selling? Cite an example of each.

7. What actions might you take when your customer gives you a clue to close?

8. How should a salesperson treat a customer who does not buy?

C·H·A·P·T·E·R

34 *Using Consumer Credit as a Selling Tool*

Lisa Lang, who owned and operated a smart dress shop that appealed to career-minded women, was disturbed. She realized that the money she had tied up in customer credit services had almost doubled during the past year, and that too much time was being spent in managing and operating her credit accounts. At lunch, she confided to her friend, Charles Chamness, "I wonder how many of my charge customers will ever pay me the money I have lent them through credit? I'm beginning to question whether I should be offering credit at all."

Charles managed a cash-and-carry sporting goods store in a neighboring shopping center and was thinking of offering some kind of credit to improve his sales volume. His response was, "I'd think twice before discontinuing credit services, Lisa. People just don't seem to want to pay with cash anymore."

This chapter discusses consumer credit from the retailer's point of view, so that you can understand the differences in credit policies of various firms and support those of the company for which you work. It deals with the factors that retailers must consider if they want to offer credit and the types of credit and collection policies they use. This chapter also explains the sources of information that retailers use to check credit applicants, the way they evaluate this information, and the procedures they use for granting credit.

■

WHY RETAIL MARKETERS OFFER CONSUMER CREDIT

The use of consumer credit is not new—but the extent to which credit is used is new. Not many years ago, "cash on the barrelhead" and "neither a borrower nor a lender be" were still commonly held values. The average consumer probably had a monthly credit account with a few local stores and may have financed an automobile purchase by using credit. Today, that same consumer probably has a wallet stuffed with cards and plates that authorize him or her to buy merchandise and services from firms such as retail marketers, public utilities, and special credit-granting companies.

Few people realize that the liberal use of credit by both businesses and consumers is one of the most important factors in the constant economic growth of our country. The United States is renowned for its leadership in producing, distributing, and consuming products and services. Our enviable position among nations has been achieved through mass production, mass distribution, and mass credit—the "three M's of American Business." Keep in mind that were it not for credit, mass distribution could not survive and production would come to a halt.

Why Consumers Use Credit

Consumers vary greatly in the extent to which they use credit. Some use it almost all of the time, some only in emergencies. Some use it mostly for big-ticket expenditures, some for everyday staple goods. Some use credit only when purchasing from a few firms, others have credit accounts everywhere—at department stores, drug stores, banks, and automobile service stations. Credit has become popular because it appeals to consumers for the following reasons:

Convenience. Many customers like the convenience of paying for an entire month's purchases at one time. Using credit is a way to avoid carrying cash on a shopping trip. Moreover, charging a purchase makes it easier for a customer to shop by telephone.

Immediate use of the product or service. Credit is an advantage to many people because it gives them the opportunity to enjoy and use costly items while spreading out the payments. This enables many people to own appliances and automobiles much sooner than if they had to save to buy them.

Possible savings. In some cases, using credit may enable people to save money. By using their charge accounts or credit cards at a time when they lack cash, customers may be able to buy items being sold at reduced prices.

Preferred treatment. Some customers use credit because they feel that as charge customers they receive better service. For example, they find that at many stores it is much easier to return credit merchandise than cash purchases. Also, sometimes

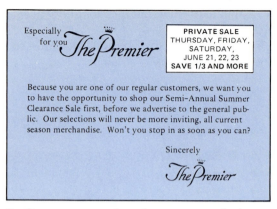

Credit customers receive advance notice of sales.

charge-account customers receive advance notice of sales and thus have the first choice of goods on sale.

Recordkeeping. Another advantage of using credit is that it's easier to keep track of expenditures. Such records indicate the items included in a purchase as well as the amount of the purchase itself. For this reason, many people who have business expense accounts use credit receipts to justify their tax deductions.

Why Retailers Offer Credit

Credit has become so important to the American way of life that about one-third of the nation's sales volume is based on credit. Retailers feel that credit gives them a number of advantages.

Customers buy more freely. Credit customers like the convenience of saying "charge it" without worrying about whether they have enough cash on hand to pay for their purchases.

Customers may be less price-conscious. Consumers who have a charge account are less likely to hunt for bargains. They will buy an article because they want it now. The average sale to a credit customer, therefore, is larger than that to a cash customer.

Charge accounts create customer loyalty. Cash customers tend to shop several sources. People who have charge accounts, though, tend to be loyal to the firms that let them buy without cash.

Credit may attract a preferred trade. Credit privileges may attract customers interested in quality, service, and style rather than those interested in price alone.

Credit builds goodwill. For some customers, the fact that the company has sufficient confidence in them to grant them credit builds confidence in the firm. In smaller firms, salespeople often know the charge customer by name, which is flattering to the customer and a big factor in building confidence and goodwill.

Credit helps smooth out business peaks. Cash shoppers tend to buy heavily on certain days when they get paid and lightly on other days. Credit customers, on the other hand, tend to buy whenever products and services are needed. Peaks in business volume are costly, and offering credit tends to level them.

∎

WHO SHOULD OFFER CONSUMER CREDIT?

There are two policy extremes in granting credit. One is not to grant credit to anyone. The other is to grant all customers unlimited credit. Obviously, there is a wide range of credit policies between the two extremes. An appropriate credit policy for a given business depends largely on the type of business. If the enterprise involves large sums of money and small levels of profit, it can't afford to give credit freely; it must give credit only to people who will be sure to pay promptly.

As with any other function of business, the steps to organize and operate a credit and collection function must be in harmony with the profit objective and general policies and plans of the business. The objective of credit and collection is to achieve maximum sales with least losses.

Which Firms Should Offer Consumer Credit?

In the opening story, Lisa Lang wondered whether she should cut back on credit services, while her friend Charles was thinking about offering credit for the first time. What information would they need if they decided to pursue their concerns? Here are some of the important questions that Lisa and Charles should be able to answer about offering customers credit:

1. What are the consumer credit offerings in this line of retail marketing? (Usually, the lower the price of goods or service, the more likely the firm is to have a cash-only policy.)
2. What credit services, if any, do competitors offer?
3. What effect will granting credit have on **cash flow**—the money coming in and going out of the business?
4. What effect will granting credit have on **working capital**—the funds used to operate the business? Money used to finance credit cannot be used for the purchase of inventory or other business purposes.
5. To whom should credit be granted?
6. How much credit, if any, should be granted?
7. What would be the cost in expenses and effort to grant the credit?

In addition to answering these questions, Lisa and Charles should also check, from time to time, whether credit does really bring the benefits it's expected to bring. And if credit is granted, what system should be used? It could be, for example, that Lisa has problems because she's not using the best system for her type of business.

Direct Credit versus Credit Card Systems

Retailers can grant credit in either one or both of the following ways: They can grant

direct credit to customers, that is, offer their own credit arrangements or they can honor one or several established credit-card systems. Their choice depends on their needs.

Direct Credit

After considering answers to the seven questions about whether to offer customers credit, retailers may decide to do so and to offer direct credit. Such a move might result in lower costs and more loyal customers. The appropriateness of the firm's credit policy depends on these factors:

- The profit margin on the merchandise or service
- The line of business and its customers
- The policies of competitors
- The phase of the business cycle that prevails at the time
- The competitive position in which the firm finds itself
- The financial and other circumstances peculiar to the business

Businesses with similar products or services, customers, and similar images usually have similar credit policies. When two firms have different merchandising policies, that difference is usually also reflected in their credit policies. Credit policies may be divided into four main categories:

1. Liberal credit granting and liberal payment collection
2. Liberal credit granting and strict payment collection
3. Strict credit granting and liberal payment collection
4. Strict credit granting and strict payment collection

Sometimes, retail marketers, like Lisa Lang, find it necessary to adjust their credit granting and collection policies. When the sizes of the losses in their consumer credit departments balloon because of the cost of borrowing money and other operating expenses, they become more selective in adding new accounts and more strict in collecting overdue payments.

External Credit Card Systems

If retailers choose the external credit-card system, they have two options: the all-purpose bank route (for example, VISA or MasterCard) or the travel and entertainment card route (for example, American Express, Carte Blanche, or Diners' Club multipurpose cards). And if retailers have an automobile-related business, they may choose one of the major oil company card systems. The more credit cards retailers honor, the more paperwork they will have to do.

Credit granted with external credit cards greatly reduces the number of decisions that have to be made by retail personnel in making a charge sale. And since credit-card companies assume much of the responsibility for collecting payment from the customer, their fee of 3 to 6 percent of the amount purchased (usually called a discount) may well be worthwhile, since it means no collection problem.

Along with the discount rates, the credit-card company establishes a firm's authorization line. The **authorization line** is the maximum amount that a credit-card company allows a customer to charge to his or her account without special approval by the credit-card company. Thus, when a customer wishes to make a purchase on a credit card, the usual procedure is first to check to be sure that the credit-card number has not been listed as a lost, stolen, or withdrawn card.

If the card is acceptable and the purchase amount doesn't exceed the firm's authorization line, the sale may be charged to the card holder. However, if the amount the customer wishes to purchase exceeds the firm's authorization line, then the salesperson must call the credit-card company in order to gain approval for the sale. At this time, the credit-card company checks the customer's balance and decides whether or not to allow the customer credit for the purchase. If the charge is approved, the credit-card company will give the firm an authorization number for the sale. Should the firm fail to obtain an authorization number for a large credit-card purchase, the firm rather than the credit-card company must bear the loss if the customer fails to pay. The firm is also responsible for checking that the customer's signature on the slip matches the one on the credit card itself.

In many areas of the country, retailers who check customer credit, frequently install a small direct-access computer in their place of business. The salesperson punches on the terminal the amount to be purchased, and the computer checks to see whether the card has been withdrawn or whether the credit company's files show that the customer still has enough credit to cover the purchase.

■

WHAT TYPES OF CREDIT MAY BE OFFERED?

Two general types of credit services offered by retail marketers are charge account credit and installment credit. Differences between the two types are based on two criteria:

1. Who owns the purchased item after the purchase agreement has been made?
2. Whether the credit arrangement covers any purchase the customer wishes to make, or whether it's limited to a single purchase.

Charge Accounts

Charge account credit is **open-account credit**, which means that the customer's account remains open, permitting the purchaser to make any number of purchases at any time, up to a predetermined amount specified in the authorization. With this type of credit line, the purchaser usually is not asked to sign a contract or provide additional security. An article bought on open account credit belongs to the purchaser as soon as the purchase is made. The seller doesn't retain ownership of the goods.

Installment Credit

Installment credit is the second major type of credit offered by retail marketers. The selling of consumer goods and services on credit with a provision for regular periodic payments after an initial down payment is known as **installment credit**. The loan is for a specific amount of money, therefore it's closed-end credit. Installment credit differs from charge-account credit in four ways: (1) The buyer usually must sign a contract agreeing to pay for the purchase; (2) a **down payment**, which is a certain percentage of the total price paid at the time the product or service is received by the customer, may be required; (3) interest and a carrying charge are paid for the use of installment credit; and (4) periodic payments must be made until the purchase is paid for.

Installment sales are usually made either by a conditional sales contract or a chattel mortgage. The difference is very important to both the seller and the customer. In a **conditional sales contract**, the seller retains title to (ownership of) the goods and may take the article back (repossess it) if the buyer fails to make a payment. A **chattel mortgage** differs from a conditional sales contract in that title to the goods goes to the buyer immediately. The seller, however, has the right to bring legal action to regain title and repossess the goods if the buyer fails to fulfill the contract by not making payments. Firms would rather be paid than be forced to repossess the goods.

Credit Cards—The Facilitators

As you know, a **credit card** is an identification card that permits the holder to charge products and services simply on the holder's signature. Its purpose is to simplify the purchasing process through the use of a plastic card that can be inserted into a machine to print the owner's name and identification number on a sales check. This card authorizes the charging of a purchase to the customer's account, which may be with the firm where the products or services are purchased or with another credit-granting agency.

Some retailers operate their own credit plans, which have been discussed. Others recognize that various nationwide and international credit organizations can help them offer credit. Sometimes a firm will honor as many as six or seven different credit plans, only one of which is its own.

Credit cards may be classified in three ways: (1) single-purpose cards, (2) travel and entertainment cards, and (3) all-purpose bank credit cards.

Single-Purpose Cards
All kinds of businesses—department stores, motel chains, car-rental agencies, telephone companies, and the like issue **single-purpose cards**. Customers don't have to pay a fee to the issuer, and they are allowed to charge their purchases, paying all or part of the cost when billed. Customers are charged interest on the remaining unpaid balance if they don't pay the entire bill. The purpose of this kind of card is to encourage customers to buy only from the company that issued the card.

Travel and Entertainment Cards
Travel and entertainment cards—such as Diners' Club, Carte Blanche, and American Express—are used mostly by businesspeople and travelers, although anyone may apply. Holders of these cards pay a yearly fee to the issuer. Retailers who honor these cards bill the credit-card company monthly. The credit-card company charges the retailers a percentage of the bill to cover handling and collecting expense. In turn, the credit-card company bills the card holder monthly, when the full amount usually has to be paid.

All-Purpose Bank Credit Cards
Large banks operate credit plans in which member retailers agree to honor credit cards issued to individuals. **All-purpose bank credit cards**, of which VISA and MasterCard are the best known, operate in much the same way as travel and entertainment cards. The bank issues a card after checking the applicant's credit rating. If they are willing to pay an interest charge, then the holders of a bank credit card can pay bills in monthly installments as in a revolving charge account, an option that's not possible with all credit-card plans. If the bill is paid in full within the billing cycle, there's no interest charge.

Lost Credit Cards
According to federal law, the maximum liability to a credit-card holder for fraudulent charges on any kind of credit card is $50 per card. Also, the holder has no liability under the law unless the credit-granting agency has taken several steps. It must (1) have informed the card holder of the $50 liability and sent him or her a stamped, self-addressed envelope with which to notify it of the loss; (2) be able to prove that unauthorized charges up to $50 were made before the card holder notified it of the loss; (3) ensure that the credit card displays the card holder's signature, photograph, or some other means of personal identification.

■

TO WHOM SHOULD CREDIT BE GRANTED?

To decide whether an applicant is an acceptable credit risk, credit grantors collect information through questionnaires, interviews, and the reports of credit bureaus, making sure that they obey the regulations regarding equal credit opportunity. Then they evaluate the applicant's credit rating on the basis of their firm's credit policy.

Obtaining Information about Applicants

The Equal Credit Opportunity Act of 1975 (ECOA) says that everyone has the right to apply for credit without fear of discrimination on the basis of sex or marital status. This means that an application will be judged only on the basis of the applicant's "credit worthiness." The two most important factors that determine credit worthiness are the applicant's income and credit history. So, in most states, questions that discriminate according to sex and marital status have been removed from application forms.

Sources of Information When retailers have known a customer for a long time and know something of the customer's background, they do very little checking into the customer's credit status. On the other hand, if there is a question about the customer's credit worthiness or ability to pay, they check the customer's credit status thoroughly. They may use all of the following sources.

1. *Credit application forms.* Usually, credit application forms are used to start the information-gathering process. The applicant is asked to fill in a questionnaire that provides basic information to help determine whether he or she will be a good credit risk. The most important information on an application relates to the following:

Employment—A credit applicant's ability to pay is usually based on the capacity to earn a steady income. The length of time a person has been employed and the position held indicate ability to pay.

Income—An applicant's ability to pay may include income from other sources such as Social Security, pensions, and alimony. Most businesses use the total income to determine the authorization line.

Capital assets—An applicant's sense of responsibility is usually indicated by whether he or she owns property, has a savings account, and carries insurance. Applications for credit usually ask whether the applicant owns or rents his or her housing and the name of the applicant's bank.

Outstanding obligations—If the applicant is heavily burdened with financial obligations, that person may not be eligible for additional

credit. The applicant is asked to list the names of loan and finance companies with whom he or she does business.

2. *Credit interviews.* In many businesses, potential credit customers, after filling in a questionnaire, are interviewed by trained personnel. The interviews are conducted in a pleasant, tactful manner so that the necessary information is obtained without offending the applicant. Questions about marital status are avoided, and interviewers are careful to avoid statements that can be interpreted as an indication of sex bias.

3. *Credit bureau reports.* Many retail marketers depend on credit bureaus for information about customers' credit credentials. A local **credit bureau** is a central office that gathers information about credit habits of consumers and provides this information in permissible ways. Local credit bureaus are often members of regional and national as-

During a credit interview, the applicant is evaluated in terms of character, capacity, and capital.

sociations such as the Associated Credit Bureaus, Inc., in Houston, Texas. Some local bureaus are privately owned. Others may be nonprofit organizations operated by the members. Besides the membership fee, there is usually a small charge for each inquiry on a credit applicant.

Credit bureaus obtain information from three sources: (1) credit applications; (2) creditors with whom the applicant has done business; and (3) public records such as bankruptcies, court judgments, disposition of lawsuits, marriages, deaths, and divorces.

Credit bureaus don't rate how good a credit risk the applicant is. They simply collect information from the three sources mentioned and report it to their clients or members. The lenders then decide whether the applicant is a good risk. The activities of credit bureaus are subject to the rules generated by the Fair Credit Reporting Act of 1971.

Credit bureaus can be friends of both consumers and businesses. Both benefit from the ease with which a credit transaction can be made, a charge account opened, or a new credit card issued. This is made possible by the voluminous files of 2500 credit bureaus throughout the country and the large number of local merchants' associations.

The Fair Credit Reporting Act of 1971 (FCRA)

This law represents an effort by Congress to regulate the gathering of information on individuals in order to protect their privacy. Before the law was passed, a consumer didn't legally have the right to know what was in his or her file. And credit grantors were not as limited in the purposes for which they could gain access to a person's record. Here are some of the essential features of present consumer rights:

■ Upon the consumer's request and proper identification, the credit-reporting agency must disclose all information in the consumer's credit file and inform the consumer about the sources of the information.

■ If an account is in dispute, the credit bureau will reinvestigate any item the consumer questions. If it's found to be inaccurate or can no longer be verified, the item will be deleted.

■ If the re-investigation doesn't resolve the question, the consumer may file a brief statement reporting his or her side of the issue, which will be included in any future reports containing the item in question.

■ Whenever consumers are denied credit on the basis of information in a credit report, the credit company must inform the consumer of the decision and also provide the name and address of the credit bureau supplying the information.

■ The law limits to 7 years the reporting of adverse information. The only exception is bankruptcy, which may be reported for up to 14 years after the event.

■ Credit bureaus are limited to providing credit reports to credit grantors for specific purposes—extending credit, review or collection of an account, employment purposes, underwriting insurance, or in connection with some other legitimate business transaction such as an investment.

Evaluating Credit Applications

Guidelines for evaluating credit applications vary from lender to lender. Two retailers with different credit policies may take completely different points of view about the same credit credentials. Nevertheless, they do have some common goals.

There are three major factors that credit grantors consider when evaluating a credit application: (1) the applicant's ability to pay, based on income and obligations; (2) the applicant's willingness to pay, determined from his or her credit history; and (3) the potential profitability of the account. When the credit manager has analyzed the information about the applicant, a decision is made to accept or reject the application and decide the amount of a limit, if any.

NAME AND ADDRESS OF CREDIT BUREAU MAKING REPORT	☐ SINGLE REFERENCE ☒ IN FILE REPORT ☐ TRADE REPORT	

NAME AND ADDRESS OF CREDIT BUREAU MAKING REPORT

☐ SINGLE REFERENCE   ☒ IN FILE REPORT   ☐ TRADE REPORT

CREDIT BUREAU OF ANYTOWN
1131 MAIN ST.
ANYTOWN, ANYSTATE 12345

☐ FULL REPORT   ☐ EMPLOY & TRADE REPORT   ☐ PREVIOUS RESIDENCE REPORT

☐ OTHER _____

	Date Received	CONFIDENTIAL
	4/11/86	crediscope® REPORT
	Date Mailed	
	4/11/86	
FOR FIRST NATIONAL BANK ANYTOWN, ANYSTATE 12345	In File Since	
	APRIL 1970	Member Associated Credit Bureaus, Inc.
	Inquired As:	
	JOINT ACCOUNT	

REPORT ON: LAST NAME	FIRST NAME	INITIAL	SOCIAL SECURITY NUMBER	SPOUSE'S NAME
CONSUMER	ROBERT	G.	123-45-6789	BETTY R.

ADDRESS: CITY	STATE:	ZIP CODE	SINCE:	SPOUSE'S SOCIAL SECURITY NO.
1234 ANY ST. ANYTOWN	ANYSTATE	12333	1973	987-65-4321

COMPLETE TO HERE FOR TRADE REPORT AND SKIP TO CREDIT HISTORY

PRESENT EMPLOYER:	POSITION HELD:	SINCE:	DATE EMPLOY VERIFIED	EST. MONTHLY INCOME
XYZ CORPORATION	ASST. DEPT. MGR.	10/81	12/81	$ 2500

COMPLETE TO HERE FOR EMPLOYMENT AND TRADE REPORT AND SKIP TO CREDIT HISTORY

DATE OF BIRTH	NUMBER OF DEPENDENTS INCLUDING SELF: 4	☒ OWNS OR BUYING HOME	☐ RENTS HOME	OTHER: (EXPLAIN)
5/25/50				

FORMER ADDRESS:	CITY:	STATE:	FROM:	TO:
4321 FIRST AVE.	ANYTOWN	ANYSTATE	1970	1973

FORMER EMPLOYER:	POSITION HELD:	FROM:	TO:	EST. MONTHLY INCOME
ABC & ASSOCIATES	SALES PERSON	2/80	9/81	$1285

SPOUSE'S EMPLOYER:	POSITION HELD:	SINCE:	DATE EMPLOY VERIFIED	EST. MONTHLY INCOME
BIG CITY DEPT. STORE	CASHIER	4/81	12/81	$1200

CREDIT HISTORY (*Complete this section for all reports*)

WHOSE	KIND OF BUSINESS AND ID CODE	DATE REPORTED AND METHOD OF REPORTING	DATE OPENED	DATE OF LAST PAYMENT	HIGHEST CREDIT OR LAST CONTRACT	PRESENT STATUS BALANCE OWING	PAST DUE AMOUNT	NO. OF PAYMENTS	NO. MONTHS HISTORY REVIEWED	30-59 DAYS ONLY	60-89 DAYS ONLY	90 DAYS AND OVER	TYPE & TERMS (MANNER OF PAYMENT)	REMARKS
2	CONSUMER'S BANK B 12-345	2/6/86 AUTOMTD.	12/85	1/86	1200	1100	-0-	-0-	2	-0-	-0-	-0-	INSTALLMENT $100/MO.	
3	BIG CITY DEPT. STORE D 54-321	2/10/86 MANUAL	4/81	1/86	300	100	-0-	-0-	12	-0-	-0-	-0-	REVOLVING $ 25/MO.	
1	SUPER CREDIT CARD N 01-234	12/12/85 AUTOMATD.	7/82	11/85	200	100	100	1	12	1	-0-	-0-	OPEN 30-DAY	

PUBLIC RECORD: SMALL CLAIMS CT. CASE #SC1001 PLAINTIFF: ANYWHERE APPLIANCES
AMOUNT $225 PAID 4/4/82
ADDITIONAL INFORMATION: REF. SMALL CLAIMS CT. CASE #SC1001--5/30/82 SUBJECT SAYS CLAIM PAID
UNDER PROTEST. APPLIANCE DID NOT OPERATE PROPERLY.

Credit bureaus compile reports like these to help retailers evaluate applicants for credit.
In this report, the applicant's credit history is given in the code shown.

Underlying their credit evaluations are the three C's of credit: character, capacity, and capital.

Character Character is the most important of the three C's. It is based on the individual's sense of responsibility in meeting financial obligations. A person who has always paid bills promptly rates high on this standard. A person who has sufficient money to pay bills but doesn't feel an obligation to pay them promptly is not considered a good character risk.

Capacity Capacity usually refers to a person's ability to earn money. It frequently means that the applicant has job skills to keep a steady job at a wage level sufficient to meet financial obligations. Wage earners who may be subject to layoffs or who already have more financial responsibilities than their earnings will safely cover are examples of those who are given a low rating on the capacity standard.

Capital In relation to credit applications, capital refers to the wealth of the applicant. This means the physical and financial assets the applicant possesses. If a person owns property or has savings or other investments that can be put up as security for an indebtedness, the person's credit potential is usually good. To most retailers, it's the least important of the three C's.

Limiting Credit Sales

When a decision is made to accept a credit application, the final decision is whether or not a credit limit is to be set on the account. If a firm decides to put a limit on the amount a customer can charge, some guidelines that help determine what this limit should be are as follows:

■ The applicant's income and that of the other members of the family whose income will be used to repay the account, and the number of dependents of the applicant

■ Other financial obligations the applicant must meet, such as house mortgage payments or car loans

■ The amount the customer can be expected to buy during the account month.

Businesses try to prevent customers from overcharging by requiring that salespeople check with the credit department for the credit rating of any person making a purchase above a specified amount, called a floor limit. Some credit cards are marked in code with the limit the customer may charge without special authorization. If the customer wishes to make a purchase above this amount, the salesperson must get authorization.

When customers apply for credit, they often wish to make a purchase immediately. Some retailers will give the customer a courtesy account with a special credit limit. This account allows the applicant to make purchases up to that amount. It is granted on the basis of the information received directly from a credit bureau. This practice is called **spot credit approval**. It is temporary. The usual full credit investigation is made before the account is finally approved.

Rejecting Credit Applications

If a decision is made to refuse a credit application, generally the person is informed in a tactful letter. Such a letter usually states that the person's application is not acceptable "at the present time." If the customer requests the reason for rejecting the application, it must be given. For example, the firm must tell the customer that the reason the credit application was denied was "based on information received from the XYZ Credit Bureau." The person can then contact that bureau for specific details about the reason for the rejection and can ask to see the credit record on file with the credit bureau. The applicant can then discuss the information in the credit file with the bureau and have included in the file any corrected information.

Define each term and use it in a sentence.

All-purpose bank
   credit card
Authorization line
Cash flow
Chattel mortgage
Conditional sales
   contract
Credit bureau
Credit card
Direct credit

Down payment
Installment credit
Open-account credit
Single-purpose
   credit card
Spot credit approval
Travel and
   entertainment card
Working capital

CAN YOU ANSWER THESE?

1. Why do consumers use credit? Why do retailers offer it?

2. Who has title to the goods in each of the two types of installment sales?

3. What are the three main types of credit cards? Who uses each type, and why do they use it?

4. What are the questions that should be answered by a retailer who is debating whether or not to offer consumer credit?

5. What services does a credit-card company offer the retail marketer?

6. What are the most common questions included in an application for credit?

7. What are the three criteria used in establishing credit limits?

8. When a credit application has been rejected, what recourse does the applicant have?

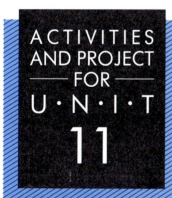

ACTIVITIES AND PROJECT FOR U·N·I·T 11

RETAIL MARKETING CASES

1. After graduating from the marketing education program at his high school, Monty Lamas took a position as a salesperson in a large sporting goods store that advertised extensively. Opportunities for advancement appeared to be excellent, and he looked forward to a prosperous future with the firm. However, during his first week on the job, Monty was disappointed with the attitudes of the other salespeople. Some of them actually seemed to avoid waiting on certain customers. They withdrew to the stockroom and often continued with their stock work

even after a customer arrived. Sometimes they would continue to chat with one another in the customers' presence. They didn't smile when waiting on their customers and appeared disinterested in their customers' problems. This behavior was particularly noticeable when teenagers or people who were not well dressed were being served. The salespeople didn't spend much time with them.

1. Was Monty right when he decided to join the company?
2. Now that Monty is an employee of the firm, what are the options available to him at this time?
3. What might happen if Monty consistently sold more than the other salespeople in the department?
4. Should Monty talk to his superior about his negative feelings toward the other salespeople?
5. Should Monty try to find another job?

2. Anita Schwartz was a senior at West High School and a marketing education student-trainee at Karstens Men's Clothing Store. Anita liked her work and hoped to pursue a retailing career after graduation. So she worked hard and studied salesmanship avidly. Her concern for customer buying problems was evident, and she began to build a steady clientele. Her sales volume continued to increase until it was frequently higher than that of several of the full-time sales workers. Anita's employer was highly pleased with Anita's work and singled her out for praise at one of the weekly sales meetings.

Soon after that sales meeting, Anita began to encounter difficulties with some of the other sales personnel. She thought that some of them were going out of their way to take sales away from her. She also noticed that two of them were unfriendly and avoided talking to her. One of the older men even seemed to make extra work for Anita.

1. Identify the true problem.

2. What are the important facts to be considered in this problem?
3. List several possible solutions to this problem.
4. Evaluate the possible results of each solution.
5. Which solution do you recommend?

3. Hugh Belling was the owner-manager of a new marina that sold pleasure boats and parts and offered repair services in a high-income suburb. After a few months in business, he decided to engage the services of an outside company—either a bank credit-card service such as MasterCard or VISA or a travel and entertainment charge-card company such as American Express or Diners' Club. Being the owner of a new firm, he realized the necessity of a good cash flow—cash income and outgo. His main concern, however, was to maintain the goodwill of present customers and, of course, to attract new ones. He estimated that the cost of services plus his bookkeeping expense for bank credit cards would be from 5 to 7 percent of gross sales and for travel and entertainment cards would run from 7 to 10 percent.

Hugh characterized his customers as follows: (a) The majority were in high income brackets; (b) they traveled extensively at home and abroad; (c) they were above average in economic understanding; (d) their family size was above average; (e) all seemed to be status-conscious; and (f) they responded to personal services.

1. What else should Hugh know about his customers?
2. What are the advantages of bank credit cards for his customers?
3. What benefits would travel and entertainment cards offer them?
4. What would Hugh gain from an affiliation with each type of service?
5. What other questions should Hugh answer before making a choice?
6. Which type of service would attract more new customers?

PROBLEMS

1. On a separate sheet of paper, write the letter of each of the following types of products and services: (a) automobile, (b) barber shop or beauty parlor, (c) corsage, (d) dry cleaning, (e) fire insurance, (f) health spa, (g) house paint, (h) motel room, (i) restaurant dinner, and (j) typewriter. Under each letter, write a selling statement or describe a selling action that would appeal to more than one of the five senses (sight, hearing, touch, taste, and smell). Appeal to as many senses as you can. After completing your list, you can add statements or selling actions contributed by other class members.

2. Rule a form similar to the following. In the left-hand column, write the letter of each of the following products and services: (0) paint, (a) automobile oil change, (b) bicycle tire, (c) electronic calculator, (d) pocket camera, (e) film processing, (f) barbecue grill, (g) car rental, (h) fast food hamburger, (i) VCR cassette, (j) dress shoes. In the right column, list for each product or service at least three related items that may be suggested to a customer who is interested in purchasing the product or service.

Product or Service	Related Items
Example: (0)	Brushes, thinner, and sandpaper

3. Rule a form similar to the following. In the left-hand column, write the letter of each of the following questions: (0) Do you have a savings account? (a) How many jobs have you held during the past 5 years? (b) Do you own an automobile? (c) How many years of education have you completed? (d) Will you supply the names of two personal references? (e) How long have you worked for your present employer? (f) What are your present financial obligations? (g) Have you ever been turned down for credit? (h) How much life insurance do you carry? (i) What is your Social Security number? Place a checkmark (X) in one of the columns to the right to indicate whether the credit interviewer is attempting to gain information regarding character, capacity, or capital by asking the questions listed in the first column.

Question	Character	Capacity	Capital
Example: (0)			X

PROJECT: AMENDING THE FEATURE-BENEFIT TABLE

YOUR PROJECT GOAL

Given a feature-benefit conversion table, reorganize and amplify its features and benefits to make it more functional and easy to use.

PROCEDURE

Now that you are acquainted with the steps of a sale and understand the necessity of accurate, functional product and service knowledge in today's competitive retail marketplace, you are ready to reshape your feature-benefit conversion table to better serve your needs in personal selling and promotion activities. Here are your directions:

1. Review the discussion of feature-benefit conversion tables in Chapter 29, pages 248–249.
2. Update the features and benefits of the table you prepared for the project at the end of Unit 10 (p. 258) with additions and cor-

rections. (If you haven't completed that project, prepare another feature-benefit [f-b] table similar to that described on p. 248.)

3. Classify each of the benefits associated with the various product or service features as follows and mark each benefit with the proper letter.

a. "O" Obvious or apparent benefit: advantage that needs little or no explanation by the salesperson.

b. "H" Hidden benefit: advantage that usually is not seen or understood without help from a salesperson or informative literature.

c. "U" Unique or exclusive benefit: advantage that is available only from your product or service.

4. Reorganize and copy your f-b table (a) listing the features of the product or service beginning with the ones that will be seen first; (b) arranging the labeled benefits in the sequence O, H, U.

5. Star each benefit labeled H and U that you think is suitable for use in a merchandise approach and/or in suggestion selling.

6. Exchange your new f-b table with a classmate who prepared a table for a related product or service. Discuss additions and corrections.

EVALUATION

Your new feature-benefit conversion table will be evaluated on its completeness and utility.

U·N·I·T 12
DEVELOPING A SALES FORCE

C·H·A·P·T·E·R
35 *Maintaining the Right Corporate Image*

Where you shop is as important as what you buy. That's the guiding principle of prudent shoppers—those consumer models who set the shopping procedure for their friends and relatives. And that's the underlying reason why retail marketers build an image that appeals to their target market consumers. Forming a favorable image is one of the most important tasks in operating a business. It's what consumers think of your enterprise that's the most important factor in bringing customers into your place of business.

Think about the stores you have been in, heard about, or whose advertising you have read. Which ones fit the following descriptions?

■ This store has real bargains. The merchandise may not be top quality, and the assortments are average. You have to wait on yourself, but you get good value for the price you pay.

■ They have the largest selection in town,

and you can charge and have your purchases delivered. Prices aren't the lowest, but they're not the highest either.

■ Just go in and let them solve your problem. They're experts, and they give you the kind of attention that's special. Of course, the prices are rather special too, but then you know that you get the best there is.

■ This firm was born out of a heavy commitment to the community in which it does business. It sponsors civic events and supports programs that are designed for us.

By matching a store you know with one of the descriptions above, you have in part defined its personality. You may not have thought of a business as having a personality, but each one does. Just as you have distinctive, individual qualities by which you are known, retail firms also make a general impression on their customers, employees, business associates, and the community in general.

UNDERSTANDING THE CORPORATE IMAGE

The impression, personality, or mental picture that is generally called to mind when a firm is mentioned is known as its **corporate image**. As suggested in Chapter 18, it is really the reputation of the enterprise as consumers and others know it.

All of the following contribute to a retail firm's image: each salesperson serving a customer, each advertisement run by the company, each assortment of goods, each display, each promotional sale, and each remark about the company by an employee (or anyone else). Management sets policy guidelines to help employees communicate to customers the desired corporate image during their daily work. All workers should follow the company guidelines to create an image that attracts and holds customers.

Before retailers can begin to create their own corporate image, they must decide on the market(s)—types of consumers—they wish to serve. Authorities generally agree that about the worst sin that a retail marketer can commit is to try to be all things to all people.

How a Corporate Image Functions

Shoppers usually patronize a firm whose image is closest to the image they have of themselves. The closer the association of the two images, the more successful the store is likely to be. Unless the firm's image is acceptable and consistent with the positive image in the minds of potential customers, they will not favor a particular establishment. Thus, each enterprise must determine its own individual niche in the marketplace and project its desired image to the potential customers in that niche.

The individual images of the members of the sales staff contribute to the image that the retail firm conveys to its customers.

The Mark of a Cloudy Image

Merchandising giants have perished because of a cloudy retail marketing image. For example, the W. T. Grant Company went out of business after many years of effective service, largely because it was unable to maintain a distinctive image among its competitors and attract enough customers to maintain profitability. Regardless of size, maintaining an image compatible with that of the selected market niche is crucial.

Thus, it is critical that entrepreneurs carefully identify the retail market niche(s) they want to serve and specifically describe the image they want to portray. In the excitement of starting a new business, it's easy to neglect this essential task; it's so enticing to add a product or service that distorts the marketing image.

The Need for a Specific Appeal

Many business policy makers operate on the basis that there is no longer a mass market, only a "class" market. Therefore, they program their promotion expenditures toward the particular "classes" of customers who are most likely to patronize their firm.

The various social classes in a community have different psychological expectations and seek different measures of satisfactions in the marketplace. As a result, only appeals to specific social classes are likely to be effective.

For example, homemakers in the lower-income group tend to look at goods and services in a functional sense; they are generally concerned with practicality and dependability. They will seek to identify themselves with the firms whose image reflects their concepts of frugality and economy. In contrast, homemakers in the upper-income group are generally more interested in the labels associated with products and services and whether or not the symbolic meaning of the seller's personality reflects their status and lifestyle. They may make purchases merely for the sake of change.

The Value of Market Positioning

Retail businesses do not exist in isolation; they must compete in the marketplace for consumer patronage with many other similar businesses. So just meeting the needs of customers is not enough.

Customers show strong preferences for a market leader. A statement by a Dayton-Hudson (Minneapolis) marketing executive illustrates the intensity of competition among soft-line retailers for consumer market leadership: "I used to think it was enough to be a trend merchant, but the competition is so very quick to be with you—even if Dayton's is first, we have less than 4 to 6 months to stay ahead of it." His aim is to find and offer trendy goods in attention-getting ways. "You have to be new and fresh, always doing something interruptive," he said. "Retailing has to be noticed."

As indicated in Chapter 12, in order to get and hold attention, retailers try to match their firm's service and behavior with potential customers' perceptions of a compatible supplier. Thus, effective market positioning ensures that customers will recognize your firm as having the qualities necessary to satisfy important needs.

SHAPING THE FIRM'S IMAGE

One important characteristic of a market is the income level of consumers. It roughly corresponds to four types of retail stores. So there are basically four major types of retail markets. These markets are those served by (1) the exclusive shop, (2) the specialty store, (3) the popular-price store, which has the largest percentage of buyers, and (4) the discount store. The figure on page 302 shows how the market for men's suits is segmented into four income-level categories that correspond to the four broad categories of stores. Note the overlapping of individual incomes among the categories.

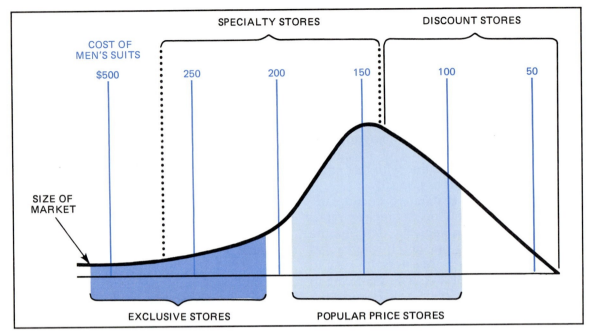

SPECIALTY STORES   DISCOUNT STORES

COST OF
MEN'S SUITS

$500   250   200   150   100   50

SIZE OF
MARKET

EXCLUSIVE STORES   POPULAR PRICE STORES

Store strategy and market segmentation.

Once retailers have decided on the consumers they wish to serve, they can change, sharpen, or shape their firm's image to meet those consumers' needs and wants. To do this, retailers work to make their company policies reflect and reinforce the desired image.

From the consumer's perspective, every store is characterized as either a prestige, promotional, semipromotional, or convenience type of enterprise. Let's look briefly at prestige, promotional, and convenience-type operations.

Prestige-Oriented Enterprises

Nieman-Marcus of Dallas, Texas, projects a strong patronage image that encourages consumers to identify themselves with the store. The market strategy of prestige stores of this kind is to base their promotional appeals first around themselves and then around the merchandise they handle. Such establishments attempt to distinguish themselves and their offerings by stressing individuality, exclusiveness, service, and prestige.

Promotion-Oriented Companies

Promotion-oriented companies concentrate on popular-priced merchandise and services, usually emphasizing savings and economy. They are cheery and bright, with plenty of signs directing customers to the various kinds of merchandise and service, and they may have well-designed self-service units.

Convenience-Oriented Firms

Convenience-oriented firms are epitomized by the 7-Eleven stores scattered about the city. The purpose of the convenience store is to supply the neighborhood with various and sundry needs for goods and services—frequently food products or repair services.

Of course, there are all shades of gray among the three main categories from which to choose, the objective being to find a niche in which to excel.

■

MAINTAINING THE DESIRED CORPORATE IMAGE

A desired corporate image for a retail marketing firm is the characterization that generates the satisfactions sought by its owners. That image should be confirmed with facts and figures, and it should be described in enough detail to serve as a guide for management in formulating operating policies. Although the desired image is durable, it is not set in concrete because it must respond to the changing market environment.

Consumer values and attitudes toward shopping may change rapidly. During prosperous times, shopping may become a form of entertainment, a way to relieve boredom and loneliness. Studies in the mid-1980s revealed that adults spent 6 hours weekly, on the average, shopping. Such activity has a major favorable impact on the economy. Yet, a slight recession could change consumer attitudes and shopping behavior. When economic conditions require that consumers restrict their purchases to the fulfillment of basic needs, the image of retail marketing changes dramatically.

Maintaining a desired corporate image is a critical management responsibility. It is sustained by all public and private customer contacts that are made through the media or by any individual associated with the firm. Thus an image, the keystone on which long-run success depends, is influenced by the four P's of the retail marketing mix and by the firm's personnel throughout the enterprise.

First, let's look briefly at some of the ways each of the familiar operating policies of the marketing mix discussed in Chapter 17 influence the general perception of a firm. Then we can explore the ways that a firm's personnel, particularly the salespeople, influence a firm's image.

Impact of Operating Policies

The four major types of company operating policies that have a direct bearing on a retail marketing firm's image are (1) the product or service it sells, (2) its pricing policies, (3) the place where the sales transactions occur, and (4) the promotion of sales and goodwill. How does each aspect of a business operation relate to the formation of a desired image? Each area of operating a business may provide opportunities for a firm to excel and gain goodwill or to falter and erode its image. To neglect one aspect of the operation in order to enhance another will defeat the firm's purpose. Careful coordination of operating policies derived from the desired image is essential.

Influence of Product or Service Policies The most important factor contributing to a store's image is the merchandise it sells; and the most important factor in building a service company's image is the quality of service it sells. Therefore, a clearly spelled-out merchandising policy or services-offered policy is crucial. A merchandise (product) policy relates to the major lines of merchandise to be carried—including the quality and assortment of goods in each line. Its counterpart in a service business would be a services-offered policy.

■ *Major lines of merchandise.* The firm's image and its patronage appeal are generally determined by its highest-priced merchandise classification. Stores are usually judged by consumers on the basis of the quality of the products handled. With some kinds of products, such as apparel and jewelry, the quality range may be great. Other considerations relating to merchandise lines that affect a firm's image may relate to policies concerning familiarity and image of brands.

■ *Depth and breadth of merchandise line assortments.* Another aspect of merchandise policy that affects the firm's image is the assortment or number of brands it carries and the number of sizes within a merchandise line. Some stores carry several brands to give customers a wide selection and stock a complete range of sizes and styles. For example, a customer called Brooks Brothers, a nationwide men's clothier known for its complete service, to ask if the store sold nightcaps. Without missing a beat, the salesperson inquired, "With or without a tassel, Sir?" On the other hand, discount stores usually restrict assortments to those items for which there is a big demand.

Influence of Pricing Policies
Relative prices are an important aspect of a firm's image, but prices are not easily controlled. With some types of goods and services, such as many food items, competition brings about nearly uniform prices in a given locality, and there is little that retailers can do about it. For other goods, such as art supplies, the price is determined largely by the cost of business operations. So a firm that offers many free services, such as the advice of knowledgeable salespeople and delivery service, has to charge more than one that offers fewer services. Chapter 51 provides an explanation of the many factors that enter into pricing decisions.

Influences of Place Policies
Although consumers have accepted the automation of retailing, modern shoppers still want convenience, comfort, and courtesy when they shop, so the physical environment is an important aspect of the firm's image. In order to keep their customers, most firms are faced with the choice of becoming more efficient in self-service techniques or more personalized in the services and shopping environment they offer. Place policies are increasingly important image builders as the trend toward shopping for fun develops.

In the realm of place policies that affect a firm's image are decisions concerning where, when, and how the products and services are to be sold, what methods and technology to use in selling and displaying them, and the appearance of the physical facilities both inside and outside the structure. Thus, if a cus-

tomer service is to be added to improve the desired image, management must consider existing costs as well as costs of the new service.

Influences of Promotion Policies
Even before a customer enters a place of business, he or she frequently has a fairly good idea of what the firm is like because of its promotion activities. Its selection of advertising media, the mix and frequency of its ads, the quality of the products and services advertised, messages in the ads, publicity articles, and word-of-mouth communication provide an idea of what to expect from a retail business.

Upon entering the sales floor, the customer's impression of the firm is influenced by displays of products, by floor decorations, and by the behavior of the salespeople. Retailers make sure that the promotional activities inside the store (floor layout, displays, and personal selling) reflect the same image as promotional activities outside the store (in the media).

Many customers judge a firm by the activities it uses to promote sales. There are many variations of the promotion techniques used by various companies. A company may do very little sales promotion of any kind. Or it may carry on frequent, aggressive sales campaigns, offer premiums or coupons, announce limited-time sales over a loudspeaker, and so on. See Chapters 38 and 44 for additional information on promotion techniques.

Impact of Personnel Policies and Practices

For purposes of clarifying the formation of a retail marketing image, another "P" has been added to the four P's of the marketing mix. This fifth "P" is personnel, for the *people* who are charged with the responsibility of implementing the policies relating to the four P's. Furthermore, it is the firm's personnel (people) who make the most vivid impression on consumers, especially during personal

A new cut above. N-M's remarkable new Quadrillion® diamond is square-cut and precision-faceted to achieve a powerful brilliance and infinite depth, creating the effect of a flawless, solid diamond set in 18kt yellow gold. (Enlarged to show detail.) Precious Jewels Salon.

Neiman-Marcus

Dallas   Fort Worth   Houston   Bal Harbour   Fort Lauderdale   Atlanta   Washington, D.C.
Boston   Chicago   St. Louis   Las Vegas   Beverly Hills   Newport Beach   San Diego   San Francisco

A store's promotional policies contribute to its image.

contacts with them. Recall how you felt about some company after a particularly good or bad experience with a salesperson or an adjustment clerk. Didn't it alter your image of the firm?

Personal Contacts Personal contacts form lasting impressions that overpower all advertising and publicity or customer services a firm can muster. Imagine how much goodwill the eminent, late J.C. Penney generated when he personally greeted customers and showed concern for their problems, often seeing personally that a particular need was fulfilled.

Salespeople, in particular, can be either the best or the most doubtful image element of a retail establishment. At one end of the spectrum, there is no better asset than the goodwill developed by salespeople who are well trained and public-relations minded—ambassadors who have merged their personal service objectives with those of the company. At the other end, there can be no worse detriment to a firm's image than an indifferent or arrogant salesperson. In the final analysis, the key contact point between the company and the customer is the salesperson or sales representative. Eliminating a salesworker to save operating costs or relying on poorly trained, part-time sales personnel may result in reducing rather than increasing sales.

Care-and-Share Mentality Most customers sense the character and objectives of retail businesses, looking beyond that of meeting their personal needs and wants for goods and services. Consumers generally carry a mental picture indicating which companies hold a **care-and-share mentality**. In terms of caring for people and sharing responsibility for their welfare a retailer's image are good, bad, or in between. Customers patronize those that are good and avoid, when possible, those that are bad according to their standards. Here are some of the things they may value when they weigh the character of a retail marketing institution.

Many retailers, both large and small, participate in activities outside of operating the business that manifest their interest in the community. They donate money, energy, and their expertise to various worthy causes and become known for being public-spirited. Their executives participate in service clubs and other community organizations. Their personnel policies and employee training programs contribute to a team spirit that makes work on the job purposeful and enjoyable; and when people have a purpose in life, they enjoy more of everything they do.

In this chapter, you've learned how retail marketers constantly work at making their firm's image match the customers they want to serve. You found out that retailers do this by tailoring their product or service, pricing, place, promotion, and personnel policies to reflect the firm's image they want to project to consumers.

In the next chapter, you'll learn about measuring sales performance to achieve the objectives of the "right image."

TRADE TALK

Define the term and use it in a sentence.

Corporate image

CAN YOU ANSWER THESE?

1. Explain why where you shop is as important as what you buy, from the customer's viewpoint and from the retailer's perspective.

2. Exactly what is the right retail corporate image?

3. Who contributes to the formation of a retail marketing corporate image?

4. What are the probable difficulties of a firm that tries to be "all things to all people"?

5. What is the relationship between a firm's corporate image and the positioning of that firm in the marketplace?

6. From the consumer's viewpoint, what are the four types of retail stores?

7. In what ways do product or service policies affect the retail marketing image?

8. Why are personnel policies and practices included among the factors in maintaining the right corporate image?

9. Explain the ways that a care-and-share mentality manifests itself.

C·H·A·P·T·E·R

36 *Measuring Sales Performance*

"Tell me, Mr. Jones, why do you want to measure the performance of your sales force?" asked the management consultant of the new business owner-manager. "To reduce my selling costs, of course," was the ready response. "Also, I'm beginning to see that there are inequities in the way we're paying our salesworkers and I'd like to give the better producers more than the less productive ones. Then too, we've been thinking about doing some sales training. Sales have been falling off a little lately."

Mr. Jones has justifiable reasons for wanting to measure **sales performance**—the generation of sales by virtue of a salesworker's behavior or "customer following." **Customer following**, or **personal trade**, refers to a customer-salesworker relationship characterized by the same salesworker serving a particular customer over a long period of time. Mr. Jones will find that there are three broad categories of reasons for measuring sales performance of his employees as he pursues his objectives.

WHY MEASURE SALES PERFORMANCE?

There are three broad categories of reasons for measuring sales performance: (1) upgrading customer sales or service, (2) reducing selling costs to increase profits, and (3) using fair compensation methods to maintain a harmonious sales staff. If Mr. Jones can find valid measures for the kind of selling that fits the desired image of his firm, he'll have the key to knowing how to develop a superior sales force. He'll also be able to retain his qualified salespeople and select competent recruits.

However, the task of measuring sales performance is a difficult one because nearly every sales job is different—the products and services vary widely, desired corporate images differ, business conditions change, and so on. Also, to make matters more difficult, there are so many criteria that can be used to evaluate the selling process. Therefore, measuring sales performance is a matter of analyzing selling jobs and individual positions to the best of one's ability. Then it's a matter of applying suitable measures (yardsticks) to an individual salesworker's assigned duties and responsibilities. Let's look at the major factors that decision makers might consider while determining the yardsticks used to measure sales performance.

DIFFERENCES IN SALES POSITIONS

The following general categories of factors influence the thinking of decision makers in varying degrees: (1) goods versus services, (2) clientele characteristics, (3) characteristics of current salesworkers, (4) present sales practices, and (5) outside forces. Because of the many variables in these categories, there is rarely any one best method of selling for an entire firm. What may be an optimum sales approach for one classification can be poor for another.

Goods versus Services

Selling methods at the retail level range all the way from complete self-service checkout of groceries to full-service selling of intangibles such as insurance. Many retail marketers deal with intangibles as well as with tangible goods; and intangibles usually defy accurate measurement. For example, services such as insurance, health spa membership, travel, and education are difficult to measure.

Also, within the realm of tangible goods there are marked variations that call for separate yardsticks of measurement. Recall the discussion of the differences in selling convenience goods, shopping goods, and specialty goods on page 237.

Clientele Characteristics

Customers in various parts of the country prefer different kinds of sales treatment. When you shop during your travels, notice the differences in sales procedures used by salespeople. For example, contrast the behavior of many New York City salespeople with that of their counterparts in the South or West.

Characteristics of Current Sales Workers

Another area of concern in selecting yardsticks of sales performance is the diverse characteristics of present salesworkers. The composition of the salesforce from the standpoint of age, special qualifications, and special assignments may be a factor to consider. Should one apply the same criteria in judging the performance of experienced and inexperienced salespeople?

Present Sales Practices

Company sales practices vary with regard to the degree of persuasion to be used. Hard sell, soft sell, and the consumer-based personal selling described in this book all have their place in retail marketing. Factors such as the products and services offered and the location of the store or shop have a bearing on the selection of the type of selling. However, using the same criteria for judging performance would be inappropriate. For example, a soft sell might not be a successful way of selling used cars in many places.

Those who measure sales performance usually consider carefully the company's current practices for evaluating the sales staff. Changing the criteria could create problems. Sometimes the older salespeople resist major changes, and a hostile attitude may defeat the purpose of any new practice.

Outside Forces

Numerous outside forces over which the decision maker has little control are taken into consideration when selecting the yardsticks with which to measure sales performance. Frequently the most important among them are the following:

- Competitors' practices
- Labor organization policies and practices
- Supply of and demand for salesworkers
- Labor laws, regulations, and licenses
- Seasonal factors
- Economic conditions (inflation, business cycle position)

Now that you are aware of the vast differences in selling positions and a number of the factors to consider when measuring sales performance, you are ready to examine the yardsticks for measuring the performance of your sales staff.

■

EVALUATING SALES PERFORMANCE

The measurement of job performance may be divided into two groups: (1) yardsticks

that can be expressed in numbers and (2) judgmental factors that are difficult to assign specific numbers.

Yardsticks Expressed in Numbers

The list below is an extensive, but not all-inclusive, list of selling yardsticks that can be expressed in numbers. It includes items that apply to all three levels of selling jobs—salesclerk, salesperson, and sales representative. Thus, some of the yardsticks will not apply to all three types of jobs. The items are not necessarily in order of importance.

- Time spent on the job
- Sales volume
- Returned purchases
- Cancelled orders
- Size of average sale
- Error record
- Number of complaints
- Number of transactions
- New accounts acquired
- Amount of profit generated

Judgmental Factors

Here is a partial list of judgmental factors that may be used as additional means of evaluating sales performance:

- Technical knowledge required
- Nonselling duties
- Personal following
- Special clientele ties
- Favorable rating by customers
- Sales group leadership
- Portrayal of the company image
- Cooperation with management
- Knowledge of the business
- Selling methods and style

Suppose you feel that sales volume is not a valid measure of performance because of differences in the prices of the merchandise being sold. You think that the salesperson who sells infants' wear, for example, is just as important as the one who sells cosmetics or

It is easy to record the number of items sold by a particular salesworker which have been returned.

junior apparel. So you look for other measures of sales performance, such as some of the judgmental factors above. Perhaps one member of your salesforce attracts a special following of customers who likely would not patronize your business if it were not for this salesperson. Notwithstanding legal or union rules, it would be prudent to credit the salesperson with the special clientele ties that have additional job performance value.

Common Errors in Measuring Sales Performance

Decision makers involved in measuring the performance of salesworkers—salesclerks, salespersons, and sales representatives—may be subject to five common errors: (1) They evaluate their sales personnel too highly on the basis of sales volume; (2) they rely too much on the number of sales made by each salesworker; (3) they compare the salesworker's present sales with past sales of a corresponding period; (4) they expect the salesworker to follow explicitly the selling methods that worked for them.

Misconceptions About Sales Volume

Usually sales volume by itself won't tell you how much profit or loss you're making on each salesworker. As indicated earlier, some in-house salespersons sell mostly sale merchandise (on which the profit is low), because it's easier to sell. And outside sales representatives do the same—moreover, they may have the authority to cut prices, which also reduces the profit.

Equally important is the fact that a large sales volume may indicate poor selling practices. Often, sales grabbers hurry their customers in order to get on to the next sale. A **sales grabber** is a salesworker who attempts to sell large quantities of goods at the expense of other salespeople in the department by waiting on customers out of turn, or by ignoring small purchases in order to serve customers buying in large quantities or purchasing more costly goods.

Misconceptions About the Number of Sales Calls or Sales Transactions

Of course, the number of sales calls made by a sales representative or the number of transactions completed by an in-house salesperson is an indicator of the salesworker's activity. But neither one tells the evaluator anything about the quality of the contact, which may be poor if the number is large in relation to sales of comparable salesworkers.

Misconceptions About Comparisons with Past Years' Figures

Comparing current sales with the same periods of the previous year is misleading unless sales are accumulated quarterly, semiannually, or annually. Some months have more working days than others. Changes in products, prices, competition, and tasks make comparisons with the past unfair to the salesworker.

Misconceptions About Selling Methods and Practices

Sales performance evaluators usually expect the salesworker to follow exactly the selling methods that worked for them when they were selling, even if they don't realize it. A successful salesworker has to be a person who is suited for the particular selling job. The qualifications for a salesworker should be determined by the selling job the employer wants him or her to do. For example, the very qualifications and characteristics that make a sales representative successful in selling one type of product or service may hamper that person when he or she tries to sell something different.

■

MEASURING SALES PERFORMANCE

Is a given salesworker an asset or a liability to your business? This is a question that ev-

ery manager must be able to answer in order to compete successfully in this technological age. Unfortunately, much more attention is given to the profitability of merchandise and services than to the productivity of salespeople.

Retail marketers in this information age make use of all the computer data and knowledge they can gather before they decide to carry a line of merchandise or offer a service. And after adopting a product or service line, the buyer is constantly fed data from computers and information from salespeople that indicate the advisablity of continuing to offer that line.

In contrast, retail salespeople are too often hired with little or no understanding of the employer's expectations. At the salesclerk and salesperson level, they are advised to "ring up all sales, be polite, and keep the area clean. If you have questions, just ask."

Usually, the new employee won't even know what questions to ask. Eventually, all employees have questions as to the owner-manager's expectations. These questions may be spoken or unspoken, but nevertheless, the questions exist. Frequently, these questions can be answered through a written job description, such as the one on page 312.

Using Explicit Job Descriptions

The use of a written job description offers several advantages:

■ It represents an informal "contract" between employer and employee, committing both parties to its provisions.

■ It provides disciplined guidelines for employee supervision and performance review, eliminating the customary pleas of ignorance concerning responsibility.

■ It reduces the chances of misunderstanding between employer and employee. The person with little understanding of what is expected on the job has little chance of fulfilling it. As a result, both owner and employee soon become dissatisfied. The owner is displeased because the salesworker is not living up to expectations. The salesworker is disappointed because of inability to understand why the owner is dissatisfied.

Amending the Personnel File

Like a retail buyer who gets positive and negative feedback on products from customers, so the job performance evaluator gathers information about a salesworker's performance. Pertinent data and information are matched with the job description and placed in the employee's file for consideration by management.

A personnel file like this, based on the yardsticks mentioned above, assists the employer and the employee when the salesworker's performance is evaluated. The job description provides a checklist so that all essential duties and responsibilities can be reviewed. Then commendations for achievements can be spotted and the need for corrective action can be identified. It is advisable for the employer and the employee to meet to discuss those areas where the employee is living up to expectations, those areas where improvement is in order, and how the improvement will be accomplished.

Developing Retail Sales Skills

Ultimately, the value of any employee is measured by that employee's productivity. How many sales dollars did he or she produce? Did the sales stay sold? Or did they lead to a high percentage of returns, cancelled orders, dissatisfied customers, or hostility among sales staff members?

Productivity can vary widely from one employee to another. A top producer will often generate two or three times the sales volume of the average producer. The top producer will develop a loyal following of customers: "people who always buy their suits from Bob because he knows what looks good on them." Best of all, this loyal following sends its friends to the retail firm.

Reviewing Sales Performance Reinforced with information now in the employee's personnel file, as suggested above, management is prepared to review the sales performance information with the salesworker. This periodic review allows the employer and salesworker to discuss each essential item in the report and to resolve any misunderstanding regarding duties and responsibilities or other essential problems regarding sales performance.

Establishing Sales Goals The review also provides an opportune time to discuss sales goals for the interviewee and, if feasible, for the unit to which he or she has been assigned. Goals give direction to one's efforts and permit the employee to evaluate his or her own progress. Through this evaluation of progress, a person can detect inefficiencies and determine any corrective action that needs to be taken. Similarly, when an objective has been achieved, the salesworker knows that he or she has done the job properly and can continue to do it in the same way.

Planning Improved Performance In those areas where a change is advisable, a mutually agreeable plan that improves or corrects the behavior in question can be made. Alternatives can be discussed—corrective measures such as on-the-job training, company training program, formal education, and so on, which have been discussed in Unit 9. However, a final word regarding formal education seems appropriate.

Company training programs are usually practical and achieve the goals for which they are intended—take advantage of them whenever possible. However, there is a difference between training and formal education.

Training usually deals with the how, the where, and the when, but it often neglects the why something is done. The answers to the first three questions help improve the skills needing improvement. But business and industry are usually not in a position to as-

JOB DESCRIPTION
RETAIL SALES—POWER TOOLS*

Function

Assist customers in the purchase of power tools.

Responsibilities and Authority

- *Have working knowledge of product line.*
  Be familiar with use and application of various power tools in order to provide reasonable technical assistance for customers.
  Be reasonably familiar with competitive products in order to point out advantages of our line.

- *Be able to present features of various tools in terms of customer benefits.*
  Close sales quickly.
  Suggest related sales such as bits with drills, blades with saws.
  Upgrade customer's purchase when appropriate.

- *Give customer service*
  Explain warranty requirements to customers.
  Assist customers in forwarding tools for repair.
  Advise customers of tool maintenance and operation tips.
  Advise customers of availability of any tools that are out of stock; follow up with telephone calls. explain credit policies to customers.

- *Follow store policies*
  Be courteous and cordial with customers at all times.
  Refer all complaints to the manager, unless they can be handled to the customer's satisfaction immediately.
  Have all customers' checks approved by manager before acceptance.

Follow store policies (continued)
  Secure bank authorization on all credit card purchases over $25.00.
  Record all sales, showing amount, department number, manufacturer, and product code.
  Collect sales tax on all sales.
  Refer all credit requests, including layaway and budget plans, to manager.
  Approve merchandise exchanges up to $10.00.
  Accept merchandise returns, whether for credit or exchange, only if original packing is available and undamaged.
  Notify manager of credit requests so that authorization can be signed by the manager in the customer's presence.
  Total sales daily, recording cash receipts, credit memos, and charge slips separately. Reconcile cash balance.
  Maintain department in a neat and orderly fashion.
  Notify manager of need for additional display stock.
  Conform with all provisions such as appearance, punctuality, working hours, etc., as described in the store's general conditions of employment.
  Read and understand all memos describing changes in store policy.

- *Make sales and profit*
  Meet with store manager to establish goals for sales and profit.
  Review department's performance with manager to establish goals for sales and profit improvement.

- *Report to appropriate supervisor*
  Report to owner

---

* Adapted from Small Business Administration: *Business Basics, Managing Retail Salespeople, A Self-Instructional Booklet*, 1019, Pp. 15–16.

A complete detailed job description clarifies the duties and authority of the position.

sume responsibility for academic learning. Therefore, they leave the matter of why to educational institutions. Thus, company training programs are usually specific in their goals. On the other hand, educational programs tend to be general in nature, emphasizing the transfer of learning to a variety of related situations when needed.

You may have heard that sometimes the most productive worker is not promoted. And this may be true for good reason. Productive workers may be *unconsciously competent*. They are excellent producers, *but they don't understand why*. So they can't analyze what they do or train their subordinates as they should.

The point here is to welcome training, but don't think that it is a worthy substitute for formal education.

TRADE TALK

Define each term and use it in a sentence.

Customer following	Sales grabber
Personal trade	Sales performance

CAN YOU ANSWER THESE?

1. What are the reasons for measuring sales performance?

2. Why is measuring sales performance a very difficult task?

3. What are the differences among selling postions that make the measurement of sales performance difficult?

4. What yardsticks for measuring sales performance can be expressed in terms of numbers?

5. What judgmental factors are used in measuring sales performance?

6. What common errors are frequently made in measuring sales performance?

7. Why do many retail marketers give more attention to the profitability of merchandise than to the productivity of salespeople?

8. What are the advantages of using a written job description when evaluating sales performance?

9. What is the basic difference between company training and formal education?

37 Coping With Change Through Personal Selling

CHANGE! Some individuals and some businesses grin and bear the rigors of change; others smile and do something about it. If you are a business manager and/or owner, your success or failure depends largely on how you view change. And if you hope to be successful in retail marketing, it's prudent to understand thoroughly the nature of change in today's social, political, and economic environment, and how it affects a retail marketing business. Once you understand these things, you can cope *creatively* with change.

■

UNDERSTANDING CHANGE

In this chapter, we shall think of change as a shift from one situation to another in the marketing of goods and services. Another word that needs clarification in this discussion is the word "cope." Webster defines "cope" as a verb meaning "to fight or contend (with) successfully or on equal terms, be a match for." That is a fitting description of the encounter that nearly every retail business must face under our private enterprise system. So, as suggested above, let's try to understand the nature and importance of change so that we too can "smile and do something about it."

In Defense of Change

The late Charles Kettering, former head of General Motors, aptly described the necessity of change in this statement: "The world hates change, yet it is the only thing that has brought progress." Without doubt, change is essential to our growth. Recognizing the importance of change in any society, our nation's founders planned our socio-political-economic system with change in mind. Obviously, the record of that system is an excellent one. And retail marketing has played an important part in building that record.

Change—A Certainty in Retail Marketing

Retail marketing is in a state of flux. It always has been and always will be—as long as competition is depended upon as a force to regulate the marketplace. Old, established lines of merchandise and long-lived services give way in popularity to the impact of new product lines and ways of rendering service. Think for a moment about how much and how fast retail marketing changes.

Customers' needs and buying habits shift. So some manufacturers try to control the retail prices of their products; others open their own stores or sell directly to the consumer; still others adopt a discount operation. A new type of competition develops—chain stores, self-service, vending machines, supermarkets, telemarketing, home television shopping, electronic shopping, and more to come (see Chapter 16).

Because changing market conditions have such a strong impact on retail marketing, successful managers must be aware of the changes going on around them. Each retail firm must be ready to respond to outside

Creative retailers regard change as an opportunity. When consumers shared a need for healthful foods that could be prepared quickly, supermarket retailers responded with self-service salad bars.

changes by making suitable and timely adjustments in merchandising and operating methods. Only by adjusting to constantly changing conditions can retail firms achieve maximum profits. In addition, adjustments to change usually require creativity and innovation—the keys to successful retail marketing.

Change Generates Creativity

What is the primary purpose of business? To some people it's profits, to others it's satisfying the needs of a variety of interested parties—customers, stockholders, or the employees of the company. To a seasoned retail marketing executive, however, the real, undergirding purposes of business are discovery, innovation, and creativity. Since the society in which we live is a creative one, the task of leaders is to further a creative attitude (mentality) in their firms. To do this, they need to recognize the power and strength that people-oriented businesses like retail marketing can generate. This strength is de-

rived from the differences among people—among customers, of course, but especially among employees. It's the responsibility of the owner-manager to communicate the creative purpose of business to the firm's employees, especially those engaged in personal selling and promotion who deal directly with consumers. Creative accomplishment is the actual day-to-day work of modern business; it's also the keystone of our business philosophy.

Competition Requires Change and Creativity

As implied in Chapter 10, competition is a situation in which two or more sellers vigorously seek to take business away from each other through price, product or service, and/or promotion. This situation suggests a race in which there are winners and losers. In many situations in retail marketing, it's a matter of who gets there "firstest with the mostest" in supplying the needs and wants of consumers.

It is very important that the entire personnel of a retail marketing firm possess a positive attitude toward our competetive economic system. If they view competition as an opportunity to exercise the creativity and initiative of a company in serving its clientele, they are likely to act rationally in a competitive situation. Thus it is the owner/manager's duty to cultivate a positive attitude toward the competitive element in retail marketing.

With a positive attitude toward the function of change and competition, you are ready to investigate the possibilities of coping with change via creative retail selling.

■

COPING WITH CHANGE VIA PERSONAL SELLING

As you already know, personal selling has given much ground to nonpersonal selling in recent decades. Likewise, the offering of customer services has greatly given way to price competition. During this strife, a split has developed, with sharp lines of distinction between full-service and self-service retailing. Here are the important differences between them from the standpoint of coping with change via personal selling.

Full-Service versus Self-Service

The greatest weakness of self-service is that customers must sell themselves. Therefore, the only way they communicate with management (except for a complaint here and there) is through their purchases. The primary advantage of full-service over self-service selling and over automated selling methods is the assistance of salespeople. Salespeople serve two broad purposes:

1. They help customers make buying decisions.
2. They provide management with feedback and offer suggestions.

Much has been said in this book (and elsewhere) about furnishing customers with purchasing assistance, but very little has been written or said anywhere about salespeople's offering suggestions and feeding back information to management. This is one of the most neglected aspects of retail management. Some authorities think that neglecting the management assistance function of personal selling is the main factor in the decline of personal selling.

Let's explore the neglected responsibility of personal retail selling. Why has this been called the "creative function" of personal selling, whereas assisting customers is referred to as the "conservative function"?

The Conservative and Creative Functions of Personal Selling

The **conservative function of personal selling** deals with passing along the heritage, so to speak. It deals with practicing what is known about the selling process. It means satisfying customers' needs and wants in customary ways. It's traditional.

The **creative function of personal selling**, on the other hand, involves innovation, discovery, developing something new, participating in the identification of changes in customer needs and wants. It may mean inventing a different way of doing something, of spotting a change that affects the business.

The remainder of this chapter deals with the application of the conservative and creative functions of personal selling to the task of coping with change in retail marketing. Let's talk about the conservative function first.

■

PURSUING THE CONSERVATIVE FUNCTION OF PERSONAL SELLING

Of the two broad functions of personal selling, the conservative function refers to furnishing customers with on-the-spot answers to their questions—the information-giving aspect of personal selling. Thus, it includes everything involved in serving customers. How do salespeople cope with change when they serve their customers?

You may have heard a salesperson say, "Customers just aren't what they used to be." That is true: They aren't. And when that salesperson elaborates, you'll know how he or she feels about change. Note whether it's "grin and bear it" or whether they "smile and do something about it." The progressive ones are conscious of current trends and receptive to them; and they are doing something about it. They see their work as an opportunity to stay young.

Focusing on Customer Wants

Recall the discussion in Chapter 16 of how consumers are becoming more interested in cultivating a personal lifestyle, and in Chapter 31 of how wants now overshadow needs. To capitalize on these changes in consumer behavior, salespeople can be coached to help management carve out a market niche—one that serves a selected aspect of consumer wants. They can do this by reinforcing a common want. For example, some progressive restaurants have added a deli that offers their popular specialties for enjoyment at home. Waiters and waitresses can then use their ingenuity in calling the deli specials to their customers' attention.

Cultivating Reliability

Recall from Chapter 16 that consumers increasingly expect retailers to stand behind their products' performance. To conform to this trend, a salesworker may be trained to be adept at stressing the use of the product, encouraging customers to follow directions on product use and care, following up on customer satisfaction, giving information about warranties, and following company policy on returned goods. Department stores, for example, have built goodwill by their liberal returned-goods policy.

Maintaining Ethical Standards

Recall from the introduction of Chapter 28 the development of ethical practices in retail marketing. Maintaining ethical standards among part-time salespeople in current markets presents a difficult problem unless workers are properly trained. Honest mistakes by poorly trained workers may be interpreted as dishonesty and reflect poorly on the firm. Having enough sales staff to reduce hurrying the customer helps to correct the problem.

Rendering Faster Service

Recall from Chaper 16 the consumer trend demanding faster service. The quality of service that salespeople provide can be upgraded by providing sales training on product and service information and on more effective sales practices.

Though convincing salespeople to accept the use of computers is often difficult, computers are being used to provide salesworkers with instant information about merchandise availability and about the features and benefits of products and services. More than 50 sales-oriented programs are available for use on personal computers.

■

APPLYING THE CREATIVE FUNCTION OF RETAIL SELLING

You will recall that the creative function of personal selling is providing management with feedback and offering suggestions. Salespeople are in a unique position to give management information about changes in the needs and wants of the customers they serve and frequently about the offerings of competing businesses.

Customers are a primary research source, as you learned in Chapter 13. You can find clues to change during a sale, and afterward, if you earnestly seek them. And, of course,

One way sales personnel help retail customers is to provide fast service.

there is much evidence of new fashions or styles, new products, and new services all around us when we choose to recognize it. First, let's look at some indications of change that can be spotted while the customer is present.

Clues During the Sale

Often during sales, customers provide clues to changing needs or preferences while telling the salesperson what they want, when they are raising objections, or upon deciding on an item. Alert salespeople are able to detect trends in style preferences during these regular steps of a sale. In small firms, information is generally passed along to management personally, whereas in large companies a special form is used.

Questioning the Customer Merely asking a customer why he or she likes a product or service may provide information that will

help the store buyer select merchandise. Department buyers and owner/managers of small businesses should budget time to serve customers personally on the sales floor in order to become familiar with the changing needs and wants of their clientele.

Preparing Want Slips Many firms provide the sales force with special forms called **want slips** which call for a description of items that are out of stock or not carried by the store. The completed forms are given to the buyer for study before reordering or when ordering new merchandise. See the illustration in Chapter 55 on page 478.

Recording Clues to Change Top salespeople frequently carry a small idea book in which to jot down observations that are easily forgotten during a busy day. A log of customer preferences also helps to individualize customer services.

Clues After the Sale

Post-sale reflections include analyzing complaints and following up on lost sales. Positive outcomes can stem from what first seem to be negative experiences.

Analyzing Complaints Complaints and returned merchandise furnish excellent opportunities for sensing changes in customer preferences. The kind of product selected for the item returned in an exchange sale signals changing preferences. If a customer returns an item to the salesworker who sold it, that individual is in a good position to explore the reason for the return and to help the customer find a suitable replacement.

Following up Lost Sales Interviewing customers who have been served by salespeople but did not purchase the item can be a good practice when skillfully executed. Usually this is done when the customer returns on another occasion, but it can be done via telephone.

Additional Signs of Change

Just as artists notice details that most people overlook, change-seeking retailers look for signals that have a bearing on their store's welfare. They keep track of their competitors' activities, but they watch noncompetitors as well for useful ideas.

Shopping the Competition **Comparison shopping**—seeing what competitors are offering in competing lines—isn't limited to professional shoppers who shop competing firms to compare their offerings and prices with those of the home business. Salespeople can become excellent comparison shoppers for the goods or services they sell, because they are likely to be better informed about the particular items they sell than professional comparison shoppers. They should be trained in the procedures of comparison shopping.

Checking with Friends Talking with friends and relatives about their experiences with the products and services offered by the firm can be fruitful if prudently done. People are usually willing to talk about things they know, such as the things they buy and the work they do.

Keeping Your Eyes Open Change is everywhere; it's just a matter of looking for it. And when you observe change, carry the thought a bit further to see how it may relate to you and your job. Dreaming can be beneficial when channeled to constructive purposes. Travel stimulates creative thinking, so take advantage of the situation when you travel and look for things that stretch your imagination.

■

DEVELOPING A CREATIVE MENTALITY

One's mentality is the mode or way of thought, mind set, or disposition one takes toward something. Our concern here is the development of a mind set (mentality) toward creativity that will encourage the exercise of creative thinking among salespeople. Hopefully, we can use this creativity to cope with human and environmental changes and compete successfully in the marketplace. Most leading salespersons and sales representatives have active imaginations, which can be put to good use in detecting changes in consumer behavior that affect retail marketing. So let's put this asset to good use. Let's gear up for creativity.

Some people seem to be more creative than others. Whether or not they were born with this trait is not a question that retailers need to answer. The important point for a retailer to realize is that creative productivity can be improved. So let's look at some of the means of doing so.

Take a Positive Attitude

Although creative people often assume the limelight, it may surprise you to know that creativity is not associated directly with any particular level of intelligence. Therefore, whether or not you choose to make use of your creative potential is purely a matter of choice—it's up to you.

Successful salespeople usually see their work as an opportunity to fulfill a purpose in life. Most likely, it's the conservative function of personal selling. They get satisfaction out of making their customers feel good about purchases. The more sophisticated salespersons and sales representatives agree with that concept. However, they have an additional purpose: They include the creative role of personal selling—offering suggestions and serving as channels for feedback to management. And this calls for creativity and initiative in perceiving changes in customer behavior and things that affect the market environment.

Study Creativity

People are usually against things they know little about! This is true for creativity as well as change. To correct this situation, the thing to do is learn as much about creativity as you can.

■ First, ask your teacher and school counselor about sources of instruction in how to improve one's creativity. Technical institutes and junior colleges frequently offer suitable courses in their day or evening school. Courses of study provide an organization of learning that is difficult to make via independent study.

■ You can supplement course work with independent study. Your public librarian can direct you and help you find productive periodical articles if you let him or her know what you need. Selective reading in the areas of sociology, anthropology, psychology, and education can be helpful.

■ Participating in buzz sessions, brainstorming, and role-playing activities often helps a learner improve his or her creativity. You can get the most value from these interesting classroom activities if you understand the nature of creativity.

■ If you are presently working in sales, try to concentrate on being creative when you engage in the steps of a sale, especially when you are doing the creative acts of making a merchandise approach, identifying wants and needs, and suggestion selling. And any of the five buying decisions offer ample opportunity for creative thinking.

Study Creative People

Associating with people and studying them is much like learning a language by speaking it; one learns unconsciously by example. Of course, learning increases if the experience is meaningful, so it's prudent to choose the people from whom you can learn.

■ If you are employed in retail marketing, you will generally find that workers engaged in promotional activities are creative. Observing the most creative salespeople in your department can also be fruitful.

■ Away from work, you can learn a great deal from watching children at play—especially young children, whose imagination often runs free. Plan your observations to include different age groups, so that you'll have a perspective that may reveal a subtle change that affects your business. Community involvement in civic projects and participating in service club and chamber of commerce activities provides opportunities to learn about pending changes as well as to observe creative behavior.

■ A final suggestion is to participate in games that call for using your creative abilities. Social games such as charades or individual games such as crossword puzzles help to stretch the imagination. Learning to be creative can be fun, so give it a try.

Creativity grows with exercise. The creativity you develop in recreational activities can be applied to your career in retail selling.

TRADE TALK

Define each term and use it in a sentence.

Comparison shopping
Conservative function of personal selling

Creative function of personal selling
Want slip

CAN YOU ANSWER THESE?

1. How does change benefit society?
2. What major changes in retail marketing have been made in the past?
3. How does change generate creativity?
4. Why should salesworkers look favorably on the phenomenon of change?
5. From the standpoint of coping with change, what is the greatest weakness of self-service?
6. What is the conservative function of personal selling? What is the creative function of personal selling?
7. How does the retail marketer develop the creative function of personal selling?
8. How is a creative mentality developed?

ACTIVITIES AND PROJECT FOR U·N·I·T 12

RETAIL MARKETING CASES

1. An interviewer taped the following statement of a salesperson. After reading it carefully, answer the questions that follow.

> Frequently, even if a customer has told me just what kind she wants, I get out other goods that she may not know about. I usually make a better sale that way, or sell two things instead of one. So many times, they only have a general idea of what they want and are perfectly willing to be turned to some other kind if you show them a variety.
>
> By showing lots of goods, talking intelligently about the class of goods you are showing, and when the sale is made, introducing something else along the line to increase the sale, you can show the customer that you are interested, friendly, and attentive. In many cases the sale you make in this way is what leads to a permanent customer.

1. What is your impression of this salesperson?

2. Is this an appropriate selling technique? What selling principles are involved?

3. Do customers really want new ideas? Under what conditions?

4. In what respects is this salesperson creative?

5. Do customers tend to judge creative salespeople as intelligent? If yes, are they correct in doing so?

6. Would this salesperson be a good source of feedback for management?

7. If you were a manager of a retail establishment, how would you encourage creativity?

2. You are the owner of a dress shop in Kentucky, and you are the exclusive outlet for your suppliers in your town. You have the reputation of selling one-of-a-kind dresses, and your typical customer believes that she has a right to expect, from your shop, an exclusive creation at a moderate price. Your styles are one of a kind in your town, but not one of a kind outside of your trading area, because they would then be too costly for your clientele. Your practice is to offer a dress in only one size or color, always keeping to what is popular in New York or California markets. However, other stores in nearby towns may also order the same size, color, and style that you have ordered. One of your customers, Mrs. Bly, recently purchased a dress from you to wear to a charity ball. At the ball, which was in another city, Mrs. Bly saw another woman wearing "her dress." Mrs. Bly has been a good customer and is known in the community as a style-setter. What are you going to do about her angry reaction to this incident?

1. Identify the true problem.
2. What are the important facts to be considered?
3. List several possible solutions to this problem.
4. Evaluate the possible results of each solution.
5. Which solution do you recommend? Why?

PROBLEMS

1. Rule a form similar to the following. In the left column, write the names of ten stores representing a cross section of those running ads in one issue of your daily newspaper. In the second column, write the kind of store it is—exclusive, specialty, popular price, or discount. In the third column, write the main image-building appeal(s).

Name of Store	Kind of Store	Image Building Appeal
K mart	Discount	Economy

2. Rule a form similar to the following. In the left column, write the letter of each of the following groups: (a) customers, (b) employees, (c) community, (d) society as a whole, (e) suppliers, and (f) competitors. Write a policy statement illustrating an ethical practice of a retailer toward each group. Give each group a priority based on its probable effect on a firm's welfare. Compare your ratings with those of your classmates.

Target Group	Policy Statement	Priority

PROJECT: SELECTING SALES PERFORMANCE CRITERIA

YOUR PROJECT GOAL

Given a retail sales job, a sample job description, and information about retail selling procedures and practices, prepare a list of potential sales performance criteria for a selected selling position.

PROCEDURE

1. Select a retail product or service marketing job at the salesclerk, salesperson, or sales representative level in the area of your choice. If you are employed in sales work, you may use the position you hold.
2. Review the Retail Sales—Power Tools Job Description on page 312. Note the five categories of responsibility and authority.
3. Make a list of the responsibilities and authority for your chosen job based on information from each of the three chapters in Unit 12. Include responsibilities in the creative function as well as in the conservative function discussed in Chapter 37.
4. Add needed categories of responsibility to those in the job description on page 312. For example, that job description does not include categories in the creative function of personal selling.
5. Enter your findings under the expanded list of categories.
6. Compare your findings with those of your classmates investigating comparable jobs and add or drop items from your list.
7. Have your instructor approve your findings before submitting the criteria to your employer for suggestions. If you are not employed, consult your instructor for advice on submitting your list to a suitable practitioner.

EVALUATION

You will be evaluated on how effectively you gathered information, compared your findings, and reported your findings.

PROMOTION

"I don't see why I have to hang all of these stupid signs in the windows," grumbled Erica. "Nobody looks at the dumb things anyway. I'd rather be tagging the new merchandise."

"Well, how is anyone supposed to know what new merchandise we've got if we don't put up these signs in the window?" Yvonne replied. "Look, the signs have pictures, and they're big enough to be seen from across the highway. I've also seen the new ads that will be in tomorrow's paper. They're really neat."

Erica and Yvonne are both part-time employees at a department store. Yvonne has been discussing two of the methods that retail marketers use to communicate to prospective customers—window signs and newspaper advertisements.

When you have completed this band, you'll know many other ways that retail marketers tell customers about their firm and the products or services it sells. In fact, that is what this band is all about: businesses communicating with potential customers through a process called promotion. You will learn how retail marketers decide what to promote and how and when to promote it. You will also learn how promotional campaigns are planned, produced, and evaluated.

U·N·I·T
13
LEARNING
ABOUT PROMOTION

C·H·A·P·T·E·R

38 *Promotion in Retail Marketing*

All of the things you do to communicate with your customers in order to sell more merchandise or services, create goodwill, build a desired image, and generally to create a competitive advantage for your business or line of products or services are classified as **promotion**. Promotion efforts may be classified as (1) nonpersonal activities such as advertising, display, and press releases and (2) personal contact activities such as selling and participation of personnel in community projects.

Let's see how this might work. Denny works at Sterling Hardware in Sterling Park. His supervisor, Carlos, has him unload bags of salt that can be used on sidewalks and driveways during the winter to prevent ice from forming. Carlos is putting up **shelf talkers**, small signs with the product name and price, on the shelves where the salt will be displayed in cut boxes. Since the first winter

storm is supposed to arrive this weekend, Carlos has arranged for ads to be run by the local radio station and in the local newspaper informing the public that Sterling Hardware has salt. Denny neatly arranges the boxes of salt on the counters to create a visual impression that the store has lots of salt. The red and white bags make a striking mass display.

But Carlos does one more thing. After work that evening, he calls all his salespeople together to explain why customers will need the salt. He then tells Denny and the others to ask each customer they will serve if they have any salt at home. This selling by suggestion is designed to sell more merchandise.

Carlos uses nonpersonal activities (shelf talkers, radio and newspaper ads, mass display) and personal activities (suggestion selling) to communicate to potential customers.

THE PROMOTIONAL MIX

Deciding which combinations of promotional categories and communication tools will be most effective in reaching the desired consumers requires careful judgment by retail marketers. When they want to reach more than one kind of consumer market, they may find that it is best to use several kinds of communication methods. The combination of communication methods that retailers use during a promotional campaign is called a **promotional mix**.

There are many methods businesses can use to communicate their sales and goodwill messages to the wide variety of customers they serve. These methods take on many forms and appeal to all five senses. The promotional methods can be arranged into the following seven groups:

1. Advertising
2. Visual merchandising
3. Publicity
4. Personal selling
5. Public relations
6. Customer services
7. Special incentives

The promotional mix varies widely, depending on the product or service being promoted, the characteristics of the desired consumer market, and the size of the promotion budget.

Advertising

Nonpersonal paid messages by an identified sponsor about merchandise, services, or ideas that retail marketers wish to communicate to customers and potential customers are called **advertising**. The tools that advertisers use to communicate their messages are called **advertising media** ("media" is the plural of "medium"). Common media include print, broadcast, and direct mail. The business pays for these services. Advertising usually accounts for the largest share of a retail business's promotion budget.

Print The most commonly used advertising medium is the newspaper—daily, Sunday, and weekly. Advertising makes newspaper publication possible. This is so because without advertising revenue, a paper would cost two or three times today's usual selling price. Other print media include magazines, shoppers, bus cards, the Yellow Pages, handbills, circulars, and billboards.

Broadcast Some businesses advertise on television and radio by sponsoring a specific program at a scheduled time. Others use short spot announcements between programs. National chains, franchisers, discount houses, and speciality stores use television regularly. Some small retail marketers advertise on local TV stations, particularly those who sell expensive items such as TVs, automobiles, and appliances. A new trend you may have noticed is the use of ads for local businesses at the beginning of a movie in your local theater. The increase in cable TV hookups will provide retail marketers with more opportunities to reach desired audiences.

Some stores use their intercom systems to call customers' attention to special sale items and various customer services; an example is K mart's "blue-light" specials. Loudspeakers may also be used by concession operators at sporting events and other recreational functions.

Direct-Mail Any form of advertising that is sent through the mail, such as promotional letters, samples, catalogs, circulars, and announcements, is **direct-mail advertising**. Promotional material, unlike the ads in newspapers and magazines, can be sent to specific segments of the market without competing with other ads. Often, promotional enclosures are sent along with monthly statements

Identify these examples of promotional methods.

to charge account customers at no additional cost in postage. This use of direct mail has increased recently, as many companies that regularly communicate with customer groups recognize the potential of these markets. For example, oil companies such as Shell or Texaco offer merchandise as diverse as wall clocks, exercise bicycles, and briefcases.

Visual Merchandising

Selling through display is part of **visual merchandising**, which includes all visual ways of promoting the business and the products and services it sells. Businesses make extensive use of displays, especially for special featured items. Largely through the imaginative use of window and interior displays, businesses show their products in ways intended to stimulate interest, to help consumers make selections, and to show how the merchandise is intended to be used.

Businesses that sell services also use displays. Travel agencies, banks, fast-food restaurants, and hotels all make use of the principles of visual merchandising to help sell their services.

Consistent visual merchandising makes McDonald's outlets easily recognizable anywhere in the world. The interior layout, furnishings, and the use of the familiar golden arches on signs and packaging are all part of the visual merchandising effort.

Window displays invite customers into the business. And once the customer is in the place of business, interior displays take over the selling task, either in part or in total, depending on the extent of self-service practiced. Regional shopping malls develop mall-wide institutional displays designed to encourage customers to visit the mall. These are often built around a seasonal theme such as Christmas or Spring. Stores inside the malls often take part in the overall mall display.

Many retail marketers such as automobile and boat distributors exhibit or display their products at fairs and trade shows. This can be a particularly effective way to attract potential customers.

Customer Services

Prompt, efficient, and courteous performance of customer services is one of the most effective promotion tools in today's retail marketplace. Often the products offered for sale are much the same in several different businesses, so customers choose the business that offers the services they want most. To attract and hold customers, many businesses promote how they handle returns and exchanges of merchandise, complaints and adjustments, alterations, delivery service, wrapping and

packing of merchandise, and repair services. Other services such as business hours, rest rooms, child-care facilities, the shopping climate on the sales floor, parking facilities, and consumer credit are also useful in attracting customers. Many retail marketers choose to offer these services at cost, at less than cost, or free of charge in order to encourage customer patronage.

During the past two decades, consumer credit has become a powerful promotion tool. Charge-account customers are often favored by retail marketers because a debtor-creditor relationship tends to play a key role in maintaining customer relationships with the business. So credit managers work with the promotion and merchandising divisions in seeking new charge accounts and in keeping charge-account customers happy. For example, J.C. Penney has offered new charge-account customers a choice of selected merchandise just for opening an account.

Publicity

Any mention of a firm, a product or service, or store personnel in the mass media in any form other than an advertisement is called **publicity**. Businesses use two types of publicity: free publicity and special-feature publicity.

You have only to read the daily paper to find some publicity items about a retail marketer. The newspapers sometimes obtain this information from news releases issued by the company. Large businesses usually employ professionals to prepare these releases. Small businesses generally depend more on a reporter employed by the medium to do the job. Such publicity may relate to merchandise promotion or aim at building goodwill for the institution. A recent Sunday newspaper included an article on a new type of fast-food restaurant that was going to open, an article on the increased popularity of skateboards among college students, and an article on fashion trends for the new school year. In each article, a particular business was used for the information and the owner or manager was frequently quoted. All these are **free publicity** because they are published without charge to the business.

By contrast, **special-feature publicity** costs the business money. This type of publicity includes fashion shows, sponsoring a bike race or a Little League team, educational programs, demonstrations, parade floats, calendars, and various gifts that advertise the business.

Public Relations

Activities performed in order to build goodwill rather than direct sales are called **public relations**. This function is increasingly important in the minds of progressive retail marketers. In no other field of distribution is success so dependent on public attitudes. So retail marketers engage in many public relations activities that, along with merchandising policies, encourage customers to patronize a business regularly. Common public relations activities include (1) institutional advertising and publicity releases, (2) improvements in store plant and facilities, and (3) contributions to community welfare programs.

Institutional Ads and Publicity Releases
People need to be told what the business does for its customers and for the community. So ads are run and publicity releases are prepared to make the community aware of the achievements and concerns of the firm.

Plant and Facilities
Many customers identify with a business because of its appearance and the good feeling they have when shopping there. Attractive, easily identifiable storefronts and signs; clean, comfortable, and attractive interiors; and a store layout designed with the customer in mind are public relations activities that are worth costly expenditures. At one time Kinney Shoes designed extra-wide parking spaces for its free-standing units. This helped ensure that the customer would not have a car door dented by another car parking too close.

Contributions to Community Welfare
Retail marketers realize that their success depends on the community. So, wisely, they improve their image by contributing to worthy causes, supporting community projects, serving as leaders of cultural movements, and supporting Better Business Bureau and consumer activities. By supporting service clubs such as Rotary, Kiwanis, Business and Professional Women, Jaycees, or Lions and in many other ways, retail marketers demonstrate their concern for the people of the community.

Special Events and Incentives

Retail marketers use **special events and incentives** to encourage sales during slow selling periods, to introduce new products or services, or to bolster the sale of certain products or services. These techniques include premiums, special price reductions, contests, free samples, and other incentives to buy. Each of these will be discussed in more detail in Chapter 40.

Personal Selling

"As a salesperson, I'm one of the most visible parts of the company." This statement by a successful sales representative for a large distributor suggests the importance of the sales staff in promotion activities. Success in promotion depends on the cooperation of the sales staff in particular, because they supply the expertise in selling the products or services to be promoted.

Personal contact with customers offers excellent opportunities for promoting sales. This is especially true when the sales staff is coached for its promotional role, as Carlos did at Sterling Hardware, in advance of a special sales event. Through wearing promotional badges, placing telephone calls, giving good service, using package inserts, and so on, the sales staff can put the finishing touches on a promotion event.

■

PROMOTION AND COMMUNICATION

The process of communication between business and customer is the same as between two people. There is a sender (the business) and a receiver (the customer). The illustration below shows how this process takes place. The business sends a message about its products, its services, or the business itself using a promotional activity, such as advertising, visual merchandising, special sales

incentives, or publicity. The potential customer receives the message by reading an ad, seeing a display, or receiving a coupon in the mail and then responds. The response may be in the form of a decision to buy or to ignore the message.

To be successful, communication must be interactive. The seller must communicate about the product or service in a way the customer will understand. The customer may ignore the message (this will happen if the message does not concern something of interest to the customer), or the customer may respond by coming to the firm and speaking to a salesperson. The customer may come into the store and make a purchase, or the customer may simply call the business for additional information. This communication process will continue as long as the business meets customer needs.

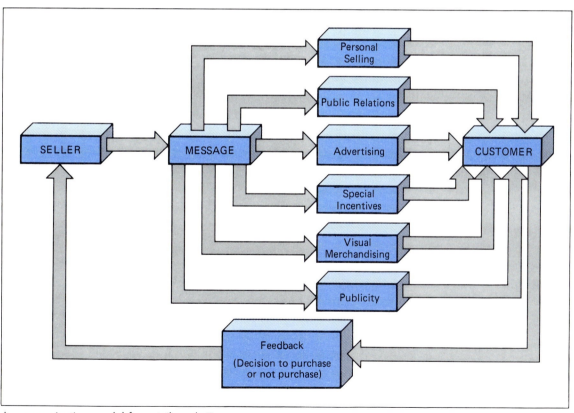

A communication model for retail marketing.

TYPES OF PROMOTION

There are two general categories of promotional activities in retail marketing: product and service promotion and institutional promotion.

Product and service promotion deals with selling products storewide or selling products of single departments. It involves using various forms of advertising, display, and other promotion tools. This is what Carlos was doing with the salt.

Institutional promotion deals only indirectly with selling products or services by building goodwill for the business (institution). The activities focus on the entire company and use devices such as image-building newspaper ads and various customer services that the firm offers.

For example, many retailers will develop promotional activities during holiday seasons (for example, Christmas and Hanukkah or the Fourth of July) to highlight the season. A business may set up a display window supporting scouting or community fund appeals.

Many businesses will encourage the use of their facilities by local schools or charitable organizations. For example, a bank may allow the senior class of the local high school to place posters announcing the forthcoming senior play in the bank's windows. The local McDonald's restaurant may actively collect donations for the Jerry Lewis Telethon.

None of these activities are designed to sell specific products or services. It is hoped that potential customers will enjoy the displays or participate in the fund drives and feel that the business is interested in the community. Business owners believe that this creates a positive image and will indirectly help sell merchandise or services.

Both kinds of promotion, product and service and institutional, may employ nonpersonal and personal methods of communicating with their audiences. Also, both may use the same tools to reach potential customers

TABLE 1 / THE PROMOTIONAL MIX

Communication Tools	Institutional Promotions	Product and Service Promotions
Advertising	*	*
Display	*	*
Personal selling		*
Customer services	*	*
Publicity	*	*
Public relations	*	
Special incentives		*

and supporters. Table 1 shows which communication tools can be used in both kinds of promotion.

HOW AIDCA APPLIES IN SALES PROMOTION

You will recall the discussion of AIDCA in Chapter 28. These letters stand for the mental stages a customer goes through in order to make a purchase. Promotion is designed to focus on each of those stages. Some ways that retail marketers use AIDCA in promotion to turn disinterested consumers into satisfied customers are shown on page 333.

A customer's attention may be drawn to an attractive picture or to a headline that mentions the brand name of a current fad in an advertisement. If you are the intended customer, you might be attracted by a picture of your favorite rock group or your favorite sports hero. Homemakers may be drawn to a new product because of coupons received in the mail. A store window displaying desired merchandise may attract the attention of passing shoppers.

Once retail marketers have the customer's attention, they will attempt to build interest in and a desire for the product or service they are selling. In a print ad, the description

Original Condition

Disinterested consumer

Attention

Newspaper advertising

Interest

Window display

Desire

Self-service display,
personal selling

Conviction

Personal selling

Action

Customer service

New Condition

Satisfied customer

Retail marketers use the various promotional media to guide customers through the
mental stages of the buying decision.

of the product or service may be designed to do this. Or the picture in the ad may be enough to create interest and desire to own the product. Displays of products in use, in-store demonstrations, and fashion shows are other examples of how the media are used to encourage interest and desire.

Depending on the nature of the product or service being promoted, customers may visit a location where the sales personnel will greet them and attempt to provide them with the products or services that will best meet their needs. Once the customer becomes convinced about the product or service, the salesperson will try to close the sale and thus move the customer to action.

Some businesses, such as mail-order retailers or self-service outlets, do not require salespeople. In these businesses, the nonpersonal types of promotion will need to address all stages of the buying process. Direct-mail businesses usually include order blanks in their catalogs or provide free numbers for customers to call. In self-service businesses, special types of displays may be used to help bring consumers to the action stage of the buying process.

∎

WHO HANDLES PROMOTION

Within a retail marketing organization, the responsibility for promotion is determined by both the size and type of organization. Many retail marketers, large and small, use the services of outside specialists.

Small Firms

In a small business, the owner or manager usually handles promotion planning. At Sterling Hardware, Carlos handled all the promotion for the store. The local newspaper helped him prepare ads. He had a printing machine in the stockroom for making small signs, and he used many signs and props provided by the manufacturers of the products the store sold. He and the sales staff usually built the displays in the store. But for spring and Christmas, he and the other merchants in the shopping center hired a freelance display specialist. The hardware store paid a fee for each display built. A freelance display specialist is not employed permanently, or full-time, by any one store.

Chain Operations

Most chain-owned organizations have a central or regional promotion director. It is this person who decides what promotional activities will be used throughout the chain or region. This person is also responsible for carrying out these activities. He or she is assisted by a group of advertising, display, and sales training specialists who take part in planning sales campaigns, are responsible for window and interior displays, and sponsor sales training programs for all store personnel. These plans are supervised by regional supervisors and carried out by local store managers. In some situations, an advertising agency may handle the advertising.

Large Department Stores

Large department stores usually have their own sales promotion staffs. Heading the staff may be a sales promotion manager and an advertising manager, and there also may be someone in charge of publicity and someone else in charge of visual merchandising. A department store usually has its own artists and display specialists and prepares all its promotional material itself.

Shopping Centers

Businesses in many shopping centers cooperate in promoting the shopping center as a whole. Large centers employ a promotion director. This person coordinates the overall publicity and advertising activities of the center and may also plan special shows and events to provide publicity for the center. This coordination enables the center to compete with downtown retailers and other local distributors in attracting customers. It is also of special benefit to the smaller stores in the shopping center, because they are able to take part in the centerwide promotions, which are planned by experts.

Yvonne and Erica, in putting up the window signs at the Glitter Boutique, were participating in promotional activities. So was Carlos at Sterling Hardware. In both instances, the businesses were trying to bring more customers into the store and to increase sales.

TRADE TALK

Define each term and use it in a sentence.

Advertising
Advertising media
Direct-mail
    advertising
Free publicity
Institutional promotion
Promotion
Promotional mix

Product and service
    promotion
Public relations
Publicity
Shelf talkers
Special events and
    incentives
Special-feature
    publicity
Visual merchandising

CAN YOU ANSWER THESE?

1. What is promotion?
2. What are the two general categories of promotion?
3. List the seven elements of the promotion mix.
4. What are common media used by advertisers?
5. What is the difference between free publicity and special-feature publicity?
6. How does promotion relate to the concept of AIDCA?
7. How is promotion handled in small businesses? In large businesses? In chain stores?

C·H·A·P·T·E·R

39 Promotion Goals

Margaret Mead, the late anthropologist, once blamed many of our economic and social problems on the advertising industry's sales tactics. But she also viewed consumer advertising as essential, saying that "you really can't live without advertising." Mead referred to the problems of the Soviet Union and what happened when it started to produce consumer goods without advertising them. Because the goods weren't advertised, Soviet consumers didn't know they were available. And they didn't buy them. Finally the Soviet government had to launch advertising programs.

There are literally thousands of choices facing the consumer in today's marketplace. And the mix of products changes constantly. Eighty percent of the products on a store's shelves today were not there ten years ago! This vast choice makes deciding which product or service to buy very difficult. One of the primary benefits of promotion to the consumer is that it provides needed information about price, availability, performance, and benefits of products and services. This information helps consumers make good buying decisions.

Promotion benefits retail marketers as well. Today's consumers are better educated and demand more information.

Promotion is often criticized because some firms are not honest in their promotional activities. Misinformation inhibits wise decision making by consumers. But industry self-regulation and government laws have reduced this problem considerably. Another criticism charges that products and services would be cheaper if sellers spent less money on promotion. This reasoning ignores the influence of promotion in increasing competition, which helps keep prices low. Competition has increased at the same time as have consumer choices. As a consequence, it is much more difficult for retailers to obtain and retain consumer loyalty. A well-thought-out marketing communications program has become a necessary expense for retailers who want to stay in business.

■

WHO SPONSORS PROMOTION?

Let's look at retail promotion in terms of sponsorship. Knowing who pays for promotion will help you understand how promotions fit into a particular retailer's plans and into retail marketing in general. There are three main sources of funds for retail promotion: (1) manufacturer and wholesaler advertising, (2) cooperative advertising, and (3) retailer sponsored promotional activities.

Manufacturer and Wholesaler Advertising

Many manufacturers and wholesalers of national brands spend large amounts of money on promoting their own brands. They spend some of that money on promotion to encourage retailers to stock their products or buy their services. But most of the money is spent on advertising to encourage consumers to buy their products from retail outlets. The purpose of this national consumer advertising is to persuade consumers to buy a particular product or service wherever it is sold. It is the product or service, not the local retailer, that is important to the manufacturer or wholesaler. The retail marketer is encouraged to stock certain products if the manufacturer or wholesaler can create sufficient demand. In some types of retailing, such as food retailing, some stores are reluctant to stock merchandise that is not heavily promoted by national advertising.

Retail marketers have little influence over the amount of national advertising their vendors prepare and purchase. However, if retail marketers maintain good communication with their suppliers, they can stay current on what items suppliers are planning to promote and when they plan to do so. This information is important in deciding what to order and how much additional promotion, if any, should be given to these products or services.

Cooperative Advertising

Advertising in which the cost is shared by the retail marketer and the supplier of the product is called **cooperative advertising**. The supplier may pay a set percentage of the advertising cost or provide a discount on future purchases. By law, a supplier must offer the same program to all retail customers.

For help in selecting your color call Clairol toll free 800-223-5800

What are the advantages and disadvantages of cooperative advertising to the retail marketer? Why do suppliers offer to share in the cost of placing ads?

Cooperative advertising may be difficult for some retailers to use. The supplier usually requires the use of ads provided by the supplier. This limits the creativity of the local retailer. Some retail marketers feel that agreeing to accept cooperative advertising tends to influence both their buying plans and their promotion plans. They feel that their buyers may be more influenced by the amount of promotional money a supplier offers than by their own estimation of what their target customers want.

Retailer Sponsored Promotion

The chief purpose of a retail marketer's ad is to attract buyers to a particular place of business. To do this successfully the retailer may promote national products. But the message is, "come to *me* to buy."

Most retail marketers prefer to depend on their own efforts to attract customers. They plan and prepare their own promotion, often with the help of media representatives. Successful retailers carefully choose the media that will most influence their target markets. A promotion program developed for a specific business, telling specific customer groups about specific service or product benefits, is likely to be more expensive than a manufacturer-supported program. But it is also likely to be more effective.

Retail Information by Nonretailers

Manufacturers, wholesalers, and retail marketers are not the only sponsors of advertising. More and more, other agencies, organizations, and institutions are competing for consumer support. Government agencies, "Be all you can be in today's Army"; charitable organizations, "Give the United Way"; public and private schools, "Vocational Education Makes Good Cents," and many others are using promotion to reach consumers. Many professionals, such as doctors, attorneys, accountants, and others, are beginning to use promotion techniques to capture their share

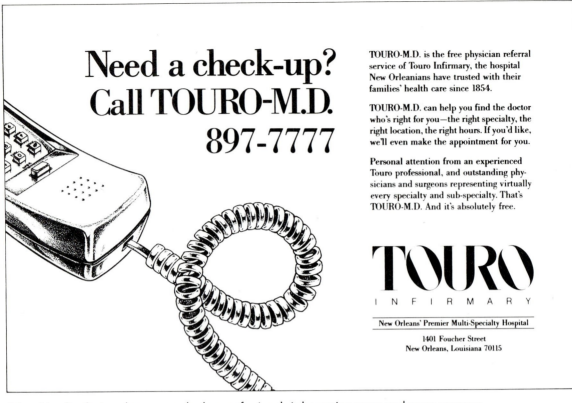

Advertising by doctors, lawyers, and other professionals is becoming more and more common.

of the consumer's dollar. All of this creates more information for the consumer to deal with. The effective retail marketer develops promotion that gains consumers' attention, builds interest and desire, and ultimately helps consumers to make good buying decisions.

■

GOALS OF THE PROMOTIONAL MIX

Each element of the promotional mix is used for a different purpose in an effort to increase profitability. By sending messages designed to build sales and goodwill, retail marketers can expand present markets and develop new ones. Promotion activities are an important factor in creating a product and service image, a company image, or a store image.

Goals of Product and Service Advertising

The main purpose of advertising a product or service is to persuade people to purchase it from the sponsor's firm. But each advertisement is usually planned to achieve one or more of the following goals.

1. *Increase sales volume.* This is a goal of all product and service advertising. Additional sales volume can increase the profitability of a business.

2. *Bring customers into the place of business.* Effective advertising will develop interest on the part of customers and encourage them to come into the place of business. Sometimes retailers use **price leaders**. These are items offered for sale at reduced prices; it is expected that customers will purchase other merchandise as well.

3. *Attract new customers.* Advertising can be targeted to market segments that are not already a part of the advertiser's clientele. For example, if Sterling Hardware (see Chapter 38) was interested in attracting more female customers (more men shop at hardware stores than women), it could create advertising to show what products and services are offered that would appeal to female consumers.

4. *Introduce new products or services.* The promotion of new fashions, the latest in ten-speed bicycles, or the most recent addition to the Burger King menu is often the aim of advertising. Ads may also be used to inform consumers about new uses for existing products. Baking soda, long used for cooking, is now advertised as a deodorant for refrigerators. Johnson's Baby Shampoo is heavily advertised for adult use.

5. *Develop a demand for private brands.* Many large retail marketers sell their own private brands of products. In addition to selling Lee jeans, Farm Fleet stores also sell jeans with a Farm Fleet label. These jeans sell for less, and although they are sometimes made by a major manufacturer, they do not carry the manufacturer's label. Farm Fleet will often advertise their brand of jeans in the same ad as Lee jeans.

6. *Reinforce user satisfaction.* Advertising is often used to remind current consumers of the satisfactions they receive from a product or service. This type of advertising is done to reduce **cognitive dissonance**, which is the doubt that a consumer experiences after purchasing a product or service. Advertisers seek to reassure consumers that they made a wise buying decision. Many retailers, such as automobile dealers, use advertising to build pride in the ownership of their product. Their advertisements tend to emphasize the status associated with their product.

7. *Level out sales volume.* Retail marketers try to increase customer traffic on light days or in off seasons. Grocery stores will spend considerable money promoting customer traffic on Mondays, typically a slow day. Most retail marketers use advertising to bring customers into their business during January, February, and July, months that are typically low in sales.

8. *Ease the job for the retail salesperson.* Well-developed advertising programs begin the sales process before the customer enters the place of business. Good ads attract consumers' attention and create interest and desire for the products and services a business offers. The job of the salesperson is made easier when the customer is pre-sold.

Goals of Institutional Advertising

Institutional advertising is usually classified as either service advertising or prestige advertising. **Service advertising** informs the public of the ways in which the retailer serves customers. Services might include the availability of credit, delivery service, free parking, and many other things. **Prestige advertising** is used to impress the customer with the "personality" of the business as a way of convincing them that this is the place to shop. The advertising may stress such distinctive characteristics of the business as quality of products, varied assortment of merchandise, the quality of the sales staff, support for local organizations (many sports shops support local Little League teams) or any other aspect of the business that will build credibility in the consumer's mind.

Much advertising by large retail marketers is designed to create the kind of image desired by the seller. Usually it will not focus on the products or services sold, but rather, on the customer orientation of the business: "K mart is your savings place," "Have it your way at Burger King"; the trendiness of the fashion department; or the market the business wants to identify with, such as "Sears is where America shops."

Goals of Visual Merchandising

The main objective of all visual merchandising activities is to increase the sale of products and services. Usually the approach is direct, through the display of merchandise or services. More recently, however, visual merchandising has been used to create or enhance a business's image. The entire selling area is now considered part of the visual merchandising effort. Retailers located in regional shopping malls recognize the necessity of distinctive displays that break through all of the visual clutter to attract potential customers into their store. That is one of the primary goals of visual merchandising—to attract the potential customers into the store.

Promotional displays increase sales in two ways. Retail marketers know that customers will buy more when they see merchandise displayed with related products in an appealing way. A good display prompts impulse buying, and it reminds shoppers of things they want to buy.

Another goal of promotional displays is to show new uses for familiar products. For example, athletic shoes are frequently displayed as part of a total fashion look in addition to having their functional features highlighted.

Displays that are used to build goodwill for the business in the minds of regular and potential customers are called **institutional displays** because they sell the institution or business as a whole. During holiday seasons, some large department stores, public utilities, banks, and hotels use displays that reflect the season rather than promoting specific goods and services. Other institutional displays may dramatize such themes as civic fund-raising drives, high school clubs, or the work of social agencies.

Goals of Public Relations

Retail marketers engage in many public relations activities, which, together with merchandising policies, encourage customers to patronize a business regularly. Common public relations activities include (1) institutional advertisements, (2) physical plant and facilities, and (3) contributions to community welfare.

Institutional Ads People need to be told what the business does for its customers and for the community. So retail marketers run ads that raise awareness of the achievements, concerns, and good citizenship of the firm. Many local retail marketers pay for advertisements saluting employees who are students in local marketing education programs. These ads show the firm's support for public education and commitment to the local community by hiring its youth and helping them prepare for a career in marketing.

Physical Plant and Facilities Many customers identify with a retail store because of its appearance and the good feelings they have when shopping there. Attractive, easily identifiable storefronts and signs; clean, comfortable, and attractive interiors; and a layout designed with the customer in mind are effective public relations activities that are worth the expenditure. Many shopping malls are taking advantage of the tremendous amount of open floor space and are inviting senior citizens to come into the mall before regular business hours for exercise classes. This costs the mall very little in additional expenditures but creates considerable goodwill.

Contributions to Community Welfare Retail marketers recognize that their success depends on the community. Wise merchants work to improve their public image by contributing to worthy causes, supporting community projects, serving on local boards and as leaders of cultural movements, and actively supporting consumer organizations.

Goals of Publicity

Publicity is different from advertising in that it is not paid for and usually not controllable by the business. Publicity is used to accomplish one or more of the following five major goals:

■ To maintain or improve the business image

- To show the business as a contributor to the community's quality of life
- To demonstrate innovativeness
- To increase awareness of the business, its products or services
- To reduce overall promotion costs

To be effective, publicity must be newsworthy if it is to be covered by the media. Having an Olympic bicyclist or sports hero spend a day in your sporting goods store signing autographs will attract the local media. Inviting the mayor to give a speech at the opening of a new shopping mall will likewise bring reporters. Major donations and unique sales are often reported in the media. Holiday parades such as Macy's Thanksgiving Day parade can receive tremendous media coverage. Television and newspaper reporters often visit restaurants or other retailers and rate their performance and quality.

While publicity can be effective, it has some drawbacks. Macy's parade, even though it receives free television time, is expensive. The publicity that McDonald's restaurant chain receives because of its support for the Ronald McDonald Houses is free, but the cost of corporate donations is large. Other drawbacks include lack of control of the message and the timing of the message. A local reporter may criticize some aspect of the business. Or the news release about the new business may not be run when it is needed.

Goals of Personal Selling

Personal selling as a form of promotion was discussed extensively in Chapter 38. It is mentioned briefly here to reinforce its role in the total promotion mix. As an important element in the mix, the goals of personal selling are to:

- Assist the customer to make a purchase
- Feed information back to the retail marketer
- Provide customer service
- Improve customer satisfaction

Special incentives may encourage customers to try a product they haven't used before.

Goals of Special Incentives

Special incentives (sometimes referred to as sales promotion) are activities and offerings designed to encourage consumer purchasing of specific items. Special incentives include coupons, sweepstakes, special pricing, gifts, and contests. Over the past decade, business expenditures for special incentives have been increasing at nearly twice the rate of expenditures for advertising. Many companies now spend more of their promotion budget on special incentives than on traditional advertising.

The goals of businesses that use special incentives are to:

- Gain the attention of and provide information designed to lead the customer to the product or service
- Provide an inducement designed to represent a value to the consumer
- Provide a distinct invitation to purchase now
- Get nonusers to try a product or service
- Encourage larger purchases by current users

■

ETHICS IN PROMOTION

Advertising as we know it today began with the first newspaper. In 1846, Volney Palmer established the first advertising agency in Boston. During these early years, there was no code of ethics and few, if any, restrictions on advertising. Patent medicine, soap, and railroad travel led the list of advertised products and services. Anyone of national prominence in any field, from the President down, was fair game for those who were willing to go to any length to sell their products and services. Many well-known figures lent their names, willingly or not, to products. At one time, the President of the United States endorsed a brand of North Carolina cigarettes.

Advertising has come a long way since those early days. Many federal and state laws attempt to define "false" or "misleading" advertising. Organized business associations and individual companies have worked out codes of ethics for promotion. These codes attempt to end practices that might be considered wrong, or unethical, even if they are not technically illegal.

Agencies That Support Honesty in Promotion

Better Business Bureaus are local commercial organizations that have drafted codes setting standards for promotion practices. These codes forbid the use of unethical practices such as offering "free" goods, making exaggerated claims about products or services, giving misleading information, giving false price lists for marked down merchandise, and bait-and-switch tactics.

Bait and switch is the practice of advertising a product or service at an extremely low price and then using pressure selling tactics to get the customer to buy a more expensive item. This is avoided by all legitimate businesses. It is also illegal in most states.

The Federal Trade Commission (FTC) is responsible for keeping firms from engaging in unethical advertising practices. It will fine persistent violators of the laws that govern truth in labeling, advertising, and selling in interstate commerce. The FTC is responsible

for laws such as the Federal Food and Drug Act, the Cosmetics Act, the Fair Packaging and Labeling Act, and the Textile Fiber Products Identification Act.

Advertising and other promotion tools are critical to the communication process between retail marketer and consumer. Therefore, it is important to maintain standards that will keep the consumer's confidence. These laws, codes, and guidelines protect both the public and the businessperson against less reputable competitors.

In the next chapter, you will be able to study in more detail the use of special incentives in promotion. In Chapters 41, 42, and 43 you will be able to examine the techniques of advertising and visual merchandising. These three elements of the promotional mix are critical to success in communicating with the buying public.

TRADE TALK

Define each term and use it in a sentence.

Bait and switch
Cognitive dissonance
Cooperative
    advertising

Institutional displays
Prestige advertising
Price leaders
Service advertising

CAN YOU ANSWER THESE?

1. How does promotion help the consumer?

2. Identify three sources of sponsorship for promotion directed toward consumers.

3. List six goals of product and service advertising.

4. Identify two types of institutional advertising.

5. Identify three goals of visual merchandising.

6. What are institutional displays used for?
7. What are three common public relations activities?
8. How is publicity different from advertising?

9. What factors contribute to the decision on what merchandise to promote?
10. What two organizations support honesty in advertising?

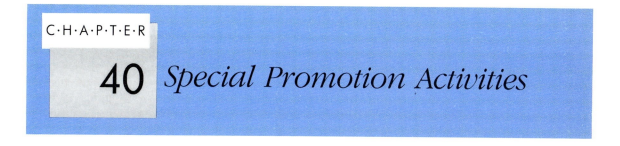

C·H·A·P·T·E·R

40 *Special Promotion Activities*

■ Arby's gave away special Christmas glassware with soft drink purchases in its fast-food restaurants.

■ The Athlete's Foot gave away a free Kaepa T-shirt with the purchase of a pair of Kaepa tennis shoes.

■ A car dealer offered to finance the purchase of new cars at 2.9 percent interest (when regular loans were 11 percent) or to fly the customer to Las Vegas for a vacation if the customer purchased a Pontiac.

■ A bank in Houston gave away a Porsche 928S sportscar with the deposit of $1 million for 5 years. If you were not interested in cars you could select a small airplane instead.

■ McDonald's Game Card, tied into the 1984 Olympics, increased average store sales by nearly 6 percent. (You scratched off the coating to uncover an event, such as pole vaulting, and if the United States won, you won a prize.)

These are examples of incentives provided to customers to encourage their purchase of a product or service. Spending by businesses on special incentives exceeded $85 billion in 1985. (By comparison, all other media advertising amounted to only $95 billion during the same time period.) These special incentives work best when used together with advertising. Special displays of a product that were tied into TV advertising sold 15 percent more than when the special displays of the product were used without TV advertising.

In retail marketing, all promotional media are important, but special incentives may provide the spark to generate action and produce immediate results. Special incentives help to make advertising more effective. In self-service businesses where there is little or no personal selling, special incentives can be used to present information to customers and move the customers toward a decision to buy.

■

TYPES OF SPECIAL INCENTIVES

Special incentives include a variety of product offers and activities. Some activities are premiums, contests and sweepstakes, and special price reductions.

Premiums

Premiums are the most often used special incentive. A **premium** is a prize or reward offered to a customer as an inducement to buy. The use of premiums has a long history. In early Rome, merchants gave away unusual trinkets to women who purchased cosmetics. In Colonial America, merchants gave away packages of needles to women customers and candy to their children to encourage patronage of their stores. The beginning of the trading cards that we know today came in 1851 when a company exchanged soap wrappings for picture cards.

Coupons   The premium with the widest use is the coupon. A **coupon** is a certificate entitling the customer to a cash discount, merchandise, or services. Manufacturers of soap, cereal, and various other products issue coupons to customers. When customers buy an item at the grocery store and present the coupon, they receive the price reduction stated on the coupon: "25 cents off Maxwell House coffee," "50 cents off Kitty Litter." The retail marketer is reimbursed by the manufacturer for the face amount of the coupon plus an additional amount for handling costs.

Local retailer marketers often distribute their own coupons or double the value of manufacturers' coupons. Others, such as automobile service businesses, restaurants, and shoe stores, often use coupons that offer two-for-one deals or other incentives.

In 1972 more than 40 billion coupons were distributed to consumers by direct mail, door-to-door delivery, newspapers and magazines, packages, or other means. In 1985, more than 180 billion coupons were distributed. They were redeemed for $2.24 billion. Quaker Oats, makers of Cap'n Crunch cereal, redeems more than 800,000 coupons a day. Coupons are an important part of marketing cereal and other food products.

Despite these impressive statistics, one of the problems with coupons is the often low

This national retailer offers coupons that can be redeemed in its shops. The shop manager supplies the information to complete the "Limit" and "Offer good" lines to the local newspaper running the ad.

rate of use. Generally, fewer than 10 percent of the coupons issued are redeemed by consumers. If a company distributes them by relatively expensive methods such as direct mail, the rate of use increases to 15 to 20 percent. The best rate of return is reached when coupons are part of the packaging. Redemption rates increase to 35 percent. Newspaper coupons have the lowest rate of redemption.

Even though manufacturers invest heavily in coupons, many small retailers do not like to use them because of the time and energy required to keep track of them and obtain reimbursement from the manufacturers.

Trading Stamps   A second premium, less used today, is trading stamps. **Trading stamps** are printed stamps that retail marketers offer to their customers in return for making purchases at their place of business. Customers collect the stamps, and when they have enough, they redeem them for merchandise supplied by the trading stamp company. Until the early 1970s, trading stamps were used by grocery stores and service stations as an effective sales incentive. However, the use of trading stamps began to fall into disfavor with both consumers and retail marketers, and today they are used infrequently.

Contests and Sweepstakes

After being in business for a few years, Kathy Touhill, the owner of a variety store, found that sales usually dropped off during January and February. Last year, she decided to try to increase sales during this slow period by offering customers an incentive to come into the store and shop. She prepared a series of postcards, which she mailed to residents in the area at regular intervals during January and February. The cards invited everyone to guess the number of cassette tapes in a huge cylinder in the middle of the store (there were 3496). The winner received a box of Valentine's Day candy, flowers delivered on Valentine's Day, and a selection of romantic music on cassette tapes. Ms. Touhill got results by using direct mail to announce the contest. This promotional activity took the sales slump out of February by arousing customer interest and increasing store traffic.

Many products and services have been successfully promoted by the use of contests and sweepstakes. While both create excitement and interest, they are different promotional activities. **Contests** are set up by companies and built around a game that usually requires a skill.

Because contests require some skill, they are not subject to state laws governing lotteries, so proof of purchase can be required. Chef Boy-Ar-Dee invited consumers to submit recipes for pizza mix along with proof of purchase. Finalists were brought in for a "pizza cook-off," which generated considerable extra publicity for Chef Boy-Ar-Dee.

A **sweepstakes** is a game of chance rather than of skill. It must be carefully planned so that it does not become an illegal lottery.

Such chance promotions are considered to be the fastest-growing category of incentives. More than $916 million was spent during 1984 on sweepstakes and games. This is 11 times the amount spent in 1972.

In a sweepstakes, you cannot require a proof of purchase. It is very important for retail marketers to seek the advice of professionals when establishing such activities. Sweepstakes involve giving away prizes to randomly selected qualified entrants. In the usual game, predetermined winning tickets are seeded among those given out. A popular sweepstakes is the Publishers Clearing House sweepstakes. This national sweepstakes is designed to encourage consumers to subscribe to magazines. To enter, you send in a form that has been preprinted with your name and address. Winners may receive over $1 million in prizes. Before you get too excited, however, remember that you have to pay taxes on any winnings. Also remember that the bigger the prize, the lower your odds are of winning.

Free Samples   A small size of an advertiser's product that is given away is called a free sample or **product sample**. Samples are designed to encourage customers to buy new or improved products. Detergents, toothpaste, and soap are often promoted in this way by manufacturers. Other products are promoted by retailers giving away product samples. A food retailer might offer product samples of a new type of cheese. Employees in a cosmetic department might offer to spray a new perfume on passing customers to introduce a new fragrance.

Samples may be sent through the mail, hung on doors in targeted communities, or handed out in stores or shopping centers. Some product samples are packaged with other products of the same manufacturer. A toothbrush might be packaged with a sample of toothpaste.

Gifts and Self-Liquidating Premiums
Direct premiums or **gifts** are items that are given away at the time of purchase. These

are sometimes referred to as *factory packs* meaning that they are packaged by the manufacturer. This form of sales incentive is popular among cereal and soap manufacturers. The prize in a box of Cracker Jacks, the whistles in Good & Plenty, or the glasses in the box of detergent are all designed to give the product greater consumer appeal. Recently, these gifts have been tied to popular TV shows, comic strips, or other media. If you buy Cheerios, you can get a Garfield the Cat reflector for your bicycle. Record albums include posters of the rock stars inside the album cover.

Self-liquidating premiums require that the consumer send in proof of purchase and a specified sum of money. The amount of money usually represents the cost of the premium to the company. Usually, the customer benefits by obtaining the merchandise at less than it would ordinarily cost, and the manufacturer is reimbursed for the cost of the premium. Although gifts and self-liquidating premiums are sponsored by manufacturers, retail marketers benefit by incorporating these incentives into their own promotions.

Direct Sales Premiums   House-to-house salespeople use premiums to create goodwill and begin a sales conversation. People involved in direct sales, such as Fuller Brush salespeople, have used this technique for years. They give the customer a vegetable brush or some other item to interest the customer in the product line.

Automobile retailers, appliance retailers, and other big-ticket-item retailers are beginning to use direct sales premiums more often. These premiums are offered to prospective customers to get them to come into the store or showroom. Small gifts such as portable radios are given to people who come in and test drive a car, for example.

Not-for-profit organizations, such as public radio and TV stations, often offer gifts bearing their logos to encourage membership and contributions.

Special Price Reductions

The two types of sales incentives that offer customers special price reductions are special sales and combination offers. When a retail marketer offers products or services at a reduction in price, it is called a **special sales event**. Department store white sales in January and August and August sales on ski equipment by sporting good stores are designed to even out sales slumps and clear older merchandise from the inventory. Hotels offer special weekend rates to fill their rooms during times when business use is light. Some movie theaters and restaurants offer special "earlybird" rates before 6:00 p.m. to encourage customer traffic when it is typically slow.

A free gift with a combined purchase is a strong incentive.

In recent years, automobile retailers have used September for end-of-the-model-year special price reductions. **Rebates**, a technique whereby the dealer or manufacturer pays the customer back a certain amount of money for buying their car, are used to increase traffic in the dealers' showrooms and sell automobiles before the next year's cars are introduced.

Combination offers allow customers to buy two products or services at a price that is less than if they were purchased separately. Supermarkets, drug stores, shoe stores, and others often make combination offers. Packages of socks, packages of cookies sold with ice cream, sparkplugs packaged with tune up kits for cars are all examples of this incentive.

As noted at the beginning of this section, sales incentives work best in coordination with other means of communication. Ziploc sandwich bags were promoted using special incentives, a 15-cents-off coupon combined with a mail-in offer of free bread with two proofs of purchase. In addition, stickers of the "beasties" from a popular movie were factory packed. Advertisements on TV and through other media supported this program. Alert local retail marketers tied into these national special incentives with special promotions of their own or with cooperative advertising.

TRADE SHOWS AND EXHIBITS

Another form of promotion that has been around for centuries is the trade show. Home shows, car shows, boat shows, and craft fairs annually attract more than 20 million people. The purpose of these shows is to bring buyers and sellers together to do business. Home shows have exhibits by interior decorators, hardware stores, lumber yards, appliance stores, air conditioning and heating specialists, furniture stores, and many other businesses that relate to the housing market. Auto shows exhibit the latest in automobile technology, including the exotic sports cars; automotive accessories, and other products related to the automobile industry.

During these shows, sellers can demonstrate their products or services to prospective customers. This provides a tremendous opportunity to develop new customers, since people who attend these shows pay to enter and are usually interested in the products being displayed. Buyers can see and compare a variety of products and services and decide which would be most useful to them. Many exhibitors include contests or sweepstakes as part of their exhibit to obtain customer names and addresses for follow-up after the show.

PUBLICITY

So-called free publicity is largely a myth, according to the Small Business Administration. But if it is carefully planned, properly prepared, and well placed, publicity can be very valuable in increasing sales.

Newsworthy Items

Publicity must be based on news. The most common form of publicity is a news release involving a company, a product, or a service. It must have interest for some group, such as stockholders, company employees, or the general public, or the media will not consider it worth featuring.

Publicity may be built around any of the following.

■ *Announcing a new product.* When the first tanning salons opened, they often generated articles in local newspapers about tanning in the "off season." When Ford introduced its Taurus line of cars, stories about the car appeared in car magazines, newspapers, and other media—including television reports. Each new microcomputer from IBM or Apple usually is able to generate a tremendous amount of publicity. Shopping centers frequently receive press coverage when a major new retailer opens a store in the mall. All the mall's retailers can benefit.

■ *Employee promotions.* Banks may announce the promotion of an employee to an important position. Insurance companies may announce the names of their top salespeople. An automotive accessories chain in Baltimore regularly announces the appointment of its new managers.

■ *Opening a new business or a new branch.* A video game parlor moves into a former gas station located near the high school.

■ *Special events.* The 100th birthday of a business, a fire sale, the change of name of a business, and many other special events may create media interest.

Publicity Releases

A standard format is followed in preparing publicity releases. A **publicity release** is a story or message about a product or a company. Publicity releases are prepared by the business owner-manager or by the promotion department in a larger firm.

A good news release will follow the five W's formula:

Who: The company or persons involved
What: The important event
When: The date and time
Where: The location
Why: The reason for the event

For example:

Who: The Taste Bud: A Unique Ice Cream Experience, Ann Hill, owner
What: Announcement of the opening of a new business with a creative approach to the marketing of ice cream
When: May 2

Where: Springfield Mall
Why: To bring New York style ice cream to the Washington market

This information should all be included in the first paragraph, which is often called the *lead*. A good lead will summarize the whole story in one or two sentences. This is necessary to capture the reader's attention and because editors may cut part of the story. The following paragraphs should provide more detail but contain less important information than the first paragraph.

■

PUBLIC RELATIONS

As you will recall from Chapter 38, any activity designed to build goodwill toward a business organization is called public relations. A good public relations program must be based on truth and integrity. Public relations efforts are usually directed toward two groups: customers and the general public.

Customer Relations

Successful retail marketers build good public relations by providing service. Retail marketers should train their sales staff to provide helpful service during and after the sale. Additional services may include credit terms and the acceptance of major charge cards, free delivery and assembly, child care on the premises (many shopping centers are beginning to provide this), a customer service department to handle problems and complaints, and extended warranties on products or services.

This consumer orientation may include the use of consumer advisory boards so that the business can stay closely attuned to consumer needs. Some businesses have appointed panels of consumers to make suggestions for improving business services and have increased sales by following their advice. Many hotels

Sesame Place P.O. Box 579, Langhorne, PA 19047

N E W S

CONTACT: PHILADELPHIA: Sharla Feldscher, 215/546-7004
             NEW YORK: Amy Friedland, 212/980-1212
             WASHINGTON, D.C.: Ann Scully, 202/659-0330

FOR IMMEDIATE RELEASE

SESAME PLACE TO CELEBRATE 'SCOUT FAMILY DAYS' IN OCTOBER

LANGHORNE, Pa., September 11, 1987 -- Sesame Place, the action-oriented children's play park, will offer scouts and their families a discount and a variety of family-oriented activities during two "Scout Family Days" weekends, Oct. 3-4 and Oct. 10-11.

During "Scout Family Days," scouts who bring membership identification to Sesame Place (and all members of their party) will receive a discounted admission of $6.75. Regular Sesame Place admission prices are $12.05 per child and $9.85 per adult (tax included). There is no minimum number for a group discount. In addition, for every 10 children in a group, one adult receives free admission (excluding tax).

As part of the festivities, scouts bringing a "leaf" decorated with a family photo, a drawing or other family identification will take home a special gift. The "family leaf" can be hand-made, a tree leaf, or other variation of a leaf.

Sesame Place is located off Pennsylvania Interstate 95 at the Route 1/Morrisville exit to Oxford Valley exit and is a 30-minute drive north of Philadelphia, 15 minutes west of Trenton, N.J., and an hour-and-a-half from New York City.

# # #

Identify the five W's in this press release.

place an evaluation form in all rooms and encourage guests to fill it out and "grade" the hotel and its staff. Guests who complete the form and make a complaint receive a prompt reply from a specially trained customer service representative.

Community Relations

Activities planned to make a company a good civic member of a community are referred to as **community relations**. Many firms build positive community relations by sponsoring activities of interest to the public, for example:

■ A bank distributed a booklet to new residents that described the community, where services were located, unique aspects of the community, and laws a new resident should know.
■ A new car dealer provided a place for a high school auto club to meet.
■ A grocery store promoted healthy nutritional habits by distributing booklets on sound eating habits, creating special displays of low-calorie meals, providing a computer station where customers could receive answers to questions about nutrition, and employing a professional nutritionist to help plan merchandising strategies.

In Chapter 38, you were introduced to Denny and Carlos at Sterling Hardware. Carlos used several promotional activities to communicate to his customers. Can you think of other promotional techniques he might have used?

In the following unit, you will have the opportunity to develop skills in the use of advertising and visual merchandising, two important tools of retail marketing communication.

TRADE TALK

Define each term and use it in a sentence.

Combination offers	Publicity release
Community relations	Rebates
Contests	Self-liquidating
Coupon	premium
Gift	Special sales event
Premium	Sweepstakes
Product sample	Trading stamps

CAN YOU ANSWER THESE?

1. How can a retail marketer increase the use of coupons?
2. Why do small retail marketers not like to use coupons?
3. What is the difference between a contest and a sweepstakes?
4. Suggest several ways a retail marketer might provide free samples.
5. Identify businesses that might use direct sales premiums.
6. What is the benefit to retail marketers of participating in a trade show?
7. What business activities can be used for publicity?
8. What are the "five W's" for writing a news release?
9. Public relations programs are usually directed toward what two groups?

ACTIVITIES AND PROJECT FOR U·N·I·T 13

RETAIL MARKETING CASES

1. Arnold had been operating The Video Connection at the Farview Shopping Center for the past two years. During that time, he had encountered problems with neighboring merchants and with the community as his business attracted a gang of unruly teenagers who came to play the video games. As a result of all the negative publicity, Arnold's business receipts began to decline as many parents kept their kids away from his business. Therefore Arnold was faced with the problems of declining sales and a poor public image.

1. What promotion goals should Arnold pursue to solve his two problems?

2. Which promotion methods would work to achieve these goals?

3. What benefits of Arnold's business would you promote?

4. What media would you recommend that Arnold use?

5. Since Arnold's business is small, who would be responsible for the promotion activities?

2. "I'm tired of it," Mike muttered. "What's the problem?" Vin asked. "Oh, I can't seem to get customers to come through the door. I've run some ads; I even paid for a radio spot. But nothing seems to make any difference. If we don't get some customers soon, we'll be out of business."

Mike is the owner of Northstar Sports, a sporting goods store. Vin is a marketing education student who is working part-time as part of his course requirements. Vin has been studying promotion in retail marketing recently and has wanted to make some suggestions about Mike's approach to promotion. But since he's only a high school student and Mike is the owner, he has been reluctant to offer suggestions.

1. Assume that you are Vin; how would you approach your boss to make a suggestion about how the business should be run?

2. What is the basic problem in this case?

3. What solutions would you propose?

4. Do you think Mike has the proper attitude toward promotion?

5. Who might you suggest Mike talk to for further help?

PROJECT: A SURVEY OF SPECIAL PROMOTION ACTIVITIES

YOUR PROJECT GOAL

Given an area of retail marketing, survey a sample of businesses on their use of special promotional tools.

PROCEDURE

1. Identify a type of retail marketing business of interest to you. Obtain the approval of your instructor for this choice.

2. Make a checklist of the types of special promotion activities discussed in Chapter 40.

3. Select a sample of businesses, preferably no fewer than four and no more than eight. Half of the businesses in your sample should be locally owned, and the other half should be either franchise or chain operations.

4. For each business selected, collect information on all of the special promotion activities used. This collection will involve interviewing people in the business who are responsible for promotion activities; reviewing ads in the local newspaper; reviewing ads on radio and TV; checking direct mail delivered to your home; visiting the businesses to see what special incentives might be used in the business.

5. Conduct the survey and summarize your findings for each business.

6. Prepare a report on the special promotion tools used and reasons for their use. The report should compare the businesses.

7. In the conclusion to your report, offer your opinion of why the businesses selected differ on their use of special promotional tools.

EVALUATION

You will be evaluated on the completeness of your survey and the thoroughness of your comparison of locally owned retail businesses to chains and franchises.

PROMOTION METHODS

41 *Developing Effective Advertising*

"You know," said Adrienne, "Ms. Cohen runs a lot of ads for this bank. But I wonder if it does any good?"

"I don't know," said Howard, "but lately a lot of people have come in asking about our new high-interest savings account. In fact, several have had the ads with them when they started asking me questions."

"You're right," Adrienne said. "Now that I think about it, I remember seeing an ad for those accounts on TV and in the *Boston Globe*."

Mr. Hanson, the teller supervisor, overheard the conversation. "Ms. Cohen does spend a considerable amount of money on advertising. But, since she began this recent advertising campaign, new deposits are up almost 13 percent."

Adrienne and Howard are tellers at the Newton Center Citizens Bank. It is owned and managed by Sylvia Cohen. They were discussing one of the critical questions of retail marketing: How much does advertising help business?

■

HOW ADVERTISING SELLS

Whether you are selling banking services, ice cream, skateboards, automobiles, clothes, or hotel rooms, advertising is an important tool in communicating to potential customers. But what makes a good ad? What is the retail marketer trying to do with advertising? These and other questions will be discussed in this chapter. Advertising is used to help move a customer through each of the five mental stages of AIDCA.

Attracting Attention

To be effective, an advertisement must be seen or heard, or both. In order to attract attention, advertisers use sharp contrasts through illustrations, white space, color, motion, sounds, position, time slots, and so on. Some advertisers even scent their advertising messages so as to attract attention by means of a pleasant fragrance. Perhaps you have seen one of the "scratch 'n' sniff" ads.

In printed media, attention is usually drawn to the ad by the headline. Advertisements must compete with the news, sports, comics, and other features in newspapers and with the feature articles in magazines. Readers will not pay attention to an ad unless the headline attracts their attention. The headline expresses the major single idea that the advertiser is trying to communicate. One expert claims that 60 to 70 percent of the effectiveness of an ad can be attributed to the headline. It should summarize the primary benefits of the merchandise or service being advertised.

The headline draws attention; it can begin the selling process. It influences the reader to read the rest of the ad. To accomplish this, the headline must be targeted to the people who may buy the product or service. It should promise a benefit, contain news, or provoke curiosity. And a successful ad usually includes an active verb in the headline.

The best headlines usually promise a benefit. The benefit promised must be related to the needs of the market segment the business is trying to attract. Ms. Cohen may have used a headline such as "Make Your Money Work for You" to demonstrate the benefit of a high-interest savings account.

Another strategy would be to provoke the reader's curiosity. A recent ad for Domino's Pizza used the headline, "This deal is so big, we couldn't keep the lid on it."

Stimulating Interest

Attention is brief. If the consumer's attention can be held for a length of time, interest can be developed. The initial attention to the ad can be held by appealing to the self-interest of the customer. People are always interested in merchandise and services that satisfy their needs and wants. Ads that put the potential customer in the picture using the product or service create interest. Also, descriptions used in the ads should use words, phrases, and symbols that have meaning to the prospective customer.

Building Desire

Appeals to the emotions as well as to reason are used to lead the customer from interest in the merchandise or service to a desire for it. Among the buying motives appealed to are: curiosity, imitation, companionship, pride, ambition, desire for good health and beauty, desire for comfort, desire for pleasure and fun, and excitement. The particular buying motive appealed to depends on the types of merchandise being offered and the nature of the target audience. It should use the "you" approach; that is, it must answer the question that is always in the customer's mind: How will I benefit from owning this? The bank customer might ask: Why should I put my money in this bank? What will this bank do for me that a competing bank will not?

Copy   If the job of the headline is to catch the reader's attention, the job of the copy is to create interest and hold it. By appealing to the reader's self-interest and emphasizing fea-

In outdoor advertising the headline must not only capture attention, it must deliver the message.

tures that bring benefits, copy arouses interest and desire for the product or services advertised. Good copy will follow the thought of the headline and get the main point across in the first paragraph. Copy should include brand name, model number, specifications, price, and benefits.

Good advertising works the same way as a good salesperson: It translates the features of the product into benefits using language that customers can understand. It shows what the customer will gain from product features, thereby giving the customer a reason to buy.

Developing effective copy for an ad requires skill, creativity, and an understanding of your customer. Whether you work with an advertising agency, a media sales representative, or create your own ads, using the following guidelines will help you develop more effective copy:

KNITS REALLY FIT

Knits fit your lifestyle.
Knits are easy-wear, easy-care solutions to the big problem of what to wear for a **very** busy day.

Knits fit your figure.
Whether smooth jersey or cotton knits or the more textured sweater knits, they're feminine, flattering and can hide as well as highlight!

Knits fit your budget.
Knits are affordable alternatives to suits and other day-dressing options . . . especially with Cohoes' everyday low prices.

And does Cohoes have knits!
Knits are big fashion news this season and we knew you would want them. So we have them—knit dresses, skirts and tops—but the best go first so make your choices now and just wait for the compliments.

COHOES
WORTH A TRIP FROM ANYWHERE

43 MOHAWK STREET COHOES, NEW YORK (518) 237-0524
COHOESCARD MASTERCARD VISA
MON WED THURS SAT 9:30-5:30 TUES FRI 9:30-9:00 SUN 12:00-5:00

Good advertising copy translates product or service features into customer benefits.

■ Make each word count. Keep sentences short. Get right to the point. Use short, familiar, concrete words.

■ Remember, about seven times as many people will read the headline as will read the copy, so put what you have to say in the headline.

■ Be consistent. Choose a theme and a style and stay with it. Use a logo for quick recognition.

■ If your intent is to get action now, put a benefit in the headline. If you are trying to build image, use a brand name in the headline.

■ Modify the copy to take advantage of the medium. For example, in print ads, a brand name in large print will not need to be repeated. However, in a radio ad, the name must be repeated again and again.

■ In print ads, put the key words at the beginning and end of sentences. In radio and TV ads, other sentence structures can be used, and key words can be emphasized by the announcer's voice.

■ Thirty-second commercials are more than half as effective as one-minute ones, and therefore more economical. A full page advertisement will not get twice as much attention as a half-page ad.

Illustrations   It is often said that one picture is worth a thousand words. This statement is especially true in advertising. Although the headline may be the most effective part of an ad, illustrations can communicate more information more accurately than words. This knowledge of the significance of pictures is the basis of catalog advertising.

Consumers are exposed to pictures far more often than they are to printed copy, and they pay more attention to pictures. Because illustrations are now so commonly used as a means of communication, people have become more critical of what they see. For this reason, advertisers have become more skilled in the way they prepare and use illustrations.

In an effective ad, there should be one dominant visual element to attract attention and guide the reader's eye movement through the ad. Other tips for effective use of illustrations include:

1. Consider what your ad is selling and the medium you are using when choosing between photographs and drawings for illustrations. Generally, photos are useful for advertising such items as houses, cars, and electrical appliances. Photographs reproduce well in magazines. Newspaper ads for fashion apparel frequently rely on line drawings for an effective presentation.

2. Rectangular photographs get more attention and are more convincing than other shapes.

3. Photographs used in newspapers should be black and white and have very little gray.

4. All pictures and art work should face into the ad.

Gaining Conviction

Advertising may convince interested customers to buy by reinforcing claims that are made for the product or service advertised. A warranty, testimonial, or illustration may convince a prospective customer to make a final decision to buy. Sears warranties Craftsman brand hand tools to be replaced if they fail for any reason, regardless of how long the customer has had them. This warranty is designed to gain the confidence of potential customers in the quality of Craftsman tools.

Inducing Action

Advertising may call for immediate action. Incentives to encourage action may include the use of coupons, combination pricing, or gifts.

The concluding paragraph should stimulate the customer to buy now. For example:

■ At these prices, you'll be smart to stock up now.

- Now is the best time to buy.
- 2.9% financing definitely ends Saturday.
- Limited supply.

The store address, phone number, hours of operation, and other necessary information are included at the end of the ad to help the consumer take buying action.

■

TARGETING YOUR ADVERTISING

Understanding your **target audience**, the customer you are trying to reach with your advertising, will help you shape and direct your communication efforts. There are two steps in the process of targeting your advertising: (1) developing a customer profile and (2) developing your message.

Developing a Customer Profile

If Socrates were alive today, he might say, "Know thy customer." This is critical to the success of promotional efforts in retail marketing. You can understand your customer better by asking a series of questions about your past customers (those who no longer patronize your business), present customers (those who currently patronize your business), and future customers (those whom you would like to patronize your business). Critical questions include:

- Where do they live?
- How old are they?
- Are they male or female or both?
- What is their annual income?
- How do they perceive your business? Your merchandise and services?
- What customer services do they value the most?
- Why do they buy from you rather than a competitor?
- What are their buying patterns?

Market research can answer many of these questions. Such research may be as simple as filling out a customer information card on each of your customers or as sophisticated as some survey procedures used by professional market research firms. Regardless of how it is collected, market information is necessary to develop effective ads.

Developing Your Message

Based on your customer profile, you can begin to develop the appropriate message. To a large extent, the characteristics of the promotional form determine the message. A shopping bag usually contains the business logo or name; a billboard will have no more than 12 words and an illustration (after all, it has to be read at 55 mph or faster); a full-page, one-item newspaper ad can deliver more content in the message.

Ads can say many things about a business, its merchandise, and services. No effective ad will emphasize more than a single theme, however. The first step in developing the message for your ad is to develop alternative messages that can be compared. Each of these can then be pre-tested and rated on desirability, exclusiveness, and believability.

The message must say something desirable or interesting about the product, service, or firm. Because many brands or businesses might be able to say the same thing, the message must also say something exclusive—that is, something the other businesses or brands cannot say. If you have prepared a product or service analysis (as discussed on pages 245–246) or a feature-benefit table (as shown on page 248), you can easily identify the point to highlight in your message. Finally, the message must be believable to the consumer. If these three elements are present in the messaage, it will create a distinctive ad. Distinctiveness is important because the consumer is bombarded with hundreds of messages daily. Distinctive ads, repeated often, can cut through the clutter of messages.

COMPONENTS OF PRINT ADS

Retail marketers are heavy users of print ads. This is even more true of small retailers. Because of this, it is important to look more closely at how print ads are assembled.

The five parts of a retail advertisement are the **headline** (which states the main idea of the ad), **copy** (words or text), the **art** (illustrations), the **logotype** (identification of the sponsor), and the **layout** (arrangement of the headline, copy, art, and logotype). Ads may consist of only copy and a logotype or only art and a logotype; but more commonly, ads contain all three.

The layout is used like a blueprint to plan the ad. The main reason for preparing the layout is to ensure that the proposed ad will fulfill the desired objectives. An advertising layout shows what the elements look like, how they are arranged, and where the emphasis lies. Its role is to attract the attention of prospective customers and stimulate their interest as their eyes are led from one element to the next.

Considerations in Layout Development

Given the purpose and the allotted space for the proposed ad, there are several important concerns to keep in mind as the layout is planned. These are: the type of business; the strategy or objective of the ad; the needs, wants, and values of the targeted audience; and the mood or atmosphere to be generated by the ad.

Type of Business Businesses may be classified as promotional, semipromotional, or nonpromotional. These classifications are derived from the image each business strives to attain. This desired image will influence the type of ads the business will use.

Special value is the main appeal of a promotional business. The emphasis is on price, sales, clearances, special purchases, and discounts. This group of businesses includes the major discounters and off-price stores. Cost-Cutters Hair Styling, K mart, Target Drug Stores, and Kuppenheimers are examples of this type of business.

Semipromotional businesses alternate between sales offerings and regular-price marketing. They tend to have regularly scheduled sales events: white sales, founder's day sales, inventory sales, and so forth. Most conventional department stores and most small retail businesses fit this pattern.

Nonpromotional businesses tend to stock fashion merchandise and staple goods. They usually have prime locations, attractive facilities, and well-trained salespeople. Their advertising is slanted toward fashion or image. Boutiques and other specialty shops often use this approach.

Advertising Strategy An **advertising strategy** is a statement about the specific objective of the ad or the selling problem to be solved. You can think of advertising strategy by thinking of the purposes of promotion. Your strategy can be used as a guide to decide whether the ad achieves what was intended.

One approach to strategy is to consider the assortment of merchandise or services to be advertised. A **one-item advertisement** stresses a single item. This allows full concentration of the elements of the layout on that item. There is plenty of space to tell the full sales story. An **assortment advertisement** shows related items. Giant department stores often show a full page of coffee makers; electronics stores will show a full page of "boom boxes." Showing these assortments creates an image of the business as a complete place to shop.

Omnibus advertisements are used to show both related items and unrelated items. The intent is to show a wide variety of merchandise. For example, an automobile acces-

This assortment ad shows and describes a selection of related products. Customers can decide which item or items would best fill their needs.

sories outlet ad could be built around the theme of tuning up the family car. It might include tune-up kits, filters, oil, lubricants, and engine cleaners. A home furnishings ad could be built around curtains, drapes, carpeting, and furniture. An omnibus ad of unrelated items might show merchandise from several departments.

Targeted Audience The needs and preferences of the target audience will affect how you combine the elements of the ad layout. For example, an automobile ad targeted toward the average consumer would have more illustration than copy. On the other hand, an automobile ad for the sports car fan would contain a lot more detail about the car in the copy. Each would also respond with a different type of headline stressing different types of benefits.

Mood of the Ad   The mood desired for the ad will affect the selection of elements to be emphasized. For example, a festive mood or a holiday requires a different layout from one for a major sale or announcement of a new store opening. Moods such as joy, excitement, luxury, patriotism, richness, and so on can be created by illustrations, headlines, copy, and other elements of the layout.

Elements of a Layout

The headline, subhead, logo, copy, and illustrations are combined in a well executed ad, with the imaginative use of white space, typeface, borders, and logos to create the desired impact.

White space is the term used for the unprinted areas within the boundaries of an ad. Although it is empty space, it creates its own impact. When a design leaves a lot of white space around the copy, the impression is one of exclusiveness or special importance. This is a technique often used in ads for higher-priced merchandise. When little white space is left and the ad is filled with type and illustrations from border to border, the impression is one of excitement or bargain announcements.

Type is the lettering style used in the ad. Type is chosen to suit the mood or impression the ad is trying to portray. The right type makes the ad both readable and interesting.

The **border** is the edge around the ad. Often it is left as white space. Newspapers and magazines usually put a thin line around ads anyway, to separate them from competing ads. But the use of an unusual border can create a special impact. Repeating this border in all print ads can help identify the ad quickly in the consumer's mind as being associated with a certain business. Borders unite the parts of the ad and attract the attention of the reader.

The logotype or **logo** is a symbol that represents the business. Often it is a stylized version of the business name. Sometimes it is a picture with the business name as part of the picture. Many retail marketers combine other information with the logo. They might include business hours, addresses, and telephone numbers. To many customers, the logo serves as a signal indicating whether the ad is worth reading. A distinctive logo creates an identity and personality for the business. A logo is like a person's face: It says who you are.

In general, the headline of an ad should always be surrounded by white space. White space makes the headline easier to read.

Boxes around parts of an ad also create a visual impact. Boxes work as internal borders and organize the ad to make it easier to read.

One of the most overlooked parts of an ad is the buying information. **Buying information** includes the business address, phone number, directions, credit terms, and perhaps motto. "We will not be undersold," "In business since 1894," or "K mart is your savings place" says a lot about the business.

Finally, it is important to develop a consistent format. By arranging the elements of the layout the same way each time you run an ad, you will eventually develop a strong visual identity for your business. Retail marketers who use consistent layouts for their ads usually generate the best results.

EVALUATING ADVERTISEMENTS

Adrienne and Howard wondered about the usefulness of the advertising Ms. Cohen had run to increase deposits at the Newton Center Citizens Bank. Certainly, the fact that bank deposits had increased suggests that the ads were effective. This is known as measuring sales results, one of several ways to evaluate advertising. Ads may be evaluated before they are run, to determine consumer response, or after they have run, to determine actual results.

Post-Testing Ads

The type of research that attempts to measure the effectiveness of an advertisement after it has appeared is known as **post-testing**. Post-testing can identify the most effective ads as well as the most appealing features of those ads. This allows markets to improve their advertising. There are three types of post-testing done in retail marketing: (1) measuring sales results, (2) measuring audience recognition, and (3) measuring audience recall of ads.

Measuring Sales Results Nearly every retail marketer does a post-test of some sort on each ad that is run. In a large business, the

process is relatively formal. The advertising department may request a written report from the buyer or department head. The report would show how many units or how much dollar volume resulted from the ad. These reports may also include information about weather conditions, competitors' ads, and other promotion used along with the ads that might have affected unit or dollar volume. A moderate-size chain of automobile parts stores in Washington, D.C., runs large omnibus ads every Saturday morning for the weekend's business. On Friday afternoons, the store manager takes an inventory of items to be included in the next day's ad. Another inventory is taken on Monday morning, and the results are sent to the home office.

Many small retail marketers rely on more informal methods. They may measure the immediate response to an ad by counting coupons turned in, the increase in the number of customers entering the store, or the number of phone orders generated.

ADVERTISING RESULTS

Department _56 — Toys_
Date of Ad _Oct 14, 198—_
Media _Columbus Dispatch_
3 Day Results _Excellent_
No. of Units Sold _175_

DOLLAR SALES:
Advertised Item _$9,341_
Total Department _$21,637_

Note: *This form must be turned in to Merchandise Manager before noon the 4th day after ad has run. Merchandise Manager will initial and send promptly to Sales Promotion Manager.*

Buyer's Signature _Terry Adams_
Merchandise Manager's Initials _CP_

Successful retailers always check the results of their advertising campaigns.

Measuring Audience Recognition of Ads Recognition tests tell advertisers how readers react to their ads compared with other ads in the same publication. The consumer reviews all the ads and is asked which ads he or she remembers and if they made an impression. The ads the consumer remembers are then rated.

Measuring Audience Recall of Ads Recall tests attempt to measure what an ad actually communicated to the reader. In interviews, the readers' answers are based entirely on what they can remember about the ads without actually seeing the ads again. Both audience recognition and recall require formal research techniques that are expensive and time-consuming.

Pre-Testing Ads

Evaluating an advertisement before is it actually used is called **pre-testing**. Pre-testing is especially useful when a marketer is considering putting a lot of money into an ad campaign. Pre-testing helps the advertiser decide if the effort will be worth the expense; it also allows for necessary changes in a promotional effort before it reaches the public. Two of the more commonly used methods are opinion studies and test-area studies.

Opinion Studies   An opinion study involves questioning people or collectively questioning a group. People are asked to rate ads based on their believability, ability to attract interest, and power to persuade people to buy.

Test-Area Studies   Another way to test an idea for an advertising campaign is to try out the campaign in a small area called a **test-market**. This technique involves selecting two test-market areas that are similar in terms of size, customer characteristics, and buying power. The ad is used in only one of the areas; the second area serves as a control. After a specified time, sales of the advertised items in the two areas are compared.

Once customers have been attracted into the place of business, retail marketers have other tools to help motivate them to make a purchase. In addition to advertising, special incentives, and personal selling, retail marketers use visual merchandising to encourage sales. The next chapter will provide an overview of visual merchandising.

Assortment advertisement
Border
Buying information
Copy
Headline
Layout
Logo
Omnibus advertisement
One-item advertisement
Post-testing
Pre-testing
Target audience
Test market
Type
White space

TRADE TALK

Define each term and use it in a sentence.

Advertising strategy   Art

CAN YOU ANSWER THESE?

1. How does advertising influence the mental process a customer goes through before making a purchase?

2. "Good advertising works just like a good salesperson." What does a good salesperson do that good advertising does also?

3. List several guidelines for writing effective copy.

4. Why are illustrations so important in print advertising?

5. What does a logo do in an ad?

6. What characteristics distinguish between business described as promotional, semipromotional, and nonpromotional?

7. Explain how the target audience for an ad affects the way you would combine the elements of an ad layout.

8. What is the purpose of a customer profile?

9. What are three requirements for an effective advertising message?

10. Describe two ways that ads can be evaluated.

42 *Visual Merchandising*

At one time, the word "display" would have been an accurate description of the way retailers presented their products. But marketing practices have become more sophisticated, and so have the methods retail marketers use to promote sales. There has been much progress since the early 1900s when manufacturers first began to package their products under brand names. Today "visual merchandising" is a more accurate description of how retail marketers visually present their products, services, and the business itself to potential customers.

Visual merchandising has grown in importance due to the increasing sameness of merchandise and services among competing businesses. In fact, nearly 80 percent of the merchandise carried by any store is the same as the merchandise carried by that store's competitors. And in shopping malls, you find many competitors clustered together. It has become more difficult for stores to create a competitive advantage. Visual merchandising offers a way for a store to create a distinctive image and attract customers.

Visual merchandising as defined in Chapter 38 is selling through the use of sight only. It involves visual presentations that will create a general atmosphere that invites the purchase of goods and services. The visual presentation is designed to trigger buying decisions while the customer is on the sales floor. Visual merchandising is art expressed with color, lighting, signing, mannequins, and fixtures. To be effective, it requires careful coordination with advertising, display, special events, and merchandising.

HOW VISUAL MERCHANDISING SELLS GOODS AND SERVICES

You will recall from your study of retail selling in Chapter 28 that selling through advertising and visual merchandising is guided by AIDCA, the mental stages through which a customer passes when making a purchase. The purpose of visual merchandising is to guide potential customers through all five mental stages.

Attention

There are two kinds of attention: voluntary and involuntary. Voluntary attention exists when window shoppers purposefully view various displays, usually to learn about merchandise that they intend to purchase. Involuntary attention is unintentional observation. It is more difficult to achieve, because the display must be powerful enough to draw the potential customer's attention away from its previous focus.

If a display is sufficiently surprising and unusual, a potential customer will move to view it more closely. It doesn't matter if this result is achieved by movement, color, sound, smell, lighting, or signing. Contrast is a particularly useful way to attract the attention of a maximum number of potential customers.

Interest

A display will stimulate interest only if it highlights the product and suggests a reason for continued attention. It must relate in some way to the viewer's interests and concerns. Sometimes a display will tell a story, which is an effective device for holding the viewer's interest. Putting the customer in the display (through the use of pictures or mannequins) is an effective way to relate the product to the viewer's interest.

Desire

In order to instill desire, the customer must be made to want the product; this desire can be aroused in the following ways:

■ Demonstrate the features and benefits of the product.
■ Demonstrate the use of the product.
■ Present the product in such a way as to induce sales.
■ Explain the necessity of the product.
■ Sell the idea that this product is exactly what the viewer needs and that owning it will bring satisfaction.

Conviction

A good display convinces viewers that they want to own the product. This is especially true when the product is displayed as it would be used. For example, a set of lawn furniture may be shown in a gardenlike setting, with attractively dressed mannequins stretched out in the lawn chairs. Viewers can visualize themselves enjoying the furniture in their own back yards. The price on the show card may convince them to buy.

Action

In self-service businesses, the attractiveness of an item or its packaging may tip the scale in favor of the merchandise. Also, information on the package or labels may help the customer make a positive decision. Of course,

price tags and signs also help customers make the final buying decision.

The goal of most exterior window displays is to encourage viewers to enter the place where the merchandise or services are sold. So such displays must let the customer know where the items may be purchased and, if possible, offer some incentive for going there. Interior displays in these stores should create interest and desire and move the customer toward a buying decision.

■

THE IMPORTANCE OF A THEME

A display is used more effectively when there is careful coordination with other elements of the promotional mix: advertising, personal selling, publicity, and public relations. Merchandising personnel decide what type of merchandise will sell well at a given time. Visual-merchandising decision makers plan and build displays to promote these products and project the desired image of the business.

Many factors enter into the judgments of visual merchandisers. While planning, they must keep in mind the following points:

■ The type of business
■ The desired business image
■ The types of customers wanted
■ The season of the year
■ The display cycle of the merchandise
■ The assigned space to be used

Every display, no matter what type it is or where it is located, should get across to the viewer a clear message or basic theme. This theme should be well thought out and consistent with the overall promotion theme. The entire presentation should be built around a single idea, and viewers should be able to understand the idea immediately. All the displays in the store should be based on the same theme, such as a season or an event.

Every display should have a unifying theme in keeping with the image of the business it represents.

The royal British weddings in the middle 1980s led many stores to use royalty as a theme. Holidays, seasons, and events may provide a theme: Christmas, Easter, Spring, Fall, or Election Day.

EXTERIOR VISUAL MERCHANDISING

The public, including potential customers, is impressed with a business by its exterior appearance. If the impression is favorable, the business will gain customers. At the very minimum, a business should be sure that the outside of the store is clean and the exterior of the building is in good repair.

Visability

In thinking about the store exterior as a total visual presentation, there are several factors to consider. When Ms. Cohen had the Newton Center Citizens Bank constructed, she wanted to make sure the bank would be visible to people driving by. She located the building close to the highway and chose a design for the building that was distinctive and dignified—in keeping with the image of a bank.

Maintenance

Cleanliness communicates caring to potential customers. This includes keeping the front windows clean, the sidewalks swept, and the building in good repair. It also includes keeping the parking lot free of litter (a particular problem for fast-food stores and shopping centers). In winter, it may also mean plowing and removing snow quickly and preventing ice from forming. If there are signs in the exterior windows or on the building itself, these must be kept clean and straight. A torn paper sign, a sign hung crooked, or a bulb burned out—these are all signs that the business owner doesn't care about the customer.

The exterior of the place of business should be well lit. When bulbs burn out, they should be replaced immediately. This is important for the appearance of the business and the safety of the customers. A well-lit exterior makes customers feel safer at night.

Business Signs

Frequently, a business owner does not have control of the exact location of an outlet or its exterior appearance. It can still ensure that the business name is prominent and easily seen. This is done through the use of business signs. A *sign* is the most direct form of visual communication. Signs tell people who you are and what you are selling. We use signs to communicate many things in our society: wet paint, beware of the dog, no left turn, no smoking, and so on. Businesses use signs for two reasons: to give information about the business; and to direct people to the business location.

Signs can compensate for a poor location by substituting effective communication for poor site characteristics. You may have noticed that signs for service stations on interstate highways often tower 200 feet or more and are visible even when the station is not.

Well-designed signs perform three functions:

1. Signs attract people in your trade area.

Exterior signs provide the customer's first impression of a retail business.

2. Signs are always visable, 24 hours a day, repeating your message to potential customers. (Repetition is one of the most effective ways to get customers to remember your message.)

3. Everyone reads signs, so they are constantly communicating. Even small children quickly learn to recognize their favorite signs. (If you don't believe this, think of a small child's reaction when passing a McDonald's sign.)

In addition, signs are inexpensive. In terms of the cost of reaching 1000 adults, signs cost 11 percent of what a billboard costs. Signs are 4 percent of the cost of newspaper ads and 2 percent of the cost of radio ads.

Types of Exterior Windows

Various types of window display areas are used by retail businesses, such as elevated windows, shadow boxes, corner designs, and islands. These may be open-back, closed, or semi-open back.

Elevated Windows Elevated windows are usually 12 to 14 inches above the sidewalk level. Windows are elevated for two reasons: to prevent damage to the glass from pedestrians' feet, clean-up crews, or vibrations from passing cars; and to put the merchandise closer to eye level, where it may be seen more easily. Jewelry stores, bookshops, bakeries, and optical stores often elevate their windows 2 to 3 feet above the street level because of the nature of the merchandise they sell.

Shadow-Box Windows Shadow boxes are usually small windows and are used alone or as part of a larger window. They provide a display area for small merchandise such as jewelry, cosmetics, books, or infants' shoes. The shadow-box window permits special emphasis to be placed on the displayed merchandise.

Corner Windows Corner windows are often considered the most important areas of any business exterior. They are a central viewing point for traffic coming from two directions and are the ideal display area. People notice corner windows more than any other type.

Island Windows Island windows are usually found in locations with large, deep entrances (such as an arcade front would provide). They are separate from the rest of the building. This type of window allows the merchandise to be seen from all angles, because the customer can walk around the island display.

Open-Back Windows As the name implies, the back of the window display is open, allowing the customer to see the display as well as the interior of the store. This stimulates the passerby to come in and look around.

Closed-Back Windows Closed-back windows completely isolate the display from the store interior. The advantage of this design is that it focuses the viewers' full attention on the display. The design is used most often by department stores in downtown locations as well as in shopping malls. By controlling light-

What different impressions are made by open-back and closed-back window displays?

ing and background, dramatic effects can be created in a closed-back window.

Semiclosed-Back Window Semiclosed-back windows are closed up to the average line of vision. Most often they are used by drug stores and hardware stores.

■

INTERIOR VISUAL MERCHANDISING

Once the customer has entered the store, interior visual merchandising takes over. Aisle space and store layout are just as important as display space, because both can be used to guide the customer through the store. In Chapter 43 you will have the opportunity to study the importance of store layout in more detail.

Six types of interior displays are used by retail marketers: (1) open displays, (2) closed displays, (3) built-up displays, (4) shadow boxes, (5) ledge displays, and (6) flying displays. The choice of the interior display type depends on the type of merchandise or service to be displayed and the space available.

Open Displays

Merchandise in an open display is arranged so that customers can touch it and examine it. Merchandise may be displayed openly on a counter, rack, table, or shown on a mannequin. These displays are effective for some types of merchandise, but increase the risk of loss due to damage caused by customer handling.

Closed Displays

Closed displays are closed on all sides and allow the customer only to look. Display counters in jewelry and department stores, and floor-to-ceiling locked displays in gun stores, are examples of closed displays. This type of display is used where the merchandise is fragile, expensive, easily damaged, dangerous for small children to handle, or popular with shoplifters. You may notice that many record stores keep cassette and eight-track tapes in closed displays.

Built-Up Displays

Built-up displays use props, platforms, and other devices to make the merchandise more attractive. These displays are usually located at important traffic points: the ends of aisles in grocery stores, in front of elevators or escalators in department stores. One special type of built-up display is the island display. As the name implies, an **island display** is isolated and usually displays a single type of item, or a single item with related merchandise (golf clubs and bags, shirts and ties). Islands may be used to show a mass of merchandise to create the image that the store has lots of the item displayed. Shoe stores in shopping malls frequently use large island displays near the entrance of the store.

Shadow Boxes

A small display area that resembles a shallow box open in the front is called a **shadow box**. It is similar to the shadow box design used in exterior windows in that it allows more dramatic presentation of merchandise. Shadow boxes are most often located behind a counter. This location makes it easy to display and maintain an arrangement of merchandise that is beyond the reach of the customer. Shadow boxes are usually illuminated with lighting of greater intensity than their surrounding areas, so that they will attract attention immediately.

Ledge Displays

Merchandise is sometimes displayed on ledges, store walls, or partitions. These areas may also be used for decorations during holiday seasons or other special occasions. Displays in these areas make the store look inviting and do not clutter the aisles. And as floor space becomes more expensive and stores become smaller, it becomes necessary to use all available areas for display.

Flying Displays

The **flying display** design is used quite frequently by small fashion boutiques. The flying display consists of suspending merchandise from the ceiling using wire, hangers, and other devices. The clothing displays are arranged to give the appearance of "flying." This type of display allows for floor-to-ceiling visual presentation of color and design.

DISPLAYS IN FULL-SERVICE BUSINESSES

Full-service businesses use visual merchandising to bring customers into the store and create an atmosphere that allows the professional salesperson to take over the selling process. In department and larger specialty stores, each department usually has one or more displays featuring timely, attractive merchandise that is sold in the department. These displays are usually located at heavy traffic points, frequently at or near the most used entrance to the department. Sometimes, department displays are also located on ledges and tops of fixtures or in recessed shadow boxes. Counter and showcase displays are also popular in these locations. The way merchandise is grouped and the informative signs that describe the items aid both customers and salespeople by showing what is new or fashionable.

Displays in the interiors of these stores may be designed by personnel from either the display department or the sales department. Simple displays on counters are usually built by salespeople. More complex displays are often built by professional display personnel. A recent trend in chain stores is for displays to be designed and built in the chain's home office and shipped to the store with instructions for installation.

Most retailers will try to display related items. In clothing stores, related items of apparel and accessories, called an **ensemble**, may be displayed together. In a sporting goods store, a display of tents may show an entire campsite with cookstoves, sleeping bags, back packs and hiking clothes on mannequins, and dried food. This strategy of showing related items is designed to encourage additional sales through suggestion.

Some businesses, such as Ms. Cohen's bank, which once ignored the concepts of visual merchandising, are now beginning to recognize their value. Banks, hotels, travel agen-

Can you identify the types of interior display shown here? Why is each effective for the merchandise it promotes?

cies, fast-food restaurants, and other service businesses are now beginning to use visual merchandising techniques to help sell their products and services.

■

DISPLAYS IN SELF-SERVICE BUSINESSES

Self-service businesses such as hardware stores, drug stores, and variety stores use visual merchandising to get the customer to make a purchase with little or no assistance from store personnel. Because of the competitiveness of the grocery business, visual merchandising in supermarkets is more highly developed than anywhere else. The typical supermarket sells more than 7000 items to customers, who spend an average of 26 minutes in the store. This means that an item has to catch the customer's attention in a split second. Manufacturers of these products have become more sophisticated in their packaging and visual merchandising.

Point-of-Purchase Displays

The most effective display for self-service businesses is a point-of-purchase display. A **point-of-purchase (POP) display** is a display made of materials supplied by the manufacturer and designed to encourage impulse buying. POP displays include posters, shelf talkers, backdrops, price cards, cutouts, stands, racks, barrels, and other devices that call attention to the product. They are usually tied into the manufacturer's national advertising program and repeat messages the customers have seen on TV, in magazines or newspapers, or heard on the radio.

Grocery stores often use POP displays at the ends of aisles for products such as canned goods, paper napkins, and cookies. Many department stores use POP displays to sell cosmetics, packaged socks, and other small items.

POP displays are beginning to include advanced technology. A new design by Pills-

bury for refrigerated products such as cookie dough will allow these products to be displayed in more strategic locations in a grocery store. This POP display includes a display unit that will keep items cool for 12 hours without plugging it in. This unit has the Pillsbury Dough Boy for a backdrop. Pillsbury will provide the POP display at no charge if the grocery store orders a certain quantity of cookie dough.

A recent trend in POP displays is the use of video. One such display has a 12-inch video screen that flashes a message inviting the customer to press an automatic sensor bar and watch a brief message about a product or service.

POP displays are designed to encourage last-minute impulse purchases. Impulse items

Video displays at the point of purchase are an effective way to show merchandise such as apparel in use. This display cleverly combines the video screen with a mannequin.

such as candy, magazines, chewing gum, razor blades, and flashlight batteries are displayed in special racks, often near a checkout area. This location is a point where customers have finished their planned purchases, so these items are added to the customers' purchase rather than used as substitutes for other items.

Dump Displays

Dump displays are large bins that contain merchandise. These displays are used for small, unbreakable items such as flashlight batteries, boxes of cake mix, small inflatable toys, or ball-point pens. They often contain items that people use frequently or items in seasonal demand. This type of display presents a bargain image and encourages customers to reach in and buy the displayed merchandise. Hardware stores often use dump displays for related merchandise such as masking tape, bags of paint brushes, and painting tarps. The recent trend of low-service "box stores" in food marketing has increased the use of dump displays.

Gondolas and Endcaps

Gondolas are movable shelving units. They may be used singly to create an island; or they may be used in rows, as in grocery stores and drug stores. Because they are movable, gondolas allow for quick changes in store layout. **Endcaps** are display units at the ends of aisles. These are strategic locations and are used to highlight higher-profit merchandise or seasonal merchandise.

■

DISPLAYS IN REGIONAL SHOPPING MALLS

Regional shopping malls are large, often climate-controlled shopping centers located near or next to major highways, often interstate. Their role in retail marketing has in-

creased in the past 20 years, and they are now the dominant influence in retailing. They may house as many as 300 or more businesses and are becoming a cultural center for many communities.

Visual merchandising in a mall is different from that of smaller shopping centers or individual stores. Most people shop malls on a regular basis, which means that some types of large exterior signs for shops in the mall, for example, become unnecessary. It also means that displays must be changed more often. Most mall shoppers tend to be younger women which affects the selection of merchandise that retailers will put out front. Malls have become a hangout for teenagers, who go there to see and be seen by friends, go to the movies, or play video games. And most mall businesses do not have fronts; the entire business is visible and open to the mall shopper. This creates an additional burden on protecting and maintaining displays. Individual mall outlets are limited in their control over visual merchandising activities, because they often must tie into a mall-wide theme or special event. These and other characteristics affect visual merchandising decisions in malls.

Visual merchandising is an important part of the promotional mix. It is art, communication, selling, and a little bit of theater combined to present a business to its customers. In the next chapter, you will study the techniques used by retail marketers to create effective displays.

CAN YOU ANSWER THESE?

1. Why does "visual merchandising," rather than "display," better describe how a business uses sight to encourage customers to buy?

2. How is visual merchandising used to help move customers through the five mental stages of a buying decision?

3. List four ways that a display can create desire for a product.

4. What factors should visual merchandisers consider when planning displays?

5. How do visability, business signs, cleanliness, lighting, and exterior windows influence the impression that customers have of a business?

6. List and describe four types of exterior display windows.

7. Why would a business use an open-back window display rather than one with a closed back?

8. List and describe six types of interior displays.

9. What is the difference between the ways full-service and self-service businesses use visual merchandising?

10. How has the growth of regional shopping malls affected visual merchandising?

C·H·A·P·T·E·R

43 *Creating Effective Displays*

If you randomly group items of merchandise together in space, your result will probably not be an attractive display. When you place merchandise in the display area so that it presents an attractive arrangement, pleasing to the eye, you'll have good visual composition. When Denny was preparing a display of salt at Sterling Hardware, he was using elements and principles of design. He used signs, show cards, color, and other devices to help the customer make a decision to buy.

Design is a visual composition. Like written composition, it must have a beginning, a middle, and an end. It should tell a story. A display is a work of art, and good composition in a display depends on understanding and using the elements and principles of design.

Retail marketers design displays with specific goals. The most important goal is to sell merchandise. Another goal is to present a favorable impression to the customer. To accomplish these goals, retailers combine the basic elements and principles of design with display arrangements.

■

ELEMENTS OF DESIGN

Elements of design are important because each can influence the way customers react to a display. Positive reactions help to develop interest and desire. **Elements of design** include line, shape, size, texture, weight, and color.

Lines

Lines form the physical outline of merchandise and create moods and impressions. Vertical lines create a formal mood. Curved lines suggest informality, a sensation of free-flowing movement. Diagonal lines communicate a sense of action. Vertical lines would be appropriate for a display of tuxedos, curved lines for a display about South Sea cruises, and diagonal lines might be used in a display for all-terrain vehicles.

Shape

Shapes such as cubes, rectangles, and ovals are typical display-unit shapes. Similar shapes placed together create a feeling of harmony; different shapes put together create contrast and are used to attract attention.

Size

Merchandise that is small will not be noticed in a large display window. Jewelry items in a full window will attract little attention from passersby, but they can be effectively highlighted in a shadow box.

Texture

In display design, **texture** means the surface of the product or display unit. Textures can be shiny, dull, smooth, or rough. Texture can be used to create contrast for emphasis in a display. A wool sweater will attract more attention if it is displayed against a smooth-surfaced background.

Weight

The weight of an item of merchandise can be real weight or visual weight. Darker objects appear heavier than lighter objects of equivalent size. Size and color used together can influence the customer's judgment as to the apparent weight of the objects on display. Visual weight or real weight can be used to draw a customer's attention from one item to the next in a display.

Color

Color is perhaps the most important display element. Color is actually energy—light energy. When you walk into any color environment, you are walking into an energy force field. Color is known to cause biological and emotional changes in humans. Your blood pressure will rise if you sit under red lights and drop if you sit under blue lights.

Industries are becoming more aware of the importance of color in preventing accidents, increasing productivity, and increasing sales. Fast-food restaurants usually decorate in orange, yellow, and brown. Why? Orange makes you hungry (a biological change). Yellow and brown make you feel comfortable (an emotional change).

What Color Suggests Each basic color usually suggests certain feelings and concepts to people. This does not mean that every person sees colors in the same way or reacts to them in the same way. But it does mean that most people will tend to have similar reactions to colors. Knowing this, the display designer can use colors to influence customers.

Recent research suggests that retail stores should use warm colors (yellow, red, and orange) for show windows and entrances as well as areas of the selling floor associated with impulse buying, because these colors are "approach colors." That is, people will more likely approach an object that has a warm color than one that does not. But they will not stay long. These bright colors are best used as accents in a display and to lead the eye to the main feature.

The high visibility of yellow makes it a good background color for price tags on sale merchandise. Red lettering is also appropriate for marking a sale price.

Cool colors (blue, green, purple) are more appropriate where customers need to think about the purchase. These colors are more soothing and cause people to stay longer because they create a restful environment.

Black and white are the neutral colors. Together with brown, they are used in brightly colored displays to soften the bright effects.

Color Suggestions The following are some helpful tips in using color in display:

■ Keep the color selection simple. Some of the most interesting displays are those that use a **monochromatic** or one-color scheme. Too many colors, unless well thought out, can confuse the viewer.

■ Look for clues in the colors of the merchandise, the package, or the container.

■ Be careful when using bright colors and contrasts. The more intense a color, the smaller the area it should cover. Too much bright color may attract attention, but it may soon disturb the viewer and distract from the merchandise.

■ Try a balance of colors. If you blend two

Contrast between the color of the merchandise and the color of the background makes the merchandise stand out.

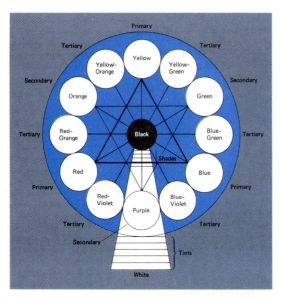

When the colors of the spectrum are arranged in a circle, they form a color wheel. Shades of a color are produced when the color is mixed with black, and tints of a color are produced when it is mixed with white.

or more colors so that the effect is pleasing, you have color harmony. The effect can be exciting or subtle. Select colors to create the mood that fits the occasion.

■ Allow sufficient space around a colorful article. Beware of clashes. Space serves as a buffer and emphasizes the featured product.

■ Light shades are easy on the eyes. They appear to deepen the display space and seemingly increase the size of the display area.

■ Emphasize contrast between the merchandise and background. Contrast in color makes a display more interesting. Contrast can be achieved by lighting also.

■

PRINCIPLES OF DESIGN

A good display results when the elements of design are arranged following basic design principles. **Principles of design** define how you place the elements together to achieve order and unity. **Unity** is achieved by having one main theme or idea as a point of emphasis or dominance, with the other elements in the display contributing to the main idea. Unity is especially important in visual merchandising, where the objective is to increase sales. Viewers may find a display pleasing to the eye, but unless there is a central point of interest that emphasizes the sales message, the display misses its target.

Order in a display means that all the parts of the display are arranged into an easy-to-understand plan, so that the passerby immediately gets the selling message of the display. The proper blending of all the design principles—emphasis, contrast, balance, harmony, proportion, and rhythm—produces displays that make the customer stop, look, and buy.

Emphasis

Emphasis refers to the point of a display that appears most dominant. Therefore, the point that is emphasized is the place at which the eye makes contact with the display. It is from this point that all eye movement flows. It is best to have only a single point of emphasis. Too many areas of emphasis in a display may lack unity and confuse the viewer. If, however, your display will be approached from more than one direction (such as a corner or island display window), it is a good idea to have a secondary point of emphasis leading the viewer to the dominant item.

Contrast

You can achieve emphasis in a display by surrounding the dominant unit with appropriate colors and similar or contrasting lines, shapes, and textures. Combining shapes, sizes, and colors so that the difference is emphasized is known as **contrast**. The dominant unit may be larger, stronger, brighter, darker, or lighter than its surroundings. Contrast is a way to create emphasis and draw the viewer's attention to the dominant unit.

Balance

There are two types of balance: formal and informal. **Formal balance** in a display means that the left half of the display is a mirror image of the right half. One or more identical items are placed on opposite sides of the axis, which is the center of the display area. The arrangement is symmetrical. Formal balance can be used in most types of displays and is relatively easy to design.

Informal balance is used to achieve balance among items that are different in size, shape, or some other element. Informal balance is visual balance in which different elements are creatively assembled to make the total display appear balanced to the viewer's eye. While informal balance can be used to interesting effect, its use requires more skill than that of formal balance.

Can you identify the examples of formal balance and informal balance?

Harmony

Combining the elements of display, lines, shapes, sizes, weight, color, and textures, into a pleasing arrangement is called **harmony**.

Proportion

The principle of **proportion** involves the relationship of one item to another with respect to size. The meaning of proportion can be explained by comparing two boxes. A box that is 1 foot wide and 2 feet high and a box that is 2 feet wide and 4 feet high have the same ratio of height to width—2:1 in each case.

The size of the display area determines the size of the merchandise that is put into it. Small items such as jewelry or perfume containers can be displayed in a small area. But large items such as snowmobiles, men's suits, or skis require a larger area for effective display. Show cards must be proportionate to the size of the area and merchandise.

Rhythm

In a design, **rhythm** is the sense of movement created by the way the various design elements are arranged. **Repetition** is the reproduction of an element of a design more than once. Similar design elements may be used several times in a display. A display of skateboards, for example, could use the same size boards and possibly the same color. A display of blue jeans for fall might use orange, brown, and yellow backdrops in a repeated sequence.

Rhythm may also be obtained in a display by arranging the pieces according to size, so that smaller items are in front and the larger ones in back. This involves **gradation**, or progression, which is the gradual change in size or color of the units in the design.

If the design consists of the same design element, inserting an item that is different in size, shape, or color produces an **interrupted rhythm**. In a display of skateboards, for example, an elevated skateboard might be used to break up the pattern and create interest.

■

BASIC DISPLAY ARRANGEMENTS

Visual merchandisers use several basic patterns of item arrangement over and over again because they are flexible and effective. These patterns can be used to create rhythm, harmony, and contrast within the display. The five most frequently used patterns are radiation, step, pyramid, zigzag, and repetition.

Radiation

In **radiation**, the elements of the design are spread out like rays from a central point. This type of design creates interest by having one dominant feature from which the other elements of the display radiate.

Step

In a **step** arrangement, either the merchandise or the fixtures holding the merchandise are arranged in a series of steps going up or down. This is a harmonious type of display that gives the feeling of motion. If a customer looks at a display of shoes arranged on ascending platforms, the customer's eyes will move naturally from one step to the next.

Pyramid

A **pyramid** display arrangement is shaped like a triangle, with a broad base that gradually tapers to a point. This type of display is used a lot in supermarkets, drug stores, hardware, and automotive accessories stores because it is easy to construct and allows for a massing of merchandise. It is also frequently used in houseware departments with boxes of cookware.

Zigzag

The arrangement called **zigzag** is similar to the pyramid arrangement except that it is not built up directly to the top. It begins with a broad base but zigs and zags its way to the top. Department stores often use zigzag displays for clothing. It is best suited to light, open displays and is usually limited to three major types of items: shoes, sweaters, shirts and skirts.

Repetition

Repetition in a display uses items of the same general nature and aligns them in exactly the same manner, either by height, spacing, or angle. Monotony can be avoided by using panels or elevated platforms or by tilting the platform.

■

MAINTAINING DISPLAYS

Displays need to be maintained properly if they are to remain effective. Displays and merchandise on display must be kept clean and orderly. This may require periodic dusting, or, in the case of shoes and clothes, regular replacement of display items so that colors do not fade.

When merchandise is sold from a display (this happens when the store is low on inventory of the display item), it should be replaced immediately by an item as close to the original as possible. A hole in the display creates a sloppy and uninviting image for the business.

Displays that are illuminated should be checked daily to ensure that all lights are working properly and that the lenses are clean. Lighting is an important part of the impact of a display and requires constant attention.

In addition to the custodial aspects of maintaining a display, other problems can also render a display ineffective.

Too Much or Too Little

There are no specific rules on how much merchandise should appear in a display area. One guideline is price. More expensive items, such as designer dresses, may be a single-item display. Low-priced, bargain stores tend to have many items in the displays—sometimes to the point of being cluttered. But discount electronics stores, self-service shoe stores, and off-price luggage stores will frequently put hundreds of items in their windows to create a bargain image.

Lack of a Unifying Theme

Whether a display is in a window or inside the store, it should be coordinated with the business-wide promotional theme. It should contribute to that theme and not detract from it.

The viewer should be able to understand the idea presented by the display in a matter of seconds. Too often, merchandise is simply placed in a display area without a selling message, or too many ideas or themes are presented at the same time. This confuses the customer and renders the display ineffective.

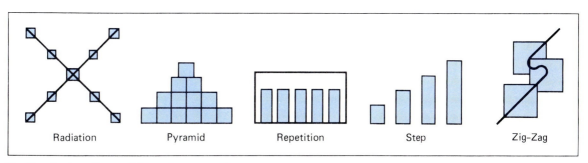

The five basic patterns of item arrangement.

Too Many or Inappropriate Props

Props are supposed to enhance the selling message. But too many props distract the viewer's attention from the central theme. There should be no question in the customer's mind as to which items are for sale.

Displays Changed Too Seldom

The timetable for changing displays depends on a number of factors: how frequently customers shop the place of business, whether customers have access to the display, the season of the year. Many interior displays are changed daily because merchandise is sold directly from them. Exterior windows may be changed from twice a week (common in shopping malls) to every other week (common in suburban stores). Christmas displays, because they are often complex, are usually not changed until the new year.

EVALUATING DISPLAYS

Judging the effectiveness of displays is not always easy. It has often been said that beauty is in the eye of the beholder. What works for one person in a display may not work for someone else. There is general agreement, however, on seven factors that all effective displays have in common:

1. *Power to attract attention.* Are the elements of display used to appeal to potential customers? Is a theme or clever idea apparent?

2. *Arrangement.* Does the display reflect the character of the business? Do show cards improve or help the display? Is there enough merchandise in the display?

3. *Cleanliness.* Are all exposed surfaces clean, fresh, and well maintained? Is the merchandise neatly displayed?

4. *Timeliness.* Are the items selected appropriate for the season and the overall promotional theme?

5. *Selling power.* Is the dominant item clearly the focus of the display? Does the lighting produce the appropriate mood? Are buyer benefits clearly shown by the presentation and/or use of show cards?

6. *Lighting.* Does the lighting enhance the colors used? Are the lighting fixtures clean?

7. *Technical quality.* Is there a unique use of display materials? Do props and other materials enhance the visual presentation?

Advertising and visual merchandising, when planned carefully and budgeted properly, can be powerful communication tools for the retail marketer. In the next unit you will have the opportunity to study the promotional planning process and how retail marketers combine the use of special incentives, advertising, and visual merchandising to develop their promotional strategies.

TRADE TALK

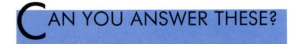

Define each term and use it in a sentence.

Contrast	Principles of design
Design	Proportion
Elements of design	Pyramid
Emphasis	Rhythm
Formal balance	Radiation
Gradation	Repetition
Harmony	Step
Informal balance	Texture
Interrupted rhythm	Unity
Monochromatic	Zigzag
Order	

CAN YOU ANSWER THESE?

1. List the six elements of design.
2. Explain how design is used in visual merchandising.

3. Why would a fast-food restaurant use orange in the customer seating area?

4. What colors might be good to use in a display to encourage impulse buying?

5. List the six principles of design.

6. What is the difference between formal and informal balance in a display?

7. What are the five basic patterns of display arrangement used by visual merchandisers?

8. Identify five typical problems that can render a display ineffective.

9. List seven factors you should consider in determining if a display is effective.

ACTIVITIES AND PROJECT FOR U·N·I·T 14

RETAIL MARKETING CASES

1. Regional shopping malls have grown in importance in recent years. They have become the new "downtown" for many communities. Because of their design, they share certain unique characteristics that affect how businesses advertise and display their products and services. Some of these characteristics include:

■ Most customers live nearby (70 to 80 percent of repeat customers live within a 20-minute driving distance).

■ Most people come to the center often. In half of the malls, 90 percent of the people who shop there come on a repeat basis.

■ Among repeat shoppers, 25 percent account for two-thirds of the mall's sales.

■ Most mall customers are women (average age is 30–50).

■ Customers enter on the average of no more than four stores on a single shopping trip.

■ Stores are designed with narrow fronts and deep selling areas.

■ Mall managers are beginning to make greater use of "internal media" such as electronic scoreboards and media walls.

Assume that you are the assistant manager for the Jeans Connection in the mall, a store that sells jeans and related casual clothing. Part of your responsibilities includes developing promotion for the business. Sales have been slow recently. Your manager has asked you what should be done to improve sales.

1. Suggest a combination of promotional activities that will help boost sales. Identify which promotional methods you would use and why.

2. Thinking specifically about visual merchandising, what conclusions would you draw from the information presented above? What visual merchandising policies would you recommend to your manager?

2. Barbara Henn works with you at the Raceway Auto Store. She has been working there for about 6 months. Yesterday, a customer came in asking about a battery she had seen advertised. The customer couldn't remember the exact price or brand name. Barbara's response was to tell the customer that she was not a mind reader, but that if she would tell her what battery was advertised, she would see if one was in stock. The customer became angry and left the store.

After the customer left, Dean Rothson, the assistant store manager, came over and asked Barbara what had happened. Barbara's response was that the customer didn't know what she wanted.

1. What are the two main problems?
2. How could Barbara have been more helpful?
3. Since the assistant store manager was nearby, what could Barbara have done?
4. Do you think the store management was partly responsible for this lost sale? Why? What would you suggest that management do to keep this problem from happening again?
5. If you were the customer, would you shop at this store again?

PROJECT: EVALUATING A RETAIL MARKETER'S PROMOTIONAL ACTIVITIES

YOUR PROJECT GOAL
Given a retail business of your choice, assess the impact of that business's promotional activities.

PROCEDURE
1. Identify a business related to your career interest. Obtain approval from your instructor before beginning the assignment.

2. Visit the place of business and collect samples of promotional materials. Develop written descriptions of promotional activities you cannot collect (radio and TV spots, for example). Be sure to collect examples of print advertising, descriptions or pictures of the store exterior, pictures or descriptions of the interior displays and other visual merchandising activities, copy for the radio or TV ads (if used), samples of special incentives, and any other promotional materials used by the business.

3. Prepare a report that includes the following:

a. Show which activities promoted products or services and which were institutional.

b. Suggest which mental stage of the buying process (AIDCA) the different promotional activities are trying to address.

c. Identify the theme of the in-store visual merchandising activities. Determine if this theme was consistent in all other promotional efforts.

d. How would you define the target audience of the business based on the promotional materials you have collected?

e. Using the suggestions for good copy on page 354 of Chapter 41, select one print ad and explain how you would evaluate the ad copy and use of illustrations. What would you change? Why?

f. From your visit and description of the store's interior, can you suggest a reason for the choice of colors used? Is it an effective use of color? What changes would you recommend? Why?

g. From your visit and description of the store's interior displays, select one display and evaluate it using the criteria provided in Chapter 43, page 378.

EVALUATION
You will be evaluated on the completeness of your analysis.

MANAGING PROMOTION

C·H·A·P·T·E·R

44 *Determining Promotion Objectives*

"Sales are down. We're just not pulling in the customers the way we were. And I'm spending a lot on advertising," said Malcolm as he closed the sales record book.

"You know," said Nora, "you really need to develop a long-range promotion plan. We've been studying how to develop promotion plans in our marketing education program. A good promotion plan requires well-developed objectives, an adequate budget, the coordination of all of the elements of the promotion mix, and effective evaluation."

Malcolm was the owner-manager of Star Fourplex, a movie theater in suburban Arlington, Virginia. Nora was his assistant manager and was enrolled in a high school marketing education program. She was also taking classes at the local community college in retail management as part of her high school program. The problem they were discussing is common to many retail marketing businesses: lack of sales. Although the solutions are never simple, many solutions involve developing a well-thought-out promotion plan. In this chapter, you will have the opportunity to consider what retail marketers have to think about as they manage promotion: objectives of the promotion, communicating with customers, the product life cycle, market segmentation, and factors that affect the choices of what to promote.

■

PURPOSES OF THE SALES PROMOTION CAMPAIGN

Promotion, as we noted in Chapter 38, is how a business communicates with its customers. The purpose of communication may be to increase sales, create an image (or change an image), or one of many other possibilities. Regardless of the purpose, successful retail marketers recognize that promotion must focus on one or more of the following objectives:

1. *To inform.* This process is similar to education in that the customer needs to learn about the business or product.

2. *To persuade.* Persuasion would not be as necessary if the retail marketer did not have competition. However, because of competition, retail marketers have to show customers why they should patronize a particular business.

3. *To remind.* Previous or current customers need to be reminded of how a business has met their needs and that it can continue to do so. You want customers to continue to buy from you rather than from a competitor.

In order to inform, persuade, or remind, the retail marketer needs to plan carefully the promotion mix. The illustration below shows the relationship between the elements of the promotional mix, AIDCA, and the general objectives of the promotion. In this model, conviction ("C") is omitted because it is generally not known when the customers reach this stage. The model suggests that advertising is relatively more cost-effective in inform-

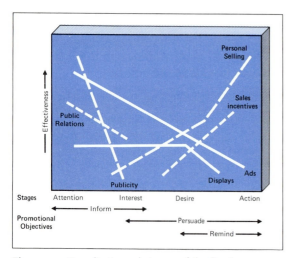

The promotional mix and stages of the buying process.

TABLE 1 / SAMPLE PROMOTION OBJECTIVES

Increase customer traffic during slow selling periods
Clear leftover merchandise at the end of a selling season
Create an awareness of new departments or services
Attract new customers
Hold onto current customers
Build the business's reputation
Build goodwill
Encourage more customers to become charge account customers
Identify the business with national brands
Explain business policies
Introduce a new product or service
Penetrate new markets

ing the public, getting attention, and creating interest than is personal selling. Personal selling is, however, much more cost-effective in persuading—moving the customer to action—than is advertising or any other element of the promotion mix.

To inform, persuade, and remind are general objectives of promotion. Businesses usually pursue more specific objectives, such as those in Table 1. The actual objectives selected will depend on the considerations discussed in the remainder of this chapter.

■

COMMUNICATING WITH THE CUSTOMER

A communication model for retail marketing was introduced in Chapter 38. Now we need to expand it a little. In the revised model on page 383, two new elements have been introduced: noise and encoding/decoding the message.

Noise is anything that reduces the effectiveness of the communication process. For example, perhaps the retail marketer cannot decide which market segment to appeal to

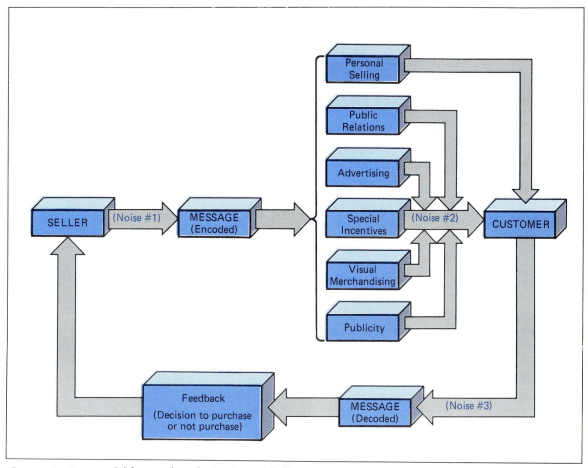

Communications model for retail marketing (expanded).

and tries to develop a general appeal message (noise #1). Or the receiver may be distracted entering the room when a commercial message comes on the radio (noise #2). Or other advertisers may make competing claims about their businesses or products and the customer becomes confused (noise #3). The customer may then decide not to buy from anyone.

Encoding the message is what is said and what words and symbols are used that will have meaning to the potential customer. **Decoding** is what the customer does to translate the message. A problem can arise when the words and symbols used by the retail marketer do not relate to the potential customer or they mean something entirely dif-

ferent than what was intended. For example, General Motors had to change the name of one of its best-selling cars, the Nova, in Spanish-speaking countries, when it was discovered that Nova means "no go" in Spanish. Retail marketers who continually run sale ads may find that they are communicating a "bargain basement image" when they were trying to say "value for the dollar."

■

PRODUCT LIFE CYCLE

Products, services, and even businesses follow a pattern of growth. The stages that a product, service, or business passes through,

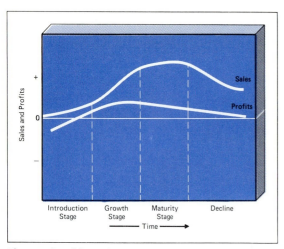

The product life cycle.

from beginning to end, are called the **product life cycle** or PLC. This curve (see the illustration above) is usually divided into four distinct stages, known as introduction, growth, maturity, and decline. Each stage has unique characteristics that affect managements decisions about promotion.

Introduction

Introduction is a beginning stage, in which sales are usually slow. Consumers are not looking for the product, and they don't know much about it. Retail marketers must invest heavily in communication activities at this stage. Promotion is used to inform potential customers about the new product, or new business, its benefits and usage. Chapter 66 discusses promotional activities for introducing a new business.

Growth Stage

Growth occurs when sales begin to take off. The retail marketers who originally offered the product or service find their profits increasing. This rise in profits begins to attract competitors. The competitors may introduce new models with unique product features and begin to attract new customers. A major goal of communication efforts during this stage is to keep the growth going as long as possible. Promotion begins to shift from informing potential customers about the product to bringing about customer acceptance and purchase of the product. Product quality and added new features are promoted as new models are introduced. Prices begin to fall in response to competition. Personal computers, for example, after going through a rapid introduction stage, are now nearing the end of their growth stage.

Maturity

The maturity stage is recognized by the leveling off of sales. Competition becomes intensive, profits decline, and prices are cut to attract business. Experts believe that most products on the market today are in the maturity stage. As a result, each retail marketer has to develop promotion strategies geared to meeting competition—to persuade customers to purchase from his or her outlet, not from a competitor. The goal in the maturity stage of the PLC is to keep the product alive.

Keeping the Product or Service Alive
A product may be kept alive in many different ways. Retail marketers may look for new market segments who have not used their products before. Carson, Pirie Scott & Co. in Chicago found a new market segment for their more expensive men's and women's clothing when they opened a basement shop with early morning hours. (This example will be discussed in more detail in Chapter 45.) The segment of busy business executives and travelers who stay at nearby hotels responded to the opportunity to shop at unusual but convenient hours. Malcolm, the owner of the Star Fourplex in our opening story, might follow the lead of other movie theaters, which have begun "midnight" shows.

Increasing the Item's Use Another
strategy is to look for ways to increase use of the product among current customers. This

might be accomplished by discounting large purchases or suggesting new uses for an older product. There is a line of movie theaters in the Midwest that promotes the use of their theaters for meetings or fashion shows. One of Malcolm's competitors offers discounts on books of movie tickets. These discounts encourage movie goers to buy more tickets and use them for movies they want to see.

Positioning   A third method of keeping a product alive is called positioning. Positioning, as defined earlier, refers to how a business or product is perceived by customers in relation to competitors. For example, consider K mart, The Gap, and J.C. Penney. Each sells clothes for teenagers, but each has a distinctly different "position" as communicated by pricing policies, visual merchandising, lines of merchandise and services provided, and promotion activities.

Using Special Incentives   It is at the maturity stage that retail marketers begin to use special incentives such as coupons, cents-off deals, contests, and gifts more aggressively. You will recall that in Chapter 40, it was stated that budgets for special incentives are increasing rapidly in relation to budgets for more traditional advertising. This is happening because most products are in the maturity stage, and special incentives are more useful in attracting value-conscious consumers to mature products. This trend will most likely continue, because the average life cycle for a product has been reduced from 3 years in the early 1960s to about 3 months today.

Decline Stage

Decline is the stage where profits and sales decrease. This decrease may occur over a long period of time (black-and-white TVs, electric typewriters, coffee), or it may occur quite rapidly (most fashion goods fall into this category). Retail marketers recognize that at some point most products and services

need to be replaced. Promotion strategies at this stage are geared toward clearing the inventory of these goods. As noted earlier, businesses also move through a life cycle, sometimes referred to as a "retail life cycle." It took department stores nearly 100 years to reach the maturity stage after they were introduced. It took supermarkets 40 years. Fast-food restaurants began in the early 1960s and reached maturity by the mid-1970s, a period of only 15 years.

Catalog showrooms have reached maturity in less than 10 years. So businesses, just like products, are experiencing the quickening of a PLC.

■

MARKET SEGMENTATION AND RETAIL PROMOTION

The traditional approach of retail marketers, being all things to all people, is not possible in today's consumer market. A business must decide which segments of the market it is serving and then attempt to match the business to the needs of these customers. Businesses have to segment their messages as well as their product and service mix. They have to know who their customers are and understand their needs and wants.

Successful retail marketers know that not all customers are alike. They may be of different ages, live in different areas, have different incomes, pursue different lifestyles, and so forth. As discussed in Chapter 12, market segmentation involves subdividing the total market into distinct groups who have distinct needs and wants in relation to a particular business. Then the retail marketer must tailor products and communication to each segment.

For example, Phil and Don own a record shop called Everly's. They know that the record business is in the maturity stage of the PLC. There are many competitors, from K mart to Sears to the corner drugstore.

Even though they grew up on rock 'n' roll music and still prefer it, they know that the market for this type of music will not keep them in business because of the intense competition. Therefore, they developed a **product mix**, the collection of products and services a business offers for sale, that will appeal to several market segments.

Based on marketing research they did in their community, they identified their segments as shown in Table 2. Because of differences in age, behaviors, and education, each segment tends to be interested in different types of music, and Phil and Don know they must communicate to each segment differently. Using newspaper ads to reach the hard rock and Top 40 segment would be a waste of money. Radio and TV would be more effective, but only those radio and TV stations that feature this kind of music. On the other hand, newspapers and popular magazines could be very effective in reaching the "classic rock oldies" segment; radio ads on selected stations would also be useful. Because public TV and public radio stations do not accept commercial advertising, Phil and Don will have to use other media to communicate to the classical music lover. Given

the size and growth potential of each segment, to which segment would you recommend the owners of Everly's give priority?

Other retail marketers have responded to new and emerging market segments by modifying their product or service mix and their promotion activities. A good example of this is the response of retailers to the needs of working women as discussed in Chapter 11.

■

DECIDING WHAT TO PROMOTE

Each element of the promotion mix has a purpose. No one element is totally effective when used alone. But the decisions of which elements to use and how much money to spend on promotion, and many other decisions, are determined in part by the merchandise or service. There are several factors that influence retail marketers' choice of product or service to promote. Carlos, whom you met in Chapter 38, chose to promote salt in his hardware store because of the possibility

TABLE 2 / MARKET SEGMENTS FOR EVERLY'S MUSIC STORE

Product	Age Segment	Behaviors	Growth
Hard rock/Top 40	10–20	Watches MTV, does not read, listens to WKAT and WBBB	Large group but declining
Classic rock oldies	30–45	Watches popular TV, reads papers and popular magazines, listens to WOLD	Moderate, but increasing
Classical	30–65	Watches public TV, reads frequently, highly educated, listens to WPUB	Small and steady
Country/western	25–60	Watches popular TV, sports fan, listens to radio while on the job, listens to WHLL	Moderate and steady
Soul	14–30	Listens to WWRB	Small and steady

of snow. He would not promote salt during the summer.

Factors That Influence Promotion Decisions

Weather, seasons, and geography influence what the retail marketer promotes. Other factors that influence this decision include the following.

Fashion and Current Demand   A business with an image of fashion leadership will advertise the newest styles. Consumers who are interested in the latest fashion trends will watch for ads from certain businesses with a reputation for fashion leadership.

Current demand may dictate what a retail marketer promotes. Fast-selling, popular items will bring customers into the store. When rock groups tour, record shops in cities they visit will advertise the group's most recent album. When movies or TV shows become popular, spin-off products become the focus of heavy advertising. These products may include anything from clothing seen in the film to lunch boxes with the main characters' pictures on them.

Current events may also influence a retail marketer's decision on promotion. In the early years of the space program, models of rockets and space coloring books were heavily promoted. Telescopes were the focus of considerable media spending by camera stores when Halley's comet passed near Earth in 1986.

Price   Price is often a factor in deciding what to promote. When merchandise or services can be promoted at discount or below the competition, most consumers take note because everyone is interested in a good deal. Discount retailers, such as Target Drug, Best Company, Pic 'n Pay shoes, Best Buy, and others feature products and services that have already gained customer acceptance. Because

This ad is part of a campaign featuring customers who represent the target market.

of their buying strategies and business policies, they can sell their products at prices below those of more traditional stores. These types of businesses attract the customer who is willing to put up with less service and fewer salespeople to get a good price.

Brand   Private brands require constant promotion to gain customer acceptance. **Private brands** are brands that the retailers put on their own products. A common strategy to build a market for private brands is to run ads comparing the national brand to the private brand, pointing out differences in price and comparable features and benefits. Sears, for example, has been very successful in promoting its private brands of Kenmore appliances and Craftsman tools.

What Not to Promote

Many retailers face the problem of overstocks of some merchandise. Often this is a result of poor buying decisions, or perhaps the item was simply a slow seller. The temptation is to advertise these items. Generally this is not a good idea and may leave the potential customer with a negative image of the store as one that sells unfashionable or out-of-date merchandise.

Popular products that are not adequately stocked should not be promoted. Nothing is more frustrating to a customer and more likely to create bad feeling than being brought into a store for an item that is out of stock. Issuing rainchecks will not always make the customer happy. If low stock is a problem, then the fact that supply is limited should be noted.

No product or service should be promoted that has not been carefully thought through and planned for. This means that all products and services to be promoted should be brought to the attention of the sales staff and other store personnel.

Malcolm's problem at the Star Fourplex theater was a result of a lack of understanding of promotion. Like many people, he thought that all he needed to do was advertise. What Malcolm needed was a plan that would incorporate all elements of the promotion mix: advertising, visual merchandising, special sales incentives, publicity, and public relations. Such a plan should be based on well-thought-out objectives that include such factors as the PLC, market segmentation, potential problems in communicating to potential customers, and factors that influence promotional decisions.

What would you recommend to Malcolm about market segmentation? Where in the PLC are movie theaters? How should this affect Malcolm's decisions on promotion? If you can answer these questions, you are well on your way to understanding management's complex task of promotion. In the next chapter, you will have the chance to study the basic promotion planning questions asked by all retail marketers.

TRADE TALK

Define each term and use it in a sentence.

Decoding	Private brands
Encoding	Product life cycle
Noise	Product mix

CAN YOU ANSWER THESE?

1. What are three broad objectives of a promotion campaign?

2. Which element of the promotion mix is most cost effective in obtaining the customer's attention?

3. What might interfere in the communication process between the retail marketer and a potential customer?

4. What are the four stages of the PLC?

5. At which stage of the PLC does the retail marketer concentrate on persuading the public to purchase from his or her business instead of a competitor?

45 *Establishing a Promotion Budget and Schedule*

Nora's suggestion to Malcolm, the owner-manager of the Star Fourplex movie theatre, was that he needed a promotion plan. A good plan, she noted, has objectives, a budget, and elements of the promotion mix that are all coordinated. In the last chapter, we examined how objectives can be developed from awareness of the product life cycle, knowledge of market segments, and other factors such as desired business image, current demand, seasons and holidays, current events, and pricing strategies. Regardless of the source, a sound promotion plan begins with a statement of objectives.

Once the objectives for a promotion plan have been established, the retail marketer must make five decisions:

1. How to allocate the overall budget
2. How to schedule promotion activities
3. What promotion mix to use
4. What message to send
5. How to determine whether the promotion objectives have been met

In this chapter, you will have a chance to examine what the retail marketer needs to consider to make decisions 1 and 2. Decisions 3, 4, and 5 are discussed in Chapter 46.

∎

HOW TO ALLOCATE THE OVERALL BUDGET

There are a number of methods for determining the amount of money to spend on promotion activities. The four most common are the affordability method, the percentage-of-sales method, the competitive parity method, and the objective-task method.

The Affordability Method

The affordability method is the least effective but most often used method, particularly by small business owners. The retail marketer first allocates funds for all other business expenses and then uses what is left over for promotion. One problem is that the amount of money left over may be inadequate to do any good. Another problem is that it leads to inconsistency of effort. Because budgeting is not tied to objectives, the amount of money spent will vary from one fiscal period to the next. This inconsistency makes it very difficult to plan long-range promotion activities.

The Percentage-of-Sales Method

Like the affordability method, the percentage-of-sales method is simple to calculate and simple to understand. The retail marketer simply decides what percentage of revenues he or she wants to spend on promotion. Typical percentages are between 1 percent and 4 percent for retail firms. By contrast, cosmetic manufacturers spend between 20 percent and 25 percent of revenues on promotion. Stores located in shopping centers are usually required to maintain some agreed-upon level of advertising. The advantage of the percentage-of-sale method is that promotion expenditures vary with what the company can "afford." The disadvantage is that it may lead to inconsistency of effort in promotion as revenues rise and fall from year to year.

The Competitive Parity Method

Some retail marketers set their promotion budgets to match those of their competitors. This is referred to as **competitive parity**.

The advantage of this method, one could argue, is that setting a budget this way takes advantage of the collective wisdom of the industry. The disadvantage is that there is no guarantee that a retailer's competitors know any more than he or she does. A second disadvantage is that this method does not account for specific objectives a particular firm may have for its campaign.

The Objective-Task Method

The objective-task method is one of the best methods for retail marketers. Using this method, objectives are clearly defined and then a budget is established to meet these objectives. For example, Malcolm may set as an objective that 35 percent of the people in the businesses trading area will recognize the Star Fourplex. He might project the costs shown in Table 1.

The advantage of this method is that objectives are clearly identified, spending is related to the completion of specific tasks, and the success of the campaign can be readily

evaluated. The main disadvantage is that it is very difficult for some retail marketers to identify objectives.

■

THE PROMOTION BUDGET

Promotion plans are usually made up of several budgets and schedules. There may be a separate budget for advertising, one for special incentives, and one for visual merchandising. In other cases, all promotion activities may be designated under a single budget plan. Regardless of the budgeting method, the total budget will be allocated to different elements of the promotion mix. In large firms, committees with members from various store departments plan what emphasis, and how much money, to spend on advertising, visual merchandising, special incentives, publicity, and public relations.

For example, in 1984, Carson, Pirie Scott & Co. added a new department to its Chicago department store called "Corporate Level." This department was designed to attract the executive set. The merchandise mix assembled for this department included exclusive, higher-price brand lines. In addition, the store instituted unique hours of operation for this department, opening as early as 7:00 a.m. Management developed a promotion plan with the goal of attracting more young, fashion-oriented men, a target market for the

TABLE 1 / OBJECTIVE: 35 PERCENT NAME RECOGNITION

Subobjective	Task	Cost
Gain awareness of men	Use four quarter-page image ads in four successive Friday afternoon sports editions	$2000
Gain awareness of motorists	Rent eight billboards in strategic locations around the city	1700
	Use ten 30-second radio spots during the afternoon rush hour	1000
Gain awareness of pedestrians	Hand out flyers in shopping centers	500
	Total budget	5200

Holmes has all the newest, best fitting beachwear to beguile on a tropical isle . . . shown, only a few of the bright hued styles we've netted for your summer of '87! All swimwear of nylon/Lycra® spandex. A. GABAR® tank with bow detail at low back, black, 6-14. Please wash with Woolite®. **$40**. B. HARBOUR CASUALS® tropical print ruffle bikini with ruffle bandeau top, multi-brights, 6-14. **$42**. Matching woven cotton big shirt coverup; S,M,L. **$44**. C. BILL BLASS® leopard print tank with buckle, navy/white, 8-14. **$48**. D. ROXANNE® 40's retro draped sheath has optional straps. Proportioned bra sizes 32-40 B,C,D, magenta. **$52**. E. LA BLANCA® high-waisted side-tie bikini has french cut legs and bandeau top, jade/black, 6-14, **$36**. F. WEAR ABOUTS® cotton gauze beach coverup camisole dress with staggered hemline; peacock blue, XS,S,M,L. **$57**. Misses' Swimwear

you've got it All
you've got
HOLMES

The promotional budget allocates a certain percentage to each medium. By using several media, such as newspaper advertising and window displays, the retailer increases the opportunities to reach the customers.

Corporate Level. The specific goal of the campaign was to increase annual volume in these lines by 20 percent. They allocated their budget in the following way:

Promotion Media	Percentage of Budget
Newspaper advertisements	45.0%
Broadcast advertisements	22.5
Catalogs	22.0
Visual merchandising	10.0
Special sales incentives	00.5

SCHEDULING PROMOTION ACTIVITIES

Most retail marketers work out promotion schedules in two stages. First they make a series of decisions regarding how often to promote, and then they develop a promotion calendar for a six- or twelve-month time period.

Retail marketers find that promotion schedules are most effective when they are worked out to accomplish a specific goal, such as shown in the example above. The planned-for goal is more likely to be reached when several elements of the promotion mix are used. For example, a fashion boutique might include advertising, visual merchandising, special sales incentives, publicity, and a fashion show combined with a special mailing to preferred customers to start off the Christmas-Hanukkah buying season. Coordination of all the elements is critical to the success of any promotion campaign.

Scheduling Decisions

Promotion scheduling usually involves a number of decisions and choices. The first decision relates to how to schedule promotion over the course of a year or the usual consumer buying cycle. This decision has to take into consideration the seasonality of the products and services offered. For example, for many retail marketers, 70 percent of the year's business is conducted during the 6 weeks between Thanksgiving and Christmas. A retailer might choose to use a scheduling technique known as **massed effort**. In this case, a store with 70 percent of its sales in a 6-week period would spend 70 percent of its promotion budget during or around these 6 weeks. Many stores follow shopping patterns in allocating and scheduling promotion using massed effort.

Grocery stores use a massed effort centered around days of the week. They know that almost 75 percent of grocery shopping is done on Thursday, Friday, and Saturday, so they mass their advertising on Wednesday and Thursday (about 80 percent of expenditures) and concentrate on newspaper ads, many using coupons.

However, a retail marketer might try to even out this pattern by building sales in another part of the week or year. Some retail marketers in the fast food industry evenly allocate promotional expenditures over the entire year. This scheduling decision is referred to as **distributed effort** in promotion.

Another set of decisions relates to scheduling promotion over shorter periods of time. There are two basic decisions involving the reach of the promotion effort and the frequency of promotion.

Reach of the message refers to the number of people who will be exposed to one or more promotion messages. Some products have a very specialized audience. For several years, Cabbage Patch dolls were in short supply and in great demand. Toy stores, department stores, and other retailers who had these dolls in stock tried to reach as many people as possible with the message that they had this highly demanded item. It was not necessary to constantly repeat the message.

When promotion is scheduled to reach many people, but only once or twice, it is called **extensive coverage**.

Frequency is a measure of how often a customer is exposed to a promotion message. If a new toy store opens just before Thanksgiving, the toy retailer will probably want to keep the store name before the public. The strategy in this case will be to increase the frequency at which potential customers hear the new store's name. A strategy relying on repetition using selected promotional elements is called **intensive coverage**.

Sources of Calendar Information

As noted in Chapter 44, there are many opportunities to schedule promotion events. Table 2 lists some of the possibilities.

Malcolm, as manager of the Star Fourplex, should know that there are several different seasons for movies. The Christmas season usually sees the release of many movies aimed at the family audience. The end of the school year is marked by the release of films aimed at the school-age market. The beginning of the school year is the time when more serious films aimed at an older segment of moviegoers are released. This knowledge should help him plan his promotion calendar for the year.

TABLE 2
POSSIBLE EVENTS FOR PROMOTION

Business-Oriented Events	Society-Oriented Events
Grand opening	Back-to-school
Business anniversaries	Mother's/Father's Day
Moving sale	Sporting events
Going-out-of-business	Graduation day
Clearance	Seasons and holidays
Pre- and post-inventory	Outdoor activities
End of model year	Elections

Another source of information that Malcolm could use to develop his promotion calendar would be to study past records to identify busy time periods. Past experience is usually a good indicator of future business behavior. Promotions are usually scheduled to begin prior to the beginning of a busy time period. So if Malcolm can identify past busy time periods, this will help him identify when to begin and when to end major promotion efforts. The key is to find the time when each group of potential customers is most likely to buy and to encourage buying at the appropriate time. That is why Christmas ads for department and apparel stores appear in early November, back-to-school ads appear in early August, and so forth.

Malcolm should be careful in relying on past records, however, because some outside force, such as bad weather, may have affected sales. Also, this year could be different because of new competition, road construction, and many other outside factors. Past sales records should be used only as a guide in planning.

Developing a Promotion Calendar

A **promotion calendar** is a written timetable for a long-range promotion plan. It should indicate:

- When the promotion activity will occur
- What merchandise or service will be promoted
- Which promotional activity will be used
- Who will be responsible for the activity
- How much is budgeted

Generally, the promotion calendar uses a regular calendar format with months, weeks, and days and special places for all the necessary information. Although it is important to develop a detailed plan, it is also important to remain flexible and permit revision should conditions require a change.

The promotion calendar Malcolm developed for the month of June is shown on page 394. His goal was to increase sales by 20

Promotional Calendar

June, 19 – –
(month, year)

Last year, June, 19 – – produced <u>14%</u> of average total sales
(month, year)

Total sales for ___June___ last year were <u>$70,000</u>
(month)

	MONDAY	TUESDAY	WEDNESDAY	THURSDAY	FRIDAY	SATURDAY	SUNDAY
Sales goal	1	2	3	4	5	6	7
$77,000	Direct mail first mailing		*Times* ad starts	WROC radio starts WROL radio starts		*Times* ad stops	WROC radio stops WROL radio stops
Promotion budget	8	9	10	11	12	13	14
$2310			*Times* ad starts	WROC radio starts WROL radio starts		*Times* ad stops	WROC radio stops WROL radio stops
	15	16	17	18	19	20	21
			Times ad starts	WROC radio starts WROL radio starts		*Times* ad stops	WROC radio stops WROL radio stops
	22	23	24	25	26	27	28
	Direct mail second mailing		*Times* ad starts	WROC radio starts WROL radio starts		*Times* ad stops	WROC radio stops WROL radio stops
	29	30					

Budget allocation:

	%	$
Print Adv.	25	578
Dir. Mail	20	462
Radio	25	578
TV		
Visual Mdsing.		
Special Incen.	30	693
Other		

Promotional calendar for the Star Fourplex.

percent during the summer months. He sought to do this by increasing use of the movie theater by a market segment already known as heavy users—young adults. His strategy included an intensive coverage of the 25-to-35 age group (his target market). His message was that the Star Fourplex was the best bargain for summer entertainment. His plan called for the use of coupons offering one free movie admission for every five paid admissions and special pricing for late night shows. He intended to use a local newspaper with wide readership among this age group to distribute the coupons, along with direct mail flyers. Two radio stations with listeners in this age category were to be used in this campaign. Using the "objective-task" method, he calculated that it would require $2310 per month to obtain a 20 percent increase. Based on movie industry averages, he allocated his budget as follows:

Promotion Media and Strategy	Percentage of Budget
Newspaper advertisements Repetition of theme	25%
Special incentives Direct mail coupons	45
Radio advertisements Repetition of theme	30

Malcolm will need to prepare a similar calendar for each month of the year. This same type of calendar would need to be developed for a single retail business, a chain of retail businesses, or a shopping mall. In the next chapter, you will have the opportunity to find out how Malcolm can better choose which elements of the promotion mix to use; how to tailor the promotion message; how he might coordinate the promotion effort with suppliers, staff, and outside agencies; and finally, how he might evaluate the overall promotion campaign.

TRADE TALK

Define each term and use it in a sentence.

Competitive parity	Intensive coverage
Distributed effort	Massed effort
Extensive coverage	Promotion calendar
Frequency	Reach

CAN YOU ANSWER THESE?

1. What are the five basic promotion questions that a retail marketer needs to answer?

2. List the four methods for calculating a promotion budget and the advantages and disadvantages of each.

3. How does a distributed promotion effort differ from a massed promotion effort?

4. Give an example of when intensive coverage might be a good strategy.

5. Give an example of when extensive coverage might be a good strategy.

6. Why would Carson, Pirie Scott & Co. choose not to use coupons in their promotion campaign for the Corporate Level described in this chapter?

7. What drawbacks are there in using past records in planning sales promotion?

CHAPTER

46 *Implementing the Promotion Plan*

Many businesses fail every year because of their management's inability to develop and implement a total, comprehensive promotion plan. In addition to decisions about objectives, the overall promotion budget, and scheduling promotion, a successful promotion plan must also include the message to be delivered; the promotion mix; and the way to determine whether the plan is appropriate. As part of this decision-making process, the successful retail marketer also must consider how to coordinate the promotion mix with suppliers and employees. This process, called **promotional strategy,** is management's way of achieving its overall marketing objectives using promotion. In this chapter, you will see how to put a promotion campaign together.

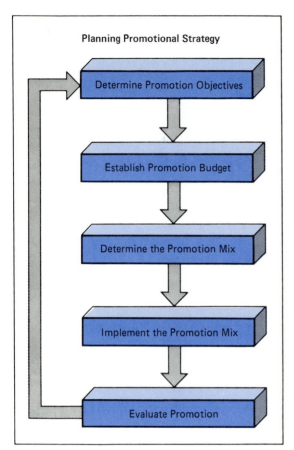

Planning promotional strategy.

■

WHAT MESSAGE TO USE

In Chapter 41, you were introduced to the concept that an effective promotion message is targeted to a specific segment and can be judged on three elements: desirability, believability, and exclusiveness. Messages should be developed and selected based on their desired effect on the consumer and then judged by these three criteria.

Desired Effect

When consumers are moving through the mental stages of the buying process, they will react to elements of the promotion mix. These stages are also sometimes referred to as the **hierarchy of effects**. Retail marketers usually have specific objectives they are trying to accomplish at each stage.

As shown in Table 1, the objective at the awareness and interest stages is to provide information. The most effective elements of the promotion mix at these stages are advertising, publicity, window displays, and certain special sales incentives such as premiums and point-of-purchase displays.

At the desire level, retail marketers attempt to change attitudes and feelings about the firm or the products and services it offers by the business. In the initial stages, advertising concentrates on use of slogans, jingles, and descriptions; advertising at this stage tries to demonstrate the advantages of one product over its competition. During the "burger wars" of the early 1980s, Burger King tried to show the advantages of its method of cooking hamburgers over McDonald's methods. The promotion objective was to change consumer's attitudes or feelings about the advertised products. This type of advertising is usually combined with personal selling, publicity, and product demonstrations.

Retail marketers try to move the customer through the conviction and action stages by using point-of-purchase displays, advertising that focuses on special pricing, last-chance offers, and testimonials. Personal selling is the most effective element of the promotion mix at this level. In addition, direct mail and telemarketing are often combined with the other promotion elements. For more complex products or services (personal computers or insurance), personal selling is more effective in changing attitudes and stimulating desire to own than the nonpersonal elements such as advertising.

Creating the Message

There are many things that could be said about any product, service, or business. In order to select the best message, the retail

TABLE 1 / STAGES OF THE BUYING PROCESS AND PROMOTION OBJECTIVES

Stage of the Buying Process	Promotion Objective	Promotion Elements
Awareness		Advertising, slogans, jingles, descriptive ads
	Provide information	Visual merchandising, window displays, interior displays
Interest		Special incentives, premiums, point of purchase
Desire	Change attitudes or feelings	Advertising, competitive ads, argumentative copy, status appeals, image ads
		Personal selling
		Special incentives, product demonstrations
		Publicity
Conviction	Stimulate desire to own	Advertising, price appeal, last-chance offer, special pricing
		Direct mail
Action		Personal selling

marketer must consider what the target market seeks from the business in terms of benefits or rewards and how the consumer may best be shown these benefits.

Most buyers will respond to one of four groups of benefits (sometimes referred to as buying motives). These are rational, sensory, social, or ego satisfaction. Consumers can be

shown these benefits in any of three ways. The benefits can be shown as a result of the experience of using the product. The product can be shown in use. Or the product can be shown without reference to use.

Using a decision matrix like the one in Table 2, a retail marketer could develop 12 possible messages. For example, the message

TABLE 2 / MESSAGE CREATION MATRIX

Visualization	BENEFIT			
	Rational	Sensory	Social	Ego Satisfaction
Results of Use Experience	"Gets clothes cleaner"		"Lets you get closer"	
Product in Use Experience		"More raisins in Post Raisin Bran"		"Anyone who thinks the shortest distance between two points is a straight line, hasn't driven a Porsche"
Incidental to Use Experience				"Levis 501 Jeans"

"Gets clothes cleaner" is a rational benefit promise that follows from a results-of-use experience. The TV ads for Levi's 501 Jeans create an image of the wearer (ego satisfaction), and the jeans are not actually the focus of the viewer's attention (incidental-to-use experience). Much of the promotion directed toward the teenage market emphasizes the social benefits of owning the promoted product and service. Why do you think this is so? The long-running ads for breath mints showing social approval for having clean breath uses the message, "Lets you get closer." After all, how close could you get with bad breath?

Executing the Message

Once the message has been developed and evaluated, the retail marketer must decide the best way to deliver the message. This usually involves decisions about style. The more commonly used styles include:

Slice of life: Shows a person using the product in a realistic setting (family enjoying frozen dinners)

Lifestyle: Shows how the product fits into an idealized lifestyle (sports car alone on mountain road)

Fantasy: Creates a fantasy about the product use (woman sprays on a perfume and suddenly becomes irresistible to men)

Mood-image: Creates a mood around the product without actually discussing the product (cigarette advertising that mentions the health hazards of the product only in the legally required warning)

Musical: Uses songs and jingles (a favorite of the soft drink companies)

Personality: Creates a character to represent the product or service (Ronald McDonald, Mr. Clean, the Jolly Green Giant)

Technical expertise: Emphasizes the skill and care the business puts into serving the customer (a national muffler company that claims to be the "car care experts")

Scientific evidence: Uses surveys (nine out of ten doctors) or other test evidence to

Geoffrey the giraffe represents the image or personality of Toys "R" Us.

support claims that the advertised product or service is better (toothpastes and mouthwash)

Testimonials: Someone the target market would trust endorses product use (celebrity, expert, or ordinary person)

WHAT MEDIA TO USE

The experienced retail marketer recognizes that each medium has advantages and disadvantages. These advantages and disadvantages have to be considered when selecting media for use in a promotion campaign. In addition, the media habits of the target market, the nature of the product or service being advertised, the nature of the message, and the relative cost all have to be considered as well.

Media Habits of the Target Market

All media have good points, but the key question to the retail marketer is which medium or mix of media will best meet the promotion objectives. As the promotion plan is developed, the advantages and disadvantages of various media will need to be considered. Table 3 shows how to compare advantages and disadvantages.

It is possible to identify which media will most likely offer the opportunity for message exposure. For example, hotels will benefit from advertising in travel magazines and by using billboards on interstate highways. Why? If the product is hobby items (stamps, coins, models), specialized magazines will be appropriate media to use. The local newspaper will probably not be of much value.

It is critical to the success of promotion that the target market have the opportunity to be exposed to the message. The first thing that happens to a message in the communication process is that it may be screened out because of the lack of opportunity for exposure. If the target market is not exposed to the message, there is no opportunity for a response.

The Nature of the Product or Service

Some products need to be demonstrated to be shown to their best advantage; others can be shown effectively with line drawings or the use of words alone. When Polaroid cameras were introduced, there was a heavy use

TABLE 3 / ADVANTAGES AND DISADVANTAGES OF MEDIA

Medium	Advantages	Disadvantages
Newspaper	Flexible Timeliness Local market coverage Broad acceptance High believability	Short life Poor reproduction Difficult to target
Magazines	Can segment based on geographics/demographics Selectivity Credibility High-quality reproduction Long life	Long lead time for ads Some wasted circulation
Radio	Mass use High selectivity Low cost Allows for last-minute changes	Sound presentation only Low audience attention Brief exposure
TV	Combines sight, sound, and motion High attention factor Can demonstrate product features	High cost Less audience selectivity Fleeting exposure
Direct mail	Audience selectivity Flexibility No ad competition Can personalize	High cost "Junk mail" image
Billboards	Flexible High repeat exposure Low cost Low competition	No audience selectivity Fleeting message Difficult to measure response
Bus cards	Low cost Color Well read	Difficult to measure response

of television because this was a product that people had to see in use. Expensive fashion items are shown to better advantage when color is available. This suggests the use of magazines.

Some products or services are expected to be advertised in certain media. It is no accident that you rarely see ads for Rolls Royce cars in the local newspaper. The image is not appropriate. On the other hand, few local pizza parlors advertise in *Seventeen* magazine. In assembling the promotion mix, consumer behavior in searching out information about classes of products and services needs to be considered.

The Message

A message designed to inform the public of a major sale occurring in 2 days will require the use of newspaper or radio or both. For a message containing a great deal of technical information (about microcomputers, for example), radio would not be very useful, but direct mail and magazine ads would be.

Cost

The final consideration regarding the choice of media is the cost. However, it should not be just the total cost but the cost to reach each potential customer. This is usually considered on the basis of cost per thousand exposures. For example, if an ad placed in a national magazine costs $50,000 and reaches 10 million readers, is it a better or a worse deal than an ad placed in another magazine that costs only $15,000 but reaches 2 million readers? This decision is made by dividing the $50,000 and the $15,000 by the number of readers in thousands:

$$\text{Cost per thousand} = \frac{50{,}000}{10{,}000{,}000/1000} =$$

$5.00 per thousand readers

$$\text{Cost per thousand} = \frac{15{,}000}{2{,}000{,}000/1000} =$$

$7.50 per thousand readers

As you can see, even though the retail marketer would spend more money up front for the first magazine, he or she would reach more readers at a lower cost. While this is an important consideration, the retail marketer must also consider who reads the magazine, what their reading habits are (do they look there for ads?), and what images the magazines portray.

There is no one mix that is best for every retail business. The target audience, their media habits, costs, the nature of the product or service—all affect decisions on what promotion media to use. Look at the differences in percentage of budget spent on various media between the national companies shown in Table 4.

TABLE 4 / PERCENT OF BUDGET SPENT ON VARIOUS MEDIA

	Sears	Walgreens Drugstore	Jewel Supermarkets	Western Motels
Newspaper ads	82%	82%	50%	X
Magazines				X
Radio	10%*	18%*	10%	
TV			40%	
Direct mail				
Circulars	8%**			
Special incentives				
Billboards				X

X means percentages are unknown but indicates where money is spent.
* Percentage includes radio and TV expenditures.
** Percentage includes direct mail and circulars.

To maintain customer traffic during store renovation, this retailer used a special incentive and newspaper advertising.

COORDINATING THE PROMOTION CAMPAIGN

The development of a promotion campaign must be a coordinated effort if it is to be successful. Regardless of the size of the firm or its organizational structure, one individual should have final authority over all major decisions. Large retail marketers like Sears or J.C. Penney usually have a vice-president responsible for promotion. This person is in charge of visual merchandising personnel and advertising personnel. Additionally, the same person will be the primary contact with outside ad agencies. The personal selling function is usually the responsibility of the store manager. The successful coordination of promotion involves the person responsible for nonpersonal promotion, the individual responsible for personal selling, outside ad agencies, and possibly the vendors or manufacturers.

Working With the Staff

The salesperson, the final contact with the customer, must be informed of the forthcoming promotion campaign. Special training may be needed if the promotion involves new products or services. This training might involve learning about the product features and benefits. Cashiers should also be included in this training so they will be able to offer suggestions to customers at their registers. In addition to training, simple techniques such as hanging current ads next to where employees sign in will help alert them to promotion activities.

Personnel in the warehouse and stock area must also be informed of any special event so that they can be sure items are stocked in sufficient numbers and that correct prices are on the products.

Display workers will need sufficient advance notice so that they can create or remake the interior and exterior displays to coordinate with the theme of the promotion. Often this lead time may be several months.

Working With Suppliers

As discussed in Chapter 39, many suppliers, vendors, and manufacturers support promotional efforts by local retail marketers by sharing the cost of advertising through cooperative advertising.

While newspaper ads are the most used medium for cooperative advertising, some radio and TV ads are beginning to be used as well. In addition, some manufacturers permit retailers to create ads as long as the manufacturer's product and logo are used exclusively in the ad.

In addition to working with suppliers on advertising, it is also important to have good relations so that merchandise can be delivered on time and in sufficient quantities. Suppliers are usually more willing to help out local merchants who are current in paying their bills and who have had a long-standing relationship.

DETERMINING WHETHER THE PROMOTION PLAN IS APPROPRIATE

While business spends millions on promotional activities, it has been estimated that no more than 1/5 of 1 percent of the total spent on promotion is spent on finding out how effectively the other 99.98 percent was spent. Ultimately, the evaluation of the impact of the promotion plan must rely on the objectives established at the beginning. Techniques for evaluating the effectiveness of individual advertisments were discussed in Chapter 41.

In addition to measuring the effectiveness of individual promotion activities, it is important to evaluate the promotion plan before implementing it. Let us now consider the points on which the plan as a whole can be judged.

Product or Institutional Objectives

A good plan begins with objectives, which should be stated in such a way that they can be measured. This part of the plan identifies the direction for all promotion activities. Examples of measurable objectives include:

■ Adding a specific number of customers from a new market segment
■ A specific increase in sales
■ Promoting awareness of certain brands
■ Introducing new services to the existing market
■ Presenting new fashion trends to a select group of customers

These objectives should result from a careful assessment of overall business strategies and company objectives.

Budget

It is essential that a budget of sufficient size be established for the promotional campaign.

What do you think are the objectives of this ad?

The retail marketer will have to determine the cost and expected benefits to the business, and these can then be evaluated in relation to the budget.

Strategies

The combination of techniques used by retail marketers to achieve marketing objectives is often referred to as promotional strategy. The strategies to be used should be detailed in the promotion plan. The plan should identify the message or theme and the desired positioning for the business. For example, is it a bargain image that is desired? Or does the firm wish to position itself as an alternative to national chains? There are many possible positions to take in the market, but it is necessary to identify the most desirable one. Inability to do this has caused many companies to go out of business.

All strategies should contribute to the accomplishment of one or more of the objectives identified. The retailer should review previous successful promotion strategies and reuse those that meet current objectives.

Responsibility

Once the specifics of the promotion campaign have been established, someone has to be assigned responsibility for carrying out the plan. Usually specific individuals are assigned, although it may be appropriate to assign responsibility to a department; the department then assigns specific individuals to each task. The absence of assignment of specific tasks to individuals can just about guarantee failure of the plan.

Timing

The proper timing of promotion can make the difference between success and failure in a campaign. If ads break too soon or too late, if the sales staff is not prepared ahead of time, if the displays are not put up at the right time, the promotion campaign will most likely not meet the objectives set for it. Although many promotional campaigns follow traditional patterns, the alert retail marketer will be quick to spot trends. For example, the "back-to-school" season used to start in early August and finish by the end of September. However, the trends toward year-round schooling and the wearing of more casual clothing (sneakers and blue jeans) to school has caused major changes in back-to-school promotions. The back-to-school season starts much earlier now and continues farther into the school year.

It may also be appropriate to plan an innovative approach to timing. A small department store in upstate New York recently held a Christmas sale in mid-July, complete with Santa and his reindeer, snow, and Christmas carolers strolling through the store.

Evaluation

In addition to evaluating the effectiveness of individual components of the promotion program, the promotion plan should include evaluation of the overall campaign. Consumer advisory panels may provide feedback on their feelings about the campaign. Recently, a new strategy has been developed to determine customer opinions and attitudes toward a service or product. The **focus group technique** uses small groups of consumers (six to nine individuals) in a process similar to brainstorming to provide an in-depth analysis of consumer attitudes.

The key to successful promotion planning is to be sure that each element of the promotion mix—advertising, visual merchandising, special incentives, publicity, public relations, and personal selling—is carefully thought out before the campaign begins. The business's promotion plan is of concern to all levels and areas of management. Retail marketers are in business to make a profit. Profits are made by providing products or services that meet the needs of a target market: those that are priced right and are available at the right time and location. Finally, benefits must be communicated to the target market using the most appropriate mix of promotion activities. To be successful, the promotion plan must be targeted, comprehensive, and well planned.

TRADE TALK

Define each term and use it in a sentence.

Focus group technique   Promotional
Hierarchy of effects   strategy

CAN YOU ANSWER THESE?

1. How does the hierarchy of effects influence the promotional mix?

2. Which medium, advertising or personal selling, is more effective for moving a customer for a microcomputer to the action stage? Why?

3. What two considerations can be used to create a decision matrix for generating a message?

4. Name five possible "styles" that a promotion campaign might use.

5. List the advantages and disadvantages of each promotion medium.

6. What are the five major considerations for a retail marketer in selecting the mix of media to use?

7. Why does a promotion plan need to specify timing?

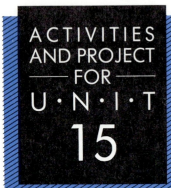

ACTIVITIES AND PROJECT FOR U·N·I·T 15

RETAIL MARKETING CASES

1. Kathy Ralston is the manager of the Encounter Bookstore, located at the Kansas City airport. It is actually a branch of a large chain of bookstores. She has done extensive research into the reading habits of travelers (they prefer paperback fiction, magazines, and newspapers). Since her product mix is much different from that in the other bookstores in the chain, she does not benefit from their promotion efforts—primarily newspaper ads.

1. What media would you recommend to Ms. Ralston?

2. Briefly outline strategies you think might be useful to her.

2. You were introduced to Malcolm, the manager of the Star Fourplex movie theaters in Chapter 44. Movie theaters are considered to be in the maturity stage of the PLC.

Some even argue that they are already in decline.

1. Assuming that Malcolm is managing a business in the mature stage of the PLC, what would you recommend to him as promotion strategies?

2. How might he position his theater in the market?

3. How would this position change if you determined that movie theaters are in the decline stage?

PROBLEMS

1. Select a product and a service of interest to you. If you are employed, select a product and service from your place of employment. Identify the ways in which it is promoted. Track the promotion activities for the selected product and service for a period of 1 month.

■ What changes in promotional activities have you observed?

■ Explain how well you think these activities are coordinated.

■ What differences in promotion activities did you find between the product and the service? (For example, compare the types of ads, the content, the message, and so on.)

2. Assume that it is now early September. You are responsible for raising $1000 for a class trip to visit Macy's department store in New York. Your promotion budget is $100. You may obtain merchandise on consignment (school T-shirts, Christmas trees, and so on), or you may sell a service (lawn mowing, curb painting, and so on). You may market only to other students in the school.

■ Identify a product or service you could retail.

■ Identify the methods you would use to promote the product or service.

■ Suggest an overall theme (message) for your promotion campaign.

■ On what would you spend your $100?

PROJECT: PREPARING A PROMOTION CAMPAIGN

YOUR PROJECT GOAL

Working with two other students as part of a three-person management team, consult with your instructor and identify a small local business that retails products and/or services of interest to your management team. Develop a promotion plan for the business for a minimum of a 6-month period.

PROCEDURE

1. Make an appointment with the manager or owner of the small business to discuss the outlines of the promotion plan.

2. Prepare a set of questions for the interview. The purpose of this interview is to collect all the information you will need to develop your promotion plan. Consult with your instructor on the final list. You will probably want to touch on the following:

    a. Objectives for the campaign

    b. The stage in the PLC for the services and/or products

    c. The business's competition

    d. The market segments served by or sought by the business

    e. The selected business's desired market position

    f. Budget

    g. Evaluation of the plan

3. Develop a plan for the promotion campaign based on your interview. The final plan should address the items in Procedure 2 above. Each item should be developed as a separate section of the report. In addition, your plan should specify the strategies you recommend. This section should include a discussion of the message or theme of the campaign and how you intend to carry this through by using various elements of the promotion mix (advertising, visual merchandising, direct mail, special sales incentives, and so on). Remember, all you recommend must stay within budget.

4. Prepare at least two print ads and two broadcast ads for the campaign. Pre-test the ads using any of the techniques described in Chapter 41. Prepare sketches for all visual merchandising activities proposed. Create mock-ups of or describe any other promotion activities you plan to use (coupons, publicity, public relations, and so on). Suggest how you might evaluate the potential value of these activities.

EVALUATION

The completed project will be evaluated by the owner or manager and by your instructor using the criteria for promotional plans outlined in Chapter 46.

MERCHANDISING AND OPERATIONS

Jim Barkley is a merchandise receiving and checking trainee. Kelly Redman is a merchandise buyer trainee. Doug Smith is an owner-manager of his own sporting goods store. They all have similar merchandising responsibilities. These responsibilities relate to the flow of goods and services to that all-important person, the customer.

In this competency band, you will understand how Jim, a new retail marketing employee, receives and checks merchandise, performs stockkeeping tasks, maintains inventory security, and processes merchandise and sales transactions. You will learn, as Kelly did, to understand pricing policies, to calculate prices, and to work with various inventory control systems. In the concluding chapters, you will observe Doug Smith as he develops and follows a merchandise buying plan for his sporting goods store.

Through this competency band, you will obtain a clearer understanding of the merchandising functions involved with providing the customer with the right goods and services at the right place, at the right time, at the right price, and in the right quantities. In addition, you will obtain valuable career planning information for a variety of merchandising occupations.

PROCESSING THE PRODUCT OR SERVICE

47 Receiving and Checking Merchandise

Jim Barkley was concerned about his new job. He had recently been hired as a receiving and checking trainee. Jim's original job application goal was to acquire a position as a salesperson. Since the sales positions were filled, Jim accepted a position in the receiving and checking department. He now wondered if he had made the right decision.

Mr. Jones, the supervisor of the receiving and checking department, sensed Jim's concern. During his initial orientation and training Mr. Jones began the discussion by saying:

I can understand your apprehension about working with the various forms, reports, equipment, and merchandise. This department is really the life support of the sales departments. If we don't process the merchandise quickly and accurately, they can't sell it. In fact, receiving and checking merchandise is so important that all our management trainees begin with their initial training assignment in this department.

■

UNDERSTANDING THE MERCHANDISE FLOW

The merchandise flow begins when a store buyer orders goods from a supplier, who may be a manufacturer or wholesaler. Merchandise is ordered by using a written **purchase order**. This is a written agreement between the buyer and seller on which complete information about the kind and quantity of goods wanted and the terms of the purchase are recorded. (Preparation of the purchase order is explained in Chapter 55.)

To move the incoming merchandise from the receiving area of the sales floor, retailers must develop a system. The system must (1) assemble or consolidate the orders, (2) receive the goods properly, (3) check the goods, (4) mark the goods for sale, and (5) distribute the goods to the proper selling area of the store. Depending on the size of

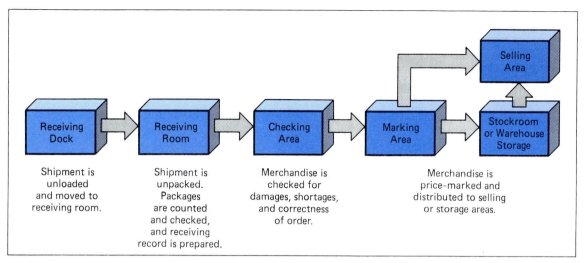

Retailers must develop a system for moving goods from the receiving area to the selling floor.

the store, the steps in the system may be very simple or very detailed.

Using Consolidator Services

Mr. Jones explained to Jim that in this store the services of a consolidator are being used more and more. A **consolidator** is a person or group of people, employed either within or outside the store, who put together merchandise orders from many suppliers. The orders are then shipped to the store at one time by one carrier. A **carrier** is any form of transportation, such as a train, truck, or airplane.

To explain to Jim how consolidators do their job, Mr. Jones discussed the ready-to-wear coat department:

> The coat buyers place orders through the consolidator to several different coat manufacturers. The consolidator then fills the orders from these manufacturers and sends one large coat shipment to the store in a single truck. (In certain cases the consolidator just arranges transportation for several orders that the buyer has placed with different suppliers.) The consolidator can save time, transportation, and receiving and checking expenses involved with several smaller shipments from different suppliers.

Mr. Jones also explained that to further speed the flow of the merchandise to the sales floor, the consolidator carefully unpacks the coats from the suppliers and hangs them on racks installed in the carrier's trucks.

Using Computerized Receiving Systems

Suppliers' invoices are forwarded to the store's computer center by the consolidator. Magnetic price tickets are then prepared from these invoices by computerized equipment. A **magnetic price ticket** is a ticket that is printed in magnetized ink. The magnetic particles within the ink are arranged in such a way that a variety of merchandise information can be read by a computer. (See Chapter 48 for examples of such tickets.)

Mr. Jones continued:

> When the coats arrive in the receiving area, they are moved off the truck racks directly onto racks suspended from the ceiling of our receiving area. After the magnetic tickets are attached to the coats, the coats are moved on overhead racks to our store shuttle trucks, which are equipped with similar overhead racks. This computerized and automated system allows the consolidator and our store

receiving personnel to move goods from the manufacturer to the selling floor in a shorter period of time.

◼

INVOICE INFORMATION

Mr. Jones showed Jim an invoice for an order of leather jackets and said:

When the supplier is ready to ship goods either to the store or to the warehouse, an invoice is prepared and mailed to the store. An **invoice** is a bill for the goods that specifies the description, quantity of items, how and when the shipment was made, and the terms of payment.

Jim, let's review this invoice from top to bottom. We will compare the supplier's invoice with our original purchase order to note any differences or discrepancies. I'll explain each item in the invoice along with important points to consider.

INVOICE

WILD WEST CLOTHES
13 1st St N.
DENVER, COLORADO 56300

SOLD TO	SHIP TO
The Western Wear Shop 189 Colt Street Cheyenne, Wyoming 567000	SAME

DATE	DATE SHIPPED	SHIPPED VIA	YOUR ORDER NO.	DEPT. NO.	TERMS	NO. OF PCS. 3	INVOICE NO.
3/15	3/16	TEC	1426	56	8/10, Net 30, EOM	WEIGHT 65 lbs	No. 246

Returns and Claims: None accepted after 10 days from receipt of goods.

Style No.	Description	Qty. Ordered	Qty. Shipped	Qty. B/O	Unit Cost	Extension
47	Western Leather Jackets	10	8	2	60 00	480 00
48	Western skirts	6	6		40 00	240 00
NOTE: B/O's will be filled by 3/20					INVOICE TOTAL	720 00

An invoice is a bill specifying what was ordered and the terms of the sale.

Sold to and Ship to

The name and address of the purchaser (*sold to*) and the place where the goods are to be delivered (*ship to*) are filled in near the top of the invoice. If the delivery address is different from the business office address, both sets of lines must be filled in. If both addresses are the same, only one address has to be filled in.

Invoice Date and Date Shipped

The *invoice date* tells when the invoice was written by the supplier. The *date shipped* is also very important. This is the date when the vendor ships the goods to the retailer. The invoice date is often used to determine when payment is due or when discounts may be taken. Many times a store will receive the vendor's invoice ahead of the merchandise. If the vendor ships the merchandise too early, the accounting department may record the order in the wrong selling month. This causes the merchandise department to be credited with either too much or too little inventory on hand within a selling period. **Inventory** is another term used to describe merchandise available for sale. Early shipment can distort the records for a department's selling period.

In some cases, if merchandise isn't received by a certain date, the store has the right to cancel or return the order to the vendor. These things are agreed to by the buyer and the vendor prior to the writing of the invoice. It is the receiving department's responsibility to alert merchandise buyers and managers to possible violations or variances in the purchasing contract conditions.

Shipped via

The **shipped via** entry shows which transportation company will deliver the merchandise to the business. Increasingly, retailers are using computer terminals to check the status of incoming shipments. By inputting a code word meaning "shipping inquiry," a traffic supervisor can contact the mainframe computers of all the merchandise shippers and carriers that are used. Within a few seconds a listing of all shipments being processed or actually being transported for the company will be available on the computer screen and on a hard-copy printout. This listing will include carrier numbers, vendor identifications, carton or package counts, weights, and invoice references. This information is very helpful in planning receiving and checking activities.

Order, Department Numbers, and Terms

The *order identification number, department number*, and *terms* are entered in the retailer's computer data bank. This data bank is a helpful reference when checking the status of lost, incomplete, or delayed invoices. The terms 8/10, net 30, tell the store that the supplier will give an 8 percent cash discount if the bill is paid within 10 days of the invoice date. The total amount of the invoice (net) is due within 30 days of the date of the invoice. The supplier offers this discount to encourage prompt payment.

Number of Pieces

The word **pieces** is used to mean packages, cartons, containers, bales, and so forth. The number of pieces tells the purchaser the quantity of items being shipped on a certain invoice.

Mr. Jones told Jim:

> We must check the total number of pieces received from either the invoice, the delivery receipt from the carrier, or the **bill of lading**, which is the contract document between a shipper and a carrier. We usually don't begin the process of receiving and checking merchandise until we've received the total number of pieces shipped. Sometimes we have had to contact the supplier or

carrier to locate missing or split-order shipments. Occasionally, the missing piece will arrive in a later shipment.

Weight and Freight Rates

Both the supplier and the store need to check the *weight* and *freight rates*. Mr. Jones continued:

> Once we have assembled the correct number of packages in a shipment, we check to make sure that the proper freight rates and charges for shipment weights have been made. If the shipment has arrived in good condition and everything is satisfactory, we sign for the shipment. But if containers are damaged and the shipment is short—or there are any other discrepancies—claims are made to the shipper or carrier. In most cases, we make a note on the bill of lading as to the damage or the shortage before the carrier leaves the premises. Because stores lose money if they can't prove claims for damages or shortages, receiving department personnel must count and check shipments carefully. Receiving personnel either pay the shipping charges to the delivery person or approve the delivery receipt and send it to the office for payment.

Quantity Ordered, Shipped, and Back-Ordered

"Qty. ordered" means "quantity," which reminds the business of the number of each item that has been ordered. "Qty. shipped" shows the business how many items the supplier is shipping and billing the business for. "Qty. BO (**back-order** items)" means that the supplier does not have enough stock to send all the goods ordered. The supplier is back-ordering (BO) jackets that it cannot send with this shipment. They will be shipped at a later time. It is important to know when these back-orders will be shipped. If necessary, the back-order should be cancelled if the items are shipped after the selling season is completed.

The date of the anticipated back-order should be noted on the invoice. If it is not, the receiver should contact the supplier and inform the selling department of the anticipated date of the back-order.

Unit Cost, Extension, and Invoice Total

The quantity shipped multiplied by the unit cost should equal the total extension cost figure. The invoice uses the term **extension** to mean the same as total cost of all items that are alike. The invoice total is found at the bottom of the invoice. It is the total price of all the merchandise included on the invoice. The cash discount is figured on this amount.

■

MAINTAINING RECEIVING RECORDS

In addition to the invoice, other types of receiving records may be maintained, such as an apron record, or a simpler record called a receiving log.

Using Apron Records

Many stores use a type of receiving record called an apron. An **apron** is a series of receiving records. These records are assembled into one order file from the time the merchandise was ordered until the time it is paid for. The information entered on the apron includes the department number, the order number, the terms on the order and on the invoice, the routing, and the date the shipment was checked. Often this information is entered into a computer and can be viewed on a video screen or can be printed on a receiving form. The apron statements are checked against the original purchase order to see that the quantity and description of the items are the same as ordered, that the price is correct, that the proper cash discount has been given, and that the shipping instructions were followed.

An important use of the apron is to prevent internal theft within the store. This record accompanies the merchandise from the receiving area to the selling floor. On the selling floor, the content of the shipment can again be checked by sales personnel to make sure that no goods have been lost, misdelivered, or stolen.

An advantage of the apron system is that it guards against paying duplicate invoices, because the apron is made out only when the shipment is received. It is also used when the goods are marked and stored. The apron serves as a permanent record because copies of the delivery receipt, the store's original order, and the vendor's invoice are usually attached to the merchandise and stored in a computer program. (See the illustration below.)

Maintaining a Receiving Log

Some stores log or enter the invoice information in a **receiving log**, which is the record of all shipments received. The information entered includes the number of parcels, the time and date of the delivery, the name of the vendor, the weight of the goods, the shipping charges, and the name of the delivery firm. The invoice is usually mailed to the store by the vendor on the same day the merchandise is shipped. The invoice number and the price of the merchandise are entered in the receiving book when the order is received.

■

CHECKING SYSTEMS

Jim worked in the receiving department for several weeks. Mr. Jones then approached

INVOICE APRON

REC CLK	SHIPPER OR VENDOR	SHIPPED FROM	REC VIA (CARRIER)	CARRIER'S No.	PCS	WT	CHGS	DEPT	KEY-REC No.	DATE REC
RC	MORRIS UNIFORM CO.	N	E	18330	2	20	95	5	1001 SHORT 01 DAMAGE 01	1/7

CORRECT DEPT	TERMS	DUE DATE	VEND INVOICE REF	TOTAL RETAIL	TOTAL COST	DISCOUNT	DEDUCT TRANSP	MDSE CKD BY	DAY
5	8 10 EOM	2/10	75164	363.75	250.00	20.00	WE PAY	CR	7

APPROVED FOR PAYMENT BY	DAY	MFGR. OR HOUSE CODE	PURCHASE ORDER NOs
Howard Smith	8	F10	4537

MFGR'S STYLE OR LOT NUMBER	30	32	34	36	38	40	42	COLOR	TOTAL QUANTITY RECEIVED
1408	2	2	2	1	1	1	1	BLK	10
		2	3	2				BR	7
				2	2	2	1	GRY	7

ORIGINAL

ATTACH INVOICE BELOW THIS LINE

OTHER PATENTS PENDING

DO NOT DESTROY! ACCOUNTING MADE FOR EACH KEY-REC

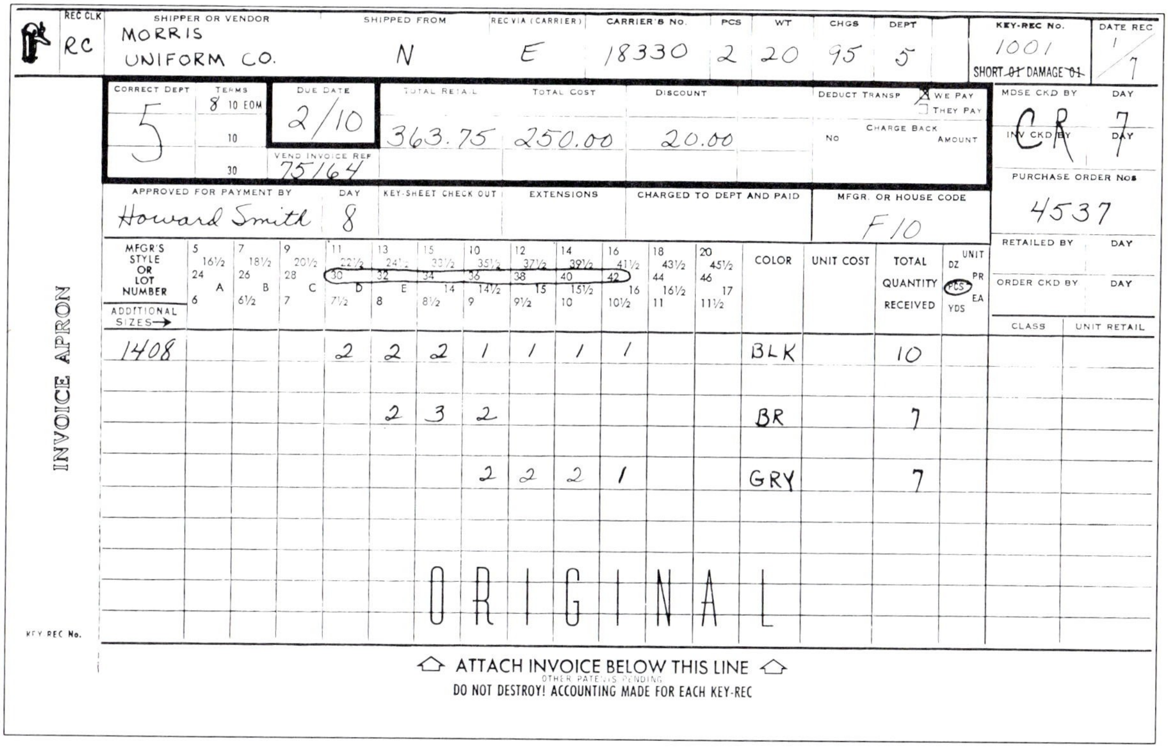

This receiving record is also called an apron. It provides important information about the goods received.

Jim about working with Lucille Anderson in the checking department. This department adjoins the receiving area, so packages do not have to be moved very far. In some small stores, goods are checked on the sales floor, but most stores do not allow merchandise to go to the selling floor until it has been checked. Sometimes, checking on the sales floor may be a safety hazard or an inconvenience to customers. Moreover, receiving records made out on the sales floor may not be as accurate, because sales personnel may be rushed during busy selling hours.

Stationary Tables

Lucille explained the different systems used in checking merchandise. When stationary

Checking merchandise may require opening all shipment containers to insure merchandise condition.

tables are used, the merchandise is unpacked, checked for quantity and quality, and price-marked by one person in an area from which the goods move directly onto the selling floor. A disadvantage of this system is that salespeople or buyers usually have access to this area. Sometimes they take needed merchandise off the tables without notifying the appropriate people. When portable tables are used, the merchandise is checked and then rolled to a separate marking room. From the marking room, the tables are moved to the stockroom or sales floor.

The Bin and Other Receiving Systems

The bin system divides the receiving room into receiving, checking, and marking sections. Merchandise is placed in the bins in the various sections. The bin method prevents removal of merchandise until it has been checked and marked, but it involves further handling of the merchandise.

Some stores use a conveyor-belt system, which moves goods from the receiving section to the checking section, then to marking, and finally to the stock areas.

■

METHODS OF CHECKING MERCHANDISE

Lucille told Jim that merchandise is checked for both quantity and quality. The **quantity check** is a count of the merchandise, and it is usually done by the checker who opens the cartons, removes the merchandise, and counts each item. This check is the most important in the receiving operation.

The **quality check** determines if the merchandise is of the quality ordered by the store. It may or may not be done immediately after the goods are received. In small stores this may be done by a salesperson who has a knowledge of quality and values or by the owner or manager. In large stores, the buyer usually purchases a sample in the vendor's showroom. When the merchandise is received, it is checked against the sample. Some merchandise is checked by quality inspectors, who may use standards and specifications established by the government, the manufacturer, or the retailer. Quality checks are usually made for big-ticket items such as appliances, furniture, and electrical equipment.

If the vendor is a regular and reputable supplier of the store, the quantity check is often more important than the quality check. The three common methods of checking quantity are the direct check, the indirect or blind check, and the spot check.

Direct Check

The **direct check** is used when markings, notations, and numbers on packages are compared directly with the invoice information. Packages are opened and inspected for quantity and quality as identified by the invoice. Advantages of the direct check method are:

1. It is a fast and economical system because a manufacturer's invoice is used.
2. Merchandise can be rechecked because it is still in the receiving area.

Disadvantages are:

1. The checker may not count or may be careless, as the amount is already known according to the supplier's invoice.
2. Manufacturers' invoices may not be available, causing a delay in checking.

Indirect Check

Using the **indirect** or **blind** check method, the checker completes a dummy invoice based on an actual inspection of the shipment. A **dummy invoice** is a blank invoice form that has no merchandise information on it. The checker simply completes the invoice based on merchandise information available at the time. Or, the checker may receive an invoice with merchandise infor-

mation preprinted and can then fill in the quantity of items received. Only when the checker completes this form is a comparison made with the quantities indicated on the original invoice. Advantages of this method are:

1. A more accurate quantity check is achieved.
2. Checking can be partially completed before the vendor's invoice is received.

Disadvantages are:

1. It is more expensive and time-consuming, as the checker has to complete a form and check this form against an invoice.
2. If the merchandise is checked without the vendor's invoice and moved to the selling floor, it is impossible to check for shortages when the vendor's invoice arrives.

Spot Check

The checker selects one or a few packages at random when the **spot check** method is used. The checker compares the quantity and quality of random packages with the invoice. If errors are found in the random check, the entire shipment is checked. Advantages of the spot check method are:

1. It is a more economical method of checking larger shipments.
2. It speeds up checking of seasonal items.

Disadvantages are:

1. Certain errors in the quantity or quality of the total shipment may remain undetected. The spot check may miss specific errors.
2. It is difficult to determine errors if spot checking is not done frequently enough.

RETURNING GOODS TO THE VENDOR

Next, Jim was assigned to work in the returned-goods section of the receiving department. Jim's main responsibilities during this assignment were to pack return shipments, schedule returned goods transportation, and notify the vendor of the return.

In some cases, when shipments were lost or damaged, Jim filed a claim, which means that a bill is presented to the carrier for the loss or damage. Jim kept report forms that were filled out in the receiving room as soon as damaged goods or invoice discrepancies were found in a shipment. These forms contain information such as the date of the report, the name and address of the shipper, the purchase order number, the method of shipment, and the amount of loss or damage. Jim sent the forms to the store's traffic office, which took care of filing the claim. The store filed a claim against the carrier if it was certain that the carrier was at fault. If there was some doubt, the claim might be filed against the vendor (manufacturer or wholesaler).

■

DISTRIBUTING GOODS

After Jim had become experienced with various types of receiving, checking, and returned-goods procedures, he was introduced to the methods of distributing goods to the departments within the main store and to the branch stores in shopping centers. Jim learned that the purchase order shows where goods are to be delivered within the store, since the purchase order shows the department that ordered the goods. When goods are to be sent to different stores from a warehouse, a buyer fills out a **distribution form**. This form indicates the quantity of goods to be sent to each store and the goods to be kept in reserve stock in the warehouse.

After three months of employment in the receiving department, it was time for Jim's initial job performance review. During this review, Mr. Jones evaluated Jim's progress and training. He asked Jim, "What's your opinion about your job in the receiving department?"

Would you agree with the answer Jim gave—that the job was certainly more interesting and challenging than he had thought it would be? Possibly yes, because in this chapter you've learned about the merchandise flow, computerized receiving systems, invoices, inventory reports, claim forms, shipping policies, and receiving logs. So now, like Jim, you should have a better understanding of why management trainees often get their initial training in the receiving department.

In the next chapter, you'll learn about other processes that merchandise must go through on its way to be sold—marking and stockkeeping.

TRADE TALK

Define each term and use it in a sentence.

Apron	Inventory
Back order	Invoice
Bill of lading	Magnetic price
Carrier	ticket
Consolidator	Pieces
Direct check	Purchase order
Distribution form	Quality check
Dummy invoice	Quantity check
Extension	Receiving log
Indirect or blind	Shipped via entry
check	Spot check

CAN YOU ANSWER THESE?

1. Retailers often develop a system to get the incoming merchandise from the receiving area to the sales floor. What are five possible steps in this system?

2. What services do consolidators provide a retailer?

3. What are four types of merchandise information contained on an invoice?

4. Copies of what receiving documents are usually attached to the apron records? Why are these documents useful?

5. What are four types of information contained in the receiving log?

6. What are an advantage and a disadvantage of the direct check? The indirect check? The spot check?

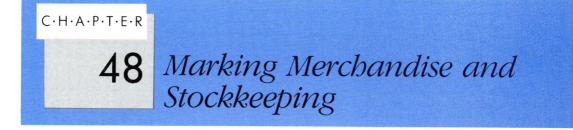

C·H·A·P·T·E·R

48 *Marking Merchandise and Stockkeeping*

Jim Barkley was curious. He had been assuming more responsibilities in the receiving and checking department. His job was becoming more interesting and challenging as he worked with the different merchandise receiving and checking procedures and records. His department had just received a shipment of merchandise that already had the individual price tags attached. Jim thought:

> I understand the price figure on this merchandise tag, but all these other letters, numbers, and markings must have a certain meaning. I'll ask Mr. Jones what all these mean at our next department training meeting.

At the training meeting, Jim asked this marking related question. Mr. Jones, his manager, explained that the store was automating and computerizing its marking procedures to reduce the time involved in getting merchandise from the receiving department to the selling floor. Stores lose sales and profits if the merchandise isn't available to customers. In this chapter, we will cover these topics Mr. Jones presented in the training session.

■ What a price ticket really says
■ Ticket information and codes
■ Computer-based marking systems
■ Marking methods and equipment
■ Stockkeeping practices

■

WHAT A PRICE TICKET REALLY SAYS

A computer-based marking system may use several futuristic-appearing devices. One of these is an **automatic reading scanner**, also called an optical scanner, which resembles a ray gun. This scanner sends a variety of merchandise information from the magnetized ticket to an electronic cash register, often called a terminal. In turn, the terminal feeds this information to either a minicomputer located in the store or to a larger computer located at a regional headquarters. This system makes the following needed information available to retailers:

■ What and how much merchandise is selling
■ How much merchandise and when to reorder
■ The sales productivity of individual salespeople

- The percentage of cash versus credit sales
- The results of various comparisons between past and present sales
- Other types of desired information

In certain cases, after a predetermined level of inventory has been reached, the computer can be programmed to write automatic reorders of needed merchandise.

Ticket Information and Codes

Mr. Jones held up several price tickets and said, "Let's identify the different markings on these various tickets. The markings on a ticket usually include such information as the price, merchandise classification, department, manufacturer, style, model, color and size, and the selling season in which the merchandise was received into stock."

The NRMA Classification

Mr. Jones pointed to a price ticket with several letter and number codes. He explained that the National Retail Merchants Association (NRMA) is a group of merchants who developed a standardized merchandise classification system. Members of this association are encouraged to use the same merchandise codes on pricing tickets. These codes enable suppliers and retailers to obtain and maintain merchandise information

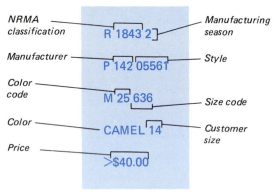

NRMA classification — R 1843 2 — Manufacturing season
Manufacturer — P 142 05561 — Style
Color code — M 25 636 — Size code
Color — CAMEL 14 — Customer size
Price — >$40.00

Elements contained on a basic price ticket. Why are color and size presented in both coded and noncoded formats?

through the use of computerized systems and equipment.

The price ticket on this page uses the NRMA classification system. On this ticket, the classification identifies a woman's jacket (R 1843). The manufacturing season is indicated by the last number (2) of the NRMA classification. This number represents the selling season for which the manufacturer shipped the merchandise to the retailer. In this case, the number (2) indicates the summer selling season. The manufacturer is specifically identified by the letter and numbers P 142. The color and size code are presented in both coded (M 25 636) formats for the terminals (electronic cash registers) and decoded information (CAMEL 14) for the customers.

Cost Codes "If the retailer wants to indicate the cost of merchandise on the ticket," Mr. Jones continued, "a cost code is used." A **cost code** is usually a code word or phrase of ten letters and related numbers. The following example shows a typical cost code:

$$\text{M O N E Y} \quad \text{T A L K S}$$
$$1 \ 2 \ 3 \ 4 \ 5 \quad 6 \ 7 \ 8 \ 9 \ 0$$

If this code is used, the letters NAY on a ticket would mean that the item cost the retailer $3.75. An eleventh letter, such as X, may be added to represent a decimal point. In this case, the coding for $3.75 would change to NXAY, and $375 would be NAYX. It is possible to include a cost code using the NRMA classification system.

Computer-Based Marking Systems

Mr. Jones explained that the store uses a computer-based **Universal Vendor Marking (UVM)** system on its price tickets. The word "universal" means that many manufacturers, suppliers, and retailers have agreed to use a common coding system that can be understood by the various companies that buy and sell goods. The UVM system is used primarily by manufacturers, suppliers, and retailers of general merchandise items. The **Universal Product Code (UPC)** system is used mainly by manufacturers, suppliers, and retailers of food and drug items. This code is also appearing on an increasing range of general merchandise items and has become more widely used than the UVM system.

The UPC System

Mr. Jones distributed samples of both UPC and UVM price tickets. He explained the UPC price ticket by calling attention to a set of numbers and a series of thick and thin lines.

"The ten numbers across the bottom of the symbol," he explained, "provide the same information as the lines in the symbol." The automatic scanner reads the meaning of the lines into the cash register. You can interpret the numbers accordingly: The first set of five lines and numbers identifies the manufacturer. The second set of five lines and numbers identifies the product. The price of the merchandise is stored in the computer. When the scanner reads the price ticket, the computer identifies the product and the price is recorded on the cash register. (See the illustration below.)

It is possible to change merchandise information and prices by entering the new data into the computer. These changes eliminate the time and expense of changing individual price tickets.

The UVM System

Mr. Jones explained, "The UVM price ticket resembles the more common price tickets. If you look closely at the numbers and letters on this price ticket, you'll notice that the shapes of the markings are different from normal printing. These shapes are in the form of standardized **optical character recognition (OCR)** markings. These are magnetically coded markings that can be read by many different scanners, electronic registers, and computers. An advantage of the UVM system is that it can be read by automated scanners as well as by the human eye."

Simply stated, OCR-A is a type style equally as readable as that used in the publishing of this text, with one important unique characteristic—it is also completely acceptable to

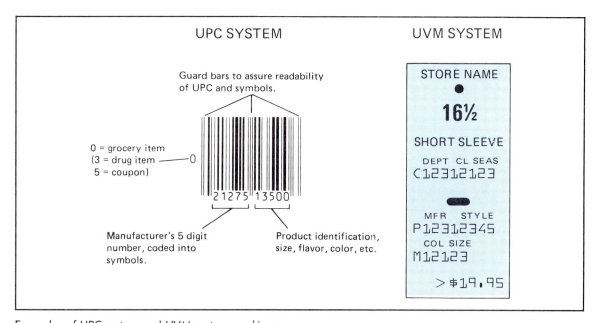

Examples of UPC system and UVM system markings.

computer-controlled reading devices, such as "wands" or "scanners." Here is a sample of OCR-A, the characters used in the NRMA voluntary identification standard:

```
A C D M N P R V X Y
1 2 3 4 5 6 7 8 9 0
≠   >   .     /     "
```

Human and computer interpretation of this price ticket is relatively easy. The "C," "P," and "M" are used to identify each of the components in the merchandise description.

```
C 1 0 4 2 2 0 1 2
P 4 6 3 0 1 3 1 4
M 4 5 1 9 6
16½ X 36
$15.00
```

■ The "C" line identifies Department 104, Class 22, and Season Code 012 (12th week in the year).
■ The "P" line represents vendor (or supplier) number 463, style 01314.
■ The "M" line, color code 45, identifies light blue, size code 196.
■ 16½ X 36 means shirt size (the actual shirt size is printed for the customer's convenience in a non-OCR-A style of print).
■ The price ($15.00) is printed in OCR-A for both human reading and machine processing.

The above illustration indicates the identification of merchandise according to the stockkeeping unit description commonly known as an *SKU*. The SKU is an individual merchandise description which usually includes the style, color, and size. With the OCR-A standard price ticket there is complete flexibility in the amount of marking detail included. In addition to the SKU infor-

mation, OCR-A marking may identify department, class, price, vendor and/or style.*

Marking Methods

Marking may be done by hand or by machine. A variety of methods may be used, including ink stamps, colored pens, grease pencils, and various kinds of tickets, tags, and labels. The method used is determined by the kind of equipment the store has available and the kind of merchandise to be marked. In some cases, every item is not marked. Instead, the price is indicated on a price list on the shelf or bin where the item is stored.

Item Marking   Mr. Jones now showed the employees a variety of different marking equipment and materials. He held up several marking pens and pencils and said, "These grease pencils or colored pens are the simplest types of markers used for fast-moving, lower-priced items. Supermarkets, self-service, or smaller businesses often use this fast, simple, manual marking method.

"In our larger business, however, we print and punch price tickets and tags with computerized marking equipment. Our markers program computerized machines to mark and attach tags and tickets automatically." (The illustration on page 421 shows a variety of price tickets.)

In-Store Pricing of Merchandise   Frequently, merchandise is priced after it arrives in the store. The person who sets the price at this time has the advantage of up-to-date market informtion on which to base that price. Also, a shipment of newly arrived merchandise items, such as jeans, can be inspected for variations in style and quality and then priced accordingly. The items can also be sorted into different price groupings based on their sales appeal.

---

* National Retail Merchants Association, "OCR-A Marking System: Its Application as Today's Marking Technology," *Receiving, Marking, and Coding Merchandise* (New York: NRMA, 1986), p.64.

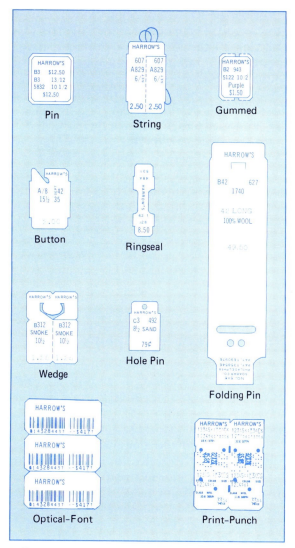

Different types of price tags.

Labels (top to bottom, left to right): Pin, String, Gummed, Button, Ringseal, Wedge, Hole Pin, Folding Pin, Optical-Font, Print-Punch

Nonmarking saves time, labor, and the cost of price tags. It's also useful in times of rapid price increases, because it eliminates the need to re-mark merchandise when a price adjustment is made. In certain areas, however, consumer protection groups have opposed nonmarking practices. They contend that nonmarking may mislead or misinform customers regarding the true price of the merchandise.

Vendor Marking   More and more, suppliers or vendors premark merchandise with the appropriate price and item identification information before delivering the merchandise to the store. This premarking service offered by some suppliers or vendors is called vendor premarking, or **preticketing**.

In some cases, the store supplies the prepared tickets and the vendor puts them on the merchandise. In other cases, the vendor both prepares and attaches the tickets. Sometimes the price is a nationally advertised one that the manufacturer has printed on the package.

When a vendor prepares the price tickets, the store's code or the vendor's own code, which the store then adopts, may be used. The tickets may be prepared with all the necessary information on them, or they may have space to insert code numbers, which the store adds when it receives the shipment. In either case, the service speeds up the flow of merchandise onto the selling floor by eliminating some of the preparation work the store needs to do.

In addition, marking at the vendor level is much more accurate than marking at the store level. In stores, too many different types of equipment and too many different people may be involved in the production of the tickets. There is neither uniformity nor continuity. But at the level of the wholesale supplier, a single marking machine operated by a single operator produces the same ticket in long continuous runs for merchandise shipped to all stores, whether in New York or California.

Nonmarking   When the price is not put on the item itself but appears on a price list or bin holding the item, the system is known as **nonmarking**. Some retailers have eliminated the markings of many items, such as packaged groceries, drugs, notions, and small hardware items. Instead, retailers put these items on containers, trays, or shelves that show the price. Also, for goods such as tires and storage batteries, retailers may post price lists in the area where the goods are sold.

Re-Marking Changing a price or replacing a ticket that has been removed or a mark that has become illegible is known as **re-marking**. Re-marking is required, for example, when merchandise is returned by the customer with the price ticket removed.

Merchandise may be re-marked by (1) putting a new ticket on the merchandise, (2) removing the old price and showing only the new price, or (3) using the original ticket and showing both the old and the new price. Store policy determines the method of re-marking. If merchandise was marked down for special sales such as bargain days, holiday sales, or store anniversaries, the unsold items may be re-marked with their original prices. Re-marked tickets must contain the same information as the original tickets and keep the same season numbers or letters, so that there will not be any confusion about the length of time the merchandise has been in stock.

In a small store, the manager decides which merchandise should be re-marked. In a large store, the buyer or head of the department must fill in a form regarding the change in price. Salespeople may do the re-marking under the supervision of the head of the receiving department or the buyer. Re-marking machines are used by some stores to do the work faster and more economically than it can be done by hand.

■

STOCKKEEPING PRACTICES

Mr. Jones continued the training session by saying, "After the merchandise has been received, checked, and marked, we must decide where to stock the merchandise. In our business we utilize in-store and/or warehouse stockkeeping plans."

In-Store Stockkeeping

The primary goal of in-store stockkeeping is to place the stock (merchandise) as close as possible to its selling point. Most retailers follow the plan of in-store stocking. This plan maximizes the amount of display and forward stock and minimizes the amount of stock in reserve.

Display stock is stock placed on display fixtures that customers can examine directly. **Forward stock** is backup stock that is temporarily stored on the sales floor near its selling department.

Reserve stock is backup stock stored farther from its selling department, usually in a central stockroom. Because reserve stock frequently is hard to obtain during busy selling seasons, most retailers prefer to limit stock in this area. Reserve stocks usually are moved to forward or display stocks as quickly as possible.

Warehouse Stockkeeping

Warehouse stockkeeping is often used in addition to or in place of in-store display, forward, and reserve stocking. Bulky merchandise such as furniture and appliances usually requires warehouse stocking. The retailer must often limit the amount of this type of display stock on the sales floor. Seasonal products, such as artificial Christmas trees or water skis, are typically held in warehouses until the appropriate selling seasons.

Many retailers find it desirable to use central warehouses and large distribution centers that serve several stores. The receiving, checking, marking, and stocking functions are carried out at these regional facilities. A recent development in the use of central warehousing facilities is to place less emphasis on storage and more emphasis on distribution. The overall goal of these central facilities is to keep the merchandise moving from the producer or manufacturer to arrive "just in time," when the retailer and consumer need it. The amount of merchandise storage required and inventory financial costs are thereby reduced by this **in-time method of distribution**.

Examples of (left) forward stock, (middle) reserve stock, and (right) under-the-counter stock.

COMPUTER NETWORK SEARCHES

Growing numbers of chain store retailers use a computerized inventory control network to reduce inventory storage and lost sales. If a customer requests an item that is out of stock in an individual store, information shown on the price tickets is input into the store's computer terminal. This terminal is connected to a network of similar stores within a district or region. Stores that have this requested item of merchandise in stock are identified. A mail order for the item is automatically processed by the computer ter-minal. In many cases the merchandise is delivered to the customer's home within 24 hours of the computer search.

STOCKKEEPING REQUIREMENTS FOR MERCHANDISE FLOW

Regardless of where stockkeeping occurs, four requirements are necessary for successful merchandise flow: accessibility, security, controllability, and housekeeping. When temporary stockouts occur on the sales floor, sales personnel should be able to replace display stock with minimal time and effort from either forward or reserve stocks. If merchandise is not on the selling floor, a strong temptation exists for sales personnel to inform customers that the shortage is permanent. Merchandise that has been properly received, checked, and marked must be placed near the selling area. Receiving and checking and sales personnel must cooperate during sometimes hectic selling seasons to ensure that unnecessary errors or damage are reduced.

Security and controllability go hand in hand. To avoid unacceptable inventory losses, merchandise must be protected from customer (external) theft and employee (internal) theft. (These topics are covered in Chapter 49.) Security also involves limiting access to the merchandise to authorized personnel. Careful maintenance of all records is a security and control responsibility as well.

Housekeeping prevents damage from dust, breakage, deterioration, and misplacement. When goods become dirty or damaged, retailers may have to lower prices and possibly take a loss. Proper care of stock can reduce markdowns and increase profits. A neat, well-organized stockroom and/or sales area can help in reducing misplaced merchandise. Two important benefits of good housekeeping are improved employee morale and more positive customer impressions. Mr. Jones pointed out the following effective housekeeping practices posted on the employee bulletin board:

If you open it, close it.
If you move it, put it back.
If you turn it on, turn it off.
If you make a mess, clean it up.
If it belongs to someone else, get permission to use it.
If you use it, take care of it.
If you borrow it, return it.
If you break it, repair it.
If you don't know how to operate it, leave it alone.
If you can't fix it, call someone who can.

Mr. Jones concluded the training session with these comments:

Now you should understand that marking and stockkeeping involve various types of decisions and procedures. The accuracy and timeliness of these functions are critical if the merchandise is to flow smoothly from the supplier to the consumer. Modern computerized technology can assist all of us in performing these merchandising functions.

TRADE TALK

Define each term and use it in a sentence.

Automatic reading scanner
Cost code
Display stock
Forward stock
In-time method of distribution
Nonmarking
Optical character recognition (OCR)
Preticketing
Re-marking
Reserve stock
Universal Product Code (UPC)
Universal Vendor Marking (UVM)

CAN YOU ANSWER THESE?

1. What are four points of information that a computer can tell a retailer from an analysis of product markings?

2. Explain how a cost code is organized according to letters and numbers.

3. What are the differences between the UPC and UVM price ticketing systems?

4. What is the major advantage of the OCR marking system over the regular printed or marked price tickets?

5. When do goods need re-marking?

6. What are the advantages of the in-time method of distribution of merchandise?

7. What four elements are necessary for successful merchandise flow?

Mr. Vance, the security officer at Jim Barkley's store, asked Jim this question:

> Let's assume that an average of one candy bar selling for 50 cents was stolen or "misplaced" every day for a year in our store. Also, let's assume that our store realizes an average 3 percent net profit. What would be the dollar volume of sales needed to recover this yearly loss of sales?

$0.50 × 365 days = $182.50 lost sales
$182.50 is required in net profit to replace these lost sales.
$182.50 = 0.03 × sales needed to replace the lost profits

Therefore,

total sales needed = $\dfrac{\$182.50}{0.03}$ = $6,083.33

The sales needed would be $6,083.33, which is a lot of sales to replace that one candy bar "shrinkage" per day.

Mr. Vance continued their discussion of the importance of maintaining security and controlling theft by pointing out the following:

> According to a recent national report, merchandise losses and extra security costs add an average of 2 to 3 percent to everything sold by major department stores, grocery, and drug chains. Since many retail stores earn only 3 to 5 percent net profit each year, it is evident that shrinkage could consume this profit.

The term **shrinkage** is commonly used in business to mean the difference between the amount of merchandise that **should be** in stock according to records and the amount of stock that a physical inventory (count) reveals *is* in stock. This shrinkage is usually caused by shoplifters (external theft), employees (internal theft), mistakes due to recordkeeping and processing errors, and vendor or supplier theft. (This chapter will discuss external and internal theft.)

■

DETECTING AND PREVENTING THEFT

Mr. Vance extended an invitation to Jim. "How would you like to accompany me on your day off as I spend the day on my job as security officer? I know you have a possible interest in a store security career. I'm sure you'll find it interesting and educational."

Forms of Theft

When the day arrived, Jim met Mr. Vance in his office.

> Before we visit the stockrooms and sales floor I want to ask you a question. Do you know the legal definitions of the different forms of theft, namely, shoplifting, larceny, embezzlement, and pilferage? As security officers and retailers we need to be able to describe these offenses accurately to law enforcement officials. The evidence required and the penalties involved vary for each type of offense.
>
> **Shoplifting** is a crime that occurs when a person, usually a customer, steals merchan-

dise from a store. When an employee steals merchandise from the store for which he or she works, the crime of **larceny** is committed. The theft of money by an employee is called **embezzlement**, and **pilferage** is a type of stealing done by hiding merchandise in shopping bags, purses, pockets, and other places of concealment. In any case, all these forms of theft, regardless of what is taken or who takes it, are crimes punishable by law.

Types of Thieves

How would you describe the typical shoplifter? If you described a particular age group or a predominant sex, you would be both right and wrong. Studies done by a major retail department store indicate that shoplifters represent approximately similar percentages of age groups and sexes with one exception. Shoplifters under 20 years of age account for more than 40 percent of the thieves apprehended. Offenders come from all walks of life. They may be first-time "thrill-seekers" or veteran professionals.

Professional Shoplifters Fortunately for retailers, most shoplifters are amateurs rather than professionals. Mr. Vance told Jim that professional shoplifters are people who enter a store knowing what and how they plan to steal. They usually have a customer, or "fence," for the stolen merchandise. Sometimes they work in teams. One-fourth of all shoplifting is done by professional shoplifters. Included in this group are drug addicts, who may have to steal between $100 and $1000 worth of merchandise daily to support their drug addiction.

Professional shoplifters use a variety of sophisticated techniques. As sleight-of-hand experts, they can, without being noticed, snatch items from counters and pass these items to accomplices. Shoplifters come equipped with coats and capes that have hidden pockets and slits or zippered hiding places. By reaching through the slits in their clothing, shop-

lifters can snatch articles directly from open displays without being seen. Often, the open coat itself prevents the shoplifter's actions from being seen. Professional shoplifters tend to concentrate on high-demand, easily resold consumer goods such as televisions, stereos, and other small appliances. The pro may case a store or department well in advance of the actual theft. Professionals may be hard to prosecute. They may belong to underworld organizations that are very effective in raising bail and providing defense in court.

To all appearances, professional shoplifters are average, polite customers who don't like to take chances. If they fear discovery or conditions are not favorable for shoplifting, they won't try to steal but will wait for a "sure thing." They can be deterred from theft by effective layout and alert personnel.

Kleptomaniacs A **kleptomaniac** is a person with an abnormal impulse to steal. Kleptomaniacs often have no control over this desire, and many of them are very practical

Shoplifters are on the lookout for store personnel; retailers should be equally alert.

and skillful thieves. They usually have little or no actual use for the items they steal, and in many cases they could well afford to pay for them. Medical or physical treatment is sometimes required for kleptomaniacs.

"Thrill" Shoplifters Some people steal not for real gain but because they get excitement from the very act of stealing. Sometimes they steal "for kicks" or because they have been dared to do so. Many "respectable" people fall into this category. They have not planned their theft, but a sudden chance (such as an unattended dressing room or a blind aisle in a supermarket) presents itself, and the shopper succumbs to temptation. They may enter stores in gangs to distract salespeople. When salespeople are suspicious of a group, they should request assistance from associates or managers.

Juvenile Offenders Because a higher percentage of shoplifters are apprehended in the younger age groups, retailers must be aware of certain behavior patterns. Juvenile offenders may steal on a dare or simply for kicks. Frequently they expect that store owners and courts will go easy on them because of their youth. They may enter stores in gangs in an attempt to confuse sales personnel. Shoplifting is usually the first type of theft attempted by juveniles, and it may lead to more serious crimes. Juvenile theft should be pursued and prosecuted through the proper legal channels.

Shoplifting Techniques

Shoplifters use a variety of techniques. Shoplifters are often described as (1) boosters, (2) diverters, (3) blockers, (4) sweepers, (5) walkers, and (6) wearers.

1. Boosters are shoplifters who shove merchandise into concealed areas of parcels and/or clothing. *Booster boxes* are carefully constructed boxes that appear to be authentic,

tightly wrapped packages, but which contain trap doors that allow the shoplifter to slip merchandise into the boxes quickly and easily.

2. Diverters are members of a team of shoplifters who attempt to divert the attention of the store's personnel while a partner shoplifts. Diverters use several techniques to attract store personnel's attention. They include (a) engaging the sales person in conversation, (b) acting suspicious, (c) creating an attention-grabbing disturbance by fainting, falling, or fighting, and (d) requesting merchandise that requires the salesclerk to go to the stockroom.

3. Blockers obstruct the vision of store personnel while they or a partner shoplift. In a team effort, the blocker simply stands between the salesperson and a shoplifting partner. Working as a single, the blocker might employ a topcoat draped over an arm and use it to shield the shoplifting activities of the other hand.

4. Sweepers simply brush merchandise off the counter into a shopping bag or some other type of container. Typically, sweepers reach over a counter—apparently to examine a piece of merchandise—but in the process of bringing their arm back they sweep merchandise off the counter and into the container.

5. Walkers have perfected the technique of walking naturally while carrying concealed merchandise between their legs. Shoplifters who have developed this skill are capable of carrying, in a completely natural way, both small items such as jewelry and large items such as small appliances.

6. Wearers try on merchandise, then wear it out of the store. The *open wearer* is a bold shoplifter who tries on a hat, coat, or some other piece of clothing, removes the tags, and then openly wears it while shopping and exiting the store. It is the boldness of this technique that makes it successful.

Several other shoplifting techniques are also used by both amateur and professional shoplifters. *Carriers* walk in, pick up a large piece of merchandise, remove the tags, affix a fake sales slip, and walk out. *Self-wrappers* use their own wrapping paper to wrap store merchandise before removing it from the store. And *price changers* pay for the merchandise, but only after taking a shoplifters' reduction by altering the store's price tag, switching store price tags, or removing the store's price tag and substituting realistic fakes.

PROTECTING STOCK FROM THEFT

"If shoplifters use all these different techniques, how can we as employees detect and prevent shoplifting?" asked Jim.

"Well, Jim, it is a challenging and important responsibility. Let me suggest several important precautions and practices," replied Mr. Vance.

Following Customer Service Practices

At this point during the meeting, Jim asked Mr. Vance what they should do to improve detection and prevention of shoplifting. Mr. Vance answered that employees must continually watch merchandise and people and:

1. Keep in mind that ordinary customers want attention, while shoplifters do not. When busy with one customer, salespeople should acknowledge other customers with a polite remark, such as "I'll be with you in a minute." Such attention can make a shoplifter feel uneasy, but it pleases ordinary customers. Remember that shoplifting is more likely to occur during the busy, rush periods of the day or week.

2. Always give a receipt. If store rules require that you staple a customer's receipt to a bag or box, do so without fail. This prevents shoplifters from obtaining refunds and

credits on stolen items if receipts are required for returns.

3. Observe customers carrying unwrapped packages. Offer to wrap or bag the merchandise. This will not offend a true customer. It will, however, discourage a shoplifter.

4. Do not give the impression that you distrust customers, but always be alert to their movements. If possible, never turn your back on customers, even when seeking merchandise for them.

5. Be alert to people who wear loose coats, capes, or bulky dresses. Also, watch individuals who carry large purses, packages, umbrellas, and shopping bags. Those who push baby strollers and collapsible carts also bear watching.

6. In clothing departments, beware of the "try-on" shoplifters. They try on an item for size, as it were, and then, if they feel no one has seen them, walk out wearing the garment. Salespeople should keep a check on the number of garments carried into the fitting rooms. Thieves often try to sneak in extra garments, beyond the number permitted.

7. Be especially alerted for "teams"—thieves who pretend not to know each other. One of the team will distract the clerk's attention from the partner. One team member will cause a fuss, ask unreasonable questions, create an argument, or even stage a fainting fit while a partner picks up the merchandise and escapes.

8. Know your stock. Keep your stock in good condition. By paying attention to new stock and the orderly appearance of your displays, you can more readily detect missing stock. A messy department attracts shoplifters. Thieves will assume that the salespeople will not be able to miss the item in time to catch them before they leave the store.

9. Know how to obtain authorized help promptly if you suspect someone of being a shoplifter. Most stores have a way of letting other personnel know about a suspected shoplifter. Some have security personnel you can call; others have a special number that can be used to alert the manager.

Using Surveillance Systems

Mr. Vance explained that the store security department now uses a closed-circuit television system to monitor sales areas, entrances, exits, and storage areas. He went on to say that, periodically, security guards use selected observation posts and one-way mirrors that allow them to watch activities on the sales floor without being detected. Occasionally the security guards assume the role of customers to check sales and stockkeeping security practices.

One of the newer security systems that some stores have installed to protect merchandise involves electronic detection equipment. When this equipment is used, each article is tagged or labeled with a plastic device. When the article is paid for, this device, which is often hidden, is removed or deactivated by the salesperson. If the customer attempts to leave the store with an article without paying for it, the hidden device will trigger an alarm as the customer passes through the electronic detection equipment.

However, there is a legal danger in using electronic devices. If the cashier forgets to remove the pellet device, an innocent shopper may be stopped outside and falsely detained. At the very least, this can be very embarrassing for both the customer and the store.

Improving Store Layout

"Stores such as ours," Mr. Vance explained, "take a number of preventive measures against theft. Shoplifters like crowds, open counters, and displays near exits or in corner areas. A store's layout can discourage or encourage shoplifting. For example, high fixtures and tall displays that give visual protection to shoplifters will encourage theft. To destroy such protection, set display cases in different layout arrangements.

"Keep small, high-priced items out of reach, preferably in locked cases," Mr. Vance continued. "Keep valuable and easy-to-hide items at counters where salespeople are in attendance. Or better yet, encourage customers to ask a salesperson to show such items from the display fixtures."

Observing Apprehension and Arrest Policies

A question that salespeople often ask is, "What should I do if I actually catch a shoplifter stealing merchandise?"

Most stores have specific store policies regarding the responsibilities of employees and managers with respect to apprehending shoplifters. Salespeople should check with their managers to get a clear understanding of the store's policy.

Managers should also instruct employees about what they are to do when they observe a theft by a shoplifter. This training should be given periodically, at least once every 3 months. The knowledge will help prevent legal problems in addition to catching offenders.

There are certain principles and practices that many stores follow regarding shoplifting apprehension and arrest. But the most important guideline to follow is to be certain; otherwise you risk a false-arrest lawsuit. Never accuse customers of stealing or try in any way to apprehend shoplifters. When you see what appears to be a theft, keep the suspect in sight and alert your manager immediately. The police or the store security personnel should also be notified.

Many states have passed "shoplifting laws," which, among other things, deal with apprehending shoplifters. Apprehension in many states doesn't necessarily have to begin outside the store. Sometimes, shoplifters can be apprehended if they are observed in the process of concealing merchandise. Shoplifters are generally apprehended in the store if the merchandise involved is of substantial value.

Certain store policies recommend apprehending shoplifters outside the store. For one thing, apprehension of this kind strengthens the store's case against a shoplifter. Then, too, a scene or any type of commotion that a shoplifter may cause interferes with the store operation. In most cases, store security or management personnel will handle these types of apprehensions. It's very important for employees to inform such personnel immediately, so that apprehensions can be made before the shoplifters escape. If necessary, when supervisory or designated antishoplifting personnel are not available, a good approach to use when stopping a suspect is to speak to the person and identify yourself. Then say: "I believe you have some merchandise that you've forgotten to pay for. Would you mind coming back to the store to straighten this matter out?" Never touch the suspect, because the contact could be considered roughness or rudeness.

Some organizations in large cities have control files on shoplifters who have been caught. The local retail merchants association or chamber of commerce can inform retailers about the services available in their area. These files can be checked to see whether the person caught has a record. As mentioned earlier, shoplifters often claim to be first offenders. And they are likely to remain "first offenders" if retailers allow them to leave the store without obtaining positive identification or referring names to the police and local retail merchants' associations.

■

PREVENTING EMPLOYEE THEFT

Actually, in certain businesses a more serious cause of shrinkage has been internal employee theft. It is estimated that over half of all merchandise shortages are related to employee theft. Employee dishonesty regarding merchandise, cash, and time are important security considerations.

Theft of Merchandise

Theft of merchandise may range from simply pocketing an item to larger-scale stealing con-

cealed by accounting manipulations. The most common types of theft by retail employees include:

■ Taking merchandise from the store
■ Passing out merchandise to accomplices
■ Conspiring with employees in nonselling areas—such as the warehouse, stockroom, and dock—to remove goods
■ Giving discounts to friends or other unauthorized people
■ Giving unauthorized markdowns to themselves or others
■ Writing a fake sales slip and picking up merchandise on the receiving dock
■ Smuggling goods out of the store in trash
■ Eating food without paying for it
■ Switching the price ticket of lower-priced merchandise to a higher-priced item before purchasing it
■ Taking supplies and equipment, such as a wrench or a roll of tape

Theft of Cash

Cash in a retail business is handled by salespeople, cashiers, bookkeepers, and credit department personnel. There are many opportunities for dishonest employees to steal. Dishonest employees usually steal cash by doing the following:

■ Ringing a no-sale. A *no-sale* occurs when a cashier voids the sale after the customer has left and pockets the cash given by the customer.
■ Overcharging. Overcharging the customer means charging more than the regular price or charging regular prices for sales merchandise so that the cash overages can be taken.
■ Making false entries or setting up false credit accounts. Such errors in the store's records and books serve to conceal thefts.
■ Making improper refunds. Giving refunds to accomplices or recording fictitious refund slips.
■ Taking cash. Cash can be taken from the cash register or from petty cash.
■ Falsifying payroll records. Pay rates and number of hours worked can be faked.

Theft of Time

The misuse of time by employees can be as costly to a business as the theft of merchandise or cash. Suppose that an employee's hourly rate is $5.00 and the employee is late or wastes an average of 15 minutes per day. The resulting loss would total over $325 in just one year. Table 1, below, shows the dramatic effects of employee theft of time.

Other examples of the misuse of time include (1) excessive absenteeism; (2) fraudulent claims for worker's compensation, which is payment received for job-related illnesses or accidents; and (3) punching time cards or signing out for other employees.

■

INTERNAL LOSS PREVENTION TECHNIQUES

"In our business we have an active loss prevention program," Mr. Vance explained to Jim. "From our experience we have learned that there is no such thing as a typical dishonest employee. In fact, the dishonest person is often the person least likely to be suspected."

Watch for Signals of Employee Theft

An alert manager will be aware of the following signals or characteristics of employees who may be thieves:

■ Employees who have financial problems
■ Employees who have spending habits that could not be covered by their earnings alone—for example, expensive clothes, gambling, or an expensive hobby
■ Employees who arrive early or stay late when there is no need
■ Employees who are unhappy, dislike the boss or the company, and complain about being underpaid or overworked
■ Employees who place merchandise or materials in unusual places, such as near exits, close to rest rooms, or in concealed corners
■ Employees whose cash register records frequently show errors
■ Employees who make many alterations in inventory records, void slips, refund receipts, and other documents

Build Positive Employer-Employee Relations

A sense of honesty and loyalty to the firm in all employees helps to prevent employee theft. Many managers are reluctant to tackle internal security problems because they are afraid of bad publicity. Some feel that it will create poor employee relations. But honest employees will not be outraged by efforts to curb dishonesty. An alert manager will have definite personnel policies, such as:

■ Screening new employees carefully and insisting on references that can be checked
■ Informing all prospective employees of an active internal loss prevention program

TABLE 1 / YEARLY COST OF 5 MINUTES LOST TIME PER DAY PER EMPLOYEE

Number of Employees	Hourly Wages		
	$ 4.50	$ 6.50	$ 9.00
10	1,912.50	2,762.50	3,825.00
50	9,562.50	13,812.50	19,125.00
250	47,812.50	69,187.50	95,625.00

■ Establishing a program to show that management views dishonesty as both immoral and illegal

■ Urging employees to be alert for illegal activity and to report it to management, perhaps through a "secret witness" program

Take Action in Every Case

When managers discover dishonest employees, they should deal with the situation swiftly and very visibly. Managers should take this action to discourage other employees from similar actions. Most businesses have a fixed course of action to be followed, which might include:

1. Having fixed policies about discipline for dishonesty

2. Apprehending suspects in strict accordance with the law—the police department may be of assistance

3. Terminating employment and proceeding with prosecution of the employee

Crime consists of three basic elements: a criminal, a victim, and an opportunity. For internal loss in a business, the criminal is a dishonest employee, the victim is the business, and the opportunity is as large as the owner or manager will permit. Theft and stock shortages can be significant, as these losses can account for more than 50 percent of net profit. All managers and employees have a responsibility to prevent, detect, and control these needless expenses.

Define each term and use it in a sentence.

Blockers	Pilferage
Boosters	Shoplifting
Diverters	Shrinkage
Embezzlement	Sweepers
Kleptomaniac	Walkers
Larceny	Wearers

CAN YOU ANSWER THESE?

1. What are the differences between larceny, embezzlement, and pilferage?

2. Name the major types of shoplifters. What type do you think is responsible for the largest losses? Why?

3. What recommendations were given to salespeople concerning effective customer service practices that can reduce shoplifting?

4. What recommendations were given concerning the apprehension of suspected shoplifters?

5. Describe the different ways by which employees can steal merchandise.

6. What are some of the common types of cash thefts?

7. What are some of the common ways that employees misuse time?

50 *Recording Sales Electronically*

Jim Barkley had been transferred from the receiving and checking department to the sporting goods department. On the sales floor he learned how the merchandise and service flow was completed.

ELECTRONIC POINT-OF-SALE SYSTEMS

Alison Jordan, the sporting goods supervisor, told Jim about the electronic **point of sale (POS)** systems. As she explained, the electronic POS system is an integrated computer system, which means that all of the store's cash register terminals and data input equipment are linked with a large, mainframe computer. This system allows the retailer to check customer credit electronically, compute the sale, furnish customer receipts, maintain inventory records, automatically reorder items in short supply, provide up-to-date financial statements, supply sales trends and analyses, and calculate salesperson productivity reports. The electronic POS system consists of three basic components:

1. The input devices, such as electronic cash registers, data scanning devices, and other telephone and data transmission devices

2. The central or mainframe computer

3. The output devices, such as printers, and data display terminals and monitors

Let's consider how these components function, how you as a salesperson input the data, and what information or output is available from the POS system.

THE ELECTRONIC CASH REGISTER

Electronic cash registers perform many functions automatically, such as calculating sales taxes; computing customer change; totaling and extending quantity purchases; and subtracting refunds, returns, and credits.

Retailing Applications

There are a number of different electronic cash register models, with many different retailing applications. The simple ones are like adding machines with drawers. The more complex computerized registers, often used in supermarkets, produce a sales slip that lists by name each item purchased. Department store computerized registers produce a completed sales check instead of a sales slip. Some registers will not process a charge sale unless the customer's credit check is acceptable. Electronic cash registers are beginning to be used to transfer customers' funds automatically from their checking accounts to pay their bills. The "cashless society" may be a reality in the future.

Inputting Information

There are several means for inputting or entering information or data into an electronic cash register.

Manual Entry   In most stores, salespeople manually depress keys to record the required sales information. Item amounts are entered on a 10-key cash register/numeric pad. Other data are entered on department and transaction keys conveniently surrounding the numeric pad. The data are often stored on magnetic tape for input into a computer.

Wand Reader Entry   In other systems, price tags are encoded with Universal Price Code (UPC) or Universal Vendor Marking (UVM) information (see Chapter 48). Each tag contains merchandise and pricing data that is read by manually sweeping the wand reader across the encoded tag, as shown below. The cash register terminal to which the wand is attached automatically computes the sales total, the sales tax, and the change due to the customer. Data from the tag and terminal are recorded on magnetic tape. This tape can then be processed by a computer located in the store. In other places of business, information from the tape is communicated by telephone lines to a central computer for processing.

Laser-Beam Scanning Devices   In certain stores, primarily supermarkets, a **laser beam scanner** is built into each checkout counter. The cashier slides each merchandise item's UPC price tag symbol over the scanner. The scanner sends the code data to the central computer. Almost immediately the item's price and description are flashed on a viewing screen at the checkout counter. If the code marking is damaged or smudged, the scanner will not read it. The cashier must then manually input the code number into the keyboard of the register. In any case, the computer has stored vital merchandise information.

The modern electronic cash register is equipped to accept data input manually as well as by a wand reader or built-in scanner.

How a laser beam scanner works.

Other Data Input Systems Other systems provide a batching or grouping of merchandise and sales information. When a sale is made, the salesperson simply removes the price ticket or a portion of the ticket. This tag is placed in a box or collection point. At the end of the day the ticket stubs are processed by a reader that records data onto a computer magnetic tape. After the computer analyzes the data, merchandise reports are prepared to reflect the day's transactions.

CASH REGISTER RESPONSIBILITIES

No matter what type of data input or electronic cash register system is used, a salesperson who works with the register, has certain responsibilities. These responsibilities include:

1. Processing different types of sales transactions
2. Following general rules for cash register use.
3. Making change correctly
4. Opening and closing the cash register
5. Guarding the register against theft

Processing Sales Transactions

The two most common types of sales transactions are cash and charge sales. Salespeople may also handle COD sales, layaway or will-call sales, and discount sales. Every transaction involves the use of cash, a sales check, or both.

Cash Sales When a customer pays for merchandise with money or a check, the transaction is a **cash sale**. Each store has its own procedure to use when accepting checks. In most cases, the customer is asked for one or more forms of identification. Some reliable documents are a driver's license, a company

identification card, a passport, a credit card, and a check guarantee card. A **check guarantee card** is a card issued by a bank that ensures the store against loss provided that the check doesn't exceed a specified amount.

The cash sale is almost always rung up on a terminal. The slip of paper from the terminal roll that is ejected from the machine and shows the dollars-and-cents amount of the sale is called a **register tape**. It's usually given to the customer as evidence of the purchase.

Often, a **sales slip** or sales check may be used to record a cash sale. Sometimes the store wants to collect more information than is recorded on most register tapes. Sales slips are also used to record a customer's address and delivery instructions. Another use for a sales slip in a cash sale is to provide a more detailed receipt for the customer. The receipt is either a copy of the sales slip or a small portion of it, known as the "stub." Stores that use sales slips for cash sales often use the terminal to stamp the sales slip. This way the terminal tape becomes an accurate record of all the business done each day.

Charge Sales Many stores offer some form of credit service. When customers buy on credit, they charge merchandise to their accounts and pay for it later. In a **charge-take sale**, customers take the merchandise with them at the time of the sale. In a **charge-send sale**, the merchandise is delivered to customers.

Because charge customers have the use of a store's merchandise before they pay for it, stores require some form of customer identification for every charge sale. In the most common type of charge transaction, the customer presents to the salesperson a charge plate or credit card. This is usually a plastic card with the customer's name and account number printed on it in raised letters. It's valid only when signed by the customer. The salesperson uses the card to imprint the customer's name and account number on a sales check. It's the salesperson's responsibility to compare the signature on the charge plate or credit card with the one on the sales check.

If a bank card can be accepted, the salesperson may be required to check a **credit-card bulletin** before completing the sales check. The bulletin is issued on a weekly basis and lists the account numbers of credit cards that should not be accepted for charge sales. Many stores that accept bank or business credit cards have computer telephone hookups to customer credit records. By calling this record source, the salesperson can obtain authorization to accept or decline a credit sale.

There is usually a limit to the amount a customer can charge without authorization from the store's credit department or the credit card company that issues the card. This is called the **floor limit**. For purchases below the floor limit, the salesperson generally has the authority to approve a credit sale.

Layaway or Will-Call Sales If a store withdraws an item from stock and holds it in storage for a customer, it is a **layaway** or **will-call sale**. In return for this service, the customer must leave a deposit and must pay the total price plus tax within a certain amount of time. When the payments are completed, the customer receives the merchandise. If the customer does not complete the payments within the time allowed, the merchandise is returned to stock.

Discount Sales A **discount sale** is a reduction in price to special classes of customers. The most common discount sale is the employee discount. It's usually a reduction in price between 10 and 25 percent. When a discount sale is made, the sales check is made out in the usual way. Then the discount is subtracted from the recorded price before the sales tax is added. Employees and any other customers who qualify for a discount must properly identify themselves in order to receive it.

COD Sales If a customer pays for merchandise when it is delivered, it is called a **COD (cash-on-delivery)** sale. COD service is usually used for goods ordered by tele-

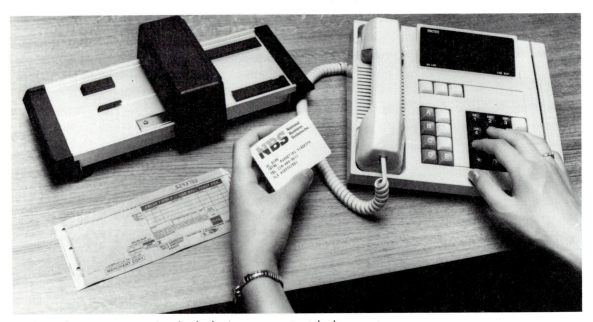

Credit card transactions can be checked using a computer-telephone system.

Unit 16   Processing the Product or Service

phone or mail. Some customers may also use COD service when they are actually shopping in a store but would rather pay for a purchase at the time it is delivered. It is the salesperson's responsibility to establish the fact that someone will be there to accept the merchandise when it is delivered. Some stores require a deposit on COD sales to ensure that the customer will accept the goods when they are delivered. In addition, there may be a delivery charge for COD items.

General Rules for Cash Register Use

The following procedures are applicable to any register and have stood the test of time.

Keep Your Cash Drawer Orderly   Arrange your cash drawer, which is also called a **till**, so that all the bills are face up and in the same direction. One common way to arrange bills is to place the $20 bills in the first compartment on the left. Then place the $10 bills in the compartment to the right of the $20 bills. The $5 bills, and then the $2 and $1 bills, are placed to the right of the $10 bills. Because the $2 and $1 bills share the compartment on the far right, place the $2 bills, if you must handle them, underneath the $1 bills. It's always a good idea to crumple new bills and straighten them out so that you won't accidentally give out two bills instead of one. The coins should be arranged in the cash drawer in a similar manner, with silver dollars and half-dollars in the first compartment on the left. Then put the quarters in the next compartment, followed by the dimes, nickels, and pennies.

Always Have Sufficient Change   Make sure early in the day, when you are less likely to be busy, that you have enough coins and bills in your cash drawer to make change. This will help you avoid unnecessary delays that annoy customers. If you need change, be sure to follow the store procedure for obtaining additional change.

Record Sales Carefully and Accurately
Take care to record accurately all the information that your store needs to collect, not just the dollar amount of the sale. You may be asked to record such things as a salesperson number, department number, product codes, prices, tax, and an amount tendered. The **amount tendered** is the amount received from the customer.

If you should happen to make a mistake in recording a sale be sure to correct it immediately. Follow your store's procedure for recording the correction.

Do Not Group Sales   Most stores require that each sale be recorded separately. If you ring sales of different customers together, store records become inaccurate. They show that one customer was served instead of several. The grouping of sales may also reflect unfavorably on your honesty.

Be Very Careful in Handling Receipts
The receipt, or sales slip, is very important because it is an official record of the sale. It provides the customer with proof of the purchase in case the merchandise has to be returned or exchanged, and it protects the store against accepting returned goods that were purchased elsewhere. It also gives charge customers accurate records of what they purchased from your firm when they are asked to pay their bills.

Follow the required procedure for handling the receipt. Some stores enclose it with the merchandise, others attach it to packages, and still others hand it to the customer. If a customer will not wait for a receipt, ring up the sale immediately and comply with store policy regarding the receipt.

Build Customer Goodwill   Make a habit of looking at the customers as you thank them. Smile and call them by name if you've seen the name on the credit card. Showing customers that you're pleased to serve them and that you hope they will return soon builds goodwill.

Making Change

Cash register terminals in most retail stores have a change-computation feature. After you ring up the total of the sale, you register the amount of money received from the customer. The machine computes the change due the customer. This change is registered in the indication window. Both you and the customer know exactly how much change is due the customer. Using $7.63 as an example of a total sale and $10 as the tendered amount (for payment), you would handle the sale in the following way on a change-computation register:

1. Subtotal the order after all items and taxes have been registered.

2. Register the denomination of the bill or check tendered, which is $10 in this example, on the amount keyboard. Press the amount-tendered key.

3. Complete the register operation by opening the cash drawer with the appropriate key or bar. This key is called the change key or the balance-due key.

4. The amount of change to be given, $2.37, will appear in the indication window at the top of the register. Build your change to $2.37 by taking out the bills first and then the necessary coins. You would take out two one-dollar bills, one quarter, one dime, and two pennies.

5. Announce to your customer, "Your change is $2.37." Proceed to count the amount into the customer's hand.

6. Should the exact amount of $7.63 be given you in payment of the bill, register $7.63 as the amount tendered. The indication window will show that no change is due the customer.

Opening and Closing Activities

At the start of each day, the employee in charge of opening the register must get the change fund from the store's accounting office. He or she must then count the money to be sure that it's the correct amount. If it's over or short, this fact should be reported to the person in charge. The money must then be arranged in an orderly way in the cash drawer.

At the end of each day, each salesperson and each cashier is expected to account for the day's sales and money. They prepare a summary of the sales handled during that day and submit it to the proper store department. A record or summary of sales made during the day is known as the **tally**. Salespeople who use books of sales checks keep a daily tally of all sales. Each time a sales check is written, the sales information is entered on a tally sheet. Then, at the end of each day, the salesperson adds up the tally sheet and gives it to the department manager together with the carbon copies of the sales checks.

In many stores the cash registers keep an automatic tally of the sales punched into them. An employee in charge of a register writes down this amount, counts the money in the till, and fills in whatever report forms the store requires. The employee also removes the machine's tape and sends it to the accounting office. In any case, all cash is bagged and taken to the cashier's office or picked up by the cashier's staff. Often the change fund for the next day is bagged separately from the day's receipts. That way the change fund is ready for the next day's business.

Guarding the Register Against Theft

If possible, everyone in a store should be trained to prevent theft of money and merchandise. Theft hurts the retailer, the employees, and the customers. Short-change artists and counterfeiters, for example, are constantly trying to cheat retail business firms.

Cash registers play a vital part in recording sales. As an employee who handles a cash register, you should know how to recognize and deal with potential thieves. Some of the tips that stores give their cashiers follow.

Never Leave Your Cash Drawer Open

Whenever you leave the register, be sure that the drawer is closed and latched. If you have a key to lock the register, be sure to use it. An open drawer invites a dishonest person to steal. It's also very easy for a thief to ring the register and steal the contents of the cash drawer.

Watch for Customers Who Try to Confuse You

Short-change artists may try various tactics to confuse you when you're making change. They hope that you'll make mistakes in their favor. Such a person may, for example, interrupt while you're counting change and ask that a larger bill be changed. Another short-change artist may use the ploy of remembering some small item to add to his or her purchase or wanting to exchange one purchase for another.

Ignore Interruptions

The best way to protect yourself against short-change operators when you're handling cash is to ignore all interruptions. Always finish counting change first, no matter what question is asked of you. If a customer asks to add another item to the sale or to make an exchange, treat it as a new transaction. Follow the store's procedure at all times, and don't try other methods of cashiering that customers may suggest.

Beware of the Marked Bill

You may have difficulty with short-change artists who work in pairs. Often, they try the marked-bill trick. One member of the team may buy an item and pay for it with a $5 bill that is marked with an ink blot or some other distinguishing mark. Later the other team member may buy some article for a small amount and pay for it with a $1 bill. After you have put the $1 bill in the register, the second customer may try to convince you that he or she had presented a $5 bill. The customer can identify it as having a certain mark. When you look in the till and find the $5 bill with that mark, you may believe you have made a mistake. So make a habit of examining both sides of every bill you handle. If there is any unusual mark or tear, call the customer's attention to it. This indicates to the customer that you are well trained and that the short-change attempt had better be dropped because it will probably be unsuccessful.

Be Alert for Counterfeit Money

Counterfeiting is on the rise, so you should be prepared to receive and reject counterfeit money. In order to guard against accepting counterfeit money, you should (1) become more familiar with what genuine money really looks like, and (2) learn how to recognize money that is counterfeit.

There are several places to look on paper money for signs of counterfeiting. One of the more obvious signs of counterfeiting is the portrait with the oval background. The portrait should be lifelike and stand out sharply from the background. The lines in the pattern of the oval background should be sharp and unbroken. They should look like a fine screen. If the portrait is dull, blurry, or lifeless and blends in with the background, the bill may be counterfeit. This is also true if the lines in the background of the oval are broken. A second obvious thing to look at on a bill is the paper it's printed on. The paper used for genuine currency has tiny red and blue silk fibers mixed in with the paper.

Stores usually advise their employees specifically on how to spot counterfeit money. Pay attention to what you're told to look for. Also, make sure that you know the procedures for dealing with someone who's passing counterfeit money, whether intentionally or unintentionally.

Never Accuse a Suspect Finally, no matter how sure you are that someone is trying to commit a theft, never accuse that person of the attempt. Instead, notify a supervisor or a member of the store's security force at once. These people are trained to know what to do and should be able to handle the situation discreetly.

■

SALES CHECKS

Certain retailers use sales checks in addition to cash registers to record sales. A sales check has these two main purposes. (1) It gives the customer a receipt that's useful in case the merchandise has to be returned. (2) It gives the retailer information that's vital to the operation of the store.

The information recorded on the sales checks is used by a number of departments. Buyers use the information to help them decide how much and what kind of merchandise to order. The credit department uses the information to bill charge customers. The people in charge of delivery use the infor-

mation to determine what merchandise to deliver to whom. The accounting department uses the information to update records, prepare tax reports, and prepare reports for management's use. Inventory records may be updated from the information recorded on sales slips. If these departments are to understand and use the information on sales checks, all salespeople must be familiar with the forms and procedures for preparing them.

Sales Check Procedures

The procedure that a store uses to complete sales checks depends on the type of sales check that it has and on store policy. Every time a salesperson writes up a sales check, all the appropriate blanks for that type of sale should be filled in. Details should never be left to be filled in. Most salespeople develop a set order in which they put down the information on a sales check. By following this order faithfully, they avoid leaving out any of the information needed.

Each sales check is numbered and should be used in the proper order. If a salesperson makes a mistake on a sales check, the check

QUAN	CLASS	MERCHANDISE 6388588	AMOUNT	
1	12	Turtleneck Sweater - blue	47	95
1	23	Pleated Skirt - tweed	115	95

BROWNING'S DEPT. STORE
1845 Center Avenue
Des Moines, Iowa 50314
6388588

ACCOUNT NUMBER 0 5 2 — 3 7 — 1 4 L

CHG. TO M Mrs. Catherine Lacey

STREET 1729 Grand Ave.

CITY Des Moines, STATE IA 50300

SEND TO M

CUSTOMER SIGNATURE:	I agree to pay the total amount shown on this sales slip in accordance with my credit agreement with you.		SUB TOTAL	163	90
X Mrs. Catherine Lacey			TAX	13	52
GIFT WRAP ☐	GIFT BOX ONLY ☐		SHIP CHGS.		
CARD ENC. ☐	☐				

DATE	DEPT.	SOLD BY	HOW SOLD			TOTAL	
9/4	801	744	AMOUNT REC.	OTHER	CHG. ✓	177	42

STREET APT. NO.

CITY STATE

INSTRUCTIONS

DATE	DEPT.	SOLD BY	HOW SOLD			AUTH.
9/4	801	744	CASH	OTHER	CHG. ✓	OK

Why is the sales check important to both the retailer and the customer?

must be voided or nullified by an authorized person. Then, it is turned in at the end of the day with the store's copies of the sales checks. Sales checks must never be destroyed unless this is specifically authorized.

Sales Check Records

There are a variety of sales check records used by different retailers. The most common records are sales books and sales registers.

Sales Books Some stores use sales books that contain three copies of each sales check. The original is kept by the store for its records and the duplicate is the customer's copy: it goes with the merchandise. The triplicate copy is a tissue-paper copy that remains in the sales book.

Sales Registers Other stores and a large number of service establishments use sales registers instead of sales books. The salesperson or order clerk fills out the sales check, which is in the register. When the check is completed, the handle on the side of the register is turned. The complete sales check then rolls out, a carbon copy is retained in the register, and a new blank sales check rolls into place for the next sale. Whenever possible, increasing numbers of businesses, large and small, are converting the sales check records to a computerized information storage and retrieval system.

Alison Jordan, Jim's supervisor, concluded their discussion by saying:

Jim, we realize that because you are a beginning salesperson, there are many sales transactions and cash register terminal procedures you have to master. I suggest that you study the cash register training materials carefully. Observe the experienced sales associates as they process customer transactions. Above all, if you are uncertain about any aspect of cash register operations, be sure to ask. You can appreciate the many effects of cash register errors on the entire recordkeeping system. We should, however, view this computerized system as an electronic tool that can speed up and improve the accuracy of the sales transaction process. We can thereby offer our customers greater personal attention and service.

TRADE TALK

Define each term and use it in a sentence.

Amount tendered	Floor limit
Cash sale	Layaway or will-call
Charge-send sale	sale
Charge-take sale	Laser-beam scanner
Check guarantee	Point-of-sale (POS)
card	system
COD (cash-on-delivery) sale	Register tape
	Sales slip
Credit-card bulletin	Tally
Discount sale	Till

CAN YOU ANSWER THESE?

1. What are different devices used to input information or data into an electronic cash register terminal?

2. Name the types of sales transactions and describe the differences among them.

3. Describe some special features of computerized registers and show how each feature can save time for the salesperson.

4. What are some general rules to follow when handling a cash register?

5. Describe the typical opening and closing activities for the salesperson who deals with the cash register.

6. What are some tips for protecting money against theft?

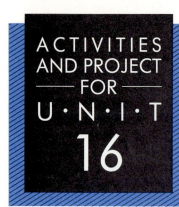

RETAIL MARKETING CASES

1. You are the owner of a small sewing and yard goods store. Your store carries a very extensive line of notions, including buttons, zippers, and binding. Much of the merchandise is sent to you in large cartons, and you have not been counting each piece of merchandise as it is received from the vendor. Instead, you have only been checking total cartons received against the invoice. Because your store shortages have increased, you have decided to be much more complete with your receiving process. To begin with, you are going to check the calculations on each invoice for accuracy yourself.

   1. For the invoice on page 443, calculate and check the total amount for each item purchased, calculate the gross amount of the invoice, determine the total discount, and figure the net amount of the invoice.

   2. What action would you take if your checking indicated that some figures calculated by an employee were different from those on the invoice?

   3. How could you ensure that your receiving process resulted in correct counts?

2. You have just been hired as a salesperson in a record store in a shopping mall. On the first Saturday afternoon, your store is very busy, as a special record promotion is being offered. While assisting a customer, you observe two customers studying a record album. Suddenly, one of the customers slips the album under a trench coat and rapidly walks out the door. You try to hurry through the crowd of shoppers to catch the "customer." By the time you reach the door, the individual has disappeared.

You report the theft to two of the other more experienced salespeople. Their response shocks you about as much as the theft.

"Oh, that happens all the time. We have to expect some thefts. The management anticipates it; they just add a percentage for stock shortages and theft to the markup. The cost is just passed on to the customers. The last time a shoplifter was prosecuted, the judge threw the case out of court because of lack of evidence. Besides, we shouldn't get involved in all the hassle for a mere $9.95 album."

   1. What do you consider to be the major attitude problems in this store?

   2. What are the important facts to be considered?

   3. What are possible solutions to the problem that managers and employees can work together on?

   4. How could the results of each solution be evaluated?

INVOICE NO.	4546

The New England Fabric Mart
Concord, New Hampshire 03301

SOLD TO: Bond's Yardage House
152 State Street
Yorktown, Indiana 47396

DATE: October 10, 19--
YOUR ORDER NO.: 0612
TERMS: 2/10, n/30
VIA: Midman Trucking Company

QUANTITY	DESCRIPTION	UNIT PRICE	AMOUNT	
1 gross	ABC assorted zippers	$0.29 each	$ 34	76
12 cards	3/4" white buttons, style 24	1.10 each	13	20
6 dozen	Assorted colored carpet thread	2.15 each	144	90
6	S419 beach bags, assorted striped	4.50 each	27	00
		Gross amount	$ 95	86
		Less 2% discount	1	92
		Net amount due	$ 93	94

3. After you finish giving change from a $10 bill for a $7.39 purchase, the customer insists that she gave you a $20 bill. When you tell her that you believe she is mistaken, she says that she is sure she gave you a $20 bill. She also says that she had written a phone number on it. She then asks you to look at the top $20 bill in your register till. When you look at the bill, sure enough there is a phone number written on it. You are still sure, however, that the customer gave you a $10 bill.

1. What would you say to the customer at this point?
2. What other options do you have?
3. How could this problem have been prevented?

PROBLEMS

1. Rule a form similar to the following. In the left column, list five items of merchandise with which you are familiar, either as a consumer or a seller. Assume that you are responsible for inspecting incoming goods. In the right column, record the features of this item that you would inspect. Discuss your completed list with your employer or a retailer to identify additional features to inspect.

Item	Inspection Features
Example: Transistor radio	Damage to case, working condition, sound

Amount of the Sale	Amount Tendered	Change Due	Bills and Coins Returned						
			$5	$1	$0.50	$0.25	$0.10	$0.05	$0.01
$36.75	$40.								
0.69	1.								
3.79	5.								
8.46	10.								
43.25	50.								
16.83	20.								

2. Indicate how you would return change to a customer using a register that computes the change. Remember to use the fewest number of coins and bills possible. Rule a form similar to the one at the top of this page to indicate the bills and coins you would return.

3. Your department head has requested that you use your creativity in designing a distinctive price ticket for a new line of merchandise. You may select a merchandise line that you are familiar with for this assignment. Your department head requests that the ticket design reflect the basic identity of your merchandise line. In addition, the layout of the price ticket should provide for manufacturer identification, merchandise classification, department, cost code, size, style, color, and selling price.

PROJECT: PLANNING A RECEIVING AND MARKING DEPARTMENT

YOUR PROJECT GOAL

Given a retail business of your choice, identify what activities must be done to properly receive, check, mark, and distribute merchandise to the selling floor.

PROCEDURE

1. Design a physical layout for the receiving and marking department for the above functions. Include within your layout the receiving dock, receiving room, checking area, marking area, and stockroom or warehouse storage area. Keep in mind the logical flow of merchandise from the receiving dock to the storage or selling area.

2. Also include within your layout needed equipment and fixtures, such as overhead distribution tracks, conveyor belts, storage bins or racks, tables, marking machines, or other related equipment.

3. Draw the plan on a large sheet of paper using an appropriate scale.

4. Study the receiving and marking department of your firm or other businesses to obtain ideas for your project. Contact your instructor for additional references, if necessary, to complete the layout plan.

EVALUATION

You will be evaluated on the completeness and appropriateness of your layout plan for the kind of store and merchandise line you selected.

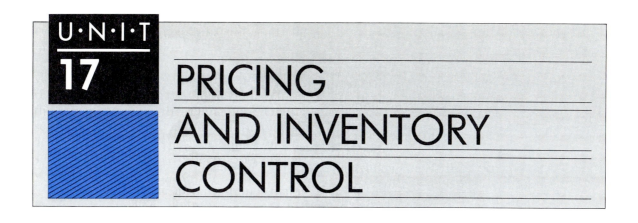

U·N·I·T 17
PRICING AND INVENTORY CONTROL

C·H·A·P·T·E·R 51 *Understanding Pricing Policies*

Kelly Redman was hired as a merchandising buyer trainee in the sportswear department of a retail clothing store. She had previously been employed as a part-time salesperson in the accessories department of another store.

She eagerly anticipated her new responsibilities as a merchandise buyer. She realized that she had a lot to learn regarding "behind-the-scenes" merchandise buying decisions.

The first assignment that Mrs. Genelli, the sportswear department head, gave Kelly was to conduct a comparison study regarding merchandise and prices offered by the store's major competitors. After studying the competitor's advertisements and "shopping" several of their stores, Kelly discovered that even though in several cases the merchandise was exactly the same, the prices varied considerably. She told Mrs. Genelli, "I wonder what factors influenced our competitors to charge different prices. You would think that the customers would naturally shop where the prices are lower."

■

THE ROLE OF PRICING DECISIONS

Mrs. Genelli responded to Kelly's comments by saying:

> One of the most important decisions a retailer makes is the determination of the right prices of the goods and services. The *right price* is one that consumers are willing and able to pay and retailers are willing to accept in exchange for merchandise and services. The right price allows the retailer to make a fair profit. The customer, in turn, receives value satisfaction from the sale. The right price can attract customers to the store. It can serve as an incentive to make a decision to buy. It can encourage people to return to the store as customers.

Let's consider with Kelly and Mrs. Genelli those factors that influence the pricing decisions and the various pricing policies available to retail businesses.

■

FACTORS THAT INFLUENCE PRICING DECISIONS

Every business faces the problem of how high or low to set prices. When stores set the price for a particular product or service, they usually consider these factors: (1) customer reaction, (2) competition, (3) supply and demand, (4) possible future markdowns, and (5) laws regarding pricing. Certain goods such as staple or basic items are often not influenced as much by these factors. Prices of trendy fashion merchandise, however, are often greatly affected by these factors.

Customer Reaction

How will customers react to prices that are higher than those of the competition? Will they recognize the advantages of a product and pay a premium price? Can they be persuaded by salespeople that the product is worth a little more? What if the product is no better than that offered by competition? Or what if there are no significant advantages either in the merchandise or in the service, delivery, or credit terms offered? In this case, how large a price discount will be necessary to attract customers away from competition? How much will it cost to tell the market that this comparable product is offered for a lower price? If prices are raised or lowered, retailers often have to figure on extra promotion costs, either to overcome customer reluctance to pay a higher price or to inform the customer of possible savings.

Goods with fashion appeal, unusual items, and products that have been improved are all sought by the customer, and a retailer can take these desirability features into consideration when setting prices. Fashion-conscious customers are anxious to buy the latest styles and are willing to pay the price for them.

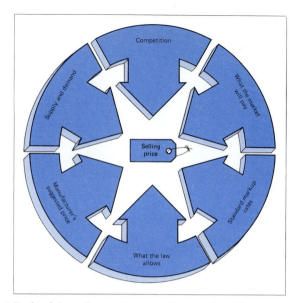

Each of these factors has an effect on the selling price of goods and services.

This is particularly true in the clothing field, where fashions change often and where high-fashion items are desired by people who wish to be distinctive. When a fashion is new and different, higher prices can be charged for it. However, when that fashion reaches the peak of its life cycle, the point at which it is mass produced for mass distribution, it will have lost its distinctiveness and the price must be reduced.

A store's target market, its image, decor, merchandise purchases, advertising, and selling objectives determine, and must be consistent with, its pricing objectives. For example, if the store has an image of selling medium- to high-quality merchandise at a high price, and the clientele expects and purchases this quality, it would be disastrous to attempt to sell low-quality, inferior merchandise at medium or low prices. The customers would reject the merchandise, causing a shift in the image of the store. The reverse is also true. Should the store "trade up" to a point at which customers object because they cannot afford the new prices, the store's image will change, causing a downturn in sales.

Competition

Just as Kelly was given the assignment of comparing competitive prices, so, too, must retailers keep themselves informed of competitors' prices. Setting prices according to competitive levels is popular among some retailers because it can be simpler to administer. A list of trade-area competitors and their merchandise prices is basically all such retailers do to make pricing decisions. The basic decisions to be made are whether to price below, at, or above competitors' price levels. Factors involved in making these decisions are discussed in the section of this chapter on pricing policies.

Supply and Demand

When the demand for products and services is greater than the supply, retailers can charge higher prices. But when the supply exceeds the demand, prices should be set low. For example, when seasonal fruits and vegetables first reach the market in the spring, supply is low and people will pay higher prices. But as the year advances and more new produce appears on the market, the price has to be lowered. Sometimes retailers experiment with new products by offering them at introductory discounts. Then, if the demand justifies reordering additional merchandise, they will often set the price at the regular levels.

Possible Future Markdowns

Retailers seldom expect to sell an entire stock of a product at full price. Some items spoil, get damaged, become soiled, or go out of fashion; they must either be discarded or sold at a reduced price. Other items with a fashion appeal or a seasonal appeal have a limited period of popularity. Stock still in the store at the end of that demand period needs to be marked down if it's to be sold. Perishable goods—such as fresh meat, vegetables, and bakery products—are subject to both aging and spoilage. Products that are beyond their peak of freshness can sometimes be sold at a reduced price, but spoiled goods have to be discarded.

Retailers may offer three types of price reductions. Using the terminology suggested by the National Retail Merchants Association, these are as follows:

1. A **sale** is an offer of goods at a lower price than the retailer normally charges. Sales may run for a limited time, after which the items return to their higher prices. If the sale is not limited in time, the item should be marked to show that the price was "formerly" or "originally" charged. The use of these terms tells the customer that the items will not be returned to the higher price.

2. A **clearance** is a sale that a retailer uses to remove leftover items from the selling

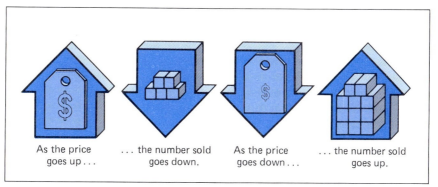

As the price goes up... / ... the number sold goes down. / As the price goes down... / ... the number sold goes up.

The best selling price is *not* that which produces the highest gross profit per sale or results in the largest number of units sold. The *best* selling price is that which makes the biggest *total* contribution to gross profit from *total* sales.

floor. Clearance items are not returned to their former prices. Customer purchases are usually final, and merchandise is not returnable.

3. A **special purchase** refers to merchandise that the retailer was able to acquire at a low cost. Savings are passed on to customers by pricing the goods at less than the customers would expect to pay.

Laws Regarding Pricing

There are federal, state, and local laws that apply to pricing. The federal laws are concerned mainly with preventing deceptive pricing and pricing that would tend to kill competition within a given market. State laws may specify the prices below which a retailer may not sell a product. Local laws, when they exist, are likely to reinforce or strengthen the state or federal laws. (See the discussion of unfair trade practices in Chapter 15.)

■

DETERMINING PRICING POLICIES

After retailers have considered the various factors that might affect prices, their next step is to determine specific types of pricing policies.

Fixed or Variable Pricing

In the majority of stores, the one-price policy is followed. Under the **one-price policy**, goods are sold at any given time to all customers at one price, which is marked on the goods. All customers are treated alike. They do not have a choice of the price they will pay, but they can decide whether or not they want the item at that price. The one-price policy has several advantages. It builds customer confidence in the store, saves time, and can be used in self-service stores.

Under the **variable-price policy**, the price paid by a customer at a given time for a certain item is determined by a bargaining process between the customer and the salesperson. This means that customers may pay lower or higher prices for the same merchandise, depending on how skillful they are at bargaining. Variable pricing is used in some smaller, single-line stores and in sales situations where a trade-in allowance is involved, as with automobiles.

The variable-price policy gives the seller an opportunity to be flexible in dealings with customers. By lowering the price, the seller may attract new customers or increase the volume of sales. In most retail stores, however, variable pricing would disrupt the orderly sales transactions that contribute to the smooth, profitable operation of the store.

Competitive Pricing

The retailer must use judgment and experience when competitive prices are used as reference points for pricing decisions. The basic policy decision is whether to price below, at, or above competitors' price levels.

Pricing Below Competition Price Levels To price below competition, retailers must not only secure merchandise at a lower cost, they must also keep operating expenses as low as possible. Lower-price retailers usually stock and sell "presold" or "self-sold" merchandise, thereby reducing advertising and personal selling expenses. Typically, these retailers sell name brands at the lowest prices to build traffic and to promote a low-price image. For many standard items, low-price retailers stock private brands that consumers cannot easily compare with other retailers' private brands and on which they can receive high margins at the lower prices. Additionally, these retailers keep their service offerings at the minimum levels necessary to sell the merchandise. Any nonessential services they offer carry a separate, additional charge.

Pricing below competition is not without its risks. This aggressive price-setting strategy often leads to pricing wars that put considerable strain on the profitability of all competing retailers within the trading area. Also, retailers who rely primarily on price competition as their principal merchandising strategy find that if that strategy fails, they cannot very easily reposition themselves against higher-priced retailers who have a variety of competitive weapons (such as large assortment, various services, and selective promotion strategies).

Pricing at Competition Price Levels

The second method of competitive price setting is to sell a merchandise item at the "going" or traditional price. Pricing at competition levels implies that the retailer has, in general, decided to deemphasize the price factor as a major merchandising tool. Instead, the retailer has decided to compete on a location, product, service, and promotion basis. Competitive price parity does not necessarily imply that the retailer matches every price exactly. Usually this policy involves setting prices that are within an acceptable range of the competitive standard.

Although competitive pricing is a relatively safe and simple method of establishing retail selling prices, retailers must watch the competitive situation to avoid missing a pricing opportunity. If a competitor makes a small price reduction in key merchandise that another retailer is offering, and that retailer does not make an equivalent price reduction, the second retailer stands to lose considerable sales volume and profit. As a result, price equality among retailers is a common practice that does not "rock the boat."

Pricing Above Competition Price Levels

When retailers set prices above those of competitors, then they must include several of the following consumer benefits: (1) many free services, (2) higher-quality merchandise, (3) exclusive merchandise, (4) personalized sales attention, (5) plusher shop-

ping atmosphere, (6) fully staffed stores, (7) a prestige image, (8) superconvenient locations, and (9) longer store hours. In other words, retailers of higher-priced merchandise must provide consumers with a total product having features that give consumers the psychological benefits they expect from buying, using, and possessing the product. Many exclusive specialty shops and some department stores engage in price-setting strategies that establish prices above those of less prestigious competitors.

Price Lining

Many stores have definite price lines that are used in pricing merchandise. **Price lining** means setting up a limited number of prices at which merchandise will be offered for sale. For example, a store may sell $79, $99, and $149 suits. The buyer looks for merchandise that meets the standards of quality for each of these three price lines, and cost prices are sought that allow for a sufficient markup.

One of the most apparent advantages of price lining is that it avoids confusing customers with a number of prices; therefore it makes buying easier. Since stores with definite price lines sell goods at the prices that they have found to be most popular with their customers, the stock moves quickly.

On the other hand, price lining may make it difficult for a store to adjust its prices to meet the prices of the competition. During periods of inflation and deflation, retailers may face the alternatives of changing either the prices of the lines carried or the quality of the merchandise within each line.

Odd-Cent Pricing

Some retailers believe that prices have a psychological effect on customers and that **odd-cent pricing** will encourage people to buy. This pricing is based on the belief that customers feel, for example, that $2.95 is much lower than $3 because they pay more attention to the dollar figure than to the cents figure. These retailers also believe that odd prices such as 49 cents or 97 cents will bring in a greater volume of sales than prices of 50 cents or $1. Bargain-oriented stores like odd-cent pricing, but prestige stores and stores that sell higher-priced merchandise seldom use it except during sales events.

Leader Pricing

To attract consumers into their stores, some retailers often price certain items (called "leaders") just above their delivered cost price. Usually the price covers part, but not all, of the expense of handling the item. A **loss leader** is an article that is actually sold for less than its cost to the store, including the cost of delivery.

Retailers use leaders on the theory that once customers are in the store, they will purchase other items. Some believe that leaders create the impression that all the store's prices are low. Food stores often select items from different departments in the store and use them as leaders: for example, coffee, canned fruit juices, and soaps. Drug stores feature photographic film, over-the-counter drugs, toiletries, and candy.

Sometimes loss leaders are used by a store that actually carries only a very limited stock of the articles advertised at the low price; this practice has been criticized as a bait-and-switch tactic by both customers and manufacturers. Customers object when the small supply runs out and the store tries to sell substitute merchandise at a higher price. National brands are used as leaders because their quality and retail prices are well known. So manufacturers object to the use of their products as "bait" to attract customers.

■

EVALUATING PRICING GOALS

A retailer's pricing goals can be evaluated by determining whether the following were

achieved: (1) a certain percentage of return on investment, (2) a desired gross profit on merchandise investments, (3) a projected share of the market, or all three.

Achieving Return on Investment

The dollar amount of the net profit realized for each dollar invested in a business is a company's return on investment. Return on investment is probably the most common goal and yardstick used by retailers. This goal is a much more accurate measure of the effectiveness of any business operation than simple net profit. Two companies can earn identical net profits, but one may have a much better return on investment than the other. For instance, one firm may have $100,000 worth of inventory, equipment, floor space, promotion, and sales force invested in a product line that produces a $15,000 net profit. Another firm may be able to produce exactly the same net profit for an investment of only $85,000. The second firm achieves a greater dollar return on investment because its management controls the relationship of prices, expenses, and merchandise investments more effectively.

Acquiring a Desired Gross Profit on Merchandise Investment

Gross profit on merchandise investment is the gross profit made on every dollar invested in average inventory of a merchandise item or line. It provides retailers with a way of comparing the profitability of various merchandise items. And this enables them to make decisions about whether to increase or decrease the inventory carried or the prices charged.

Gross profit on investment is calculated by dividing the gross profit realized from an item by the dollar amount invested in the average inventory of that item:

$$\text{Gross profit on merchandise investment} = \frac{\text{Gross profit on item}}{\text{Investment in average inventory of item}}$$

Investment in average inventory of item is determined by multiplying the number of units of average inventory by the cost of a unit. **Average inventory of item** is the midpoint between the highest inventory, which occurs right after a new shipment is received, and the lowest inventory, which usually exists just before a new shipment arrives.

Assume that for 3 months the gross profit (profit before expenses are deducted) for portable television sets was $1500. Also assume that the average inventory investment was $4500. The average inventory is calculated by adding the high and low values of inventory investment during this period and dividing by 2. In this case,

$$\frac{\$6000 + \$3000}{2} = \frac{\$9000}{2} = \$4500$$

The gross profit on investment can then be calculated as follows:

$$\text{Gross profit on investment} = \frac{\$1500 \text{ gross profit}}{\$4500 \text{ average inventory of item}}$$

This means that a gross profit of 33 cents is made on every dollar invested in average inventory of this line of television sets. Retailers can compare the gross profit on investment of individual items, lines of merchandise, or the total store sales with past sales periods or with other stores. This comparison enables retailers to evaluate the profit performance, inventory investments, and price levels of certain merchandise. Merchandise lines that have a lower gross profit on investment than other lines may be reduced in quantity or discontinued.

Realizing a Share of the Market

An important pricing objective of retailers is to either get a certain projected share of the market or to maintain the share of the market they currently hold. A **share of the market** is a part of the total sales available for a

product or service in a certain sales area, territory, or region. Retailers project or plan to realize a certain share of the total market for a given sales period. This projection is usually expressed as a percentage (10 percent, 20 percent, for example) of the total sales considered to be available in a city, area, or region.

A retailer with a new product, a new department, or a new store may price goods at lower levels for a short time to attract customers. While this policy will not result in maximum profit, it may enable a new retailer to build up a share of the market that will eventually lead to a profitable operation.

In somewhat the same way, a retailer may have to set lower prices to keep a share of the market if competitors are offering strong price competition. This, however, is the way price wars begin, and most retailers try to avoid such situations. In a price war, all the retailers involved suffer and none wins.

All retailers must be aware of the ever-changing influences affecting price decisions. There are many ways to evaluate whether certain marketing goals have been achieved by various pricing policies. Obtaining a sufficient profit on merchandise investment and an adequate share of the market are necessary for the continued success of new businesses as well as for the survival of established retail firms.

TRADE TALK

Define each term and use it in a sentence.

Average inventory of item	Price lining
	Sale
Clearance	Share of the market
Gross profit on merchandise investment	Special purchase
Loss leader	Variable-price policy
Odd-cent pricing	
One-price policy	

1. Describe three characteristics of the "right price."
2. What are the factors that affect pricing decisions?

3. What are the advantages and disadvantages of a variable-price policy?
4. What are the advantages of price lining, odd-cent pricing, and leader pricing?
5. How can the gross profit on investment be used by a retailer to analyze merchandise operations?

C·H·A·P·T·E·R 52 *Calculating Retail Prices*

Kelly Redman's training session involved a meeting with Mr. Janko, the merchandise manager of the store softlines division. One of Mr. Janko's responsibilities is to review and approve the pricing decisions made by the various department supervisors. He began his meeting with Kelly by asking her this question: "Could you tell me the difference between markup and profit in your department? Also, do you understand the different kinds of markups and markdowns we use?"

■

UNDERSTANDING MARKUP, PROFIT, AND PRICING OBJECTIVES

Kelly answered Mr. Janko's questions by saying, "According to my marketing education course, **markup** is the difference between the factory or wholesale cost of a product and its initial retail selling price. A **markdown** is a reduction in this retail price. Profit is what is left from the markup amount after all expenses are paid. I really don't know all the different types of markups and markdowns the store uses."

Very good, Kelly. You are certainly correct in your understanding of the basic difference between markup and profit. Many people confuse these two terms. Markups for certain products may be quite high—on some items as much as 50 percent or more. It is generally not understood that the percentage of profits for most American businesses is in the neighborhood of 3 to 5 percent of sales. Recent surveys show that most people continue to think that net profit is about 10 times that much.

It is out of the markup that businesses must

get the money to pay all the costs of running the business. This includes salaries, mortgage or rent payments, utility bills, advertising, promotion, credit costs, interest, and all our administrative expenses. If a company made only 2 cents on a sales dollar in one year, you can see that the amount of the markups or markdowns can drastically affect this relatively small net profit. Let's use my office blackboard to describe the calculations of the various markups and markdowns. Before we explain our pricing strategies and calculations, let's first define what pricing is. **Pricing** is a course of action that involves setting a price or changing a price upward or downward to achieve a marketing objective. Such objectives may include attracting larger numbers of customers, reducing excess amounts of stock, introducing new products, or closing out year-end stocks of merchandise.

■

CALCULATING MARKUPS

Calculating markups and markdowns could be viewed as the process of pricing translated into mathematical terms. It is very important mathematics, for a retailer measures success or failure by figures—cost figures, sales figures, price figures, expense figures, and profit figures.

These calculations begin with the retailer's income statement, which is prepared at regular intervals. This statement, completed at the close of a year, enables the retailer to estimate closely sales, costs, and desired profit for the coming year. This information enables the retailer to determine the markup needed to arrive at the retail prices.

To arrive at a selling price that will yield a profit, the retailer begins with sales. Suppose that the estimated sales for the coming year are $100,000, the cost of the merchandise to be purchased is $60,000, the total estimated operating expenses are $36,000, and the retailer desires to obtain a net profit of 4 percent on sales.

The retailer now knows the gross profit on sales (40 percent) that is needed to make the desired profit. **Gross profit on sales**, or **gross margin**, is an accounting term that expresses the difference between net sales and net merchandise costs.

Category	Volume	Percent
Income from net sales	$100,000	100
Less cost of merchandise sold	60,000	60
Gross profit on sales	$ 40,000	40
Less operating expenses	36,000	36
Net profit	$ 4,000	4

Calculating the Dollar Markup

The merchandise that retailers purchase from wholesalers or manufacturers is billed to them at the cost price. To arrive at the selling price, the markup is added to the cost price. For example, if a shirt costs a store $3 and is sold for $4.50, the markup is $1.50. This markup is called **dollar markup** because it is expressed in dollars and cents.

The relationships among cost price, retail price, and markup are shown below.

Cost + markup = retail
$3.00 + $1.50 = $4.50

Retail − cost = markup
$4.50 − $3.00 = $1.50

Retail − markup = cost
$4.50 − $1.50 = $3.00

Calculating the Markup Percentage

In the formulas above, markup is expressed in dollars. In retailing, however, markup is often expressed as a percentage of either the cost price or the retail price. The formulas on page 454 are used to find what percentages of the retail price and the cost price the markup is.

Finding Percentage of Markup on Cost	Finding Percentage of Markup on Retail
Known:	**Known:**
Markup: $1.50	Markup: $1.50
Cost: $3.00	Retail: $4.50
Method:	**Method:**
$\text{Markup on cost} = \dfrac{\text{markup in dollars}}{\text{cost in dollars}}$	$\text{Markup on retail} = \dfrac{\text{markup in dollars}}{\text{retail in dollars}}$
$\text{Markup} = \dfrac{\$1.50}{\$3.00}$	$\text{Markup} = \dfrac{\$1.50}{\$4.50}$
$\text{Markup} = 50\%$	$\text{Markup} = 33.3\%$

Comparing Markup Percentages Based on Cost or Retail

Large retailers usually express markup as a percentage of the retail price rather than the cost price. Small retailers or stores that will bargain on prices may state markup percentages on the basis of cost. Markup percentages are usually based on retail prices because expenses and other items such as profits are commonly expressed as a percentage of retail sales.

If markup percentages are expressed in the same way, they can be compared with markup figures in other departments of the store or with other stores in the same line of retailing. The National Retail Merchants Association (NRMA) publishes an annual report of average markups and expense percentages for many different stores in the nation. By using markup and expense figures based on the retail price, retailers can compare a store's operations with national average reports such as the NRMA's.

You'll notice that the percentage of markup based on the retail price (33⅓ percent) is lower than the percentage of markup based on cost (50 percent). In either case, calculating a percentage figure for markups makes it possible to compare markups for several items or lines of merchandise even though the individual cost and retail prices may be different.

■

CALCULATING DIFFERENT TYPES OF MARKUPS

Now that you understand dollar and percentage markup calculation, we will illustrate different types of markups. Let's view the elements of markups as building blocks, because one depends on the other for support.

The Initial Retail Price and Initial Markup

Mr. Janko drew a rectangle on the blackboard and explained. The first element, or building block, is the cost of the merchandise. For example, an item that cost $30 would be represented by a block labeled "Cost of merchandise: $30."

The second building block is the first or **initial markup** of $20, which is added to the "cost" building block. These two blocks added together equal the **initial retail price**.

Initial retail price = cost of merchandise + initial markup
$50 = $30 + $20

Additional Markup

In certain cases, the initial markup may not be adequate to cover the cost of the merchandise expenses and the desired profit. In such cases, an additional markup is calculated. **Additional markup** is a price increase made after the initial markup is established. These additional price increases (markups) are common during periods of inflation, when a product is in short supply, or when its wholesale cost has increased. In our example, a building block of $10, the additional markup, is placed on top of the block for the initial markup.

Second retail price = cost of merchandise + initial markup + additional markup
$60 = $30 + $20 + $10

Markup Cancellations

Markups may not only be increased but occasionally reduced. A **markup cancellation** is a reduction in the retail price of an item some time after an additional markup has been made. Retailers sometimes make such changes because of a competitor's price reductions, too much inventory on hand, or resistance of customers to higher prices. A markup cancellation of $5, using the same pricing figures as in the previous example, follows:

Final retail price = cost of merchandise + initial markup + additional markup – markup cancellation
$55 = $30 + $20 + $10 – $5

■

USING MARKDOWNS AS A SELLING TOOL

A markdown is a reduction of the initial retail price. Retailers mark down for a variety of reasons, the most common of which are to attract customers, to move slow sellers, and to clear out odds and ends of stock and shopworn goods. The need to mark down goods is a frustrating problem to retailers. All of them would like to sell their goods at their

Retailers take into consideration the pricing strategy required for each item of merchandise.

initial markup prices. Still, they recognize that a certain percentage of markdowns is inevitable.

Markdowns hurt retailers because they cut into the amount of markup planned for an item and therefore, eventually, into the net profit earned by that item. However, no retailer has yet found a way to avoid markdowns. So experienced retailers plan for markdowns when the original price is established. The original price is set high enough to include anticipated markdowns as well as operating expenses.

Markdown Percentages

As with markups, markdowns can be stated in percentages. The **markdown percentage** is computed by dividing the initial retail price into the markdown allowed:

$$\frac{\text{Markdown}}{\text{Initial retail price}} = \frac{\$10}{\$50} = 20\%$$

The effect of a markdown on price may be shown as follows:

Second retail price = cost of merchandise + initial markup – markdown
$40 = $30 + $20 – $10

Markdown Cancellations

A **markdown cancellation** is an upward price adjustment on a markdown already taken. The most common example occurs when a price is restored to its initial retail level after the goods have been marked down temporarily for a special sales event. In the example below, the $30 cost of merchandise was added to the $20 initial markup, resulting in a $50 initial retail price. Then a $10 markdown was subtracted from the $50 initial retail price, resulting in a $40 second retail price. The $10 markdown was then canceled, which restored a $50 final retail price.

Final retail price = cost of merchandise + initial markup − markdown + markdown cancellation
$50 = $30 + $20 − $10 + $10

■

TIMING MARKDOWNS

It's difficult for someone new in retailing to decide when markdowns should be taken. Sometimes, retailers who delay this decision a few days find that the goods that were to be marked down can now be moved only by being offered below cost. And if retailers continue to wait, the goods may deteriorate, become shopworn, and tie up space and money that could be more wisely invested in new stock. Through experience, retailers learn to mark down goods quickly when there is evidence that they are not going to move.

Automatic Markdown System

Some stores use an automatic markdown system. An **automatic markdown system** is a plan that sets a time period during which an item is offered at its original price. If the item hasn't sold at the end of that time, it must be marked down by a given percentage. For example, Filene's department store in Boston offers merchandise in several price lines on different floors of the store. If the merchan-

dise doesn't sell at a certain price on a given floor, it is eventually moved to the basement. There, markdowns are taken for a fixed period of time. If this time period expires and the merchandise still has not sold, it is given to charity.

Multiple Pricing Plans

Certain retailers, particularly supermarket owners, use a **multiple pricing plan** for markdowns. This means that the price is reduced when several items are sold at the same time. For example, soap may be sold at 30 cents a bar or 59 cents for two bars.

Experience and observation help retailers to determine the percentage of markdowns that must be taken. Usually the markdowns must be large enough to move the goods. One large markdown is generally more effective than several small ones.

■

EVALUATING PRICING GOALS

A term that retailers use to evaluate the realization of various pricing goals is the **maintained markup** or **net markup**. This markup is the difference between the cost of the merchandise and the actual price at which it is sold. This actual selling price may include various markups and markdowns. The following example shows how pricing goals and maintained markups are evaluated.

For instance, suppose that a store with projected net sales of $100,000 and a projected initial markup of 40 percent had the following actual pricing changes:

1. Additional markups (AMU), 5%
2. Markup cancellations (MC), 3%
3. Markdowns (M), 10%
4. Markdown cancellations (MC), 5%

What would be the actual or maintained markup percentage? The following computations would be necessary to calculate this percentage:

$$5\%(AMU) - 3\%(MC) - 10\%(M) + 5\%(MC) = -3\%(\text{net pricing change})$$

$$40\%(\text{initial markup}) - 3\%(\text{net pricing change}) = 37\%(\text{maintained markup})$$

In this case, even though the initial markup (pricing goal) was 40 percent, the actual pricing markup (maintained markup) realized was 37 percent. Managers and merchandisers should analyze reasons for differences in the initial and maintained markups. Such information can enable them to set realistic future pricing goals and to take necessary corrective action.

TRADE TALK

Define each term and use it in a sentence.

Additional markup	Dollar markup
Automatic markdown system	Gross profit on sales or gross margin

Initial markup	Markdown percentage
Initial retail price	Markup
Maintained markup or net markup	Markup cancellation
Markdown	Multiple pricing plan
Markdown cancellation	Pricing

CAN YOU ANSWER THESE?

1. What is the definition of pricing presented in this chapter?

2. Why do most businesses calculate markup as a percentage of the retail price rather than as a percentage of the cost price?

3. What is the difference between the initial and the maintained markup?

4. What are examples of how markdowns can be used as selling tools?

5. How does an automatic markdown system operate?

6. Which is generally more effective, taking several smaller markdowns or one larger markdown? Why?

C·H·A·P·T·E·R

53 *Inventory Control*

Kelly Redman had been appointed as an assistant buyer for the sportswear department. She had just finished waiting on a disappointed customer. The customer had seen an advertisement for a very popular new style of sweater. Since the department did not receive the promotional sweaters in time for the sale, Kelly had to do a lot of explaining to unhappy customers. Being out of stock during peak sales periods is unfortunately not an unusual situation in retailing. Kelly wondered, "How could we do a better job of merchandise planning and inventory control?"

There are many inventory control systems and procedures that can assist retailers like Kelly in answering this question. In this chapter, inventory control systems, stockkeeping units (SKUs), merchandise coverage, unit and dollar control, merchandise lists, and physical and perpetual inventory systems are explained. An understanding of these merchandising "tools" is important for every buyer, department head, or retail manager.

■

INVENTORY CONTROL SYSTEMS

Inventory control is the coordination of the supply, physical condition, storage, distribution, and recording of merchandise goods. Retailers have such systems to maintain merchandise quantities adequate for current needs without too much oversupply or loss. Successful retailers organize an inventory-control system to keep informed on the status of merchandise for a certain period—such as a month, a selling season, or a year. Such a system provides retailers with information concerning the status of the goods at a specific date—the end of the month, for example.

Importance of Inventory Control

Recent merchandising trends have made careful inventory control more important than ever before. Reliable inventory control provides retailers with information for meeting competition, regulating the amount of stock, and calculating taxes. Intense competition has increased the need for retailers to find out exactly what customers want today and to determine what they are likely to want tomorrow. Only by identifying and measuring customer demand, as indicated by what sells and what doesn't, can retailers offer attractive merchandise to their customers.

Today, to devote the maximum amount of space to selling, more and more retailers are reducing the size of their storage and other nonselling areas. They are keeping their reserve stock in warehouses in low-rent areas and shipping to the store or directly to customers as required. Chain stores are relying with increasing frequency on central warehouses rather than keeping their reserve stock in the store or a neighborhood warehouse. When retailers keep less stock at the retail outlet, they need close inventory control to make sure that the store doesn't run out of stock.

Retailers usually pay federal and state income taxes on the basis of net profit earned. Some state and local governments also collect personal property taxes on the inventory on hand. But only when inventory records are properly organized will state and local government accept them as a basis for

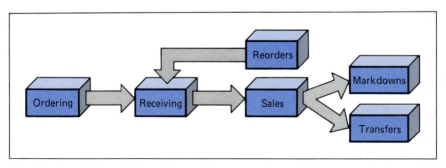

A computer system tracks inventory status.

figuring taxes. So, obviously, the lower the inventory, the less tax retailers have to pay.

Inventory Control Systems by Units and Dollars

Unit control is an inventory-control system based on the number of items of merchandise rather than on the dollar value of the merchandise. This system shows how many items (units) of each type of merchandise are on hand or on order or have been sold. This information may be classified by type of merchandise and by size, color, style, model, and so on. Since the increased use of computers, retailers can keep track of many classifications of merchandise information.

Dollar stock control is an inventory-control system that records data about merchandise in terms of money. This system identifies how much the goods are worth in terms of either cost or retail prices. Such information is very important, because buyers must know the dollar value of stock on hand and on order when making decisions about the funds required to reorder needed goods.

In actual practice, both unit control and dollar stock control are necessary if buyers are to have sufficient information for inventory control decisions. This chapter focuses on unit-control systems.

Stockkeeping Units (SKUs)

With the increase in the amount and variety of merchandise assortments a stockkeeping system of identifying and classifying merchandise was developed. The stockkeeping unit (SKU) system enables merchants to analyze and plan assortments within product lines. An **SKU** unit is one distinct, individual type of item carried by a store. For example, a gallon of white interior latex paint is one SKU, while the same paint in red is another SKU.

To determine an SKU in men's shirts, the number of collar sizes is multiplied by the number of sleeve lengths and by the number

of colors stocked. The number of SKUs for a man's shirt with an assortment of color sizes, sleeve lengths, and colors is then calculated as follows:

7 collar sizes $\times$ 4 sleeve lengths $\times$ 4 colors = 112 SKUs

If one unit of this style is ordered, such as red in size 16×33, one SKU exists. If 39 more of the identical items are received, there would be 40 units on hand but still only one SKU. If 10 red shirts and 10 yellow shirts in the same size (16×33) are ordered, then two SKUs exist. The SKU classification system helps buyers to determine and analyze the sales rates of specific assortments of merchandise according to combinations of sizes, models, prices, colors, and quality offered within each line. For example, with the men's shirts, a buyer could analyze the comparative sales of certain colors of shirts to determine which colors to reorder and which to mark down.

SKU merchandise information is inputted, stored, and retrieved through the use of computer terminals and computer data-storage systems. This information allows the retailer instantly to evaluate the current status of individual merchandise items or product lines.

Merchandise Coverage

Merchandise coverage is the basic amount of merchandise to have on hand and on order to satisfy customer demand. A store may, for example, have a merchandise coverage policy of carrying only the most popular sizes, colors, materials, and brands. Stores that decide to concentrate on a few selected styles and prices are said to have a **depth of stock**. Examples of depth of stock include:

Color: 8 units of white, 6 units of black, 4 units of blue, etc.
Size: 8 units of size 8, 12 units of size 10, 12 units of size 12, etc.
Price: 20 units of price $6.95, 25 units of price $7.95, etc.

Stores that offer a wide variety in merchandise lines are said to have a **breadth of stock**. Examples of breadth of stock include:

Color: white, black, blue, red, etc.
Size: 6, 8, 10, 12, etc.
Price: $6.95, $7.95, $8.95, etc.
Fabric: cotton, wool, silk, synthetic, etc.
Pattern: solid, check, plaid, stripe, etc.
Brand: A, B, C, D, etc.
Style: $10\times$, $20\times$, $30\times$, $40\times$, etc.
Model: 2250, 2260, 2270, 2280, etc.

Balancing the breadth and depth of inventory without keeping too much money tied up is a central problem for a buyer. A balanced stock satisfies the demands of most of a store's customers and returns greater profits for the amount of money invested.

ASSORTMENT PLANS AND LISTS

A department or store that's often out of stock finds itself constantly ordering small quantities on a rush basis or losing sales. The rush orders involve extra expenses, such as telephone and delivery charges. There are three kinds of inventory control lists that keep a buyer informed so that rush orders or out-of-stock conditions can be avoided: model stock plans, basic stock lists, and never-out lists.

Model Stock Plan

A **model stock plan** is a preplanned list of items, established by store or department policy, that are always kept in inventory. Model stock lists reflect store policy concerning the number or variety of assortments. They indicate whether a store aims to carry a full range of styles and brands or only the most popular items. For example, many prestige department stores have rather extensive model stock lists, in keeping with their policy of offering customers a broad selection. This policy is designed to attract discrimi-

nating customers who like a variety of choices and are willing to pay for this service. On the other hand, mass merchandisers usually have very limited model stock lists. These limited lists are based on a policy designed to attract customers who prefer lower prices and are willing to forego wide merchandise assortments and services.

Since fashion can be highly changeable, model stock plans for fashion merchandise may be subject to frequent adjustment as the season progresses. Model stock plans for most staples, however, are usually adjusted only a few times a year, since such merchandise changes little in its basic characteristics. Its demand is usually predictable.

Basic Stock List

Many retailers dealing in staple goods—such as groceries, hardware, drugs, cosmetics, and stationery—use basic stock lists to maintain tight control over merchandise. A **basic stock list** shows the minimum amount of stock that should be on hand for each type of goods sold and the quantity that should be reordered when ordering is done. A basic stock list identifies the items that should never be out of stock. This is quite different from a model stock list, which shows the range of goods that should be carried.

At regular intervals—either daily, weekly, or monthly—buyers or assistant buyers count each item and enter the amount for each item on the basic stock list. By checking the quantity on hand against the minimum amount that should be in stock, buyers can determine when and how many units to reorder.

Never-Out List

The **never-out list** is a specially created list of merchandise items that are identified as key items or best sellers for which the retailer wants extra protection against the possibility of a stockout. Due to the high level of demand for these items, many retailers establish rigid stock requirements. For exam-

BASIC STOCK LIST

Store __30__   Dept. __7__   Effective Date _____ 4/15 _____   Page __2__

Vendor Westco Apparel / Address 924 Belmont	Item Description	Style	Size	Color	Pkg.	Retail	Min Qty	Max Qty	
Chicago, Illinois	Men's over–the–calf	63	small	black	2/pkg.	4.98	4	12	1
	100% nylon stretch			gray	2/pkg.	4.98	4	12	2
Representative Sandra Baker	socks			brown	2/pkg.	4.98	4	12	3
Address 416 Harris Boulevard				navy	2/pkg.	4.98	4	12	4
Oakland, California			medium	black	2/pkg.	4.98	6	16	5
Phone 286–5188				gray	2/pkg.	4.98	6	16	6
Coverage Period __7__ Weeks				brown	2/pkg.	4.98	6	16	7
Delivery Period __2__ Weeks				navy	2/pkg.	4.98	6	16	8
Method of Count [XX] Group Mgr. [ ] Vendor			large	black	2/pkg.	4.98	5	14	9
				gray	2/pkg.	4.98	5	14	10
__x__ 1. First Week / 2. Second Week				brown	2/pkg.	4.98	5	14	11
___ 3. Third Week				navy	2/pkg.	4.98	5	14	12
___ 4. Fourth Week									13
___ See Additional Information Below									14
Additional Information									15
									16
									17
									18
									19
									20
									21
Emergency Orders: [XX] Call Vendor									22
[ ] No Emergency Orders									23
Requisition must be mailed from store by Wednes. of count week									24
Minimum Model Allowed									25

A basic stock list.

ple, a retailer might specify that 99 percent of all items on the never-out list must be on hand and on display at all times. Stockouts of these key items result in permanent loss of sales. Typically, the consumer will simply not wait to purchase best sellers. Never-out lists can include fast-selling staples, key seasonal items, and best-selling fashion merchandise. The never-out list is maintained through regular and frequent revision. Many chain organizations expect individual store managers to have a near-perfect record in maintaining the stock levels for merchandise on the list. Even a moderate number of stockouts of merchandise on the list is considered an indication of poor management.

PHYSICAL INVENTORY SYSTEMS

Under a **physical inventory** system, buyers take an actual count of merchandise to determine the exact quantity on hand. In addition to keeping records of the unit sales of each item, buyers obtain the sales figure by adding any merchandise received to the opening inventory and subtracting the closing inventory. This sales figure is based on an actual physical count of the merchandise. The count may be lower than the sales figure obtained from a perpetual inventory record, such as a cash-register tape. The difference between sales recorded on a tape and sales based on a physical inventory is usually due to shortages from theft, improper checking of incoming merchandise, errors in cash-register operation, or damaged and unsalable merchandise. Some of the more commonly used physical inventory systems are (1) tickler control, (2) reorder control, and (3) visual control.

Tickler Control

A system by which buyers figure the entire inventory for a given period by counting portions of the stock at regular intervals is called **tickler control**. The term "tickler" comes from another system that buyers use, called a tickler file, which reminds them when to take stock counts for each type of merchandise. Tickler control is also referred to as a "rotated inventory," because the stock counts occur on a rotated, or staggered, basis.

Tickler control is used most often for staple merchandise. The unit-control card usually shows the maximum amount of stock that should be on hand and on order when goods are reordered. Each time buyers take a count or inventory of an item, an order is placed to cover the difference between the maximum stock and the amount of stock on hand and on order. For instance, maximum stock for an item may be 20 pieces, and the buyer may take a count every month. If the monthly count shows that there are 15 pieces in stock and none on order, the buyer places an order for 5 pieces.

Maximum stock, 20
Stock on hand, 15
Stock on order, 0
Stock to order, 5

Reorder Control

A type of physical inventory system that doesn't involve regular counting of stock is

Careful inventory control is very important to retailers. Here, inventory is being checked at a supermarket (left) and in a warehouse (right).

Unit 17   Pricing and Inventory Control

called **reorder control**. Buyers may use it to control items such as hosiery, gloves, blouses, and shirts that are stocked in boxes, bins, or drawers. A card, slip, or gummed label containing necessary reorder information is used to mark the minimum stock point under reorder control. When the stock reaches this level, the reminder card, slip, or label appears and is removed and sent to the buyer, who makes use of the data in reordering.

Visual Control

Visual control by **color coding** is another inventory-control technique that can assure good rotation. This inventory control technique is used by retailers dealing in perishable or seasonal merchandise, such as grocers or discount mass merchandisers. With this method, a record is kept of the date on which a shipment of merchandise was received, and a color is assigned to the shipment. The price tag or label placed on the item will be the assigned color. For example, the first shipment may have blue tags, the second one green tags, and so on. When a price is applied directly to the merchandise by a marking pen, the color used is the same as that assigned to the shipment.

Once the system has been in operation for more than one shipment, buyers can tell at a glance which merchandise has been in stock the longest. Besides helping with stock rotation, such color coding helps to reveal slow- and fast-moving items, thereby identifying merchandise ready for reduced-price sales.

■

PERPETUAL INVENTORY SYSTEMS

Taking a physical inventory is a tedious and costly job. This is why many retailers take inventory only once or twice a year. Even so, to market goods competitively, retailers need information about sales and stock on hand that is much more current than the figures

PERPETUAL UNIT-CONTROL RECORD

Style Men's knit golf shirt

Size 15½ 36

Unit Cost 5.95

Minimum Order Quantity 8

Delivery Time 1 week

Date	Qty. On Hand	Qty. On Order	Qty. Recd.	Qty. Sold	Qty. Returned	Balance
4-7	28			3		25
4-21	25			1		24
5-5	24	8			2	26
5-19	26		8	4		30
6-2	30			3		27
6-16	27		2	1		28
6-30	28				1	29

A perpetual inventory control record.

obtained in the last physical inventory. For most categories of merchandise, a monthly updating of inventory information is important. For some categories, such as food and apparel, weekly and sometimes even daily updating is needed. A **perpetual inventory system** produces this kind of updated information. The aim of this system is to keep inventory records in agreement with inventory actually in stock.

Manual Systems

A manual system of perpetual unit control is maintained by the retailer's accounting or inventory-control personnel. These individuals continuously record merchandise data on **perpetual unit-control records** for individual merchandise items. These records are updated regularly to indicate current orders, receipts, and customer returns (additions) as well as sales, shortages, and damages (subtractions).

As you can observe on the unit-control record for men's knit golf shirts above, the following information is readily available:

■ Items currently in stock
■ Sales trends over a 3-month period
■ High and low sales months
■ Comparative figures for the previous year
■ Wholesale costs and retail prices
■ Delivery information: what has been ordered, what is in, and how long it takes to obtain a fresh supply

- Minimum quantities
- Ordering quantities

The number of units received into stock is obtained from records furnished by the receiving department or clerk. Information on the number of units sold can be gathered using a number of manual systems, such as:

1. *Point-of-sale tallies* (sales personnel keep track of the number of units sold by making a tally mark on a merchandise list after each sale);

2. *Price-ticket stubs* (sales personnel remove information stubs from price tickets when the merchandise is sold and collect, sort, and tally the number of units sold); and

3. *Cash-register stubs* (sales personnel remove information stubs from receipts before giving them to customers; these stubs are then used to determine the number of units sold).

Computerized Systems

Computerized systems of perpetual unit control accomplish the same tasks as manual systems except that they are faster, more timely, and more accurate. The use of computer-based electronic data-processing equipment allows the retailer to convert merchandise data on sales, purchases, and stocks into useful information automatically. Several automatic systems are available, including tag, card, and point-of-sale systems. (A *tag system* uses prepunched merchandise tags containing basic assortment information that are attached to each merchandise item.) These tags are collected when the item is sold and sent to a data-processing facility where the information is fed into the computer. *Card systems* are similar to tag systems except that sales personnel record assortment information directly onto punched cards or scanner cards, which are then fed into the data-processing system and used for unit-control purposes. *Point-of-sale (POS) systems* use cash registers or terminals capable of transmitting assortment information (style, price, color, material, and so on) directly to the central data-processing facility as the sale is being recorded.

■

WHICH INVENTORY SYSTEM IS BEST?

As mentioned previously, both unit and dollar stock-control systems are necessary to provide the buyer with sufficient inventory control information. This is also the case regarding physical and perpetual inventory systems. Both systems are necessary. Each system offers the "best" information in certain circumstances.

The main advantage of the physical inventory system is that it is more accurate in determining inventory quantity and value at a particular time. Its chief disadvantages are that (1) it is costly and time-consuming and (2) it can provide accurate information only right after the inventory is completed.

The main advantage of the perpetual inventory system is that records can be updated frequently and at any time. It's also readily adaptable to the use of automated and computerized information systems. Its chief disadvantages are that the system depends on the accuracy of the information provided and that it's expensive to maintain the necessary records. A perpetual inventory system doesn't reveal shortages, damaged merchandise, or losses due to shoplifting.

For these reasons, retailers usually rely on a perpetual inventory system to keep track of staples and merchandise of lower unit cost. To control high-unit-cost items, retailers usually use both a periodic physical inventory and a perpetual inventory.

If Kelly and her retail associates use effectively the many inventory control systems and procedures that are available, then they will have to explain out-of-stock conditions far less often. It should be remembered that the ideal inventory control system for any retailing operation is the one that produces all the information that retailers need (and no more) to merchandise goods efficiently. Unnecessary additional information is not only confusing but wastes the time and money spent in collecting it. The ideal inventory control system also produces information when the retailer needs it—neither too early, which would mean that unnecessary or inappropriate information was produced, nor too late, which would give only outdated and useless information.

TRADE TALK

Define each term and use it in a sentence.

Basic stock list	Inventory control
Breadth of stock	Merchandise coverage
Color coding	Model stock plan
Depth of stock	Never-out list
Dollar stock control	Perpetual inventory system

Perpetual unit-control records
Physical inventory
Reorder control

SKU
Tickler control
Unit control

CAN YOU ANSWER THESE?

1. What trends in retailing cause inventory control to be more important than ever?
2. What are two reasons why dollar stock control is important?
3. What is a basic use of the SKU?
4. How does a model stock plan differ from a basic stock list?
5. What are three types of physical inventory systems?
6. What are three types of manual perpetual inventory control systems?
7. For what reasons would you as a retailer use a perpetual inventory system? A physical inventory system?

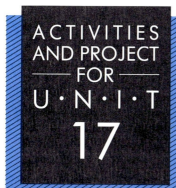

ACTIVITIES AND PROJECT —FOR— U·N·I·T 17

RETAIL MARKETING CASE

Johnson's Hardware is receiving strong price competition on its small, power hand tools from a nearby discount store. The discount store sells the same national line of hand tools. In addition, the discount store handles a lower-quality, lower-priced brand of hand tools. The following table compares the selling prices for the two stores for comparable models of power sanders and drills:

	Johnson's	Discount Store
Brand A sander	$29.95	$25.95
Brand B sander	Not handled	$19.95
Brand A drill	$25.95	$21.95
Brand B drill	Not handled	$19.95

Johnson's is concerned for two reasons: (1) Sales are being lost on a price basis, and (2) certain customers do not realize the advantages of shopping at a full-service hardware store.

1. What merchandise promotion and pricing alternatives are available to Johnson's Hardware?

2. What recommendations would you offer Johnson's Hardware?

(1) Pricing Policy	(2) Firm Name	(3) Merchandise	(4) Reasons for Policy
Variable	Sam's Used Auto	1984 Chevrolet Corvette	Customers accustomed to bargaining, value of used cars difficult to determine

PROBLEMS

1. In Kelly Redman's department $7000 worth of sportswear was sold. Because she wished to see if she could calculate the gross profit on merchandise investment, she obtained the following inventory and sales figures from Mrs. Genelli:

a. Merchandise on hand during the peak inventory period = $7000

b. Merchandise on hand during the low inventory period = $5000

c. Cost of sportwear sold = $4000

See if you can solve Kelly's problem.

2. Rule a form similar to the one below. In column 1, list the different types of pricing policies commonly used by retail firms: fixed, variable, price lining, odd-cents pricing, leader pricing. In column 2, list the names of stores in your community that would be likely to use each policy. In column 3, give examples of merchandise that would be priced according to each policy. In column 4, state reasons why particular stores would use certain pricing policies for the merchandise named.

3. The cost figures of various items are: (0) $4.00, (a) $12.00, (b) $9.00, (c) $120.50, (d) $53.75, and (e) $1056.00. Corresponding in order to these cost figures are the following desired retail prices of these items: $6.00, $18.50, $22.00, $189.95, $82.50, and $3095.00. Rule a form similar to the following one, and in the left-hand column write the letter of each of the cost figures. In the next column, write the desired selling price corresponding to the figure. Then, for each item, calculate the markup in dollars, the markup as a percentage of cost, and the markup as a percentage of retail price, and list these in the last three columns.

Cost of Item	Desired Selling Price	Markup In Dollars	Percent of Cost	Percent of Retail Price
Example: (0)	$6.00	$2.00	50%	33⅓%

4. The cost figures of various items are (0) $10.00, (a) $18.00, (b) $96.50, (c) $200.00, (d) $35.20, (e) $22.50, and (f) $4.95. Corresponding in order to these cost figures are the following initial markup percentages used on cost: 20 percent, 46 percent, 44 percent, 36 percent, 18 percent, 42 percent, and 9 percent. Rule a form similar to the following one, and in the left-hand column write the letter of each of the cost figures. In the next column, write the initial markup on cost corresponding to the figure. Then calculate the selling price and the markup in dollars for each item and list these in the last two columns.

Cost of Item	Initial Markup	Selling Price	Dollar-Markup
Example: (0)	20%	$12.00	$2.00

5. A buyer made purchases of $16,000 and initially priced the goods at $30,000 for resale. Markdowns of $800 were taken during the selling period. Discounts on goods bought by employees totaled $300. Shortages of $500 occurred. Calculate answers for the following questions:

a. What was the initial markup in dollars?
b. What was the initial markup percentage based on the selling price?
c. Assuming that all of this merchandise sold, what was the maintained markup in dollars?
d. What was the actual maintained markup percentage realized?

6. You are in charge of maintaining the unit-control cards for a hardware department. Your department uses a perpetual unit-control system. From the following information, determine how many units of hammers should be ordered. The maximum stock can be 30 hammers.

a. June 1: quantity on hand, 20
b. June 3: quantity ordered, 10
c. June 4: quantity received, 8
d. June 10: monthly quantity sold to date, 6
e. June 10: quantity returned to date, 1

7. For the same situation as Problem 6, determine the stock on hand at the end of the

month. The unit-control card provides the following information:

a. June 30: quantity on order, 10
b. June 30: quantity received, 5
c. June 30: quantity sold, 4
d. June 30: quantity returned, 2

PROJECT: COMPARISON SHOPPING

YOUR PROJECT GOAL

Assume that you work in a department offering a line of merchandise of your choice. Also assume the buyer believes that a new line should be added. You are asked to check out competitors to find out what they are offering in terms of items, brands, styles, and price ranges.

PROCEDURE

1. Choose a merchandise line and type of store that fits your training station or your career goal.
2. Determine the location of at least two stores that offer this line and that are competitors.
3. On a separate sheet of paper, rule a form like the following or a form of your own design. Then comparison-shop in both stores.

Store _____
Name of item _____
Quantities/brands/styles carried _____
Price ranges _____
Assortment (wide or narrow) _____
Comments _____

4. Prepare a comparison shopping report form for all stores in which you shop and prepare a memo to your buyer. The memo should not be more than two pages in length and should cover the following points:
a. Where you shopped.
b. What the competition is offering.

c. What your recommendation is. Should the buyer add or drop a price line? Should price lines be used that are the same as other stores or that are different from them? Give reasons for your recommendations.

EVALUATION

You will be evaluated on the completeness of the information in your comparison shopping reports, on the clarity and directness of your memo, and on the value of your recommendations based on the facts you present.

PROJECT: ANALYZING INVENTORY CONTROL FORMS

YOUR PROJECT GOAL

Given a retail store of your choice or the store in which you are currently employed, determine the types of inventory-control forms that are now being used.

PROCEDURE

1. Select one line of merchandise that is being handled by the store being considered.

2. Interview the department manager, buyer, or your supervisor concerning the inventory control forms used to record orders, sales, markdowns, returns, and so on.

3. Write a brief report describing the inventory-control method used. Include in your report examples of the various business forms used. Indicate how and when entries are recorded on these forms.

4. Be prepared to present an oral report to the class describing the inventory-control forms and entries made on the forms.

EVALUATION

You will be evaluated on how accurately and completely you have described the inventory-control forms.

U·N·I·T 18 DEVELOPING MERCHANDISING STRATEGIES

C·H·A·P·T·E·R 54 *Analyzing Stock Turnover*

Doug Smith owned a motorcycle and snowmobile business called the Moto-Ski Shop. He was very concerned about the spring ending inventory of snowmobiles. During the past selling season he had been offered a quantity purchase "deal" for a larger number of snowmobiles than he normally sold in a year. Unfortunately, the city's largest employer cut back on its work force and the area received a below-average amount of snowfall.

Doug sought the advice of Mr. Jenkins, a Small Business Administration counselor who had managed a similar business. Mr. Jenkins asked Doug, "What were your stockturns for the snowmobile line for the past 3 months?"

"I'm not sure," said Doug. "All I know is that sales were slow and that I have too many left over. I wonder if I should consider drastically reducing the snowmobiles and expanding the downhill and cross-country ski lines next year. I know that I need to develop a

better inventory analysis system. Could you help me set one up?"

■

THE MEANING OF STOCK TURNOVER

Mr. Jenkins replied, "Before you make inventory decisions to increase or decrease your lines of merchandise, you need to calculate the **stock turnover** or 'stockturns' as it is often called." This is the number of times a quantity of stock or inventory is turned into sales during a given period of time. Stock turnover can be figured for a week, a month, a selling season, a year, or any other period. It can be calculated for the store as a whole, for each department within a store, for each classification of merchandise, or occasionally for a particular item of merchandise. Stock turnover is calculated in terms of units or dollars or both.

Determining Stock Turnover by Units

Stock turnover by units is the number of times that the average units of stock on hand have sold out and been replaced during a selling period. "Average units of stock on hand" means the usual amounts of stock that are kept on hand during the selling period. (Various methods of computing average stock are described later in this chapter.) The rate of stock turnover by units can be computed by dividing the total number of units sold by the average number of units of merchandise in stock. This calculation is illustrated as follows:

$$\text{Stockturn in units} = \frac{\text{sales in units}}{\text{average units of stock on hand}}$$

Let's determine the unit stockturn of Doug's snowmobiles for the past 3 months. From the inventory and sales records, the following information is computed:

Average units of snowmobiles on hand = 10
Total units of snowmobiles sold = 15
Number of unit stockturns for 3 months = 1.5 (15 ÷ 10)

Doug knows that the snowmobile inventory has been turning over at the rate of 1.5 times for a 3-month period. He can use this number to identify the lines of merchandise that have turned over at a faster or slower rate. In some cases, to increase profit, Doug may decide to order more of the motorcycles that have been selling at a faster rate. In other cases, he may decide to reduce or eliminate slower-selling snowmobiles.

Computing Average Stock

Determining total net sales volume for the period is a simple matter of referring to the

sales records. Determining what the average stock on hand is during a particular period requires more effort. The general formula is:

Beginning inventory + ending inventory ÷ 2 = **average stock**

If Doug Smith's beginning inventory was 9 units, and the ending inventory was 11 units, then the average units of stock on hand was 10 units (9 + 11 ÷ 2 = 10). Suppose that Doug had a beginning inventory of $27,000 and ended the year with $33,000 worth of goods. Adding the figures $27,000 + $33,000 and dividing by 2 gives an average dollar value of stock on hand of $30,000. These two examples illustrate how the average stock can be computed both by units and by dollars.

Computing Quarterly and Yearly Average Stock

These calculations are satisfactory methods to use if the period of time involved is short. The figures will be accurate enough when

Computer printouts provide stock turnover information.

calculating stock turnover for a week or a month. However, the method will not be accurate for a period longer than a month, such as a quarter, a season, or a year. In the case of a year, for example, most retailers try to carry their smallest inventories at the end of the year or the selling season, particularly if those inventories are subject to tax.

A more useful way to figure an average inventory for a period of a year is to use the inventory figures for the beginning of each month in that year. The 12 monthly figures plus the ending inventory for the last month of the year are added, and the resulting sum is divided by 13. This method is more accurate because the monthly changes in inventory are taken into account. This consideration of monthly variations is important. In some stores, for example, the amount of inventory changes widely because of the seasonal nature of sales, such as for motorcycles and snowmobiles.

Determining Stock Turnover by Dollars

Stock turnover by dollars is a measurement of the number of times during a given period that the retail dollar value of the average inventory is sold and replaced. To determine the stockturn in dollars, the following calculation is used:

$$\text{Stockturn in dollars} = \frac{\text{dollar sales of merchandise for the period}}{\text{average retail dollar value of the merchandise on hand}}$$

Note that in this calculation, the average dollar value of the merchandise must be at the retail, or selling price, value if the correct stockturn in dollars is to be obtained. Similar values (retail sales and retail value of merchandise on hand) must be used to calculate a correct stock turnover.

Doug can calculate the average dollar value of his snowmobile inventory by reviewing the inventory records. The beginning inven-

tory of snowmobiles was valued at $27,000 and the ending inventory was valued at $33,000. The average dollar value of merchandise can be calculated to be $30,000. Doug determines from his records that the dollar sales of snowmobiles for the period was $45,000. By using dollar figures rather than unit figures, he can also determine that the stockturn for the snowmobiles was 1.5 ($45,000 ÷ $30,000). Unit and dollar stockturns should result in the same number if the proper calculations are made.

USING THE COST OR RETAIL METHOD OF INVENTORY VALUATION

Some retailers keep records in terms of cost figures; others keep records in terms of retail figures. Stock turnover can be figured either in terms of cost figures or retail figures, depending on the kind of bookkeeping the retailer uses.

The Cost Method

Many small stores use the **cost method of inventory valuation**. This means that all records are kept on the basis of the actual cost value of the merchandise. This is the older of the two methods. It is popular among retailers with very rapid turnover of merchandise, such as supermarkets, where retail prices may change several times within a given week. For small stores, it's the easier of the two ways of keeping records. Less information needs to be collected and calculated when the cost method is used.

The Retail Method

Most retailers use the **retail method of inventory valuation**. This means that records are kept on the basis of the retail value of the merchandise. This method enables retailers to record a more current estimate of the value of the inventory. The current retail selling price is usually a realistic price, the price that retailers believe customers will pay for the merchandise. This price is adjusted upward or downward on the basis of such factors as economic conditions, supply of and demand for the merchandise, and competition. For these major reasons, this method is widely used by retailers.

ANALYZING STOCK TURNOVER RATES

Turnover rates themselves are of little importance unless retailers know what they mean and how to analyze them. For example, the rate of stock turnover within a store or any of its departments can be compared from one year to the next. And this comparison will suggest whether the right items are being bought and promoted. You can also compare rates of stock turnover with the rates of similar stores. If turnover rates are different from the average of other similar stores, it's necessary to determine why.

Variations in Turnover Rates

Table 1 shows examples of key yearly business ratios and demonstrates how stock turnover varies depending on the type of business. Even though grocery stores may have a yearly turnover of 16.8 for all merchandise, it is obvious that the meat or milk lines require an almost weekly turnover to prevent spoilage. More detailed information regarding specific merchandise turnovers is available from professional publications.

The rate depends on a number of factors. First, what assortment does the store wish to carry? Some stores carry huge assortments with many items that sell very slowly. Customers expect to find whatever they want

Turnover rates vary—antique stores may carry huge assortments of merchandise with many items that sell very slowly.

and expect to pay a price for this service. Some stores carry only a limited line of goods that are best sellers. And they expect to lose some sales when they don't have everything customers want. Some stores are located near suppliers and can get stock replacements quickly. Others are not, so they must order far in advance.

Benefits of Increased Stock Turnover

Increased stock turnover rates generally reflect good merchandise planning and control. Several benefits exist for retailers with a high rate of stock turnover. They include:

1. *Higher profits.* A rapid stock turnover results in an increase in sales and a corresponding decrease in inventory. A higher return on inventory investment is realized.

2. *Greater sales.* A rapid stock turnover allows the retailer to adjust merchandise assortments according to the changing needs of the target market.

3. *Lower inventory expenses.* A quick stock turnover helps to reduce inventories and, therefore, reduce such inventory expenses as interest and insurance payments, storage costs, and taxes on inventory. Sales promotion costs are reduced since a new and fresh selection of merchandise tends to sell itself.

4. *Fresher merchandise.* With a rapid stock turnover there is more frequent replacement of merchandise. A continuous flow of new and fresh merchandise comes into the store.

5. *Fewer markdowns and less shrinkage.* A fast stock turnover is associated with a faster rate of sales. Losses resulting from style or fashion obsolescence and soiled or damaged merchandise are reduced.

Disadvantages of High Stock Turnover

A store may lose sales and decrease profits if it tries to maintain too high a rate of turnover. If the inventory becomes too low or too restricted in variety, the store may often be out of stock on some items. Sales and customer goodwill will be lost. To keep a complete assortment of goods, most retailers also stock some items that sell more slowly. While this leads to a slower turnover for the complete stock, the store satisfies its customers and maintains its sales volume. A high rate of turnover may also increase the costs of ordering and receiving, because more frequent orders and shipments are made. Finally, retailers may lose quantity discounts if only small quantities are ordered.

INCREASING STOCK TURNOVER

Merchandising decisions have a direct effect on stock turnover. The following merchandise strategies can help to increase stock turns.

Improved Buying

When buyers know what customers want and follow an appropriate plan, stock turnover

TABLE 1 / MERCHANDISE TURNOVER RATES (Selected Retail Businesses)

Book store	4.1 times
Clothing and furnishings, men's and boys'	3.5
Department stores	4.6
Florists	16.7
Furniture stores	4.5
Gasoline service stations	31.3
Grocery stores	16.8
Hardware stores	4.7
Hobby, toy, game shops	3.7
Jewelry stores	2.4
Radio and television stores	5.8
Retail nurseries, lawn and garden supply stores	5.5
Shoe stores	3.2
Sporting goods/bicycle stores	3.6
Variety stores	3.6
Women's ready-to-wear stores	4.3

Source: *Industry Norms and Key Business Ratios,* Dun & Bradstreet, Murray Hill, N.J., 1986–87.

will increase. Buyers can find out what customers want by spending time on the selling floor, consulting with customers and salespeople, and studying reliable market information. And by carefully following a plan, buyers can purchase goods in sufficient quantities without overstocking a department or store.

Better Pricing

Pricing goods too high leads to slow stock turnover. If this situation occurs, buyers or retailers should immediately mark down the goods to a price that will cause customers to buy. A general rule is to make the first markdown the "best" markdown to stimulate customer buying.

Accurate Stock Control

Accurate stock control helps to increase turnover. It shows which items are selling well

One way to increase stock turnover is to mark down the price of merchandise.

and which are not. Stock control also indicates the maximum number of items that should be in stock. This eliminates buying too much stock, which reduces stock turnover. Also, accurate records are necessary to calculate stock turnover.

Efficient Stockkeeping

Turnover can be increased by efficient stockkeeping practices that reduce damages in handling and assembling. Proper stockkeeping procedures protect merchandise from soiling, spoilage, and water, heat, or age damage—all of which prevent rapid turnover. Prompt restocking of shelves will prevent the store from running out of floor stock and keep turnover rates high.

Coordinated Promotion

Stock turnover can be increased by buyers who use a coordinated plan for advertising, display, and personal selling. Advertised items that are both displayed in store windows and promoted by sales personnel on the selling floor arouse the customer's interest and increase sales. To ensure that salespeople give correct information regarding promotion campaigns, retailers should offer their sales staffs training in selling techniques. Promotions lose their effectiveness when the sales staff is not adequately trained or informed.

Other Considerations

Obviously, stockturns are only general guidelines. There are certain considerations why retailers can't strictly adhere to them with respect to specific items. These considerations include the following:

1. Minimum quantities of an item may have to be purchased. Because of such purchases, the average inventory cannot be reduced enough to maintain the stockturns desired.

2. An opportunity to obtain quantity discounts on large volume purchases may exist.

In cases where it pays to take the discount, the average stock on hand will be larger, causing the stockturns to be smaller than desired.

However, the lower cost of the purchase garnered from a quantity discount may enable the buyer to reduce the retail price. This, in turn, may increase sales volume and increase the stock turnover.

Doug Smith, as well as other retailers, large and small, must keep informed of the turnover of merchandise. With today's frequently changing customer preferences for new product models, styles, and colors, retailers can't tie up their selling space in yesterday's outdated merchandise "dogs." Stock-turnover analysis is a valuable merchandising tool that helps retailers to make buying, pricing, stockkeeping, and promotion decisions.

T RADE TALK

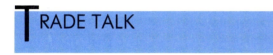

Define each term and use it in a sentence.

Average stock	Cost method of inventory valuation
Retail method of inventory valuation	Stock turnover by units
Stock turnover	
Stock turnover by dollars	

C AN YOU ANSWER THESE?

1. How is stock turn by units calculated?

2. How is the average stock figure calculated for a year period?

3. How is stock turnover by dollars calculated?

4. What advantages are there to a retailer in having a high stock turnover? What risks?

5. What are four strategies for increasing stock turnover?

6. What are two reasons why retailers can't adhere strictly to planned stockturns?

CHAPTER
55 *Buying for a Profit*

Doug Smith had made an important merchandising decision. He had decided to add a new skiing department, with skis, skiwear, and accessories, to his motorcycle and snowmobile store. He believed that his customers would buy downhill and cross-country ski equipment, as his store was located near ex-

cellent ski slopes and resorts. He also believed that related skiwear and accessories would complement his ski equipment.

Since Doug had never handled this type of merchandise before, he called again upon the advice of Mr. Jenkins, his business counselor. Mr. Jenkins cautioned Doug by saying, "Be-

r business hasn't handled these lines
ou need to consider several mer-
g policies and determine certain
s before you add the new merchan-

■

CONSIDER MERCHANDISING POLICIES

Merchandising policies affect the planning and buying of a merchandise line or assortment. Merchandise image, brand policies, and pricing policies all affect buying decisions for a business.

Merchandise Image

In Doug's business, motorcycles and snowmobiles as well as a repair service had been the primary emphasis. Could he extend the personality or image—the way customers feel about the business—to new lines of products?

Doug should ask these questions:

1. What kind of business are we?
2. What kind of business do we want to become?
3. Who are the customers (target market) we want to attract?
4. Will we gain or lose certain customers because of merchandise changes?
5. Will our image be blurred or confused by offering different products or using different merchandising techniques?
6. What special kinds of advertising, display, and promotion(s) are necessary to communicate our desired image?

Brand Policies

Doug will have the choice of selecting international, national, private, and in certain cases, unbranded or custom-made ski equipment and clothing. Rossignol, Elan, and Olin are internationally known brand names for skis.

Obermeyer, Fera, and Roffe are brand names for knowledgeable ski clothing customers. Retailers who carry national brands know that their customers recognize brand names. This works to the store's advantage, largely because it means that less selling effort will be needed. A disadvantage is that the wholesale cost of such products is usually higher. However, manufacturers of national brand merchandise advertise nationally and locally, all of which benefits the retailer.

Private brands carry the label of an individual store. The store usually has a manufacturer make the items for it according to predetermined specifications. The wholesale price for private-labeled merchandise is generally lower than that of nationally branded merchandise. However, private brands must be advertised more extensively by the retailer because they are not nationally known.

Custom brand products are "tailor-made" to satisfy unique customer tastes, requests, or whims. Custom brand offerings for skis, as well as customized clothing, automobiles, vans, motorcycles, and so on, are a growing type of merchandise. Often new, smaller businesses will add special-appearance features, trim, or accessories to regular products. A disadvantage of custom brands is the relative expense of carrying or producing such products and the limited number of potential customers.

Pricing Policies

Most retailers have a specific pricing policy that sets both minimum and maximum retail price lines for merchandise. Using these price lines, buyers determine if a particular choice of merchandise at a certain wholesale price will meet planned expense and profit requirements. For example, a supplier offers to sell skis to Doug at a wholesale price of $240. Similar skis have been selling at a retail price of $300. The retailer knows that a markup of 30 percent of the retail price, or $90 ($300 × 30% = $90), must be obtained to cover necessary expenses and obtain a profit. For the $300 price line of skis, this ski line is too expensive unless the wholesale price is renegotiated. By establishing retail price lines, the buyer—in this case Doug—has a guide to use when selecting individual items or assortments.

Price lining also helps simplify stock control. Price lining, as discussed in Chapter 51, means setting up a limited number of price categories for a given type of merchandise. By having an established price line, the buyers can determine the popularity of various types of merchandise. When markdowns are necessary, customers can more readily recognize savings from established price lines. Price lining also reduces confusion in the customer's mind regarding regular and sales prices. Established price lines do contribute to a store's image in terms of a customer's being able to more easily identify the prices and qualities of merchandise carried.

■

TYPES OF BUYING PROCEDURES

"Doug, as we discussed earlier, a wise retailer needs to establish certain types of buying procedures." Mr. Jenkins advised Doug to consider the following types of buying procedures for the various merchandise handled by his business. He may use a certain type of procedure based on the unique aspects of the merchandise line.

Replenishment Buying

Some types of stores use a basic stock list in preparing an assortment of staple merchandise (goods that should always be kept in stock). When the merchandise on hand reaches this amount, a **replenishment order**, or replacement order, of the goods is made to cover projected sales for a specified sales period. In Doug's business, motor oil would be an example of goods ordered by a replenishment procedure.

Many large retail chains prepare **seasonal information sheets (SIS)** or never-out stock lists for stores in their districts. These lists inform local managers of the quantities and types of preplanned shipments of staple merchandise. Managers can adjust or cancel such shipments if they can offer valid reasons for doing so. With the increased use of electronic cash registers connected with computers in district or home buying offices, staple merchandise is centrally bought and automatically replenished whenever possible.

Anticipation Buying

Anticipation buying is acquiring new goods that may not have been previously available for sale. Buying new, fashion ski clothing is an example of anticipation buying. In this situation Doug would not have past sales records to use as a guide in making purchases. So he would have to make a logical analysis based on supplier information, articles in trade magazines, recommendations by sales personnel, and knowledge of competitors' purchases. For untested merchandise, many buyers are cautious regarding their anticipa-

Personal computers help small business owners keep track of their inventory, and by analyzing the data, the retailer knows when to reorder.

tion buying. They will buy a limited quantity early in the selling season to obtain the reactions of sales personnel and customers. By following this practice, they can avoid overstocking with slow-selling merchandise. They will still have enough time during the selling season to order additional items for which a strong demand exists. In this case, since Doug is adding new merchandise lines, anticipation buying is very wise.

Consignment Buying

Goods sold **on consignment** remain the property of the seller. Buyers don't have to pay for the goods until the store sells them. Buyers assume the responsibility for safeguarding the merchandise and maintaining it in a salable condition. Any merchandise not sold may be returned to the seller. This is a desirable arrangement when retailers don't want to invest money in goods that may not sell. Manufacturers often ship on consignment to encourage retailers to stock their line. New products are sometimes introduced on a consignment basis. Consignment buying also has disadvantages. The price for such merchandise is higher, and there may be difficulties between the retailer and the seller about damages or returns.

Memorandum Buying

When vendors sell goods to buyers on the condition that buyers may return any unsold goods, the goods are said to be sold **on memorandum**. For example, if a vendor ships goods to a store on May 1 "on memorandum until June 15," the buyer may return any unsold goods by June 15. The title of the goods passes to the buyer, but losses are not suffered on items that are not sold. The buyer must, however, pay for the goods when they are billed, and refunds are allowed for goods returned. Doug would need to negotiate these terms with a vendor.

■

ASSESS CUSTOMER WANTS AND NEEDS

In Doug's buying decision regarding adding new merchandise lines, he cannot rely on last season's record as a guide in planning merchandise assortments. Instead, he must assess the current pulse or buying temperature of customers to identify preferences and reactions to new and established products. Buyers have two valuable means to assess this—want slips and customer contact.

Use Want Slips

To learn about the demand for items temporarily out of stock, retailers use want slips. The key to a successful want-slip procedure lies with the salesperson's careful recording of customer requests. (See the illustration below.) Before deciding to buy new items appearing on want slips, buyers must decide whether such items appeal to enough customers to increase sales and whether they are in line with the type and quality of goods usually carried.

Want slips record customers' requests for items that are not in stock. They help a buyer or manager to discover customer preferences.

Contact Customers

Although the obvious way to find out what customers expect a store to handle is to ask them, few firms do this. Some larger stores conduct fashion counts to observe what people are wearing. There are, however, several ways to obtain customer feedback. One is to distribute a questionnaire to people as they shop in the store. A questionnaire may be sent to credit customers, asking them what kinds of goods and services they would like the store to handle.

Another way to find out what the customer wants is through use of a consumer panel. Businesses of all sizes can organize a small group of customers who advise management on new products, styles, store policies, and other issues. For example, stores that sell primarily to teenagers have successfully used panels of young people to keep management aware of teenage wishes. (Additional discussion of marketing research techniques is included in Chapter 13.)

■

SELECT THE ACTUAL MERCHANDISE

There are many factors that influence a buyer's decisions concerning merchandise assortments. The final decision, however, will depend on the buyer or store owner-manager's thorough analysis and judgment. The buyer also considers the following questions regarding merchandise selection.

1. *The quality of the products.* Are the products of the quality that the store's customers expect? Is the quality obvious, or must it be explained to the customers? Will the quality result in customer satisfaction, or will it bring complaints, adjustments, and additional service calls? Has a testing laboratory evaluated the quality of the merchandise? Is the merchandise quality consistent with the store's image?

2. *The reputation of the manufacturer/supplier of the product.* Does the manufacturer or supplier have a reputation for prompt deliveries? Is the manufacturer's stock large enough to let orders be filled quickly? What credit terms and returned-goods allowances does the supplier offer? Does the manufacturer maintain a uniform quality of goods? Is the firm likely to go out of business and leave the buyer without replacement stock or parts?

3. *The profit potential of the product.* Will the product stimulate repeat business? Can the product be sold at a low markup as a trade builder? Will the product promote the sale of related items? Can the product be sold in large amounts and thus earn quantity discounts that add to profits?

4. *The retail price of the product.* Does the product fit the store's price lines? Will the spread between the retail price and the cost price provide enough margin for adequate profits? Are the retail prices in line with the merchandise plan for the department?

5. *The promotional support needed by the product.* Is national advertising available from the manufacturer (supplier)? Can the firm "tie into" the advertising through local and in-store promotions? Are promotion devices such as coupons, banners, demonstrations, and allowances for local advertising available? How much advertising or other promotion effort must the store provide?

6. *The sales support needed by the product.* Will the supplier provide sales training for sales personnel? Will the item need much effort by sales personnel to overcome sales resistance? To what degree is the item "presold" to customers through the use of manufacturer's or suppliers' advertising and promotion?

7. *The package utility of the product.* Does the package have visual sales appeal? Does the packaging protect the goods in storage and delivery? Does the shape of the package make it easy to store and wrap?

8. *The relationship of the product to existing lines.* Does this item duplicate something in the retailer's present line or assortment? Does this item compete with another in price and quality? Should this item be purchased to replace one now carried?

Mr. Jenkins summarized his comments by saying to Doug, "Buying the right products or services may appear to be like looking into a crystal ball. However, the more you look at the wants and needs of your customers in relation to the kind of business you would like to be, the clearer your buying decisions become. You can thereby increase your chances of buying the right products to realize a profit."

TRADE TALK

Define each term and use it in a sentence.

Anticipation buying   On consignment
Custom brand   On memorandum
Replenishment   Seasonal Information
order   Sheets (SIS)

CAN YOU ANSWER THESE?

1. What are four examples of questions that a buyer could ask regarding a desired merchandise image?

2. What is an advantage and a disadvantage of: (a) national brands, (b) private brands, (c) custom brands?

3. What are two advantages of price lining?

4. What is an advantage of: (a) replenishment buying, (b) anticipation buying, (c) consignment buying, (d) memorandum buying?

5. What are four ways that a buyer can obtain information concerning the wants and needs of customers?

CHAPTER 56 *Obtaining the Best Terms*

"Now that I have decided on the actual merchandise that I wish to buy, how can I obtain the best deal?" This is an underlying question that any retailer such as Doug Smith would ask when negotiations are begun with suppliers. Before negotiations can begin, however, satisfactory sources of supply must be identified and various terms of the purchase need to be agreed upon before necessary purchase orders can be issued. In this chapter, various discount options, payment arrangements, and delivery schedules are explained.

■

LOCATE SOURCES OF SUPPLY

Numerous sources of supply, called merchandise resources, exist for retailers, large or small. These sources offer various services and benefits, depending on the buying needs of the individual retailer:

- Manufacturers' sales representatives, who visit the retailer's place of business
- Wholesalers, often located in larger, central trade areas, who offer such services as storage, financing, and delivery
- Central markets, where resources of similar merchandise are grouped together within an area
- Buying offices, where market information and service are provided to client stores
- Trade association shows, where various distributors display and demonstrate their goods
- International markets, which are located in other countries or are represented by sales personnel in this country

Sales Representatives

Manufacturers' or suppliers' sales representatives who visit stores like Doug's can be valuable merchandising consultants. These representatives often show samples of the latest merchandise and offer suggestions concerning advertising, display, and sales techniques. Because clients are visited in a geographic area, the sales representatives can often provide current information concerning market trends and may offer predictions. Over a period of time, buyers come to depend on certain sales representatives for reliable market information and merchandise supply. These representatives have developed positive relationships with buyers because they have consistently provided dependable product quality, good service, and reliable information.

Wholesalers

Small, independent retail stores also often use the services of wholesalers. Many small-store buyers find it convenient to buy large amounts of goods from wholesalers. **Wholesalers** buy large quantities of merchandise from manufacturers, store the goods in large warehouses, and sell them to retailers in the desired quantities.

Buyers can save time when buying from a wholesaler because they can purchase a large number of different items at one time. Wholesalers usually give quicker deliveries and better credit terms than manufacturers. However, because they are intermediaries, their prices are usually higher than those of manufacturers. Since most wholesalers do a local business, they can advise retailers on merchandising problems and offer useful market information about price trends, new merchandise, and the supply of goods that are in demand.

Central Markets

Buyers preparing to buy do so in their own stores or through visits to the market (locations where merchandise is offered for sale). For most soft-line merchandise, the biggest part of the buying is done on these "trips to the market." Most large cities have a central market where manufacturers of various goods display them periodically. One such market is the Chicago Apparel Mart. It is set up like a shopping mall; the representatives of large manufacturers staff displays where buyers can inspect their merchandise lines. In addition, national shows such as the housewares show in Chicago, the electronics show in Las Vegas, and the furniture show in Dallas are major buying opportunities for retailers.

The number of visits to a market depends on (1) the buyer's nearness to the market, (2) departmental sales volume, (3) market conditions, (4) whether the store has resident buyers (agents permanently located at the market), and (5) store policy. It is the purpose of these trips to purchase merchandise and/or to obtain information on what suppliers are offering, compare ideas with other retailers, and generally get a feel for trends in fashion.

Buyers often visit manufacturers' showrooms in central markets to obtain the best merchandise selections and terms.

Buying Offices

Stores cannot afford to send buyers to the central market as often as they would like. So to maintain contact with the central market, some stores use the services of **resident buying offices**. These offices are located in central market cities and provide information for client stores. There are two types of resident buying offices. The **independent buying office**, sometimes called a "salaried office" or "fee office," is an organization that is independently owned and operated and that actively seeks out noncompeting stores as clients. The **store-owned buying office** is an organization entirely owned by the chain or other stores that it represents.

A buying office is organized in much the same way as the merchandising division within a store. There are merchandise managers, often a fashion coordinator, and market representatives. A **market representa-** **tive** is a specialist in one segment of the market. This representative learns all about this segment and makes that knowledge known to the buyers of client stores.

Trade Association Shows

Doug was offered the following suggestions by Mr. Jenkins, his business counselor, regarding attendance at trade association shows. "When you're at the central market, attend the introductory showings of the new product lines. During this introductory show, notice the reactions of your competitors and other buyers to detect positive or negative reactions to the new models, styles, accessories, and so on. Perhaps you'll be able to determine certain trends so that you can either increase or decrease your planned orders for individual items. You'll need to keep in mind the unique characteristics of your customers and your local market so that you are not overly influenced by the exhibitors or other buyers."

International Markets

Buyers searching for unique, quality merchandise such as sporting goods, arts and crafts, china and crystal, and electronic products use international markets as a major source of their supplies.

Buyers who use international markets have a very interesting career touring the markets of various countries, attending the trade shows in world trade cities, and negotiating with suppliers from different cultures. These buyers must be knowledgeable about import regulations, currency exchange requirements, market trends, and different business practices. In certain cases, firms hire an overseas agent or importer to provide international buying services. Increasingly, U.S. exporters are taking part in central market exhibits and trade association shows throughout the world.

■

NEGOTIATE TERMS OF THE SALE

A retailer such as Doug may have to negotiate with different suppliers for a certain line of merchandise that they all offer. It's not necessarily wise to purchase merchandise from the supplier who offers the lowest price. Buyers must consider the following when negotiating the terms of the sale.

1. *Discounts.* Buyers can frequently negotiate discounts if they buy large quantities, if they pay cash, or if they buy goods early in the season.

2. *Dating.* The length of time buyers have before a bill must be paid greatly affects the amount of cash needed during the trading process.

Delivery. When merchandise arrives on schedule, the store avoids losses due to stock shortages or the rental of extra storage space. Therefore buyers must carefully consider the means of delivery so that the store can save money on transportation.

Types of Discounts

Manufacturers and other suppliers offer several types of discounts to stimulate business and encourage prompt payment of bills. The immediate availability of cash and the quick movement of goods make the granting of a cash discount worthwhile to the supplier. For the buyer who can meet the terms of the sale, the benefits of a discount are obvious. The four most common types of discounts are (1) cash, (2) quantity, (3) trade, and (4) seasonal.

Cash Discounts   Refer to the purchase order to Leatherwood Shops on page 484. Terms of a **cash discount**, which is given for early payment, are indicated on the purchase order. If Doug was offered a 2 percent cash discount, which is shown as 2/10, n/30, the 2 represents the amount of the discount, and the 10 represents the deadline for taking the discount. The 30 represents the number of days within which Doug must make full payment. If Doug had cash available, he should pay within 10 days of the invoice date, or May 16 (May 6 plus 10 days). At that time, he would write a check for $2058. If he paid the bill after the 10 days, he would have to pay $2100 by June 6.

$ 2100	$2100
× 0.02 (cash discount)	− 42 (cash discount)
$ 42.00	$2058

Quantity Discounts   A **quantity discount** is a reduction in price given to retailers who buy in large quantities. If Doug buys a gross (144) of an item instead of a dozen, he might receive a 5 percent discount. The manufac-

Leatherwood Shops 498 Jackson Street Richmond, Virginia 23200					
Ski Shop 861 First Avenue Big Sky, Montana 59000			Purchase Order No. 2315 Date May 6, 19__ Ship Via Freight, F.O.B. By Sky Terms 2/10, net/30 Date Needed May 10, 19__		
Quantity	Stock No.	Description		Net Price	Amount
24	563	Ski jacket, Style 654 Tan, Size 38		$40.00	$960.00
12	385	Ski jacket, Style 781, Navy Blue, Size 38		45.00	540.00
10	471	Ski jacket, Style 229, Brown Size 38		60.00	600.00

APPROVED BY *Douglas Smith, Owner*

A purchase order.

turer or supplier can save manufacturing, selling, storage, and delivery costs by selling items in larger amounts. The retailer obtains a price savings.

Trade Discounts

A **trade discount** is a reduction in price given to a certain class of buyers who perform a needed distribution function. A manufacturer gives a wholesaler a larger discount because the wholesaler provides storage and transportation services. The wholesaler performs needed services that retailers could not supply because of their limited storage and transportation facilities.

Seasonal Discounts

A reduction in price given to those who buy before the usual selling season is called a **seasonal discount**. By paying for fall clothing during April, for example, the buyer may deduct 10 percent from the price on the invoice. The manufacturer or supplier can keep employees working on a regular basis rather than just during the selling season. A seasonal discount reduces the sup-

plier's needs for storage and provides cash for year-round operations. The buyer receives a savings in price.

Types of Dating

The term **dating** refers to the length of time for which sellers extend credit to buyers. The length of dating depends on three factors: (1) the length of the marketing period, which is the time it takes the retailer to sell the article; (2) the length of the selling season; and (3) competitive conditions (for example, a long-established manufacturer may offer different terms from those offered by a manufacturer who is trying to enter the market).

Buyers must negotiate datings because they are interested in dating that allows a longer period of time for taking discounts or for making payment. And sellers must negotiate because they want prompt payment. The most common forms of dating are ordinary and advanced.

Ordinary Dating   Terms such as net 30 or net 60 mean that payment of the invoice must be made within 30 or 60 days of the invoice date. If payment is not made by those dates interest or penalties are added to the total invoice payment due.

Advanced Dating   **Advanced dating** is a method of setting a date following the invoice date to identify when the terms of the sale begin (receipt of goods).

Extra, EOM (end-of-month), and ROG dating are common types of advanced dating.

Extra dating can be expressed as 2/10-60x n30 (x stands for extra). In this case, the retailer has 70 days from the date of the invoice in which to take the discount (10 days plus 60 days) or 90 days in total in which to pay the bill.

Notice that the retailer has 60 extra days before the ordinary dating of 2/10, n/30, begins. Assume that on Leatherwood Shop's purchase order, 60x n30 appeared in place of 2/10, n/30. For the purpose of taking the discount, the invoice date would change from May 6 to July 6.

EOM (end-of-month) dating does not begin until the end of the month of the date shown on the invoice. For example, an invoice dated September 2, with terms of 2/10 EOM n.30, would mean that the cash discount could be taken through October 10. Because the net date calls for 30 days, the bill would have to be paid by October 30.

ROG (receipt-of-goods) dating does not begin until the goods are received in the store. Assume that an invoice was dated September 2, showing 2/10 ROG n.30. If the goods were received by September 10, the store could take the discount if it paid any time before September 20.

If the retailer chose not to take the discount, the bill would have to be paid by October 10. The net period is measured from the date of the receipt of the goods.

Table 1, on page 486, summarizes the dating terms we have discussed.

Types of Delivery

Delivery dates are very important to the retailer, because stock must arrive before customers want it. Buyers can also arrange staggered delivery so that stock shipments are scheduled to arrive at various times. Such arrivals don't overtax the store's storage space. The means of shipment determines not only the speed of delivery but also the cost. Large retailers, such as chains, sometimes buy in carload lots to save money.

When arranging delivery, buyers try to have vendors pay for transportation so that ownership of the goods is assumed only when they reach the store. With this arrangement, buyers save the cost of insurance expenses to protect the shipment because they are not yet the owners of the goods.

Vendors, on the other hand, try to pass these costs on to the buyers' stores. So vendors and buyers must bargain over what is known as the FOB shipping point. The FOB (free-on-board) point determines (1) the point from which the buyer pays the transportation charges and (2) when legal ownership of goods or **title** passes to the buyer.

FOB shipping point and FOB store are the points most commonly used as means of determining who pays for the transportation charges. When **FOB shipping point** is used, the vendor (seller) has title to the goods and responsibility for them until they are delivered to the carrier (the transporting firm). Then the title passes to the buyer, and the transportation charges are paid by the buyer from that point.

When **FOB store** is used as the determining point, the vendor pays all transportation charges. The title passes when the shipment arrives at the buyer's store. For large quantities of goods and long hauls, FOB store point saves the store a great deal of money both in shipping costs and insurance.

TABLE 1 / DATING TERMS

Future Dating Terms	Selected Examples	Explanation of Examples	
		Cash Discount Terms	Net Invoice Terms
Net	Net 30	No cash discount allowed	Net amount due within 30 days of invoice date
Date of Invoice (DOI)	2/10, net 30	2 percent discount within 10 days of invoice date	Net amount due within 30 days of invoice date
End of month (EOM)	2/10, net 60, EOM	2 percent discount within 10 days of the first day of the month following the invoice date	Net amount due within 60 days of the first day of the month following the invoice date
Receipt of goods (ROG)	4/10, net 45, ROG	4 percent discount within 10 days after receiving the goods at the retailer's place of business	Net amount due within 45 days after receiving the goods at the retailer's place of business
Extra	3/10-60 extra, net 90	3 percent discount within 70 days of invoice date	Net amount due within 90 days of invoice date

ISSUE THE PURCHASE ORDER

After negotiating with several merchandise resources at the central market, Doug is now ready to issue purchase orders for specific merchandise. A purchase order is a contract between the buyer and the supplier. This important document must be completed carefully so as to avoid mistakes or disagreements.

The purchase order on page 484 contains the following information:

- Purchase order number
- Date of the purchase order
- Vendor's name and address
- Shipping or delivery instructions
- Date of desired delivery
- Terms of sale

- Description of the merchandise, including quantity, stock number, unit price, and total price
- Signature and title of the person authorizing the purchase

EVALUATE MERCHANDISE RESOURCES

Because of the number and variety of suppliers involved, many stores maintain records evaluating buying experiences with individual resources. These records are called **resource files**. Records of individual purchases are kept on file cards, the card for any given purchase listing the vendor (supplier), the vendor's address, the name of the sales representative, the merchandise offered, and the

```
                          RESOURCE FILE

Merchandise: Posters (movie and rock stars)

Resource: Design for Tomorrow, Inc.      Terms: Cash discount - 2/10
          270 Randolph Road                      Quantity discount - 4% per gross
          Paterson, New Jersey  07512            FOB store

Contact: George M. Wilson, President     Prices: See attached price list.
```

Season	1988	1989	1990
Fall	3,000	7,000	9,000
Spring	5,000	8,000	
Total	8,000	15,000	

```
General Comments: Prompt delivery; very cooperative; generous
                  replacement policy, alert to new ideas.
```

An accurate and up-to-date resource file is very helpful to a buyer.

terms, prices, and delivery schedules involved. There is also a note of whether the delivery was prompt, whether the merchandise was of uniform quality, and whether it sold well. Finally, any other remarks that might influence future buying from this vendor are added.

Doug discovered that selecting and evaluating merchandise resources and negotiating the terms of the sale are challenging and exciting experiences. He now realizes that there are many factors to consider when making buying decisions for his business and—most importantly—for his customers.

TRADE TALK

Define each term and use it in a sentence.

Advanced dating	EOM dating
Cash discount	Extra dating
Dating	FOB shipping point
FOB store	Wholesalers
Independent buying office	Resident buying office
Market representative	Seasonal discount
Quantity discount	Store-owned buying office
ROG dating	
Resource files	Title
Trade discount	

CAN YOU ANSWER THESE?

1. What is an advantage of using each source of supply described in this chapter?

2. What are three "terms" that a buyer negotiates when purchasing goods?

3. What are four different kinds of discounts offered retailers?

4. What are three kinds of dating that allow the buyer extra time to pay the bill and still take a discount?

5. The FOB point determines what two important aspects of the buying contract?

6. Name four pieces of information a buyer would record on a resource file.

57 *Preparing the Merchandise Plan*

Doug Smith was both pleased and disappointed. The addition of the ski line to his Moto-Ski Shop had been a great success. In fact, he was out of stock in most of his cross-country skis. He had placed a reorder for these skis, but the supplier said he couldn't guarantee delivery until the end of January.

The ski clothing was another matter. Doug and his sales staff had been primarily "hardline" merchandisers (motorcycles, snowmobiles, service and repair). Merchandising clothing was a new and challenging experience for all concerned. Doug obtained a quantity discount "deal" on a line of private-brand ski clothing. Unfortunately, the quality and assortment selection of the clothing had not been satisfactory. A competitor, the Ski Chalet, had a much better selection of quality skiwear at lower prices. The ski clothing addition was definitely a disappointment.

Doug decided to visit his cousin, Susan Davis, who had managed a successful sporting goods and sportswear store for the past 5 years. Her store, the Sports Inn, is located in a nearby city close to several major ski resorts.

After listening to Doug's merchandising problems, Susan asked this question: "What type of merchandising plan have you been using?" Doug admitted that his plan had been hit and miss. When he sold out of stock, he reordered. Generally he had been reacting to situations. He was determined to improve his planning so that he could take advantage of merchandising opportunities.

■

WHAT IS A MERCHANDISE PLAN?

Susan offered this example when explaining a merchandise plan:

> A merchandise or buying plan is like a road map. It enables you to identify your destination (your planned sales), the route to follow (your planned beginning and ending inventory), and changes in the route that you may have to take (markups, markdowns, and additional purchases).

A **merchandise plan**, or sales budget, is a projection (or estimate) in dollars of the sales goals of a department, a merchandise line, or an entire store. The merchandise plan is usually made for a definite period of time. Included in the merchandise plan are the monthly sales anticipated by the store, the amount of stock on hand at the beginning and end of each month, and the planned amount of reductions, such as markdowns and shortages.

With this information, you can determine how much money can be used to purchase merchandise. By knowing the amount of money available for purchases and the expected income from sales, you're prepared to take care of financial needs as they arise.

A small business owner, such as Doug Smith, is frequently in close touch with all phases of the store's operations. By being on the job, the owner deals directly with customers every day. Owners of small businesses know that their store's success depends on how well it meets customer needs and lives up to customer expectations. In a single-owner operation, a very basic merchandise plan will guide the merchandising activities.

In a larger business, the merchandising division develops a detailed merchandise plan. This plan helps buyers select merchandise at the right time, thus keeping sufficient stock on hand to meet customer demand. The plan also helps in coordinating the merchandising activities of the various departments in the store so that each department earns a profit. In addition, information from the merchandise plan helps top management judge the efficiency of the executives responsible for the various merchandising operations.

In a service business an owner-manager will prepare a similar plan to identify anticipated sales, necessary supplies and equipment to have available, and various expenses of doing business. The process of completing a business plan is similar to a merchandise plan used by a retailer who sells goods.

■

DEVELOPING A MERCHANDISE PLAN

A merchandise plan allows the retailer to calculate the amount of dollars that can be invested in inventory at a certain time. There are two basic questions that need to be answered when making this calculation:

1. How much money is to be spent?
2. On what merchandise should the money be spent?

Some retailers, such as Doug, answer these questions by spending all the money they have available at the beginning of the selling

season. Others spend money until they no longer see merchandise that they want to stock. A more intelligent approach to buying is to:

1. Plan the open-to-buy (OTB), or the amount of purchases (in dollars) to make throughout a selling season.
2. Plan the proper stock assortment (in dollars *and* in units) for an upcoming selling season.

Open-to-Buy Planning

Open-to-buy (OTB) is a calculation of the amount of merchandise that can be received into stock during any given period without exceeding the planned closing stock level at the end of that period. Most buyers always try to have an open-to-buy amount. It enables them to (1) restock when needed, (2) keep new merchandise coming in to attract customers, and (3) take advantage of an unexpected opportunity to make a good buy. Open-to-buy, for example, helps buyers when some items are selling especially well. If buyers are open to buy, they can place orders immediately. So if they miss an item that customers want, they have funds available to buy a supply.

The procedure in OTB planning is essentially a top-down approach. A planned dollar purchase figure is the end result. Merchandise needs are planned by departments and by classifications of merchandise (stereo sets, bicycles, downhill skis, and so on).

Using Doug's ski clothing merchandise classification as an example, let's calculate the open-to-buy dollar amount for the winter selling period. Merchandise budgeting to arrive at this OTB requires four determinations:

1. Planned sales
2. Planned reductions (markdowns and shortage)
3. Planned ending inventory
4. Planned beginning inventory

Calculating OTB—Beginning of Sales Period

The dollar amount of the merchandise ordered for the selling period must equal the planned sales, plus planned reductions, plus the amount of merchandise planned for the end of the selling period. This process is described in the following formula:

Planned sales + planned reductions + planned ending inventory – beginning inventory = total merchandise needed (OTB—beginning of period)

Suppose that Doug thinks he will have $7500 sales of ski clothing for the period. He expects to have $300 in reductions and $4700 in inventory on hand at the end of the season. He expects to have available $4000 in inventory at the beginning of the period. Therefore, Doug's open-to-buy (total merchandise needed) at the beginning of the period is $8500:

Planned sales	$ 7,500
+ Planned reductions	300
+ Ending inventory	4,700
	$ 12,500
– Beginning inventory	–4,000
Total merchandise needed (OTB)	$ 8,500

Calculating OTB—During the Sales Period

Now suppose that Doug wants to determine how much money is still available to buy ski goggles on any given day during the selling period. To find his open-to-buy, he will need to know the following:

1. The inventory of the merchandise on hand that day (He finds his inventory to be $100.)
2. How much merchandise is on order that has not been delivered by the vendors (Outstanding orders for October amount to $300.)
3. Planned stock for the first of November (He wants to end the month with $150 in inventory.)

4. Planned sales for the month (Estimated sales are $500 for the month of October.)
5. Shortages and planned markdowns (Shortages and planned markdowns for October are $60.)

What is Doug's open-to-buy on that particular day in October? The difference between what he has ($100 + $300) and what he needs ($150 + $500 + $60) is $310. So Doug is still open to buy $310 for the remainder of October.

Assortment Planning

Assortment planning is the second method of merchandise planning commonly used in conjunction with open-to-buy (OTB) dollar planning. An **assortment plan** is the complete range of merchandise within a merchandise classification. In terms of men's shirts, for example, the range of prices, styles, colors, patterns, and materials that are available for customer selection is the assortment plan.

The weakness in OTB planning is its lack of a way of determining how many items in a classification or department should be purchased. Since customers buy in units—one pair of sunglasses, one fishing rod, one scarf—buying plans should reflect unit purchases. To overcome this weakness, assortment merchandise plans are developed. The planning procedure in assortment planning is essentially a bottom-up, rather than a top-down (OTB) approach.

Using the assortment planning procedure Doug, for example, would determine how many dollars to spend for specific units of merchandise. His assortment plan might identify purchases for 12 dozen ski stocking caps, 10 dozen ski goggles, 15 dozen Elan ski bindings, and so on, until all needed merchandise units have been planned for the coming season. An advantage of assortment planning is that, before placing purchase orders, a buyer must think in terms of a balanced assortment of merchandise in units. This more detailed buying plan is of great help when going to market or purchasing from other sources.

In the ideal situation, the total of the assortment plan purchases equals the total dollar amount arrived at through the OTB plan. If the figures aren't similar, the retailer must reevaluate both plans. Have adequate or excessive units or assortments of stock been planned? Are the open-to-buy planned purchases realistic, adequate, excessive? One procedure is, therefore, a check on the other. Consequently, wise buyers use both merchandise planning systems.

■

ELEMENTS OF A MERCHANDISE PLAN

Regardless of whether the open-to-buy and/ or assortment merchandise plan is used, the retailer (buyer) must carefully plan the following elements of a merchandise plan:

1. **Planned sales**—the anticipated amount to be sold
2. **Planned stock**—the amount to be on hand at the beginning of the month (BOM) and the end of the month (EOM)
3. Shortages and planned markdowns—the reductions in planned sales due to markdowns or shortages
4. Retail purchases—the amounts to be ordered
5. Planned markup—the amount of markup needed

Planned Sales

The first and most important element of a merchandise plan is the volume of sales forecast for the period. All other figures are based on those planned sales figure. If a large error

MOTO-SKI SHOP MERCHANDISE PLAN		PRODUCT CLASSIFICATION Ski Caps				
Factor	Year		Sept.	Oct.	Nov.	Total
Sales, dollars	Last year (actual)		500	400	350	1,250
	This year (planned)		500	500	400	1,400
Stock, beginning of month dollars	Last year (actual)		100	100	100	300
	This year (planned)		150	200	150	500
Shortages and planned markdowns, dollars	Last year (actual)	Markdowns	25	25	20	70
		Shortages	25	25	20	70
	This year (planned)	Markdowns	30	30	25	85
		Shortages	30	30	25	85
Retail purchases, dollars	Last year (actual)		550	450		
	This year (planned)		610	510		
Initial markup, percent	Last year (actual)		40	40	40	
	This year (planned)		40	40	40	

A merchandise plan.

is made when the sales volume is being projected, the entire merchandise plan will be inaccurate.

The reason for beginning the merchandise plan with a sales forecast is that the volume of expected sales often determines such factors as:

1. Changes in variable expenses. **Variable expenses**, such as sales commissions or delivery costs, change in direct relation to changes in sales.

2. Changes in fixed expenses. **Fixed expenses**, such as rent, heat, and lighting, do not vary in direct relation to sales. However, if there is a substantial increase in sales, these expenses may increase. For example, a sales increase realized because a new credit program is being offered could affect accounting costs.

3. The need for new funds. Increased inventory and operating funds will be needed to accommodate projected sales increases.

4. Increases (or decreases) in present other expenses, such as storage, display, delivery, or needed salary expenses.

When forecasting sales volume, retailers must consider: (1) past sales, (2) general business conditions, (3) competition, (4) trends in customer demand, and (5) any significant changes in the store's operations or policies.

Past Sales   Analyzing past sales records is useful because they are an indication of what future sales may be. Accurate and complete sales records, including charge accounts, show what types of goods, styles, colors, prices, and quantities customers have bought. Comments regarding why sales on a particular day or period were exceptionally low or high should be analyzed. Adjustments in planned sales may be made because of unusual weather or business conditions in the previous year.

General Business Conditions   When business conditions are good and employment is high, sales may increase or remain at the usual level. Sales often decline when customers are worrying about their next paycheck or when they fear a recession may be developing. Retailers can subscribe to professional trade magazines or special services that provide information on national or regional economic conditions. Area newspapers and bulletins issued by banks, trade associations, and chambers of commerce report local business conditions. Large retail firms maintain their own research departments, which prepare reports on both national and local business conditions and on trends in the consumer market.

Competition   Changes in the nature of the competition affect a buyer's planned sales. For example, if a new sporting goods store opened near Doug Smith's place of business, he would have to revise his sales estimates. The modernization or expansion of an existing store or a change in a competing store's promotion policy may also reduce a buyer's planned sales. On the other hand, if a competitor loses popularity with customers or becomes financially unable to keep the stock demanded by customers, the planned sales estimates should be increased.

Trends in Customer Demand   Changes in customer tastes strongly affect sales. Increased interest in sports means increased sales in sporting goods and active sportswear. From time to time, a fashion trend creates a heavy demand for an item. A buyer should beware of a sudden change in sales. A trend or fad can disappear from the scene as rapidly as it arrived.

Changes in Operations or Policies   Changes in the layout of a store can make one merchandise line more accessible or more attractive to customers and thus open the possibility of more sales. The establishment of a storewide trading-up policy would probably mean a decrease in the sale of lower-priced merchandise and an increase in the sale of higher-priced merchandise.

The larger the business and the more diversified the stock carried, the more complicated it is to project future sales volume, and the higher the risk that predictions will be inaccurate. A small business like the Moto-Ski Shop can often feel the "pulse beat" of what customers want and of community changes and other conditions within the market area. A large store, just because of its size, may lose this feel for customer wants and must depend more on reports such as those given by data processing systems.

Planned Stocks

A buyer's next step in preparing a merchandising plan is to determine the stock required to meet the planned sales volume. This is the factor entitled "Planned Stock Beginning of Month" on the merchandise plan for the Moto-Ski Shop, shown on page 491. The buyer wants sufficient stock on hand to meet customer demand. At the same time, the buyer does not want to invest more money than is available for such purchases.

Although Doug Smith expects to sell $500 worth of merchandise in October, he does not need to have $500 in stock on any given day. He may be able to reorder during the month. Experience has shown him that he must have between $100 and $200 in stock at any given time. Since he expects relatively greater sales in early October, according to his estimate, his first month's stock must be $200. He also plans to have stock worth $150 on hand at the end of the month to carry into November, as is indicated by the merchandise plan.

Shortages and Planned Markdowns

The third section of a merchandise plan involves reductions in sales due to markdowns or shortages. Very seldom, if ever, does the entire stock of each item sell at its original price. For example, Doug Smith knows that he must feature certain accessory merchandise at lower prices to encourage customers to come into his shop. Therefore, he allows $30, or 6 percent of October sales, for planned markdowns.

ENTIRE STOCK OF CHILDREN'S
WINTER OUTERWEAR
20% OFF
THE TICKETED PRICE

FOR GIRLS 4-14 . . . bombers, stadium length jackets and coats in poplins, wool blends and more. Also find this season's latest fashion details. Famous makers in the group.
Little Girls 4-6x, Orig. $30-$104 .... $24-83.20
Big Girls 7-14, Orig. $37-$106 .... 29.60-84.80

FOR TODDLERS 2-4 . . . boys and girls snowsuits in exciting fall colors. Find a variety of fashion details and several famous makers including London Fog, Weathertamer and more.
Orig. $60-$72 .... $48-57.60

LITTLE BOYS 4-7 . . . heavyweight parkas and bombers from London Fog, Pacific Trail and others. Find fashion details. All easy care fabrics. Orig. $55-$66 .. $44-52.80

BIG BOYS 8-20 . . . find Pacific Trail, London Fog and others. Choose parka or bomber styles with fashion details. Easy care fabrics.
Orig. $60-$80 .... $48-$64

Sale ends Mon., Oct. 8.

Toddlers, Dept. 180. Boys, Depts. 183, 440. Girls, Depts. 170, 181.
CHARGE IT WITH YOUR STERN'S OR AMERICAN EXPRESS CARD.

Retailers plan—and customers expect—markdowns at particular times of the year.

Seldom, if ever, does a month go by without a few customers taking merchandise without paying for it. In addition, damaged and faulty merchandise all contribute to shortage expenses. Therefore, although Doug can order stock several times during the month, he still allows $30, or 6 percent of October sales, for shortages. Thus, his total shortages and planned markdowns for October are $60.

Retail Purchases

Careful planning of purchases helps retailers make sure that the right amount of stock is on hand at the right time. No retailer can afford to be either overstocked or understocked. Planned purchases will also vary according to selling season. A decision to buy 1000 snow tires in April to be sold in May, for example, would be an unwise one.

Let's refer again to the example of Doug's merchandise plan. Planned sales for October ($500) minus the difference between retail stock on the first of October and the first of November ($200 − $150) plus shortages and planned markdowns for October ($30 + $30 = $60) equals the planned purchases for the month of October. Look at the calculations in the merchandise plan. See whether you understand how Doug decided to buy $510 worth of merchandise.

Planned Markup

The planned markup is a guide for pricing merchandise as well as for ordering goods that will sell at a given price. It also helps retailers determine the profit margin. (As explained in Chapter 52, the initial markup is the difference between the wholesale cost and the initial selling price given the merchandise.) The markup is commonly expressed as a percentage of the initial selling price (markup on retail). So if the initial retail price for an individual item is $2 and the wholesale cost is $1.20, the difference is 80 cents. Initial markup is 80 cents, or 40 per-

cent ($0.80 ÷ $2) of the initial retail price, $2.

Retailers must be sure that the average markup established for the store is achieved at the end of the planning period. Not all departments in a store operate on the same markup. Fads, high-fashion items, and items that have a low stock-turnover rate require a high markup. Goods that are highly competitive must be sold at a low markup.

■

CONVERTING TO COST FIGURES

Note that, so far, all the elements of the merchandise plan have been figured at retail. Of course, as a buyer, Doug does not pay retail prices when he makes purchases. To determine the amount of money that he can spend at cost, he must adjust the retail figure by the amount of initial markup planned. If the initial markup is 40 percent, the planned $510 of retail purchases for October should be multiplied by the complement of the retail markup (that is, 60 percent). In this case, $306 worth of goods can be purchased at cost price ($510 × .60). This is the actual dollar amount that Doug will pay for purchases in October.

If more goods are on hand and more merchandise on order than Doug estimated he would need for October, he would be overbought. He would not be open to buy. Until Doug took some steps to reduce his stock or to cancel a part of the merchandise on order (sometimes this is permitted, sometimes it isn't), he would not be in a financial position to buy anything during the rest of October. This could be disastrous if he began to run low on some of his best sellers.

Susan concluded her visit with Doug by saying:

So, Doug, there are merchandising planning "tools" that you can use to make important buying decisions. You can appreciate that no one tool or system can provide all the answers to the questions of what should I buy and how many dollars should I spend. However, by applying a top-down (open-to-buy) and bottom-up (assortment planning) approach to merchandise planning, you have a means of evaluating your dollar and unit plans. Just remember that your merchandise plan is a needed road map to assist your business in arriving at its destination of planned sales. If you continually refer to your merchandise plan, your next selling season should be more successful. Good luck.

TRADE TALK

Define each term and use it in a sentence.

Assortment plan	Planned sales
Fixed expenses	Planned stock
Merchandise plan	Variable expenses
Open-to-buy	

CAN YOU ANSWER THESE?

1. What two basic questions are asked when calculating the amount of dollars to invest in inventory?

2. What is a difference between the open-to-buy and assortment planning processes?

3. What are the elements needed to calculate the open-to-buy amount at the beginning of the sales period? During the sales period?

4. If the calculations of total dollar amounts between the open-to-buy and assortment planning are significantly different, what should the retailer (buyer) analyze?

5. What are four factors to consider when planning sales forecasts?

6. How do planning markdowns help achieve a profit for retailers?

7. Why do retailers convert the retail planned purchases to cost figures? Explain the procedures.

ACTIVITIES AND PROJECT —FOR— U·N·I·T 18

RETAIL MARKETING CASES

1. Rick Santana has been assigned the position of buyer for his school store this month. In reviewing the merchandise promotion materials received by his teacher-coordinator, he discovers an interesting brochure from a national supplier describing monogrammed T-shirts. The supplier will furnish T-shirts and will imprint slogans or designs requested by the customers. The store has never handled this line of merchandise before. Develop a questionnaire for potential customers that would aid Rick in deciding whether to add this product line to the store's clothing assortment. On a separate sheet of paper, list at least six points or questions you would include in this questionnaire.

2. A department buyer planned sales of $33,000 for a month, markdowns of $1200, and shortages of $600. At the beginning of the month the stock totaled $30,000 at retail value and was to be reduced to $24,000 by the month's end. On the tenth day of the month, the retail value of goods received was $4500, and goods on order for delivery in the month amounted to $7500 at retail.

1. What purchases should have been planned for the month?
2. What was the OTB on the tenth day of the month?

PROBLEMS

1. Doug Smith's business recorded its total sales and stock inventory from January 31 to June 30 as follows:

Date	Sales	Stock
Jan. 1	$30,000	$40,000
Feb. 1	26,000	42,000
Mar. 1	26,000	40,000
Apr. 1	42,000	60,000
May 1	48,000	60,000
June 1	40,000	50,000
June 30	60,000	75,000

On a separate sheet of paper, calculate the stock turnover for the period from January 31 to June 30.

2. At the central market, you are negotiating for discounts and dating terms with suppliers. You wish to analyze these terms to determine:

a. The amount due if the discount is taken

b. The date when the total amount of the invoice is due

Rule a form like the one on page 497, and use it to complete your analysis.

3. You are a buyer in the coat department of one of your town's leading department stores and are in the process of planning total sales for the period. Sales planning in your store is usually done for a 6-month period, with monthly sales reflecting the store's past sales experience. It is anticipated that the department will sell $120,000 for the 6 months from February to July. Calculate the planned sales for each month on the basis of the following estimated percentages of total sales for each month: February, 36.4 percent; March, 34.2 percent; April, 15.9 percent; May, 6.4 percent; June 4.8 percent; and July, 2.3 percent.

4. The swimwear department has net sales of $100,000. The beginning-of-the-month inventory was $30,000. The end-of-the-month inventory was $20,000. The jewelry department has net sales of $30,000. The beginning-of-the-month inventory was $10,000. The end-of-the-month inventory was $20,000. Which department has the more rapid stock turnover? Which department produces the greater sales return based on inventory investment?

5. A line of automobile air filters sells at the rate of 160 weekly. A reserve stock of 320 is considered necessary, and delivery usually requires 2 weeks.
How many items should be ordered when the stock reaches a level of 250 and 200 are on order?

Amount of Invoice	Date of Invoice	Terms	Amount Due If Discount Is Taken	Date When Total Amount of Invoice Is Due
$500	Sept. 1	2/10, n/30		
$400	Aug. 1	3/10, n/45		
$850	Jan. 1	2/10, n/30, 60 extra		
$1200	July 1	2/10, n/30, EOM		
$3600	Aug. 1	6/10, n/30, EOM, 60 extra		

PROJECT: ANALYZING CURRENT MERCHANDISING PRACTICES

YOUR PROJECT GOAL

Given magazines, newspapers, trade journals, employer training materials, and so on, prepare a written summary report describing current merchandising practices related to one of the topics covered in Unit 18: analyzing stock turnover, buying for a profit, obtaining the best terms, or preparing the merchandise plan.

PROCEDURE

1. Refer to the "Trade Talk" terms at the end of each chapter in Unit 18 for possible merchandising topics.

2. Contact your instructor or employer for possible reference materials.
3. Organize your report using this outline:
    a. Reference selected for study
    b. Date of reference
    c. Title of article or materials
    d. Merchandising practice described
    e. New, interesting, or unique aspects of the merchandising practice.

EVALUATION

You will be evaluated on the completeness of your report.

PLANNING FOR ENTREPRENEURSHIP

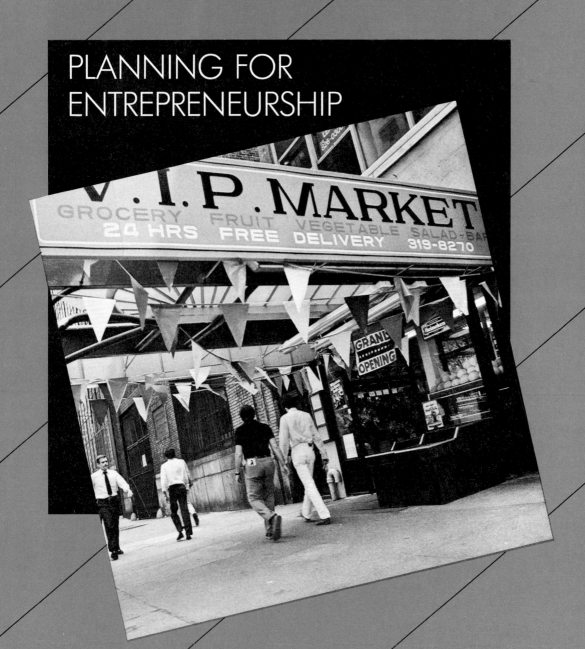

Connie Lee and Brent Ness are recent graduates of a Marketing Education program. They have a dream of someday owning and managing their own music store. They enjoy music and wish to pursue a career helping other people (their customers) enjoy music. You could say that they are future entrepreneurs. An entrepreneur is a person who organizes, manages, and assumes the risk of a business or enterprise.

Often dreams remain dreams unless they are acted upon. In this competency band, Connie and Brent attempt to make their dreams a reality through the development of a business plan. This plan includes such elements as assessing business alternatives, developing a marketing plan, selecting the business location, planning the business design and layout, preparing personnel organization charts, and planning and obtaining financing. All these necessary planning steps lead to that exciting day of their grand opening.

Connie and Brent's business planning experiences will help you gain valuable insights into the development of your own new business plan. If owning a business is not your immediate career goal, you can benefit from these planning experiences in several ways. You can plan a business that you would like to be employed in or manage. Or, you can keep your business plans as a future career alternative. Who knows? Someday you may own and manage that dream business of yours.

BEGINNING YOUR BUSINESS PLAN

C·H·A·P·T·E·R

58 *Identifying Your Business Opportunities*

Stop! Before you go on to the next paragraph, think of the name of a business—any business—that produces or sells any product or service.

Chances are, you thought of a large corporation such as General Motors, Sears, McDonald's, or U-Haul. Yet large corporations make up a very small portion of the total number of businesses in the United States today. By far the largest percentage of American businesses are small. Moreover, a majority of individuals are employed by small businesses.

Interestingly, we deal mainly with small businesses in our daily lives. Why, then, didn't we think of a small local firm—the Fish and Pet Shop or Dave's T-Shirt Shack—when we were asked to name a business? Perhaps because these firms are small and not widely known, we take them for granted.

■

WHAT ARE THE OPPORTUNITIES IN SMALL BUSINESS?

The Small Business Administration (SBA) defines a **small business** as "one which is independently owned and operated for profit and is not dominant in its field."* There are about 14 million businesses in this country. Close to 90 percent of businesses are small, and many are new—up to 8400 new businesses are started in a typical week. The makeup of the small-business sector of Amer-

---

* *The State of Small Business, A Report of the President to the Congress*, May 1986, The U.S. Small Business Administration, p. xi. U.S. Government Printing Office, Washington, D.C., 1986.

ican business is constantly changing. While some businesses are starting, others are being taken over by larger firms, and many, unfortunately, are closing their doors. What does all this mean? It means that small businesses offer ample opportunities for individuals who aspire to become entrepreneurs.

Small Businesses Offer Career Options

Small businesses are responsible for providing a higher percentage of new jobs and career options than large businesses. According to some estimates, new career opportunities created by small businesses account for more than 60 percent of all new jobs in a given year.

Evidently, there are many career opportunities in small business ownership and management. Here are some examples of individuals who are considering launching a new business:

Maria is now 18 and has just graduated from her high school's marketing education program. She plans to remain at her training station to learn more about the business so that someday she can own her own hobby shop. Maria is very skilled in several craft areas. She wishes to convert these hobbies into a lifelong career.

Bill, 17, has just been selected to serve as a manager of the school store in his high school. Bill is excited about this opportunity, as his father has said that if he wished, he could someday become a partner in the family owned business. Experiences obtained ordering merchandise, planning promotions, and managing the school store's operations will pay off in Bill's future career.

Jim, 16, operates and manages his own lawn service business. During the past summer, he cut lawns for more than 15 customers on a monthly service contract basis. He has purchased another, larger, riding lawnmower and a used delivery truck. He plans to hire two of his friends to cut the lawns so

that he can devote more time to developing additional lawn service contracts. Jim plans to study horticulture and marketing in college. He is already on the way to becoming a successful entrepreneur.

Susie, 18, has just completed a visit with the school counselor regarding her possible career plans. She has analyzed her interests and discussed her personality profile tests. Susie has a desire for independence, a willingness to find and accept a challenge, and is often bored with routine types of activities. Susie realizes that she would be happiest where she could eventually be her own boss. She plans to continue her education after high school. In her college program she wishes to become involved in a business internship with a franchise firm where she can gain merchandising and management experiences. Someday she hopes to manage her own franchise business.

At age 19, John Shorb was a successful entrepreneur, managing his own lawn service.

Acquiring the Entrepreneurial Spirit

Maria, Bill, Jim, and Susie have what is sometimes called the **entrepreneurial spirit**—the desire to create a new venture or business. Researchers have suggested that a variety of personal characteristics, such as independence, self-confidence, determination, creativity, and ability to take calculated risks, all contribute to the entrepreneurial spirit.

As you recall from Chapter 9, an entrepreneur is defined as one who organizes, manages, and assumes the risks of a business or enterprise. Even if you do not at present consider it realistic to start your own business, you should be aware of the fact that large corporations seek individuals who possess this entrepreneurial spirit. In many larger retail firms, individuals are often responsible for their own department or enterprise. These employees are called **intrapreneurs**.

For some people, becoming a successful entrepreneur can be compared to climbing a ladder. An initial step to climb this career ladder is to obtain managerial experiences. A new firm's success depends on the abilities of the owner-manager. The owner-manager must be able to direct the firm's personnel, develop its marketing strategies, plan its finances, and supervise its day-to-day operations. This owner-manager must handle sales, advertising, purchasing, pricing, and a variety of other business functions. The knowledge and ability to do so are most often acquired by working for other firms in the same kind of business. Through such experiences it is possible to gain the confidence that builds your entrepreneurial spirit.

■

WHY PLANNING IS SO IMPORTANT

Successful entrepreneurs must be planners *before* they can become new business own-er-managers. Planning a new business begins with gathering and evaluating data, studying trends, identifying potential markets, assessing competition, estimating costs, and many other activities. After analyzing available information, a written business plan should be developed that outlines a detailed course of action for starting and operating a new business.

Unfortunately, too many eager entrepreneurs push ahead impulsively, without paying much attention to planning. The result is frequently business failure. Adam Osborne, the entrepreneur who started the Osborne Computer Corporation, is such an example. His company manufactured an innovative, portable computer. A lack of planning regarding how to meet new competition forced the company into bankruptcy. Today, other computer firms successfully market portable computers.

Planning, in effect, reduces unnecessary, foolish risks. A successful entrepreneur can be more accurately described as a "risk reducer" than a "risk taker."

■

CRITERIA FOR EVALUATING NEW BUSINESS OWNERSHIP POSSIBILITIES

In this unit and those that follow, you will be given the opportunity to plan your own business. This business may handle any product and/or service of your choice.

Assignments and projects at the end of each unit will assist you in completing a written business plan. Various planning checklists and questions will enable you to follow planning processes used by many new business owner-managers. During the initial phase of your business planning you will need to answer the important questions discussed in the following paragraphs.

What Are Your Interests?

A major reason you may want to open your own business is that you want to be doing the kind of thing you like to do. This might include your current interest in some particular line of products or services.

You may love beautiful clothes, for example, or you may be a sports enthusiast. Or perhaps you recall enjoyable times shopping for something you like. Whatever product or service you choose to sell, it should be something you will be interested in and enjoy being around. After starting the business, you'll be spending most of your waking hours with these products or services, displaying them on shelves or repairing certain items, reading about them, and explaining them to customers. They'll really become a part of your life, so choose your business idea with care.

What Is Your Past Experience?

Not only is interest in a particular type of business important, but knowledge and experience will also be valuable as you progress in retail marketing. The more you know about the products and services you are going to be marketing, the easier it will be to sell them. For example, if you're going to open a bicycle shop, it will be useful to know about the various models—which ones are designed for street use or racing, how to figure out the various gear ratios, and the unique features of each model. You should enjoy biking and take an active interest in the latest developments in bicycle technology. You will thereby be able to answer questions your customers might ask. Also, your enthusiasm for whatever you sell will influence your customers. You will find it a lot easier to sell products and services that you value and enjoy.

The best experience would be actually to work in the type of business you plan to open. By working as a salesperson you can get first-hand knowledge in dealing with that particular type of clientele. You can observe your manager and the other salespeople to see how they handle difficult customers, or how they turn a "just-looking" customer into a final sale. You may also get a chance during this time to learn a great deal about the products you're selling, to observe changes in fashions and customer needs, and to become aware of general marketing trends.

What Business Do You Really Want to Be In?

In considering new business alternatives, a major question to answer is: What business should I really be in? This question may initially seem silly. "If there is one thing I know," you may say to yourself, "it is what business I want to be in." Some owner-managers have gone bankrupt and others have wasted their savings because they did not accurately define their businesses. Actually, they were confused about what business they really were in and strayed into unfamiliar, dangerous ground.

Consider this example. Mr. Amos, on the West Coast, maintained a lakeside dock. He also sold and rented boats. He thought he was in the marina business. But when he got into financial trouble and asked for outside help, he learned that he was not just in the marina business. He was in several businesses. He was in the restaurant business with a dockside cafe, serving meals to boating parties. He was in the real estate business, buying and selling lots. He was in the boat repair business, buying parts and hiring a mechanic as demand arose.

Mr. Amos was trying to be too many things and couldn't decide which venture to put money into and how much return to expect. What slim resources he had were unnecessarily divided. Before he could make a profit on his sales and get a return on his investment, Mr. Amos had to decide what business he really was in and concentrate on it. After much study, he realized that he should stick to the marina format—buying, selling, and servicing boats.

Decide what business you are in and write it down—define your business. To help you decide, think of answers to questions like: What do I buy? What do I sell? What products or services do people want? What is it that I am trying to do better or more of or differently from my possible competitors? Write down your answers to questions such as these when deciding the priority goals of your new business.

What Is The Market Potential?

New York City probably has at least one specialty store of every type that a large, diversified population might require. But in a smaller market many of those stores would die from lack of customers.

Why is this the case? All of us need to buy shoes, clothes, and food on a fairly regular basis. On the other hand, how many of us are interested in exotic pets, stamp collecting, or kite building? If only a small percentage of the population in a trading area are potential customers for a particular item, one needs a large population on which to draw.

Suppose you plan on opening a clothing business and you learn that your market area already has three shoe stores, five clothing stores, and two general merchandise department stores. Can it support another clothing-related business? Possibly. Perhaps your market area could use another clothing store that appeals especially to teenagers, one that sells mod clothing for high school students or one that features sportswear. Look for a potential business in your market area which does not now exist and for which there is a real need. Maybe a lot of people shop outside this area because there is no local business that offers desired items or services.

It is vitally important to make sure that you have a potential clientele large enough for your business. Even in a big city, where the chances of finding customers are better, make certain that your business will be located near potential customers. You should be able to identify who these potential customers are—by age, location, income, education, and buying habits.

Who Is Your Competition?

It's important to analyze your competition in any location. If you are going to open a gift shop, how many other shops are in the area, what kinds of gifts do they sell, how popular are they, how well operated are they? Don't think that the lack of any evident competition is a ticket to sure business success. The fact that there is no craft-supply store in your town may simply mean that your town can't support one. If you're thinking of a new kind of business (which your city doesn't already have), first try to learn if anyone has tried that type in the past and failed. Visit similar businesses in other market areas.

Is Your Business Idea a Fad?

Ask yourself what kinds of businesses are in abundance today that you did not see 2, 5, or 10 years ago. How about the T-shirt shop, the boutique, the health-food store? How many of these businesses will make it in the future? It's hard to tell how long a fad will last, or whether something new is here to stay, but you should at least consider such things. You'll also have to take into consideration what the larger businesses are doing to your market area. For example, have many furniture warehouses that offer discount prices taken customers away from the standard furniture stores? If you are thinking of opening a stereo equipment store, study what effect such big chains as Sears Roebuck and Montgomery Ward might have on your market potential. Be aware of marketing trends and fads and how they might affect your business in the future.

SHOULD YOU CONSIDER BUYING A GOING BUSINESS?

Some of the advantages of buying a going business are that it will save you the time and effort of setting up your own store with equipment and stock. You will probably start with ready-made customers who have grown accustomed to buying at this store. The owner should give you the benefit of previous business experience by explaining the daily operation of the store. If the store already has a good reputation, you can profit from having loyal customers.

There are, however, possible disadvantages to buying a going business. The present owner may be asking too high a price for what is actually being offered. You should ask yourself these questions: Does the business have a negative reputation? Is it in an undesirable or declining location? Is it poorly equipped? Is the store filled with a lot of unsalable merchandise? If the answer to any of these questions is "yes," you would have many headaches if you bought that business. Try to find out why the current owner wants to sell the business.

SUMMING UP

It's important that you take the time to choose carefully the type of business you'll open. Of course, you'll want to work with a kind of merchandise or service in which you have some interest or knowledge, or both. The more you know about the products and services and the more experience you've had using and selling them, the better chance you will have for success.

You must also take into consideration the sales potential of your market area. In a larger city there will be greater opportunity for spe-

Buying a franchise is an alternative to starting a new business or buying a going business.

cialization and variety of merchandise than in a smaller market area. Additionally, you should consider the characteristics of the population—age, education, location, income, interests, and so on. Even the climate and recreational facilities are important considerations, especially for stores that specialize in sporting equipment and outer clothing.

Once you have matched your interest and experience with the needs of the market area, you will have to analyze carefully your potential competition. If your town has five gift shops barely struggling to survive, opening a sixth one is asking for trouble. Finally, be careful not to open a business at the peak of a particular fad. Such a business may either have a very short life span or you may end up being smothered by discount prices of the larger stores.

6 Open for Business

5 Acquire the Money You'll Need

4 Put the Business Down on Paper

3 Make Sure There's a Market Opportunity

2 Select a Business That's Right for You

1 Make the Self-employment Decision

The steps that lead to the opening of your own business.

In the remaining chapters and units of this band you will be given opportunities to develop a written plan for a business of your choice. Even though you may not start your own business in the near future, the experiences in developing this business plan will help you in acquiring that "entrepreneurial spirit" necessary for success in any business.

TRADE TALK

Define the following terms and use each one in a sentence.

Entrepreneurial spirit   Small businesss
Intrapreneur

CAN YOU ANSWER THESE?

1. How has the Small Business Administration defined a small business?

2. List five personal factors that contribute to an individual's degree of "entrepreneurial spirit."

3. What is the first step on the career ladder leading to becoming an owner of your own business?

4. What are three examples of planning information and data required when developing a new business?

5. What is meant by the statement, "A successful entrepreneur can be more accurately described as a risk reducer than a risk taker?"

6. What are three important questions that should be answered when evaluating new business possibilities?

7. According to what three characteristics can the potential customers of a new business be identified?

8. What are two advantages and two disadvantages of buying a going business?

C·H·A·P·T·E·R

59 *Developing Your Business Plan*

Brent Ness and Connie Lee plan to be married after they complete their educations. They both wish to work together someday in the development and management of their own business.

"We've got this great idea!" they explained to their local banker, Mr. Ramos. "Of course, we'll need to borrow a certain amount of money before this idea can become a reality," they admitted.

Mr. Ramos, an experienced small business loan officer, continued to listen to Brent's and Connie's new business idea. He then asked them a very important question. "Do you have your ideas written down in the form of a business plan?"

"Well, not really. How should we do that?" was the response of both Brent and Connie.

Mr. Ramos introduced the importance of a written business plan by saying:

The business plan is very important if you need to borrow money or seek investors to get your business going. Bankers, like myself, or investors will want to study your plan to see if your business promises to be profitable. Only then will they consider loaning you money or investing in your company. The business plan gives you a guide to follow in planning and managing your business. The business plan should not be an afterthought, nor should it be fixed in concrete. It should be changed as conditions in the marketplace change. Let's review the basic organization of a business plan. I'll also show you a summary of an actual business plan so that you can better understand the total plan.

■

HOW IS THE BUSINESS PLAN ORGANIZED?

A **business plan** outline or framework generally has five major sections:

1. A description of the business
2. The marketing plan
3. The personnel organization plan
4. The financial plan
5. The business plan summary

Section 1. A Description of the Business

Section 1 introduces the reader, such as a potential financial lender, to the business by stating the name of the business, the name(s) of the owner-manager(s), the occupational experiences of the owner-manager(s), the type of business, and the product or service to be sold.

Section 1 also describes the proposed or actual business location, its features, and how it supports the marketing plan. (See Chapter 61—"Selecting Your Business Location.") The building and its layout for selling products or offering services are also included. (See Chapter 62—"Planning the Business Design and Layout.")

The names and business backgrounds of advisors or consultants who have assisted you with your business plan are often included in this section. Providing this information improves the credibility of your business plan.

Section 2. The Marketing Plan

Section 2 tells the reader how the product or service will be marketed to make a profit. It describes your potential customers, their buying habits, and their location. Your competition is analyzed in terms of the marketing methods used and share of the market. In this section you should discuss how your business will be superior or unique in relation to the competition. Most important, you should identify your marketing strategies for attracting and retaining customers. The development of the marketing plan is discussed in Chapter 60.

Section 3. The Personnel Organization Plan

In Section 3, you will discuss how you plan to organize and manage the business. This section includes information about your man-

agement personnel and their qualifications. You will describe the needs for employees and how you will employ, pay, train, and supervise them. An organization chart for the business should be included. Also mentioned are any personnel policies involving employee benefits. Chapter 63 focuses on ways to develop the personnel organization plan.

Section 4. The Financial Plan

This section tells the reader how you expect to use the loan or the investment in your business. It includes an operating or profit-and-loss statement, a balance sheet, and a projected cash-flow statement. These statements, as well as steps in preparing the overall financial plan, are discussed in Chapter 64.

Section 5. The Business Plan Summary

The business plan summary should contain only two or three pages and review the main points of the business plan for the reader. In many cases the potential financial lender will want a concise, one-to-two-page abstract or review of the major reasons why it would be advantageous to provide financial backing.

■

A SAMPLE BUSINESS PLAN SUMMARY

A sample "Business Plan Summary" describing the proposed *Railroad Station Restaurant* highlights essential elements of a business plan. Each element of the business plan summary would be described in more detail in the main body of the plan. (Succeeding chapters of this text discuss how to plan and develop these elements.)

BUSINESS PLAN SUMMARY

Description of the Business

Name of Business. Railroad Station Restaurant

Owner-to-be. Jacques Aslan; to operate the business as a sole proprietor with plans to incorporate in the near future.

Occupational Experiences of the Owner-Manager. Mr. Aslan has over twelve (12) years of restaurant management experience, ranging from maitre d' at Venetos in San Francisco to his current position as manager of the Colony Kitchen in Vallejo. He has supervised as many as forty (40) people, managed a dining room seating one-hundred-twenty-five (125), and been responsible for full management of several restaurants.

Type of Business. A 1920-style railroad restaurant (an old-fashioned theme restaurant), a small antique/gift shop, and a banquet operation.

Location. To be located at the intersection of Highway 29 and Canyon Road; serving a trade area that extends roughly twenty-five (25) miles in all directions and includes the communities of Vallejo, Fairfield, Napa, Sonoma, and Calistoga. These communities are prime market areas for an attractive, medium-priced, table-service restaurant.

Marketing Plan

Potential Customers. The market area comprises an estimated population of 250,000. The traffic count on Highway 29 adjacent to the site is 19,500 per day. The traffic count on Canyon Road adjacent to the site is 20,000 per day. The demand for "concept" restaurants offering a total experience in dining is high in this relatively affluent area.

Competition. The theme, atmosphere, decor, excellent service, and food will provide an attractive alternative to the limited-menu fast-food chains common to the area. At the present time, there are a limited number of full-service banquet restaurants within a 10-mile radius of the proposed location. The nearest competition offering banquet services are the Sheraton and Holiday Inn located in the city of Napa.

Marketing Strategies. The restaurant is designed to function as a one-stop, full-service tablecloth restaurant that will serve, feed, and entertain the motorist trade on Highway 29 and the local population of the Napa Valley area. Lunch and dinner service will include a complete meal, appetizers through dessert. The restaurant will feature a full line of fresh food prepared on the premises by a highly qualified chef. Railroad Station Restaurant's reputation will be based on the careful selection and skillful preparation of fine foods, graciously served in a distinctive dining room. Names of entrees will be derived from early Napa-Vallejo railroad historical events and will be matched by the interior decor. Prices will be moderate to attract the family and middle-income tourist customers.

The restaurant will include a fireplace and follow the station house decor. The gift shop will serve as a tourist information center for travelers to Lake Berryessa and the towns of Sonoma and Calistoga. It will merchandise gifts, touring maps, and early railroad souvenirs, including historical train books and photographs. The banquet operation will offer a complete lunch and dinner menu for business, industries, special groups, and parties. It will feature hors d'oeuvres, fruits, hot entrees, and desserts.

Personnel Organization Plan

There will be a staff of approximately thirty (30) full/part-time employees at time of start-up. Personnel levels will be adjusted after the first few months of operation and will fluctuate with seasonal variations in patronage. (An organization chart as well as individual job descriptions are included in the main body of the business plan.)

Financial Plan

Sources of Finances. A three-party investment plan is proposed. Mr. William G. Elliott of Vallejo will arrange for the construction of the 5000-sq.-ft. restaurant on leased property at Highway 29 and Canyon Road. Mr. Elliott will equip and furnish the restaurant to specifications satisfactory to Mr. Aslan. Mr. Aslan, upon approval of his loan, will enter into a lease agreement with Mr. Elliott. The china, kitchenware, inventory, minor furniture, and equipment will be provided by Mr. Aslan. (Refer to the proposed lease and layout sketch of the building in the main body of the business plan.)

Records and Controls. Both food and beverage sales will be recorded and controlled with electronic registers to ensure control over sales, expenses, and profits. Accounting and financial statements will be prepared by a certified public accountant. (See the Financial Plan section of the Business Plan for the proposed Operating [Income and Expense] Statement, Balance Sheet, and Cash Flow Statement.)

The business plan summary provides a quick reference for potential lenders.

As you can see, this Business Plan Summary is intended to provide an overall understanding of the major aspects of a new business. References are made to additional detailed plans, charts, layouts, budgets, and other documents in the main body of the business plan.

■

SUGGESTIONS FOR DEVELOPING A BUSINESS PLAN

A business plan serves as a map to owning and operating a small business. It is a description of what a business does, how it operates, how it is managed, and how it functions financially. It helps identify the strengths and weaknesses of the proposed business.

As the future owner-manager of a new business, your responsibility is to plan the details of every part of the proposed venture. You need to collect information carefully and organize your findings using a well-organized format. After you have prepared the business plan, you will be able to find out whether or not you can make a profit, and, if so, when this is likely to happen. Thus, you will probably see the need for changes that can be made on paper before the business opens and before you make costly mistakes.

Use Experienced Business Advisors-Consultants

"Two heads are better than one," goes the old saying. As a new business owner-manager it is critical that you seek the advice of an experienced business advisor or consultant. You should contact a present or former business owner-manager who is operating or has operated a business similar to the type and size that you are planning. Your instructor can often provide information regarding the names of such individuals.

An experienced business consultant can provide valuable advice in developing a business plan.

The Small Business Administration (SBA) can be another source of business advisers or consultants for your new business. A business consulting service entitled SCORE/ACE is offered through the SBA offices. **SCORE** stands for the Senior Corps of Retired Executives. **ACE** stands for the Active Corps of Executives. Both groups of executives are willing to offer business counseling on a voluntary basis to both new and existing small businesses. There is no charge to the prospective entrepreneur. SCORE/ACE counselors have assisted high school and college students in the completion of entrepreneurship-business plan projects. The services of these individuals may be requested by contacting the local Small Business Administration Office.

Another source of helpful advice in either identifying a potential new business idea or developing your business plan is your current employer or supervisor. These individuals are also often very willing to assist students with business-related assignments and projects.

Suggested Business Plan References

You may wish to refer to the following publications, which provide ideas for specific types of business plans: *Business Plan for Retailers* or *Business Plan for Small Service Firms*, Small Business Administration (SBA). Copies of these publications are available from SBA field offices or from the Superintendent of Documents, Washington, D.C. 20402. In addition, the Distributive Education Clubs of America (DECA) offers a written entrepreneurship competitive event that provides a suggested business plan format. You may wish to obtain a booklet entitled *Utilizing DECA's Entrepreneurship Event*, available from DECA Related Services, 1908 Association Drive, Reston, Virginia 22091. There are a variety of other business plan references that you may wish to use. See your instructor or librarian to obtain such references.

Organizing and Writing the Report

The business plan will be received more positively if it is well organized and easy to read. Here are some suggestions to achieve these aims.

1. Use a looseleaf notebook with dividers to assemble the information for the various sections of the business plan.
2. List the business plan section headings on divider pages in this notebook.
3. Assemble information for each section.
4. Present complicated data in some type of chart or graph.
5. Prepare organizational charts in graphic form.
6. Describe the data or information in each chart or graph with a series of short explanatory sentences.

A business plan will read best if it is written in direct conversational language, as it would be described orally to a prospective investor or lender. Write only the essential information without cluttering sentences with adjectives. Use short, single-topic paragraphs with simple, familiar words. Make every word count. Avoid slang.

The business plan should be carefully typed with clear headings, plenty of "white space," and a well-designed cover page. A functional binder or heavy duty notebook will make a good impression on the reader.

A business plan may need to be revised several times before it is completed. Even the best of writers go through a number of revisions before they publish their writing. Ask someone who knows how to write clear reports to assist in editing the final draft.

Just as Brent and Connie have a challenging and exciting task writing their business plan, so too does anyone developing a "great idea" for a new business. It should be remembered that writing a business plan can help you develop as a future owner-manager. It can give you valuable experience organizing information and solving problems regarding business policies, organizations, and operations. Such experiences, over a period of time, can help increase your managerial ability to make wise decisions. This ability greatly improves your chances for career success employed as a manager for a firm or as an owner-manager of your own business.

TRADE TALK

Define each term and use it in a sentence.

ACE	SCORE
Business plan	

1. List five possible business descriptors that could be included in the Description of the Business section of a written business plan.

2. List three possible marketing descriptors that could be identified in the Marketing Plan section of a business plan.

3. Give three types of information contained in the Personnel Organization Plan.

4. What three types of financial statements are often included in the Financial Plan section?

5. What does a Business Plan Summary provide a potential financial lender?

6. What services do SCORE and ACE counselors offer potential business owners-managers?

7. List five ways to make a business plan well organized and easy to read.

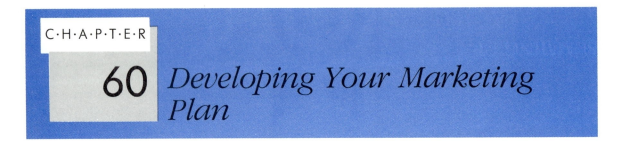

C·H·A·P·T·E·R

60 *Developing Your Marketing Plan*

Diana Randell opened her own specialty furniture store, Natural Products, featuring handcrafted items. She found a location for the store in a shopping center in a large Midwestern city. Diana identified her target market as young, upper-income professional people. Sometimes such customers are called "yuppies." Many of the targeted customers were style-conscious consumers living in the condominium buildings of the neighborhood or commuters and shoppers from the surrounding suburbs.

When the store first opened, the prospective target market customers whom Diana had identified did not shop in the store as expected. Instead, college students and low income renters were her primary customers. They were not interested in the store's furniture lines, but they purchased art pieces and accessory furniture items to enhance their rooms and apartments. They generally did not spend enough money on the more expensive furniture to maintain the business at a profit. Diana soon found that she was overstocked in the higher-priced furniture items.

Diana then invested heavily in promotion directed toward her original "yuppie" target market. Through selective use of radio and a local cultural-events magazine, she was able to inform the market about her store. Shortly after this promotional emphasis, more of her originally planned, higher-income target market customers began patronizing the store. And her business started showing a profit.

Diana Randell's experience illustrates important marketing concepts that are vital for new business success—select specific target markets; identify the needs of targeted customers; and satisfy their needs through appropriate marketing strategies. One of the biggest challenges that owner-managers of new businesses face is to develop marketing plans for their products and services.

The success of the beginning business depends on the entrepreneur's ability to build a growing body of satisfied customers. Modern marketing plans incorporate the marketing concept explained in Chapter 11. This concept directs managers to focus their efforts on identifying and satisfying customer wants and needs—at a fair profit.

■

APPLYING THE MARKETING CONCEPT

The marketing concept stems from the importance of customers to a business firm. It implies that *profitable sales volume* is a better company goal than maximum sales volume. To implement the marketing concept, a new business must:

■ Use market research
■ Identify target markets
■ Study the market potential

Use Market Research

In order to plan marketing strategies successfully, accurate information about the market is imperative. Frequently, a small market research survey, based on a questionnaire given to present customers and/or prospective customers, can disclose problems and areas of dissatisfaction. Also, a need to offer new products or services may be identified. Here are some important questions that could be answered by designing a market survey for a new business:

■ Who are the people that are most likely to buy from my new business?
■ What are their primary needs and uses for the products or services?
■ Are some needs more important than other needs?

■ What other products and services or brands might customers consider to satisfy their needs?
■ What do customers identify as the advantages and disadvantages of each of my competitors' products and services or brands?
■ Are some customers more dissatisfied than others with competitors' products and services?
■ Who will be my best customers?
■ How can they be identified?
■ Where are they located?
■ How do they typically shop for this type of product or service?

Identify Target Markets

Merchandise is of little value if it remains on a store shelf. Service equipment is of little value if it remains idle. Therefore, one of the most critical tasks in developing a marketing plan is choosing a target market that will consume those products and services.

Owners of new businesses frequently have limited resources to spend on marketing activities. Hence, concentrating new business marketing efforts on one or a few key market segments is important to maintaining profitability. Therefore, when operating your new business you should follow these practices:

Maintain customer segmentation. Identify and promote to those groups of people who are most likely to buy what you are selling. You will recall that Natural Products eventually did identify and promote its products to customers who would purchase the more profitable furniture items.

Maintain geographic segmentation. Develop a loyal group of customers in your home geographic territory before expanding into new territories. Natural Products did apply additional promotion efforts to attract the targeted local customers.

Maintain product segmentation. Promote existing products and services intensively before introducing a lot of new products and services. Natural Products initially pro-

Discovering customer information requires studying population trends.

moted and sold the less profitable decorative accessories, causing an overstocked condition in the furniture line.

Study the Market Potential

Enough customers must be available to support a successful, long-term business operation. Therefore, the business manager/owner should study the market potential very carefully before going very far in developing the new business.

While studying the market data, it is important to recognize the difference between the total potential of a market and the amount of that market the business in question can expect to capture. The **total market potential** is the total amount expected to be spent by *all* customers in *all* businesses selling similar products and services in a given geographic area. The market share is the percentage of sales that an individual business might obtain. Most new businesses moving into a competitive market will not be able to obtain a very large market share for at least several years.

Estimating the market share for a business is not a simple or exact task. It requires collecting the facts about your target customers *and* estimating their patronage versus that of your competitors. An owner-manager can, however, gather needed customer data from census information, business publications, chambers of commerce, professional associations, and other sources. Most markets can be reasonably estimated with information available to new businesses.

DECIDING ON THE MARKETING MIX

After the target market and the potential market share for the business have been determined, key marketing mix decisions are made. Key marketing mix decisions relate to (1) products and services, (2) pricing, (3) place, and (4) promotion.

Products and/or Services

Effective product strategies for a small business include (1) concentrating on a narrow product or service line, (2) developing a highly specialized product or service, or (3) providing a product or service package that includes an unusual amount of service. The quality of products to be sold, the features of those products, and the services and guarantees to be provided must be determined.

Price

Determining price levels and/or pricing policies (including credit policy) is a major decision affecting total sales. Generally, higher prices mean lower volume and vice versa. However, small businesses can often command higher prices because of the personalized service they can offer. Related pricing decisions to be made include whether to extend credit, to give discounts, or to accept trade-ins.

Place

Small retailers frequently view place decisions as they relate to both the location of their business and their customers. Oftentimes a low-cost business location may mean that additional promotion must be done to inform and attract customers.

A new business owner-manager's major challenge is to identify, evaluate, and select the best available site. This business site must profitably serve the needs of the target market. Chapter 61 provides information about where and how to choose a desirable business site.

Place decisions also relate to the use of distributors (sources) when a retail marketer purchases stock to be sold. Whether a new business should obtain its merchandise directly from producers, manufacturers, wholesalers, and/or other types of suppliers is an important place decision. Supplier services, delivery and transportation charges, and financing possibilities influence place decisions.

Promotion

The promotion decision area includes advertising, personal selling, and other promotional activities. In general, high-quality salesmanship is a must for small businesses because they cannot advertise heavily. Many small retailers advertise in the Yellow Pages. Direct mail is an effective, low-cost medium of advertising available to small businesses. Whether television, radio, newspapers, or other promotion strategies are the best ways to advertise are important promotion decisions.

Examples of Marketing Mix Decisions

An example of marketing mix decisions that the owner-manager of a small bicycle shop makes when considering the addition of a more expensive racing bicycle to the store's product lines is described as follows:

Product decisions. Racing bicycles are naturally more expensive and require much product knowledge and selling effort. The types of racing bicycles are limited, requiring the store to carry only a few models. Therefore, adding this product line may not require excessive inventory costs.

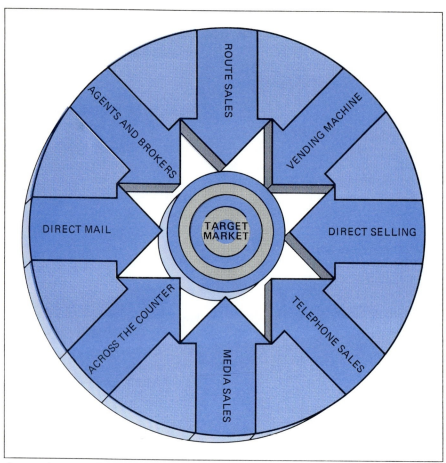

Once a business planner decides on the target markets, a final decision must be made; namely—how will I get my goods or services into the hands of my customers? There are eight possible ways to solve that problem.

Price decisions. The prices of racing bicycles may be higher than for recreational bicycles because there are fewer competitors. Because of the higher prices, the retailer must determine if projected sales and profits justify adding the product line.

Place decisions. The distribution of racing bicycles is primarily through specialized sporting goods stores. Recreational bicycles are distributed by a variety of retail outlets. The small bicycle shop needs to consider this competition.

Promotion decisions. The advertising for racing bicycles would have to be directed toward a unique target market using creative advertising copy and promotions. Advertising for regular recreational bicycles would be addressed to a more traditional target market.

There are many factors to consider when making marketing mix decisions. The more you know about your customers, the easier it will be to make those decisions. Your marketing mix will determine whether your new business can provide something that is different from the competitors' products, more satisfying to your customers, and more profitable to your new business.

WRITING THE MARKETING PLAN

The final step of marketing planning is to develop an actual written marketing plan. Marketing plans may be brief or quite lengthy, but they should contain enough information to direct the business's marketing efforts. Your marketing plan does not include enough detail if readers are not sure of the marketing activities that must be accomplished or how they will be evaluated. Even a small business should develop a written marketing plan. It forces an owner to think carefully about the planning period and what needs to be done during that time. It also shows relationships among all the firm's activities. The major parts of a marketing plan include the following:

Market Description

The target market(s) to be served should be described in detail. Descriptions of customer characteristics such as age groups, income levels, locations, product and service preferences, and unique aspects should be identified.

Marketing Objectives

Marketing objectives of the firm for a particular period of time should be recorded. These objectives should be written specifically so that they can be evaluated in measurable terms. Percentage or numerical increases or decreases in sales, expenses, profits, market share, and number of customers are examples of how objectives can be measured.

Competition

Competitors, their products and services, customer groups served, market share, and unique marketing strategies should be described. Ways your business can meet competition should be included.

Environment

Any factors in the marketplace that could affect the company's success should be described. The economy, state and federal laws and regulations, new products, population changes, and other influences should be described if they might influence the business.

Marketing Mix

Each major element of the marketing mix should be described (the customer, product or service, price, place, and promotion decisions). Marketing activities related to each mix element should be identified, timetables for completion of activities developed, and responsibilities assigned. This section will vary in length, depending on the size of the business, number of employees, and amount of marketing activities planned.

Budget

An anticipated budget should be developed to show how funds will be spent for major marketing activities. If possible, this budget should identify how funds will be spent during each month of a marketing season.

USING THE MARKETING PLAN

Obviously, it will take time to complete the planning of marketing activities for a new business. It is tempting for a business person to omit much of the planning or to spend little time at it. But care spent in planning marketing activities will reduce the time required to accomplish those activities. Also, it should result in more profitable operations. Finally, a marketing plan will provide information for the owner-manager to use in checking the performance of the new business. Problems can be identified and corrected more easily if a written marketing plan is available.

Define the following term and use it in a sentence.

Total market potential

CAN YOU ANSWER THESE?

1. What does the marketing concept imply that a new business should do regarding sales volume?

2. What are four types of questions that could be included in a marketing research study for a new business?

3. What are three practices of segmenting a market for a new business?

4. Why is it important for a new business to analyze the total market potential realistically?

5. What is one example of a marketing mix decision that could be made with respect to: (a) product and/or service, (b) price, (c) place of distribution, and (d) promotion.

6. What are the six major parts of a marketing plan?

BUSINESS PLAN ASSIGNMENTS FOR U·N·I·T 19

BUSINESS PLAN ASSIGNMENT 1: EVALUATING YOUR OWN BUSINESS OPPORTUNITY

Directions: Evaluate a potential business opportunity that you are considering. Answer the questions listed below. Refer to previous chapters in your text concerning advantages and disadvantages of various forms of business ownership. Collect additional information from your teacher, your present employer, or outside resources such as the chamber of commerce, Small Business Administration, owner-managers of similar businesses, government publications, and other sources. Assemble your assignments and information in a folder or notebook to be included as part of your overall business plan for your new business. If owning a business is not your goal at this time, plan a part-time business or a business that handles products or services in which you may wish to pursue a career.

On separate sheets of paper, list each of the following questions and answer them as completely as possible.

EVALUATING YOUR OWN BUSINESS OPPORTUNITY

1. What type of business do you plan to organize (retail, service, franchise, an existing business, a part-time business, a new business, etc.)?

2. What are your reasons for this choice of a business (existing or unique needs for the business, trends, developments, market potential, etc.)?

3. What type(s) of products or services are you going to emphasize, specialize in, feature in your business? What are your reasons for these decisions?

4. Who are your major competitors for your business? How can your products or services be competitive in your market area?

5. What are your experiences, interests, or unique qualifications that will assist you in being successful in this particular type of business?

6. What are ways that you can prepare for management/ownership of this type of business? (Some ways to consider are education required, on-the-job training programs, internships, beginning as a part-time business, management training, other.)

7. Identify the information or advice that you have obtained from others in this type of business.

8. Overall, what do you believe will be the most challenging, interesting, rewarding aspects of managing and owning the type of business you have chosen to organize?

9. What additional information are you seeking to assist you in making a decision regarding the type of business you wish to start? (Discuss this question with your teacher to obtain possible sources of such information before you begin your search.)

BUSINESS PLAN ASSIGNMENT 2: DEVELOPING YOUR BUSINESS PLAN

You have just been introduced to the elements that make up a business plan. In addition, you have reviewed a sample business plan summary. At this point in your new business plan development, you should begin a more detailed description of the business (Section 1 of the business plan). Answer the following questions on separate sheets of paper. Include your answers in separate folders or insert them in your business plan notebook.

A DESCRIPTION OF THE BUSINESS

1. What is the name of your business? Why did you choose this name? What identity or marketing image benefits does the name possess or communicate to your potential customers? (You may wish to modify or change your business name later on as you develop your business plan.)

2. What are the sources of information (publications, names of advisors) that you have used or plan to use in the development of your business plan?

3. Other information to be included in the description of your business can be completed after studying future chapters.

TABLE OF CONTENTS ASSIGNMENT

To assist you in organizing the content of your business plan, you should develop a tentative table of contents. You may wish to review the business plan outline included in Chapter 59, the major elements of the Railroad Restaurant business plan summary, or other business plan formats suggested by your teacher. You should include the major headings and subheadings that you believe are appropriate for your type of new business. Consider that eventually you will wish to obtain financing for your new business. This table of contents will be a tentative "road map" for planning your new business. As you study the following chapters you may wish to revise this table of contents.

The overall intent of this assignment is to provide you with a better understanding of the elements of a business plan. You will study how to identify potential customers and how to design marketing strategies to better serve their wants and needs.

BUSINESS PLAN ASSIGNMENT 3: DEVELOPING YOUR MARKETING PLAN

After you have decided on a certain type of business to organize, you will need to develop a marketing plan. The marketing plan as discussed in Chapter 60 identifies the following:

1. Your business target market
2. Marketing mix strategies (product and/or service, price, place/distribution, and promotion decisions) to achieve your marketing objectives

It is suggested that you obtain information regarding your new business from such sources as owner-managers of similar businesses, Small Business Administration officials and/or publications, trade magazines, and visits to area businesses.

Complete as many of the following questions and projects as you can at the present time. You will be inserting certain sections of the marketing plan as you complete future chapter projects. At this time it is important that you be aware of the various marketing strategies that need to be included in a business plan.

TARGET MARKET STRATEGY QUESTIONS

1. Describe the potential customers who are most likely to be attracted to your new business (age, sex, income levels, buying habits/preferences, unique characteristics, population trends, etc.).
2. What are the needs and wants of these customers that your products and/or services will satisfy?
3. What is the total estimated market size in terms of numbers of potential customers and projected sales dollars? What estimated percentage or share of this total market would you plan to realize at the end of the first year? Three years? These estimates may be difficult to make for a new business. Planned or estimated sales, however, are necessary for a new business. Obtaining financing and preparing projected financial statements depend on these estimates. SBA publications, the Robert Morris and Associates Publication *Annual Statement Studies,** and owner-managers of similar businesses are sources of information for these market and sales estimates.

PRODUCTS AND SERVICES STRATEGY QUESTIONS

1. What quality, variety, and style of products or services will you offer your customers?
2. What are advantages and disadvantages of competitors' products, services, or brands?

---

* *Annual Statement Studies*, The Robert Morris Associates, 1616 Philadelphia National Bank Building, Philadelphia, Pennsylvania 19107.

3. How are your products, services, or brands superior to or different from your competitors'?

4. Identify suppliers who will provide specific merchandise or materials for your products and/or services. Consult with owner-managers of similar businesses or your instructor for supplier information and catalogs.

5. Describe the type of customer services you will offer. Examples of services are delivery, merchandise return adjustment and/or repair, credit, customer/product/service information, and other unique services.

PROMOTION STRATEGIES

Refer to the project activity described at the end of Unit 13, "Learning About Promotion," page 351. For your business plan include those types of special promotion tools identified in this project that you would use in the first month of your new business operation. Include a brief explanation of your reasons for using each promotion tool. It is sug-

gested that you rule a monthly calendar to identify types of promotions, timing and length of promotions (days), and estimated costs of each promotion.

PRICING STRATEGIES (POLICIES)

Refer to Activities and Projects for Unit 17, Problem 2, page 466. Rule a form similar to the one described in Problem 2. List the different types of pricing policies you would follow for different kinds of merchandise or services offered in your new business. Include the type of pricing policy, the merchandise or service, and your reasons for the different pricing policies. You may wish to review these policies described in Chapter 51.

PLACE STRATEGIES

You will describe your place strategies in Business Plan Assignment 4 at the end of Unit 20. When you have completed Assignment 4, add it to the Marketing Plan section of your Business Plan.

U·N·I·T
20
ORGANIZING YOUR BUSINESS OPERATIONS

C·H·A·P·T·E·R

61 *Selecting Your Location*

There are two often-repeated sayings that apply when selecting the location for a new business: "Fish where the fish are!" and "Location! Location! Location!" The first saying applies to locating near the area where most of the customers reside. The second is used by real estate personnel when appraising the value of a home or a business.

Locating almost any place of business is a very important task, because the wrong decision can cause a business to fail almost before it gets started. Too often, the site is chosen because a building or parcel of land is vacant or because the site is located close to the home of the owner. These can be poor reasons for selecting a business location.

Location is more important for some types of businesses than for others. Choosing the right location is a crucial decision for those businesses that must persuade customers to come to the business site to fulfill their needs. Clothing stores, dry cleaning establishments, and automobile service stations all depend a great deal on customer traffic. These types of businesses must locate near their customers in order to earn a profit.

For other types of retail goods and service businesses, however, location may not be as important in attracting customers. Stores that sell high-cost products such as furniture, major appliances, and automobiles often attract customers to their places of business. Service businesses such as repair and rental businesses, as well as service businesses that come to the customer's home, can be located "off the beaten path" and still generate high sales. Their customers are willing to spend time searching for the product or service offered by such a company.

STEPS IN LOCATING A NEW BUSINESS

Brent Ness and Connie Lee had both worked in a music store full-time since they graduated from the retail marketing program at

Alexandria Technical Institute almost 5 years ago. They finally managed to secure $30,000 (money they saved, plus bank and government loans), and planned to meet their shared career goal of opening their own music store. They knew that their first step was to seek out a good business location.

If Brent and Connie were like many retail business owners who select a location, they probably used a combination of factors and methods in making their selection. Some of the things they considered were personal reasons, such as climate and the need to be close to family and friends. Other things they considered were business and personal contacts in the area.

The three major business-location selection steps followed were:

1. Choosing a viable community
2. Selecting the trading area
3. Evaluating the specific site

■

CHOOSING A VIABLE COMMUNITY

Large companies devote a great deal of time and study to the problem of selecting new locations. Brent and Connie and many other small retailers may be unable to do as extensive a job of selecting a viable community. A *viable community* is one that will provide an adequate and profitable sales volume for a business. When planning the location of a small business, the following three general factors are used to determine the best geographic area or city for the business: (1) economics, (2) population, and (3) competition. Brent and Connie needed to consider these factors when selecting their new business location.

Economic Considerations

A major concern in planning the location of a small business is the economic strength of the area. Therefore, the future of the area should be studied in terms of the stability of its economic base. The type of industry in the region influences its economic welfare. Agriculture, manufacturing, and commercial trade are the major types of industry that form an economic base. Some areas depend on one industry, while others have a balance of business establishments, which ensures economic stability. A study of the industries in an area should answer the following questions.

■ Do townspeople depend on one industry or a single business for their jobs? Or does the community have a variety of supporting industries?
■ Is the industry in the area healthy?
■ Is the business of the community seasonal in nature?
■ Are industries moving in or are they locating elsewhere?

Other economic factors are also important when locating a business. Good highways and railroad facilities contribute to business success. The availability of public utility services and a well-trained labor force are positive factors. Local taxes are an economic factor influencing business success.

Population Considerations

A second general factor that affects the potential of a business location is the nature of the population. Because the income of individuals determines the demand for goods and services, owners of small businesses should gather information about the income patterns of the region. Population trends should also be reviewed. The growth, decline, or stability of the population, as well as the standard of living, are items of interest.

Potential entrepreneurs should gather economic information about the population in the area selected. Specific questions to be answered include:

■ What is the average income of the potential customers?

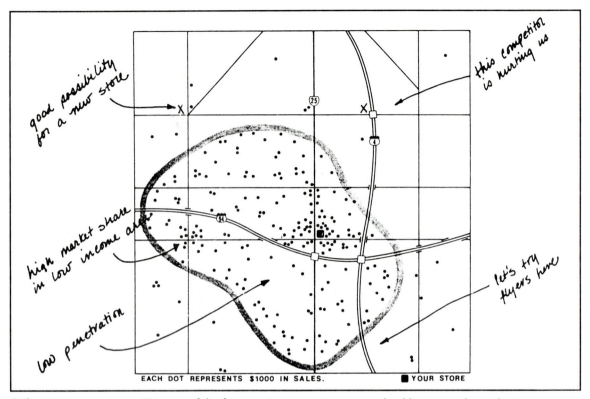

"Where are my customers?" is one of the first questions an entrepreneur should answer when selecting a location.

■ Is there a mixture of income levels (low, medium, high) in the area, or does the area have predominately one income level?
■ What are the employment/unemployment trends?
■ Do most people own or rent their homes?
■ What changes have occurred in the population in recent years?

Competition Considerations

The third general factor affecting the choice of a business location involves the number and type of competitors or potential competitors. The number of competitors is important, because an area can support only a limited number of competing businesses. If too many of the same type of business locate in the same area, they may all have limited sales and several may not survive.

A small business owner can determine if the competition is alert and up to date by driving through the area and visiting a number of retail outlets. The presence of chain stores, franchises, and other major firms should be noted. You should know not only how many competitors do business in your sales market, but also where they are located.

You should also find out how many businesses similar to yours have opened or closed in the past 2 years. Indirect competition that provides similar kinds of goods and services is another factor to analyze. Investigating the competition in a geographic area is a vital step in planning a business location. Questions similar to the following should be answered.

■ How large are the competitors?
■ What do their customers think about the

products or services offered by the existing establishment?

■ What type of management—cooperative or cut-throat—exists in the area?

■ If there is little or no competition, why not?

■ What is the history of businesses like yours in the area?

Three conditions favorable to opening a new firm are: (1) the absence of similar firms when a need for such firms exists, (2) the presence of poorly managed companies, or (3) an expanding market. A study of your competition will indicate if any of these conditions exist.

■

SELECTING A TRADING AREA

To evaluate the potential sales volume of a geographic business area, Brent and Connie defined their trading area. A **trading area** is the geographic area from which a business draws its customers. An individual business trading area is considered by the Small Business Administration to be the geographic area in which about 70 percent of the store's customers live.

Measuring the trade boundaries for an existing retail facility is much easier than doing this for a new business. However, studies of the trading area for similar existing businesses can provide an excellent measure of the probable trading area for a proposed retail business. Existing firms can analyze credit and delivery records and interview people who live in the area. Table 1 summarizes factors to consider when selecting a community and a trading area.

Brent and Connie, like most prospective retailers, studied these three basic types of locations: central shopping districts, neighborhood shopping areas, and planned shopping centers.

TABLE 1 / FACTORS TO CONSIDER WHEN SELECTING A COMMUNITY AND TRADING AREA

1. Population characteristics
   a. Total population of community
   b. Age and income distribution
   c. Average education level
   d. Percent of residents owning homes
   e. Disposable income of residents
   f. Nature and type of employment
   g. Race, nationality, and religion
   h. Lifestyle and social class
   i. Purchasing habits
   j. Stability of income
   k. Population trends

2. Economic considerations
   a. Dominant industry
   b. Diversification of industry
   c. Seasonal fluctuations of employment
   d. Growth projections for new industry
   e. Business trends

3. Competition
   a. Number and size of existing competitors
   b. Strengths and weaknesses of competitors (including quality of products and services)
   c. Potential competition
   d. Trends in competition

4. Costs and availability of support services
   a. Personnel—both management and employees
   b. Services such as transportation and delivery, credit, and promotion
   c. Rent, taxes, licenses, and other fees

5. Costs and availability of locations
   a. Number and types
   b. Opportunities for both leasing and owning
   c. Zoning and other restrictions
   d. Access to transportation

Central Shopping Districts

Central shopping districts are the main commercial areas in a city. They are generally located on main thoroughfares and often include several city blocks in medium or large cities. Government offices, financial institutions, and professional offices provide a market for the district's retail and service establishments. Many types of consumer goods and services are available in this type of shopping location. However, major department stores provide the drawing power. Theaters, restaurants, and stores sell a variety of goods and services that increase the customer traffic.

The major advantage of the central shopping district is the drawing power of the numerous retail and service establishments. Pedestrian and vehicular traffic is heavy, making it a good location for stores that sell convenience items. The advertising and sales promotions of the individual stores draw additional customers from a large trading area. Recently, through urban renewal and revitalization projects, the downtown areas of many cities and towns have been made more attractive. Often rental or real estate prices are lower than in suburban shopping centers, to attract new businesses into the downtown area.

A major problem in some central shopping districts is the deteriorating quality of life. High crime rates, vacant stores, and traffic congestion are unpleasant facts of life in some cities and towns. Other problems include high operating costs and heavy competition.

Neighborhood Shopping Areas

Scattered throughout cities and towns are small clusters of retail firms. These clusters are located along busy streets in areas that have high population densities. Clusters of this type are known as **neighborhood shopping areas**.

Small branches of major department store chains often locate in these areas. Grocery stores, fast-food establishments, and automobile service stations are very common. Bakeries, hardware stores, shoe stores, bars, and luncheonettes are also typically located in these areas.

These areas are attractive to small business owners because of their lower rents and operating costs. Additionally, the personal contact with friends and neighbors is enjoyable and accounts for a great deal of repeat patronage. A well-balanced assortment of stores also tends to act as a drawing card. The major drawback of neighborhood shopping areas is that they draw customers from a relatively small trading area. Neighborhood shopping centers may not be large enough to support some specialty businesses. These shopping areas will support only smaller stores.

Shopping Centers

Clusters of businesses in a planned shopping area are known as *shopping centers*. They have grown with the increased use of the automobile. Shopping centers are usually located on the outskirts of a city or town near a major highway. The three basic types of shopping centers are neighborhood, community, and regional.

Neighborhood centers, sometimes called strip centers, are designed to serve a trading area within a 5- to 10-minute drive of the center. A supermarket or chain drug store is often the largest store in the center. The remaining stores in the center usually sell convenience goods. Variety stores are very common in these centers.

Community centers attract customers who are willing to drive 20 minutes or so to the center. Very often a junior department, variety, or discount store is the major business. This major store will attract customers to the other stores in the center. A complementary offering of convenience and shopping goods, along with several service offerings, is commonplace. Drug stores, hardware stores, dry cleaners, and laundromats are typically located in these types of centers.

A **regional center** is usually an enclosed mall and has two or more department stores as the primary customer attraction. These stores are often known as **anchor stores**.

The Cannery, in San Francisco, is a planned shopping center converted from a factory. What are the advantages to a retailer of locating in such a shopping center?

Customers will drive from 40 minutes away or even more to shop at some regional centers. A wide range of services, convenience goods, and shopping goods are available. Chain stores and franchise outlets predominate. Banks, restaurants, and movie theaters will also be located in regional centers.

The major advantage of shopping centers is their ability to attract customers. This drawing power is enhanced by a planned tenant mix, pooled advertising and promotion programs, and ample parking. Shopping centers attempt to create an attractive and appealing overall atmosphere. Many centers sponsor promotional events, such as new car shows, to attract potential customers.

The cost of space in a shopping center can be high. Also, if you are a member business, you will give up some of your independence,

since most stores are required to maintain uniform hours. You may be limited in your advertising and promotional programs in that they must meet center standards. Maintenance costs are often beyond the control of member stores.

■

EVALUATING THE SPECIFIC SITE

After considering economic, population, and competition factors you are now ready to evaluate a specific site for your new business. A logical process of narrowing this selection from a general to a more specific site is discussed in the following paragraphs.

Using a Feasibility Study

Large businesses often use a feasibility study when selecting a business site. A business site **feasibility study** is an evaluation of location factors that can affect the success of a business. Small businesses can identify those factors that are most appropriate for their unique situations.

When evaluating alternative locations for a new business, two or three broad geographic areas should be studied. As these general areas for business locations are analyzed, several promising sites should become evident. These locations are then surveyed to gather information on economic, population, and competitive conditions. Market characteristics, such as the income, occupation, and education of the population, should also be gathered. The permanency of the population in the area is an important consideration. Factors such as the number and location of potential customers are critical for the success of your new business.

Establishing Business Site Criteria

After one or two sites have been identified as promising, the evaluation of the market po-

tential of specific sites within those areas should begin. Criteria for rating each site should be established at this time (see Table 2). The nature of your business—retail, wholesale, or service—will determine the specific criteria chosen.

Using a form similar to Table 2 will aid you in making an organized comparison of the many factors involved in evaluating alternative business sites. Some criteria may not apply in all site evaluations but you will be able to effectively compare the rankings of the criteria for each possible location.

Conducting a Pedestrian Traffic Survey

Another planning tool to use when selecting a business site is a pedestrian traffic survey. This survey can give you a reasonable estimate of potential sales volume. By interviewing passersby you can determine which ones would be most likely to patronize your business.

If you are considering buying an existing business, you will also need to know how many people pass the site during business hours and how many of those are potential customers. One way to estimate numbers of

TABLE 2 / BUSINESS SITE SELECTION CRITERIA

	Location 1			Location 2			Location 3		
	Low		High	Low		High	Low		High
Rental or purchase terms	1	2	3	1	2	3	1	2	3
Competition in the trading area	1	2	3	1	2	3	1	2	3
Compatibility of neighboring businesses	1	2	3	1	2	3	1	2	3
Neighborhood atmosphere	1	2	3	1	2	3	1	2	3
Site history	1	2	3	1	2	3	1	2	3
Customer accessibility to site	1	2	3	1	2	3	1	2	3
Traffic volume	1	2	3	1	2	3	1	2	3
Parking availability	1	2	3	1	2	3	1	2	3
Zoning restrictions	1	2	3	1	2	3	1	2	3
Other criteria (identify)	1	2	3	1	2	3	1	2	3
Total rating points									

potential customers is to divide the people passing by into three categories: those who enter the store, those who may become customers after looking in the window, and those who pass without entering or looking.

It is also important to classify passing traffic according to the time of the day when people are passing your business location. The time of day when customers are passing can often give you a good idea of their purpose, and you will want to gauge your traffic study accordingly.

Conducting an Automobile Traffic Survey

Automobile traffic flow data can be obtained from the city engineer, planning commission, highway department, or even an advertising agency. But you will want to supplement that information with some observations of your own. Check out the commercial vehicle traffic, times when shifts get off work at nearby industries, and increased traffic flow for special events or activities.

You can classify automobile traffic according to the reason for the trip. There are work trips, shopping trips, and pleasure trips. Careful observation and even some interviews with drivers can help you make the right site decision. It may be possible to decide on the type of customer you are most likely to serve and select a business site accordingly.

■

ENSURING THE VALIDITY OF A SITE SELECTION

An important step in selecting an appropriate business site is to use available references and data. Many sources of free or inexpensive business location information are available. A small business owner can obtain data to conduct a preliminary feasibility study from these sources. The U.S. Government

Printing Office is a valuable source, which publishes the following references:

Statistical Abstract of the United States. This annual publication includes national demographic data on such items as population and income.

County and City Data Book. Data for any city or county with a population over 25,000 are included in this source. Also in this book is information concerning the number of businesses, number of families, number of multifamily and single-family housing units, and average income.

The Survey of Current Business. A useful monthly publication that includes monthly sales volume for various products and services, economic information (including unemployment data), and articles on subjects such as changes in consumer buying habits.

The Small Business Administration publishes a number of free publications entitled *Small Marketers' Aids* and *Management Aids* explaining how to conduct customer traffic counts as well as criteria for locating a new business. An additional source of information is provided by the *Survey of Buying Power*, published yearly by Sales and Marketing Management.

TRADE TALK

Define each term and use it in a sentence.

Anchor stores
Central shopping districts
Community centers
Feasibility study
Neighborhood centers
Neighborhood shopping areas
Regional center
Trading area

1. Give some examples of economic factors that could be considered when deciding on a new business location.

2. What information regarding population would you want to know when selecting a business site?

3. What factors would you consider as most important regarding competitive businesses?

4. Define an individual business trading area.

5. What are two possible advantages and two disadvantages of a central shopping district?

6. What are three advantages of a neighborhood shopping area?

7. What are strip shopping centers?

8. What four factors do you consider to be the most important business site criteria?

9. What were tips offered when conducting either a pedestrian or automobile traffic survey?

C·H·A·P·T·E·R

62 *Planning the Design and Layout*

Brent Ness and Connie Lee had selected the location for their new music store. They were excited about planning the design and space layout for their new business. They wanted their music store's exterior appearance to invite customers to come in and shop for musical instruments, sheet music, tapes, and records. Their planning discussion included the following:

> Why don't we design our exterior store sign in the shape of a large guitar? Perhaps we could paint sheet music notes on the entire wall of our building. Let's install larger front window displays so that our merchandise and fixtures can be seen clearly by customers in their automobiles or on the street. We want our store to project a musical personality or image appealing to high school and college age students.

As Brent and Connie continued their plans for their new business, they sought the advice of Jason Arnas, a store planner and interior designer. Mr. Arnas offered these suggestions:

> Interior decoration is the primary means by which the desired impression is created inside the store. Everything that surrounds the customer once that person has entered your store—the walls, the ceiling, the floor, the fixtures, the signs, the merchandise—are elements contributing to the customer's impression of the business personality.

■

CREATING A BUYING ATMOSPHERE

The personality of a business should stimulate a certain customer buying atmosphere. This atmosphere is developed through layout, fixtures, decorations, lighting, color, and use of space. Stimulating buying atmospheres for different target customers include the following:

- Friendly and exciting for the young shopper
- Clean and cheerful for the family shopper
- Formal and pleasant for professionals
- Quiet and plush for the prestige shopper

Communicating the right buying atmosphere, then, is a problem of how best to convey to customers what the retailer wants them to see and feel.

■

BASIC STORE LAYOUTS

The arrangement of the store's equipment, fixtures, and furnishings is known as the **store layout**. It has an important influence on sales, since it shows where the various merchandising activities are handled and where equipment, fixtures, and furnishings are located. Developing an efficient layout has always been a challenging task. But in some newer retail stores it is considerably more challenging because of the trend toward smaller stores and reduced nonselling areas. In designing the interior layout of a store, several basic layouts are commonly used: *the grid layout, the open layout, the enclosed layout,* and *the zone and cluster layout.*

The Grid Layout

The **grid layout** is a rectangular arrangement of displays and aisles that run parallel to one another. The size and shape of display areas and the length and width of the traffic aisles are generally the same throughout the store. This layout is used most frequently by supermarkets, variety, and discount stores. The grid layout offers several advantages:

- It allows the most efficient use of selling space of any layout pattern.
- It simplifies shopping by creating clear, distinct traffic aisles.

- It promotes routine and planned shopping behavior necessary for self-service stores.
- It reduces some of the problems concerned with inventory and security control.
- It allows more efficient stocking, marking, and housekeeping.

The major disadvantages of the grid layout are the unexciting shopping atmosphere and lack of privacy that may be created. For these reasons, the grid pattern is not appropriate for most shopping-goods and specialty-goods retailers.

The Open Layout

The **open layout** provides for a complete open sales space surrounded by outside walls. All fixtures are usually kept below eye level or are designed to permit visibility throughout the sales floor. Most discount merchandise stores and drug stores use the open-plan concept. It provides better staff interselling as well as better visibility for all departments on the floor.

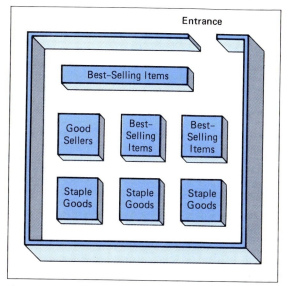

This simple grid layout is a rectangular arrangement of displays and aisles. Notice that the best-selling merchandise is near the entrance.

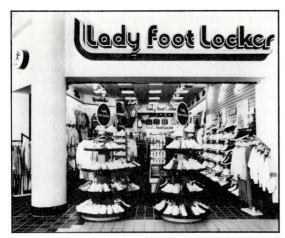

The open layout provides customer visibility throughout the store.

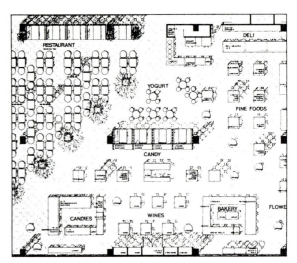

The enclosed layout subdivides merchandise classifications so that each merchandise category has its own "shop" within the store.

The layout design improves salesworker coverage, security, and exposure of merchandise. It reduces, however, the separation of merchandise departments. The lack of physical separation of merchandise departments lets unrelated merchandise rub shoulders, which may cause customer confusion in locating merchandise.

The Enclosed Layout

The **enclosed layout** design subdivides merchandise by classifications so that each merchandise category has its own "shop" within the store. Each category has its own identity, style, color, and ambience. This plan arose from the success of specialty stores using "boutique" design techniques largely borrowed from Europe.

This plan usually results in higher construction costs when adapted as a concept in a full-line department store. It requires wall separations between shops, which in turn call for more individual shop staffing and greater security safeguards. Flexibility of the enclosed layout is limited, and later changes are costly due to the need for structural remodeling. The enclosed layout has, however, been particularly successful in prestigious retail store merchandising. Higher-priced merchandise

lines are necessary to support the additional related overhead costs.

The Zone and Cluster Plan

Most businesses need to keep the costs of operation down, as well as provide a degree of layout flexibility and security. These layout needs have led to the increasing popularity of the **zone and cluster plan.** This plan incorporates the best features of the open and closed layout concepts. The sales floor is divided into large areas of associated merchandise groups, rather than into small, individually merchandised boutiques. High wall dividers or high-rise fixtures separate the zones, providing separate departments for related merchandise. The departments within the zone are divided by mobile clusters of fixtures. Each zone contains flexibility and allows for security, cross-coverage by the sales staff, and supervision. The zone and cluster plan permits a change of styling and layout in each zone. The overall store layout looks as if a series of specialty stores with associated merchandise were placed next to each other.

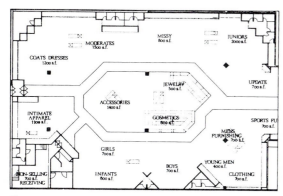
The zone and cluster layout plan features areas of associated merchandise groups.

FACTORS INFLUENCING STORE LAYOUT

Several factors influence store layout. These considerations are as follows:

■ Sales per square foot of selling space
■ The relative value of selling space within a store
■ Coordination of related merchandise
■ Desire for increased aisle impact
■ Ideas from store design resources and consultants

Sales per Square Foot of Selling Space

The layout of the store has a direct relationship to the dollar amount of sales per square foot. This amount is calculated for the store as a whole and for each department within the store. As costs of operating the store continue to increase, it becomes even more important for each square foot of floor space to be as productive as possible.

Here are a few general rules of store layout that may increase sales per square foot:

1. Concentrate stock in the smallest space possible without giving it a crowded appearance.

2. Use arrangements that encourage as much self-service as the store and merchandise will allow.

3. Place related items within a department and related departments within the store near each other to encourage suggestion selling.

4. Locate impulse goods near entrances and aisles where traffic is highest. Locate convenience goods, which customers buy frequently, near high-traffic locations. Locate shopping goods, which the customer usually wants to examine carefully, away from entrances and major traffic areas.

Profitability Ranges for Selling Space

All retailers must be concerned with realizing maximum profit from available selling space. The calculation of profit per square foot provides an indication of how much profit was realized on an item of merchandise from each square foot of selling space it occupied. This calculation helps to determine how much space should be allocated to each item. *Profit per square foot* is calculated by dividing the gross profit of an item—or merchandise line—by the area of selling space devoted to that item. The procedure for computing profit per square foot is as follows:

$$\text{Profit per square foot} = \frac{\text{gross profit on item or merchandise line}}{\text{square feet of selling space}}$$

Assume that a merchandise department made $4000 in gross profit last year on portable radios. The selling space for the line was 200 square feet of shelf and floor space. What is the profit per square foot for the radios? It can be figured as follows:

$$\text{Profit per square foot} = \frac{\$4000 \text{ gross profit}}{200 \text{ square feet of selling space}} = \$20$$

To obtain the highest profit from available selling space, retailers must study each merchandise line to determine which provides the highest, as well as the lowest, profit per square foot. To do this, they figure the profit per square foot for the fastest- and slowest-moving items. The difference in these profits per square foot for the fastest- and slowest-moving items is called a *profitability range*. In certain cases, even low-profit items justify space allocations to attract customers or provide a more complete assortment of merchandise. When laying out a store the owner-manager often has to make both objective as well as subjective decisions.

The Relative Sales Value of Store Areas

Each area of a store has a relative value. The front-right layout space has the most sales value, then the front center, the right middle, and the left.

Rear portions of stores are generally the least trafficked, suggesting that these areas should be reserved for staple goods and for service and repair customers.

Since shoppers tend to move to the right and middle of the store, the most salable and valuable merchandise should be placed there. This location is also the appropriate place for convenience and impulse items. These items can also be scattered throughout a store, using mid-aisle displays or other arrangements. As customers pass along the aisles to find specific goods on their shopping lists, they are often enticed to add some of these impulse items to their purchases. Seasonal goods are often placed directly in front of checkout stations. Such products include Christmas cards and decorations or lawn, patio, and garden equipment (in spring and early summer). On the selling floor, well-planned use of space can make shopping easier for the customers. At the same time, it can reduce confusion by making merchandise easier for customers to find.

Coordination of Related Merchandise

Presenting related merchandise in one area coordinates the customer's shopping and leads to suggestion sales. Towels coordinate better with bathroom accessories such as shower curtains, bath mats, and soap dishes than they do with table linen. Similarly, sheets and pillow cases relate best to blankets, pillows, and mattresses.

Today's customers are oriented toward buying fashion items by coordinating merchandise: gloves with handbags, handbags with shoes, blouses with skirts and slacks, ties with shirts, and even sportswear with sporting goods. Placing two or more coordinated merchandise classifications close together to conform with the customer's buying habits generates sales that might not materialize if the related goods were away from one another.

By placing all classifications related to one merchandise category together in one area, as in the zone and cluster plan, or all on one floor, the planner creates "merchandise worlds," such as a "fashion world" or a "home furnishing world." The same approach can even be extended to incorporate utility merchandise such as hardware, auto supplies, do-it-yourself materials, and garden equipment.

Desire for Increased Aisle Impact

A trend in department-store layout is the formation of wider and shallower departments so that goods can be presented with more aisle impact. Wider aisles enable customers to examine merchandise without being jostled or feeling that they are in the way. Increasing numbers of stores have little room for back stock. They emphasize fully exposed hanging merchandise. The result is a faster stock turnover of fewer units of merchandise.

Other general guidelines that should be observed when laying out the selling floor are these:

Wide aisles and large areas of open space create a luxurious environment suitable for high-priced merchandise.

■ Remove unnecessary barriers, such as walls and counters, that prevent maximum circulation by customers.

■ Encourage maximum customer traffic by careful placement of elevators, escalators, customer service areas, and high-demand merchandise that customers will seek out. Locate these areas away from major traffic aisles so that customers are drawn through the store, past as many types of goods as possible.

Store Design Resources and Consultants

Retailers setting up new stores need all the designing help they can afford. They may consult architects who specialize both in designing the basic structure of a store building and in preparing detailed interior floor plans.

Manufacturers of equipment, fixtures, and furnishings offer consulting aid in planning interior designs that make use of the products they supply. Making visits to other stores, looking through trade magazines, and talking with trade association experts are other ways in which retailers can obtain new design ideas. It should be remembered, however, that the ultimate success of a design depends on the imagination of each retailer in applying the design ideas to the available space.

■

EQUIPMENT, FIXTURES, AND FURNISHINGS

Everything within a store aside from merchandise and people falls into the categories of equipment, fixtures, and furnishings. *Equipment* includes a variety of apparatus that is built into or used in the store. Lighting, heating, and plumbing units, elevators and escalators, business and sales machines, storage shelves and bins, and merchandise carts are all equipment.

Fixtures are closely related to equipment and are sometimes classified under that general heading. But they are usually considered separately because of their very direct and important influence on the selling effort. *Fixtures* include the shelves, counters, and racks used on the selling floor to display merchandise for sale.

Furnishings are the furniture, carpeting, and decorative elements within the store. Equipment, fixtures, and furnishings should blend in with the store image and not distract the customer's attention from the merchandise.

Equipment

Lighting, air conditioning, and heating are standard features in offices and factories as well as in stores. In the retail store, however, these types of equipment not only create a comfortable working environment but also give indirect support to the selling effort by making the store attractive to customers.

Perhaps the most important equipment in the store is the lighting equipment. With the increasing costs of utilities, stores have not been able to save money on lighting. Some stores that have experimented with reducing the wattage in their incandescent lights have increased it again because they felt that dull lighting was having a negative effect on business. Good lighting offers these advantages:

■ It attracts customer attention and makes the interior of the store visible to passersby.

■ It reveals the true color, texture, luster, and other qualities of merchandise.

■ It can help to separate sections of the store visually.

■ It helps reduce mental fatigue among workers and promotes store cleanliness and neatness.

■ It helps create the type of image desired by the management.

Fixtures

The types of fixtures a store chooses depends on the type of merchandise to be sold and the merchandising policies of the company. Regardless of type, however, all fixtures perform three general functions: (1) They project the store image, (2) they promote the sale of merchandise, and (3) they provide protection for merchandise. Today, the more portable and flexible fixtures are, the more popular they are.

Fixtures may project a prestige image of an exclusive store where the selling policy calls for the assistance of salespeople. The merchandise in such stores is seldom set out where a customer can examine it without the help of a salesperson. Instead, it's displayed under glass (or, in the case of apparel, even kept off the selling floor in a storage area).

An important trend in fashion merchandising is to expose merchandise more fully.

This means that increasing numbers of retailers are displaying merchandise so that the front of the item can be seen instead of only the shoulder and sleeve. When as much merchandise as possible is hung on special rods that descend like waterfalls from wall or floor fixtures, the merchandise can face outward instead of sideways. Retailers have found that a customer will be at least twice as likely to buy a garment if it is hung face-out instead of sideways.

Supermarkets and self-service drug stores use self-service fixtures throughout most of their selling areas and put hardware, records, cosmetics, small items of apparel, and other

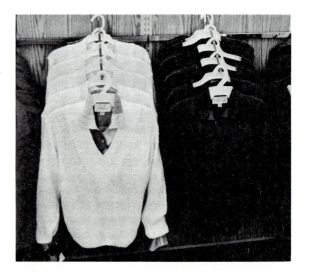

Different kinds of merchandise require different kinds of display fixtures.

prepackaged goods on them. There are fixtures with unbreakable glass and steel sidings for very expensive items. Other fixtures display frozen foods while keeping them at the right temperature.

Furnishings

Some items of furniture, such as desks and file cabinets, are designed to help store personnel do their jobs. Most furniture in the selling area of a store is intended for the comfort of customers. Any store that offers customers a pleasant place to relax will find that people come in to do just that—and that many people will stay to buy. In general, the higher the quality of the goods and the more time and money the customer is expected to spend, the more places there will be for the customer to sit down and relax.

Carpeting also invites customers to stay in a store. It makes shopping easier on their feet, absorbs noise, and looks attractive. Carpeting was once used only by prestige stores, because its upkeep was costly and it didn't stand up well under heavy traffic. However, modern carpeting is as durable and easy to maintain as any other kind of floor covering. Decorative furnishings—including the paint or paper on the walls, pictures and murals, dividers and planters—also attract customers and help to shape the store image.

■

EVALUATING STORE DESIGN AND LAYOUT

When a business owner-manager plans the design and layout of either a new building or remodels an existing building, it is helpful to evaluate the layout in terms of the equipment, fixtures, and furnishings. In addition, the owner-manager should evaluate the store layout in terms of how the equipment, fixtures, and furnishings contribute to the related merchandise or service activities.

1. Equipment, Fixtures, and Furnishings Evaluation

■ Does the layout contribute to the efficient use of equipment?

■ Is sufficient space allocated for nonselling, stock, and service areas?

■ Do aisle and counter arrangements stimulate a circular traffic flow so that customers have access to the entire store?

■ Are fixtures low enough and signs placed so that the customer can locate departments and merchandise?

■ Do fixtures (and their arrangement), signs, lettering, and colors all create a coordinated and unified effect?

■ Are ledges and cashier-wrapping stations kept free of boxes, unneeded wrapping materials, personal effects, and odds and ends?

■ Are the furnishings attractive and coordinated with the color and design of the store?

■ Are entrances and exits adequate and safe for customers and employees?

2. Related Merchandise or Service Activities Evaluation

■ Is the sales productivity of space—vertical as well as horizontal—considered when locating merchandise?

■ Is the merchandise in each category arranged according to its most significant characteristic—color, style, size, or price?

■ Are impulse items mixed with demand items?

■ Are signs for advertised goods prominent, to inform and guide customers to their exact location?

■ Are both advertised and nonadvertised specials displayed at the ends of counters as well as at the point of sale?

■ Are both national and private brands highlighted in arrangements and window displays?

■ Is each merchandise category grouped under a separate sign?

■ Are service areas clearly identified and in a logical merchandise-related area?

When Brent and Connie planned the design and layout of their music store, they considered the image and buying atmosphere of their new business. They attempted to relate all design elements, both interior and exterior, to the merchandise and services being offered. When they planned their store design and layout, they wanted to be creative and drafted several alternative layout plans. Their plans allowed for flexibility, change, and growth of their new business. They considered that their customer and business needs would change for each selling season. Business Plan Assignment 5 at the end of Unit 20 will allow you to apply many of the design and layout principles discussed in this chapter.

TRADE TALK

Define each term and use it in a sentence.

Enclosed layout
Grid layout
Open layout
Store layout
Zone and cluster layout

CAN YOU ANSWER THESE?

1. What is the current trend with respect to the design and layout of new retail stores?
2. What are three advantages of the grid layout?
3. What are two advantages of the open layout?
4. What type of layout subdivides merchandise classifications to produce a "shop" within a store?
5. What is a disadvantage of the enclosed layout?
6. What is done to the sales floor to create a zone and cluster plan?
7. What three general rules of store layout may increase sales per square foot?
8. Each area of a store has a relative value. List the following store areas in order of sales value from most to least valuable: front-center, right-middle, left, front-right.
9. All fixtures perform what three general functions?
10. List two questions that could be asked regarding whether a store layout is adequate.
11. List two questions that could be asked concerning the merchandise layout.

CHAPTER

63 *Preparing Your Organization Plan*

"I like working here. I know what I am supposed to do and what I am responsible for. Everything runs smoothly."

"This business is total chaos. Employees are confused about who does what. Everyone blames someone else for the goofups,"

These contrasting situations can exist in any business, large or small. As the owner-manager of a new business, you face a continual challenge to plan and organize the duties and responsibilities of your employees. These employees are the most important resource of your business. In fact, the success or failure of a business is determined largely by how well your employees do their work and how well their work is coordinated. Finding the right person for each position and providing thorough training and managerial leadership are therefore of the utmost importance.

There are several tools that an owner-manager can use to plan and organize the business personnel. In this chapter you will study such planning tools as:

1. Job analysis
2. Job descriptions and job specifications
3. Organizational charts
4. Personnel policies

Each of these tools will be described, and suggestions will be made about their use.

◾

JOB ANALYSIS

Before you hire a new person, you must know exactly what work you want that person to do. You must also ask yourself, "Do I have too many employees? Too few? Am I expecting people to do more than they possibly can?" The answers to these questions can be found by analyzing the tasks each person does.

Understanding the Purpose of a Job Analysis

Job analysis is a method for obtaining important facts about a job. Specifically, job analysis seeks answers to four major questions:

1. *What* physical and mental tasks does the employee perform? Examples: Plan, compute, direct, sell, promote, assemble, analyze.
2. *Why* is the job done? This is a brief explanation of the purpose and responsibilities of the job, which will help relate the job to other jobs. Examples: Ring up sales so the assistant manager can balance the books. Determine slow stock sales to determine necessary markdowns, etc.
3. *How* is the job done? The methods used and the equipment or supplies involved are identified. Examples: Use a tax table and cash register, ring up sales, use available sales/inventory data, compute merchandise turnover, etc.
4. *What* qualifications are needed for this job? The knowledge, skills, and personal characteristics required of an employee for a certain job are listed. Examples: Having a college degree, a pleasant personality, being able to supervise a merchandise department, being able to analyze computerized reports, etc.

Conducting A Job Analysis

A job analysis does not have to be very rigorous or complex. It will require a note pad and pencil and a little time and patience on your part. An easy way to begin a job analysis is first to think about the various duties, responsibilities, and qualifications required for the position in question. Jot down this information on a note pad or on a job analysis outline (see page 540). You may then want to talk to a manager or a person who now holds the job in order to complete details about the job. You could even ask the manager to list the duties and responsibilities of the job as well as qualifications believed to be needed for the job. You should then check the replies, correcting and adding information where necessary. Naturally, the more information included in a job analysis, the more it will benefit your new business operations.

When conducting a job analysis, remember that it is important to describe the job and the requirements of the job rather than the employee performing it. The present employee may be overqualified or underqualified for the job or simply have characteristics that are not required for the job. It is also a good idea to keep in mind the ultimate goals of a job analysis: to simplify and improve employee recruitment, training, and development. Job analyses can be used as a basis for salaries and wage rates.

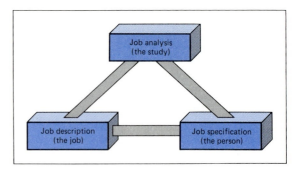

■

WRITING A JOB DESCRIPTION AND SPECIFICATIONS

After a job analysis has been conducted, it is possible to write a job description from the analysis. A **job description** is that part of a job analysis which describes the tasks and responsibilities of the job and how the job

relates to other jobs in the business. A **job specification** is a description of the desired personal characteristics and qualifications required for a certain job. The diagram above demonstrates the relationship of job analysis to job description and job specification.

In addition to their usefulness in explaining duties and responsibilities to the applicants, job descriptions and specifications can help with:

Recruiting—job descriptions and specifications make it easier to write advertisements or notices announcing the job opening, or explaining the job to an employment agency.

Interviewing of applicants—job descriptions and specifications can be used as guidelines when asking applicants questions about their abilities.

Training and development of new employees—having the duties of each job clearly defined identifies what knowledge and skills have to be taught to new employees so that (1) important skills are learned first and (2) the training is comprehensive.

Coordination—job descriptions, when they are available, can help to assure that people know what is expected of them and that their activities are coordinated.

Setting wage rates and salaries of employees—by specifying the relative amounts of work required and qualifications needed for different positions, fairer wage rates and salaries may be established.

Employee relations—Fewer misunderstandings will occur about the respective duties and responsibilities of each person's job.

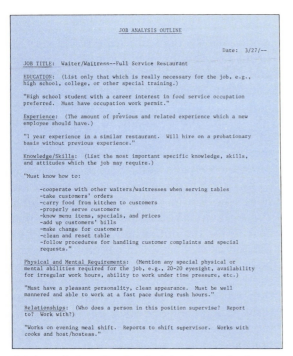

A job analysis outline for the job of waiter/waitress in a full service restaurant.

WHAT IS AN ORGANIZATION CHART?

An organization chart is a visual device that shows the structure of a business and the relationships among employees and their responsibilities. An organization chart indicates each employee's area of responsibility and the person to whom the employee reports. These charts provide for a clearer understanding of the division of responsibilities. By understanding an organization chart, employees have some idea of where and how they fit into the business.

Organization means exactly what it says—organizing a business so that it operates effectively and efficiently. It involves setting up a structure that will give order to the tasks a business must conduct to achieve its objectives.

As an owner-manager of a new business, you are required to define, group, and assign responsibility to others. This organization should divide the work load fairly among the employees. Organizing the work of a small business is a necessity if personnel, equipment, and supplies are to be in the right place at the right time. To organize responsibilities logically, you must group tasks to be done into individuals jobs. You must also define how one job relates to another.

How Can the Business Be Organized Effectively?

The following guidelines will help you as you organize the responsibilities of your business.

1. Organize responsibilities into jobs based on the business goals.

2. Place one supervisor in charge of each major department or operation.

3. Define authority clearly so that everyone understands to whom he or she is accountable.

4. Encourage decision making at the lowest possible level.

When developing an organizational chart for your business, remember that each business varies. The work of some types of businesses may fluctuate almost daily. Even though activities are different for each type of business, some basic degree of organization must exist.

An Example of the Organization Process

The Rose Flower Shop is involved in the following major activities. For purposes of this example, not all of the business activities of the shop are listed.

- Buying flowers
- Cutting flowers
- Caring for the flowers
- Operating and maintaining equipment in the store
- Making displays or arrangements
- Making sales
- Delivering flowers and related products
- Handling maintenance of shop
- Handling flowers by wire
- Keeping records
- Advertising and promoting
- Hiring and training employees
- Handling telephone sales
- Pricing merchandise
- Monitoring inventory

When organizing this business you would define each activity, group similar activities, and assign authority and responsibility. For each of the departments and individual jobs identified in this organization chart, specific job descriptions and specifications would be developed. The various activities would then be assigned to specific departments and individuals. An example of the result of these organizing steps is the organization chart for the Rose Flower Shop shown on page 542.

PERSONNEL POLICIES

Written personnel policies are important managerial tools that can be used to identify personnel standards, procedures, and benefits. These policies are often organized in the form of an employee handbook. This handbook is referred to during initial employee orientation and training. In addition, the handbook is a valuable reference for clarifying business policies when personnel problems or questions arise. When developing your personnel policies, you should include all matters that would affect employees, such as employment procedures, wages, fringe benefits, vacations, time off, grievances, promotion, and even termination policies. You may

wish to consider written policy decisions for the following areas.

Hours of Employment. Consider the number of hours to be worked per week, the number of days per week, evening and holiday work, and the time and method of payment for both regular and overtime work. Unnecessary payment of overtime at premium rates is a source of needless expense. By planning ahead, you may be able to organize your employees' work to keep overtime to a minimum. When peak periods do occur, you can often handle them by using part-time help paid at regular rates.

Wages. The majority of the employee's earnings should come from a base salary competitive with the pay offered by other similar local firms. It may be possible to supplement the base salary with some form

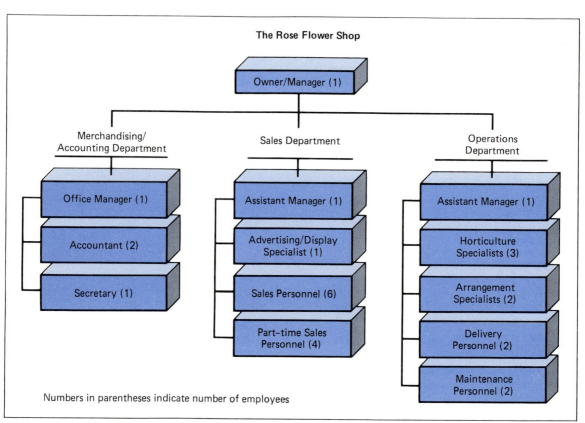

The organization chart for the Rose Flower Shop.

of incentive, such as a small commission or quota-bonus plan. Whatever plan you use, be sure each employee understands it.

Fringe Benefits. You may consider offering your employees discounts on merchandise, free life insurance, health insurance, a pension plan, and tuition reimbursements.

Vacations. How long will vacations be? Will you specify the time of year they may be taken? With or without pay?

Time Off. Will you allow employees time off for personal needs, emergencies in the family, holidays, special days such as election day, Saturday or Sunday holidays?

Training. You must make sure that each employee is given adequate training for the job. In a small store, the training responsibility normally falls to the owner-manager. If you have supervisors, however, each of them should recognize the importance of being a good trainer and should schedule time to train new people.

Grievances. You may expect conflicts with your employees for various reasons. The best course of action is to plan for them and establish a procedure for handling grievances. Consider the employee's rights to demand review, and establish provisions for third party arbitration.

Promotion. You will want to consider such promotion matters as normal increases in wages and salaries, changes of job titles, and criteria for promotions.

Personnel Review. Will you periodically review your employees' performance? If so, what factors will you consider? Will you make salary adjustments, training recommendations?

Termination. Even though this is a distasteful matter to many managers, it is wise to have a written policy on such matters as layoffs, seniority rights, severance pay, and the conditions warranting discharge.

When you have developed your personnel policies, write down the policy on all matters that affect your employees and give each one a copy. Matters such as those above should be standardized and not left to the whim of a supervisor.

■

THE IMPORTANCE OF DELEGATING

You have just studied several business organizational tools such as job analysis, job descriptions and specifications, organization charts, and personnel policies. A study of organizational tools would not be complete without considering the important managerial concept of delegation of authority. Managers delegate authority because they cannot perform all activities themselves. Managers, in delegating authority, free themselves of small tasks and can concentrate on making plans and decisions. Delegating authority also helps employees gain experience in managing. It improves morale, because employees' attitudes improve when they believe that they are making vital contributions to a firm's success.

In delegating authority, managers should remember two things. First, although a manager makes an employee responsible for a task, the ultimate responsibility is still the owner-manager's. The employee is responsible to the manager, but the owner-manager is accountable for the success of the business. Second, authority must be given with responsibility. In other words, an employee who does not have the authority necessary to get the job done should not be asked to do the job. The amount of delegation extended depends on the complexity of the tasks to be performed, the amount of time available for performing them, the confidence the manager has in the employees, and the number of employees the manager supervises. In effect, a successful organization/delegation business plan reinforces the saying, "People support that which they help create."

TRADE TALK

Define the following terms and use each one in a sentence.

Job analysis   Job specification
Job description

CAN YOU ANSWER THESE?

1. What are four major questions that a job analysis attempts to answer?

2. When conducting a job analysis, what is important to describe?

3. What does a job description include?

4. What does an organization chart show?

5. What were three guidelines mentioned to help in organizing the responsibilities of a business?

6. How can an employee handbook be used in a new business?

7. What are five examples of business personnel matters that personnel policies should cover?

8. What are two important points that managers should remember when delegating authority to employees?

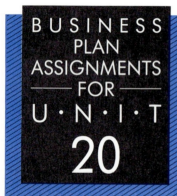

BUSINESS
PLAN
ASSIGNMENTS
— FOR —
U·N·I·T
20

BUSINESS PLAN ASSIGNMENT 4: SELECTING YOUR BUSINESS LOCATION

Directions: An exciting challenge confronts you — selecting your new business location. As you know, it is a very important planning decision that you will have to live with for as long as your business exists at this site. The following assignments are provided so that you can make a wise choice of business location. Consult with your teacher regarding additional information or assistance you require.

1. Obtain a copy of a telephone book or a city directory. Also, obtain a copy of a city or area map. The chamber of commerce or city government offices should have this information.

2. Identify specific trade area(s) on the local map that you believe would provide enough customers to support your new business.

3. Evaluate three possible business locations using Table 2 on page 528.

4. Write out answers to the following questions. Include your answers in your business plan.

    a. What business conditions are adequate to support your type of business in the site you are considering?

b. What kind of people will want to buy what you plan to sell? What are people like who live in the area?

c. What are the number, type, and size of competitors in the area?

d. Why does the area need another business like the one you plan to open?

e. Have you checked and found adequate utilities, parking facilities, police and fire protection, housing, schools, and other cultural and community activities?

f. What is the opportunity for growth and expansion of your business?

g. What is the occupancy history of this building? Does the location have a reputation for failures? (Have businesses opened and closed after a short time?)

h. Why have other businesses failed in this location?

i. What are the terms of the lease?

5. Conduct a customer traffic count of potential customers passing by your proposed new business site. Refer to suggestions regarding how to conduct such counts described in Chapter 61. Contact your advisor for additional recommendations.

6. Be prepared to discuss with your fellow classmates and advisor the major reasons for having chosen the specific location for your new business.

BUSINESS PLAN ASSIGNMENT 5: PLANNING THE BUSINESS DESIGN AND LAYOUT

Directions: An owner-manager must consider the needs of products handled, services offered, employees, and customers when planning the design and layout of a new business. Such considerations include customer buying habits and service, image, product orga-

nization and displays, utilization of available space, security, and separation of major activities. Your assignment is to plan the design and layout of your new business. Steps that you may wish to follow to complete this assignment include the following:

1. Visit several businesses that are similar in type and size to the business you plan to start. If possible, discuss with the business owner or manager the layout features that are most satisfactory and those that need changing or improving. Take notes or sketch layout features that you believe could be adapted to your business.

2. Obtain fixture and equipment catalogs and price lists from local or national suppliers. Seek names and addresses from your teacher, employer, or a local business owner. Identify fixtures and equipment needed for your business. Prepare a list of such items including an itemized price list and total budget. Local building or remodeling contractors might supply cost and labor estimates for your design and layout project.

3. Prepare a scale drawing of your business layout using graph paper. Determine the dimensions for various offices, merchandise departments, storage areas, service departments, and other areas. Consult with the drafting or industrial education teacher in your school to obtain suggestions concerning the scale drawing of your layout. You may wish to use pieces of colored construction paper cut in blocks or shapes corresponding to various areas or departments of your business. You may arrange and rearrange these pieces until you are satisfied that you have found the layout most appropriate for your business. Show the layout to fellow students, business owners or managers, and your teacher for their suggestions. You may wish to identify various areas or departments within your business layout by either labeling or coding these elements. You may wish to obtain sample fabric swatches, carpet samples, wallpaper or paneling materials, or color schemes to include with your layout plan.

All of the above information and plans should be included as a section of your overall business plan.

BUSINESS PLAN ASSIGNMENT 6: ORGANIZING YOUR BUSINESS PERSONNEL

Directions: Your employees are the most important asset of your business. As the owner-manager of your new business, you have several important organizational questions to answer.

1. What types of personnel are you going to hire?

2. How are you going to organize the efforts of your employees?

3. What responsibilities are you going to assign to each employee?

To answer these questions the following business organization assignments should be made:

1. Draw an organization chart for your new business, identifying specific job titles and numbers of employees needed for each job title. Also, organize your business according to different departments and/or activities. Identify job titles of individuals who will manage or be responsible for the departments and/or activities.

2. Prepare a job description for yourself as the owner-manager of your new business. Refer to the format of a job description in Chapter 63. Interview the owner-manager of a similar business to obtain ideas for this job description. Identify those duties and responsibilities that are most important and should not be delegated to others.

3. Design a job performance evaluation form. Consider factors in the sample job description in Chapter 63 as ideas for items to include in this evaluation form.

C·H·A·P·T·E·R

64 *Understanding Financial Statements and Ratios*

By now, Connie Lee and Brent Ness had completed many of the very important plans pertaining to their new music business. They had developed their business plan to include products or services handled, marketing strategies, business location and design, and personnel organization and policies. In short, they were on their way to realizing their new business ideas, dreams, goals. Great! But now they had to plan for and pass that critical final examination before their new business could become a reality. The final examination for any new business consists of understanding and preparing necessary financial statements and loan applications. In this case a banker, financial lender, or other source of necessary funding would conduct an examination of their financial plan.

In this chapter Mr. Baker, their financial lender, explains the basic components of the two most frequently used financial statements—the balance sheet and the operating or profit-and-loss statement. In addition, Mr.

Baker explains how to interpret information on these statements through the use of ratio analysis. **Ratio analysis** is simply a study of relationships between different business factors. Examples of ratio analysis will be discussed later in this chapter.

Connie and Brent visited Mr. Baker in his office to discuss a loan application for their new business. Mr. Baker asked them if they were familiar with such financial statements as a balance sheet and a profit-and-loss statement. Connie and Brent admitted that it had been some time since they had studied these statements in their high school accounting class. A review would be helpful.

■

THE BALANCE SHEET

The first statement a potential lender will require is a balance sheet. A **balance sheet** is a statement that tells what you own and what you owe at any one time. It is like a photograph of your business on one day. Most likely, balance sheets prepared for three days in a row will have different figures. Financial information about a business or about your personal finances changes every day. You receive income periodically and you pay bills periodically. In effect, you manage a flow of cash just like a new business.

If your cash is always in motion, why is the balance sheet so important? The balance sheet helps you control this cash flow by keeping you informed about your financial resources (what you own) and your debts (what you owe). The balance sheet is a tool used to determine whether the business is solvent. A business is said to be **solvent** when it has the ability to pay all of its debts.

Mr. Baker showed Connie and Brent a balance sheet that had been prepared for Bill's Bicycle Shop (see the illustration below). As you will notice, the balance sheet has three main parts or components: (1) assets, (2) liabilities, and (3) net worth (also called eq-

uity). All balance sheets are based on the following formula:

$$\text{Assets} = \text{liabilities} + \text{net worth}$$

Assets must equal liabilities plus net worth. In other words, the total of those items on the left hand of the balance sheet (assets) must exactly equal the total of the right side of the balance sheet (liabilities and net worth). The main components of this type of financial statement must balance. The total of the assets for Bill's Bicycle Shop is $80,000. This amount is the same as the total of the liabilities and net worth. If this total did not equal $80,000, then there probably was an error in the accounting process. You could say that this balance sheet would be "out of balance."

Assets

Assets are anything the business owns, including cash on hand, equipment, real estate, and inventory. **Current assets** include cash and anything that can be changed into

```
                          BILL'S BICYCLE SHOP
                            Balance Sheet
                            May 30, 19___

         Assets                            Liabilities and Net Worth

Current Assets                          Current Liabilities

  Cash                    $14,000         Accounts Payable      $18,000
  Accounts Receivable  $ 7,000            Notes Payable           2,000
    Less allowance for                                          $20,000
    doubtful accounts     1,000
  Net Accounts Receivable   6,000
Total Current Assets      $20,000
                                          Total Current Liabilities      $20,000
  Inventory            $ 9,000
    Less allowance for
    inventory loss        1,000 $ 8,000   Long-Term Liabilities
                                            Mortgage              $30,000

Fixed Assets
                                          Total Long-Term
  Land                    $ 7,000           Liabilities                  $30,000
  Building             $40,000
    Less allowance
    for depreciation      4,000 $36,000   TOTAL LIABILITIES              $50,000

  Equipment           $10,000             Equity (Net Worth)
    Less allowance                          Owner's Equity               $30,000
    for depreciation      1,000 $ 9,000

  Total Fixed Assets      $52,000

TOTAL ASSETS              $80,000         TOTAL LIABILITIES              $80,000
                          =======         AND NET WORTH                  =======
```

The balance sheet shows the assets, liabilities, and net worth of the business.

cash within 12 months. In addition to cash on hand or in the bank, current assets include accounts receivable (what people owe you) and inventory. **Fixed assets** are those items that usually cannot be changed into cash within 12 months. They are items the business acquired for long-term use. Fixed assets include land, buildings, machinery, equipment, and company vehicles.

Liabilities

Liabilities are the debts of a business. Liabilities might include loans, credit notes, income taxes, and mortgages. **Current liabilities** include anything you owe that can be paid by using a current asset. Current liabilities are usually due within 12 months. Current liabilities include income taxes, loans, and bills due to creditors. A **long-term liability** includes any debt that will not be paid within 12 months. A mortgage is an example of a long-term liability.

Net Worth

Net worth is the owned and retained earnings portion of the business. Net worth is what is left over after liabilities have been subtracted from assets. It is the owner's investment in a partnership, or an individual's investment in corporate stocks. Assets, liabilities, and net worth are the essential components of any balance sheet.

■

THE PROFIT-AND-LOSS STATEMENT

The **profit-and-loss statement** is a record of the activities of the business for a certain period of time. This statement is similar to a student report card. It shows where satisfactory business progress is being made as well as areas of needed improvement. There are a number of names for the profit-and-loss statement, one of which is the *income statement*. Profit-and-loss statements are usually developed at the end of an accounting period, that is, at the end of the month or at the end of the fiscal year. Profit-and-loss statements have five major components: (1) total sales, (2) cost of goods sold, (3) gross profit, (4) expenses, and (5) net profit. Each of these components provides important financial data about the firm.

1. *Total sales* includes both cash and credit sales. They do not include sales tax collected or the sales figures for products returned.

2. The **cost of goods sold** is the amount that it costs you to buy or produce the goods that you sold. The cost of goods sold is calculated by (a) taking a beginning inventory; (b) adding materials or products purchased during the accounting period; and then (c) subtracting inventory remaining at the end of the accounting period.

3. *Gross profit* is the amount of profit made from sales before operating expenses are deducted. Gross profit is calculated by subtracting the cost of goods sold from the total sales.

4. *Expenses* include all costs involved in running the business. Examples of expenses include advertising, insurance, and employee wages.

5. Net profit is your profit or loss at the end of the accounting period. Net profit does not include taxes you must pay on the business. An example of a profit-and-loss statement for Bill's Bicycle Shop is illustrated on page 550.

■

PREPARING A PROJECTED PROFIT-AND-LOSS STATEMENT

Mr. Baker, the banker, continued his discussion with Connie and Brent by saying:

```
                        BILL'S BICYCLE SHOP

                      Profit-and-Loss Statement

                  For Period Ending May 30, 19__

Sales                                                 $ 95,000      100.0%

Cost of Goods Sold

   Beginning Inventory            $ 18,000
   Purchases                        50,000
   Cost of Goods Available
      for Sale                                $ 68,000
   Less Ending Inventory                         3,000

Cost of Goods Sold                                    $ 65,000       68.4%

Gross Margin                                          $ 30,000       31.6%


Expenses

   Salary of Owner                         $  2,000                   2.1%
   Other Salaries                             5,000                   5.3%
   Rent/Mortgage                              1,000                   1.1%
   Advertising                                  800                   0.8%
   Delivery                                   1,100                   1.2%
   Supplies                                   1,600                   1.6%
   Telephone                                  1,000                   1.1%
   Utilities                                  2,000                   2.1%
   Insurance                                  1,500                   1.6%
   Loan Repayment                             4,000                   4.2%
   Legal & Professional Fees                    500                    .5%
   Miscellaneous/Other                        2,100                   2.2%

Total Expenses                                        $ 22,600       23.8%

Net Profit Before Taxes                               $  7,400        7.4%

Estimated Income and Sales Taxes                         3,200        3.3%

Net Profit                                            $  4,200        4.4%
                                                      ========       ======
```

This profit-and-loss statement serves as a report card for Bill's Bicycle Shop.

To lend money to your new music store we will need a projection of the monthly profit or loss for the first year. This statement provides an estimate of when your business will begin to make money and how much it will make. This information is important to a lender, since loan repayments are generally obtained from business profits.

The projected profit-and-loss statement is fairly easy to construct if you:

1. List your estimated gross sales on a monthly basis. Estimated sales can be based upon a share of the market, an industry average for your size business, or a dollar sales goal.

2. List the costs of the merchandise (or service) you estimate will be sold monthly.

3. Subtract the costs of the merchandise (or service) from your estimated gross sales. The resulting figure is your gross margin or profit.

4. Itemize the monthly operating expenses.
5. Total the monthly operating expenses.
6. Subtract the monthly operating expenses from the gross margin or profit. The resulting figure is the net profit or loss for the month. Losses are shown by putting parentheses around the number. For example, a $4800 loss would be listed as ($4800).

The projected profit-and-loss statement for Bill's Bicycle Shop is provided in the illustration on this page. As you can see, the owner is projecting a loss of $4800 for the first month of operation. Sales are estimated to be higher during May, the second month, because of spring sales. Therefore, a profit is estimated for the month. The third month shows an equal amount of gross profit even though sales are projected to increase. Net profit, however, is projected to decline in June due to increased expenses. The reason for this projection is that the cost of goods sold is expected to increase as well as certain expenses.

BILL'S BICYCLE SHOP

Projected Profit-and-Loss Statement

	April	May	June
Gross Sales	$ 80,000	$ 95,000	$110,000
Less Cost of Goods Sold	60,000	65,000	80,000
Gross Profit	$ 20,000	$ 30,000	$ 30,000
Expenses			
Salary of Owner	$ 2,000	$ 2,000	$ 2,000
Other Salaries	5,000	5,000	5,000
Rent/Mortgage	1,000	1,000	1,000
Advertising	750	750	900
Delivery	1,000	1,000	1,200
Supplies	1,500	1,500	1,700
Telephone	1,000	1,000	1,000
Utilities	2,000	2,000	2,000
Insurance	1,500	1,500	1,500
Taxes	3,000	3,000	3,500
Loan Repayment	4,000	4,000	4,000
Legal and Professional Fees	1,000	1,000	800
Miscellaneous/Others	2,700	2,700	2,900
Total Expenses	$ 24,800	$ 25,800	$ 27,500
Net Profit or (Loss)	($ 4,800)	$ 4,200	$ 2,500

This projected profit-and-loss statement covers a three-month period.

METHODS OF CALCULATING FINANCIAL STATEMENT RATIOS

Ratio analysis is a means of analyzing the figures that appear on financial statements. This analysis enables the manager to compare the past and present performance of the business. It can also help a manager compare the performance of the business to the performance of another firm or to the industry as a whole. Such comparisons are essential to future planning, because they reveal the strengths and weaknesses of the business operation. A ratio is computed by taking two selected figures from the financial statements and expressing one figure as a percentage of the other. The percentage of advertising dollars a business spends in relation to sales is an example of a ratio analysis. The following ratios compare figures from the profit-and-loss statement and the balance sheet for Bill's Bicycle Shop. As you study each of these ratios, however, remember that many small business owners today use computers to help them manage finances. When reading this section, think of ways that the computer could be used to help calculate financial ratios for Bill's Bicycle Shop or for your own small business.

Return on Investment

The **return-on-investment ratio** shows the return obtained on the owner's investment in the business. Compute this ratio by dividing the net profit figure by the owner's net worth figure and express the result as a percentage.

$$\frac{\text{Net profit}}{\text{Net worth}} = \frac{\$4200}{\$30,000} = 14\%$$

This figure should be larger than the return the owner could get by investing the money elsewhere. Bill's Bicycle Shop should receive an adequate return on investment because of the time, effort, and risks involved in owning and operating a business.

Net Profit to Sales

The ratio of net profit to sales is computed by dividing the net profit figure by the sales figure.

$$\frac{\text{Net profit}}{\text{Sales}} = \frac{\$4200}{\$95,000} = 4.4\%$$

A reduced net profit on sales can be caused by (1) poor pricing policies, (2) high operating costs, or (3) a combination of both factors. To determine which of these factors is causing a low net profit, the business owner could compare ratio data with similar businesses. These data are published in such sources as the *Annual Statement Studies* of The Robert Morris Associates, Small Business Administration Publications, or *The Small Business Reporter*, published by the Bank of America. Addresses for these companies are given in Business Plan Assignment 1.

Current Ratio

The **current ratio** is computed from the balance sheet. It answers the question of whether the business has enough current assets to pay its current liabilities (debts). *Current assets* are generally considered to be cash and net accounts receivable. *Current liabilities* are accounts payable and notes payable. Current ratio is computed by dividing the current assets by the current liabilities. A current ratio of 2 (assets) to 1 (liabilities) is generally considered acceptable. You can see that Bill's Bicycle Shop has an unacceptable current ratio. Current assets should be increased and/or current liabilities should be reduced to improve this ratio.

$$\frac{\text{Current assets}}{\text{Current liabilities}} = \frac{\$5,000}{\$20,000} = .25$$

Debt to Net Worth

Another important ratio is debt to net worth. This ratio is significant because banks look at it in determining your creditworthiness. This is not the only ratio banks look at, but it gives some indication of whether you are capable of borrowing additional funds. In the case of Bill's Bicycle Shop, the total liabilities (debts) are $50,000 and the net worth is $30,000. The debt-to-net worth ratio is computed by dividing total liabilities (debt) by net worth:

$$\frac{\text{Total liabilities (debt)}}{\text{Net worth}} = \frac{\$50,000}{\$30,000} = 1.66$$

This ratio means that there is $1.66 of total liabilities (debts) to be paid for every $1.00 of net worth. This is not a very favorable ratio if additional borrowing of money is needed. In time Bill's Bicycle Shop would wish to increase its net worth so that both current and long-term liabilities could be more easily paid.

Equity Trends

Business owners also like to know what has been happening to the business over a longer period of time. One way to do this is to analyze what has happened to the owner's equity (net worth) over several years. If Bill's Bicycle Shop's financial statements contained the following data for 2 years, the rate of change in net worth could be determined.

	Year 1	Year 2
Total assets	$80,000	$100,000
Total liabilities	50,000	60,000
Total net worth	30,000	40,000

You can see that net worth increased $10,000, or about 33.3 percent based on the year before:

$$\frac{\$10,000}{\$30,000} = 33.3\%$$

There are many other ways to check the financial strength of a business. If you decide to take beginning and advanced courses in accounting, you will learn more skills in topics like cost accounting, auditing, and managerial accounting. These ratio examples were intended to provide you with some ability to analyze financial ratios and statements. It is generally advisable to obtain the services of an accountant to assist you in preparing and analyzing various business ratios. In any case, it is very advantageous for an owner-manager to understand and use such ratios.

■

MAINTAINING CASH FLOW

Cash is a problem for many small marketers. Comments such as, "I never seem to have enough cash. Often I have to delay paying one creditor to pay another," are not uncommon for owners of new small businesses. The secret of controlling cash can be stated in one word—balance. A firm should aim to have just the right amount of cash on hand—never too little and never too much for its needs. If a business has too much cash on hand, it may be missing opportunities for investing in new or additional inventory, equipment, or facilities. The process of identifying and controlling these receipts and expenditures of cash is known as **cash flow management.**

Results of Undercapitalization

When a business has excessive pressure for cash, it may be **undercapitalized.** A business is undercapitalized if it does not have enough funds to pay current operating expenses or to purchase needed inventory or equipment. Such a chronic shortage of cash can lead to disaster, because the owner cannot pay the firm's bills when they are due. The business may go broke because its owner lacks the financial resources to meet the sud-

It is possible to have too much cash on hand. If excess cash is invested wisely, a business can grow.

den demands of new competition. Often, more capital is needed because the present investment does not generate enough cash to keep the business financially healthy.

Controlling Cash Flow

Control of cash involves two options. The first is having the right amount of cash on hand to pay bills. The second is using any excess cash wisely. With excess cash on hand, certain loans can be paid off earlier to reduce interest expenses. Or the business owner may purchase additional inventory or equipment to increase sales income.

Financial control, day-to-day and month-by-month accounting, should inform an owner-manager of the balance of cash flow. An accounting system can indicate how much money is available, how much is needed to pay bills, and whether there is either a shortage to be made up or a surplus to be invested. In the latter case, it may be wise to take prudent business risks—as many successful business owners do—in order to enable cash balances to produce necessary income and profits. Such risks could involve purchasing additional merchandise or equipment to expand customer sales or service.

Mr. Baker concluded his discussion of financial statements by saying to Connie and Brent:

> We have reviewed basic components of the balance sheet and the profit-and-loss statement. In addition, we have considered certain important ratios and cash flow management. These owner-manager's tools are important for the operation of a successful business. I suggest that we set up an appointment to discuss how to prepare a loan application for your new music store. During our meeting we'll review how that very important loan application is evaluated.

TRADE TALK

Define each term and use it in a sentence.

Balance sheet
Cash flow
   management
Cost of goods sold
Current assets
Current liabilities
Current ratio
Debt-to-net worth
   ratio
Fixed assets
Liabilities
Long-term liability
Net profit
Net worth
Profit-and-loss
   statement
Ratio analysis
Return-on-investment
   ratio
Solvent
Undercapitalized

CAN YOU ANSWER THESE?

1. What are the three main components of a balance sheet?

2. What are two examples of current assets? Fixed assets? Current liabilities?

3. What are the five major components of a profit-and-loss statement?

4. What information does a projected profit-and-loss statement provide a potential lender?

5. What information do the following ratios provide: return-on-investment ratio; current ratio; debt-to-net worth ratio?

6. Why is cash flow management important to the owner-manager?

CHAPTER
65 *Obtaining Financing*

At their appointment to discuss obtaining business finances, Mr. Baker greeted Connie Lee and Brent Ness by saying:

Financing a new business means getting the money necessary to start it and keep it going. If you were planning a 2000-mile trip in your enough gas money for the first 500 miles? Probably not. Yet many people do this with respect to financing a new business. Their chances for success are very limited. Money is the necessary fuel that powers the business. Just as a car will not run without fuel, neither will a business run without money.

■

BUSINESS FINANCIAL NEEDS

The first step in preparing your financial plan is to determine the reasons for which money is needed. *Business financing* involves obtaining necessary funds for business costs and expenses. These costs and expenses are start-up costs, operating expenses, and personal expenses.

Start-Up Costs

Start-up costs are usually expenses that occur only when getting the business off the ground. Once your business is started, you may not have these expenses again. Some examples of start-up costs are the following:

■ Fixtures and equipment
■ Starting inventory
■ Deposits for rents and utilities
■ Equipment for instrument repair
■ Business licenses and permits
■ Certain legal fees
■ Advertising for the grand opening

Table 1 shows a worksheet to help you figure start-up costs. When Brent and Connie open their music store they will have many start-up costs. They will have to buy display fixtures for musical instruments, racks for sheet music, secured glass cases for cassette tapes, as well as cash register terminals and office equipment. They will also have to buy or rent a building; pay for various licenses and permits; and budget for their grand-opening promotions. These are just a few of the possible start-up costs. Most lenders will require that a new business prepare

TABLE 1 / START-UP COSTS WORKSHEET
(Costs You only Have to Pay Once)

Furniture, fixtures, and equipment: Refer to supplier's catalog prices.	_____
Decorating and remodeling: Talk it over with a contractor.	_____
Installation of fixtures and equipment: Talk to suppliers from whom you buy these.	_____
Starting inventory: Suppliers will help you estimate this. For total amounts, use typical ratio to sales.	_____
Deposits with public utilities: Find out from utility companies.	_____
Legal and other professional fees: Lawyer, accountant, and so on.	_____
Licenses and permits: Find out from city offices what you have to have.	_____
Advertising and promotion for opening: Estimate what you'll use.	_____
Accounts receivable: What you need to buy more stock until credit customers pay.	_____
Cash: For unexpected expenses or losses, special purchases, etc.	_____
Other: Make a separate list and enter total.	_____
Total: Total estimated cash you need to start with.	_____

SOURCE: Adapted from Wendell O. Metcalf, *Starting and Managing a Small Business of Your Own* (Small Business Administration, Washington, D.C., 1973)

STATEMENT OF BUSINESS START-UP COSTS

Name of Business The Music Store

	Total Funds Required	Sources of Funds Owner	To Be Financed
Fixed Assets	$	$	$
Building			
Delivery vehicles	12,000	6,000	6,000
Equipment fixtures, and/or furniture	16,000	2,000	14,000
Building improvements	4,000	1,000	3,000
Other _____			
Subtotal, Fixed Assets	$32,000	$ 9,000	$23,000
Prepaid Items and Deposits			
Rent deposit	$ 1,500	$ 1,000	$ 500
Utilities and telephone deposit	200	200	0
Insurance payments	500	500	0
Taxes, licenses, and fees	500	500	0
Other _____			
Subtotal, Prepaid Items/Deposits	$ 2,700	$ 2,200	$ 500
Preopening Expenses			
Advertising and promotion	$ 400	$ 400	$ 0
Hiring and training employees	500	500	0
Legal and accounting services	500	500	0
Other _____			
Subtotal, Preopening Expenses	$ 1,400	$ 1,400	$ 0
Inventory and Supplies			
Inventory purchased	$ 8,500	$ 2,500	$ 6,000
Supplies	1,500	1,500	0
Subtotal, Inventory and Supplies	$10,000	$ 4,000	$ 6,000
Working Capital			
Fund for customer credit	$ 500	$ 500	$ 0
Fund for miscellaneous (petty) cash	1,000	1,000	0
Total operating expenses (Refer to assignment 7)	8,000	2,000	6,000
Other _____			
Subtotal, Working Capital	$ 9,500	$ 3,500	$ 6,000
Total Funds Required	$55,600	$20,100	$35,500

Connie and Brent prepared a statement of business start-up costs to show lenders how much money they needed to borrow and why.

a statement of business start-up costs. The funds to be provided by the owner and to be financed for each item are identified.

Operating Expenses

Operating expenses occur after the business has been started. They are necessary to get the business on its feet. Many businesses take a few months to perhaps a year or longer to begin to show a profit. Some examples of operating expenses are:

Inventory	Monthly rent
Repairs to equipment	Payroll
Supplies	Utilities
Insurance	Taxes
Advertising	Delivery

Once a new store is open, there will be regular operating expenses. Merchandise will have to be purchased. Employees' wages, sales taxes, monthly rent payments, and much more will have to be paid. It is important to determine how much money will be needed each month to operate the business. Table 2 is a worksheet that can help you determine your operating expenses.

Personal Expenses

Personal expenses are those expenses that are necessary for you to live. The money you need to start and operate the business is important, but don't overlook the money you need for personal or living expenses. Here

TABLE 2 / OPERATING EXPENSES WORKSHEET

Monthly Expenses	Column 1: Your estimate of monthly expenses based on sales of $_____ per year	Column 2: Your estimate of how much cash you need to start your business	What to put in column 2*
Salary of owner-manager	$	$	2 times column 1
All other salaries and wages			3 times column 1
Rent			3 times column 1
Advertising			3 times column 1
Delivery expense			3 times column 1
Supplies			3 times column 1
Telephone expense			3 times column 1
Other utilities			3 times column 1
Insurance			Amount required by insurance firm
Taxes (and Social Security)			4 times column 1
Interest			3 times column 1
Maintenance			3 times column 1
Legal and professional fees			3 times column 1
Miscellaneous			3 times column 1

*Thse figures are typical for one kind of business. You have to decide how many months to allow for in your business.
SOURCE: Adapted from Wendell O. Metcalf, *Starting and Managing a Small Business of Your Own* (Small Business Administration, 1973).

are some examples of personal and living expenses to consider:

Rent or mortgage payment
Clothing
Food
Utilities

Transportation
Medical bills
Insurance
Entertainment

As mentioned earlier, many new businesses will not be profitable right away. Sometimes it may take from 1 to 3 years for a business to become profitable. The owner of a new business may not be able to take enough salary from the business to cover personal living expenses. You must plan for these expenses when planning your total finances for your new business. Sometimes people will start a new business while working on another job. They may rely on a spouse who earns money from an outside job. These financial sources help to limit the money needed to finance a new business.

■

TYPES OF FINANCING

After you determine what you need the money for, you need to determine the type of financing to obtain. There are two basic types of financing. First, many people who start businesses use some of their own money. This type of investment is called **equity financing.** Second, the rest of the money that is needed is borrowed from other sources. This type of financing is called **debt financing.** Most businesses are started with both types of financing.

Equity Financing

The main type of equity financing for most people is their savings. Some experts say that one-half of the money needed to start a small business should come from the owner. This may mean that the future owner must work and save for several years before having enough money to start a new business. Another popular type of equity financing is money from family and friends. Family members such as mothers, fathers, brothers, sisters, aunts, or uncles frequently provide money to help start a business. Friends, too, can be a good source. However, when using money from family and friends, there are a few points to consider. For example, will they want to get involved with operating the business? What happens if the business doesn't succeed? Will it ruin your relationships? Before using money from family and friends, it is important to think carefully about the possible consequences.

Partnership Financing

Equity financing can also be obtained by selling part of the business to others. This can be done in several different ways. You could go into business with one or more partners. When all the partners put in some of their own money, it is usually easier to raise the total amount needed. However, partners must be able to get along and make decisions that each accepts. Sometimes this is not easy. Many people starting their own business want to make their own decisions. This type of financing may limit decision-making options.

Incorporating the Business

Incorporating the business and selling stock is another way to obtain equity capital. Again, this may not be acceptable to the owner, since it means giving up some control of the business. Legal and tax questions also must be considered.

Venture Capital

Venture capital is money given to a business by a venture capital investment company in exchange for shares of stock in the new business. This money is usually not easy to obtain. It does come with some strings attached. Outside owners, in effect, own part of the company through their shares of stock. If enough stock is acquired, the original owners could lose control of their business. A type of venture capital is also available from small business investment companies. These companies are licensed and regulated by the federal government.

SOURCES OF FINANCING

The sources for borrowing money are limited only by the imagination of the owner. Whatever the source, lenders will usually lend money for starting businesses only to people they know and trust. Also, lenders are careful not to lend money if the risks are great. Lenders want to be sure they will not lose their money on businesses that fail. Most lenders, therefore, will want to review the business plan carefully. This plan describes the marketing strategies, how the business will be operated, how much money will be needed and how it will be used, and when the business will be profitable.

Banks

Most people think of banks when borrowing money. Although it is true that banks lend money to help businesses get started, it is not always easy to borrow from them. Banks lend money when the risk of losing it is very low. Frequently, they will lend only to their customers whom they have known for a long time.

Credit Unions

If you are a member of a credit union, you may be able to borrow there. Many times, small loans are available for personal or business uses. Some loans can be obtained with just your signature. Credit union interest rates are frequently lower than bank rates.

Commercial and Consumer Finance Companies

Both commercial and consumer finance companies may lend you money to start your business. Commercial finance companies arrange business loans. On the other hand, personal loans are made by consumer finance companies. Both types of finance companies tend to lend money to people that banks may turn down. Because they take greater risks, finance companies usually charge high interest rates.

Life Insurance Policies

Some people borrow money against their life insurance policies. This is an easy way to obtain some of the money needed to start a business. Since life insurance policy loans are based on the cash already paid in, they are not risky. Life insurance companies usually offer these loans at low interest rates. However, it should be remembered that the amount borrowed is deducted from the life insurance policy coverage available until the loan is repaid.

Savings-and-Loan Institutions

If you need to buy land or a building for a new business, you may be able to borrow the money from a savings-and-loan institution. They specialize in real estate financing. The loans they make are called **mortgages.** Their interest rates are similar to those of banks.

Small Business Administration

Another source of borrowing is the U.S. Small Business Administration (SBA). The SBA is a federal agency whose mission is to help small businesses get started and keep going. The SBA has two basic types of business loans. One type is called **bank guaranteed loans**. The money for these loans is actually provided by a private lender such as a bank. The

SBA guarantees that the loan will be paid back to the bank even if the borrower cannot do so. The SBA guarantees a percentage of the loan, not the total amount. The SBA may guarantee up to 90 percent of the loan. The lender assumes the risk for the other part. The other type of loan is made directly by the SBA. Therefore, they are called **direct loans**. SBA loans are available only if you are unable to borrow the money from a bank or other private lender. You have to try the other sources of borrowing previously mentioned before you can be eligible for an SBA loan. The SBA has other programs, too. It is wise to check with your nearest SBA office to see what types of loans may be available for your new business.

■

ALTERNATIVE SOURCES OF FINANCING

There are alternative sources of financing available for a new business. These sources include franchisors, trade credit, and factors. Although franchisors and trade credit can be used to get the business started, factors normally are not used until the business is actually started.

Franchisors

Starting a new business as a franchise, such as Dunkin Donuts or Kentucky Fried Chicken, has advantages. Buying a franchise may help you go into business for less money than if you started a similar business by yourself. Sometimes the franchisor will let you put a small cash payment down and then lend you the rest of the money needed to get the business started. Franchises are discussed in more detail in Chapter 9.

Trade Credit

Trade credit is another good source of financing. It is usually short-term credit that

suppliers provide to their customers. In small businesses, it is widely used. Many small businesses buy the products they sell or the equipment they use on trade credit. Trade credit for buying your inventory may be for 30, 60, or 90 days. Trade credit for buying equipment is frequently longer.

Factors

Factors are businesses that buy another company's accounts receivable. Suppose you started a clothing store and provided your customers with charge accounts. Customers may buy clothes from you and then take several months to pay you back. Using a factor would help you get cash in a shorter period of time to pay your operating expenses. The factor would give you the cash and take over the credit charges or accounts receivable of your customers. The factor would charge you a fee for this service. However, it is a good way of getting cash when you need it without borrowing.

■

PREPARING A LOAN APPLICATION PACKAGE

Almost all of the sources of financing require that you prepare a detailed and thorough loan application package. Potential lenders will want detailed information about the business and its chances of success so that they can determine whether you are a good risk. The presentation of this information may take many pages. Frequently, the total business plan serves as a loan application package.

Before beginning to prepare the loan application package, you should first determine what should be included. By talking with potential lenders and/or the Small Business Administration, you can identify exactly what needs to be included. The SBA suggests that the following information be supplied in a loan application for individuals starting a new business:

■ Describe the type of business you plan to establish.

■ Describe your experience and management capabilities.

■ Prepare an estimate of how much you or others have to invest in the business; justify how much you will need to borrow.

■ Prepare a current financial statement (balance sheet) listing all personal assets and all liabilities.

■ Prepare a detailed projection of earnings for the first year the business will operate.

■ List collateral to be offered as security for the loan, indicating your estimate of the present market value of each item. **Collateral** items are any assets you own that could be claimed by the lender if you do not meet loan repayments.

Other items in the loan application package are required at the discretion of the lender. Some lenders will require further information, such as copies of business property leases, income tax statements, life and casualty insurance policies, ownership papers, and other contracts. Lenders will want to review your business plan as well. Again, you can see the importance of a detailed plan.

■

HOW LENDERS EVALUATE LOAN APPLICATIONS

After you have completed the loan application package, the prospective lender will evaluate it to determine if the loan should be made. The lender's main concern is having the loan repaid according to a specified time schedule. Therefore, the lender is interested in the future prospects of your business. Will you be able to survive, grow, and become profitable? Will you be able to repay the loan? Answers to these basic questions are what the lender must determine.

Business Considerations

As the lender reviews your loan application, four general areas of the business are considered.

1. *Net earnings.* Will your business generate enough income to sustain the business with enough left over to repay the loan?

2. *The immediate and long-range business outlook.* Will there continue to be demands for your type of business in both prosperous and depressed times?

3. *Industry outlook.* Is your business a part of a growing or dying industry?

4. *The capability of your management.* Do you have the managerial skills and motivation to make a success of your business?

The Six C's of Credit Evaluation

Besides reviewing the areas listed above, the lender will evaluate an applicant using more personal criteria. In Chapter 34 we discussed "three C's of credit" applied by retailers to customers. A bank lending money to an entrepreneur might evaluate the borrower in terms of "six C's of credit." The six C's used for evaluating credit applicants are (1) character, (2) capital, (3) capacity, (4) collateral, (5) circumstances, and (6) coverage.

1. *Character* refers to the type of person you are. Some say that it is the most important asset of an entrepreneur. Lenders evaluate a person's character according to such traits as honesty, reliability, and trustworthiness. To the lender, a person with strong character will do everything possible to protect the assets and the business, and to ensure that the loan will be repaid.

2. *Capital* is the amount of money the entrepreneur has personally put into the business. The personal investment you put into the business shows the lender your faith and commitment in the growth and eventual success of the business.

3. *Capacity* relates to the skill and drive of management. A lender is interested in leadership that has clear-cut goals and a detailed plan for seeing the business prosper. An effective management will utilize the loan to assist the business to grow and succeed.

4. *Collateral* is the security the borrower puts up to insure that the loan will be repaid. Normally, tangible assets—collateral—are forfeited to the lender if the loan is not paid. The better the collateral, the more assured the lender is that the loan will be repaid.

5. *Circumstances* are other factors that lenders consider that may be beyond the control of the borrower. They must be considered because they may affect repayment of the loan. The state of the economy, the nature of the borrower's competition, and the nature of the product or service being sold are examples of circumstances reviewed by lenders.

6. *Coverage* deals with insurance protection. The lender is interested in the loan being repaid if something unforeseen happens to the owner of the business. Insurance that covers the death of the borrower or losses due to physical damage, liability, or theft help guarantee that the loan will be repaid.

The thorough lender will weigh the applicant's character, capital, capacity, collateral, circumstances, and coverage very carefully before making a loan to any prospective entrepreneur. Knowing these six C's of credit should help you plan your loan application package and explain your financial plan to a lender. At the end of their discussion Mr. Baker provided a business loan application form for Connie and Brent. They prepared a statement of business start-up costs and completed all the sections of their business plan. These items, along with the filled-in financial loan application form, provided a comprehensive loan application package for their lender to evaluate.

This total process of obtaining financing for a new business may appear to be time-consuming and demanding. You could compare this process to a comprehensive examination in one of your high school courses. An entrepreneur who receives loan approval from a lender has passed a critical test for his or her new business.

TRADE TALK

Define each term and use it in a sentence.

Bank guaranteed loans	Mortgages
Collateral	Operating Expenses
Debt financing	Personal expenses
Direct loans	Start-up costs
Equity financing	Trade credit
Factors	Venture capital

CAN YOU ANSWER THESE?

1. For a new business of your choice, what are four examples of possible start-up expenses? Operating expenses? Personal expenses?

2. What is the basic difference between equity and debt financing?

3. What is a disadvantage of partnership financing?

4. Describe four sources of financing a new business (advantages and/or disadvantages).

5. What is an SBA guaranteed loan?

6. What is a difference between trade credit and factor credit?

7. What are four types of business information that could be included in a loan application package?

8. List the "six C's of credit" and give an example of each.

66 Planning Your Grand Opening

Connie Lee and Brent Ness were informed by Mr. Baker that their loan application had been approved. They were excitedly sharing the good news with Mrs. Johnson, the owner of a small craft shop. Mrs. Johnson started her new business a year ago. She offered these suggestions to Connie and Brent:

The most memorable day of your new business life will be the day you open your new music store. All the planning you have done is going to be subjected to two tests:

1. Getting the customers to come to the store
2. Serving them in a way that they will become steady customers

If you would like, I can share several ideas that helped make the grand opening of my business a success.

REVIEW YOUR DESIRED BUSINESS IMAGE

Mrs. Johnson made these suggestions to Connie and Brent:

As I understand it, you plan to have your business grand opening promotion in 6 weeks. The first step in planning this grand opening is to analyze once more your desired business image. What do you want people to think of when they think of your music store: high quality, name brands, unique merchandise, extra services, pleasant surroundings, courteous sales personnel, reasonable prices, the latest hits? Once you have chosen your desired business image, consider the promotion of this image as an overall objective of your grand opening.

CONSIDER MARKETING MIX VARIABLES

After you have reviewed your desired business image, you should also consider the marketing mix variables involved with the grand opening promotion. As you will recall (Chapter 11), the major marketing mix variables (product, price, place, and promotion) all relate to serving the wants and needs of the customer. Planning a new business grand opening is, in reality, planning a major marketing promotion. Answers to the following questions will assist you in developing this promotion:

1. Who are the target market customers (primary wants and needs, ages, incomes, education levels, locations, unique aspects, etc.)? This has been identified previously in your business plan, but should be constantly reviewed.

2. What product or service promotions will be featured? What are the unique qualities, models, styles, assortments, and so on, that will be highlighted for the opening day? Why would your target market customers prefer your merchandise or services to those of your competitors?

3. What price promotions, such as discounts, specials, coupons, or loss leaders, will be offered for what products or services? Have competitors' prices and policies been analyzed?

4. What place promotions, such as business location information, business name identity, exterior signs, billboards, direct mail, or special promotions, will be used?

5. What promotion strategies, media, and budgets will be planned? (This question will be discussed in more detail later in this chapter.)

Determining the answers to the above marketing mix questions will help you plan specific promotion strategies for your grand opening.

■

DEVELOP THE GRAND OPENING PROMOTION STRATEGIES

A *strategy* is a plan of action designed to achieve a specific goal or objective. Since you have reviewed your desired business image, it is now time to plan *how* you will implement your grand opening promotion strategies.

Use Sources of Assistance

A new business owner-manager may feel somewhat overwhelmed by the many challenges of opening a new business. As Mrs. Johnson said when she continued her discussion with Connie and Brent: "There are many sources of assistance that can help you answer the marketing mix questions. In addition, they can help you when actually conducting the grand opening." The following sources are available:

Suppliers, Wholesalers, or Vendors
Suppliers, wholesalers, or vendors are the first sources of help that you should consider when planning the grand opening of your new business. They have been through many openings with their customers. Their ideas can be extremely useful. Sometimes wholesalers or vendors will provide one or more of their sales representatives to help you greet customers during the first few days. Their experience is reassuring to have available when the unexpected but inevitable problems arise in your beginning business operations.

Many manufacturers will provide promotion materials for exterior or interior displays, including backgrounds, reprints of national advertising, and other aids. Some companies even offer initial window display dressing services, either free or for a fee. Most new retailers want to dress the windows themselves, but not everyone has the talent to do this. These company display specialists can offer that "professional look" to both window and interior displays.

Community Resource Personnel
Inform the local chamber of commerce or comparable organization of your business's opening. Many shopping centers, business associations, or communities designate certain individuals as "goodwill ambassadors" to greet and promote new businesses. These individuals are often willing to cut the opening day ribbon and to assist with other promotional events.

It may be possible to invite a local or regional celebrity connected with an item that you are selling. This celebrity could greet customers and sign records, books, or promote special merchandise. If the business or the community is too small for that kind of promotion, invite the mayor or some other local official. Their presence will likely result in free newspaper coverage as well.

Select the Media

When it comes time to advertise your grand opening, you will have to make up your mind media or combination of media is going to be best for your store—newspaper, radio, television, direct mail, or whatever other approach will suit your professional needs. Part of the answer will be determined by media cost and expected results. As a small retailer just starting out, you are not likely to be able to afford expensive media promotions. Your first advertising, most likely, will be done by the local newspaper, radio, and/or television stations.

Newspapers Newspapers offer the advantages of local coverage and effective timing of advertisements. The results of a grand opening ad are often measurable, particularly when customers clip out coupons and bring them to the business.

For a new business your grand promotion ad should be prominently located within the newspaper. The ad should introduce customers not only to the new business itself, but also to the specific products and services that you are featuring. An appealing, eye-catching business logo or slogan can be used to promote the grand opening. This logo or slogan can be continued in future promotions. Use a simple layout for your ad that will draw the reader's eyes through its features—graphics, illustrations, copy, price, and so on—directly to the name and location of the business. Since you are a new business, you don't want to keep your business name and location a secret from your target customers!

Basically, your grand opening ad should highlight certain product or service features and benefits that will entice potential customers to visit your store and not your competitors'. Certain service businesses may offer discounts or special coupons for introductory inspection, service, cleaning, or repair. Also, highlight in your grand opening ad any special events that will be featured. Contests, free refreshments, entertainment, and drawings are examples of such attractions. You may need some expert help unless you have a talent for laying out and writing distinctive newspaper advertising. Of-

Grand Opening!

The newest and most exciting concept in furniture buying in the country is opening its 3rd store in the Metroplex in Oaklawn. The Fort Worth and North Dallas stores are joining in the celebration with special savings of **15-50% off**. EXPRESSIONS is a unique place where you can design the furniture you've always wanted.

Sofas, sleepers, sectionals, chairs. By using more than 100 frame styles and over 600 designer fabrics, all on display in our showrooms, you'll create pieces that will bear the stamp of the person who matters most—you.

Simply visit EXPRESSIONS and take a good look around. Match fabric to frame, and the finished piece—built by EXPRESSIONS own factory—is yours in just 45 days.

CUSTOM   FURNITURE
EXPRESSIONS

Most small businesses announce their opening in local newspaper ads.

ten the newspaper representatives will assist you in planning, writing, and laying out effective ads.

Radio

Radio can be a very appropriate medium for a grand opening promotion. It goes everywhere—into homes, into offices, and other places of employment, into cars as people drive to and from work, often called **drivetime.** Radio offers immediate and flexible scheduling, comparatively low rates, and few production costs. To help liven up the grand opening, you can hire a radio personality for an on-site or remote broadcast or program featuring your business and special promotions.

When you choose airtime for your grand opening promotion, consider your target market. At what time would your most likely customers be listening to a particular radio station? Like a business, radio stations also have an image and target markets (country western, rock, contemporary, easy listening, classical) to whom they direct their programming.

Television

Television has the obvious customer appeal of both sight and sound. For the smaller retailer, television costs of production of commercials and airtime may be too expensive. It is possible, however, to participate in cooperative advertising programs whereby the supplier or manufacturer shares a percentage of the advertising costs. You may be able to coordinate your grand opening product or service promotions with national advertising campaigns featuring the same items. In any case, television media representatives can assist you in planning such advertising.

Direct Mail

A direct-mail campaign can be an excellent way of introducing a new business. It can be as simple as a postcard, or as elaborate as a full-color brochure or catalog. Manufacturers often provide material that you can use for direct mail advertising purposes.

There are, in addition, advertising c___ nies that specialize in direct-mail promotio___ you can afford one of them, it is advantageous to have such specialists do the promotion job for you.

Direct mailings in advance of your opening will help to draw customers. They can simply go to residents and boxholders in your postal zone. If your business is one that deals in a specialty item, you will be able to buy a list of potential customers in your area from a customer list supplier. Advertisements in local papers announcing the opening are essential, unless you are located in a city so large that a small firm's ad would be lost. In any case, analyze your community, identify the customers that you wish to contact for the grand opening, and find the best way to reach them.

Other Grand Opening Promotions

Find out whether the Welcome Wagon or similar organizations operate in your community. Representatives from these organizations help identify and welcome new customers that have moved into a community. They provide shopping information, merchandise coupons, and promote businesses who subscribe to their services. You can make special offers to newcomers by inviting them to visit your new place of business to get acquainted.

The Yellow Pages telephone directory is a proven advertising medium for new businesses. Commercial telephone subscribers are listed automatically. It may be worthwhile to spend a little money and have your business listed in boldface, or even in a small display ad.

Depending on the kind of business you are starting, free soft drinks or coffee and doughnuts may be appropriate for opening day. Or you may be able to arrange for a special demonstration of a product being sold. In other words, exercise your ingenuity and think of as many special promotions to attract people to your business on opening day as you can.

UTILIZE VISUAL MERCHANDISING

Visual merchandising is especially important for a successful grand opening. Some retailers think that it is one of the most important kinds of introductory promotions to utilize. It is a direct link between the prospective customer and the business. If what the customers see on the exterior signs and display windows persuades them to come into the store, then they are likely to buy something whether it is an item they saw in the window or not.

Interior Appearance

A wise merchant once said, "Successful retailing involves the sale of goods and services that won't come back to customers who will." Service businesses also want customers to return. In either case, the interior appearance of a business can contribute to or detract from the image desired. The type of business operated should suggest the "look" you want to project. Various departments or locations within a store should take on the atmosphere of the specific products or services. A floral shop or gift boutique, for example, should look and smell appealing. A music store such as Connie's and Brent's should have a definite image projecting the type of music enjoyed by their desired customers. It is very important that the various departments or areas of the store be clearly identified. Remember that your business layout is new to your customers. In-store signs or directories can be very helpful in directing your customers.

When planning a grand opening, special attention should be paid to the attractiveness, neatness, and arrangement of merchandise displays. In effect, everything should be "spic and span," because with a new business that first impression must be a positive impression. As the saying goes, "There is no such thing as a second chance for a first impression."

Exterior Signs

Signs represent your business image. Signs are the most direct and continuing form of visual communication available. They give information about your store and build your image. They are a relatively inexpensive means of advertising, are easy to use, and are always at work for you. When special merchandise items are displayed on an exterior sign, sales on these items increase. Small Business Administration studies have shown that people do read and remember what appears on signs.

To promote your business effectively, your signs must be noticeable and readable. The sign's design, therefore, is important. The colors, lettering, shape, symbols, harmony, and lighting of the sign must be coordinated to communicate the desired impression and understanding of your business and its products and services.

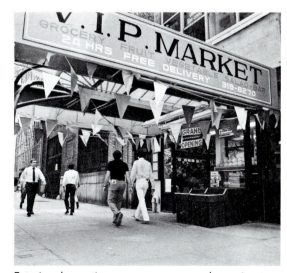

Exterior decorations announce a grand opening to passersby.

CONDUCT A PRE-GRAND OPENING

Many new businesses hold a pre-grand opening or dress rehearsal before their "official" grand opening. The purpose of this pre-grand opening is to allow management and personnel to try out the policies, procedures, equipment, cash registers, terminals, computers, inventory control systems, and so on, to determine if there are any mistakes or problem areas. Such mistakes or problem areas can be identified and necessary corrections made before the business is open to the general public.

Oftentimes, employees' relatives, friends, or special customers are invited to this "sneak preview." They may be given special discounts or invitations to participate in this preview. Reactions and recommendations obtained from these individuals can be helpful in improving the official grand opening.

Mrs. Johnson concluded her discussion with Connie and Brent regarding grand opening promotions by emphasizing these points:

1. Review your desired business image. This image can serve as the basis for the overall goals and objectives of your grand opening promotions.

2. Consider the marketing mix variables (product, price, place, and promotion) as you decide your promotion strategies.

3. Recognize the needs, wants, and preferences of your target market customers when planning your grand opening.

4. Select the various media and promotions available after evaluating their unique advantages and applications.

5. Remember the importance of customer first impressions when developing your business's interior appearance and exterior signs.

6. Have a "trial-run" pre-grand opening to discover any problem areas.

Connie and Brent had worked very hard in preparing their new business plan. The grand opening is the beginning of the realization of their new business ideas and dreams.

TRADE TALK

Define the following term and use it in a sentence.

Drivetime

CAN YOU ANSWER THESE?

1. In what ways can a business image relate to the planning of a grand opening promotion?

2. List four examples of marketing mix questions that can be asked when planning a grand opening promotion.

3. Give three examples of assistance that suppliers, wholesalers, or vendors can offer a new business.

4. What are the unique advantages or uses of newspapers, radio, television, and direct mail with respect to a grand opening?

5. Why is visual merchandising especially important for a new business?

6. What is a major benefit of conducting a pre-grand opening?

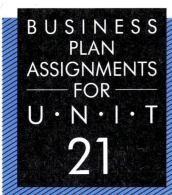

BUSINESS PLAN ASSIGNMENTS FOR U·N·I·T 21

BUSINESS PLAN ASSIGNMENT 7: PREPARING FINANCIAL STATEMENTS

In this unit you studied the financial statements required by both new and established businesses: (1) the balance sheet, (2) the profit-and-loss statement, and (3) the projected profit-and-loss statement. Using the following forms as references, prepare the following required financial reports for your new business:

1. Beginning balance sheet
2. Projected forecast for three months' profit-and-loss statement

To obtain information for the preparation of these reports, you may wish to contact your instructor for copies of the Robert Morris Associates Publication, *Annual Statement Studies,* or *The Small Business Reporter,*† published by the Bank of America. These publications furnish average percentage ratios for revenues and expenses of many different types and sizes of businesses.

Annual Statement Studies, The Robert Morris Associates, 1616 Philadelphia National Bank Building, Philadelphia, Pennsylvania 19107.

†The Small Business Reporter, Bank of America, Department 3120, P.O. Box 37000, San Francisco, California 94137

In addition, Small Business Administration representatives, various bank or lending institution officials, or owner-managers of similar types of businesses can provide valuable information and/or recommendations for your proposed financial plans and statements.

BUSINESS PLAN ASSIGNMENT 8: PREPARING A LOAN APPLICATION PACKAGE

Directions: Your new business cannot open its doors unless adequate financing is available. A loan application package is necessary to convince a prospective lender that your business should be provided necessary funding. In completing this loan application package, you should provide the following information and data:

1. Prepare a statement of business start-up costs. Refer to the form provided in Chapter 65 as a reference. You may modify this form to suit your individual business needs. Note that this form requires that the sources of the financing be identified—either by the owner or to be financed by others.

BEGINNING BALANCE SHEET   Name of Your Business_____

ASSETS

Current Assets
  Cash funds

                                                      $_____

Inventory and Supplies
  Merchandise inventory $_____
  Supplies   _____

    Subtotal, Inventory and Supplies   _____

Prepaid Expenses
  Deposit, telephone and utilities   _____
  Deposit, rent   _____
  Taxes, licenses, and fees   _____
  Insurance   _____
  Legal and accounting fees   _____
  Advertising and promotion   _____
  Other_____   _____
  _____   _____

    Subtotal, Prepaid Expenses   _____

Fixed Assets
  Building improvements   _____
  Fixtures and furniture   _____
  Equipment   _____
  Other_____   _____
  _____   _____

    Subtotal, Fixed Assets   _____

TOTAL ASSETS $_____

LIABILITIES

Current Liabilities
  Accounts and Loans payable (due within 1 year) $_____

    Subtotal, Current Liabilities $_____

Long-Term Liabilities
  Accounts and Loans payable (due after 1 year)   _____

    Subtotal, Long-Term Liabilities   _____

TOTAL LIABILITIES $_____

NET WORTH

Owner Equity $_____
Other Investor Equity   _____

    Subtotal, Net worth $_____

TOTAL LIABILITIES AND NET WORTH $_____

PROJECTED PROFIT-AND-LOSS STATEMENT FOR 3 MONTHS

Name of Business ——————————————

——————— to ———————
(Date)   (Date)

	Month One	%	Month Two	%	Month Three	%
Sales	$		$		$	
Beginning inventory						
Inventory purchased						
Total merchandise available for sale						
Less: Ending inventory						
Cost of goods sold						
Gross profit (Sales − Cost of goods sold)						
Less:						
Operating expenses						
Rent						
Depreciation						
Repairs						
Salaries and wages						
Payroll taxes/fringe benefits						
Taxes, licenses, fees						
Insurance						
Legal and accounting fees						
Bad debts						
Telephone						
Utilities						
Supplies						
Security						
Advertising and promotion						
Interest						
Postage and freight						
Delivery						
Miscellaneous (specify)						
————————						
————————						
————————						
Total Expenses						
Net Profit before Taxes (gross profit − total expenses)						
Federal Income Taxes						
Net Profit						

2. Prepare a summary of the sources of the financing of your new business. Explain your reasons for choosing these sources of business financing.

3. Identify your specific credit references by name and relationship. Explain your reasons for choosing these individuals as your credit references.

BUSINESS PLAN ASSIGNMENT 9: PLANNING YOUR NEW BUSINESS GRAND OPENING

The long-awaited day will soon be here—the day your new business will have its grand opening. To have a successful grand opening you must complete the following plans. You may wish to consult with a new business owner-manager who has just conducted a grand opening. Or you may wish to visit a media representative (newspaper, radio, television, or advertising agency) to obtain pro-motional grand opening ideas. Your own cre-ativity certainly should be applied when planning this grand opening. The following activities will assist you in conducting a suc-cessful grand opening:

1. Prepare the copy and layout for a grand opening newspaper advertisement. Feature special merchandise, prices, services, promo-tions for your new business. Prepare a bud-get estimate for the cost of this advertise-ment. Identify the dates and size of this advertisement.

2. Prepare a radio or television commer-cial for your grand opening. Include similar information for this ad as described in Activ-ity 1.

3. Design a sketch of an exterior sign or billboard for your new business. Include ap-propriate logo, colors, lettering, graphics, and other business, product, or service in-formation. You may wish to contact a sign or billboard business to obtain ideas.

4. Use your creativity in planning a special promotion that will attract customers to your grand opening. Describe the merchandise or services featured, the supplies required, per-sonnel needed, costs, and creative aspects of this promotion.

INDEX